DATE DUE

LGBTQ America Today

Advisory Board

Bear Bergman
Judith Butler
Eli Coleman
Paul G. Crowley
Judith Halberstam
Michael Horberg, MD
Karen C. Krahulik
Edward Stein
Claude J. Summers
Yvonne Yarbro-Bejarano

LGBTQ America Today

An Encyclopedia

Volume 3: P–Z

EDITED BY JOHN C. HAWLEY

EMMANUEL S. NELSON, ADVISORY EDITOR

GREENWOOD PRESS
Westport, Connecticut • London

Library of Congress Cataloging-in-Publication Data

LGBTQ America today : an encyclopedia / edited by John C. Hawley.
   p. cm.
  Includes bibliographical references and index.
  ISBN 978–0–313–33990–5 (set : alk. paper)—ISBN 978–0–313–33991–2 (v.1 :
alk. paper)—ISBN 978–0–313–33992–9 (v.2 : alk. paper)—ISBN 978–0–313–
33993–6 (v.3 : alk. paper)
  1. Sexual minorities—United States.   2. Sexual minorities—Encyclopedias.
I. Hawley, John C. (John Charles), 1947–
  HQ73.3.U6L43   2009
  306.76—dc22   2008029726

British Library Cataloguing in Publication Data is available.

Library of Congress Catalog Card Number: 2008029726
ISBN: 978–0–313–33990–5 (set)
     978–0–313–33991–2 (vol. 1)
     978–0–313–33992–9 (vol. 2)
     978–0–313–33993–6 (vol. 3)

First published in 2009

Greenwood Press, 88 Post Road West, Westport, CT 06881
An imprint of Greenwood Publishing Group, Inc.
www.greenwood.com

Printed in the United States of America

The paper used in this book complies with the
Permanent Paper Standard issued by the National
Information Standards Organization (Z39.48–1984).

10 9 8 7 6 5 4 3 2 1

For Antonio

And to the memory of Pat Arnold, Bill Dobbels, Neal Callahan, Jim Pollock, Mike Barry, Tom Naughton, Pete Davis, Skip Bacon, Lawrence King, Diego Vinales, Sakia Gunn, Rashawn Brazell, Gwen Araujo, Matthew Shepard, Gary Matson, Winfield Mowder, Harvey Milk, Fred C. Martinez, Jr., Scott Bernard Amedure, Arthur Carl Warren, Robert Hillsborough, Eddie Northington, Danny Lee Overstreet, Allen R. Schindler, Jr., Bill Jack Gaither, Steen Keith Fenrich, Teena Brandon, Robbie Kirkland, Barry Winchell, Chanelle Pickett, Jacob Lawrence Orosco, Amanda Milan, Joey Lipitz, Bill Clayton, Bruce David Michaels, Bobby Griffith, Robert Sevigny, Andrew Anthos, Victoria Arellano, and the many others.

Contents

P

Born in Endicott, New York, essayist, theoretician, and cultural critic Camille Paglia is currently professor of humanities and media studies at the University of the Arts in Philadelphia. Author of *Sexual Personae: Art and Decadence from Nefertiti to Emily Dickinson* (1992, Penguin), *Sex, Art and American Culture: Essays* (1993, Penguin), *Vamps and Tramps: New Essays* (1994, Vintage), and *Break Blow Burn* (2006, Penguin), she is a controversial intellectual and critic known for her academic adulation of Madonna (the singer), her scorn for **identity politics,** and her embrace of androgyny as the paradigm of beauty. Early academic appointments included a literature professorship at Bennington College. Her opinionated art-historical book, *Sexual Personae*, contains this now-notorious announcement: "If civilization had been left in female hands we would still be living in grass huts" (Paglia 1991, 38). She is also noted for writing in the same book, "There is no female Mozart because there is no female Jack the Ripper" (Paglia 1991, 247).

Paglia deliberately distanced herself from the feminist movement with her position on date rape: she views female victims as culpable. Aggressive males are only fulfilling their chthonic destiny, she says. Her feminist critics have objected to her assessments of women and their pretensions toward power, calling her characterizations "contemptuous." Recalling Freud's contention that primitive man prided himself on being able to put out a fire by urinating on it, she comments, "Male urination really is a kind of accomplishment, an arc of transcendence. A woman merely waters the ground she stands on" (Paglia 1991, 12).

Paglia's media presence is widespread. Her frantic delivery, extravagant body language, and comically self-aggrandizing statements are emblematic. She has redeemed herself somewhat for both the Left and the Right with the publication of

Break Blow Burn, a catholic selection of poetry accompanied by her own passionate and refined analytic essays.

Further Reading

Adnum, Mark. 2006. "Cruising with Camille: An Interview with Camille Paglia." *Bright Lights Film Journal* 54. Available at: http://www.brightlightsfilm.com/54/paglia.htm. Accessed August 22, 2008

Booth, Alison. 1999. "The Mother of All Cultures: Camille Paglia and Feminist Mythologies." *Kenyon Review* 21 (1): 27–45.

Paglia, Camille. 1991. *Sexual Personae: Art and Decadence from Nefertiti to Emily Dickinson.* New York: Vintage.

Sally Eckhoff

Chuck Palahniuk (1962–)

Chuck Palahniuk came to international attention after David Fincher's 1999 film adaptation of Palahniuk's first novel, *Fight Club* (1996). A 1986 graduate of the University of Oregon's School of Journalism, Palahniuk resides in Portland, Oregon, where he attended **Tom Spanbauer**'s "Dangerous Writing" workshop. There Palahniuk refined the minimalist style that he now utilizes in his fiction. *Fight Club* met with critical acclaim, winning the 1997 Pacific Northwest Bestsellers Association Award and the 1997 Oregon Book Award.

Palahniuk's eight novels tend to focus on alienated and marginalized protagonists, like his nameless narrator from *Fight Club* or Victor Mancini from *Choke* (2001). Palahniuk's stories often follow an epistolary form, where his narrator describes the actions of another, more important character. His novels also contain some sort of literary twist that gives the reader a surprise at the end of each book. A Palahniuk short story, "Guts," which appears in *Haunted* (2005), won considerable media attention in 2003 for causing more than 70 people to faint during Palahniuk's readings while on book tour.

Issues of contemporary alienation are the central theme of all of Palahniuk's fiction, which explore the nature of individual isolation in a variety of different subcultures. Themes revolving around sex, gender, and relationships are often inherent in his narratives. He also plays with themes of romance and love, but often does so in ways that defy conventional definitions or portrayals of relationships.

Palahniuk also publishes a number of nonfiction essays, interviews, and travelogues. The bulk of his essays are colleted in *Stranger than Fiction* (2003) and *Fugitives and Refugees: A Walk in Portland, Oregon* (2002). He has a devoted fan following, and he is the subject of a documentary, *Postcards from the Future: The Chuck Palahniuk Documentary* (2003).

Further Reading

Goodlad, Lauren M. E. 2007. "Men in Black: Androgyny and Ethics in *The Crow and Fight Club*." In *Goth: Undead Subculture*, ed. Lauren M. E. Goodlad and Michael Bibby, 89–118. Durham, NC: Duke University Press.

Mendieta, Eduardo. 2005. "Surviving American Culture: On Chuck Palahniuk." *Philosophy and Literature* 29 (2): 394–408.

Jeffrey A. Sartain

Parents, Families, and Friends of Lesbians and Gays (PFLAG)

On April 15, 1972, Morton Manford participated in a demonstration at the New York Hilton Hotel. A 21-year-old junior at Columbia University and leader of a gay activist group on campus, Manford joined others of the Gay Activists Alliance and interrupted a reporters' organization's annual dinner to speak out against the discrimination against gay people in the media. The response was violent: between 10 to 15 activists were injured, including Manford. His parents, Jeanne and Jules, saw the attack on the evening news and were outraged. Jeanne responded to the injustice by writing a letter to the editor of the *New York Post* in which she explained that she knew her son was gay and that she loved him. Her public display of solidarity with her son did not end there.

Due to the incident at the hotel, Morton had gained some notoriety, especially since his alleged perpetrator, the president of the Uniformed Firefighters Association, Michael J. Maye, was headed to trial because of his misconduct that evening. When Jeanne marched with her son in the Christopher Street Liberation Day parade in June of that year, they received additional attention—making the sign she carried more poignant and potent. The sign urged "Parents of Gays: Unite in Support for Our Children." That day, reporters asked Jeanne to provide a quote about her allegiance to her gay son, while gays and lesbians participating in the march asked her if she could talk to their parents. During the march, son and mother agreed that a parent support group was needed. In March 1973, the newly formed New York City Parents and Friends of Gays held its first meeting at a church; approximately 20 people attended. This meeting marked the beginning of Parents, Families, and Friends of Lesbians and Gays, otherwise known as PFLAG.

Between 1973 and 1979, groups like the one started by Jeanne Manford began springing up throughout the country, providing mutual support for parents of lesbians and gays. The emergence of these safe havens for parents reflected the overall development of the LGBTQ movement in America during the 1970s. As the movement continued to grow, activists planned for a National March for Gay and Lesbian Rights to take place in Washington, D.C., on October 14, 1979, marking the 10th anniversary of the Stonewall Riots. It drew more than 100,000 people from around the world, including parents who had been organizing support groups throughout the country. The national march provided an opportunity for them to meet each other for the first time. Parents participating in the march came together and held a press conference in support of their gay children.

After the march, the parents continued to meet and share information, and by 1981 participants decided to launch a national organization, known then as

Parents FLAG. Members decided to locate their headquarters in Los Angeles and nominated Adele Starr as Parents FLAG's president. Starr was the mother of a gay son and was very active in Los Angeles in advocating for the tolerance for gays and lesbians and providing support to parents. By 1982, the organization was officially known as the Federation of Parents and Friends of Lesbians and Gays, Inc., comprising approximately 20 groups, incorporated in California, and granted nonprofit, tax-exempt status. Its mission was to provide a safe space for dialogue for parents of gays and lesbians, to distribute information to educational institutions and faith-based organizations, and to establish itself as an information source for the general public.

During the 1980s, the organization grew even on a meager budget. Parents FLAG responded to the growing antigay crusade, the AIDS epidemic, and the public's growing interest in gay and lesbian issues. In 1988, it had nearly 200 local chapters throughout the nation, including in conservative states such as Nebraska, Minnesota, and South Dakota. That same year, Parents FLAG relocated its headquarters to Washington, D.C., and hired its first paid executive director, Paulette Goodman. The move to Washington contributed to its boost in visibility and increasingly national focus. In Massachusetts, chapters helped pass the first Safe Schools legislation in the country.

As Parents FLAG continued to grow, it tried to keep with the growing diversity of the LGBTQ community and issues. In 1993, Parents FLAG restructured. The organization changed its name to Parents, Families, and Friends of Lesbians and Gays (PFLAG), created an affiliation process for chapters, and decided that board seats should be elected positions. It also added **bisexuals** into its mission. As PFLAG evolved into a membership organization, it continued to support parents and speak out for their gay children in national debates about gays in the military, the right to marry, and HIV/AIDS awareness. It also continued to inspire legal change when a PFLAG family brought about the Department of Education's ruling that Title 9 protected gay and lesbian students against discrimination at school. In 1998, PFLAG added **transgender** people and families to its mission and work.

Currently, PFLAG is an ally-centered organization with over 500 chapters throughout the United States in addition to chapters abroad; it provides support and education and advocates for LGBTQ civil rights and legal protections. The core mission of the organization is to provide support both to the family and friends and to LGBTQ people before, during, and after **coming out.** Recently, PFLAG added two more groups they support: transgender people and straight spouses of LGBTQ people. PFLAG in particular deals with the coming out process by providing support to those who are planning to come out and those who are faced with others outing experience. They support all individuals impacted by the process through local chapters, a story center, publications, and a Web site. Issues they address include sexual orientation, gender identity and expression, transgender, intersex people, the flexibility of sexual orientation, the process of coming out, what not to say to someone coming out, how to support someone, and how to locate others in the area from whom to get support.

PFLAG's vision, mission, and strategic goals are to encourage society to be more tolerant of people, including those of diverse sexual orientations and gender identities. They promote the well-being of LGBTQ people and their families and friends through support. They do their best to inform the public and advocate to end discrimination and secure the rights of those with diverse orientations and identities. In addition to providing support, PFLAG educates the public in order to promote equality and safety for LGBTQ people and their families. These programs include general efforts such as national and local scholarship programs and voting drives and more specific initiatives such as the Bringing the Message Home Project, started in 2002. In gearing up for a major lobbying effort between Mothers Day and Fathers Day, PFLAG members are taught how to lobby and to have effective meetings with legislators. They are also trained on increasing voting registration in their neighborhoods and are educated on how to monitor court decisions.

As the organization's constituency broadens, PFLAG often creates educational initiatives and programs to facilitate its growth, the most notable program being the Families of Color Network (FOCN), which was established in 1999. FOCN informs local PFLAG chapters on matters of cultural differences regarding LGBTQ issues. The network is a collective group that works together to make ethnic communities safe for LGBTQs through education and is broken down into subnetworks. Such subgroups include FOCN—African American, Asian American, Latino, Native American, and Cross Cultural. Each deals with issues specific to its community while working together to promote cross-cultural synergy.

Another example of PFLAG's continued effort to broaden its membership and educate the public is its new program (2007) aimed at building connections with the straight community, Straight for Equality. They are hoping to provide straight people with the tools and means to make an important contribution to the fight for civil rights for LGBTQ people. Objectives of the project include creating forums for meaningful discussion about LGBTQ issues and informing straight people about the importance of personal choices and action.

PFLAG is also an advocate for fair treatment of LGBTQ people and their families in regards to issues related to family, workplace, hate crimes, military issues, and reparative therapy. As LGBTQ people became more vocal and visible about their choice of being or becoming parents, PFLAG responded by not only supporting those individuals but also advocating for fairness under the law—such as the right to adopt and/or be a foster parent, custody and visitation, and more immigration rights for same-sex couples in order for families to stay intact.

In the workplace, LGBTQ employees face discrimination and unequal benefits. PFLAG promotes overall equality and fairness at work by supporting the federal Employment Nondiscrimination Act (ENDA) while advocating for the act to cover sexual orientation and gender identity. PFLAG also pushes for equal employee benefits such as same-sex partner health and retirement benefits and the family medical leave opportunity by urging local representatives to stand up against discrimination in the workplace.

PFLAG obviously has many members who are parents, and one of the organization's top priorities is making schools safe for gay, lesbian, bisexual, and transgender youths. In order to protect these young people, PFLAG advocates for the passage of legislation to protect students from bullying and harassment for both sexual orientation and gender expression. Also, they argue for a change in sexual education so that it can be more comprehensive. Since states receive federal funding for sexual education based on abstinence-only-until-marriage curriculum, all critical information about LGBTQ individuals has the potential to be edited out because of this heterosexist premise for instruction. In 2000, the organization launched the initiative From Our House to the Schoolhouse, which focused on curbing **homophobia** in schools. PFLAG members also advocate change in schools by meeting with school administrators, supporting Gay/Straight alliances, providing college scholarships to LGBTQ students, and working with PTAs and other groups.

PFLAG continues to be a major advocacy group for civil rights pertaining to the LGBTQ community, rallying around legislation guaranteeing the end of discrimination for LGBTQ people at work and in the military, marriage equality, parents' rights, safe schools, and providing a voice against conservative antigay campaigns such as reparative therapy. It also informs the public through publications and endorsements of informational material. PFLAG has its own online store where one can purchase books, videos, or even logo-adorned boxer shorts. At the same time, it has maintained its grassroots sensibility and has stayed true to its initial intent, that of providing support to parents of gays and lesbians. As an ally-focused group, PFLAG is a unique and essential element of the LGBTQ community.

Further Reading

Bernstein, Robert. 1995. *Straight Parents/Gay Children: Keeping Families Together.* Emeryville, CA: Group West.

Beyette, Beverly. 1981. "Homosexuality and the Churches: Clergy to Participate in Ecumenical Lunch of Parents, Friends of Gays." *Los Angeles Times* (May 29): Section C, 1.

Pace, Eric. 1972. "Official Accused of Assault: City Aide Says He Saw Gay Intruder Being Attacked." *New York Times* (April 25): 11.

Parents, Families, and Friends of Lesbians and Gays Web site. Available at: http://www.pflag.org. Accessed July 14, 2008.

Aimee Klask

parents, LGBTQ

Before the 1970s, few people outside of the gay community knew of the existence of lesbian and gay parents. Indeed, the term "gay parent" was seen as an oxymoron, a physical and social impossibility. In the past three decades, both the perception and the reality of LGBTQ lives have changed dramatically. Although no accurate data exist, widely cited figures suggest that between 20 and 30 percent of lesbians are mothers. Further, untold numbers of gay men have become parents, in heterosexual relationships prior to **coming out,** in coparenting arrangements with female friends, and through adoption, fostering, and surrogacy. The 2000 U.S. Census reports that same-sex couples live in 99.3 percent of U.S. counties. Same-sex couples raising children live in 96 percent of the nation's counties. Widely cited estimates suggest that there are between 3 and 8 million gay and lesbian parents, raising between 6 and 14 million children.

Prior to the 1980s, the vast majority of gay parents were lesbian mothers seeking custody of their children conceived within heterosexual relationships prior to their coming out. These women often lost custody to their ex-husbands, as courts routinely ruled that being gay or lesbian automatically rendered a parent "unfit." Even when a lesbian mother was successful in retaining custody, she often faced punitive conditions, such as a judicial order not to reside with a same-sex partner. The legal struggles of lesbian mothers were the first distinctively lesbian legal issue of the 1970s. Organizations like the National Center for Lesbian Rights trace their origins to these early struggles to secure custody rights for lesbian mothers Many gay fathers limited their parental claims to access and visitation, recognizing the resistance they faced in terms of both gender and sexual orientation. Even those gay fathers who secured access to their children often faced punitive restrictions. Custody and access battles are not an artifact of the past, as untold numbers of lesbians and gay men still have children within heterosexual unions and face discriminatory practices as they try to secure their parental rights after coming out.

By the late 1970s and early 1980s, increasing numbers of lesbians began to use donor insemination to conceive a baby. In this population explosion, sometimes termed the "lesbian baby boom," many lesbians relied on sperm donations from gay male friends. As the AIDS epidemic decimated gay communities, many lesbians turned to sperm banks to secure sperm screened for HIV and other sexually transmitted diseases. While they often encountered discriminatory practices, countless lesbians became mothers, both as single mothers and in partnerships with other women. At the same time, many gay men were also becoming parents, through adoption, fostering, and surrogacy.

For decades, lesbians and gay men have fostered and adopted children as single parents, not revealing their sexual orientation for fear their applications would be rejected. By the late 1980s, however, increasing numbers of openly lesbian and gay women and men turned to adoption to form a family. Every state in the United States permits unmarried individuals to adopt; Florida alone explicitly limits that right to heterosexual individuals. In an individual adoption, an individual, unmarried person adopts a child placed for adoption by his or her biological parent or parents, who have agreed to give up all of their parental rights. These adoptions may take place through a child welfare agency, a public or private adoption agency, or consensual arrangements between private parties. Adoptions must be approved by a court and generally include a home investigation by child welfare authorities.

Foster parenting has long provided an avenue for gay men and lesbians to become parents. Because of the shortage of foster homes and the growing number of children in need of care, officials have often been willing to overlook an applicant's sexual orientation in order to find a placement for a child. Discriminatory legislation, however, can prevent lesbians and gay men from fostering children or from securing those relationships through adoption. Such policies contribute to the crisis in foster care as an estimated 500,000 children are currently in foster care, 100,000 of them waiting to be adopted. Policies on fostering by gay men and lesbians vary locally and on a state-by-state basis, with decisions regarding eligibility largely left to local child welfare officials and family court judges.

Surrogacy (an arrangement whereby a woman is contracted to serve as gestational host for a child who she will relinquish at birth) provides a route to parenting that allows for the possibility of a genetic relationship between the child and one of the parents, via donor insemination with the prospective father's sperm. Though complicated by legal and ethical considerations, surrogacy has enabled lesbians and many gay men to become parents.

For lesbian couples and gay male couples who will be raising children, securing the legal rights of the nonbiological (or nonadoptive) parent is important. Couples can seek a joint adoption, a legal procedure in which both partners simultaneously adopt a child who has no biological or preexisting adoptive relationship to either party. However, many states have laws and policies that expressly prohibit joint adoption by same-sex couples. In those jurisdictions, the nonlegal parent is forced to take additional legal measures to secure his or her parental rights. One method is second-parent adoption, a process whereby a same-sex partner can adopt her or his partner's biological or adoptive child without terminating the first legal parent's rights. Second-parent and joint adoptions protect children by giving them two legal parents, thereby entitling them to a range of financial benefits, including health insurance coverage, inheritance rights, Social Security benefits, and child support. Second-parent adoptions ensure that either parent can consent to medical treatment or visit the child in a hospital emergency room. Finally, second-parent adoption ensures that the nonbiological parent can continue to have a legally recognized parental relationship if the couple separates or if the biological (or adoptive) parent dies or becomes incapacitated.

To help secure their legal rights and to combat the isolation of parenting, lesbian and gay parents have formed support groups across the country. These range from monthly potluck get-togethers to national and international organizations. Political organizations like the National Center for Lesbian Rights and Family Pride have joined with the **American Civil Liberties Union (ACLU)** and others to change discriminatory laws and to fight for full civil marriage rights. Because civil marriage is a legal status that automatically confers over a thousand federal rights and benefits and hundreds of additional state rights and benefits, many lesbian and gay parents have campaigned for marriage rights. Marriage is a social and cultural institution that is recognized as an expression of a couple's commitment to each other, something researchers have indicated can be beneficial for children's emotional security. As of 2006, same-sex couples are legally permitted to marry in the Netherlands, Belgium, Canada, and Spain. On May 17, 2004, Massachusetts became the first state in the United States to allow same-sex couples to marry.

In these campaigns, LGBTQ advocates have faced considerable opposition. Since Anita Bryant's Save Our Children campaign overturned Dade County's gay ordinance in 1977, rights for lesbian and gay parents have been under attack. The Defense of Marriage Act, signed into law by President Clinton in 1996, and efforts to amend the U.S. Constitution to ban same-sex marriage are among the attempts to limit the rights of lesbian, gay, transgendered, and bisexual people.

Opponents of same-sex marriage have shifted their focus from overtly homophobic attacks on individual lesbians and gay men to the dangers that same-sex marriage and parenting allegedly pose for children. Opponents argue that same-sex parenting threatens the rights and the best interests of children, carrying such risks as child abuse, gender confusion, and growing up to be gay. None of these claims have been supported by scholarly research. In the past two decades, hundreds of studies have examined the effect on children of growing up in a same-sex family. The research has demonstrated overwhelmingly that children of lesbian and gay parents are as psychologically healthy and well adjusted as children of heterosexual parents on virtually every measure. Accordingly, numerous health and child welfare organizations have condemned discrimination against LGBTQ parents and have issued statements supporting second-parent and joint adoptions by lesbian, gay, and bisexual couples. These include the American Psychological Association (1976), the American Academy of Pediatrics (2002), the American Psychiatric Association (2002), and the Child Welfare League of America (2000).

The presence of lesbian and gay parents and their children in lesbian and gay pride parades, school concerts, and even the White House Easter Egg Hunt has greatly increased the visibility of LGBTQ people. Lesbian and gay families challenge homophobic images of lesbian and gay lives. They expand notions of family and of what is best for children. For these reasons, however, they also represent a threat to those who seek to uphold the "traditional family." Despite this opposition, LGBTQ people are welcoming children into their lives and, in the process, transforming the LGBT movement and the communities and neighborhoods in which they live.

See also Children, LGBTQ; Family law, Adoption, and Custody.

Further Reading

Arnup, Katherine. 1999. "Out in This World: The Social and Legal Context of Gay and Lesbian Families." *Journal of Gay and Lesbian Social Services* 10 (1): 1–25.

Bernstein, Mary, and Renate Reimann, eds. 2001. *Queer Families, Queer Politics: Challenging Culture and the State*. New York: Columbia University Press.

Bernstein, Robert A. 2005. *Families of Value: Personal Profiles of Pioneering Lesbian and Gay Parents*. New York: Marlowe and Company.

Clunis, Merilee, and Dorsey Green. 2003. *The Lesbian Parenting Book: A Guide to Creating Families and Raising Children*. San Francisco: Seal Press.

Hequembourg, Amy L. 2007. *Lesbian Motherhood: Stories of Becoming*. Binghamton, NY: Haworth.

Katherine Arnup

Pat Parker (1944–1989)

Pat Parker was an African American, feminist, lesbian poet, performance artist, and health worker. An activist involved with the Black Panther Party, the Black Women's Revolutionary Council, and the Oakland Feminist Women's

Health Center, Parker is known as one of the first African American authors to write about lesbian experience in poetry and performance pieces. After **coming out** in the 1960s, Parker helped establish the lesbian press known as the Women's Press Collective. She authored essays, an album of verse with **Judy Grahn,** and five collections of poetry. Parker became known as a political poet often cited for polemical narratives, as well as for her use of African American vernacular, including call-and-response oral traditions, in her verse. Many of Parker's poems explore African American experiences, gay and lesbian concerns, and issues of violence against women. For example, "Being Gay" examines family **homophobia,** while "My Lover Is a Woman" observes racism within an interracial lesbian relationship. The poem "Straight Folks Who Don't Mind Gays but Wish They Weren't So Blatant" critiques heterosexual privilege and compulsory heterosexuality, while the poem "Where Will You Be" calls readers to fight gay and lesbian oppression. "Movement in Black," the title poem of the collection that contains the works from Parker's three earliest collections (*Child of Myself, Pit Stop, Woman Slaughter*), is considered to be her most well-known piece in its portrayal of black women's struggles. The poem "Womanslaughter," which Parker read in Brussels at the 1976 International Tribunal of Crimes Against Women, documents the murder of her sister by a former husband. Throughout her life, Parker worked for social justice, as she also strived to connect African American and lesbian communities.

Further Reading

Alexander, Ilene. "Pat Parker." *Voices from the Gaps*. Available at: http://voices.cla.umn.edu/vg/Bios/entries/parker_pat.html. Accessed July 14, 2008.

Annas, Pamela. 1982. "A Poetry of Survival: Unnaming and Renaming in the Poetry of Audre Lorde, Pat Parker, Sylvia Plath and Adrienne Rich." *Colby Library Quarterly* 18: 9–25.

Folayan, Ayofemi, and Stephanie Byrd. 1993. "Pat Parker." In *Contemporary Lesbian Writers of the United States: A Bio-Bibliographical Critical Sourcebook*, ed. Sandra Pollack and Denise D. Knight, 415–419. Westport, CT: Greenwood Press.

Howe, Florence. 1999. "Movement in Black" (review). *The Women's Review of Books* 17 (2): 12.

Jeannette E. Riley

Peter Parnell (1953–)

Peter Parnell, born in New York City, is a playwright and screenwriter whose plays include *QED, The Cider House Rules, Flaubert's Latest, Hyde in Hollywood, An Imaginary Life, Romance Language, The Rise and Rise of Daniel Rocket,* and *The Sorrows of Stephen*. Parnell has also written extensively for such television shows as *The West Wing* and *The Guardian* and, most recently, has coauthored the noted children's book *And Tango Makes Three*.

Parnell's work largely focuses on themes of coming of age and the inevitable clash between youthful romanticism and hard-edged reality. This is most explicit in 1978s *The Sorrows of Stephen*, modeled after Goethe's *The Sorrows of Young Werther*, and 1982s *The Rise and Rise of Daniel Rocket,* about the ostracization of a boy with the ability to fly, a metaphorical treatment of the issues facing LGBTQ **youth.** Themes of disease and mortality are also prominent in Parnell's work, most notably in *Flaubert's Latest* (1992), which deals explicitly with AIDS, and *An Imaginary Life* (1993), in which the protagonist grapples with issues of identity, mortality, and midlife disappointment. Parnell's most commercially successful and widely produced plays have been his adaptations; his best-known work, *QED,* is a biographical drama centered on the life of physicist Richard Feynman that Parnell developed in partnership with veteran actor Alan Alda based on Feynman's memoirs.

Further Reading

Berson, Misha. 1996. "I Can't Believe We Staged the Whole Thing." *American Theatre* (March): 6–7.

Oliver, Edith. 1992. "L'Auteur dans le Connecticut." *The New Yorker* (July 6): 57.

Will Curl

passing

Passing is a sociological term that describes the act of obtaining recognition as a member of a social group other than one's own. For example, one could pass as a different ethnicity, race, gender, sexual orientation, social status, and so on. The verb *to pass* has been used in this context since about the Modern period. An example of this phenomenon in terms of race is Nella Larsen's novel, *Passing,* which chronicles the lives of two light-skinned African American women and the ways that their ambiguous racial phenotype impacts how they are viewed and classified by others. This article, however, will speak mainly to passing in terms of gender and sexuality.

It is essential to note that passing, in terms of gender and sexuality, is related to a discussion of the fluidity of gender, the importance of identity creation and recognition, and authenticity. All of these facets contribute not only to the success of passing but also to a discussion within the LGBTQ community about its implications. Passing generally involves physical modification to the body or modification of mannerisms. To pass successfully would mean that the person who is trying to pass appears as though he or she fits into a desired niche. Clothing, hygiene, mode of speech, and personal habits may all be adapted in order to pass as the desired persona or identity.

Infamous historical instances of passing include accounts of women who passed as men to join the military. While men have passed as women as well, male-to-female passing draws questions about gender and power. Whereas women gain agency when they transition to men, men lose agency if they become women, and therefore these cases are not as famously documented or explored. Women have passed as men in the military for a very long time historically; however, this does not necessarily indicate their sexual orientation.

In terms of sexual orientation and gender identity, passing is linked to idea of the **closet,** which describes the ultimate state of personal repression for members of the LGBTQ community. For example, a homosexual or bisexual person may try to pass as straight, or differently gendered, for a variety of personal and/or social reasons, possibly to avoid stigmatization or harm. Passing is ultimately a private experience that necessarily takes place in public.

For a subjugated person, passing can represent a demonstration of resistance against authority, or be an act of self-protection. **Leslie Feinberg** describes passing as a means of self-protection in her semi-autobiographical novel, *Stone Butch Blues*. Her character Jess is a **butch** lesbian who decides to take hormones and pass as a man in order to stop being physically and sexually harassed by members of her community and by the police. While she finds that she is not harassed as a man, Jess is not entirely comfortable passing and chooses to discontinue hormone use. As a transgender man, Jess can be viewed as reinforcing the heterosexual norm, bringing to light the idea that passing, while a personal act, is also highly public.

Because the recognition of specific physical indicators is required, passing necessitates categorization, although such categorization should never be taken as essential; it can be both reassuring and detrimental. The umbrella term *queer* is often used to describe those who align themselves with a nontraditional sexual or gender identity. Different subcultures exist within the queer community, and people who are passing cannot be lumped into one category; rather, the personal nature of passing makes the experience difficult to pin down.

A transgender person might seek to pass as a member of the opposite biological sex, though he or she may not take steps to become physically "true" to that sex; a transsexual person is generally a person who seeks or has successfully sought hormone therapy and/or sexual reassignment surgery. Others who seek to pass as the other-gendered may include, but are certainly not limited to, drag kings and queens, butch lesbians, and femme gay men. While it is generally understood that passing entails becoming or becoming like the opposite biological sex, the **queer theory** introduction of the term *genderqueer* does allow for more intricate subcategorization.

Passing is linked to debates about authenticity and the relevance of authenticity. Third-wave **feminism** and queer theory explore the idea of gender as a social and/or cultural construct and insist on the fallacy of biological determinism. More specifically, the most recent schools of criticism question the link between what it is to be biologically *male* and what it is to be *masculine;* and conversely between what it is to be biologically *female* and what it is to be *feminine*. Because of their instability and inconsistency, the innate biological factors that make a human being male or female, masculine or feminine, have been challenged in recent years. This has led to, among other conclusions, the idea that gender is fluid and, as a socially constructed (or human-made) identity, can be chosen, created, or even altered, rather than simply adhering to the gender that one has been assigned at birth.

Judith Butler in particular has paid close attention to the idea of passing in her groundbreaking work on gender **performance.** Once she had deconstructed the shaky premise of biological gender, she was free to point to the unfair categorizing through stereotype of those who did not fit into the dominant cultural ideas of sex and gender. Butler was one of the first feminist theorists to shed light on the incoherence of gender as a stable signifier. She pointed out that the naturalness of biological gender is simply an idea reinforced by those who wish to maintain the sexual norm, which is maintained through a dominant cultural dialogue. Not only is normative gender enforced but compulsory heterosexual desire is as well. Butler sees the aim of feminist theory as criticism and demolishment of these means of subjectivity, which would make passing a more culturally and socially acceptable act.

Gender performance, then, is the continuous repetition of certain acts that reinforce the ideas of maleness or femaleness, and of masculinity or femininity. Because sex and gender have no citable origin or because the original is an unstable construct, the result is simply a copy of a copy that will never live up to its heteronormative ideal. Therefore, Butler stresses the irony of **drag,** the performance of something other than what is "real"—and proposes that drag performance and passing (although the two are certainly not identical) are, as with biologically determined gender, subject to the discourse or cultural constructs that designate and therefore suppress people according to the dominant norms of gender and power. The difference between drag and passing manifests in the irony of drag—drag lends parody to gender, mocking gender's lack of stable origin, while the act of passing can be seen as a striving toward an essential norm. It is precisely this thrust toward gender **essentialism** that passing aims to achieve. While drag is usually a conscious performance, passing is more performative, an unconscious and continuous reiteration of qualities that signify a specific identity.

The obsession with realness in successful passing is based then, at least in Western tendencies, on the link between identity and visibility. The ability to read gender on the body essentially validates, or makes real, identity. Consequently, discussion of invisibility has also centered on this idea. Because, for example, a femme lesbian woman can sometimes be read as a straight woman, this renders her sexuality invisible; essentially she is passing as straight, whether intentionally or not.

Invisibility is an issue not only for some members of the homosexual community, but also for some members of certain ethnic groups, such as Italians or Jews, whose ethnicity cannot be immediately or certainly located on their bodies. Theorists sometimes use the term *illegibility* interchangeably with invisibility. In rhetorical practice, identity erasure is extremely detrimental because it results in a lack of written record and eventually a lack in proof of existence or realness.

Although Judith Butler has mainstreamed the fallacy/instability of gender within the academy, in practice, passing is very much associated with being as true as possible to the desired gender. While feminist and queer intellectual discussion tends to center around gender fluidity, the pertinent issue for someone who is passing is not fluidity, but rather crossing to the other side of the sexual binary, even as scholars seek to dissolve this binary. While drag can be seen as ironic and fluid in that to succeed in drag one must generally leave a hint of one's "innate" gender visible, passing is completely the opposite and prefers for "biology" to remain hidden.

Because passing requires the recognition of what is visibly real (or not), identity creation and detection can become a source of anxiety. Passing is a struggle to be visible—but visible in a deliberate light. It also forces the model of the real to be revealed as fantastic, or unstable, even as there was no stable model of gender or other identity to begin with. For a man to pass as a woman, or a gay person to pass as straight, is to question what gender is at all; what makes a woman a woman, and so on? The act of passing sets in motion the fluidity of gender cited in theoretical discourse and, at the same time, can defy the notion of fluidity by fitting neatly into a heterosexual normative model.

The attempt to pass as an authentic member of the opposite gender clearly poses some dilemmas. Gender can be viewed as both repressive and productive—in that it is capable of producing meaning, vocabulary, and language. While meaning is created by the person attempting to pass ("I am a woman!"), meaning is also created by the spectator ("Yes, you are," or "You are in drag/masculine woman/lesbian," etc.). Sometimes, members of the group that a nonmember is trying to pass as a member of become offended by the inorganic, or fantastic, replication of their likeness. For example, transgender people were not, until very recently, allowed to attend the Michigan Womyn's Music Festival because they were not biologically female. Controversy still surrounds the issue of who "counts" as a real woman, pointing to the discursive and socially constructed nature of gender.

Kate Bornstein has also challenged the authenticity of gender. By pointing out the multiple interpretations of maleness and femaleness, and the legitimacy of claiming something outside of this binary as one's gender, she points to not only the harmlessness of passing, but the irony of the weight that gender carries in Western society. Through passing and other forms of gender transgression, gender becomes entirely malleable and challenges the dominant ideals of gender and sexuality. If one views gender as a continuum, with maleness and femaleness somewhere on the spectrum, without seeing spectrum as a binary, then passing is a part of the whole, and not outside the realm of gender and sexual possibility.

In terms of transgender versus transsexual people and passing, disagreement has arisen both from members of the LGBTQ community who do not attempt to pass, and from those who do. Arguably, transsexuals may be beyond the point of passing, but transversely, they can remain in a constant state of *trying* to pass, as their gender is given double-take readings by those they encounter. In some cases, different groups, for example, cross-dressing gay men and lesbians versus male-to-female and female-to-male transsexuals, have each laid claim on the authenticity or realness of their identity. The difference between identifying as transgender versus transsexual may be mainly steeped in medical rhetoric: generally transsexual people identify as those who have had or want to have sexual reassignment surgery or who take hormones to achieve their desired gender. Those who identify as transgender people may or may not engage or wish to engage in this practice, but still identify in opposition to their biologically assigned gender.

Authenticity is at stake, and even within the *other*-category of "genderqueerness," a contest over realness exists. Successful passing requires the *recognition* of the person attempting to pass by members of the group they are trying to pass as. Passing transgender persons may view passing transsexuals as sell-outs or traitors to the queer subcategory. Tranversely, transsexual persons may view passing transgender persons as too afraid to make a medical transition.

The somewhat ambiguous subcategory of transgender allows for gender fluidity under the heading of *queer*, because transgender as a category of identity can embrace a host of genderqueer variations that may overlap or incorporate each other, as opposed to the discursively stricter categories of homosexuality and transsexuality. However, unlike homosexuality, affects related to transgenderism are currently pathologized in the psychiatric health care manual, the *Diagnostic and Statistical Manual of Mental Disorders*, fourth edition (*DSM-IV*). Related to transgenderism, and the proclivity for passing and even pursuing transsexuality, are gender identity disorder and gender dysphoria. These categories explain and make deviant, in medical discourse, genderqueer tendencies. While homosexuality was removed from pathology in 1974, gender identity disorder and gender dysphoria, despite protest, remain listed as mental illness.

The classification of transgenderism as mental illness is problematic for members of the transgender community who want to pass without changing their sex: most medical doctors do not understand the transgender position (as they have been taught to view it as pathological) and therefore will often recommend sexual reassignment surgery whether it is suitable to the patient's desires or not. For people who live their lives outside the sexual binary and are content to present themselves this way, this is not a feasible solution, and the suggestion not only is a gross misinterpretation of the patient, but also undermines the agency and goals of passing.

Passing is not simply a medical or superficial arrangement, however; it is deeply imbedded in cultural practice and social interpretation. Some postoperative transsexuals claim their new identity in the same way a biological member of the same sex does, and some refer to themselves as trans- (man or woman); but in all cases, gender identity relies on interpretation and social identification. *Readability* is the ability to "see through" the attempt at passing—to be read is to be unsuccessful. No matter the medical alteration or modified mannerism, if one can be read as a parody, one has not passed.

The act of passing implies an amalgamation of the personal and the private, along with both an intra- and extra-community struggle to define the real. Passing is not based in deception, though it can be interpreted by those reading it as such; instead, passing is about identity creation and self-definition. Within the lenses of queer theory and third-wave feminism, the act of passing also points to both the amorphous nature of gender and its constantly reinscribed normative ideals. Sometimes, it is a matter of survival, other times a personal choice. Passing at its most essential is the act of realizing desire.

Further Reading

Battle, Juan, Cathy J. Cohen, DorianWarren, Gerard Fergerson, and Suzette Audam. 2002. *Say It Loud: I'm Black and I'm Proud*. NewYork: Policy Institute of the National Gay and Lesbian Task Force.

Bornstein, Kate. 1998. *My Gender Workbook: How to Become a Real Man, a Real Woman, the Real You, or Something Else Entirely*. New York: Routledge.

Halberstam, Judith. 2005. *In a Queer Time and Place: Transgender Bodies, Subcultural Lives.* New York: New York University Press.

Nestle, Joan, Clare Howell, and Riki Wilchins. 2002. *Genderqueer: Voices from Beyond the Sexual Binary.* Los Angeles: Alyson Books.

Sanchez, Maria Carla, and Linda Schlossberg, eds. 2001. *Passing: Identity and Interpretation in Sexuality, Race, and Religion.* Sexual Cultures: New Directions from the Center of Lesbian and Gay Studies, ed. Jose Esteban Munoz and Ann Pellegrini. New York: New York University Press.

Smith-Rosenberg, Carroll. 1989. "Discourses of Sexuality and Subjectivity: The New Woman, 1870–1936." In *Hidden from History: Reclaiming the Gay and Lesbian Past,* ed. Martin Duberman, Martha Vicinus, and George Chauncey, 264–80. New York: New American Library.

Melanie Beaudette

Robert Patrick (1937–)

Born in Kilgore, Texas, Robert Patrick's several hundred productions off-off-Broadway in New York (the first was *The Haunted Host*, Caffe Cino, 1964) led to several dozen publications of plays in many languages and one worldwide success (*Kennedy's Children*, London, 1975). He has also published a greatly romanticized and fictionalized novel of the early days of off-off-Broadway, *Temple Slave* (1994), and an autobiography in the form of movie critiques, *Film Moi* or *Narcissus in the Dark* (2001). Travels to encourage small theaters and school theaters in the United States and abroad from 1973 through 1990 led to his being nicknamed Johnny Theatreseed and receiving the 1980 International Thespian Society's Founders Award for services to theater and to youth. Other Awards and honors include the Show Business Award for the 1968–1969 season (for *Fog, Joyce Dynel*, and *Salvation Army*); the Omni One-Act Award in 1973 for *Angel, Honey, Baby, Darling, Dear*; nomination for a special *Village Voice* Obie Award in 1973; first prize in 1973 for *Kennedy's Children* in Glasgow, Scotland, from the Citizens Theatre's International Play contest; a Rockefeller Foundation playwright-in-residence grant in 1973; a Creative Artists Public Service grant in 1976; inclusion of *My Cup Ranneth Over* in *Best Short Plays 1979*; the Janus Award in 1983; a *"Blue-Is-for-Boys* Weekend" proclaimed by Manhattan Borough presidents (1983 and 1986); and the Bill Whitehead Award for Lifetime Achievement in Gay and Lesbian Literature in 1996. The La Mama Archives and the Billy Rose Collection at the Lincoln Center Library of the Performing Arts (both in New York City) maintain extensive archives of his work and life.

Further Reading

Stone, Wendell. "Robert Patrick Bio." Available at: http://hometown.aol.com/rbrtptrck/myhomepage/fan. Accessed July 14, 2008.

Douglas Turnbaugh

Emma Pérez (1954–)

Emma Pérez, born in El Campo, Texas, is a noted professor, historian, creative writer, and feminist theorist. Her experiences of oppression and survival growing up Chicana in the contested space of South Texas is reflected in her literary, theoretical, and historical writings. In 1982, Pérez was one of the founding members of *Mujeres Activas en Letras y Cambio Social* (MALCS), an organization comprised of working-class Chicanas involved in higher education and struggles for social justice. Pérez earned her doctorate in history from the University of California, Los Angeles, in 1988 and is an associate professor of ethnic studies at the University of Colorado.

Pérez first published her widely reprinted essay, "Sexuality and Discourse: Notes from a Chicana Survivor," in the seminal anthology *Chicana Lesbians: The Girls Our Mothers Warned Us About* (1991). In this essay, Pérez theorized *"un sitio y una lengua"* (a space and a language) that affirm Chicana sociosexual agency while rejecting colonialism and capitalist patriarchy. *Gulf Dreams* (1996), Pérez's first novel, is set in a fictional rural Texas coastal town where the Chicana narrator falls into unrequited love with her childhood friend, "the young woman." The narrative in this novel weaves between a loose linear structure with characters trapped in desire, abuse, and omnipresent racism and the realm of dreams where the narrator confronts repressed memories and begins to imagine a future where love is possible. Pérez's recent work *The Decolonial Imaginary: Writing Chicanas into History* is a historical, theoretical interrogation of the elision of Chicanas in Chicano historiography. *The Decolonial Imaginary* is considered a key text in the fields of historical methodology, Chicano/a studies, and postcolonial studies. Currently, Pérez is working on two creative projects: a historical novel entitled *Forgetting the Alamo, or, Blood Memory* and *Las Shameless Sisters*, which she describes as a "chica lesbian lit" novel.

See also Chicana feminism; class.

Further Reading

Alarcón, Norma, ed. 1993. *Chicana Critical Issues*. Berkeley, CA: Third Woman Press.
de la Torre, Adela, and Beatriz M. Pesquera, eds. 1993. *Building with Our Hands: New Directions in Chicana Studies*. California: University of California Press.

Lena McQuade

performance artists

Performance art is vital to queer history and culture for the aesthetic space it provides queer politics, queer identity interrogation, and the expression of queer voice. The body of work that falls under the tenuously defined field of performance art is by no means fixed or stable, drawing influences from a multitude of disciplines, such as film, dance, visual art, literature, theater, and social protest. Although the foundations to what is termed performance art can be traced throughout history, the genre is commonly identified as emerging following World War II. At this historical moment, occurring almost simultaneously in Japan, the United States, and Europe, many visual artists sought directly to interrogate the physical body as the site of artistic form and content. The body brought the artist closer to life experience, as physical process was emphasized over the production of commodified objects. Performance art practices emerged in the years following the Holocaust and Hiroshima, a historical moment that forced many people, including visual artists, to reconsider the depths of human destruction and bodily vulnerability. By engaging in the immediacy of the material body, rather than the art object, performance art ushers in discussions of time, space, and audience relationship. Challenging formalist purity, embracing the body as a site for artistic inquiry and exploration is loaded with social and political content that cannot be erased from the form. The urgency that is inherent to live performance has a tradition in queer politics, such as guerrilla street performances and political actions of groups like **ACT UP** and **Queer Nation,** as well as numerous solo LGBTQ performance artists.

Post–World War II, performance art was explored and articulated in many artistic movements over the next several decades, such as Dadaism, Futuri, the Gutai Group, the Bauhaus, Fluxus, abstract expressionism, Kaprow's "happenings," and the work of **John Cage** and Merce Cunningham. Performance art, by its very nature, is fleeting, limited to the time and space shared by audience and artist. It toys with the boundaries of art and life, theatricality and identity. The elusive practice of performance art is unique in its refusal to define itself through traditional art disciplines. Unlike painting and sculpture, which were heavily steeped in white, patriarchal, and heterosexist traditions, performance art became a site where women, gays and lesbians, and artists of color could freely cultivate their own voices and aesthetic practices.

Fluxus artist Geoffrey Hendricks's work mirrors a shift in gay history, as he grew up in pre-Stonewall America and, like many gay men and woman, attempted to lead a heterosexual life by marrying and raising children. In 1971, he created a series of works that mirrored the new claimed visibility that Stonewall represented. In Flux Divorce, Hendricks and his wife of 10 years, Bici Forbes, **came out** as gay and lesbian in a grand gesture. They took division of property to an extreme performance in their backyard, slicing all of their assets into halves, including their home, their furniture, and their marriage certificate. In Dream Event, Hendricks spent 48 hours in bed, within a gallery, sleeping, fasting, and recording his dreams. Embodying the motto of "out of the closets, into the streets," this piece played with boundaries between the public and the private. Hendricks symbolized his coming out in Body/Hair, where he shaved his entire body, from the neck down, in a gesture of renewal.

There is a community of contemporary queer artists like Hendricks who approach performance from a strong visual arts perspective. Mel Andringa, codirector of Legion Arts (originally Drawing Legion in the 1980s), blurs art history and

autobiography, using the biographical information of famous artists in history in relation to his own personal experiences. Andringa's work incorporates live painting that comments on a constructed history of art that silences and erases queer presence. Legion Arts, founded by Andringa and F. John Herbert in 1991, is an independent, nonprofit, grassroots organization dedicated to producing and presenting multimedia performance. Mark McCusker founded the Iowa-based artist collective Habeas Corpus, whose work is strongly tied to the immediacy of the body itself as the site and creator of art making. Extending from the proliferation of body art from the 1970s and early 1980s, Habeas Corpus, including McCusker and husband Darrell Taylor, continue producing work that centralizes the body, while incorporating multiple forms of media. Habeas Corpus defines itself through its dedication to community building and service to multiple social groups that are underserved or marginalized.

Although by no means discrete, a second body of contemporary performance work follows a narrative tradition. Foundational to the intensified interest in performance art in the 1970s was the feminist assertion that "the personal is political," which informed a strong shift toward queer autobiographical work in the 1980s. The personal narrative became a tool for queer performers to speak their own desires, loves, and experiences, seeking to disrupt master narratives of heteronormativity. In the wake of the AIDS epidemic, and the government's despicable silence for years following the initial outbreak, much performance work responded with overt expressions of anger, outrage, mourning, and loss. Diamanda Galás's Plague Mass explores the anguish, sorrow, pain, and terror of the AIDS epidemic, to which her brother, playwright Philip-Dimitri Galás, was lost. Using her operatically trained three-and-a-half-octave range, she howls and wails with piercing agony, interweaving biblical text, to unleash a haunting indictment against the Roman Catholic Church and society as a whole.

Performance forefronts the artist's body, offering a space where silenced populations, such as queers of color, can interrogate and explore dominant discourses. Cuban American lesbian performance artist Alina Troyano, more commonly known by her stage persona Carmelita Tropicana, strategically uses humor and **camp** for political intervention. Creating a persona that adopts an over-the-top Cuban accent and exaggerated showgirl costuming, Tropicana plays off the 1950s Cuban stereotypes of Ricky Ricardo and the Club Tropicana. Marga Gomez (see **comedians**) began her career as a stand-up comic in the 1980s. Gomez is the writer and performer of several comedic performance pieces, which parody and deconstruct representations of Chicanas and lesbians. Monica Palacios, the Latin Lezbo Comic, uses stand-up comedy, along with dramatic monologue and autobiography as a means of articulating, examining, and theorizing the complex tensions of Chicana, lesbian, and female identity. Justin Chin is a performer/writer whose work is an ironic and potentially psychotic exploration of queer Asian bodies and cultural hybridity. Performer Luis Alfaro's work began in the 1980s on the West Coast and garnered him national attention as a performer, playwright, and poet, as a recipient of a McArthur Foundation Fellowship, and as a member of the New Dramatists. Alfaro's work, strongly influenced by his upbringing in downtown **Los**

Angeles, eloquently and fearlessly interrogates intersections of race, class, gender, and sexualities.

Throughout the 1980s, several important performance spaces emerged that provided artists a home to build community and experiment with voice and form. The WOW Café, which began in 1980 as an international women's theater festival, has remained dedicated to its mission of "the empowerment of women through the performing arts" (Martin 1996, 42). Self-described as a "home for wayward girls" with a stage that Holly Hughes suggests is "not much bigger than a g-spot" (Hughes and Román 1998, 13), the WOW Café was a foundational space for such female artists as Karen Finley, Terry Galloway, Marga Gomez, and Hughes. Also in 1980, Charles Moulton, Charles Dennis, and Tim Miller founded P.S. 122, transforming an abandoned public school in New York into a performance center that has remained a vital site for experimental work for over 25 years. In the late 1980s, Miller and writer Linda Frye Burnham founded the Highways space in Santa Monica, California.

While the notion of mainstream performance art is fairly oxymoronic, a 1990 political debate surrounding National Endowment for the Arts (NEA) funding and obscenity ushered Tim Miller, Holly Hughes, Karen Finley, and John Fleck (the "NEA Four") into the national spotlight. Each of the four received federal grants, which were refused for approval by NEA chair John Frohnmayer under the "general standards of decency and respect for the diverse beliefs and values of the American public" (Schlossman 2002, 251). A congressional committee, following North Carolina Senator Jesse Helms's campaign to restrict funding to Robert Mapplethorpe and Andres Serrano, drafted these standards. The standards denied funding to art that "may be considered obscene, including, but not limited to, depictions of sadomasochism, homoeroticism, the sexual exploitation of children, or individuals engaged in sex acts and which, when taken as a whole, do not have serious literary, artistic, political, or scientific value" (Stiles and Selz 1996, 274). The NEA Four sued for the reinstatement of their grants, as well as a rewording of the charter. While the 1993 decision awarded the artists their grants, the "decency" charter remains.

Each of the NEA Four produced work that explicitly engages with issues of sexuality (three of the four identify as gay or lesbian). Lesbian performance artist and playwright Holly Hughes entered the art world as an abstract painter, but shifted to satirical, campy narrative productions about contemporary life as a lesbian. An early performer at the WOW Café, Hughes's often-controversial work offers an unflinching view of lesbian culture, as well as her personal experiences with family, loss, and **homophobia.** Her work seeks to challenge social taboos and has been both criticized and praised from inside and outside the queer community. Tim Miller studied dance with Merce Cunningham in the 1980s in New York and began developing a series of pieces over the last few decades surrounding themes of gay male desire, personal narrative, the body, and LGBTQ issues. Both an artist and an outspoken activist for the queer community, Miller's work balances outrage with vulnerability, politicized rant with intimate audience interaction, and it strategically uses nudity in a climate where AIDS and homophobia stigmatize the gay male body. In more recent work, Miller explores issues of gay marriage and citizenship.

Karen Finley does not identify as gay or lesbian, but her controversial body of work is a wailing, unforgiving, and unsettling indictment of homophobia, conservativism, violence toward women, and female objectification. In earlier works, such as her collaborations with the Kipper Kids, Finley was highly controversial for her use of body, bodily fluids, bodily excrement, and various food materials to disrupt and comment on the purified and sexualized consumption of the female body. Finley is one of the few performance artists to achieve some mainstream success as a regular guest on Politically Incorrect, on club remixes in the 1980s, and playing a doctor in the film *Philadelphia*. Within a few months' span, Finley was featured in *Playboy* and awarded *Ms.* magazine's Woman of the Year Award.

John Fleck's performance work engages in social critique in less overtly activist forms than the rest of the NEA Four. Coming from a Los Angeles tradition, and working with artists like Rachel Rosenthal, Fleck's work uses metaphor, poetry, self-effacing humor, rants, improvisation, song, and sound to craft a series of works that gained attention in clubs in Los Angeles's 1980s punk scene. Although a gay male, he contends that his work is more about gender than sexual identity, interrogating masculinity, femininity, dysfunction, and contemporary culture.

Another prominent queer performer from the 1980s Los Angeles punk scene is Vaginal Crème Davis (name inspired by Angela Davis), who performs radically resistant "terrorist" drag. While a punk artist, Davis's work examines issues of black, Chicana, and queer identity through multiple personas, sometimes accompanied by her Motown-inspired backup singers, the Afro Sisters. One of her many personas, Clarence, is a militiaman who she performs in white face, a stringy black beard, and lipstick. Davis uses humor, camp, and shock to construct an unapologetically queer, highly sexualized, and identity-resistant performance that calls out the purified, mainstream-friendly drag queens like RuPaul. In one performance, Davis is reported to have inserted an entire apple pie into a participant's rectum and then had him defecate it onto an American flag.

As with the NEA Four, media attention to performance art has traditionally been limited to sensationalism and misrepresentation. Ron Athey, an HIV-infected performance artist, drew a tremendous amount of publicity for incorporating blood in his work. In a performance at the Walker Center in 1994, Athey used surgical paper to make blood prints from small incisions made on the back of Daryl Carlton. These prints were strung up on a clothesline above the audience, on a pulley, for audience display. The media falsely reported that these images dripped blood on the audience, who then frantically scrambled in a panic. As this performance was NEA funded, these false reports were further exploited for political gain. The media's sensationalism, in spite of the absence of any threat to the audience, testifies to the fear and ignorance surrounding gay male bodies and HIV transmission as late as 1994. Although Athey had been performing since 1981, exploring themes of sacrification, ritual, religious iconography, his Pentecostal upbringing, and sadomasochism, the 1994 controversy led to a denial of funding or access to publicly funded spaces in the United States.

While performance art usually forefronts the artist's body and rarely achieves mainstream attention outside of sensationalism, there is one interesting exception to both of these tendencies. Wayland Flowers is the puppeteer behind the sarcastic, campy, unattractive, tiara-wearing, old-crone cult character "Madame." Flowers performed with his adult-themed puppet in gay bars and clubs, offering biting commentary on men and sex, similar to the style of many drag queens. Soon "Madame" became a television regular, appearing on talk shows, *Laugh-In, Solid Gold,* and *Hollywood Squares,* and eventually landed her own show in the 1980s, *Madame's Place.* While "Madame" was far more famous than her creator, and Flowers's body was always absent from these performances, Flowers remains an important figure in early gay performance for his highly successful mediation of camp humor into American households. Flowers brought risqué sexual innuendo, bawdy gay sensibility, and gay desire to mainstream audiences in a time when gay and lesbian voices were strongly censured in popular culture. Flowers, a victim of the AIDS epidemic, died in 1988 with little public attention to the man behind "Madame."

John Epperson is most known as the creator of the "glamour goddess" Lypsinka, the New York–based drag queen who is famous for her meticulous lip-synching cabaret act. She began her career performing in her own off-Broadway show, and since that time, Lypsinka has had several follow-up cabaret shows, has appeared in multiple advertisements, is a regular at Wigstock, and has appeared in several films. Epperson has also performed the solo piece Show Trash as himself, performing and reflecting on his own voice and identity.

Performance art continues to develop, define, and redefine itself early into the new millennium. From subversive entertainment, like the Backdoor Boys, a drag king parody of boy bands, to the continued emphasis on autobiography, to the extensions of performance art that remain situated in the visual arts, performance remains a space of potential disruption, intervention, and invention of sexual identities. Although the form has no clear boundaries, informing, stealing from, and influencing dance, music, theater, stand-up, and the visual arts, performance remains a space for experimentation, politicized aesthetics, and the forefronting of the queer body.

Further Reading

Hughes, Holly, and David Román, eds. 1998. *O Solo Homo: The New Queer Performance*. New York: Grove Press.

Martin, Carol. 1996. "The WOW Café." *A Sourcebook on Feminist Theatre and Performance* 1(3): 42–51.

Muñoz, José Esteban. 1999. *Disidentifications: Queers of Color and the Performance of Politics*. Minneapolis: University of Minnesota Press.

Román, David. 1998. *Acts of Intervention: Performance, Gay Culture, and Aids*. Bloomington: Indiana University Press.

Schlossman, David A. 2002. *Actors and Activists: Politics, Performance, and Exchange among Social Worlds*. New York and London: Routledge.

Solomon, Alisa. 1985. "The WOW Café." *The Drama Review: TDR* 29(1): 92–101.

Stiles, Kristine, and Peter Selz, eds. 1996. Theories and Documents of Contemporary Art: A Sourcebook of Artists' Writing. Berkeley: University of California Press.

Yenawine, Philip, Marianne Weems, and Brian Wallis. 1999. *Art Matters: How the Culture Wars Changed America*. New York: New York University Press.

Dustin B. Goltz

performativity

A concept introduced by American philosopher and queer theorist Judith Butler, performativity offers an explication of how we come to be gendered and sexual subjects, though it has been taken up and applied to other aspects of **identity** as well, such as race, class, and ethnicity. Butler argues that gendered identities are not something that we *are* in some natural or innate sense, but rather something that we *do*, and that it is only as these repeated acts of "doing" gender become sedimented over time that one comes to be a man or a woman (or a **butch** or a **femme** or **transgendered**, and so on). Performativity has been tremendously influential on contemporary understandings of gender and sexuality both inside and outside of the academy. Within the humanities and social sciences, it has been a foundational concept in **queer theory** in that it emphasizes the constructedness and contingency of gay and lesbian identities; this represents a shift away from the more identity-based paradigm of earlier gay and lesbian scholarship that emphasized the fixity and persistence of those identities.

Butler's earliest iterations of the theory of performativity emphasized its theatrical aspects, using the example of **drag** as the model for the acquisition of gender per se and not just gay and lesbian identities, but also normative genders. A parodic repetition of the norm can have the effect of undoing or unseating that norm by exposing it as an impossible ideal, though not all performances of gender are parodic. "Gender," she writes, "is a kind of imitation for which there is no original" (Butler 2004, 1). Butler emphasizes that those instances of gender that would seem to be least hyperbolic are just as performed as more apparently theatrical genders, and that normative identities, too, are comprised of a set of labors that attempt to achieve an impossible ideal. But heterosexuality covers the tracks of its own performance and conceals its nature—a series of ritualized repetitions of acts in accordance with a norm. In this way, heterosexuality becomes *naturalized*. Butler notes that the consolidation of heterosexuality as "natural" comes only after homosexuality is diagnosed as pathological. The dismissal of queer gender roles as imitative or debased copies of heterosexuality (for instance, the charge that a **butch** is only pretending to be a man) installs heterosexuality as primary only retroactively and with recourse to a previously existing homosexuality, since the notion of "original" necessarily relies on the idea of a copy. Butler insists that both gender norms and sexual norms work coercively even though they are not primarily experienced as prohibitive; these norms reactively install themselves

Quentin Crisp, well known for the self-conscious creation of sexual dissidence by his dress and manner. Photo by Robert Pruzan, courtesy of the Gay, Lesbian, Bisexual, Transgender Historical Society, San Francisco.

as foundational and original in order to discipline more wayward forms of gender, even as the emergence of those wayward or errant forms of queer gender occasion and therefore precede heterosexuality itself.

In each of these instances, gender is not given or fixed but is capable of being changed, reworked, and embodied differently in each instant that it is performed. Gender is a constant practice, rather than a final accomplishment. But we are so accustomed to understanding markers of identity as material aspects of personhood that we read those performances of gender as if they were occasioned by something called "sex" rather than the other way around. The performance of gender, particularly when it is unthought and seamless, causes us to posit a causal "thing" behind it, called "sex." In fact, Butler claims, this structure works in the opposite way: that instead of a material reality called "sex" causing the behaviors of gender, the repeated behaviors of gender lead us to conjure up material sex as a probable cause of "compulsory heterosexual identities, those ontologically consolidated phantasms of 'man' and 'woman' are theatrically produced effects that posture as grounds, origins, the normative measure of the real" (1990: 24–25).

Gender is an action rather than a thing, or more properly a thing that comes to be so only *through* action as gender itself becomes literalized at the level of the body through its performance. Gender is comprised over time through repeated and ritualized actions that *more or less* conform to cultural expectations about how men and women should behave (differently!), and those repeated actions coalesce into something that is misrecognized as natural (hence "naturalized") or as an essential substance. There is no "I" who might ponder and reflect on how to instrumentally perform her gender; there is no pregendered agent who might act to choose gender, but rather becoming a gendered subject is the effect of this performance. As Butler claims, citing Nietzsche, there is no doer behind the deed.

The roots of Butler's theory of gender performativity can be genealogically traced and schematized through four different regions of philosophical thought. *First* is the notion of becoming a woman in the feminist philosophy of Simone de Beauvoir and Monique Wittig. *Second* is the category of the linguistic performative as it is articulated in analytic philosophy. *Third* is Derrida's idea of deconstruction. *Fourth* is the relationship between power and subjectivity, encompassing not only the reconfigured topography of the self offered by psychoanalysis, but also by a certain strain of social theory, typified by Foucault and Althusser. Common to all of these approaches is an insistence on the importance of language to our self-understanding.

BECOMING A WOMAN

Butler's understanding of gender as *becoming* is in part derived from a feminist tradition in philosophy that understands "woman" to be not simply a condition of ontological givenness. It has been argued that all feminist understandings of gender have some point of origin in Simone de Beauvoir's assertion that "One is not born a woman, but becomes one." Beauvoir's intervention offers a corrective to the nearly ubiquitous masculine presumption of the Western subject, and challenges the understanding of "woman" as a naturally and eternally fixed essence. Beauvoir claims that the category of "woman" is an historically contingent cultural achievement, a provocation that continues to inform current debates about the nature of sex, gender, and sexuality (see **essentialism vs. constructionism** debates). Butler also engages a number of other feminist thinkers, particularly Monique Wittig, who insist that as there is a normative idea of sexuality already embedded in the very notion of male or female, a **lesbian** is not a woman; she is disqualified because she violates the normative insistence that women, in order to be "proper" women, must be heterosexual. Performativity builds on these traditions by suggesting that gendered being is a matter of becoming, but also by offering a way to explain *how* one becomes a woman or a man.

THE LINGUISTIC PERFORMATIVE

The most salient, and perhaps the most misunderstood attribute of the theory of performativity is its emphasis on creation, its insistence that the performance of gender brings about gender itself. This aspect of performativity *as a theory* can best be understood as originating with J. L. Austin, a linguistic philosopher who distinguishes two kinds of speech acts: constative and performative utterances. Constative utterances are descriptive utterances; they describe or name things in the world. Most of our language, Austin says, is constative, but there is a special category of speech acts that Austin terms performative. A statement is performative when it does not just *refer to* or *describe* something, but rather it *enacts* and *achieves* the very thing that it purports to describe. Austin offers the marriage vow ("I thee wed"), vows in general ("I promise"), and apologies ("I'm sorry") as examples of performative utterances. In each of these instances, a speaker's utterance is not simply reporting on a marriage vow, a promise, or an apology, but actually enacting them through speech. Butler takes up this idea and utilizes the performative beyond a strictly linguistic framing to argue that gender works in just this way; she shows that how we speak about gender and the norms that regulate it have the effect of bringing about a gendered subject, one who does not preexist those norms. She has also analyzed the performative nature of political discourses on homosexuality, including homophobic hate speech and the military's "don't ask, don't tell" policy, in *Excitable Speech: A Politics of the Performative* (1997).

DECONSTRUCTION AND ITERABILITY

Another crucial aspect of performativity is its engagement with the deconstructive theory of Jacques Derrida and Paul DeMan. Still at issue are questions of language and of creation, but the stakes of language shift from the contractual and logical emphasis of analytic philosophy to the more literary methods of continental philosophy. Performativity in this domain becomes a practice of reading or interpretation rather than defining the parameters for a specific set of utterances. It has been suggested by Angela McRobbie, for example, that *Gender Trouble* is itself a performative text that enacts the very trouble it describes in the fields of philosophy, feminist theory, and lesbian and gay studies.

In his essay on Kafka's "Before the Law," Derrida asks after a paradox at the heart of subject formation, a paradox that Butler will read as central to the project of becoming a legible self through performing gender: we misapprehend as an essence that which is produced as an effect of what we ourselves enact or perform. Derrida suggests that we become subjects of the law through this misrecognition; Butler suggests that the law of gender works in this same way, and that the relationship postulating sex as the cause of gender relies on a similar misapprehension. We can therefore understand performativity to be a specifically deconstructionist (and generally poststructuralist) endeavor in several ways. There is a resistance to understanding structures—of gender, of sexual organization, of kinship, and so on—as absolutely determinative and determining. Performativity understands there to be an intervention possible at the structural level of gender; indeed, understanding gender as performative secures the space for that intervention. Social structures of gender enjoin us to certain norms, but we can become gendered in excess or defiance of (though never *independent from*) those norms, particularly if we are queer or genderqueer. Thus, a pure structuralism would not be able to carefully account for those identities and lives that are not normatively gendered and heterosexual. Deconstruction and performativity both insist that there are fissures in regulatory norms, and regulatory norms are always haunted by that which they repudiate and expel—a haunting that draws the norm and its excluded other inexorably together. (This last insistence on the generative power of the negative is perhaps properly attributed to the Hegelian strain in Butler's thought rather than the Derridian.) Butler terms that structure through which intelligibility of sex and gendered subject positions are distributed and regulated the "heterosexual matrix," and also insists that there can be life outside of these norms.

Performativity also maintains a deconstructive relation to the binary oppositions of man/woman, male/female, sex/gender, nature/culture, and homosexual/heterosexual by dislodging their hierarchical relation to one another and disclosing their mutual dependence. Butler emphasizes that these categories do not describe isolated and unrelated modes of being but rather do their work only in relation to one another. Because of the way performativity reworks and challenges binary oppositions, it helps us understand how seemingly unrelated categories of sex and gender might be compatible—for example, for a female-bodied person to identify with and present as masculine or even as a man. This capacity to perform a gender seemingly at odds with bodily morphology reminds us that these categories are conjoined from habit rather than necessity, that there is no necessary way in which gender must follow from sex. Indeed, Butler offers a critique of the distinction between sex and gender in her insistence that those things that we *are* are inextricably related to those things that we *are not*, and that any category of identity relies for its force and coherence on a limitless field of proximate but disallowed categories. Heterosexuality, for example, needs a concept of homosexuality against which it constantly articulates and distances itself, even as that repeated and anxious comparison is itself a close and constitutive relation. All categories of identity need this idea of the "constitutive outside" in order to function like norms, and this is especially true in the realms of gender and sexuality.

SUBJECTIVITY AND THE LOCATION OF POWER

Performativity is also concerned with questions of power. The idea of power is implicit throughout these other approaches: a performative speech act, for example, must be uttered at the proper time and place before the right audience in order to be a felicitous rather than infelicitous utterance—in order for it to *work* as a performative. The conditions of that utterance are always a matter of power. For example, if I am a lesbian parent, the claims I might make to parenthood with respect to my child or my partner's child might fail to be performative to the extent that the state is invested in sanctioning only heterosexual kinship as legitimate, refusing to recognize my kinship ties in my family as legitimate.

On the question of power, the theory of performativity has been influenced by the work of Michel Foucault. Foucault's insight about power is that it operates not only to prohibit but also to produce and that the operation of power is always at work in the cultural field, never more so than when we say "yes" to an identity or subject position. The very names with which we are allowed to identify, the subject positions available to us, are inscribed within a cultural field of power from which we can never fully disentangle ourselves. Instead of understanding power as outside the subject and acting on her, a dominating and restricting force that acts mainly to restrict behavior, Foucault insists that power shapes what we are able to become in an affirmative sense and that we are always implicated in its workings.

Although much separates Freud and Foucault as thinkers, Freud might be understood as asking this same question at the level of the psychic rather than the social: how is it that we internalize powerful figures of prohibition such that prohibition seems to be located internally rather than externally imposed? In fact, Butler uses these accounts to supplement each other, and the theory of performativity can be understood as splitting the difference between Freud and Foucault. Freud's explication of the subject as an internally partitioned psyche, comprised of identifications external to it and consolidated by repetitions both conscious and unconscious, offers a way to understand how those laws, prohibitions, and powers external to the "me" and other than "myself" nevertheless come to reside inside of me. And yet for Freud this landscape of internal dynamism is situated within an almost-static external universe, a social world that seems quite fixed.

Foucault, in turn, who explicitly rejects a theory of the psyche, offers a canny reading of the ways that culturally particular formations of power shape the domain of intelligibility and what a self can become. And yet without a more nuanced sense of the topography of psychic life, his formulation of repetition can feel both mechanistic and determinist. Butler tempers Foucault's relentless insistence on the power of social norms with Freud's equally unremitting focus on the *failure* of social norms and the psychic consequences of those failures.

RECEPTION

Butler's theory of performativity is first explicated in her 1990 book *Gender Trouble*, and several of Butler's subsequent works were dedicated to revising and elucidating the theory, clarifying the relationship between performativity and bodily materiality in *Bodies That Matter* (1993), between performativity and politics in both *Excitable Speech* (1997) and *Contingency, Hegemony, Universality* (2000), often in response to critiques. The most widely circulated critiques of performativity have tended to fall into two camps, one that argues that performativity is problematic because it treats gender as a matter of inconsequential play (too much freedom), and the second, which argues that the emphasis on gender norms is too deterministic and robs the subject of agency (too little freedom). These criticisms reflect the fact that Butler wants to insist on the importance of both the power of social norms and also the capacity to live life outside of those norms—and to iterate them in ways that cannot be predicted in advance. It is a desire to retain the tension between these two forces that leads her to define gender as "a practice of improvisation within a scene of constraint" (Butler 2004, 1).

Further Reading

Butler, Judith. 1990, 1999. *Gender Trouble: Feminism and the Subversion of Identity*. New York: Routledge.

Butler, Judith. 1993. *Bodies That Matter: On the Discursive Limits of Sex*. New York: Routledge.

Butler, Judith. 1993. "On the Being of Gayness as Necessary Drag." In *The Lesbian and Gay Studies Reader*, ed. Henry Abelove, Michèle Aina Barale, and David M. Halperin. New York: Routledge.

Butler, Judith. 1997. *Excitable Speech*. New York: Routledge.

Butler, Judith. 1997. *The Psychic Life of Power: Theories in Subjection*. Stanford: Stanford University Press.

Butler, Judith. 2004. *Undoing Gender*. New York: Routledge.

Butler, Judith, Ernesto Laclau, and Slavoj Zizek. 2000. *Contingency, Hegemony, Universality: Contemporary Dialogues on the Left*. London: Verso.

Derrida, Jacques. 1992. "Before the Law." In *Acts of Literature*, ed. Derek Attridge, 181–220. New York: Routledge.

Krolokke, Charlotte, and Anne Scott Sorensen. 2005. *Gender Communication Theories and Analyses: From Silence to Performance*. New York: Sage.

Loxley, Simon. 2006. *Performativity*. New York: Routledge.

McRobbie, Angela. 2005. *The Uses of Cultural Studies*. London: Sage.

Sedgwick, Eve Kosofsky. 1985. *Between Men: English Literature and Male Homosexual Desire*. New York: Columbia University Press.

Sedgwick, Eve Kosofsky. 1990. *Epistemology of the Closet*. Berkeley: University of California Press.

Gayle Salamon

Perverts Undermining State Scrutiny (PUSSY)

Perverts Undermining State Scrutiny (PUSSY) is a disbanded anticensorship, pro-sex feminist affinity group in **OutRage!,** a queer direct-action group based out of London. PUSSY included lesbian members of Feminists Against Censorship, lesbian artists, writers and cultural workers, women sex-trade workers, and gay male members of OutRage! In 1991, PUSSY emerged in response to the censorship of

Della Grace's book of lesbian pornography, *Love Bites,* and the second issue of the lesbian sex magazine *Quim.*

PUSSY was a group that applied academic theories to their social and **political activism.** It argued for the protection of lesbian pornography by emphasizing its difference from heterosexual pornography, especially insofar as the former mimics and parodies, rather than imitates, gender norms and heterosex practices. The argument that lesbian pornography creates an autonomous space for lesbian sexuality was also shared and expressed through the activism and writings of Gayle Rubin and Pat (now **Patrick**) **Califia.** Theories that distinguish between mimesis and mimicry can be found in the works of Judith Butler (1990, 1993), Judith Halberstam (1998), and Homi Bhabha (1994).

England's Labour Party was PUSSY's main target regarding official censorship, particularly Dawn Primarolo's Location of Pornographic Materials Bill. PUSSY also fought against censorship and exclusionary tactics imposed by antipornography feminists and some lesbian and gay spaces such as **bookstores** and **bars.** Furthermore, while working under OutRage! on issues like **HIV/AIDS** awareness, PUSSY also challenged its gay members to embrace feminist issues, highlighting the existence of sexism within gay male culture and the need for cross-gender alliances.

Further Reading

Smith, Anna Marie. 1992. "Resisting the Erasure of Queer Sexuality: A Challenge for Queer Activism." In *Modern Homosexualities: Fragments of Lesbian and Gay Experiences,* ed. Kenneth Plummer, 200–216. London: Routledge.

Smith, Anna Marie. 1993. "Outlaws as Legislators: Feminist Anti-Censorship Politics and Queer Activism." In *Pleasure Principles: Politics, Sexuality and Ethics,* ed., Victoria Harwood, David Oswell, Kay Parkinson, and Anna Ward, 20–40. London: Lawrence and Wishart.

Smith, Cherry. 1996. "What Is This Thing Called Queer?" In *The Material Queer: A LesBiGay Cultural Studies Reader,* ed. Donald Morton, 277–85. Boulder, CO: Westview Press.

Jennifer Tyburczy

Carl Phillips (1959–)

Carl Phillips is widely recognized as a major contemporary American poet. A prolific writer, he has published eight books of poetry, as well as a collection of essays titled *Coin of the Realm,* and has received many awards and honors.

Phillips's first book, *In the Blood* (1992), immediately established his distinctive voice, and his work since then has been remarkably consistent in both its themes and its style. A writer who is both black and gay, Phillips (like his contemporary **Reginald Shepherd**) does not write in ways that fit into established categories of black literature. To the very small extent that his poems engage material traditionally thought of as "black," they do so in an oblique and almost offhand manner, indicating that he finds his socially defined blackness to be neither the most important nor the most interesting thing about himself.

Homosexual desire is much more central to Phillips's work. Again, though, his work does not deal with questions of gay identity but with the workings of desire within and between individuals. (Indeed, his poems have tended to move further and further away from social specificity into a landscape of the mind.) In Phillips's work, the barriers between people are much more internally generated than externally imposed. Phillips uses sexuality to explore the connections and distances between lovers and to investigate the often difficult relations of body and mind and of matter and spirit: sex sometimes joins and sometimes separates body and soul. Phillips's poems are full of lovers who, however physically intimate they are, find themselves at an emotional remove from one another. The closeness of two male lovers, skewed mirror images, often ironically emphasizes how far apart they are.

Further Reading

Bennett, Juda. 2003. "Carl Phillips." In *Contemporary Gay American Poets and Playwrights: An A-to-Z Guide*, ed. Emmanuel S. Nelson. Westport, CT: Greenwood Press.

Hennessy, Christopher. 2005. *Outside the Lines: Talking with Contemporary Gay Poets*. Ann Arbor: University of Michigan Press.

Rowell, Charles H. 1998. "An Interview with Carl Phillips." *Callaloo* 21 (1): 204–17.

Shepherd, Reginald. 2005. "Carl Phillips." *The Greenwood Encyclopedia of African-American Literature*, ed. Hans Ostrom and J. David Macey Jr. Westport, CT: Greenwood Press.

Thomas, Max. 2000. "Mighty Lines." *The Iowa Review* 30 (2): 169–75.

Reginald Shepherd

philosophy and ethics

Philosophy is primarily considered an academic discipline, frequently called the "first" discipline, for the roots of many academic fields of study can be traced back to philosophical origins and debates. Philosophy deals with the analysis, critique, and ultimate establishment of coherent intellectual, political, and moral beliefs in an effort to create systems of thought that are consciously and deliberately moving toward the personal and social goals of truth and justice. There are numerous branches of philosophy including political, legal, and social theory; logic and game theory; metaphysics, or the study of reality; epistemology, the study of knowledge; the philosophy of religion; and ethics, which involves the examination of moral beliefs from secular and/or religious positions. There are no doubt LGBTQ philosophers contributing to every branch of philosophy. However, because of the contemporary climate of increased activism and debate about queer rights in the political sphere in the United States and abroad, particularly since the **Stonewall Riots,** perhaps the most visible and greatest impact from members of the queer community in the field of philosophy is found in the realms that deal with social, cultural, political, and ethical problems.

Social philosophers take interest in problems that deal with the nature of the state and society, fields ripe for the concerns of contemporary debates around sexuality and gender identity. Among the most historically notable U.S. social philosophers is W.E.B. Du Bois, whose thinking attended to questions around the principles of civil rights, democratic participation, social pluralism, race and racism, and other fields. Du Bois's contributions to the discipline are significant to the LGBTQ rights philosophers, particularly as they relate to contemporary struggles for equality and justice. Contemporary social philosophers also draw their intellectual lineage (in agreement or disagreement) from the combined influences of critical theory and poststructuralism. Critical theory is largely inherited from the rich intellectual traditions of the German thinker Jürgen Habermas, and poststructuralist thought is highly influenced by French philosopher and psychologist Michel Foucault. Habermas's exhaustive considerations of social dominance and analysis of social transformation lend themselves to any liberatory efforts, as does Foucault's attention to power and the shaping of concepts in historical patterns of thoughts. Both investigative methods emphasize a context-dependent approach to considering truth, which is a posture of exceptional use when questioning, challenging, and attempting to revise and change existing cultural norms and biases, as many contemporary LGBTQ philosophers are doing. The direct engagement with existing societal problems characterizes the work of social philosophers, who avoid considering "imagined" or hypothetical problems in favor of responding to actual policy-based and experientially grounded political and cultural debates.

Since the multiple dimensions of social philosophy respond to real societal problems, the field is rife with probing analyses that relate specifically to the daily lives of gays, lesbians, bisexuals, and transgendered people whose rights are openly undermined, questioned, and debated as the struggle for civil and social equality remains an active part of the U.S. political landscape. Since at this time the U.S. government has made more efforts at exclusion than inclusion for LGBTQ people, the struggle for political gains in the queer community is largely taking place in small overlapping fields of interest ranging from academic circles, legal analysis, and grassroots activism.

In keeping with the practical analysis embedded in the framework of social philosophy, the presence of inquiry in the field about LGBTQ issues emerges largely as those issues have become more publicized, politicized, and debated. Philosophical anthologies and articles dealing with LGBTQ issues reached a heyday in the mid-1990s. No doubt these contributions were in large part a response to the hotly debated U.S. Supreme Court decisions directly impacting the LGBTQ community. The 1988 *Bowers v. Hardwick* decision established that homosexuals do not have a right to sexual privacy, contradicting rights established for single and married heterosexuals in decisions from 1965 and 1972. In *Romer v. Evans* (1996), the Supreme Court determined that governments could not exclude LGBTQ people from seeking legal inclusion in civil rights matters. However, the large failure of legislative efforts at the national level to include specific protections for LGBTQ people against discrimination and harassment and to provide equal rights has led to a widespread grassroots approach, taking place at the level of states and often municipalities. The legal barriers facing LGBTQ rights activists and scholars are tremendous, and while these court decisions relate primarily to partnership, family, and privacy, there are numerous other legal fields under exploration surrounding issues of workplace discrimination, hate crimes and harassment, and other spheres of importance.

At this point, numerous significant contributions to written work in the field of LGBTQ philosophy and ethics have emerged amid these challenges to legal precedents, increased cultural awareness, and attention. A brief overview of this work includes Sarah Lucia Hoagland's *Lesbian Ethics: Toward New Value* (1988); Richard Mohr's *Gays/Justice: A Study of Ethics, Society, and Law* (1988); Timothy F. Murphy's *Gay Ethics: Controversies in Outing, Civil Rights, and Sexual Science* (1994); Claudia Card's *Adventures in Lesbian Philosophy* (1994); Richard Peddicord's *Gay and Lesbian Rights: A Question of Sexual Ethics or Social Justice?* (1996); and *Writing against Heterosexism* (2007), a special issue of *Hypatia: A Journal of Feminist Philosophy*. Simultaneously, the work of the **National Gay and Lesbian Task Force,** the **Human Rights Campaign,** and other national LGBTQ organizations has fueled the political scholarship with direct action, research, and grassroots efforts across the nation to improve overall participation by the LGBTQ community with the political process and has documented the efforts of these struggles. Furthermore, additional institutional recognition of the importance of LGBTQ studies in philosophy is identifiable specifically in the field and practice of academic philosophy through the establishment of a Society for Lesbian and Gay Philosophy and a standing Committee on Lesbian, Gay, Bisexual and Transgender People in the American Philosophical Association (APA). These institutional efforts reflect a disciplinary interest in the advancement of LGBTQ visibility, recognition, and inclusion.

Due to the (currently) contested nature of LGBTQ rights in social, political, and personal settings, it is also worth mentioning the methods of argument commonly used and how opposition to LGBTQ rights is typically framed. Opponents of LGBTQ rights frequently employ philosophic arguments based on myths and cultural assumptions about sexuality. One source that contributes to the maintenance of myths about LGBTQ people stems from religious traditions in the West. Dominant Western religions that uphold a strict definition about sexual morality typically identify the "intent to procreate" and a "commitment through marriage" as quintessential in sexual ethics. Both of these expressed commitments are impossible for LGBTQ-identified individuals. Since debate is at the heart of social philosophy as a means to respond to cultural issues, the opponents to queer rights are frequently critiqued. A philosopher often cited for severely antiqueer arguments is Michael Levin, whose work exemplifies the reductionist efforts to minimize and eliminate the potential "personhood" of queer-identified folks. *Personhood* is a philosophical term employed as a shorthand notion to link those features that establish an individual's status as a morally relevant being. When antiqueer theorists and groups reduce people to a single axis of identity (their sexuality and gender identity), this negates the recognition of individuals' complexity or multiple identities (in ethnic or racial identification, gender identity, physical ability, religious affiliations, and other social groups or family membership, for instance). The reductionist approach to assessing queer rights, as such, reinforces the social status of hetero-sexual privilege as normative, and the (queer) other is effectively marginalized. Notably, like many antiqueer thinkers and political activists' approaches, Levin's work explicitly deals with only male homosexual identity, basically ignoring and rejecting from serious consideration the social issues raised by questions of rights for lesbians, bisexuals of any gender, and trans-identified people. As such, reductionist positions against queer rights like these often take a rigid stance postulating that male homosexuality is representative of the whole queer community. The erasure of lesbian, bisexual, and transgender possibility is evident throughout many reduc-tionist attempts to present caricatures of queer possibility by substituting focused attention, frequently on particular subgroups as generic for the whole population of the LGBTQ community.

Ethics, closely related to social philosophy, is another fundamental branch of study typically understood as consisting of three core areas: meta-ethics, substantive ethics, and applied ethics. Meta-ethics, the most abstract form of inquiry, deals pri-marily with the analysis of morality through the assessment of logical and linguistic aspects of the moral domain. Substantive ethics focuses on creating and evaluating moral theories and their attempts at creating guides for ethical decision making; these approaches within the field center around determining the courses for right and wrong actions, rather than evaluating language or semantics as in metaethics. Applied ethics, then, deals with practical applications of moral theories, profes-sional ethics codes, and attempts to assess real-world problems from ethical frame-works. The fields most consistently applicable for LGBTQ inquiry are substantive and applied ethics, which engage in considerations and analysis of the perceived defensibility of the rightness or wrongness of actions and the means to approach contemporary moral dilemmas from professional, cultural, and personal perspec-tives, respectively. The aforementioned books primarily fall into these categories of ethical analysis.

The domain of lesbian ethics grows directly out of work in feminist ethics. Ap-proaches to feminist ethics are considered a branch of work within the larger body of ethics. Specifically, feminist ethicists have developed extensive critiques of tra-ditional Anglo-European, liberalist assumptions about the primary role of individu-alism and autonomy as well as the preference for reason and logic over emotion. Many feminists approach ethics with a close examination of the major influence of power dynamics through the multiple lenses of oppression, including sex, gen-der, sexuality, and social categories of experience including race/ethnicity, ability, socioeconomic class, and others. Since traditional Euro-American approaches to ethics have historically tended to dismiss women's experiences and moral reason-ing styles, feminist ethics can be viewed as an attempt to remedy the sexism found in many of those frameworks. Feminist ethics, broadly considered, reframes ethical inquiry along questions that emphasize women's realities, seeking nonsexist ap-proaches to evaluating moral theory. In general, feminist ethics tends to emphasize notions of connection, community, interdependence (mind-body, self-community/environment); it is a relatively young field, still undergoing vast theoretical and popular revisions and reformations, as is the field of lesbian ethics.

While the diversity of topics that lesbian ethicists grapple with is vast, a consistent theme within this breadth of analysis is an assessment of interlocking systems of oppression. Foundational throughout lesbian ethics is a keen attention to multiple injustices/oppressions and their deep interdependence. A highly influential radical feminist whose work has contributed to this attention is **Gloria Anzaldúa,** who authored *Borderlands—La Frontera: The New Mestiza*, originally published in 1987. This text has since become a classic in Chicano, feminist, LGBTQ, and cultural studies, for its attention to the complexities of living at, within, and among the borders (both literally and symbolically through forms of privilege/oppression). Claudia Card's significant work in philosophy spans substantive/normative analysis and ethical application and practice, dealing with notions of evil, in/justice, and social issues. Chris Cuomo's work also reflects a deep reflection about forms of oppression and privilege, and recently her analysis has extended beyond the human to include a careful examination of the relationships between environmental ethics and feminist ethics.

Lesbian philosophers have also written widely on topics in epistemology and creative knowledge-construction, particularly as attempts to create and nurture alternative learning models. Among other realms of inquiry in lesbian ethics and philosophy is an analysis of the social construction of desire, including attention to the production of pornography. Sarah Lucia Hoagland's 1988 book, *Lesbian Ethics: Toward New Value* seeks to rethink the domain of ethics and uses lesbian experiences as the lens through which to reconstruct and reshape ethical considerations. Additionally, studies of the power of language and naming, semiotics, have also emerged as they relate to the construction of sexual labels. This approach to ethics deepens and complicates concepts that are typically taken for granted in nonfeminist analysis. Monique Wittig, a French novelist and theorist, analyzed gendered language conventions and sexuality in her fiction and nonfiction. Wittig's canonical *The Straight Mind* is a collection of her essays released in 1992.

Further Reading

Anzaldúa, Gloria. 1987. *Borderlands/La Frontera*. San Francisco: Aunt Lute.

Association for Feminist Ethics and Social Theory. Available at: http://www.afeast.org/. Accessed July 14, 2008.

Callahan, Joan, Bonnie Mann, and Sara Ruddick, eds. 2007. "Writing against Heterosexism." Special issue, *Hypatia: A Journal of Feminist Philosophy* 22 (1).

Card, Claudia, ed. 1991. *Feminist Ethics*. Lawrence: University Press of Kansas.

Card, Claudia, ed. 1994. *Adventures in Lesbian Philosophy*. Bloomington: Indiana University Press.

Card, Claudia. 1995. *Lesbian Choices*. New York: Columbia University Press.

Cuomo, Chris. 1998. *Feminism and Ecological Communities*. New York: Routledge.

Cuomo, Chris. 2003. *The Philosopher Queen: Feminist Essays on War, Love, and Knowledge*. Lanham, MD: Rowman & Littlefield.

Estlund, David M., and Martha Nussbaum, eds. 1996. *Sex, Preference, and Family: Essays on Law and Nature*. New York: Oxford University Press.

Fuss, Diana, ed. 1991. *Inside/Out: Lesbian Theories, Gay Theories*. New York: Routledge.

Hoagland, Sarah Lucia. 1992. *Lesbian Ethics: Toward New Value*. Palo Alto: California Institute of Lesbian Studies.

Human Rights Campaign. Available at: http://www.hrc.org. Accessed July 14, 2008.

Moraga, Cherrie, and Gloria Anzaldúa, eds. 2002. *This Bridge Called My Back: Writings by Radical Women of Color.* 3rd ed. San Francisco: Third Woman Press.

National Gay and Lesbian Taskforce Issues. Available at: http://www.thetaskforce.org/issues. Accessed July 14, 2008.

Pharr, Suzanne. 1988. *Homophobia: A Weapon of Sexism.* Little Rock, AR: Chardon Press.

Rich, Adrienne. 1980. "Compulsory Heterosexuality and Lesbian Existence." *Signs: Journal of Women in Culture and Society* 5 (4): 631–60.

Thomas, Laurence, and Michael E. Levin. 1999. *Sexual Orientation and Human Rights.* New York: Rowman & Littlefield.

Wittig, Monique. 1992. *The Straight Mind.* Boston: Beacon Press.

Erika Feigenbaum

photographers, men

F. Holland Day (1864–1933) can be understood both as a forerunner of later gay photographers of male nudes who was perhaps ahead of his time in some ways and also very much a product of his own Victorian time. He published the work of fellow photographer Baron Wilhelm von Gloeden and in his own photography worked in the pictorial tradition, specializing in male nudes in pastoral settings, images of ethnically "exotic" youths in idealized preindustrial tableaux and religious imagery. His homoerotic renditions of the Saint Sebastian theme hovered on the boundary of socially acceptable image making, while his most famous work, "The Seven Last Words of Christ," crossed it. For this latter work, the artist fasted to near emaciation and took an elaborate series of self-portraits as Christ, which included depictions of the crucifixion itself. This series may have been controversial even had they been the work of a devout and unquestionably heterosexual photographer. Coming as they did from Day, around whom swirled rumors of sexual deviance, drug use, and general decadence, they were considered scandalous.

COMMERCIAL PHOTOGRAPHY

Duane Cramer is among the photographers who work primarily as a commercial and magazine photographer. His rich, technically polished work is popular and highly sought after. He also has a body of work, however, that is more personal and documents his extended family. This work can be seen as something of an archaeological project, uncovering layers of history of a large African American social network, and something like an archival project, that is, a record of historical documents.

George Daniell (1911–2002) was a commercial photographer best known for his celebrity photographs, but he also photographed dockworkers, fishermen, swimmers, dancers, and other athletic men. His subjects were both actual athletes and sturdy workingmen whose highly developed, masculine bodies were the natural result of daily physical labor rather than the cultivated atmosphere of the gym, pool, or ballet barre. His was an early photographic celebration of the beauty of the male body that would be influential for the generations of photographers of male nudes and seminudes who would follow.

Bruce Weber (b. 1946) has produced extensive commercial work and specializes in glamour photographs of celebrities and beautiful typecast young men. Weber's career has spanned nearly half a century; it is perhaps his professional longevity as well as the visual appeal of his work that has gained him an increasingly secure place in the world of art photography.

Herb Ritts (1952–2002) originally studied economics at Bard College. Like Daniell and Weber, he began work as a celebrity portrait photographer. He is best known for his extremely stylized and idealized images of men. One of his most famous photographs is *Fred with Tyres*, in which a sculpted Adonis gazes into the camera, casually holding a truck tire in either hand. Ritts's work has been celebrated for its beauty but also criticized for its portrayal of unapologetically perfect specimens of manhood and the disturbing undercurrent that such stark admiration of "superior" types evokes. His books include *Men/Women*, *Duo*, and *Notorious*.

Duane Michals (b. 1932) was originally a commercial and fashion photographer but took a turn into figurative allegories. He is known for his narrative sequences on contemporary versions of mythic themes. His works often focus on the "grand" themes including love and death, but they do so with a sardonic twist that keeps them from seeming heavy-handed. He regularly incorporates text into his photographs. His books include *The Portraits of Duane Michals*, *Eros and Thanatos*, and *Questions without Answers*.

Greg Day trained as an anthropologist and photographer at Rutgers University. He began his career photographing the civil rights movement in Atlanta and the Gullah people of the South Carolina low country. Later, he photographed performance artists and architecture in New York City and Berlin. In 1978 he relocated to San Francisco, developing a reputation as a gay erotic photographer. His books include *Metamorphose* and *Pacific Kouros*. His work is held by the Smithsonian Institution in Washington, D.C., the Schwules Museum in Berlin, the Tom of Finland Foundation in Los Angeles, and the Gay and Lesbian Historical Society in San Francisco. He currently lives in Palm Springs, California.

CHRONICLES OF QUEER CULTURE AND DOCUMENTARY PHOTOGRAPHY

Daniel Nicoletta (b. 1954) is a photographer of LGBT and queer history, culture, and counterculture. Born in New York City and raised in Utica, New York, he lives and works in San Francisco, having arrived in that city in the mid-1970s as a young man and taken a job at Harvey Milk's camera store on Castro Street. He photographed the exploding gay scene in the city at that time, shooting Milk's campaign photographs as well as documenting the seminal queer **performance** groups, the Cockettes and the Angels of Light. An accomplished studio photographer as well as a community documentarian, his work over the years has emphasized portraits of well-known and obscure **drag queens,** tattooed men and women, and underground celebrities. His film work has included *Sex Is . . .* and *The Times of Harvey Milk.*

John Rand (b. 1956) is a Los Angeles–based documentarian of the **bear** subculture. In contrast to the photographers who promote classical images of male beauty, Rand is personally invested in a project of countering the hegemony of the cliché image of the gym-toned hairless gay urban male. This is not to say that the subjects of Rand's photographs are not beautiful; rather they suggest that the boundaries of male beauty can be expanded to include a wide range of men, including the heavy and hirsute.

Robert Giard's (1939–2002) best-known work is a series of portraits of gay and lesbian writers. Rather than confining his scope to particular bodies, he focuses on capturing images of the men and women who have contributed their literary voices to the culture. He has published this project in book form as *Particular Voices: Portraits of Gay and Lesbian Writers.*

Los Angeles–based photographer Patrick "Pato" Herbert specializes in capturing images of everyday street life in a straightforward documentary style. Herbert is invested in the communities that he photographs, particularly those of ethnic minority youth, whose disenfranchisement he combats through active involvement. He has done collaborative work with community organizations and taught at the junior high school as well as the college level. His intimate portraits of young people testify to his close involvement with them. The children and teens in his photographs have none of the self-consciousness that could result from a more distanced investigation of their daily lives. A politically committed artist and activist, since 2002 he has been associate director of education and prevention for the AIDS Project Los Angeles.

SEX-RADICAL PHOTOGRAPHY AND CONTROVERSIAL SUBJECT MATTER

In the years after World War II, images of male physical beauty circulated both underground as well as in the mainstream through such venues as the Athletic Models Guild. After **Stonewall,** imagery became both more explicit and more political. Many gay male photographers deal in sexually explicit imagery. Some of this work has found eager, if contested, acceptance in museums and other venues that stamp it with the mark of high art. Some remains largely subcultural. And much of it has influenced and continues to influence commercial and advertising work.

Self-described sex-radical photographer Mark I. Chester (b. 1950) lives and works in San Francisco, where he specializes in documenting the radical fringes of the gay male erotic world. Chester, who also works as a commercial photographer, depicts his subjects expressing their own edgy sexuality, which often involves **leather,** BDSM, and other nonvanilla fare. His style is simple and elegant, and this tends to foreground the photographic subject rather than the photographer.

New Orleans–based George Dureau (b. 1930), also known as a painter, specializes in black-and-white portraits of men and youths who are marked by perceived imperfections, including dwarfism, missing limbs, and even various visually

Robert Mapplethorpe. Photo by Robert Pruzan, courtesy of the Gay, Lesbian, Bisexual, Transgender Historical Society, San Francisco.

apparent social stigmata. Through Dureau's lens these "defects" are transformed into a unique sort of ambiguous beauty. Dureau was a major influence on Robert Mapplethorpe, but whereas Mapplethorpe's work maintains a certain emotional distance that comes of his nearly regimental formalism, Dureau's work has an intimacy and immediacy that can be simultaneously engaging and disturbing.

Although Robert Mapplethorpe (1946–1989) was well known in art circles from the 1970s, he came to mainstream prominence during the censorship debates of the late 1980s. The controversy surrounding his show "The Perfect Moment" was sparked by protests from Senator Jesse Helms of North Carolina and the American Family Association, a socially conservative Christian organization led by the Reverend Donald Wildmon. In a sense, their protest catapulted Mapplethorpe to a level of fame beyond any he had previously enjoyed. In "The Perfect Moment" Mapplethorpe forefronts his trademark painstaking formalism in an exhibit that features sexually explicit subjects side by side with flowers and nudes. Mapplethorpe died of AIDS in 1989.

One of the artists embroiled in the National Endowment for the Arts funding controversy of the late 1980s, David Wojnarowicz (1954–1992), survived a troubled youth in which he used his wits on the streets, to achieve critical success as an artist. He also gained political effectiveness as an activist when he sued Donald Wildmon of the American Family Association for illegally reproducing artwork. He was a prolific artist with a range of interests and styles. His work sometimes included explicit gay imagery. He is considered one of the leading voices of his generation and is another artist whose career was cut tragically short by his early death from AIDS. His series include "Arthur Rimbaud in New York" and "Tongues of Flame."

Ken Probst was born in Switzerland but lived in America for almost his entire life. His book (por ne-graf'ik) is his documentary-style take on the pornography industry in California. Rather than focusing on pornography per se, it examines the business of pornography. His style is reminiscent of modernism, with careful attention given to line, form, texture, and abstraction.

Ajamu (b. 1963) works largely with his own body as the subject of representation. He takes a political stance in creating work that often intentionally transgresses received notions of race and gender and explores forbidden territories. He consciously interrogates notions of normal bodies and appropriate desire by redeploying problematic historical themes such as the carnival sideshow. In "Auto-Portrait as Armless and Legless Wonder" from the series "Anti/Bodies a Spectacle of Strangeness," he appears as a human torso, a disturbing colonial artifact in what appears to be a Victorian-era drawing room. A cultural activist as well as a practicing artist, he founded the Black Male Artists Group in the Brixton Arts Collective in 1991 and more recently cofounded ruckus! Federation Ltd., an organization devoted to the promotion, exhibition, and preservation of black LGBTQ cultural production.

Female-to-male (FTM) transsexual photographer Loren Cameron (b. 1959) specializes in self-portraits and portraits of other transsexual men and women. Cameron began his photographic career when he decided to document his own transition from female to male, and soon expanded his project to include other transsexuals. A sculpted bodybuilder with a mere 8 percent body fat, Cameron's nude self-portrait series "God's Will" questions the intersections of the natural and the artificial. He also aligns the agency of the creature with that of the "creator," invoking and opposing arguments of the religious right that certain types of agency are only within the purview of the divine will. In his current work, "Flex for Me!," he trains his lens on gay and bisexual transmen. Books include *Body Alchemy: Transsexual Portraits*.

SELF-PORTRAITURE

When a photographer turns the lens on himself, he creates, in a sense, another self. That self is frozen in time at the place and time when the photograph was taken, and this ability of the photograph to "capture" a moment forever may add to the popularity of self-portraiture among photographers.

Lyle Ashton Harris (b. 1965) was educated at Wesleyan and Cal Arts and has often worked productively within the genre of self-portraiture. He uses the artificial to address constructed categories and to challenge established **stereotypes.** In a series of collaborations with other artists, including his brother, the filmmaker Robert Allan Harris, who is also gay, he has created photographic self-portraits in which he and his collaborators engage in various types of gender, racial, and class "cross-dressing" in the context of the "family portrait" format.

Mark Morrisroe (1959–1989) specialized in portraits, especially self-portraits. In a long-term project, he recorded his own naked body as it changed over a period of 12 years. During this time, he transformed from a vibrant youth into a sick, skeletal man. He used the media of Polaroid® photography for this project, and the immediacy of this form of photography adds to the emotional range of this somewhat informal work.

Nigerian-born Iké Udé (b. 1964) lives and works in New York City. In addition to being a photographer, Udé is a writer and a publisher and the founder of *aRude* magazine. Udé also works in film, video, and television. Udé is less a photographer per se than a critically based multimedia artist who uses photography as one medium among many to interrogate the proliferation of images and identity in media culture. His books include *Beyond Decorum: The Photography of Iké Udé*.

Although born and raised in a rural Georgia fundamentalist community, Crawford Barton (1943–1993) became one of the preeminent photographers of gay San Francisco in the 1970s. Actively involved in, as well as documenting, this time of sexual liberation, his images were among the first to portray men, with their consent, as erotic objects for other men to desire, idolize, and emulate. Barton pioneered the style of male imagery that currently pervades in fashion advertising to men. Courtesy of the Gay, Lesbian, Bisexual, Transgender Historical Society, San Francisco.

FORMAL, CONCEPTUAL, AND GENRE PHOTOGRAPHY

Robert B. Flynt (b. 1956) lives and works in New York City. His work evokes a neosurrealism. He uses digital technologies to create images that evoke alternative processes of earlier eras, including collage, double exposure, and other darkroom techniques. He also includes found images from outside photography, which add to the collage-like effect of his work. His books include *Compound Fracture*.

Peter Hujar (1934–1987) lived and worked in New York; his body of work included a wide range of subject matter, but he is particularly remembered as a portraitist. An artist whose work is deeply psychological, he regarded all of his work as a form of self-portraiture. Neglected for some time after his premature death, his work is beginning to attract the attention that it deserves. Books of his work include *Portraits in Life and Death* and *Animals and Nudes*. He died of AIDS in 1987.

Jack Pierson (b. 1960) lives and works in New York, Provincetown, Massachusetts, and Los Angeles, California. His work covers a range of styles and concerns, from his conceptual work involving found objects and installation art to his more recent sun-drenched portraiture. His work is often evocative of the snapshot tradition, and individual pieces sometimes include blurring that adds to the sense that the images are hastily constructed and may be capturing a fleeting moment. His books include *All of a Sudden*, *The Lonely Life*, and *Every Single One of Them*.

Arthur Tress (b. 1940) was born in Brooklyn and lives and works in Cambria, California. His early work was in documentary photography. His more recent and better-known work is surrealistically tinged erotica. His series include "Dream Collector," "Shadow," and "Theater of the Mind."

A Vietnam War veteran, New York–based photographer Al Baltrop (b. 1948) was born in the Bronx. He studied briefly at the School of the Visual Arts but is largely self-taught. He attracted attention in the 1970s with his photographs of the emergent gay urban lifestyle of **bathhouses, bars,** and discos in the period after Stonewall and before AIDS. His later work continues in a documentary tradition but with a harder edge: he focuses on the dirty underside of the dream, capturing street queens, homeless youth, and other edge-dwelling Manhattan denizens.

Further Reading

Bright, Deborah, ed. 1998. *The Passionate Camera: Photography and Bodies of Desire*. London and New York: Routledge.

Cooper, Emmanuel. 1990. *Fully Exposed: The Male Nude in Photography*. London and New York: Routledge.

Ellenzweig, Allen. 1992. *The Homoerotic Photograph: Male Images from Durieu/Delacroix to Mapplethorpe*. New York: Columbia University Press.

Waugh, Thomas. 1996. *Hard to Imagine: Gay Male Eroticism in Photography and Film from Their Beginnings to Stonewall*. New York: Columbia University Press.

Jordy Jones

photographers, women

During the early 1970s, 20 years after the beginning of the resurgence of feminism in the United States and in the midst of the modern lesbian and gay movement, photography provided a means for some LGBTQ women to visually communicate their personal and introspective analyses of issues and societal standards surrounding issues such as gender, sexuality, race, and femininity. Many women have continued this pursuit, and the result is the development of a significant body of photography from LGBTQ women. Throughout the past 35 years, they have continued to challenge the very definition of "woman photographer."

Early women photographers of the LGBTQ community were inspired by the women around them. They wanted to document their lives, sexuality, and bodies, as they understood them. Joan E. Biren (better known as JEB) was one of those pioneers. During the age of radical feminism and the emergence of women-only communities, photography for her was a way in which to express herself outside of the male-dominated realm of language. Her images during the 1970s and 1980s set the standard for lesbian photography by representing a wide range of women of different ethnic backgrounds, ages, and abilities. Her collections of photos include *Eye to Eye: Portraits of Lesbians* (1979) and, more recently, *Making a Way: Lesbians Out Front* (1987).

JEB was not alone. Other early women photographers included Cathy Cade and Tee A. Corinne. They too were inspired by the women's liberation movement and the desire to document their community. Cathy Cade sees it as her lifelong mission to end the oppression that women experience from sexism by making women more visible. Throughout her career, Cade's work has featured women participating in political demonstrations, women in nontraditional work, and lesbians giving birth and raising children.

Tee A. Corinne's photography also celebrated women and the female body, from a woman's perspective. In 1975 she self-published *The Cunt Coloring Book*, which featured sketches of female genitalia. At the time, the book was seen as very radical and controversial because of its descriptive imagery. Throughout her career, Corinne continued to play a pivotal role as a woman photographer. In the early 1980s she moved to southern Oregon and became part of a community of lesbians and other women who were self-consciously creating and documenting a radical woman-only culture. While there she produced a series of photos called the *Yantras of Womanlove* (1982), which were explicit images of lesbian sex. She used the technique of arranging multiple prints into yantras to conceal their explicitness and models' identity. She also was the cofounder of the one-of-a-kind *The Blatant Image: A Magazine of Feminist Photography* (1981–1983). Corinne was a pioneer in making erotic lesbian photography from a lesbian perspective. Photographers such as Judy Francesconi are also well known for their sensual imagery and erotic lesbian photography.

As women photographers document their communities, they often archive their own lives in the process. Perhaps one of the best examples of this is the well-known slide show and subsequent book *The Ballad of Sexual Dependency* by Nan Goldin. Goldin grew up middle-class in Maryland during the 1950s. When her eldest sister, Barbara, killed herself when she was 18 and Nan was 11, Goldin attributed it to the conservative standards placed on women. She ran away from home and developed an interest in photography while exploring the gay subculture of Boston and visually documented the lives of her roommates, who were **drag queens.** Goldin ultimately moved to New York City and lived in a loft on the Bowery, immersing herself in the city's underground club scene. Her first photo shows were at these underground venues; she would show her images spanning over a decade as slide shows set to music. From these early slide shows emerged a 700-picture, 45-minute show called *The Ballad of Sexual Dependency*, her most famous work. The show became a book (published in 1986); central to both was her relationship with her then-boyfriend, Brian, her bisexuality, and the lives of her friends, many of them drag queens and **transsexuals.** Goldin's work was gritty, raw, and successful. It ultimately transcended this subculture to enter the mainstream art world.

During the 1980s and 1990s, the promotion of lesbians' visibility in LGBTQ women's photography included the pluralizing of the image beyond the white lesbian. Inspired by this pursuit are Hulleah Tsinhnahjinnie, Laura Aguilar, Jean Weisinger, Theresa Thadani, and Zone Paraiso Montoya. One of the best-known works from Hulleah Tsinhnahjinnie is a hand-colored photograph she created for the cover of *Living the Spirit: A Gay American Indian Anthology* (1988). The image featured a woman in fringed clothing and traditionally bound hair standing beside a motorcycle. Tsinhnahjinnie's placement of Native Americans in the present with her photograph is meant to challenge the stereotype of Native Americans as not being modern, while, at the same time, it also places Native American women center stage when discussing gay American Indians.

Laura Aguilar's photography also pushes the color line of LGBTQ women's photography. Aguilar is motivated by her desire to show positive images of Latina lesbians and to document their lives. One of her well-known photographs is "In Sandy's Room" (1989). It depicts a Latina woman trying to find relief from the heat. Another photographer providing another perspective is Jean Weisinger, an African American photographer based in Oakland who travels throughout the world to document the lives of women globally. At home, her portraits of Alice Walker and **Audre Lorde** have been widely published. Other women photographers known for featuring women from specific ethnic groups within the LGBTQ community include Theresa Thadani and Zone Paraiso Montoya, both lesbian photographers whose work often features Asian and Pacific Islander lesbians.

LGBTQ women photographers also blend the quest for representation with one's own process of self-reflection and questioning. Hanh Thi Pham, a Vietnamese refugee now living in California, uses photography to examine issues of gender and sexuality that she experienced in her exiled Vietnamese family. Gaye Chan, an immigrant from Hong Kong, is currently exploring immigrant narratives in relation to Hawaii (where she lives now).

Many LGBTQ women photographers use the camera as a weapon, hoping to bring about political and social change. Two such photographers are Linda Kliewer and Laurie Toby Edison. Motivated by how, as a child, all she saw were negative images of lesbians and gays, Kliewer has documented her gay and lesbian middle-class community in Oregon for nearly 15 years. In fact, she served as cinematographer for *Ballot Measure 9* (1993) an award-winning film about the fight against an antigay measure in Oregon. Edison, a bisexual activist, took to photography to help push her agenda of challenging body image issues. Her publications *Women en Large: Images of Fat Nudes* (1994) and *Familiar Men: A Book of Male Nudes* (2003) feature intimate images of nude women and men (respectively). She is motivated not by eroticism but rather by her aim to undermine stereotypes.

When the HIV/AIDS epidemic hit Europe and the United States, Tessa Boffin, a photographer and **performance artist,** was the first British lesbian artist to produce work in response to it. Her book *Angelic Rebels: Lesbians and Safer Sex* (1989) placed lesbians into the public discourse of the epidemic. Boffin's role in the LGBTQ community both in the United States and abroad was extensive. In 1991, she coedited with Jean Fraser *Stolen Glances: Lesbians Take Photographs;* it was the first collection of its time.

As the HIV/AIDS epidemic pushed LGBTQ women further into the public space, what they found there became the very focus for some photographers. Jill Posener is a lesbian photographer who has been motivated by her own activism since her early days as a radical feminist in the 1970s. And yet, instead of taking images of her community of activists or demonstrations in which they participated, she prefers to document the symbols of those protests. Her images include lesbian slogans on advertising billboards. Sue Schaffner and Carrie Moyer created Dyke Action Machine (DAM), a public art collaboration that critiques mainstream culture by inserting lesbian images into a recognizably commercial context in public spaces, like a bus station.

Chloe Atkins and Trista Sordillo are photographers motivated by public disclosure. Atkins's monograph *Atkins: Girls' Night Out* (St. Martin's Press, 1998) was an attempt to document bar culture in the lesbian community. In addition, Atkins won an award in California for a billboard showing a lesbian couple, with the caption "Another Traditional Family." Meanwhile, Sordillo, while attending school at the University of California, Santa Cruz, photographed a series called "Lesbian Visibility Series" (1995), which documents lesbians in public spaces.

As LGBTQ women photographers explored the doctrine of postmodernism during the 1980s, 1990s, and 2000s, the very notions of "public," "sexuality," and "gender" came into question. Photographers such as Deborah Bright explored the "public space" of already-existing material from pop culture, most notably film stills. In her series "Dream Girls" (1989), she placed herself in well-known films, interjecting a male-looking lesbian into the narrative, making visible both lesbians and lesbian identity.

Postmodern ideals also inspired some LGBTQ women photographers to publicly challenge the standards of sexuality and gender performance placed on them by past generations of LGBTQ women. Cathy Opie is a photographer who empowers self-identified butches and dykes. In the late 1980s and mid-1990s Opie gained national attention for her large portraits of "dyke daddies," female-to-male transsexuals (FTMs), and gay male performances. Drag king culture and performances have also become the muse for photographers such as Erin O'Neill.

Still, some photographers question the very notion of gender and sex itself. Born Debra Dianne Wood, Del LaGrace (also known as Della Grace or Del LaGrace Volcano) lived the first 37 years of her life as a woman. For about 20 of those years, she was known as a lesbian photographer. She is best known for her photographic monograph of lesbian sexuality, titled *Love Bites* (1991). Given the aggressive sadomasochistic imagery in the images, the book was seen as controversial and was censored in both mainstream and lesbian/gay communities. Since then Grace's identity has metamorphosed from lesbian to hermaphrodyke to transman to intersexed. Grace identifies herself as a gender-variant visual artist while she continues to push the boundaries of expected behavior for lesbians and transgendered people. Her recent work focuses on the transformation of the body once it is liberated from a binary understanding of sex and the problematizing of male-dominated transgender culture through the use of portraits of drag kings.

Some photographers question the very existence of reality itself. At the very edge of postmodern LGBTQ photography are Jill Casid and Maria DeGuzman. In 1991, they created SPIR: Conceptual Photography. They called themselves a queer feminist partnership and worked with others to produce photo-text pieces and sequences to challenge myths, stereotypes, and notions of identity construction. In 2003 they split, and DeGuzman went on to create Camera Query, a project similar to SPIR. Still committed to making a statement about an idea or concept through images, Camera Query is dedicated to conceptual photography. This type of photography uses many formats and procedures—image taking, computer manipulation, and something with text. Both SPIR and Camera Query place issues important to the LGBTQ community at the forefront of their work by dealing with issues of gender performance, sexuality, and identity.

While LGBTQ women's photography has grown and evolved, lesbian photographers still have a precarious relationship with the mainstream art world, making the coming-out process usually a cause for some debate, forcing many LGBTQ women photographers to negotiate in some way between their public and professional lives. One of the most famous American contemporary photographers today, Annie Leibovitz is one of those women. Famous for her celebrity portraits and work in advertising, Leibovitz's career began in 1970 when she began working for *Rolling Stone* magazine. Since then, she has had an amazing career. She has worked for *Rolling Stone*, *Vanity Fair*, and *Vogue*. She has also worked for many advertising campaigns, including those of American Express and The Gap. Recently, she created a series of portraits of less-famous people, including a series of people with AIDS and the victims of the war in Bosnia. This recent work was inspired by her relationship with Susan Sontag (1933–2004). For over a decade the two were close companions but never came out as a couple. That changed somewhat in 2006, when Leibovitz published *A Photographer's Life: 1990–2005*. The publication included both professional and personal images. Through this work, an accompanying traveling exhibition, and a slew of interviews, Leibovitz has redefined her relationship with Sontag as a love story. Her disclosure has been the center for much debate in both the LGBTQ community and mainstream America.

The ever-expanding number of LGBTQ women photographers reflects artists' past efforts to visually communicate their own self-image, expectations, and sensibilities. Their images reveal a process of community building and questioning of both self and society. As LGBTQ women photographers continue to push notions such as gender, sexuality, and woman to their breaking points, they watch in anticipation to see if and how these notions will give.

Further Reading

Boffin, Tessa, and Jean Fraser, ed. 1991. *Stolen Glances: Lesbians Take Photographs*. New York: Pandora Press.

Hammond, Harmony. 2000. *Lesbian Art in America: A Contemporary History*. New York: Rizzoli International.

Rosenblum, Naomi. 1994. *A History of Women Photographers*. New York: Abbeville Publishing.

Aimee Klask

Leah Lakshmi Piepzna-Samarasinha (1975–)

Leah Lakshmi Piepzna-Samarasinha is a spoken-word artist, poet, educator, and Sri Lankan activist whose art and activism document the lives of queer and trans people of color, abuse survivors, mixed-race people, and diasporic South Asians and Sri Lankans. The daughter of a Sri Lankan father and an Irish-Ukrainian mother, her work focuses both on her personal identities and on justice for Sri Lanka and all places under siege from multinational corporate greed, sexism, and homophobia. After leaving Worcester, Massachusetts, where she grew up, she attended Eugene Lang College and the New School for Social Research in New York, where she admits that she "ended up learning a lot more from the student, squatter, spoken word, women of color and queer/trans of color movements" (Leah Lakshmi Piepzna-Samarasinha Web site). Since 1997, she has performed her spoken-word poetry throughout North America and has particularly focused on issues of social justice for the queer community and immigrants. Currently residing in Toronto, Piepzna-Samarasinha teaches writing and recently authored *Consensual Genocide* in 2006, hailed by Anna Camilleri as "urgent, sumptuous writing that demands, and deserves, a wide audience" (book jacket); she frequently contributes to feminist, queer, and social justice publications like *Bitch, Colorlines,* and *Colonize This!* She also coordinates queer-of-color spoken-word shows through her company, brownstargirl productions, including her most recent show, called Grown Woman Show, which debuted in August 2007. She also cocreated the Asian Arts Freedom School for Asian and Pacific Islander youth in Toronto, is an active member of the Canadian Sri Lankan Women's Action Network, and recently launched Mangos with Chili, a touring cabaret group featuring queer and trans people of color.

Further Reading

Leah Lakshmi Piepzna-Samarasinha Web site. Available at: www.brownstargirl.com/bio.html. Accessed July 14, 2008.

YAAHA: Youth Advocating for Anti-Homophonia Awareness. Available at: www.yaaha.org/links.html. Accessed July 14, 2008.

Breanne Fahs

piercing, tattoos, and scars

Body modifications—including piercings, tattoos, and scarification—have a long tradition in many cultures as elements of ritual and markers of group identity. Most societies throughout history have adopted some form of body modification, from simple earlobe piercings to the *moko* facial tattoos worn by the Maori of New Zealand. Even Ötzi the Iceman, a 5,000-year-old mummy found in the Austrian Alps, sported multiple tattoos and stretched earlobe piercings.

Yet while humans have been remarkably consistent in their embrace of body modification, the specific forms and associated meanings have varied widely across cultures. Some societies have emphasized the arduous process as a rite of passage, an element of religious ceremony, or a means of achieving altered states of consciousness, whereas others have focused on the end product as a symbol of social standing—either a badge of elevated rank or a marker of outsider status.

In contemporary Western societies, piercing and tattooing have been adopted by "outlaw" subcultures including pirates, sailors, bikers, criminals, gang members, and rock-and-roll musicians. These customs thus came to be associated with the lower socioeconomic classes, although in other times and places they were the purview of the wealthy elite. Yet despite their recognition as symbols of subcultural affiliation, piercings and tattoos have gained widespread mainstream acceptance over the past two decades, with the LGBT community at the forefront of this trend.

Visible body modifications often serve to set people apart from normal society, while at the same time symbolizing membership in a particular subgroup. For many gay men since the 1960s, ear piercing has functioned as a nonverbal signal and a form of public coming out. As ear jewelry was primarily associated with women—although in many other cultures both men and women pierced their ears—sporting an earring was a subtle way to express one's femininity.

As countercultural heterosexual men began to adopt earlobe piercing in the 1960s and 1970s, much was made about which side an earring was worn on and what that conveyed about one's sexuality. The most common convention was for gay men to wear an earring on the right and straight men on the left, though this varied from community to community. Adding to the confusion, piercing on one side or the other was also used to signify "top" (left) or "bottom" (right) sexual roles. But as ear piercing gained wider popularity among gay and straight men alike in the 1980s and 1990s, it lost much of its symbolic value as a sexual signifier.

As earlobe piercing became commonplace, those wishing to set themselves apart began sporting piercings elsewhere on the face and body. A parallel trend—and one with considerable overlap—was the growing popularity of body modification within a sexual context. This included permanent nipple and genital piercings intended to increase sensitivity or enhance a partner's pleasure, as well as temporary "play" piercings, cuttings, and brands. These practices were most strongly associated with **sadomasochism** (S/M), with a smaller subculture using intense bodily sensation to pursue spiritual ends. Within an S/M context, body modification encompasses both an interest in pain and the acknowledgment of the historical use of tattoos and brands as markers of nonconsensual slavery or ownership and of genital piercings as chastity devices.

Body modification in the LGBT community derives from several intersecting strands. One of the first well-known gay male tattoo artists was Samuel Steward, who wrote homosexual erotica under the pen name Phil Andros. Steward, who quit his teaching job and took up tattooing in Chicago in the 1950s, collaborated with Alfred Kinsey, providing the sex researcher with information about the nascent gay male S/M subculture.

An organized gay male body modification community—overlapping with the S/M and motorcycle scenes—arose in the late 1960s and early 1970s in California. One of the earliest pioneers was Doug Malloy (also known as Richard Symington), who made his fortune with the Muzak Corporation. During his travels and through gay and fetish publications, Malloy made contact with many people who shared his interest, including Sailor Sid Diller, gay tattoo artist Cliff Raven, Jim Ward, Fakir Musafar, and Mr. Sebastian.

Ward first met men with piercings through the gay S/M scene in New York City in the 1960s. He decided to pierce his own ears and nipples and before long began doing piercings for friends and acquaintances; this continued after he moved to Los Angeles and met Malloy and his circle. Ward refined his piercing techniques through trial and error and—since none was commercially available—designed and produced his own piercing jewelry. In 1975, with financial support from Malloy, he started the first piercing business, Gauntlet Enterprises. Gauntlet published *Piercing Fans International Quarterly (PFIQ)* magazine and opened the first-ever storefront piercing parlor in West Hollywood in 1978.

Fakir Musafar (also known as Roland Loomis) began exploring various forms of "body play" such as piercing, self-tattooing, and corseting as an adolescent in the 1940s. Though primarily heterosexual, he found kindred spirits among the gay men in the California S/M and body modification communities. Musafar, Ward, and other "modern primitives"—a term coined by Musafar—began performing Native American rituals involving intense bodily sensation, including the sun dance (in which the dancer pulls against flesh hooks in the chest until they tear through the skin), as documented in the 1985 film *Dances Sacred and Profane*. Musafar later published *Body Play* magazine and brought awareness to the modern primitive scene through his teaching and performances.

Mr. Sebastian (also known as Alan Oversby) was the best-known proponent of tattooing and piercing among the gay male community in London. In 1987, he and 15 other men were charged with assault after police obtained a film of them engaged in S/M (Oversby was seen piercing a penis). The resulting Operation Spanner case went on for a decade, finally losing an appeal before the European Court of Human Rights.

Though not to the same degree as the gay male body modification community, lesbians also took an interest in tattooing, piercing, cutting, and branding. One key pioneer, Raelyn Gallina, began doing nipple and female genital piercings and cuttings at the request of friends in the early 1980s; like Ward, she developed new techniques and designed and made her own piercing jewelry.

As the S/M scene became increasingly "pansexual" and subgroups came into greater contact in the 1980s and 1990s, more heterosexuals began embracing body modification within a sexual context, though this was not a new concept. In Pauline Réage's 1954 novel *The Story of O*, for example, "O" receives a labia piercing from her master to symbolize her submission.

Body modification became one of issues in the 1980s feminist "**sex wars**" over S/M and other forms of stigmatized sexuality. While some condemned piercing and cutting as mutilation, others defended them as a way to reclaim one's own body. With the advent of the AIDS epidemic, practices associated with blood took on a new and often disturbing significance.

In the mid-1980s, Musafar began collaborating with V. Vale and Andrea Juno of RE/Search publications on a book about the modern primitive subculture. RE/Search started out in the late 1970s documenting the punk scene, which also included many people who sported tattoos and piercings (though this was often driven by shock value—e.g., safety pins through the cheeks—rather than specifically sexual or spiritual motivations). The 1989 book *Modern Primitives* brought awareness of tattooing, piercing, and scarification to a wide audience and ushered in a new level of popularity beyond the S/M scene.

The LGBT community was among the first to embrace the newfound popularity of tattooing and piercing in the late 1980s and early 1990s. Many favored the contemporary black-work style based on tribal and Celtic designs, while others expressed their identity with triangles and other gay symbols. Popular piercings of the day included the upper ear cartilage, nose (both nostrils and septum), lips, labret (chin), tongue, eyebrows, navel, and nipples. Tattoos and facial piercings became part of the informal uniform of "in-your-face" activist groups such as **ACT UP, Queer Nation,** and the **Lesbian Avengers.**

By the mid-1990s, tattooing and body piercings had entered the mainstream, worn by celebrities, supermodels, and professional athletes. Madonna's popular book *Sex* (1992) included several photographs featuring body piercings. Tattoos on women largely lost their "bad girl" stigma. Tattoo parlors moved out of their traditional low-rent enclaves, while body piercing emporiums cropped up in urban centers and small towns alike. When Janet Jackson flashed her breast during the 2004 Super Bowl halftime show, she was wearing a pierced nipple shield originally designed by Gauntlet.

Such widespread acceptance led to some scorn and resentment among early aficionados, who felt that this popularity diluted the meaning and symbolism of body modification and that many of the newcomers—motivated by fashion— did not share their deeper sexual and spiritual understandings of the practices. Ironically, however, much the same accusation could be directed against the early adopters, who appropriated traditional tribal practices outside their original cultural contexts.

Today, more than half of college students have at least one piercing, according to a recent survey (though most are probably ear or navel piercings). In 2006, the

Journal of the American Academy of Dermatology reported that nearly one-quarter of U.S. residents ages 18–50 had a tattoo; since these cannot be easily removed like piercings, their ubiquity is destined to endure. Scarification, cutting, and branding never gained widespread popularity, and more extreme forms of body modification remain the purview of the most dedicated; thanks to the Internet, however, such practices are no longer underground.

Further Reading

Featherstone, Mike, ed. 2000. *Body Modification.* Thousand Oaks, CA: Sage Publications.

Pitts, Victoria. 2003. *In the Flesh: The Cultural Politics of Body Modification.* New York: Palgrave Macmillan.

Vale, V., and A. Juno. 1989. *Modern Primitives: An Investigation of Contemporary Adornment and Ritual.* San Francisco: RE/Search Publications.

Liz Highleyman

pink triangle

In the visual code applied in concentration camps under the German National Socialist regime, prisoners were identified by means of colored badges: red (political prisoners), black "antisocials"), purple (Jehovah's Witnesses), brown (gypsies), green (professional criminals), blue (emigrants), and yellow (Jews). A pink triangle badge five centimeters wide, sewn onto prisoners' uniforms, identified men interned as homosexuals on charges related to §175 of the German penal code.

While alternative markers for homosexuality existed—the number 175, referring to the respective legal paragraph, or a yellow band worn on the arm with the capital letter "A," interpreted as standing for *Arschficker,* a crude reference to anal intercourse—the pink triangle served as the main means of identification. Between 1933 and 1945 approximately 50,000 men were sentenced with regard to §175, and it is assumed that 5,000 to 15,000 of them were interned.

Under the leadership of Heinrich Himmler, **homophobic** head of the SS, the Nazi regime specifically targeted male homosexuals from the mid-1930s. The lives of gay men and, to a lesser degree, lesbians were under threat. Lesbianism was not considered a punishable offense, but in some cases women were interned because they were involved in lesbian relationships. Female camp inmates were, however, generally not marked with the pink triangle. But while speculative statistics and claims of a persecution of homosexuals on a genocidal level, with hundreds of thousands of victims, have been put forward, the persecution of homosexuals—unlike in the case of Jews—did not occur according to a plan of eradication. As research and personal

The rallying cry of "Never Again!" on a sign reminding us that thousands of homosexuals, forced to wear pink triangles, were killed by the Nazis in concentration camps during World War II. Courtesy of the Gay, Lesbian, Bisexual, Transgender Historical Society, San Francisco.

---

accounts have shown, inmates wearing the pink triangle were situated at the very bottom of the camp hierarchy. Lacking support, suffering from isolation, and subject to hard labor and, in some cases, scientific experiments and castration, their mortality rate was high. It remains impossible to assess the number of homosexuals who perished in concentration camps, but it is estimated that about 60 percent of those wearing the pink triangle died. To these victims needs to be added an unknown number of gay men who died outside the camps—for instance, at the cruel eastern battlefront, to which many released homosexuals had been sent.

While other victims were rehabilitated and received reparations, those camp survivors who had been branded homosexual by the Nazis continued to be criminalized. In the newly founded Federal Republic of Germany, homosexuality remained a punishable offence and §175, enlarged under Nazi rule to allow for easier prosecution, remained in force until 1969. Only in 2002 did the German government repeal sentences. Research into the persecution of homosexuals under National Socialism has to date uncovered individual histories of those forced to wear the pink triangle; many of these individuals had long remained hidden due to the homophobic environment in postwar Germany. Despite misgivings of some Jewish representatives, who speak of an exploitation of Holocaust imagery, the gay movement in the 1970s adopted the pink triangle as a symbol of **gay rights,** indicating awareness and, as evident in public memorials, remembrance of the persecution of homosexuals under National Socialism.

Further Reading

Grau, Günter, ed. 1995. *Hidden Holocaust? Gay and Lesbian Persecution in Germany, 1933–45.* Trans. Patrick Camiller. London: Cassell.

Heger, Heinz (pseudonym of Josef Kohut). 1994. *The Men with the Pink Triangle: The True, Life-and-Death Story of Homosexuals in the Nazi Death Camps.* Rev. ed. Boston: Alyson.

Lautmann, Rüdiger. 1981. "The Pink Triangle: The Persecution of Homosexual Males in the Concentration Camps in Nazi Germany." In *Historical Perspectives on Homosexuality,* ed. Salvatore Licata and Robert Petersen, 141–60. New York: Haworth.

Plant, Richard. 1986. *The Pink Triangle: The Nazi War against Homosexuals.* New York: Henry Holt.

A. B. Christa Schwarz

David Plante (1940–)

Born in Providence, Rhode Island, David Plante is the author of over a dozen novels that address the complexities and numerous variations of male homosexuality. Of both French Canadian and Indian descent, Plante often focuses on male sexuality and its variations, but also spirituality and its role in the sensual. Following the 1970 publication of *The Ghost of Henry James* (his first novel), he has come to be regarded as one of the most important contemporary gay American writers, particularly because of his experimental style and willingness to explore variations of sexuality. His novels immediately following *Henry James—Slides* (1971), *Relatives*

(1972), and *The Darkness of the Body* (1974)—present characters that, while often not overtly, struggle toward the formation of a coherent gay identity.

Plante is perhaps best known for his much-acclaimed Francoeur Trilogy, which is comprised of *The Family* (1978), *The Country* (1981), and *The Woods* (1982). Daniel, the trilogy's sexually ambiguous narrator, serves as both the focal point for the trilogy as well as a touchstone for understanding the other characters and relationships among the members of the Francoeur family.

In matters of sexuality as well as life, a lack of definitiveness and clarity seems to characterize Plante's depiction of the world. In *The Foreigner* (1984) and *The Catholic* (1986), he shifts from the Francoeur family slightly, although both novels connect to the trilogy in significant ways. *The Catholic*, in particular, offers a graphic and turbulent portrait of homosexuality. Male protagonists in *The Foreigner*, *The Accident* (1991), and much of his other work often appear to fail to recognize their own desire, suggesting the fluid and complicated nature of all sexuality, regardless of orientation. This idea also appears in Plante's nonfiction work, *Difficult Women* (1983), a memoir of his relationships with Jean Rhys, Sonia Orwell, and Germaine Greer. Fictional or not, Plante's work evinces an awareness of and a staunch belief in the possibility of multiple identities, sexual and otherwise, being encapsulated in a single individual. For Plante, it seems, there is no singular definition or aspect when it comes to human nature or character.

His 1994 novel, *Annunciation*, explores the fluid nature of human character in more brutal circumstances—deception, suicide, and rape—and the possibility for redemption therein. Throughout the novel Plante interweaves the stories of Claire O'Connel and Claude Ricard, portraying sexual ambiguity and dissatisfaction, the search for meaning in the face of violence and loss, as well as the role of religion in personal identity in the modern world. More recently, Plante published *The Age of Terror* (1999), which chronicles the research of Joe, a 23-year-old obsessed with a photo he finds of a Russian hanged by Nazi troops during World War II. Set in the Soviet Union and relying heavily on flashbacks, the book explores contemporary Russia and its possibility for an improved future.

Plante's most recent work finds him continuing to explore elements important to all of his work: sexuality, spirituality, self-discovery, personal and familial relationships, and the possibility of synthesizing those disparate elements. *American Ghosts* (2005) is Plante's memoir exploring his desire to reconcile his heritage and physical desire with his quest to find a fulfilling spirituality. Indeed, Plante's ultimate conclusion in his memoir is that writing itself becomes a spiritual activity of sorts, offering an interesting perspective on a career of creating characters whose appeal is often based in a lack of clarity. Important for his stylistic innovation as much as thematic content, Plante is a prolific writer who was nominated for the National Book Award and regularly contributes essays and reviews to publications like the *New Yorker* and the *Paris Review*. He currently owns homes in New York and London and teaches at Columbia University.

Further Reading

Dukes, Thomas. 1993. "David Plante." In *Contemporary Gay American Novelists*, ed. Emmanuel S. Nelson, 309–15. Westport, CT: Greenwood Press.

Kaiser, John R. 1983. "David Plante." In *Dictionary of Literary Biography Yearbook 1983*, ed. Matthew Joseph Bruccoli and Jean W. Ross, 298–304. Detroit: Gale.

Nye, Robert. 1976. "David Plante." In *Contemporary Novelists*, ed. James Vinson, 1088–89. New York: St. Martin's.

J. G. Adair

playwrights

American theater has been dominated by gay playwrights, composers, directors, choreographers, and designers. Three of the most important playwrights of the 1950s, **Tennessee Williams, William Inge,** and **Edward Albee,** were gay, although only Williams cautiously opened the closet door in his major plays. Throughout his half-century career, Albee has argued against gay playwrights writing what he called "ghetto drama" and has challenged them to write plays about other subjects than sexual orientation. Yet his most recent and, arguably, best work, *The Goat, or Who Is Sylvia* (2000), shows how **homophobia** may reside in even the most sexually unconventional families. Despite Albee's proscription, the history of queer drama is primarily one of depictions of the LGBTQ community, particularly when it was ignored or vilified by the mainstream media.

Lesbian and gay theater began as alternative theater. Gay theater began in the early 1960s in Greenwich Village with a group of young playwrights who presented their work at Joe Cino's coffeehouse, Caffe Cino, in Greenwich Village, which became a center for alternative theater. Robert Patrick, **Lanford Wilson, Doric Wilson, William Hoffman,** among others, had their work premiered on the tiny stage at the Cino, as did young straight playwrights like Sam Shepard and John Guare. Some of these playwrights moved to more lucrative venues; others remained on the fringe. All of them were seeking to create not only gay theater but also an edgier form of American theater than that offered by Broadway. The Cino playwrights' works offer the most vivid, often bittersweet pictures of the price gay men paid for internalizing the prevailing homophobia or of the challenges of developing relationships and an ethos in the urban gay underground. (See, in particular, Robert Patrick's *The Haunted Host* and Lanford Wilson's *The Madness of Lady Bright*, both 1964.)

After the closing of Caffe Cino in 1968, its playwrights found other venues through LaMama Experimental Theater, founded by lesbian Ellen Stewart; The Other Side of Silence, a gay **theater company** founded by Doric Wilson; The Glines; the producing team Richard Barr, Clinton Wilder, and Edward Albee, champions of alternative drama; or the Circle Repertory Company founded by Lanford Wilson and Marshall Mason.

The most commercially successful early gay drama, **Mart Crowley**'s *The Boys in the Band* (1968; film, 1970), began its life in the commercial theater. While later critics attacked Crowley's picture of self-hatred among a group of New York gay men, the play echoed the themes of alienation and dysfunction among gay men found in the Caffe Cino plays without stressing that the root cause of its characters' malaise was homophobia and the price of living in the **closet,** not their sexual orientation. Structurally, Crowley's play was quite influential on other gay playwrights, and many plays followed that depicted a group of urban gay men spending an evening in a living room. David Dillon's commercially successful *Party* (1992) turned Crowley's truth game into a pretext for nudity, and Jonathan Tolins's *The Last Sunday in June* (2003) is both an homage to and a spoof of the genre.

One of the most consistent voices to come out of the 1960s gay theater has been **Terrence McNally,** the most successful and prolific writer in bringing gay men into mainstream theater. His hit comedy, *The Ritz* (1974), was successful enough to transfer to Broadway (a first for a comedy set in a gay **bathhouse**) and later become a film. For 40 years, McNally has been an articulate voice of the aspirations and crises of the gay community. McNally's major works provide a minihistory of gay New York, from the comic queens of *The Ritz,* to the obsessed opera queens of *The Lisbon Traviata* (1985), to the AIDS-era works *Andre's Mother* (written for television, 1990) and *Love! Valour! Compassion!* (1994). His presentation of Jesus as a gay man in *Corpus Christi* (1997) led to nightly protests. Recently McNally took on the issue of gay marriage in *Some Men* (2007). Even McNally's hit play about diva Maria Callas, *Master Class* (1995), and the long-running musical, *Kiss of the Spider Woman* (1992), with a score by the gay songwriting team, John Kander and Fred Ebb, have connections to gay culture.

At the same time as young gay playwrights were finding their voices at Caffe Cino, a campier, **drag** theater was developing first through Ronald Tavel and John Vaccaro's Theater of the Ridiculous and its offspring, **Charles Ludlam**'s Ridiculous Theatrical Company. Mixing B movies and other pop culture artifacts with spoofs of high culture, these productions centered on the drag diva turns of the leading performers Tavel, Ludlam, and, later, **Charles Busch.** Ludlam, the most celebrated of the ridiculous performers and creators, was not a conventional drag queen. His elegant gowns did not hide his chest hair or his body fat. One never forgot that a man was playing a woman. The Ridiculous tradition continues with its current practitioner Lypsinka (John Epperson), and elements of their style can be found in later plays. One queer drag artist, **Harvey Fierstein,** managed to move from the fringe to Broadway with his *Torch Song Trilogy* (1981), which he wrote and starred in (and which was later turned into a film), and with his book for the hit musical *La Cage aux Folles* (1983). Both works can be seen now as early arguments for gay marriage, and *La Cage aux Folles,* with its elaborate drag acts, brought the **camp** subtext of many ostensibly heterosexual musicals to the surface.

Lesbian theater never moved into the mainstream as gay male theater did. There is no lesbian equivalent in commercial theater to gay writers like Mart Crowley, Terrence McNally, or **Tony Kushner.** Indeed, lesbian writers and performers had to battle against both homophobia and the privileged position men held in the theater. As a result, **performance art** has become a major creative force in the lesbian artistic community. Nonetheless, there have been a number of important playwrights, although their work has not received the attention that male playwrights

Angels in America: The Millennium Approaches (Original Broadway Production). By Tony Kushner. Directed by George C. Wolfe. Shown: Joe Mantello, and Stephen Spinella. Courtesy of Joan Marcus/Photofest.

have received. Pioneer and mentor Maria Irene Fornes began her career as part of the playwrights group at Judson Memorial Church, started by Reverend Al Carmines, himself a writer and composer. Fornes's writings chart the lives of a variety of women, gay and straight, white and Latina. **Jane Chambers**'s series of plays about lesbians in the 1970s, including *A Late Snow* (1974) and *Last Summer at Bluefish Cove* (1980), validated women's communities and love. To a great extent, lesbian theater has been driven by the radical performing groups of the 1970s such as Split Britches and the Five Lesbian Brothers. In 1976, the WOW Theater Festival began in New York as a showcase for lesbian performing groups. Latina playwright, poet, and essayist **Cherrie Moraga** is the most celebrated of the younger generation of lesbian playwrights. In works like *The Hungry Woman: A Mexican Medea* (2002), Moraga bridges Chicana, feminist, and lesbian politics. In the twenty-first century, some of the most commercially successful American plays center on female protagonists, but only one (Margaret Edson's *Wit*) was written by a woman, and that play, penned by a lesbian, only hints at the sexual orientation of its protagonist.

As lesbians and gay men began to demand a place at the table in American society, theater groups were founded west of the Hudson. Theater Rhinoceros in San Francisco and Bailiwick Repertory Company in Chicago were the largest of a number of theaters either devoted exclusively to queer theater or making the promotion of gay and lesbian drama part of their agenda. Theaters such as Medusa's Revenge in New York, the Red Dyke Theatre in Atlanta, and the Lavender Cellar in Minneapolis were devoted to plays and entertainments by and for lesbians. Such theater provided an outlet for playwrights and performance artists as well as an important meeting place for the lesbian and gay community when mainstream theater, film, and television offered no positive representations of their lives. Adventurous publishers realized there was a reading audience for plays by gay and lesbian writers, particularly since gay and lesbian **bookstores** such as A Different Light in San Francisco and New York, the Oscar Wilde Bookshop in New York, Lambda Rising in Washington, D.C., and OutWrite in Atlanta had also become a crucial part of urban gay culture. By the beginning of the twenty-first century, some of these shops had been forced to close as many gay and lesbian couples moved out of the **gay ghettoes** and the giant bookstore chains and Internet sites captured the reading market.

The AIDS epidemic struck the gay community in the early 1980s, and for the next decade much of gay male drama was devoted to responses to the AIDS crisis.

William Hoffman's *As Is* (1985) moved from Greenwich Village to Broadway to television and **Larry Kramer'**s *The Normal Heart* (1985) was produced at the New York Public Theater. Hoffman's *As Is,* a depiction of a gay couple dealing with AIDS, was the first AIDS play to be performed on Broadway. **Robert Chesley'**s *Night Sweat* (1984) and *Jerker* (1985) are among the most powerful and angriest of the dramatic responses to the AIDS crisis. **Christopher Durang'**s *Laughing Wild* (1987) offered an angry, yet funny diatribe against homophobia and indifference in the midst of the AIDS epidemic. Lesbian playwright **Paula Vogel'**s playful tribute to her late brother, *The Baltimore Waltz* (1992), has been one of the most performed dramas of the AIDS era. These angry, often funny, deeply moving works are representative of a large body of drama presenting the AIDS crisis as the community saw it, as opposed to the many television dramas depicting a person with AIDS, and homosexuality as a family problem conveniently eliminated by the patient's death. As AIDS became less of a death sentence, works like Tony Kushner's *Angels in America* (1992) could depict a person with AIDS as a heroic survivor. Kushner's mammoth work, which moved from small theaters to the National Theater of Great Britain to Broadway and finally to HBO, became a kind of summation of gay politics of its time, confronting the perils of the closet and the political danger to gay people caused by closeted conservatives and conservative American religion, the impotence of the Left, AIDS as a gay disease, and the inevitability of acceptance of gay men and women into the body politic. The one thing *Angels in America* did not show is a positive view of loving gay relationships. Nonetheless, it stands as the most brilliantly written of gay plays and, in its mix of domestic realism with more experimental theatrical forms found in earlier queer drama, forms a powerful influence on younger writers.

A number of gay playwrights have been active in the past two decades. **Paul Rudnick,** who moves back and forth from stage to film, wrote a series of funny plays, from the AIDS comedy *Jeffrey* (1993) to the mock-biblical *The Most Fabulous Story Ever Told* (1998). Richard Greenberg's *Take Me Out* (2003), which won the Tony for Best Play in 2004, used the coming out of a baseball star to raise issues about race, homophobia, and isolation in America. Throughout Greenberg's career, in plays like *Eastern Standard* (1988), *The American Plan* (1990), and *Three Days of Rain* (1998), he has placed gay characters in his dramas of loneliness in contemporary America. Neal Bell's *Spatter Pattern* (2004) depicts the relationship between a murderer and a man overcome by grief and rage at the death of his lover. **Craig Lucas'**s *Dying Gaul* (1998, later made into a film) is an angry portrait of the relationship of a **bisexual** Hollywood producer, his wife, and a young writer who is reluctant to change the gay couple at the heart of his screenplay to a heterosexual couple. Douglas Carter Beane's *The Little Dog Laughed* (2006) is an equally devastating satire on the Hollywood closet. After over 20 years on the road, queer performance artist Tim Miller continues to insist on anger and action in his celebrated one-man shows.

Paula Vogel is the most produced of contemporary lesbian playwrights. In works like *And Baby Makes Seven* (1986), *Hot 'n' Throbbing* (1992), *The Minneola Twins* (1996), and *How I Learned to Drive* (1997), Vogel has placed lesbian characters in satires of the values that diminish same-sex relationships, lesbians, and women.

Like many queer playwrights, Vogel is always defying realistic theater and experimenting with new techniques of representation.

Across the country, other dramatists were dealing with the experiences of non-white queer people. **Chay Yew**'s *A Language of Their Own* (1995) is a touching picture of the lives and loves of gay Asian Americans in the age of AIDS. **Guillermo Reyes**'s *Men on the Verge of a His-panic Breakdown* (1994) and *Deporting the Divas* (1996) dramatized the perils of the closet in the Latino community. In the 1980s and early 1990s, the group *Pomo Afro Homos* offered theatrical snapshots of the life of the African American gay community.

Since the success of *La Cage aux Folles* in 1983, a number of musicals have outed the gay subtext always just below the surface in musicals. **William Finn**'s *March of the Falsettos* (1981) and *Falsettoland* (1990), musicals about the coming out of his antihero, Marvin, and Marvin's loss of his lover to AIDS, were combined on Broadway in 1992 as *Falsettos* and had a respectable run. The camp musical reviews based on the late Howard Crabtree's outlandish costume designs, *Whoop-de-Doo* (1993) and *When Pigs Fly* (1996), were off-Broadway hits. *Zanna Don't* (2003) is a fanciful picture of a high school where gay is in and straight is definitely out. Major gay characters are crucial to the hits *Rent*, *Avenue Q*, *Altar Boyz*, and even *Mamma Mia*.

In the twenty-first century, a number of the adventurous, small theater companies that championed gay theater have found it difficult to survive. Gay audiences now have cable channels like Logo and Here specializing in queer entertainment. Gay and lesbian soap operas *Queer as Folk* and *The L Word* were on premium cable (two of the most important gay playwrights—Jonathan Tolins and Canadian Brad Fraser were involved with these series), and the brilliant HBO series *Six Feet Under* (produced by gay writer Alan Ball) featured a gay couple. Logo's *Noah's Arc* offers a comic picture of the tribulations of African American gay men while commenting on particular issues for that community, from the hypocrisy of many black churches to HIV. Of course, television being television, all the characters on *Queer as Folk* or *Noah's Arc* are relatively affluent. The one character that remains invisible is the poor queer. Independent queer cinema flourishes and is readily available on DVD. Why would an author write for theater, where there is little chance of getting a play produced, when he/she can make a low-budget gay film that will be available for home viewing? The Internet, too, offers many attractions for gay people and has redefined notions of entertainment and community. In this age of competition with all the media, some theaters and producers understand that variations on the hit *Naked Boys Singing* will bring in audiences that otherwise are not interested in theater (one major gay theater even offers *A Naked Christmas*). Still, four plays by gay playwrights Douglas Carter Beane, Paul Rudnick, Terrence McNally, and Craig Lucas opened at major New York theaters in the 2006–2007 season. Prominent queer playwrights are on university and conservatory faculties mentoring the writers of the future. In the twenty-first century, the issue for gay playwrights is, as it is for their straight colleagues, the future of serious live drama in America.

Further Reading

Bernstein, Robin, ed. 2006. *Cast Out: Queer Lives in Theater (Triangulations: Lesbian/Gay/Queer Theater/Drama/Performance)*. Ann Arbor: University of Michigan Press.

Clum, John M. 2000. *Still Acting Gay: Male Homosexuality in Modern Drama*. New York: St. Martin's Press.

Sinfield, Alan. 1999. *Out on Stage: Lesbian and Gay Theatre in the Twentieth Century*. New Haven, CT: Yale University Press.

John M. Clum

Kenneth Pobo (1954–)

Kenneth Pobo, born in Illinois, is a widely published poet in American little magazines, in small presses, and on literary Web sites. His books include *Musings from the Porchlit Sea* (1979), *Ordering: A Season in My Garden* (2001), *Introductions* (2003), *Glass Garden* (2008), and eleven others. Much of his best work remains uncollected, including poems about alter-ego Aaron Stern in his creative thesis at University of Wisconsin–Milwaukee (UWM) (PhD granted in 1983); his peers in the creative writing program at UWM included **Nuala Archer** and **Henri Cole.** Pobo is associate professor of English at Widener University.

The pop iconography of top-40 music transforms into a muse for Pobo; *Evergreen* is named after a song on *Cellophane Symphony* (Tommy James and the Shondells, 1969). As in the work of **David Trinidad,** Pobo's **camp** style weds innocence to the pop tune. Another influence was D. H. Lawrence's *Pansies* (1929), a book of poems attacking human stupidity. Lawrence "allowed me to be free to say things I didn't think I ever could say" (interview, 2007). The title *A Barbaric Yawp on the Rocks* indicates Walt Whitman as a progenitor. Other gay influences include Frank O'Hara and Mutsuo Takahashi.

Pobo's poetry—in both free verse and traditional forms—contemplates the past, explores nature, engages politics, and invents or explores characters (including a series on Red Riding Hood in *Introductions*). The tone shifts from humor to anger: in "Special Rights" (*Bay Windows*, 1993), he writes, "I have the right to be attacked/the right to be fired (cause unstated)/...the right to stand on Camac Street/looking down at my lover,/pistol-whipped, unconscious." He writes poetry of witness, as well as poetry of contemplation. Because Pobo's work is scattered through myriad magazines and chapbooks, a new and selected edition of his work is needed to gauge his achievement as a poet.

Further Reading

Lawson, D. S. 2003. "Kenneth Pobo (1954–)." In *Contemporary Gay American Poets and Playwrights: An A-to-Z Guide*, ed. Emmanuel S. Nelson, 363–68. Westport, CT: Greenwood Press.

Michael J. Emery

poets, gay

It is important to consider two conflicting approaches to the study of poetry. One is that poems be read as "organic wholes," divorced from their historical context and their author's biography. However, another tendency—especially evident in the 1970s—was to emphasize the relationship of "art" to a wider social and political context, with this approach fueled by the writings of marginalized poets. It is therefore important to recognize the influence of cultural history (as well as the personal biographies of poets) on modern gay poetry. It is also important to identify shared themes and styles (as well as differences) between poets that, along with the adaptation of traditional forms, assist us in understanding the notion of a gay aesthetic. Indeed, some poets were grouped together in so-called schools.

Influenced by British Romantics like William Wordsworth, Walt Whitman (1819–1892) advocated individualism, the necessity for a retreat from society into nature, the joy of the senses, and homosexual mystic union; he occupies a prestigious position hovering over the literary landscape as the "father of American gay poetry." **Hart Crane**'s poetry in the early twentieth century is also significant; in a country where the (homosexual) artist was alienated, he sought a means of giving voice to a more pluralistic "American" identity.

However, gay poetry has been most prominent in the United States since the 1950s, a decade marking a development from Crane's work, which, when it did explore homosexual desire, did so mainly in a coded metaphorical fashion, and which saw homosexuality (though physical) as a means to the spiritual. The 1950s witnessed the emergence of the Beat writers who reacted against conformity to the white heterosexual middle-class values so characteristic of the decade. First meeting at Columbia University in **New York City,** the Beat writers discussed the need to express more radical (if not necessarily homosexual) experiences in a direct, angry tone. Nevertheless, Allen Ginsberg's (see **San Francisco Bay Area Poets**) homosexuality came to the fore in his poems, where he bluntly referred to sexual activity using shocking slang. **Harold Norse,** influenced by Ginsberg, is often described as a Beat writer since he veers between writing about the exotic and writing about activities such as masturbation and desire in a conversational tone. So a newer gay aesthetic was apparent. In these ways, the Beat writers were influenced by another of the most important figures shaping modern poetry, William Carlos Williams, who, in 1944, wrote (with slight echoes of Crane's view) of the need to capture a representative American voice and to employ freer poetic forms in order to do so. The **New York School of Poets** can also be situated in relation to the 1950s with wit being one of their characteristics, again evidencing a gay aesthetic; Frank O'Hara's use of **camp** was partly a reaction against conservatism. Another group situated in relation to the 1950s is the Black Mountain School, who had attended North Carolina's Black Mountain College (1933–1957), an experimental institution in the arts. Artists of this school, such as **Jonathan Williams,** were associated with the avant-garde since their work ran contrary to the mainstream; they practiced new artistic techniques that had a definite social function.

Allen Ginsberg. Photo by Robert Pruzan, courtesy of the Gay, Lesbian, Bisexual, Transgender Historical Society, San Francisco.

The rebellious 1960s, when marginalized groups used their voices to expose their individuality, have had an impact on gay poetry to the present day. As a result of **Stonewall,** much gay poetry has become (sometimes with hesitation) confessional, where we must look to the personal histories of poets set against this wider context. Occasionally, poetry has taken on the quality of **autobiography** in verse, as in the case, in the early 1990s, of Alfred Corn, who had grown up in the 1950s and 1960s. The emergence of the gay individual from the **closet** is, moreover, a theme in the later work of **Henri Cole.** Gay poetry further deals with themes of humanity and of homosexual desire. This is evident in the poetry of **Edward Field, Rudy Kikel,** and **Carl Phillips.** Field's poems, for instance, influenced by Whitman (and, like those of Alfred Corn, making reference to classical Greece), emphasize the majesty of the created world and of the sexual stirring of the self away from society's constraints.

While this entry, by its very definition, seeks to group gay poets together, each gay poet is a unique individual, a fact recognized by the individual entries on various gay poets, and we must again look to personal histories and note the impact that these have had on gay poetry when considering that poetry has also been written by gay men from other minority groups, with an individual having multiple cultural identities. Living in a country where white heterosexuality is considered the norm, **Maurice Kenny**'s status as both gay and of Native American descent informs his work, which concerns the manner in which people cross cultural boundaries. Conversely, much more recently in the poetry of Carl Phillips and **Reginald Shepherd,** ideas of their "blackness" play a marginal role. Gay men have also been located within different religious persuasions; for example, converting to Catholicism was a means by which Canadian American poet **Daryl Hine** attempted to escape his homosexuality, as dealt with in his 1970s autobiography in verse.

Stylistically, post-1960s gay poetry differs from much poetry of the 1950s. Writing largely in the first person, many poets continue the trend set by the Beat writers of breaking free from the shackles of older, more ordered forms of verse, emphasizing a conversational style appropriate to the down-to-earth subject matter. This natural rhythm of speech is also important to Maurice Kenny's poetry in locating the work within a Native American, as well as a gay, tradition. However, gay poetry does not completely abandon both traditional and ordered forms of verse, and individual gay poets are not consistent in the use of one particular form throughout their oeuvre. **Richard Howard** appropriated the traditional Victorian form of the dramatic monologue (most commonly associated with Robert Browning), in which a speaker addresses an unheard person in a conversational manner and we must deduce that speaker's motives, important in conveying that all of us, in one way or another, put on masks. Later, Howard turned to a poetry of dialogue between two speakers, reclaiming voices from the past. More recently, Henri Cole, despite writing in a self-reflexive manner of abandoning formal techniques, has appropriated and adapted the traditional ordered form of the sonnet, as has **J. D. McClatchy,** while probing the harm we do to those we love.

Historically, the onslaught of **HIV/AIDS** in the early 1980s, and the stigma associated with the disease—fueled politically, by the church, and by society at large— also had an immeasurable impact on gay poetry. There was a haunting silence in discourses surrounding AIDS, as the victims were frequently regarded as subhuman. President Ronald Reagan would not publicly speak the word AIDS for five years, while the church saw many of the victims as having engaged in immoral homosexual behavior. Against this context one can place both the **Names Project AIDS Memorial Quilt** (itself a woven texture, memorializing the dead through words and pictures and giving the disease a human face) and gay AIDS poetry (which to some extent paralleled this aesthetic strategy). For poetry served as a choral record to the human devastation wrought by the disease and, unlike the AIDS memorial quilt, immortalized the very voices of those afflicted with the disease, thereby making evident that which society had largely repressed. Even the elegies to loved ones (the emergence of an old poetic form) are not only personal but also have the political effect of putting a human face to the disease. Themes—at once personal and political—are not only of institutional homophobia by the government and church, resulting in the individual's alienation, but also of a lost youth and gay subculture and, as with much gay poetry, ideas that make us all human (love and death), here giving a face to the disease, amid the occasional use of the impersonal vocabulary of medical science. Tonally, the voices in this poetry shift between the extremes of wit, sentimentality, and anger, while, formally, this poetry further challenges the notion of the need for an ordered poetic language, consisting as it often does of chaotic outpourings of grief. So again poetry was appropriate for communicating gay sensibilities and capturing the emotions attached to AIDS. Poetry, like the play and the short story (see **HIV/AIDS** impact on literature), was an ideal type of literature for providing a swift testament of one's suffering or that of loved ones afflicted with AIDS, as well as commenting on political oppression; these ideas inform the poetry of **Walter Holland, Paul Monette,** and **D. A. Powell,** among others. Even the 1997 AIDS poetry of Rudy Kikel, which was deeply personal, blurs this line between art and politics, which, along with more universal themes, causes gay poetry to occupy such an important place in U.S. LGBTQ culture.

Further Reading

Caplan, David. 2005. *Questions of Possibility: Contemporary Poetry and Poetic Form.* New York: Oxford University Press.

Charters, Ann. 2003. *The Portable Beat Reader.* New York: Penguin.

Foster, Edward H. 1994. *Understanding the Black Mountain Poets.* Columbia: University of South Carolina Press.

Holland, Walter. 2000. "A Poetry of Crisis, A Poetry of Witness." In *Body Positive.* Available at: http://www.thebody.com/content/art31284.html. Accessed July 14, 2008.

Martin, Robert K. 1998. *The Homosexual Tradition in American Poetry.* Iowa City: University of Iowa Press.

Andrew O'Day

poets, lesbian

However one chooses to define lesbian poetry—the sexual identity of the poet, the themes and perspectives of the poem, or lesbian readers' identification with certain poets and poems—in American letters, lesbian-authored or "-identified" poetry has an articulate and distinguished tradition that dates at least as far back as the mid-nineteenth century, with erotic lyrics such as "Wild Nights, Wild Nights" and "Her Breast Is Fit for Pearls" that Emily Dickinson wrote to her sister-in-law, Susan Huntington Gilbert Dickinson. While the determination of Dickinson's sexual identity remains conjectural, these and other poems articulate lesbian passions that are not, in some sense, less real for being, perhaps, fantastic or even mythical. Indeed, the continued reliance of lesbians on textual as opposed to geographical community has drawn acute attention to the textual construction of lesbian identity, although the same holds true for all cultural identities. The mythic structures surrounding the ancient Greek poet, Sappho of Lesbos, who invented the sublime lyric love poem and from whom lesbians have derived their name—and the continuously contested definitions and referents of this overdetermined name—bear witness to the privileged place that poetics have had in the histories, theories, and legends of lesbian identity. However, despite the renewed evocations of the name lesbian, in American letters this term refers as often to the institutions of romantic friendship between women and to women's political and social activism, as to the mythic structures surrounding the "founder" of lesbian poetry and "identity." On the whole, an interweaving of the personal and erotic with the public and political has characterized American lesbian poetics, resulting in an enabling exchange between personal passion and political engagement that redeems eros from solipsism and politics from abstract jargon and flat propaganda.

Such interweaving of the erotic and personal with the public and political informs the earlier twentieth-century modernist poetics of lesbian or bisexual writers otherwise as diverse from one another as Amy Lowell, Edna St. Vincent Millay, Angelina Weld Grimké, Marianne Moore, and H. D. Lowell, who dedicated the erotic verse of "Pictures of a Floating World" and "Decade," among others, to her longtime partner, the actress Ada Russell. Another imagist, the bisexual poet H. D., had passionate romances with several women, most notably the English writer Bryher, and her mythopoetic and melodic verse explores recurring lesbian themes such as the longing for a protective maternal goddess, or an analysis of her fears of self-erasure and self-aggrandizement in relationship to her lover in "Toward the Piraeus." Like H. D., Millay was bisexual, although quite arguably far more invested in women than men. In "A Few Figs from Thistles," she asserts that women have the right to sexual pleasure but no obligations to fidelity. At the same time, in her verse play, *The Lamp and the Bell*, Millay idealizes—perhaps because the play arranges for their tragic separation at the hands of a male suitor—the romantic bond between two stepsisters, about whom another character declares, "I vow I never knew a pair of lovers/More constant than these two." Marianne Moore, although apparently celibate, excoriates what she terms the "enterprise" of heterosexual union in "Marriage." Her high-hearted pith contrasts sharply with the near-Victorian melancholic rue expressed by the African American lesbian poet, Angelina Weld Grimké, over her frustrated erotic and romantic longings for another woman in poems such as, for instance, "Naughty Nan." The longing for love from and for another woman, whether represented as a maternal, a sisterly, or an openly erotic object, with this desire extended into the domain of social relations, remains the core defining desire of "lesbian" poetics.

However, the sumptuously playful, joyous, and innovative paeans to lesbian love composed by the leading lesbian modernist, Gertrude Stein, along with the incisively defiant song lyrics of blues artists such as Gertrude "Ma" Rainey, Bessie Smith, and Gladys Bentley, which deserve inclusion in the traditions of American lesbian poetics, not only rearticulate lesbian desire and segue into later lesbian poetics but also develop new means of representing the relationship between the personal and the public spheres. Stein's "Lifting Belly," an elaborate exploration of the delights of lesbian passion that remains, alongside "Tender Buttons," among the masterpieces of American lesbian poetry, is set or, rather, counterpointed, against the madness of World War I, which rages outside the domain of the lover's bedroom—a stark and telling contrast between creatively fecund woman-on-woman pleasure and the sterile angst of the "rule of the fathers" that Stein parodies in poems such as "Patriarchal Poetry." Black blues song lyrics such as "B. D. Women Blues" humorously characterize "bull daggers" as "rough" women who can drink their whiskey and "sure can strut their stuff," while Ma Rainey, in her delightfully tongue-in-cheek treatment of the open secret of lesbian desire in "Prove It on Me Blues," sings, "They must've been women, 'cause I don't like no men." Stein, like the African American women blues artists, can be said to mark an essential departure from the past—in their unapologetically robust articulations of lesbian desire, their refusal of "high romantic" melancholic sentiment and anomie, and most of all in their recognition of the very public and political significations of "private" lesbian desire. If we postulate, as supported by the evidence, the recurrence in women of an intense and primal desire to receive from and give to women forms of love that are risked in the name of meaning, then it is entirely likely that women poets recognized similar passions in other women poets and identified them within their tradition. The late lesbian modernist poet **Elizabeth Bishop,** and her contemporary **May Swenson,** established the foundations for the explicitly lesbian poets who emerged as an important collective voice in the mid-1970s and who included **Adrienne Rich, Olga Broumas, Audre Lorde, Judy Grahn,** and **Irena Klepfisz,** among others.

Bishop began her long poetic career, which spanned from the 1920s to the 1970s, by avoiding identification with various poetic schools and choosing obscure places such as Florida, Brazil, and Nova Scotia over the familiar haunts of New York City and Paris. Both she and Swenson adumbrate what later became the lesbian poetic ethos of care, reserve, and anti-incorporative love toward nature, animals, and, in Bishop's case, native cultures. The narrator of Bishop's "The Fish" literally lets her catch "off the hook," and in the late narrative poem "The Moose," the unexpected appearance of an enormous female moose in the road delivers the passengers in a bus from their tedious self-absorption and concerns. Bishop lived for some time in Brazil, where she had a long-term lesbian relationship with Lota de Macedo Soares and wrote numerous poems evoking lesbian subjectivity—the joys of shampooing another woman's hair, native women who flee from the rapacious conquistadores, the home she shared with Soares enveloped in protective rain and fog, and magical dolphins. In her late poem "In the Waiting Room," the child narrator describes how she becomes aware of her "difference" and her estrangement from her culture while gazing at the photographs of seminaked African women in *National Geographic*, presented to her "Western" gaze as embodiments of racial backwardness "captured" by the same culture that, beyond the office walls, prosecutes World War I—a conflict that a number of lesbian poets evidently see as the eclipse of Western culture. Bishop refused to identify as lesbian but poured languages of lesbian subjectivity and ethics into her poetry. In contrast, **Muriel Rukeyser,** who had committed her poetry to social justice, helped create the image of her late volume *Speed of Darkness* (1968) as her **coming out.** Rukeyser declared, "No more masks! No more mythologies!" but remained deeply apprehensive over removing her heterosexual mask, as evidenced in the poem "Kathe Kollwitz," where she proclaims that "if one woman told the truth about her life," the "world would split open." Bishop even refuses to be included in what she characterized as the "segregated" 1973 anthology of women poets *No More Masks!*, suggesting that, if Rukeyser had imbibed **homophobia,** Bishop had, perhaps, gone one step further, confusing her ethical detestation of allegory with both **identity** and identification and, therefore, declining, in public, social bonds with other women and remaining blind to the ethical implications of a voice that had time and history but not the moral and social obligations to others conferred by identity.

For most of the twentieth century, lesbianism had been reduced to an allegorical figuration of pathology, maladjustment, mistaken gender, and failure, but lesbian feminists claimed for lesbians the right to self-representation or, at least, to representations that differed from the fantasies of heterosexual men. According to Mary J. Carruthers, the map of lesbian poetics was redrawn in 1978, the year in which Rich's *The Dream of a Common Language*, Lorde's *The Black Unicorn*, Grahn's *The Work of a Common Woman*, and Broumas's *Beginning with O* were published. Carruthers argues persuasively that these poets differ fundamentally from their predecessors, examining social, psychological, and aesthetic life at the level of metaethics. Their poetry cannot be approached through psychoanalysis or confession, and their ethics, not confined to the dimensions of the personal or experiential, can be articulated only through myths that structure intricate poetic images of "lesbian relationship." In other words, while earlier lesbian or bisexual poets, such as Lowell or H. D., had evoked mythemes of Sappho—as founder, mother, creator, lover—they could not name her identity or theirs, which meant that location depended on images and associations derived from the scene, not the persons. Lesbian "identity" depended on context. The lesbian feminists, many of whom had once been heterosexual, addressed the issue of value in language and decided that little in the culture of environmental catastrophe, trivialization, violence, coercion, and deceit commanded their respect. At the heart of this new lesbian mythopoetics was the lesbian as someone who, rejecting deceit and avowing buried myths, could articulate the ethical call for women to shatter the silence between them caused by privatization, denial, and shame and to construct a new language. Lesbians needed new foundations on which to articulate themselves, foundations that could envision the creation of social rather than merely private textual space. Grahn reclaimed Sappho, wrote the essential literary historical narrative of lesbian poetics, and, in "Edward the Dyke," written two years before the American Psychiatric Association removed homosexuality as a mental illness in 1972, defined lesbianism as "Cinnamon toast poetry. Justice equality higher wages. Independent angel song. It means I can do what I want." Broumas evoked Sappho, Lorde the women warriors of ancient Dahomey, Rich accomplished women who had been marginalized or compromised by sexism, and the Jewish lesbian feminist poet Irena Klepfisz the Tribe of Dina. The title of Klepfisz's poem *"Etlekhe Verter Oyf Mame-Loshn*/A Few Words in the Mother Tongue" suggests the importance attached to locating the ancestral maternal language that could supersede the languages of pathology, shame, marginalization, and secrecy. However, eventually the freedom granted to self-represent resulted in a questioning, sometimes of the meaning of the term lesbian, and sometimes of the authenticity of the term itself.

Most believe that this lesbian feminist mythopoesis had faded by the mid-1990s in the face of AIDS, racist divisions, and the return of repressed gender differences embodied in **butch–femme** female clones. However, lesbian mythopoetics remain, although the emphasis has fallen increasingly on ordinary ethics, family life, and erotic expression. The Native American lesbian poet Beth Brant explains that a bald eagle that had landed near her car instructed her to write—and therefore validated the authentic "root" of her identity. **Chrystos,** vigorous in her attack on genocide, racism, and the mainstreaming of LGBT culture, uses the Native American term *two-spirit*, rather than lesbian. The Chicana lesbian poets **Cherrie Moraga** and **Gloria Anzaldúa** speak of culture and border crossing, but for Moraga no mythos can erase the consequences of "Loving in the War Years," which "calls for this kind of risking / without a home to call your own." For others, such as **Becky Birtha,** lesbianism and Quakerism are ethical choices that furnish her a home, so that in recent years she has written extensively about her experiences with motherhood. For the African American lesbian poet **Cheryl Clarke,** race matters far less as an issue than it does to **Pat Parker,** another African American lesbian poet, and Clarke populates her poems with African American cultural references and, in a marked recent trend, elaborates an explicitly erotic lesbian poetics. Of course certain writers, such as **Dorothy Allison** and **Minnie Bruce Pratt,** as Southern white lesbian poets, have not inherited an enabling lesbian mythos of which they could claim ownership. Pratt notes that the only thing of value she has inherited from her forebears is the habit of skepticism. On the other hand, Allison, who occupies the social position of someone who is poor, Southern, white, female, lesbian, and called "trash," does not shelter illusions that women are less capable than men of using religion, class, ignorance, and social status as weapons. Allison, like Pratt, in the absence of alibis, myths, or languages has taken to asserting—or taking charge of—the value of her existence by telling difficult home truths about what actually happens, although, it must be said, the absence of a tradition nudges people closer to feelings of worthlessness or rage. In "The Women Who Hate Me," Allison avers that she no longer believes in the "natural superiority" of the lesbian, for she has witnessed herself succumb to mothering desperate women, just as her straight peers mother desperate men.

The marked trends in recent time toward lesbians becoming mothers and creating families on the one hand, and lesbians creating public community through erotic verse on the other hand, indicate, along with the prominence of transgender issues, how much continues to change in relation to the function, the topics, and the audience of lesbian poetry. In *Love, Death and the Changing of the Seasons*, **Marilyn Hacker** exhibits the command of craft, form, and technique that had sometimes been missing from post-**Stonewall** lesbian poetry, but, at the same time, omits the political and social investments that had long been intrinsic to poetic articulations of lesbian identity. In this usually moving, if occasionally slick, sonnet sequence, however, Hacker tackles the hard and poignant topic of an older lesbian abandoned romantically by a younger woman. Perhaps the lack of social or even historical engagement that has characterized more recent lesbian poetics with notable exceptions reflects the need to establish the private and the public as distinct domains, or, in contrast, the general unraveling of political passion caused by too much corruption and failed policy. The lesbian community's concern with environmental degradation, violence, poor health care, corruption, and social stress will be shared as equal burdens with the general public. Future lesbian poetry will continue the dialectical dialogue with the past and articulate the voices that need to enter the past in order to shape the future. No longer oppressed by psychiatry but rather by politicized religion, lesbians will continue in increasing numbers to give birth to children and to create families that, unlike at any other point in the historical past, no longer depend on men. Possibly, the changing temporal and spatial horizons of lesbian community will favor extended prose narrative over poetry, and we will witness the elaboration of new "family plots." Almost surely, the widespread enjoyment of lesbian erotic poetry as well as the popularity of raising families will result in investment in practical ethics as opposed to the ambitions of myth.

Further Reading

Carruthers, Mary J. 1983. "The Re-Vision of the Muse: Adrienne Rich, Audre Lorde, Judy Grahn, Olga Broumas." *The Hudson Review* 36 (2): 293–322.

Comment, Kristen M. 2001. "Dickinson's Bawdy: Shakespeare and Sexual Symbolism in Emily Dickinson's Writing to Susan Dickinson." *Legacy* 18 (2): 167–81.

Faderman, Lillian, ed. 1994. *Chloe Plus Olivia: An Anthology of Lesbian Literature from the Seventeenth Century to the Present*. New York: Penguin.

Garber, Linda. 1995. "Lesbian Identity Politics: Judy Grahn, Pat Parker, and the Rise of Queer Theory." PhD diss., Stanford University.

Garber, Linda. 2001. *Identity Poetics: Race, Class, and the Lesbian-Feminist Roots of Queer Theory*. New York: Columbia University Press.

Owens, David. M. 1998. "Gertrude Stein's 'Lifting Belly' and the Great War." *Modern Fiction Studies* 44 (3): 608–18.

Corinne E. Blackmer

political scandals

Pervasive **homophobia** in American society has led to both paranoia about LGBTs invading positions of power and a frenzy of scandal surrounding even a suggestion that LGBTs had covertly been enjoying such positions. Unsubstantiated rumors rise to the level of lore when sexuality is at stake. J. Edgar Hoover's pro-clivity for wearing women's lingerie has become almost fact amid various claims. Eleanor Roosevelt's possible penchant for the ladies entered the public fray when her intimate letters to newswoman Lorena Hickok became public in 1978. Candi-dates have used the fear of homosexuality to sabotage competitors' campaigns. In two consecutive elections, Dwight D. Eisenhower's supporters used innuendo as-sociated with the less-than-macho persona of Eastern intellectual Adlai Stevenson to thrust his sexuality into question and assure political disaster. Gossip columnist Walter Winchell announced on his radio program that "A vote for Adlai Steven-son is a vote for Christine Jorgensen," the high-profile male-to-female transsexual. Nearly half a century later, politicians and pundits were still using similar tactics to create suspicion regarding opponents. Whether Karl Rove's tactic of casting Texas Democratic Governor Ann Richards as a drug-addicted lesbian or conservative talk show hosts casting verbal slurs implicating the sexuality of candidates, homophobia retains its power in creating trouble for politicians and their political futures.

Beyond the power of rumor and innuendo, substantiated accounts and casu-alties of LGBT scandal litter the American political landscape. As early as the 1920s, homosexual witch-hunting and scandal rocked Congress. A questionable attempt to ferret out gay sailors at the Naval Training Station in Newport, Rhode Island, resulted in a congressional investigation. In 1919, when future president Franklin Delano Roosevelt, then assistant secretary of the navy, requested investi-gation into the homosexual activities on and around the base, young naval recruits were instructed to engage in homosexual acts with the gay sailors, document the activity, and ultimately use it as legal evidence against them. A somewhat success-ful operation, the press publicized ensuing military and civilian trials. A livid Con-gress would form a subcommittee to deal with the scandal, laying blame on neither Roosevelt nor the sailors, but on the officers who oversaw the operation.

The 1950s brought increased hysteria regarding LGBTs in government. Shortly following Joseph McCarthy's 1950 speech regarding the threat of Communist in-filtrators, Deputy Undersecretary John Peurifoy announced the firing of a number of "security risks" from the State Department, including 91 homosexuals. Rather than appearing as part of a major crackdown, the firings highlighted a perceived in-filtration of the State Department by homosexuals. These firings would lead to the "Panic on the Potomac" and a continued degradation of the department's "pansy tint," "lavender diplomats," and overwhelming number of perceived sexual per-verts. Like suspected Communists, suspected gays and lesbians were questioned, asked to name names, and ultimately fired for immorality and susceptibility to blackmail.

Amid panics regarding homosexuals in the State Department, Eisenhower—campaigning on the slogan "Let's Clean House"—sought to demonstrate a tough policy of rooting out gays and lesbians from government service. The new head of the State Department's Bureau of Security and Consular Affairs, R. W. Scott McLeod, created the "Miscellaneous M Unit" to rid the government of undesirable moral deviates. McLeod instituted the use of polygraphs and deemed the discovery of one "offense" of homosexual behavior to be grounds for expulsion—stricter than the rule used for suspected Communists. Senator Lester Hunt found himself a victim by association of this homosexual panic, ultimately shooting himself in the course of a 1954 campaign scandal and trial regarding his son's arrest on a morals charge. Data show that an overwhelming number of individuals forced from government positions in the 1940s and 1950s for posing security risks were in fact fired for suspected homosexuality.

Political scandal continued to rock the government though the Vietnam era and into the period of the **gay rights** movement. Seeking legitimacy prior to the 1964 election, Lyndon Baines Johnson found himself in the middle of a gay scandal. On October 6, 1964, police booked LBJ's top aide, Walter Jenkins, on a sex charge for engaging in a homosexual act during a sting at the Washington, D.C., YMCA. LBJ would respond by saying, "I was as shocked as if someone had told me my wife had murdered her daughter" (Weisel 1999). Despite national publicity regarding the arrest, LBJ went on to demolish Barry Goldwater in the upcoming election (and phase out Jenkins's position).

The gay rights movement brought new light to gays and lesbians in government service. Although the government dictate that allowed for the mass firings of LGBTs would not officially be repealed until Bill Clinton signed an executive order in 1995, the ensuing years brought a new kind of scandal connected to self-proclaimed, unapologetic, and politically successful LGBTs. In 1977 openly gay Harvey Milk won a seat on the San Francisco Board of Supervisors and successfully fought to defeat legislation that would have legalized the firing of openly gay and lesbian teachers. Only 13 months into Milk's term, however, political and ideological opponent Dan White shot and killed him and the San Francisco mayor—and Milk supporter—George Moscone. Although Milk's political tenure ended both prematurely and tragically, he paved the way for openly gay political figures. In 1983 Democratic Representative Gerry Studds became the first openly gay member of Congress after the revelation of his affair in 1973 with a 17-year-old male page. Studds would stand unapologetic for his sexuality in the face of congressional censure and win reelection until 1997. Elected in 1981, Massachusetts Democrat and member of the House of Representatives Barney Frank would join Studds as an openly gay Congressman after coming out publicly in 1987. Frank survived both a 1989 scandal—involving paying for sex, hiring a male hustler as his personal aide, and discovering a prostitution ring being run out of his town home—and homophobic slurs, such as the infamous 1995 House Majority Leader Dick Armey's "Barney Fag" slip of the tongue.

Despite growing acceptance of gays and lesbians in public office, homosexual scandal continues to provide fodder for the journalists. In 2003, bloggers discovered that a journalist working under the pseudonym Jeff Gannon (also known as Jim Guckert)—who had for two years gained access to the White House pressroom under the auspices of antigay Talon News—had been registered on gay male escort Web sites such as hotmilitarystud.com, militaryescorts.com, and militaryescortsM4M. com. In 2004, married New Jersey Governor Jim McGreevey resigned from his office amid a corruption scandal after admitting he had been having a gay affair for four years. McGreevey came out just before a sexual harassment case levied by the

A SERVICE OF THANKSGIVING

for the lives of
GEORGE R. MOSCONE and HARVEY B. MILK
November 26, 1983 at Seven P.M.

Welcome to Grace Cathedral, a house of prayer for all people. We invite you to join fully in the service.

PRELUDE

Sung by the Dick Kramer Gay Men's Chorale

Veni Sancte Spiritu   Leoš Janáček
Quatre Petites Prières
  de Saint François d'Assise   Francis Poulenc
Pueri Hebraeorum   Randall Thompson

Bulletin for memorial service for San Francisco Supervisor Harvey Milk (left) and Mayor George Moscone (right), murdered by another supervisor, Dan White. Courtesy of the Gay, Lesbian, Bisexual, Transgender Historical Society, San Francisco.

man—Golan Cipel—went public. Twenty-three years after the Studds incident, Representative Mark Foley, the **closeted** Republican from Florida, stepped down from his position when salacious instant messages to an underage page were made public. Foley would attribute his lapse in judgment to alcoholism and heretofore undisclosed childhood molestation. Republican Senator Larry E. Craig of Idaho in 2007 pleaded guilty to misdemeanor charges of disorderly conduct after an undercover police officer accused him of soliciting sex in June in a Minneapolis airport restroom; Craig later recanted his plea and loudly asserted that he was happily married and not gay. A week later, he announced his intention to resign from the Senate, then withdrew his decision to do so. He was subsequently accused by other men of having had sex with them at some time. Bob Allen, a Republican state representative in Florida, was dismissed from the John McCain campaign for president in 2007 after he also was arrested on charges of soliciting sex in a public restroom.

After nearly a century of homosexual scandal, Washington—and local—politics have become more gay-friendly environments, but a pervasive sense of anxiety over sexuality still breeds scandal, innuendo, and partisan panic. Rumors of a gay network of closeted Republicans protecting the reputations of others run rampant. Politicians choose to stay closeted rather than suffer political backlash from their conservative constituents. While not the hotbed of scandal and panic associated with the Eisenhower years, American politics still suffer from a fear of queer associations.

Further Reading

Johnson, David K. 2004. The Lavender Scare: The Cold War Persecution of Gays and Lesbians in the Federal Government. Chicago: University of Chicago Press.

Kurtz, Howard. 2005. "Online Reporter Quits after Liberals' Expose." *Washington Post* (February 10): C4. Available at: http://www.washingtonpost.com/wp-dyn/articles/A12640-2005 Feb9.html. Accessed July 14, 2008.

Murphy, Lawrence R. 1988. *Perverts by Official Order: The Campaign against Homosexuals by the United States Navy*. New York: Haworth Press.

Streitmatter, Roger. 1998. *Empty without You: The Intimate Letters of Eleanor Roosevelt and Lorena Hickok.* New York: Free Press.

Weisel, Al. 1999. "LBJ's Gay Sex Scandal." *OUT* (December): 76–131. Available at: http://home.nyc.rr.com/alweisel/outwalterjenkins.htm. Accessed July 14, 2008.

Kelly Kessler

politics and activism

In the last 50 years politicians have defiantly declared their sexuality, have been outed, or, more frequently, have simply been rumored to be something other than what they claimed to be. In various of these categories some of the most notable have been Roy Cohn (1927–1986), featured as a central character in **Tony Kushner**'s *Angels in America*; Barney Frank (1940–); James Hormel (1933–); Barbara Jordan (1936–1996); James McGreevey; Carole Midgen; Harvey Milk (1930–1978); Elaine Noble (1944–), the first openly gay candidate ever elected to state-level office; Gerry Studds (1937–); and James M. Vandeventer Jr. (1963–).

Politicians have also been actively involved in raising awareness about lesbian and gay social issues. Since the **Stonewall Riots** in June 1969, lesbian and gay social movements approach politics by attempting either to expose heterosexual bias or to raise awareness about issues specific to lesbian and gay communities. A contemporary example is the debate over **same-sex marriage,** which forces both a reevaluation of the institution of marriage and an identification of inequalities embedded in marriage-related policies like insurance benefits. In order to counteract the lack of political action on a national level, same-sex marriage advocates emphasize assimilation, viewing marriage as the next plausible step toward integration. Politicians use these types of wedge issues to clearly define their values for a particular constituency. This tension between lesbian and gay social movements and values-oriented political representation defines the framework in which gay rights activists must speak.

Similar to the same-sex marriage controversy of the new century, a major concern of the previous decade was the ban on lesbians and gays in military service. One of the first domestic policy initiatives of the Clinton administration was the institutionalization of "don't ask, don't tell." This moderate political solution resulted from President Clinton's attempt to appeal to lesbian and gay activists by addressing the military's discriminatory practices while, at the same time, distancing his administration from these same special interest groups. This political maneuvering had the twofold effect of frustrating LGBTQ groups unsatisfied with the overall ineffectiveness of the policy and mobilizing the Christian Right with the support of veterans and other antigay military groups.

The politics of **HIV/AIDS** represents a different set of circumstances beyond the legal strategies pursued in response to the military-service ban. In the early

A get-out-the-vote effort in the 1970s in San Francisco. Courtesy of the Gay, Lesbian, Bisexual, Transgender Historical Society, San Francisco.

1980s, the subject of AIDS first appeared in the American press. While the response of the Christian Right organizations like the Moral Majority headed by Jerry Falwell was to frame the epidemic as "the judgment of God," the Reagan and Bush administrations' reactions were those of denial. President Clinton appointed as surgeon general Dr. Joycelyn Elders, who supported comprehensive sex education programs, although she was soon fired over a controversy regarding the distribution of condoms in schools. The subsequent Bush administration emphasized abstinence-only initiatives. Gay rights activists' responses to these lackadaisical policies were to bypass legal strategies and increase media visibility in order to foster AIDS awareness.

The development of the AIDS Action Council and other like-minded organizations moved the epidemic beyond its identity as a gay problem by addressing more general matters concerning public health and poverty. Beginning in 1979, political demonstrations and art projects like the AIDS quilt worked to raise consciousness across college campuses and in the popular media. Though AIDS awareness remains a powerful component of gay and lesbian activism, specific questions concerning support for lesbian and gay youth, **privacy rights,** the elimination of **sodomy laws,** and the passing of the Employment Non-Discrimination Act illustrate what is at stake for lesbian and gay activist groups today. These concerns do not easily enter popular discourse and must repeatedly be raised in social environments controlled primarily by reactionary politics.

Further Reading

Clendinen, Dudley, and Adam Nagourney. 1999. *Out for Good: The Struggle to Build a Gay Rights Movement in America.* New York: Simon and Schuster.

D'Emilio, John. 2002. *The World Turned: Essays on Gay History, Politics, and Culture.* Durham, NC, and London: Duke University Press.

Marcus, Eric. 2002. *Making Gay History: The Half-Century Fight for Lesbian and Gay Equal Rights.* New York: Perennial.

Murphy, Kevin P., Jason Ruiz, and David Serlin, eds. 2008. "Queer Futures." Special issue, *Radical History Review* 100 (January).

Nichols, Jack. 2004. *The Tomcat Chronicles: Erotic Adventures of a Gay Liberation Pioneer.* New York: Routledge.

Rimmerman, Craig A. 2002. *From Identity to Politics: The Lesbian and Gay Movements in the United States.* Philadelphia: Temple University Press.

Yeager, Kenneth. 1998. *Trailblazers: Profiles of America's Gay and Lesbian Elected Officials.* New York: Haworth.

Katheryn Wright

polyamory

Polyamory is the practice of having multiple relationships of a sexual or romantic nature with the knowledge and consent of those involved. These relationships take a variety of forms but share a commitment to negotiating mutually agreeable relationship boundaries through honest communication. Some view polyamory as a sexual identity, whether chosen or innate, while others view it as a sexual practice. Polyamory emerged from the free love movement of the 1960s. The most well-known example was the Kerista community, a commune that practiced group marriage over a 21-year period. This group coined many terms now used by polyamorists, such as *polyfidelity*, a commitment to sexual exclusivity among more than two individuals.

In practice, polyamory differs from polygyny and polyandry in that it rejects sexual ownership, whether mutual or unidirectional. Polyamorists aim to build relationships without sexual possessiveness or jealousy, which they regard as effects of social conditioning. In its stead they cultivate *compersion*, the pleasure derived from witnessing a partner's happiness or success in other relationships. Another difference between polyamory and other multiple-partner arrangements lies in polyamory's attitude toward same-sex attraction. Polygyny, for example, is based on a heterosexual model, in which a man has multiple wives but the wives are expected to view one another as sisters rather than potential sexual partners. In contrast, polyamory has tended to take a positive view of same-sex attraction.

While people of all orientations may practice polyamory, there is some indication that heterosexuals and **bisexual**s are more likely than gays and lesbians to adopt a polyamorous identity. A 2002 study by polyamory journal *Loving More* Magazine found that 50 percent of their 400 respondents identified as bisexual, 45 percent identified as heterosexual, and only 5 percent identified as gay or lesbian.

Feminist critics of polyamory note that while the practice challenges male ownership of women's bodies, it does not take place in an environment free from sexism and patriarchy. Unless women are empowered socially and economically, they argue, polyamory may only increase men's sexual access to women. In addition, a socialist feminist perspective suggests that the practice of having multiple sexual partners may be modeled on a capitalist premise of accumulation and consumption.

Some conservatives warn that as same-sex marriage becomes accepted, state recognition of polyamorous relationships, such as group marriage, is not far off. There is disagreement among polyamorists as to whether state recognition is desirable. Some welcome the protection and benefits, such as health insurance or inheritance rights, that state recognition could bring to their families. Some, such as the De Bruijn family in the Netherlands, have made use of available legal protections such as the *samenlevingscontract* (cohabitation agreement). Others oppose government regulation of their personal relationships and view legal recognition with suspicion. Before multiple relationships can obtain legal recognition, however, changes would need to be made to current criminal statutes that criminalize multiple marriages in many countries. A Canadian study commissioned in 2006 by the Federal Justice Department recommended that Canada decriminalize polygamy.

Further Reading

Anapol, Deborah M. 1997. *Polyamory: The New Love without Limits*, San Rafael, CA: IntiNet Resource Center.

Barker, Meg. 2005. "This Is My Partner, and This Is My…Partner's Partner: Constructing a Polyamorous Identity in a Monogamous World." *Journal of Constructivist Psychology* 18: 75–88.

Munson, Marcia, and Judith P. Stelboum. 1999. *Lesbian Polyamory Reader: Open Relationships, Non-Monogamy and Casual Sex*. New York: Haworth Press.

Strassberg, Maura. 2003. "The Challenge of Post-Modern Polygamy: Considering Polyamory." *Capital University Law Review* 31 (3): 439–563.

Margaret Robinson

pomosexual

The term *pomosexual* combines *postmodern* and *sexuality* to reflect and celebrate a multiplicity of sexual positions and desires that move beyond narrowly defined, or normative, **gay, lesbian,** and **bisexual** to include **transgendered, transsexuals,** pansexuals, metasexuals, and anyone who wants to be free of **essentialist** gender- or sexual orientation–based signifiers or **identity** labels. The term was made popular in Carol Queen and Lawrence Schimel's 1997 collection, *PoMoSexuals: Challenging Assumptions about Gender and Sexuality*, which contains essays about individuals who live beyond and across various categorical norms; for instance, male lesbians, hermaphrodykes, or those whose relationships defy current classification such as a "lesbian" female-to-male transsexual who is in a relationship with a "heterosexual" male-to-female transsexual. Pomosexual is more inclusive than **queer,** since it embraces all individuals, particularly those who are often marginalized by mainstream gay, lesbian, and bisexual men and women. Nonetheless, pomosexuality is problematic since it is still an identity signifier that does not allow individuals to truly escape any labels. As a political term, pomosexual is useful because it forces normative lesbians, gays, and heterosexuals to acknowledge the sexism and exclusion that is faced by many individuals who are marginalized from queer movements and communities while mainstream gays and lesbians seek equal rights and full cultural inclusion in the United States.

Further Reading

A postmodern sexual look. Courtesy of Shutterstock.

Ailles, Jennifer L. 2003. "Pomosexual Play: Going beyond the Binaristic Limits of Gender?" In *Bisexuality and Transgenderism:*

InterSEXions of the Others, ed. Jonathan Alexander and Karen Yescavage, 71–85. New York: Harrington Park Press.

Queen, Carol, and Lawrence Schimel, eds. 1997. *PoMoSexuals: Challenging Assumptions about Gender and Sexuality.* San Francisco: Cleis Press.

Jennifer L. Ailles

pornography in film

Often referred to as the "golden age of film pornography," the post-**Stonewall** era saw a proliferation of mainstream pornographic films and venues, especially in major cities, where queer film pornography followed a path from short films or "loops," available in public venues or by mail order, to feature-length films shown in theaters. A number of directors and studios quickly became fixtures within the industry, including directors Wakefield Poole (whose 1971 film *Boys in the Sand* initiated the contemporary gay film era), Joe Gage, Al Parker, and William Higgins and studios/distributors like Surge, P.M. Productions, Falcon, Target, and Colt, the latter dealing primarily in mail-order porn. Popular porn stars quickly became celebrities within the gay community.

By the mid-1980s, the move from film to video had resulted in both an explosion of material for the consumer and the closing of most, if not all, porn theaters. Mail-order distribution dominated for a number of years, with major studios like Falcon, Catalina, HIS Studio, Colt Studios, and eventually Titan Media offering most of the product. Once again, the gay community continued to embrace various directors and performers as celebrities, though the greater proliferation of offerings resulted in shorter tenures for such "stars." Smaller niche companies and a greater number of producers for lesbian, bisexual, and fetish pornography had growing success. The evolution from video to DVD and now to streaming Internet media has also expanded the market since individuals with video cameras or webcams can create pornography to distribute. Webcam sites, either live or recorded, are perhaps the most common and readily accessible venues for video pornography today. Internet porn has cultivated its own culture and communities of fans, producers, amateur and professional artisans, and so on. At the same time, the ease of distribution has resulted in greater problems with piracy of pornographic materials.

Queer pornography has faced the same challenges and criticism that heterosexual porn has encountered. Since the 1970s, the feminist antiporn movement, led by figures like Andrea Dworkin, Susan Brownmiller, and Catharine MacKinnon, has insisted that pornography exploits women, reaffirms patriarchal privilege and male dominance, eroticizes the humiliation of women, and reinforces the cultural values that lead to women's oppression. Many have argued that gay and lesbian pornography inherently challenges these claims: it contains members of the same sex and offers liberating images of alternative sexuality; lesbian porn can challenge the lesbian images available in heterosexual pornography, and so on. However, some have argued that queer porn replicates the problematic power dynamics of heterosexual porn—that is, privileging the dominant "masculine" role and demeaning the "feminine" role, reaffirming a vision of masculinity that depends on denigrating the feminine, and the like. Also, like heterosexual porn, queer porn has been criticized for failing to incorporate people of color, or for doing so in ways that reaffirm **stereotypes** (e.g., the dominant black male or the passive Asian male), or for relegating such porn to niche markets.

Pornography's role with respect to the community has seen ongoing debate as well. **HIV/AIDS** became a central issue impacting the entire porn industry, but there is no question that gay male porn producers realized the need to respond and educate via the porn products, and recent lesbian pornography has been especially invested in safe-sex promotion. Still, producers faced a dilemma—porn would seem a natural venue for the promotion of safe-sex practices; however, too direct or didactic an approach would undermine the erotic goal of the product. Videos since the mid-1980s often carry opening advisories about safe-sex practices, and performers generally use a condom for anal sex. Since the mid-1990s, however, gay pornography has seen an increase in depictions of unsafe sexual practices (e.g., "**barebacking**" or anal sex without condoms, cum eating, etc.), with entire studios arising as producers of such products. This trend has renewed the debate over porn's role, its responsibility to the community, and its impact on both the community and the individual consumer.

GAY MALE PORN AND ITS CULTURE

Without question, "all-male" pornography constitutes the largest category of queer porn. Some studies suggest that gay men watch porn more frequently and more readily acknowledge porn as part of their lives than do heterosexual men, though this openness might result both from gay culture's general acceptance of porn and from mainstream culture's stigmas against porn consumption. However, while the audience for gay male porn is generally presumed to be homosexual and bisexual men, studies indicate that heterosexual women often view the porn as well. Thus, although mainstream American culture generally posits males as the primary audience for pornography, a major reason that this category remains so vast likely has more to do with the symbiotic relationship between pornography and gay culture than any innate "male" drive.

Many gay men cite pornography as the primary vehicle through which they came to understand their gay identity, to discover gay sexual practices, and to learn about gay culture. In fact, for a generation of men coming out in the late 1970s to early 1980s, films like Joe Gage's *Heatstroke, Closed Set,* and his *Trucking* trilogy, Falcon's *The Other Side of Aspen,* Al Parker's *Games* and *Dangerous,* and/or William Higgins's *These Bases Are Loaded* were primers on gay sex, the art of **cruising,** and the developing post-Stonewall gay culture. Thus the educational role of porn cannot be underestimated. At the same time, as some of these films depicted, gay theaters were not simply a place to view pornographic films but also a place to meet men for sexual activity. In the 1980s, when the initial AIDS panic spread and many men curtailed sexual activity, porn became a safe outlet for sexual expression and for another generation of men to learn about sexual practices. While representations of gay men and queer culture in mainstream media have become more common since the mid-1990s, given the increasingly easy access to film pornography on the Internet, porn likely still functions as an introduction to gay sex and gay culture, though porn's depiction of that culture is necessarily limited.

Gay culture also embraces pornography rather extensively. **Gay bars** frequently play porn videos and hire porn performers as dancers. Porn "celebrities" attend numerous LGBTQ events, including political events like the March on Washington. In recent years, porn performers and promoters have produced charity fund-raisers, and various gay organizations have come to recognize the fund-raising potential of events that incorporate pornography, despite its stigma within the larger American culture. The Internet also offers a wide range of options that connect porn and the community, including webcam chat rooms (see **queer hotlines**), online porn sharing groups, profile sites, and others.

Given the integral relationship between porn and gay culture, debates have raged over the extent to which pornography reflects gay culture or informs it, debates that have been especially crucial when considering porn and its depiction of safe-sex practices. As evidence of porn's influence, for example, critics might note how in the 1980s porn veered away from showing men with body hair, preferring shaved models, and how gay culture followed suit. Supporters might counter that the shaved appearance reflected cultural preferences of the time, both in the gay community and mainstream America, and might note that once porn producers realized the market potential, body hair returned in pornography with a vengeance (see **bears**). While critics might note that certain staple porn settings, like the prison, the public restroom, or the porn theater, might reinforce cultural stereotypes about gay men as promiscuous and potentially criminal, supporters would note that staple settings such as the military and the locker room reflect the reality that gay men exist in all walks of life and challenge the notion that gay men are necessarily less "masculine," by traditional standards, than heterosexual men.

Critics have blamed gay porn for everything from fashion trends to the rise of HIV infection, claiming that porn perpetuates mainstream America's negative stereotypes of gay men as promiscuous, reinforces unrealistic expectations about sexual partners, overvalues youth and limited notions of beauty, and tells gay men that unsafe sexual practices are acceptable, an argument that has become especially virulent in the last 10 years as more barebacking pornography has been produced. In contrast, advocates would argue that individual consumers can readily distinguish between porn's fantasy and their lived realities, that porn promotes safe sex by encouraging fantasy over real unsafe activity, and that even bareback porn reflects rather than creates cultural desires.

Gay film pornography continues to evolve as gay culture in America evolves. While a good deal of current porn does focus on young male actors (i.e., "twinks"), the industry continues to respond to communal desires, offering an increasingly wider range of ages and body types (e.g., older men, "daddies," bears, musclebears) and more diverse activities (e.g., films devoted to specific fetishes). An increasing trend from major studios is to offer a standard version and a director's cut of key films, with the latter version generally offering material like **watersports,** toy play, or **fisting,** activities that will, in some markets, prevent the product from being sold or rented except via mail order or Internet download.

LESBIAN PORNOGRAPHY

To discuss lesbian film porn, one must consider both audience and what we mean by lesbian porn. Is it porn by lesbians? For lesbians? Porn that includes lesbian scenes? One could argue that American culture is rife with lesbian porn, given that so much heterosexual pornography includes lesbian scenes. However, such scenes are generally understood as being presented for a heterosexual male audience. In fact, such scenes often function as the "foreplay" before the "main event" of heterosexual intercourse. Although many "heterosexual" films include solely lesbian scenes, even those films are generally geared toward the heterosexual male's pleasure. If we consider porn produced by and/or for a lesbian audience, the volume of films reduces dramatically, though scholars have traced full-length films as far back as 1968's *The King* (directed by Looney Bear). The 1980s saw an increase in lesbian films and filmmaking, including works like Cristen Lee Rothermund's *Erotic in Nature*, but the productions by Blush/Fatale Video from the mid-1980s onward, including Debbie Sundahl's *Suburban Dykes* and *Bathroom Sluts,* became the benchmark of lesbian porn. Furthermore, as with most other pornography, lesbian pornography proliferated in the 1990s through the present day, in part because of technological advances and increased accessibility to production materials. Studios like S.I.R. productions developed during this period, and amateur lesbian porn has had a significant market presence as well.

Lesbian film porn has also had to negotiate a number of cultural issues prevalent within the lesbian community. It has consistently emphasized safe-sex practices, often more so than gay male pornography, and in a more explicitly didactic way, proof for some scholars of a significant difference in spectatorship and audience desire/expectation. It has also reflected changes in the makeup of the lesbian community, offering depictions that cover a range of settings (from initially mostly urban to more suburban), fetishes (bondage, fisting, etc.), roles (**butch–femme, lipstick lesbian, and granola lesbian,** etc.), and activities (vaginal and anal penetration, use of dildos and other toys, cunnilingus, etc.). In fact, the question of what constitutes lesbian sex has often been central both to the lesbian community and to the film pornography, debates about the status of butch–femme role-play, or about the politics of penetration and the use of dildos, which are often explored in the films and in the responses the films generate. Some have argued that lesbian porn challenges both gay male and heterosexual porn's emphasis on youth, reductive standards of beauty, and what defines erotic or arousing representations.

BISEXUAL AND TRANSGENDER PORN

As with lesbian pornography, the issue of audience must be considered when discussing bisexual pornography. Given the large number of girl-on-girl scenes in straight porn, many of those films might be considered bisexual porn as they would likely appeal to viewers seeking bisexual representations. In general, however, porn that is identified as bisexual usually refers to films that contain two or more engages in sexual activity with another man. There are, for example, "gangbang" films that depict groups of men together with a single female, which would not be considered bisexual behavior, since the focus is on the men engaging sexually with the woman. Bisexual films comprise a large market, though again it is hard to know the sex or sexual orientation of the average spectator. Additionally, many popular performers from all-male films, including Jack Wrangler, Jeff Stryker, and Peter North, made bisexual and straight films as well. Thus, for the consumer seeking bisexual depictions, the options could be more varied, depending on the individual knowledge of performers.

Transgender or transsexual pornography complicates the audience issue even further. The Internet offers an array of films and videos, for sale or download, of transsexuals engaging in sexual activity. Male-to-female transsexuals are more common in the overall market, but products with female-to-male performers do exist. There has long been a market of "tranny" or "chicks with dicks" films. However, the indicator "chicks" suggests to some that the audience for these products is not transgender viewers, but straight males with this particular fetish. Thus, it becomes difficult to speculate whether transgender viewers would look to such films to learn about the transgender life, culture, or common sexual practices, let alone to derive sexual pleasure.

In contrast to the pornographic films that comprise the gay and lesbian markets, the films that comprise the bisexual and transsexual markets do not seem to reflect these communities or to negotiate the issues central to their concomitant communities, and very little research has been done on these films. Especially transsexual films often get lumped in with fetish pornography.

Further Reading
Conway, Mary T. 1997. "Spectatorship in Lesbian Porn: The Woman's Woman's Film." *Wide Angle* 19 (3): 91–113.

Morrison, Todd G., ed. 2004. *Eclectic Views on Gay Male Pornography: Pornucopia.* Binghamton, NY: Haworth Press. Copublished simultaneously in the *Journal of Homosexuality* 47 (3/4).

Waugh, Thomas. 1995. "Men's Pornography: Gay vs. Straight." In *Out in Culture: Gay, Lesbian, and Queer Essays on Popular Culture,* ed. Corey K. Creekmur and Alexander Doty, 307–27. Durham, NC, and London: Duke University Press.

Waugh, Thomas. 1996. *Hard to Imagine: Gay Male Eroticism in Photography and Film from Their Beginnings to Stonewall.* New York: Columbia University Press.

Williams, Linda, ed. 2004. *Porn Studies.* Durham, NC, and London: Duke University Press.

Andrew Schopp

pornography stars

Gay **pornography,** a large and significant part of gay subculture, produced as one of its main phenomena gay pornography stars. A pornography star is an actor performing in pornographic films, live strip shows, and/or modeling in the nude for adult publications with great success and a huge fan following. The majority of models and performers, as they are also called, become stars overnight due to the fact that, with the appearance of home videos in the 1980s and DVDs later on, the production of feature-length porn reached over 20,000 titles a year.

The making of porn stars could be seen as a response to the mainstream, Hollywood-style star system in the film industry. In reaction to the decades-long denied visibility of gay and lesbian stars in the mainstream Hollywood film industry, the gay subculture in a duplicate move created its own stars, icons, and hard-core legends. The performers' names, the faces, and, more often than not, the anatomies became revered in the gay community even though the salaries, contractual obligations, and longevity of stardom did not match those of the mainstream film industry. The gay porn industry embraces stars and stardom in a parodic move that mocks the whole star system while at the same time bowing down and worshiping it.

Gay pornography slowly appeared after World War II, initially in the form of physique photography in magazines like *Physique Pictorial* and *Dance,* followed by a posing strap genre of physique cinema produced strictly for the home market, Bob Mizer's Athletic Model Guild wrestling films, and the gay underground/art house films of Kenneth Anger, Curtis Harrington, Jack Smith, and **Andy Warhol** that were closer to soft-core fantasies than to hard-core pornography. None of these productions was yet ready to elevate its performers to porn star stature simply because of their limited home market distribution. Once audiences became interested in attending theatrically released gay pornography in the late 1960s and early 1970s, the gay porn star was ready for his close-up.

Casey Donovan is usually considered to have been the first superstar of gay porn. He starred in Wakefield Poole's 1971 *Boys in the Sand,* the first major theatrical hit of the gay hard-core

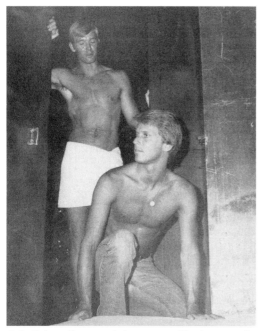

Cab Culver (lower right) was arguably the most famous and important American male porn star of the 1970s and 1980s, appearing primarily in gay adult films and videos under the screen name Casey Donovan. His appeal came largely from his natural good looks, his boy-next-door persona, and especially for his great enthusiasm for sex, both on and off the set. He became a star with his appearance in *Boys in the Sand* in 1972. Courtesy of the Gay, Lesbian, Bisexual, Transgender Historical Society, San Francisco.

porn circuit. With his clean-cut, all-American blond good looks, Donovan instantaneously established himself as an icon of a new, sexually liberated American homosexual male, happy and eager to perform as bottom in front of the gay/bi-curious eyes of America. *Unzipped,* the magazine of gay adult entertainment, named in 1998 the top 10 performers of all time—Donovan took first place, followed by Jack Wrangler, Al Parker, Fred Halsted, Leo Ford, Jon King, Rex Chandler, Jeff Stryker, Joey Stefano, and Ryan Idol. The names on this list belong either to the 1970s era of porn flicks distributed to about 50 hard-core gay porn theaters in major cities across the United States, or to the golden wave of late 1980s gay porn videotapes made for viewing in the privacy of homes. The arrival of VHS porn tapes produced a proliferation of porn stars and stardom in the gay pornographic industry. Thus, while the theatrical distribution of gay hard-core in the 1970s created the demand for stars in porn, it was the high-quantity home video market of the 1980s and afterwards that made it finally happen. If porn of the 1970s worked on emulating mainstream filmmaking production values, as well as more fully developed story lines and characterizations, later made-for-video porn abandoned the aesthetics of film production in favor of the immediacy, directness, and thirst for novelty of the new generations of porn consumers.

Within particular genres, typecasting of and role-playing by the porn stars is more often than not clearly and continuously reinforced—Casey Donovan was proud and satisfied to play a bottom in front of the camera from film to film and thus became the first exclusive bottom to achieve stardom; Jon King was another, as was Joey Stefano. On the opposite side were the exclusive tops, the dominant, aggressive, assertive bunch, and at the top of the tops is, arguably, the biggest international gay porn superstar, Jeff Stryker. Stryker never performed as anything other than the inserter or as the subject who was fellated by others. Neither his mouth nor his anus was ever offered to the other actors or to viewers of the films. Ryan Idol was another star who kept his fan base and his comparatively high salary thanks to the perpetuation of the exclusive top role fantasy he maintained. Most of the performers, however, are more versatile. The more we move to the 1990s queercore and afterward, the more we see the previously exclusive tops getting comfortable and letting themselves enjoy the bottom role in front of the cameras—for example, the hugely endowed top Tom Chase.

The early home-video porn stars often played in both gay and straight porn, and quite a few of them identified themselves as heterosexual. In the business such performers are known as "gay for pay": some of them are willing to fellate their sex-scene partners or even bottom for them if the pay is adequate.

The AIDS crisis and the precondom productions had devastating effects on the porn industry community. Many of the performers died prematurely as a result of unsafe sex practices. Gay porn industry losses were among the factors that alarmed the community and encouraged it to impose safe-sex practices on the sets and to educate consumers about the importance and pleasures of safe sex. AIDS was, however, just one of the elements that contributed to the brief fame and short lives of many porn stars. Some of them came into the industry to escape an abusive past, only to encounter abuse of a more subtle kind; some had troubles coping with the fandom, money, and attention the newfound status brought them: sex, alcohol, or drug addiction sometimes followed. Others ultimately had to face the contradictions between their real identity and their stage personas. Some, for one reason or another, committed suicide.

Porn stars remain a huge phenomenon in gay subculture—beacons of LGBTQ liberation, for some. They continue to embody the visibility and joy of queer sex on the one hand and, at the same time, are hot commodities in a culture dominated by market demands, fame, ratings, and addictive behaviors produced and reproduced by the now global markets' laws—a fittingly complex construct for our increasingly contradictory times.

Further Reading

Charon's Ferry: Death and Life in Male Erotica. Available at: http://models.badpuppy.com/archive/charon.htm. Accessed July 14, 2008.

Kinnick, Dave. 1993. *Sorry I Asked: Intimate Interviews with Porn's Rank and File.* New York: BadBoy.

List of Male Performers in Gay Porn Films. Available at: www.en.wikipedia.org/wiki/List_of_gay_porn_stars. Accessed July 14, 2008.

Rowberry, John W. 1986. *Gay Video: A Guide to Erotica.* San Francisco: G. S. Press.

Stevenson, Jack. 1997. "From the Bedroom to the Bijou: A Secret History of American Gay Sex Cinema." *Film Quarterly* 51 (1): 24–31.

Williams, Linda. *Porn Studies.* Durham, NC: Duke University Press.

Milan Pribisic

Joe Ashby Porter (1942–)

Born into a family of coal miners in 1942, Porter is an influential academic as well as an important contemporary fiction writer. Well known for splitting his personality along the lines of academia and fiction, Porter uses the name Joseph A. Porter for his scholarship on Renaissance literature and Joe Ashby Porter for his works of fiction. Porter has enforced this division throughout his career, asserting that the two endeavors are fundamentally different and require compartmentalization. Currently a professor of creative writing and Renaissance literature at Duke University, Porter studied at Harvard (BA, 1964), Pembroke College Oxford (Fulbright Fellowship, 1964–1965), and the University of California at Berkeley (PhD, 1972). Porter's works on Shakespeare include *The Drama of Speech Acts: Shakespeare's Lancastrian Trilogy* (1979), *Shakespeare's Mercutio: His History and Drama* (1988), and his edited *Critical Essays on Shakespeare's* Romeo and Juliet (1997). Porter's fiction includes the novels *Eelgrass* (1977), *Resident Aliens* (2000), and *The Near Future* (2006) and the short story collections *The Kentucky Stories* (1983), *Lithuania: Short Stories* (1990), and *Touch Wood: Short Stories* (2002). Much of Porter's work does not address homosexuality in any overt way. Indeed, *Eelgrass* contains his only substantial references to homosexuality. The novel is set on an island off the coast of South Carolina, where Carter, the novel's protagonist, experiments with all varieties of sexual experience. Although never tied directly to sexuality, Porter explores themes of rootlessness and alienation in many of his works, suggesting the complex nature of forging identity in a post-**Stonewall** world. Porter's awards include two National Endowment for the Arts Creative Writing Fellowships and a 2004 Academy Award in Literature from the American Academy of Arts and Literature.

Further Reading

Clum, John. 1993. "Joe Ashby Porter (1942–)." In *Contemporary Gay American Novelists: A Bio-Bibliographical Sourcebook*, ed. Emmanuel S. Nelson, 316–19. Westport, CT: Greenwood Press.

Halcomb, David. *Joe Ashby Porter.* Available at: http://www.english.eku.edu/SERVICES/KYLIT/porter.htm. Accessed July 14, 2008.

Jaimy, Gordon. 1991. "Porter's Stories Strip Away the Conventions of Fiction." *The Baltimore Sun* (May 12): B9.

J. G. Adair

D. A. Powell (1963–)

D. A. Powell is considered one of the leading American poets of his generation. He has published three books and is the recipient of several awards and honors. Very open about his status as a person living with AIDS, Powell, along with such writers as the late Paul Monette and the late Tory Dent, is a poet who has taken the **HIV/AIDS** epidemic not only as a (sometimes overwhelming) subject matter but also as the occasion for finding a new way of writing at the extremes, one that would be equal to (in both senses) the immensity of the AIDS crisis on a personal and a social level. His work can be harshly brutal and meltingly lyrical, sometimes in the space of a single stanza.

Reflecting an eclectic and wide-ranging sensibility, Powell's poems are kaleidoscopic and collage-like, incorporating a broad array of voices, echoes, puns, allusions, and references (some immediately apparent, some buried) in a sometimes linguistically fragmented mode, from popular music, films (both art and mass market), classical and biblical mythology, Shakespeare and Gertrude Stein and **Tennessee Williams**, and gay slang and other elements of gay subculture (including tight-fitting 501 jeans). Powell has spoken of his desire to bring all the voices of his world(s) into his poems, and of how this is both an aesthetic strategy and a way of preserving and honoring the voices of the dead, who can no longer speak for themselves. In Powell's first book, *Tea* (1998), whose title refers among other things to gay tea dances, the lyrics of gay disco songs of the 1970s and 1980s are a pervasive presence. Indeed, the book is both a celebration of and an elegy for the gay club subculture of that period, changed forever by the advent of AIDS. It is also a memorial to the poet's own lost youth and to the various dead friends and lovers with whom he shared that youth and that subculture. Powell has spoken of his desire both to elegize and to "lay waste" to the elegy, to express his emotional investments in the people, things, and places that have mattered to him (no matter how seemingly trivial or trashy) while at the same time avoiding any false idealization or nobility. "Filmography," one section of his third book, *Cocktails* (2004), whose title refers simultaneously to mixed drinks and to the pharmaceutical combinations that help keep many people with HIV/AIDS alive, revolves around various cult films (most of which have gay content), while the section called "Bibliography" irreverently but earnestly explores the often-homoerotic dimensions of the New Testament gospels.

Further Reading

Bedient, Cal. 1999. "In Search of the Torturer's House." *Parnassus: Poetry in Review* 24 (2): 315–30.

Hennessy, Christopher. 2005. *Outside the Lines: Talking with Contemporary Gay Poets*. Ann Arbor: University of Michigan Press.

Shepherd, Reginald. 2003. "D.A. Powell." *Contemporary Gay American Poets and Playwrights: An A-Z Guide*, ed. Emmanuel S. Nelson, 369–76. Westport, CT: Greenwood Press.

Reginald Shepherd

Minnie Bruce Pratt (1946–)

Minnie Bruce Pratt, a native of Selma, Alabama, is the author of five books of poetry and three works of creative nonfiction. Her works of poetry include *The Sound of One Fork, And We Say We Love Each Other, Crime against Nature, Walking Back Up Depot Street*, and most recently *The Dirt She Ate*, which received the 2003 Lambda Literary Award for Poetry. Pratt, widely known for her extensive grassroots organizing, focuses on social justice issues in her writing. Her work aggressively confronts and challenges racism and contributes to a growing body of work on white antiracist activism. Her creative work explores the complexities of lesbian identity, exposing multiple themes of oppression and marginality. Pratt's creative nonfiction includes *Rebellion: Essays 1980–1991*; *S/He*, which explores gender and identity in fierce and vivid language; and *Yours in Struggle: Three Feminist Perspectives on Anti-Semitism and Racism*, which she coauthored with Elly Bulkin and Barbara Smith. Pratt has received numerous honors for her creative work, including Creative Writing Fellowships in Poetry from the National Endowment of the Arts and the New Jersey State Council on the Arts. Her critically acclaimed *Crime against Nature*, which explores her relationship with her sons as a lesbian mother, was the Lamont Poetry Selection in 1989 and was also chosen as a *New York Times* Notable Book of the Year. Additionally, *Crime against Nature* received the American Library Association Gay and Lesbian Book Award for Literature. In 1991 Pratt was selected with two other lesbian authors for the Lillian Hellman-Dashiell Hammett Award from the Fund for Free Expression. Pratt was also a member of the editorial collective of *Feminary: A Feminist Journal for the South, Emphasizing Lesbian Visions*. *Yours in Struggle* was honored in 2004 when it was chosen as one of the 100 Best Lesbian and Gay Nonfiction Books by the **Publishing Triangle.**

Further Reading

Martin, Biddy, and Chandra Talpade Mohanty. 1986. "Feminist Politics: What's Home Got to Do with It?" In *Feminist Studies, Critical Studies*, ed. Teresa de Lauretis, 191–212. Bloomington: Indiana University Press.

Erika Feigenbaum

John Preston (1945–1994)

John Preston was known as a prolific gay writer who sought to blend literary works with explicit **sadomasochistic** sexuality. Preston's novel *Mr. Benson*, originally published as a short story in *Drummer*, is among his most well-known works. *Drummer* regularly featured Preston's work under the name Jack Prescott, while many of his books were published under a variety of pseudonyms including Jack Hild, Preston MacAdam, and Mike McCray, though these pseudonyms were at times shared with other authors. Preston holds an iconoclastic role in both literature and erotica, in part for his insistence on calling his erotic work "pornography" and for his emphasis on the craft of writing.

Also known for his work as an editor, Preston briefly held the post of editor of the *Advocate* in 1975 and took editorial leadership of *Mandate* in 1979. In his later life, Preston turned to editing anthologies. In 1987, Preston tested positive for HIV, which prompted him to edit *Personal Dispatches: Writers Confront AIDS* as part of his own attempt to grapple with the impact of AIDS on the gay community. Preston lived in various cities across the United States but settled in his adopted hometown of Portland, Maine, in 1979, where he remained for the next 15 years until his death from AIDS. Preston's personal papers are archived at the John Hay Library at Brown University.

Among Preston's fiction are *Franny, the Queen of Provincetown* (1983); *Mr. Benson* (1983); and *I Once Had a Master, and Other Tales of Erotic Love* (1984). His nonfiction includes *The Big Gay Book: A Man's Survival Guide for the Nineties* (1991); *My Life as a Pornographer and Other Indecent Acts* (1993); and *Winter's Light: Reflections of a Yankee Queer* (published posthumously in 1995, edited by Michael Lowenthal). Preston's edited collections include *Personal Dispatches: Writers Confront AIDS* (1990); *Hometowns: Gay Men Write about Where They Belong* (1991); and *Sister and Brother: Lesbians and Gay Men Write about Their Lives Together* (1994, edited with Joan Nestle).

Further Reading

Antonious, Laura, ed. 1995. *Looking for Mr. Preston*. New York: Masquerade Books.

Gambone, Philip. 1991. *Something Inside: Conversations with Gay Fiction Writers*. Madison: University of Wisconsin Press. (Contains an interview with Preston.)

Andy Inkster

Reynolds Price (1933–)

Born in Macon, North Carolina, Price was educated at Duke University and at Oxford as a Rhodes Scholar. After three years in England he returned to Duke in 1958 as a professor of English, a position he continues to hold. As a Southern writer, he has produced numerous novels, volumes of poetry, essays, and plays set in his Southern home. In recent years, Price has also become a respected commentator and authority on religion, spirituality, and faith, producing several works on these subjects. His turn toward the spiritual came after a fight against cancer that would leave him partially paralyzed. He outlined his struggle and belief that divine intervention saved his life in his novel *A Whole New Life: An Illness and a Healing* (1994).

Price's writings have consistently pushed the boundaries of the normative culture. He has not shied away from topics of race, sex, sexuality, religion, politics, or the like. The issue of sexuality in his works has been of particular interest to readers and scholars based on Price's own ambiguity around his personal sexuality. While gay characters have not played central roles across all of his writings, Price's texts have a certain **homoerotic** and **homosocial** engagement with readers. Generally nonexplicit, such themes can be felt throughout his poetry and prose. His ability to conjure such emotional responses without the erotic language of sexual engagement or love is a testament to his talent. He points to the connection of individuals, no matter what the gendered sex, as the bond that creates grace, thus making room for homosexual connectivity in a world that otherwise attempts to degrade it as the "other."

In *The Promise of Rest*, published in 1995, Price most overtly deals with homosexuality. The main character of the novel is a young gay man dying of AIDS who must return to his North Carolina home from New York to be cared for by his father, who has never fully accepted his son's sexuality, much less his son's African American lover. It is a story of love, loss, compassion, family, and forgiveness.

In his essay "The Uses of Freedom," Price notes the triumphs of the 1960s and 1970s as the sexual freedom that was present at the time. He attributes this aspect of the time with creating a turning point that allowed writers to be more open with situations of sexuality in various arenas. For Price, this was the key to unlocking his own door to writing about sexuality in a way that was not pornographic but visual, raw, and real.

Price's more prominent texts also include *A Serious Way of Wondering* (2003), *Kate Vaiden* (1986, winner of the National Critics Circle Award), *The Surface of the Earth* (1975), and *A Long and Happy Life* (1962, winner of the William Faulkner Award for Literature).

Further Reading

Hogan, Michael. 1997. "Man to Man: Homosocial Desire in Reynold Price's Short Fiction." *South Atlantic Review* 62: 56–73.

Schiff, James A. ed. 1998. *Critical Essays on Reynolds Price*. New York: G. K. Hall.

Strandberg, Victor. 2002. "The Religious/Erotic Poetry of Reynolds Price." *Studies in the Literary Imagination* 35: 61–87.

Needham Yancey Gulley

pride parades and festivals

Since the twentieth century, public events honoring the lives and contributions of LGBTQ persons have taken place across the United States, particularly in its major cities. The history of these celebratory events in America dates back at least to the 1960s, during the **homophile movement**, a reform-minded rather than revolutionary phase of the movement for LGBTQ rights. Influenced by the methods of the civil rights movement and the messages of the women's movements, advocates of **gay liberation** participated in rallies, pickets, and demonstrations designed to increase unity and bring their cause to the attention of the whole nation. For example, early Philadelphia-based protests that intended to promote a more inclusive model of democracy invoked the city's historic ties to struggles for freedom and often selected Independence Day (July 4) as a symbolic occasion in the country's rhetoric of equality and opportunity.

As the movement for gay liberation—a term once used as if referring generically to the rights of all persons living outside the normative expectations and entitlements of heterosexual culture in America—evolved, public expressions of "gay pride" became more widespread and the number of individuals participating in such events grew. An individual or group's decision to join marches and parades provided an occasion for **coming out.** In other words, as one of the slogans of the

Gay Pride Parade of 1979, San Francisco. Photo by Marie Ueda, courtesy of the Gay, Lesbian, Bisexual, Transgender Historical Society, San Francisco.

927

A 1981 Los Angeles Pride Parade advertisement. Courtesy of the Gay, Lesbian, Bisexual, Transgender Historical Society, San Francisco.

day proclaimed, the emphasis at these events was on a movement "out of the **closets** and into the streets."

One such historic and widely cited occasion, held on June 28, 1970, served both as an expression of gay pride and a recognition of the previous year's **Stonewall Riots.** The 1970 march sought to pay tribute to the efforts of all those, whether at Stonewall or since, who resisted oppression of LGBTQ people. Although estimates of the number of participants in the 1970 Stonewall remembrance differ, most describe the crowd as consisting of between 2,000 and 5,000 marchers.

One of the persons present during the Stonewall conflict, activist Brenda Howard, has been credited with the idea for the first Christopher Street Gay Liberation Day March. For this reason, during her lifetime, Howard was sometimes called the "Mother of Pride." Craig Rodwell was the first parade's grassroots organizer. On June 28, 1970, members of the Gay Liberation Front, Gay Activists Alliance, and interested others marched from New York's Greenwich Village to Central Park. Upon arriving at Central Park, marchers joined a "gay be-in" held in Sheep's Meadow. Similar events took place in other American cities, such as a "gay-in" held in San Francisco and a march conducted in Los Angeles. Together, these public events launched a new tradition.

In the years since 1970, the titles given to these pride events shifted in order better to reflect the diversity of LGBTQ America. With time, the original gay-ins came to be known as gay freedom or gay liberation marches, names indicative of the patriotic rhetoric surrounding the nation's bicentennial. By the 1980s, regular celebrations and accompanying shifts in outlook led to a more formalized approach to the presentation of annual events. Each year, June is designated as Gay Pride Month, and the day on which special events such as parades are held is sometimes referred to as Gay Freedom Day. During the 1990s, many of these events shifted their titles again to make explicit the involvement of lesbians. Pride celebrations came to be labeled accordingly, such as San Francisco's 1990 Lesbian/Gay Freedom Parade and Celebration. Since the turn of the twenty-first century, the emphasis for pride parades and festivals has been on assigning titles that reflect an even clearer message of inclusiveness, so that events such as the annual parade in San Francisco began to be described as the San Francisco Lesbian Gay Bisexual Transgender Pride Parade and Celebration.

In some respects, pride parades take some of their cues from the country's legacy of ethnic parades and celebrations. Ethnic parades and pride parades both tend to occur where large concentrations of the relevant population reside or work. For this reason, metropolitan areas and, in particular, cities with lengthy associations with gay history, such as **New York City** and **San Francisco,** are most likely to host pride parades. In recent years, however, some smaller cities and municipalities have begun their own pride events.

The parades themselves have become more elaborate over time. LGBTQ singing groups, marching bands, motorized and decorated floats, celebrity grand marshals, and other crowd-pleasing elements have become fairly standard entertainments at pride parades. As enthusiasm and numbers of participants/attendees grow, marches and parades have sometimes extended the festivities of a single day or weekend to span periods as long as a week in a given city. Such festivals may feature additional displays, speakers, events, and special guests. Sometimes dubbed "pride festivals," these celebrations typically attract visitors and reunite participants from previous years' events. Picnics, dances, parties, concerts, and other related activities help make these festivals enjoyable and socially rich occasions.

Although the initial focus of pride events was primarily on white gay men, subsequent pride parades and festivals widened both their language and their scope. In addition, pride festivals often incorporate component events dedicated to participating groups, such as women or people of color. For instance, some metropolitan areas host pride events intended to attract specific populations, such as African Americans. One example is Atlanta's Black Gay Pride Parade. In addition, some pride events have made a concerted effort to gather women in general and lesbians in particular. For example, dyke marches, which are pride assemblies of lesbians and/or bisexuals, have been conducted since 1993, when the **Lesbian Avengers** staged the first one in Washington, D.C. San Francisco's annual Dyke March features a procession from Dolores Park to the Castro District. New York City's Dyke March moves down Fifth Avenue toward Washington Square in Greenwich Village. In order to provide a counterpoint to the increasingly corporate feel of contemporary pride events, some of these smaller gatherings are deliberately less structured, less official, and less sponsored than the pride festival's central march or parade. In fact, several operate without the formalities of permits, reaffirming the concept of homosexual America as subversive rather than merely subcultural. Pride festivals may also extend hospitality to straight supporters, whether through affiliated organizations, such as **Parents, Families, and Friends of Lesbians and Gays (PFLAG),** or faith communities that have made explicit their invitation to LGBTQ communities, such as the Unitarian Universalists and the Metropolitan Community Church.

One prevalent image associated with pride parades and festivals is the **rainbow flag,** sometimes also known as the freedom flag. Originally designed by artist Gilbert Baker for San Francisco's June 25, 1978, Gay Freedom Day parade, the rainbow flag represents the pride movement with eight colored horizontal stripes. In its current form, the flag boasts six stripes—red, orange, yellow, green, blue, and violet—presenting a natural spectrum of colors to stand for the diversity of LGBTQ culture. Each color used within the flag's design also bears a symbolic association: red with life, orange with healing, yellow with sunlight, green with nature, blue with serenity, and violet with spirit. For a time, versions of the rainbow flag also featured a black stripe, envisioned as a tribute to those living with or dead of HIV/AIDS. Although Baker attempted to restore the eight-striped version of the rainbow flag during the first years of the twenty-first century, the six-striped version is the one most Americans recognize and display.

In subsequent years, other flags have been added to the sea of banners on view at pride events. In 1998, Michael Page designed the bisexual pride flag, which consists of two broad stripes, one of pink and another of blue, joined at the center by a thin band of lavender, representing the blending of the traditionally gender-coded colors of pink and blue. The transgender pride flag, created by Monica Helms, debuted in Phoenix, Arizona, in 2000. At its horizontal edges, it includes two light blue stripes, placed just outside two pink stripes surrounding a center band of white. Other flags, such as the leather pride flag (1989) and the queer pagan flag (1997), can also be seen on display during pride parades and festivals. Each of these flags offers a message of pride and a gesture of welcome. Other icons frequently associated with pride events are the 11th letter of the Greek alphabet (lambda) and the now-reclaimed and inverted image of the **pink triangle,** which had been used to identify homosexuals within Nazi concentration camps.

Even before the advent of pride parades and festivals, however, LGBTQ Americans played a part in many of the nation's marches and processions. In some instances, this involvement has taken the form of specialized planning tied to more broadly defined holiday events. New Orleans offers a case in point. Since the 1950s, gay Mardi Gras celebrations have taken place, and the city's gay Halloween tradition started in 1984. In some instances, localities have originated events that place LGBTQ life at the center of carnivals and masquerades, such as the Fantasy Fest in Key West, Florida.

Contemporary practices associated with pride events range widely. Most commingle elements of pageantry and politics. Costume, **camp** sensibilities, and **drag performance** are popular features of parades, and the carnival-like atmosphere lends itself to identity play. Self-expression also takes the form of acts of remembrance, such as memorials to those lost to HIV/AIDS, and acts of advocacy, such as raised placards and chanted slogans related to issues including funding for AIDS research and legal standing for same-sex marriage. Activist groups from **ACT UP** to **Queer Nation** have lent their numbers and their voices to pride parades.

As pride parades and festivals have grown in scale, overcome difficulties of permitting or routing negotiations, and become routinely advertised in the mainstream press, pride events have become major metropolitan events, attracting tourists, concessions, and Fortune 500 corporate sponsors. Responses to pride parades and festivals vary, including within LGBTQ communities. Some welcome the theatricality of the parades and the public presence asserted through the events that characterize pride festivals. Others worry that the visual eccentricities or the overly sexualized suggestions of those participating in parades or other highly visible events will complicate ongoing efforts to convey a notion of LGBTQ civil liberties based on the grounds that these individuals are in several major respects just like members of heterosexual America; they wish to be themselves, engage in satisfying work, help others, build their families, contribute to their communities, and leave the world a better place.

Detractors of pride parades and festivals, such as members of the gay shame movement, often point out the consumerist tendencies or outright commercialization of pride events. They warn against commodification of alternative sexual identities, exploitation of LGBTQ Americans as untapped consumer markets by merchants and sponsors, or cooptation of cultural differences within a culture of consumption. They also point out the dangers posed by LGBTQ bids for civil rights predicated on assimilation into **heteronormative** America. Such opponents prefer events they regard as more independent and confrontational, arguing that it is necessary and, at times, even healthy to offer an affront to the dominant social order.

In contrast, some viewers of the phenomenon of pride events, while acknowledging their increased commercialism compared to the early grassroots celebrations, suggest the festivities still affirm and legitimate LGBTQ America in substantial ways. From this perspective, tacky souvenirs or pricey postparade bashes supplied by opportunistic businesses clued into the profit potential at pride events still do not undermine the lasting value of pride events in terms of customs, gatherings, and communion. Even the rituals of consumption might be viewed as acts of symbolic resistance, such as a gay man in the parade who dons a T-shirt that pretends to confide: "Shh! I'm gay, but don't tell anyone." In fact, even some of the slogans overheard at parades make sport of the **stereotype** of the gay consumer. During the 1980s, for example, one such chant declared, "We're here. We're queer! And we're not going shopping!"

Other critics of pride celebrations question whether the aspects of public spectacle associated with these events typify LGBTQ life and accurately portray its diversity, and/or whether these displays and experiences are effective ways in which to promote understanding among onlookers from other communities. To be fair, few American parades held in recognition of holidays, from St. Patrick's Day to Thanksgiving Day, replicate contemporary daily life for the featured populations. Instead, they are once-a-year statements of celebration, and their embrace of excess and eccentricity might be understood on that basis.

Scholars from Lynda Johnston to Steven M. Kates and Russell W. Belk have analyzed conduct at pride parades and ceremonies at festivals as discursive events. Such studies tend to emphasize these events' role as community-building rituals, helping forge a deeper sense of both individual and communal identity. Other interpretations focus on the way pride events aim to increase the visibility of LGBTQ America and, in doing so, might hold the potential to build awareness and understanding. In fact, toward this end, some events have employed "PRIDE" as an acronym for "people rejoicing in diversity everywhere."

Recent years have witnessed a rise in popular representations of pride parades and festivals. Examples include documentary films and videos, still photographs such as those of gay activist Thom Higgins, and even children's literature. Lesléa Newman, author of *Heather Has Two Mommies* (1989), a rather controversial treatment of same-sex parenting written to a youth audience, also penned *Gloria Goes to Gay Pride* (1991), an exuberant account of a pride parade recounted from the child's point of view.

These images and texts suggest what an important part pride parades and festivals have come to play in American LGBTQ culture, identity, and history. Not simply in the United States but throughout the world, pride parades and festivals affirm LGBTQ identities and render them more visible to others.

Further Reading

Hagen-Smith, Lisa. 1997. "Politics and Celebration: Manifesting the Rainbow Flag." *Canadian Folklore* 19 (2): 113–21.

Herrell, Richard K. 1992. "The Symbolic Strategies of Chicago's Gay and Lesbian Pride Day Parade." In *Gay Culture in America: Essays from the Field*, ed. Gilbert H. Herdt, 225–52. Boston: Beacon Press.

Johnston, Lynda. 2005. *Queering Tourism: Paradoxical Performances at Gay Pride Parades*. New York: Routledge.

Kates, Steven M., and Russell W. Belk. 2001. "The Meanings of Lesbian and Gay Pride Day: Resistance through Consumption and Resistance to Consumption." *Journal of Contemporary Ethnography* 30 (4): 392–429.

Newman, Lesléa. 1991. *Gloria Goes to Gay Pride*. Boston: Alyson Wonderland.

O'Neal, Hank. 2006. *Gay Day: The Golden Age of the Christopher Street Parade, 1974–1983*. New York: Abrams Image.

Stein, Marc, ed. 2004a. "Pride Marches and Parades." In *Encyclopedia of Lesbian, Gay, Bisexual, and Transgender History in America*, 416–20. New York: Gale.

Stein, Marc, ed. 2004b. "Public Festivals, Parties, and Holidays." In *Encyclopedia of Lesbian, Gay, Bisexual, and Transgender History in America*, 456–59. New York: Gale.

Stewart-Winter, Timothy. 2006. "Gay Pride Day." In *Encyclopedia of American Holidays and National Days*, ed. Len Travers, 287–99. Westport, CT: Greenwood Press.

Linda S. Watts

privacy and privacy rights

The legal battle for and over privacy rights can in many ways be viewed as the root of our contemporary LGBTQ rights movement. Just as privacy rights have historically been a cornerstone in the fight for equality for LGBTQ communities, the right to privacy continues to be a driving force in much of its current social and political struggles. In its most simple sense, privacy rights revolve around the fundamental right to not have personal and private thoughts, actions, or ideas monitored by law enforcement or any other governmental body. Privacy rights dictate that an individual or group of people is not at risk of social or legal consequence as a result of thoughts, desires, and/or actions.

There is a widespread misunderstanding about the right to privacy within the United States. This misunderstanding stems from many citizens' assumption that the right to privacy is fundamental and, as such, explicitly covered within the Constitution. In actuality, no right to privacy is specifically mentioned in the Constitution of the United States. The right to privacy is of particular importance for the LGBTQ community, because of the frequency with which the privacy of individual community members has been violated by law enforcement and the government. The ability to maintain privacy and not be persecuted for one's **identity,** consensual actions between adults, and ideas is an area of privilege in which the queer community has made great legal strides and for which it continues to struggle.

One fundamental case related to privacy and the LGBTQ community in the United States is the 1960 case at Smith College. Three professors at the prestigious school, **Frederick Newton Arvin,** Raymond Joel Dorius, and Edward Spofford, were arrested and suspended from teaching after police uncovered gay **pornography** and diaries with accounts of living gay lives. The pornography consisted of pictures of men in their underwear and was illegal at the time. State troopers and local police from Northampton, Massachusetts, searched the men's homes. Arvin, a tenured professor at the college, was the first professor to have his home raided. After the discovery, he provided authorities with the names of Dorius and Spofford. Arvin later agreed to testify against them in exchange for a more lenient sentencing from the courts. Shortly afterward he suffered a mental breakdown and committed himself to a mental institution. Prior to the pornography conviction he was considered a top scholar in his field; however, he never recovered his former academic success and died in 1963 in the institution. Dorius and Spofford pled guilty to the possession of pornography, but the intention of their guilty pleas was to appeal the case under Massachusetts's law. Dorius and Spofford fought their convictions, and in 1963 the Supreme Court overturned the previous rulings. Smith College never issued a formal apology to the men, who lost their jobs and whose lives were destroyed by this investigation. In 2002 the school established a $100,000 Dorius and Spofford Fund for the Study of Civil Liberties and Freedom of Expression.

These raids were carried out as a direct result of the effort to rid the nation of "obscenity." The crackdown was conducted through the postal system, at the direct orders of President Dwight D. Eisenhower's postmaster general, Arthur E. Summerfield. Summerfield launched what he referred to as his "war on smut," obtaining governmental authority for the postal service to seize and examine the mail of anyone whom it believed to be trafficking in obscene materials. Eisenhower took the mail seizure further by giving police permission to search the private homes of individuals believed to possess obscene material and to seize anything they found. The justification for these raids was tied explicitly to the ideology of freeing the nation from pornography. These images would be considered tame by today's standards, but at the time they were considered detrimental to society. It is widely believed that the raids were actually part of a wide-scale **McCarthyism**-like attempt to root out homosexuals within American culture.

In the 1986 case of *Bowers v. Hardwick* the right to privacy of members of the LGBTQ community was tested even further. This is considered a landmark case in the struggle for privacy rights of queer people and a step backwards. In this case police officers entered the home of Michael Hardwick to serve an arrest warrant for nonpayment of a fine and failure to appear (an issue that Hardwick had already resolved with the courts). Upon entering Hardwick's home, the officer on the scene discovered Hardwick in his bedroom with another man. The two men were engaging in oral sex, which according to Georgia law was illegal under **sodomy laws,** which applied to both oral and anal sex. Represented by the **American Civil Liberties Union (ACLU),** Hardwick sued the state's attorney general in federal court. His attorneys argued that the sodomy law was illegal. After winning in a lower court, the state of Georgia attempted to overturn the decision and the case ended up before the Supreme Court.

In a landmark Supreme Court ruling, the court determined that homosexuals were not entitled to privacy rights concerning consensual events taking place in their own bedrooms. This ruling was particularly groundbreaking in that it rewrote precedents from the 1965 case *Griswold v. Connecticut,* where the Supreme Court had ruled that the right to privacy was implicit as part of the due process clause of the 14th Amendment of the Constitution. The *Hardwick* case did not completely reverse that ruling for all citizens—only for the gay community. The courts ruled in favor of sodomy laws and the criminalizing of consensual acts of oral and anal sex between same-sex adults. The courts refused to comment on the legality of sodomy laws in relation to heterosexual couples, as that was not the case before them. This ruling carried profound cultural weight, as the highest court in the nation explicitly declared both that the gay community was not entitled to the same privacy rights afforded to heterosexuals and that consenting adults did not have a right to partake in certain sexual activities in the assumed privacy of their own bedrooms.

Bowers vs. Hardwick remained part of federal law until the 2003 case of *Lawrence v. Texas.* On September 17, 1998, John Geddes Lawrence and Tyron Garner were discovered by Texas police to be having consensual sexual relations in Lawrence's apartment. Police entered the unlocked residence after receiving a telephone tip from a neighbor that a weapons disturbance had occurred in the residence. Lawrence's neighbor had previously been accused of harassing the men and later was found guilty of filing a false police report that led to the discovery and arrest of Lawrence and Garner. Local law enforcement officials entered the apartment with weapons drawn and, upon discovering the two men having sex, proceeded to arrest them on charges of violation of the state's sodomy laws, along with a violation of the homosexual conduct law on the books in Texas at the time.

After spending a night in jail, the two men were released on bail and began to fight what they argued was an illegal arrest that violated their right to privacy. After hearings in lower courts over the validity of the arrest and the legal basis of the Texas laws, the case was heard in the Supreme Court of the United States. The court ruled 5 to 4 that the Texas law was unconstitutional. *Lawrence v. Texas* overturned the court's previous findings in the 1986 *Bowers v. Hardwick* case by ruling that consenting adults did have an inherent right to privacy regarding sexual activity within a private residence. The courts found that it was unconstitutional for states to enforce laws that criminalized consensual activities between consenting adults. This case is considered to be a fundamental shift in the privacy rights of the

LGBTQ community. The ruling, which Justice Antonin Scalia argued was playing into a larger homosexual agenda, provided wide-scale privacy protections for the gay community. This case had particularly broad implications in that it struck down all sodomy laws as unconstitutional.

Although advances have been made in securing the legal right to privacy for the gay community, particularly in light of the *Lawrence v. Texas* ruling, the legal right to privacy remains a civil liberties concern for the community. Privacy rights of all Americans have been questioned after the instillation of President Bush's Patriot Act in 2001, but there have been specific concerns for the LGBTQ community. In 2005 news media broke a story about the federal government infiltrating and spying on various civilian groups and organizations that were believed to be suspicious; among them were some LGBTQ rights groups. Particular attention was paid to college groups, including those protesting the "don't ask, don't tell' policy. A student protest at the University of California, Santa Cruz, campus, which included a kiss-in directly in front of military recruiters, was considered a credible threat of terrorism by the government.

Government monitoring of the actions and movements of LGBTQ organizations, **activists,** and individuals is not a new phenomenon connected only to a post 9/11 American government. Government monitoring has historically been a fundamental issue for the gay rights community in the United States, dating back to the political climate of the Cold War. It is widely accepted that the Federal Bureau of Investigation (FBI) was involved in monitoring meetings of the **Mattachine Society** in 1961. The Mattachine Society was one of the nation's first gay rights organizations to be formed. The government also monitored the first public protest of the military's exclusionary policies toward the gay community. This protest occurred in 1965 and took place directly in front of the White House. At this protest, government agents reportedly took photographs of the gay and lesbian protesters to keep on file. It was not uncommon for FBI agents to routinely follow members of the community who were involved in political activism, and names of known gay rights activists were kept on record. The right to privacy for the gay community, and attempts at furthering political rights, have been compromised by the U.S. government since their inception. The infringement on the privacy of LGBTQ individuals, activists, and organizations in Cold War America should be viewed not as separate from, but as part of the McCarthyism that swept through the nation. The gay community was a prime target for what are often described as witch hunts, akin to and connected with the ones that oppressed Communists of the same era. This attempt at rooting out LGBTQ communities and individuals directly resulted in egregious privacy violations on the part of federal and local law enforcement bodies. Members of the community were not free to gather safely or to partake in consensual private acts safely within their own homes.

Relatively simple aspects of everyday life that most contemporary American LGBTQ community members take for granted were not available to LGBTQ people in the 1950s and 1960s; during the decades prior to Stonewall, privacy violations were a routine part of community members' lives. Concerns over the right to privacy can in fact be looked at as the catalyst for the beginnings of the modern gay rights movement in the United States. During the 1950s and 1960s it was routine for bars where the gay community gathered to be violently raided by law enforcement officers. The 1969 **Stonewall Riots** in New York City's Greenwich Village, which are credited as the birthplace of the gay rights movement, were a direct result of a refusal to continue to tolerate the police abuse and brutality that were inflicted on patrons as a result of their sexual orientation and/or gender identity. For example, in many places it was illegal for two women or two men to dance together, making dancing with a lover or partner in a private bar or club an illegal action if law enforcement were to arrive (which they routinely did). Gender-nonconforming members of the community who were in the bars were in additional danger from law enforcement. The right to what many would consider basic privacy was not extended to members of the community as they were strip-searched to determine whether they were wearing at least three pieces of "appropriate" gendered clothing, as failure to do so was illegal in many areas of the country.

Other contemporary concerns and manifestations of privacy rights issues revolve around transgender members of the community. The basic privacy of transgender people relating to intimate details of their lives and bodies is all too often compromised. Of specific concern is the right of transgender individuals to maintain privacy regarding their gender history, assigned sex, former names, and past, present, or future transitional status in terms of hormones and/or surgery(ies). Frequently the privacy needs of transgender people in the United States are compromised by state legal systems that often make it extremely difficult or impossible to alter identification documents such as birth certificates, Social Security cards, and driver's licenses to match the individual's gender identity and/or current name. An inability to change legal documents results in a privacy nightmare in which transgender people are basically required to come out about their gender nonconformity in order to receive employment, open a bank account, process routine traffic violations, enter a bar, or go through any number of aspects of daily life where legal proof of identification is required.

The privacy rights of the transgender community have become an even greater issue in post-9/11 America. Under the guise of national security the Bush administration considered a plan for enacting a "real ID," a required identification card for all Americans that they would be mandated to carry at all times. Dramatically different than a state driver's license or identification card, real ID would be federalized and would thus eliminate any discrepancies among state identification systems. The government argues that such an ID would greatly curtail issues related to identity theft, and it has therefore become a part of a national security antiterrorism agenda. But privacy rights of transgender individuals would be violated in key ways or rendered increasingly tenuous. Real ID cards would contain data chips that, when scanned by law enforcement, would force transgendered individuals to out themselves—at routine traffic violations, for example.

In short, the right to privacy remains a cornerstone of current LGBTQ legal, public, and political battles as well as in the lives of private individuals who daily struggle to live lives in an authentic way without persecution for who they are, how they love, or who they love.

Further Reading
Johnson, David K. 2006. *The Lavender Scare: The Cold War Persecution of Gays and Lesbians in the Federal Government.* Chicago: University of Chicago Press.
Werth, Barry. 2002. *The Scarlet Professor: Newton Arvin: A Literary Life Shattered by Scandal.* New York: Anchor.

Sassafras Lowrey

promiscuity

Promiscuity is a term applied to individuals whose sexual encounters conflict with social values or break taboos. The term is usually pejorative, used to suggest the individual engages in sexual acts indiscriminately. Women are often labeled promiscuous for sexual behavior that would be considered normal for a man. Psychologists suggest that both sex drive and attitudes toward sex are significant in predicting how many sexual partners an individual will have in his or her lifetime. Individuals with a high sex drive who hold liberal views on sexual behavior are likely to have sex more frequently and with a larger number of partners. In addition, masculine women report having had more sexual partners while less masculine men report having a higher sex drive.

One of the studies frequently cited as proof of gay male promiscuity was done in 1970 by the Institute for Sex Research. Alan Bell and Martin Weinberg interviewed predominantly gay men and women in the Bay Area of California. Of their white male participants, 75 percent reported having had over 50 sexual partners, 60 percent reported more than 250, and 28 percent reported having 1,000 or more. Of their black male participants, 77 percent reported having more than 50 partners, 44 percent reported more than 250, and 19 percent reported 1,000 or more. Bell and Weinberg acknowledge that theirs was not a representative sample. Their white male sample was recruited from **gay bars** (28 percent), **bathhouses** (7 percent), after-hours bars (6 percent), or **cruising** areas (4 percent). That 45 percent of these respondents came from these highly sexualized locales within the gay community would certainly affect the results. In addition, the study took place more than a decade before awareness of AIDS permeated gay culture in the United States.

Critics of promiscuity argue that frequent sexual encounters reduce individuals' sense of self-worth, damage their ability to bond emotionally, and increase the chance of contracting a sexually transmitted disease. Against this, sex activists argue that just as sexual intimacy bonds couples, sexual promiscuity can bond communities.

Further Reading
Brown, Norman R., and Robert C. Sinclair. 1999. "Estimating Number of Lifetime Sexual Partners: Men and Women Do It Differently." *Journal of Sex Research* 36: 292–97.
Mikach, Sarah M., and J. Michael Bailey. 1999. "What Distinguishes Women with Unusually High Numbers of Sex Partners?" *Evolution and Human Behaviour* 20: 141–50.

Ostovich, Jennifer M., and John Sabini. 2004. "How Are Sociosexuality, Sex Drive, and Lifetime Number of Sexual Partners Related?" *Personality and Social Psychology Bulletin* 30 (10): 1255–66.

Simpson, Jeffry A., and Steven W. Gangestad. 1991. "Individual Differences in Sociosexuality: Evidence for Convergent and Discriminant Validity." *Journal of Personality and Social Psychology* 60: 870–83.

Margaret Robinson

prostitution

Called the world's oldest profession, prostitution is the practice of offering sex in exchange for money, drugs, protection, or other items of value. Synonymous with the less pejorative term *sex work,* prostitution is illegal in the United States, except in Nevada. Historically, heterosexual prostitution has been the only profession in which women consistently have been able to make a living. With the advent of the Internet, the way the sex industry works has changed, especially in terms of male sex workers with male clients: the number of street prostitutes has decreased as prostitute business through the Internet has increased. All sex workers face risks and health problems, including high exposure to sexually transmitted diseases (STDs), drug use, and physical violence. In the United States, many face social stigma, the feeling of emotional exploitation, and self-destructiveness. Regarding the LGBT community, commonly a percentage of young lesbians and gay youth who come out to their parents are disowned or run away from home. Often these children turn to prostitution to survive.

Relatively little information is available on lesbians who employ sex workers for pleasure, although the scant information is coupled with the general belief that this is rare. Same-sex male prostitution with a "hustler," "rentboy," or escort involves a variety of sexual acts according to the client's requirements and sexual orientation. Both parties come to the relationship with a variety of positive and negative personal motivations. Motivations for the hustler, in addition to the financial incentive, can include physical gratification, increased social status (when taken to expensive restaurants, shows, and resorts by a client), a sense of self-worth, or rebellion against society. Clients likewise have complex motivations, including loneliness, need for physical gratification, the drive to engage in secret fetishes, or emotional issues (including issues of sexual orientation). Some male clients who identify as straight but are looking for a male prostitute prefer escorts who are preoperative transwomen. Clients include married men, gay men of all ages looking for sex, and both gay and straight couples. Clients find male sex workers on the street or in **bathhouses,** parks, and **bars.** Male sex workers can also be found through print ads and online as escorts or massage therapists, and subject-specific Internet Web sites make sex workers available to clients as well. In addition to the risks faced by all sex workers, male sex workers also risk gay bashing; those working the street and younger hustlers and escorts seem to face the greatest risk. Because of the social stigma of homosexuality, male prostitution is generally considered more degrading with male than with female clients, increasing the stigmatization and isolation for this already-marginalized group. Same-sex prostitution for bisexuals is not radically different than same-sex male and heterosexual female prostitution (as the majority of clients are male), including many of the same reasons and justifications.

Further Reading

Elias, James, Vern L. Bullough, Veronica Elias, and Gwen Brewer, eds. 1998. *Prostitution: On Whores, Hustlers, and Johns*. Amherst, NY: Prometheus Books.

Friedman, Mack. 2003. *Strapped for Cash: A History of American Hustler Culture*. New York: Alyson.

Morrison, Todd G., and Bruce W. Whitehead, eds. 2007. *Male Sex Work: A Business Doing Pleasure*. Binghamton, NY: Haworth.

Sycamore, Matt Bernstein, ed. 2000. *Tricks and Treats*. Binghamton, NY: Haworth Press.

Weitzer, Ronald. 1999. *Sex for Sale: Prostitution, Pornography, and the Sex Industry*. New York: Taylor & Francis.

West, D. J., and Buz De Villiers. 1992. *Male Prostitution*. Binghamton, NY: Haworth Press.

Mária I. Cipriani

Protestants, evangelical

The word *evangelical* transliterates *euangellion*, the Greek term for "good news" in the New Testament. This "good news" or "gospel" is the essence of the early church's preaching that, as Paul puts it, "God was in Christ, reconciling the world to God" (2 Cor. 5:19). It is famously summarized in John 3:16. Evangelicals place primary emphasis on this norming story, expounded in scripture and the ancient Christian creeds. In Europe, evangelical often simply signifies Protestant as distinct from Roman Catholic. The term became more frequently used during eighteenth-century religious revivals in England and America and came to be identified with nineteenth-century Protestant orthodoxy as over against that era's theological liberalism and the early twentieth-century's theological modernism.

All evangelicals emphasize the importance of a clear biblical basis for Christian belief and behavior, a cross-centered doctrine of God's grace and peace, personal conversion as the initial means of appropriating God's grace and peace, and lives of discipleship to Christ and service to others. Today, evangelical may conjure up images of "red-state" reactionary politics (including antigay rhetoric), but the term is not a synonym for the religious Right. Exit polls in 2006 found that evangelicals split their votes approximately 60/40 (Republicans/Democrats). A poll of Southern Baptists in 2006 found that 75 percent reject Pat Robertson's periodic announcements that God is giving him special revelations. In making the HBO documentary *Friends of God*, Alexandra Pelosi discovered that younger evangelicals say Pat Robertson, Jerry Falwell, and James Dobson do not speak for them.

In previous generations, evangelical faith was associated with populism and progressive political ideology—as in the antislavery and abolitionist movements and in the advocacy of women's voting rights. But in all eras, the theology proper, rather than any political position, distinguishes the evangelical faith. Apart from a commitment to the historic Christian gospel, there is, and always has been, a wide diversity in the distinctive details of theology and practice among the evangelicals.

There are entire denominations of evangelicals as well as many thousands of independent assemblies. And some—usually sizable—evangelical congregations exist within the more theologically liberal, so-called mainline denominations. Evangelicals meet in inner-city storefronts, small rural church buildings, and in less-structured home Bible studies as well as in huge auditoriums on the sprawling campuses of suburban megachurches. There are independent, non-church-affiliated or parachurch agencies for evangelism, missions, and broadcasting as well as for education and ministries of health and human services. Many specifically evangelical publishers serve the community.

Evangelicals in science get together as the American Scientific Affiliation, theologians and biblical scholars gather in the Evangelical Theological Society, and churches and other organizations come together under the umbrella of the National Association of Evangelicals. There are specifically evangelical academies, prep schools, colleges, universities, seminaries, and graduate schools in the liberal arts, medicine, and law. Contrary to stereotypes, America's evangelicals include outstanding scientists such as Harvard/Smithsonian astrophysicist Owen Gingrich and Human Genome Project director Francis S. Collins, world-class philosophers like Nicholas Wolterstorff and Alvin Plantinga, respected historians like Randall Balmer and Mark Noll, progressive social **activists** like Jim Wallis and Tony Campolo, and cultural icons like Bob Dylan (although Dylan told Jon Pareles in 1997 that "he now subscribes to no organized religion").

It is very difficult to estimate the number of evangelicals in the United States, but polls find that between 40 and 50 percent of Americans consistently call themselves evangelical or "born again." Although the Southern Baptist Convention is the largest typically evangelical denomination, 25 percent of Southern Baptists do not identify themselves as evangelical or born again. Among African Americans, 61 percent identify themselves as born again—the largest percentage of evangelicals in any racial group. While all evangelicals believe God created the universe out of nothing and a few believe in six 24-hour days of creation, most evangelicals affirm that the universe was formed over billions of years. While all evangelicals emphasize a personal trust in Jesus Christ as Savior and Lord, how that relationship is explained, experienced, and expressed varies. Some speak of a dramatic moment when they were born again, while others speak of a more gradual spiritual awakening. Some evangelicals—the Pentecostals and charismatic Christians—"speak in tongues," but most evangelicals do not. Evangelical groups such as the Salvation Army do not baptize or observe the Lord's Supper, but most evangelicals do. Some baptize by sprinkling and some by immersion; some baptize only adults, others baptize infants as well. Some use grape juice and plain bread for the Lord's Supper, and others use wine and wafers to celebrate the Eucharist. Some evangelicals, such as Seventh-Day Adventists, worship on Saturday, but most evangelicals worship on Sunday. Some evangelical worship services, called "contemporary," use worship teams and repetitive praise choruses rather than more traditional hymns, professional choirs, and rote ritual. Some ordain women to pastoral ministry, and some do not. Evangelicals take different positions on divorce and remarriage, pacifism, just-war theory, the death penalty, predestination, free will, end-time theology, faith healing, engagement in pop culture, and so on.

The diversity found among evangelicals generally is also apparent in evangelical approaches to homosexuality. Among evangelicals there are three basic approaches to homosexuality. Some believe a biblically based ethic can endorse committed same-sex couples. This view is known in the debate as "side A." Others hold that a biblically based same-sex relationship is not possible, so these evangelicals support only celibacy for gay men and lesbians. This view is known as "side B." While Christians on side A and side B can be at odds with each other, a respectful dialogue is facilitated at, for example, www.bridges-across.org and www.gaychristian.net. Still other evangelicals insist that side A is wrong and side B does not go far enough. This third group advocates "healing" through "reparative therapy" and prayer. Many such "ex-gay" agencies advocate heterosexual marriage for ex-gay men and women. But the ex-gay movement's many sexual scandals—involving even its leaders—and its frequent downsizing of definitions of what constitutes healing have undermined its credibility both in the general public and in the evangelical community.

Homosexuality was not on the evangelical radar screen before the 1960s. For example, the popular *Unger's Bible Dictionary* (Moody Press, 1957) had no entry on the subject. On "Sodomite," Unger correctly noted that the Hebrew term that was rendered sodomite in English did not designate residents of Sodom but rather "consecrated" or "devoted" men who engaged in the sex rites of pagan temples. And yet, in 1974, evangelical publisher InterVarsity brought out a book on singleness, *They Walk Alone*, in which author Margaret Evening specifically declined to address the rightness or wrongness of homosexual acts but affirmed that heterosexuals and homosexuals were meant to enjoy their sexuality.

With the increasing influence of the religious right in the later 1970s, evangelical publishers, including InterVarsity, began to publish books that took a very negative view of homosexuality. This opposition to homosexuality from conservative religious groups can have as much to do with allegiance to right-wing sociopolitical agendas that are shared by secular conservatives as with anything particularly Christian. Likewise, support for homosexuality from liberal church groups can have as much to do with the arguments of secular liberals as with anything Christian.

Jesus is not known to have said anything that can be construed as addressing homosexuality. However, since evangelicals place great importance on "what the Bible says," the few Bible verses that are said to address homosexuality have received much attention. But the seemingly commonsense reading of these verses in English is considered superficial, even by some evangelical scholars. For example, the late Marten Woudstra, a former president of the Evangelical Theological Society and an Old Testament scholar, argued that nothing in the Old Testament corresponds to homosexuality as it is understood today. Close examination of the Hebrew and

Greek vocabularies and the historical backgrounds and cultural settings of the texts reveal mistranslation, anachronism, and interpretative errors that render popular antigay readings and applications unwarranted. For example, though the book of Genesis affirms God's having created humans as "male and female" (Gen. 1:27), Paul, in his letter to Romans, uses this specific phrase from Genesis to contend that, in Christ, just as there is now no theological relevance in ethnic, racial, and social distinctions, the "male and female" pairing of Genesis is likewise theologically irrelevant (Gal. 3:28). The well-known story of Sodom (Gen. 19) depicts an attempted raping of strangers for the purpose of subjugation—the opposite of homosexual affection. And the prophet Ezekiel rails against that city's atrocious inhospitality (16:48–49). Some English versions of Deuteronomy 23:17–18 use *sodomite*, but this is not based in the Hebrew text, where the term used refers to "holy" prostitutes of the Canaanite religion. *Abomination* in Leviticus 18:22 means a cultic defilement. Even Jerry Falwell's *Fundamentalist Journal* acknowledged that Christians are not bound by these rules of the ancient priestly code. In Paul's letter to Romans, he engages in polemic against pagan religion and illustrates it with probable reference to prostitution that was part of the ritual in the temples of Cybele (Rom. 1:26–27). This, of course, is beside the point for homosexuality today. A word in Paul's vice list in 1 Corinthians 6:9 is apparently a word he coined, for it (*arsenokoitai*) appears in no other extant literature of his day or earlier. And since it appears in a list, its specific meaning cannot be deciphered from the immediate context. Another term in the list (*malakoi*) literally means "soft" or "weak." But it is a stretch to say it must mean "homosexual." Whatever Paul meant by these two terms, they are merely examples. The thrust of his argument is that Christians should not be dragging each other into pagan law courts to settle disputes they should settle among themselves.

Even among the religious right, there is some awareness that its approach to homosexuality has been simplistic, harsh, and obsessive. In 2006, the Christian Coalition, founded by Pat Robertson, tapped Florida pastor Joel C. Hunter to be its new head. Although he does not support gay relationships, he wanted to shift the coalition's emphasis from its heavy-handed antigay rhetoric to issues of economic and social justice and the environment. He resigned when the board disagreed. In 2006, when *Christianity Today*, the flagship journal of evangelicals, ranked the most influential authors for evangelicals over the past 50 years, several pro-gay authors were on the list, although their pro-gay positions were not noted. The author whom *Christianity Today* ranked as the most influential was the late Rosalind Rinker, author of books on conversational prayer. She was a board member of the pro-gay Evangelicals Concerned (EC) and a keynoter at EC's summer conferences in the early 1980s. Three other keynoters at these conferences were also on this *Christianity Today* list, while other keynoters have included a *Christianity Today* editor, evangelical authors, clinicians, singers, pastors, and denomination officials as well as faculty members from evangelical colleges and seminaries. One keynoter, Lewis B. Smedes, even after speaking at two EC conferences, was honored with a chair of Christian ethics designated in his name at Fuller Seminary, arguably the foremost evangelical seminary in America.

Presidents Gerald Ford, Jimmy Carter, and Bill Clinton—all self-professed evangelicals—have registered their support for gay rights. Furthermore, to the dismay of antigay social conservatives, even President George W. Bush—another self-professed evangelical—has appointed openly gay people to ambassadorial levels and other high positions in his administration. As more gay men and lesbians continue to **come out** to their evangelical families, friends, and fellow churchgoers, it will be increasingly difficult to see these real people in the religious right's **stereotypes** of homosexuals. Once an initially negative reaction subsides, it tends to be replaced with either a warm and accepting understanding or, at least, a cordial live-and-let-live arrangement. Very few families and close friends—whether evangelical or not—are willing to turn their backs on those they love, no matter how unprepared they may have been for their coming out. This more comfortable accommodation has happened with divorce in evangelical families. As more evangelicals have had to deal with divorce in their families and churches, they have became correspondingly more accepting of divorced relatives, divorced fellow church members, and even divorced pastors.

Many believe that the more evangelicals focus on their central tenet of God's free grace in Christ's death as the basis for righteousness and refrain from an uncharacteristic righteousness through asceticism, the more they will see homosexuality, as such, as theologically neutral. And the more they focus on Jesus's emphasis on the "golden rule" of neighborly love as the essence of God's call to discipleship (Matt. 7:12), and the more they focus on Paul's view of self-giving love as "the law of Christ" (Gal. 6:2), the more they will be able to be welcoming of people who just happen to be gay or lesbian.

Further Reading

Balmer, Randall. 2004. *Encyclopedia of Evangelicalism*. Rev. exp. ed. Waco, TX: Baylor University Press.

Evangelicals Concerned Inc. Web site. Available at: http://www.ecinc.org. Accessed July 14, 2008.

Myers, David G., and Letha Dawson Scanzoni. 2005. *What God Has Joined Together: The Christian Case for Gay Marriage*. San Francisco: HarperSanFrancisco.

Pareles, Jon. 1997. "A Wiser Voice Blowin' in the Autumn Wind." *New York Times* (September 28). Available at: http://www.interferenza.net/bcs/interw/97-set27.htm. Accessed July 14, 2008.

Rogers, Jack. 2006. *Jesus, the Bible and Homosexuality: Explode the Myths, Heal the Church*. Louisville, KY: Westminster, John Knox.

Ralph Blair

Protestants, mainline

Mainline Protestants, also referred to as mainstream or liberal, share a theological tradition that considers the Bible a central guide for matters of faith and practice. In contrast to many **evangelical Protestants,** liberal Protestants often maintain that the Bible should be read with reference to the historical and cultural context of its creation and reinterpreted in light of contemporary problems and historical developments. For nearly four decades, mainline Protestants have been debating the relationship between homosexuality and the church, owing largely to the increased momentum of the lesbian and gay rights movement after the 1969 **Stonewall Riots.** Central to these debates, argues sociologist Wendy Cadge, are questions concerning the interpretation of scripture, understandings of human sexuality, the organization of the family, and the requirements for participation in church leadership.

Attitudes toward homosexuality vary both across the mainline groups and within denominations. Some denominations and congregations do not welcome practicing homosexuals as fully entitled members, while more progressive denominations may wholly embrace openly gay men, lesbians, bisexuals, and transgender persons. Mainline Protestants have approached homosexuality mostly through policy debates at the denominational, congregational, and grassroots levels. Some of the most divisive debates, particularly among Methodists, Episcopalians, and Presbyterians, have addressed the ordination of practicing lesbians and gays and the blessing of same-sex unions.

Though some racial and class diversity exists, most members of mainline denominations come from white, middle-class backgrounds. Most also tend to be older and relatively well educated. About three-fourths of mainline Protestants define their political views as moderate or liberal. Mainline denominations generally include the **United Church of Christ (UCC),** the **Episcopal Church,** the Presbyterian Church, the American Baptist Churches, the United Methodist Church, the Disciples of Christ, and the Evangelical Lutheran Church in America. Many denominations actively support the National Council of Churches (previously the Federal Council of Churches), an umbrella group of mainline and liberal Christian denominations. These groups have earned reputations as progressive denominations due to their commitment to countering social problems such as poverty and racism since the turn of the twentieth century.

LUTHERAN LESBIAN
& GAY MINISTRIES

Empowering openly identified
sexual minority people
called to God's mission of
ministry and witness

www.llgm.org

Brochure for Lutheran Lesbian and Gay Ministries. Courtesy of the Gay, Lesbian, Bisexual, Transgender Historical Society, San Francisco.

EARLY ENCOUNTERS

Much research has yet to be done on religion and homosexuality before the 1970s, but historians of sexuality such as John D'Emilio have noted that religious individuals and communities gathered in the decades before Stonewall to support the **homophile movement.** As early as 1946, in Atlanta, Georgia, 85 members of the Eucharist Catholic Church met in a gay bar to celebrate Christmas Eve, making it possibly the first church organized for homosexuals. In 1948, a Unitarian minister helped found the **Mattachine Society,** a key contributor to the homophile movement, and their first national conference was located at First Universalist Church in Los Angeles in 1953.

The Council on Religion and the Homosexual was founded in 1964 through the efforts of A. Cecil Williams and Ted McIlvena, two reverends from Glide Memorial Methodist Church in San Francisco. Its mission was to promote dialogue between homosexuals and the church. In December 1967, the UCC devoted an issue of its denominational magazine to the civil liberties of homosexuals, and in 1969 the UCC's Council for Christian Social Action issued a formal statement on homosexual issues, the first time a mainline denomination had done so. The statement opposed all laws criminalizing private homosexual relations between consenting adults as well as the exclusion of homosexuals from public employment and service in the armed forces.

By the end of the 1970s, nearly all of the mainline denominations, with the exception of the American Baptists, offered formal statements on homosexuality. The Lutheran, United Methodist, and Presbyterian denominations found homosexual behavior to be incompatible with Christian teachings but have consistently supported lesbian and gay rights in the secular sphere. In 1976, for instance, the United Presbytery Church passed a resolution stating that homosexuality was a sin, though the following year they emphasized the need to support the just treatment of homosexual persons in regard to civil rights and liberties. They formally welcomed gays and lesbians as members of the denomination in 1978. The Episcopal Church also made its first statement on homosexuality in 1976, referring to homosexuals as children of God, and supported their struggles for equal protection and civil rights.

ORGANIZING IN THE MAINLINE CHURCHES

Members of mainline congregations formed independent grassroots organizations in the 1970s to support LGBT members and to lobby denominational bodies to change their policies regarding homosexuality. William Johnson founded the UCC Gay Caucus in 1972 to provide support for gay and lesbian members of the denomination. The United Church Coalition for Gay, Lesbian, Bisexual, and Transgender Concerns followed in 1973. Presbyterians for Lesbian and Gay Concerns, founded by David Bailey Sindt, first formed as the Presbyterian Gay Caucus after the denomination's 1974 General Assembly. The group advocated against the denomination's policy of not ordaining practicing homosexuals. Lutherans Concerned was also founded in 1974 to promote the understanding and acceptance of gay and lesbian members. The United Methodist Gay Caucus (later renamed Affirmation) was founded in 1975 in Evanston, Illinois, and by 1976 Louie Crew had founded the Episcopalian group Integrity in rural Georgia.

Since the 1970s, some congregations seeking to include homosexuals in their services have begun designating themselves as welcoming, affirming, or reconciling churches. The Presbyterian "More Light" congregations, the model of this movement, began when Reverend Robert Davidson wrote a statement of conscience in 1978 that provided the first step toward developing a network of congregations formally welcoming gay and lesbian members. The United Methodist Reconciling Congregation Program was organized by Affirmation in 1984. Individual congregations within the Methodist denominations can vote on whether or not to identify as reconciling congregations. With over 200 congregations and 28 campus ministries, this program includes people of all sexual orientations. Some local groups also specifically include transgender persons. The program became the Reconciling Ministries Network in 2000 and functions independently of the Methodist denomination. The Evangelical Lutheran Reconciling in Christ Program formed in 1984, and the United Church of Christ Open and Affirming Congregation Program was founded in 1986 to offer similar programs in their denominations.

Organizations opposed to homosexuality also formed in the 1980s, beginning with the Transforming Congregation Program in 1988. This group grew out of the Evangelical Renewal Fellowship of the California-Nevada Annual Conference and includes mostly United Methodist members, but Lutherans and Presbyterians have also joined. In 2002, it gained official membership status in Exodus International, the largest international ex-gay organization. Members of this movement believe that homosexuality is a sin and that the Holy Spirit can transform the life of homosexuals, eventually allowing them to live either as heterosexuals or as celibate homosexuals. Some programs offer reparative counseling for those "struggling" with homosexuality. The Presbyterians for Renewal, founded in 1989, and the Presbyterian Coalition actively oppose equal status for gays and lesbians within the denomination. Episcopal groups organized against the inclusion of homosexuals in church life include the American Anglican Council, Concerned Clergy and Laity, and Episcopalians United.

The leadership bodies of mainline denominations consistently supported secular LGBT rights throughout 1980s and 1990s. The UCC approved resolutions in its national governing body that rejected institutionalized homophobia and supported gay and lesbian families in 1983, supported privacy in 1987, and brought attention to violence against gays and lesbians in 1989. The General Convention of the Episcopal Church offered support for **hate crime** legislation in 1988. The Presbyterian General Assembly joined the UCC's Office of Church and Society to jointly file an amicus curiae brief in the 1985 Supreme Court case *Bowers v. Hardwick*, in support of Hardwick. By the 1990s nearly all the mainline denominations had passed resolutions supporting full civil right for gays and lesbians. In addition, many religious leaders, denominations, and congregational bodies signed amicus curiae briefs to show their support for gay and lesbian rights in state and federal court cases. In 1994, UCC President Paul Sherry testified before the Armed Services Committee in support of lifting the ban on gays in the military. In the mid-1990s the Episcopal denomination's Washington, D.C., office joined the Evangelical Lutheran Church, the Presbyterian Church, the United Church of Christ, and the United Methodist Church to support the Employment Non-Discrimination Act. Each of the denominations' Washington offices also supported hate crime legislation in the late 1990s.

THE QUESTION OF ORDINATION

While support for lesbian and gay civil rights outside of the church was strong, the question of whether to allow practicing homosexuals to be ordained became a divisive topic within mainline denominations. The United Church of Christ has been the most progressive on this issue, ordaining openly gay William Johnson in 1972 and openly lesbian Anne Holmes in 1977. The ordination of practicing lesbians and gays was formally accepted by the UCC in 1980, allowing local congregations to decide their own ordination practices. The Episcopal Church has permitted the ordination of celibate gays and lesbians since 1979, and the denomination has no canon law explicitly excluding practicing homosexuals from ordination. In 1997 the denomination approved health benefits for domestic partners of clergy and lay employees. Gene Robinson was the first openly gay Episcopalian to be elected bishop in New Hampshire in 2003. In contrast, the United Methodist *Book of Discipline* has excluded homosexuals from being ordained since 1980. In a move similar to many mainline denominations, the United Methodist Church passed a "fidelity in marriage and celibacy in singleness" statement in 1984, a gesture seen as intended to discourage practicing homosexuals from being ordained. That same year the *Book of Discipline* explicitly outlawed the ordination of practicing homosexuals. In 1987, Reverend Rose Mary Denman disclosed her lesbian sexuality to her bishop, and charges were filed against her. Denman lost her trial and her position in the denomination.

The Evangelical Lutheran Church of America (ELCA) stated in 1989 that practicing homosexuals were excluded from the ordained ministry. In San Francisco, this decision was challenged by St. Francis Lutheran Church, which called a gay pastor to serve, and First United Lutheran Church in San Francisco, which called a lesbian couple to serve. The following year, both congregations were tried and suspended from membership in ELCA. In the late 1990s, the Lutheran Church issued its first decision on homosexual ordination, voting to ban practicing homosexuals from clergy membership. Anita Hill, of St. Paul-Reformation Church, who had been serving as an unordained pastoral minister since 1994, had been ordained in violation of ELCA governing documents. Hill was ordained in 2001 by four bishops, one active and three retired; in that same year, the congregation was censured. ELCA initiated a four-year study of homosexuality in 2001, and the following year a call was made to remove the censure on St. Paul-Reformation Lutheran Church; sanctions that prevented members from serving in the synod office were removed, but the censure remains.

In 1985 the Presbyterian General Assembly reaffirmed their 1978 decision that practicing gays and lesbians could not be ordained. Martha Juillerat, a Presbyterian minister who resigned her ordination after disclosing her lesbian identity in 1995, initiated the Shower of Stoles Project. Juillerat requested that other ministers who had been denied ordination, forced to leave the church, or required to conceal their sexual practices send her their stoles. She initially received 80 stoles, and the number has since grown to over 800 from 13 different denominations. Juillerat displays the stoles at various annual meetings. The Shower of Stoles Project has become a nonprofit organization. At the 2006 Presbyterian General Assembly, clergy and other church officers were still required to exhibit "fidelity within the covenant of marriage between a man and a woman or chastity in singleness." However, local ordination bodies now have some flexibility when reviewing candidates who do not meet these standards. In June 2008 the Presbyterian General Assembly, meeting in San Jose, California, took two important votes that opened the door to the ordination of gays and lesbians, but the country's 173 presbyteries have a year from that date to approve or reject this assembly vote.

The American Baptist Church entered the debate on homosexuality in 1992 by stating that homosexual behavior was incompatible with Christian teaching. Debate continued within the denomination, particularly after several congregations that had publicly welcomed gays and lesbians were kicked out of regional denominational bodies. Ordination in American Baptist churches is done at the congregational level, making it difficult to assess general denominational practices. Some gays and lesbians have been ordained, but few have been called to serve within the denomination. Nadean Bishop became the first openly lesbian woman to be called to service for an American Baptist congregation in 1992. The denomination's *Commission on Human Sexuality Resources* reported in 1993 that congregations did not find homosexuality to be a concern of great priority within the denomination.

MAINLINE DENOMINATIONS AND SAME-SEX UNIONS

The performance of same-sex union ceremonies became a hotly contested issue in the 1990s. The UCC performed commitment ceremonies throughout the decade, and the UCC Board for Homeland Ministries supported same-sex marriage rights in 1996. On July 4, 2005, the UCC became the first major Christian denomination to promote same-sex marriage, deciding against discrimination on the basis of gender in its wedding policies. In 2000, the Lutheran denomination passed a resolution to minister to those in same-sex partnerships, and some ministers have been presiding over same-sex unions for years without repercussions. The Presbyterian Church declared in 1991 that homosexual relationships were not forbidden and asserted, three years later, that decisions about commitment ceremonies were the responsibility of the regional presbytery. In 2000 the highest court of the denomination ruled that ministers could bless same-sex unions so long as they were not considered marriages. The Episcopal Church, which recognized nonheterosexual living arrangements in 1991, initiated a study in 1994 on the theological and pastoral components of same-sex partnerships. In 2003 the Episcopal Church's General Convention approved the blessing of same-sex relationships, and at least 10 dioceses have official policies allowing such blessings.

Methodists have been at the center of the debate on gay marriage because of the ambiguity of their denominational policy. In 1998, Reverend Jimmy Creech was tried for marrying a lesbian couple inside a church building, a violation of denominational rules. Creech was found not guilty on the basis of a technicality: the extent to which the policy was binding on local congregations (as opposed to being a guideline) was unclear. After this trial, however, the statement on marriage in the 1996 *Book of Discipline* was clarified; it prohibited Methodist pastors from performing homosexual unions in denominational buildings. Reverend Greg Dell was later found guilty of violating this law and lost his ministerial credentials for one year. In California, 150 Methodist clergy collectively performed a lesbian wedding in 1999 to protest the new policy. Charges against participating clergy were dropped on the basis that complaints brought against them were not proper for trial. In 1997, Reverend Jeanne Knepper and other Methodist members founded the Covenant Relationships Network, which advocates for same-gender unions in the church. In 2006, Methodist youth met for the annual United Methodist Student Development Conference, where they approved 14 resolutions on the topic of homosexuality, urging the denomination to be more tolerant and inclusive of gay and lesbian members.

While homosexuality remains a largely divisive topic in most mainline denominations, as of the mid-2000s the welcoming and affirming movement includes over 900 congregations in 10 denominations spanning 46 states, Washington, D.C., and five Canadian provinces. Several groups, including the Welcoming and Affirming Baptists, Disciples of Christ Open and Affirming Ministries, Lutheran Reconciling in Christ Program, More Light Presbyterians, United Church of Canada Affirming Congregation, United Church of Christ Open and Affirming Program, and the United Methodist Reconciling Congregation Program, have been jointly publishing the quarterly magazine *Open Hands* since the 1990s. Other welcoming and affirming programs and pro-gay religious organizations include the Brethren/Mennonite Supportive Congregations Network, Episcopal Oasis, the Unitarian Universalist Association Welcoming Congregation Program, the Presbyterian AIDS Network, Presbyterian **ACT UP,** That All May Freely Serve, and the Extraordinary Candidate Program (ELCA).

Further Reading

Associated Press. 2008. "Presbyterian Assembly Votes to Drop Gay Clergy Ban." June 27. Available at: http://www.iht.com/articles/ap/2008/06/27/america/NA-REL-US-Presbyterians-Gays. php. Accessed July 9, 2008.

Cadge, Wendy. 2002. "Vital Conflicts: The Mainline Denominations Debate Homosexuality." In *Quiet Hand of God: Faith-Based Activism and the Public Role of Mainline Protestantism*, ed. Robert Wuthnow, 265–86. Berkeley: University of California Press.

Comstock, Gary D. 1996. *Unrepentant, Self-Affirming, Practicing: Lesbian/Bisexual/Gay People within Organized Religion*. New York: Continuum.

D'Emilio, John. 1983. *Sexual Politics, Sexual Communities: The Making of a Homosexual Minority in the United States, 1940–1970*. Chicago: University of Chicago Press.

"Evangelical Church in America and Homosexuality: Developments 1974 to 2002." Available at: http://www.religioustolerance.org/hom_elca2.htm. Accessed July 22, 2008.

Religioustolerance.org (Ontario Consultants on Religious Tolerance). Available at: http://www.religioustolerance.org. Accessed July 14, 2008.

Anthony Petro

protests and actions

Protests and demonstrations have been an important part of the movement for LGBT rights for more than four decades, serving both to promote gay visibility and to demand redress for injustice. Protest tactics have ranged from small pickets to mass marches to acts of civil disobedience and direct action. Throughout this period, the frequency and militancy of LGBT actions has waxed and waned in cycles reflecting the country's overall political mood, peaking in the late 1960s and early 1970s with "kiss-ins," and again in the late 1980s and early 1990s with "die-ins." Even as the LGBT movement has borrowed tactics from other liberation struggles, it has made its own unique contributions—including theatrical flair and media savvy—that in turn have been adopted by heterosexual activists.

The first organized LGBT protests took place in the mid-1960s, targeting anti-gay discrimination in the military and federal employment. In 1964, about a dozen activists, including members of the Sexual Freedom League, demonstrated outside the Whitehall Induction Center in New York City. In the spring and summer of 1965, members of the East Coast Homophile Organizations (ECHO)—cofounded by Frank Kameny, who had himself been fired from a government job—picketed in front of the White House, the Pentagon, the State Department, and the Civil Service Commission in Washington, D.C.; in New York, activists demonstrated outside United Nations headquarters to protest the treatment of gays in Cuba. On July 4 of that year, some 40 activists, including members of the **Mattachine Society** and the **Daughters of Bilitis,** staged the first of four "Annual Reminders" at Independence Hall in Philadelphia (home of the iberty Bell). Typically, these demonstrations were small and polite, featuring men in suits and women in dresses walking in circles holding signs.

A "Five Facists" display during a parade in the late 1970s in San Francisco. Photo by Marie Ueda, courtesy of the Gay, Lesbian, Bisexual, Transgender Historical Society, San Francisco.

At a meeting in Kansas City in early 1966, the North American Conference of Homophile Organizations (NACHO) called for demonstrations on Armed Forces Day to protest the ban on homosexuals in the military. On May 21, actions took place in cities including Washington, D.C., New York, San Francisco (a demonstration outside the federal building), and Los Angeles (a motorcade that included Mattachine Society cofounder Harry Hay).

Beyond these organized demonstrations, other early LGBT protests were spontaneous expressions of outrage against police harassment in bars and other gathering places. In August 1966, **drag** queens, hustlers, and runaway queer youth rioted at Gene Compton's Cafeteria in San Francisco's Tenderloin neighborhood after a police officer tried to grab a young queen, who in turn threw her coffee in his face. About 50 enraged customers hurled dishware and overturned tables, while outside a police car was destroyed and a nearby newsstand was set on fire.

In Los Angeles, a campaign of police harassment of gay bars spurred LGBT organizing and gave rise to institutions such as the Metropolitan Community Church and the *Advocate*. Shortly after midnight on New Year's Eve in 1967, police raided the Black Cat bar on Sunset Boulevard in the Silver Lake neighborhood, beating several patrons and bartenders (one of whom was left unconscious with a ruptured spleen); protests erupted outside the bar that night and continued for several days. In July of the following year, after police raided the Patch bar, patrons marched to the local police station in the early morning hours and pelted the building with flowers.

The best-known LGBT protest began the night of June 27–28, 1969, at the **Stonewall** Inn in New York's Greenwich Village. After police conducted a routine raid of the Mafia-run bar, some patrons resisted as they were hauled away, and the crowd gathered outside—which included drag queens and local queer youth—grew increasingly restive. The officers retreated inside as protesters threw coins, battered the door with an uprooted parking meter, and attempted to set the bar on fire; confrontations between police and thousands of protesters in the surrounding streets continued for the next few nights.

News of the Stonewall uprising spread rapidly, and the national climate of cultural change and political militancy provided fertile soil for the nascent **gay liberation movement**. A month later, New York activists organized a commemoration of the event featuring a march from Greenwich Village to Central Park. In June 1970, several cities held Stonewall anniversary celebrations—including an unpermitted march in Chicago, an evening parade in Los Angeles, and a "gay-in" in San Francisco's Golden Gate Park—which gave rise to the annual LGBT pride events that now draw millions of participants around the world.

As new groups such as the Gay Liberation Front emerged across the country, activists

Gay men protesting in San Francisco parade. Photo by Marie Ueda, courtesy of the Gay, Lesbian, Bisexual, Transgender Historical Society, San Francisco.

grew less interested in polite pickets and adopted more militant tactics. Many gay liberationists considered themselves part of a larger struggle that included the black power and women's liberation movements. Sizable LGBT contingents participated in antiwar marches and other demonstrations for non-gay-specific causes, which played an important role in increasing gay visibility. Gay liberation groups from more than 50 cities endorsed the April 1971 moratorium against the Vietnam War, which brought out thousands of queer protesters in San Francisco and Washington, D.C., in what the *Advocate* called "one of the largest concentrations of gay power ever assembled" (Beardslee and Kepner 1971, 1).

In the early 1970s, LGBT activists protested against a variety of institutions that perpetuated antigay discrimination. Perhaps the largest organized gay protest up to that time occurred in March 1970 when some 500 New York activists held a march and vigil for Diego Vinales, who had jumped out a window at the police station and impaled himself on a fence spike after he was arrested in a raid of the Snake Pit bar. In the fall of 1970, New York University students who were denied a permit for a gay dance occupied a dorm and were ousted by police, leading to a week of protests and riots. While the largest protests of this era occurred in the gay hubs of **New York City, Los Angeles,** and **San Francisco,** they also took place in smaller cities and towns across the country, often utilizing tactics beyond the usual pickets and marches. In Cleveland, for example, activists held a gay trash pick-up in 1971 to protest police sweeps of park cruisers.

The Gay Activists Alliance (GAA) pioneered the use of "zaps," sudden unannounced actions intended to interfere with business as usual. In their quest to obtain passage of an antidiscrimination bill, New York GAA members disrupted city council meetings, protested at the offices of recalcitrant politicians (often liberals), and repeatedly hounded Mayor John Lindsay, including chaining themselves to the furniture in his city hall office and locking themselves to a balcony and sounding air horns during his appearance at Radio City Music Hall. In April 1972, two dozen GAA members disrupted an Inner Circle dinner (a men-only affair at which political journalists hobnobbed with New York City officials) and were beaten by firefighters. With articles in popular magazines such as *Newsweek*'s "The Militant Homosexual" (August 23, 1971) and *Life*'s "Homosexuals in Revolt" (December 31, 1971), these tactics helped changed the public stereotype of gay men as weak and effeminate.

Media outlets that ignored or failed to cover gay issues fairly were also a frequent target. In 1969, activists picketed the *Village Voice* for refusing to run an ad for a gay dance. On Halloween of the same year, during a demonstration against the *San Francisco Examiner,* newspaper staffers dumped a bag of printer's ink from a window onto the protesters below, who then used the ink to mark purple handprints and "gay power" graffiti on the building and throughout downtown. New York activists protested against publishers that ran inaccurate representations of LGBT people in magazines, while those in Los Angeles focused on movies and television shows. On one occasion, GAA members invaded the office of *Harper's*, where they sang songs and offered the employees coffee and donuts.

Discriminatory businesses also came under fire, including Pacific Telephone (for its antigay hiring policies and refusal to list gay groups in its yellow pages); States Steamship Lines in San Francisco, which was picketed for weeks after the company fired gay activist Gale Whitington; and Barney's Beanery in Los Angeles, where protests continued for two decades due to its "Fagots Stay Out" (*sic*) sign.

The psychiatric establishment drew particular ire. In the early 1970s, protesters shouted down Dr. Irving Beiber and other proponents of behavior modification therapy for gays at medical conferences in San Francisco, Chicago, and Los Angeles. Activists seized the stage at the annual convention of the American Psychiatric Association (APA) in Washington, D.C., in 1971 and, in the following year, staged a guerrilla theater performance mocking aversion therapy outside a meeting in New York City; the APA finally removed homosexuality from its list of mental illnesses in December 1973.

As the LGBT movement grew, so did internal divisions. Antiracism activists protested gay groups and venues, such as bars, that excluded people of color; such demonstrations were still continuing decades later, as exemplified by the months of protests outside Badlands bar in San Francisco's Castro neighborhood in 2004. As tensions arose between some gay and lesbian activists and transgender people (particularly drag queens), Sylvia Rivera and Marsha P. Johnson founded Street Transvestite Action Revolutionaries (STAR) in 1970 in New York; the Transsexual Action Organization formed in Los Angeles the same year.

Before long, many lesbians broke away from mixed-sex gay groups to focus on feminist activism. At the Second Congress to Unite Women on May 1, 1970, in New York City, about 20 lesbian feminist activists organized by **Rita Mae Brown** (who later dubbed themselves the **Radicalesbians**) took the stage wearing "Lavender Menace" T-shirts and delivered a manifesto entitled "The Woman-Identified Woman," demanding that the women's movement take lesbian concerns seriously. Some lesbians became separatists, turning away from public protest and focusing on the creation of women-only institutions. In some cases, segments of the lesbian feminist community protested against each other over issues such as sadomasochism and the inclusion of transsexuals.

By the mid-1970s, the LGBT movement had made remarkable gains with regard to legal recognition and social acceptance, and militant protests fell out of favor. Some activists came to believe that an "insider" strategy was more effective, while others shared the growing disillusionment with the radical tactics espoused by groups such as the Black Panthers and the Weather Underground.

At the same time, the era's gay rights advances sparked a conservative backlash. In 1977, Anita Bryant and her Save Our Children campaign succeeded in repealing an antidiscrimination law in Dade County, Florida. After the defeat, LGBT communities erupted in protest nationwide. For months, enraged queers confronted Bryant wherever she appeared on her singing tour; 20 lawyers wearing black armbands with pink triangles stormed out when she performed at a legal convention in Houston, some 4,000 people protested her appearance at the Southern Baptist Convention in Atlanta, and an activist in Des Moines threw a cream pie in her face. The backlash brought many people out of the **closet** for the first time, healed old community rifts, and reenergized the LGBT movement.

The late 1970s is often characterized as an era of hedonism, disco, and sexual abandon, but the period also saw its share of actions. After openly gay San Francisco supervisor **Harvey Milk** was murdered in November 1978, the light sentence given to killer Dan White sparked the White Night Riots, in which 3,000 protesters marched on city hall, where they broke windows and burned police cars, followed by a violent police crackdown in the Castro. In the summer of 1979, gays in New York disrupted the filming of *Cruising*, which they considered **homophobic.** In October of that year, LGBT people organized the first March on Washington—the largest gay demonstration to date, with an estimated 100,000 participants—which helped solidify the movement on a national scale.

The early 1980s ushered in the **HIV/AIDS** epidemic, which decimated the community and led to the loss of many veteran activists. But it also brought formerly uninvolved LGBT people into the streets. The early years of the epidemic were largely devoted to caregiving and the creation of community services, but government inaction and the growing influence of the religious right sparked a new wave of queer activism. People with AIDS themselves took the lead, holding candlelight marches and storming the stage at the Second National AIDS Forum in June 1983 to present a set of demands known as the "Denver Principles." In 1984, as many as 100,000 queer activists turned out for the National March for Lesbian and Gay Rights coinciding with the July 1984 Democratic National Convention in San Francisco, and three years later, the **Sisters of Perpetual Indulgence** held a public exorcism to mark Pope John Paul II's visit to that city.

Another massive March on Washington took place on October 11, 1987, with a turnout estimated at half a million. The march was preceded by a mass wedding of

The People with AIDS Alliance marching in a parade in San Francisco. Courtesy of the Gay, Lesbian, Bisexual, Transgender Historical Society, San Francisco.

same-sex couples conducted by Reverend Troy Perry outside the Internal Revenue Service headquarters. Two days later, some 700 activists—including the leaders of several major LGBT organizations—were arrested in front of the Supreme Court in one of the largest-ever acts of civil disobedience, protesting the 1986 *Bowers v. Hardwick* decision upholding state **sodomy laws.** After the march, countless newly energized activists returned home to organize in their own cities and towns nationwide.

The year 1987 also saw the birth of the AIDS Coalition to Unleash Power, better known as **ACT UP.** Founded after a speech by playwright **Larry Kramer** at the gay community center in New York City, ACT UP (and the earlier Lavender Hill Mob) pioneered a new style of activism. The group's first action was a die-in on Wall Street in March of that year, and chapters soon sprung up across the country and eventually around the world. ACT UP's membership combined veteran LGBT activists, young radicals, and formerly uninvolved gay men with access to privilege and resources who were spurred into action by the prospect of imminent death.

Among its best-known actions, ACT UP disrupted several International AIDS Conferences; protested at the headquarters of the Food and Drug Administration, the Centers for Disease Control, and various pharmaceutical companies; halted trading on the New York Stock Exchange; interrupted a CBS evening news broadcast; marched on then-president George H. W. Bush's home in Kennebunkport, Maine; draped a giant condom over the home of North Carolina Senator Jesse Helms; and disrupted a mass at St. Patrick's Cathedral in New York. ACT UP/Los Angeles briefly interrupted the 1990 Rose Bowl Parade in Pasadena, and a related group in San Francisco called Stop AIDS Now Or Else (SANOE) stopped traffic on the Golden Gate Bridge. In its later years, ACT UP held political funerals (a tactic adopted from the South African anti-apartheid movement) and threw the ashes of cremated people with AIDS onto the White House lawn. As many activists joined AIDS service organizations, service provision itself became integrated with direct action in the form of needle exchanges, squatter housing for people with AIDS, and distribution of unapproved and alternative therapies.

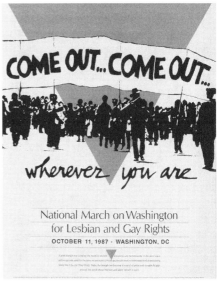

March on Washington, 1987. Courtesy of the Gay, Lesbian, Bisexual, Transgender Historical Society, San Francisco.

ACT UP spawned a number of new activist groups that shared a similar sartorial aesthetic (leather jackets, Doc Marten boots, day-glo stickers), militant tactics, and media awareness. During this era, the LGBT community was at the forefront of progressive activism and participated in several non-gay-specific struggles, including pro-choice actions and abortion clinic defense, protests against the 1991 Gulf War, and actions against art censorship. After the approval of effective HIV drugs in the mid-1990s, AIDS activism shifted to a demand for treatment access in poor countries, and queer activists made common cause with the growing global justice movement. On its 20th anniversary in March 2007, activists in New York and San Francisco attempted to revive ACT UP with protests calling for universal health care and housing for people with AIDS.

Queer Nation formed in New York City in the spring of 1990. The group gained widespread attention after activists distributed a broadsheet proclaiming "Queers Read This/I Hate Straights" at the city's pride parade, and chapters soon formed around the country. Queer Nation members held "Queer Nights Out" at straight bars, organized Suburban Homosexual Outreach Project actions at shopping malls,

A poster for the Dyke March, now a staple in many pride parades, in 1998 in San Francisco. Courtesy of the Gay, Lesbian, Bisexual, Transgender Historical Society, San Francisco.

disrupted the filming of *Basic Instinct* in 1991, protested outside the 1992 Academy Awards ceremony, and formed street patrols to counter antigay violence. In September 1991, Queer Nation members were among the estimated 50,000 protesters who took to the streets throughout the state—and even blocked a runway at Los Angeles International Airport—after California Governor Pete Wilson vetoed AB 101, an antidiscrimination bill.

The **Lesbian Avengers** formed in the summer of 1992 and eventually expanded to some 50 chapters. The Avengers distributed safer-sex information outside schools, held an "eat-out" at a Jenny Craig diet center in Boston, and released a "plague of locusts" (actually 1,000 crickets) at the headquarters of Exodus International, a religious group that claimed to "cure" homosexuals. Members of the Avengers and ACT UP organized the first Dyke March, which drew some 20,000 women on the eve of the April 1993 March on Washington. Similar groups included the Women's Action Coalition (WAC), Women's Health Action and Mobilization (WHAM), and Lesbians and Bisexuals in Action (LABIA).

The early 1990s also saw the birth of distinct bisexual and transgender movements. Bisexual activist groups such as San Francisco's BiPol and Boston's BiCEP worked for bi-visibility and joined gay and lesbian activists in antidiscrimination and AIDS-related actions. Transgender Nation formed in 1992, followed by **Transsexual Menace** and It's Time America. The most prominent ongoing transgender action was Camp Trans, a mobilization of transgender people and their allies protesting exclusion of transsexual women from the annual Michigan Womyn's Music Festival.

With the election of Bill Clinton in 1992, followed a few years later by the development of effective HIV drugs, many activists again shifted to an "insider" strategy and militant protests once more fell out of favor. As an increasing number of local governments and corporations adopted antidiscrimination policies, activists focused on the military ban and same-sex marriage. Both were key demands of the April 1993 March on Washington, which drew nearly one million people, making it one of the largest-ever demonstrations in the United States. The following June, tens of thousands turned out in New York City to commemorate the 25th anniversary of the Stonewall Riots with both a permitted parade organized by established LGBT groups and an unpermitted march in the opposite direction called by more militant activists. In 1996, queers took advantage of the Olympics in Atlanta to protest sodomy laws and antigay discrimination. Throughout the 1990s, LGBT people also took to the streets in large numbers to protest several gay bashings and murders, including those of gay sailor Allen Schindler, Brandon Teena (a transgender man), gay soldier Barry Winchell, Amanda Milan (a transsexual woman), and, most prominently, University of Wyoming student Matthew Shepard.

The turn of the millennium witnessed another LGBT March on Washington in April 2000, the inauguration of Republican President George W. Bush, and an intensified antigay backlash, while the terrorist attacks of September 11, 2001, led to an increasingly conservative and security-conscious atmosphere that discouraged militant activism of any sort. Yet LGBT people continued to fight for their rights and played a leading role in non-gay-specific activism, including the new antiwar movement. In June 2003, LGBT activists took the rare opportunity to hit the streets in celebration after the Supreme Court overturned state sodomy laws in its *Lawrence v. Texas* ruling.

As more than a dozen states have passed constitutional amendments banning same-sex marriage, gay and lesbian couples have demanded marriage licenses from city and town clerks across the country, often on Valentine's Day. Although not intended as protests per se, the large turnouts and media attention devoted to couples seeking legal same-sex marriage in Massachusetts and (briefly) in San Francisco have had a similar impact in raising queer visibility and awareness of the demand for LGBT equality.

Further Reading

Beardslee, D., and J. Kepner. 1971. "Thousands Protest War: Gay Lib Marches in S.F." *Advocate* (May 26–June 8): 1, 6.

Carter, David. 2004. *Stonewall: The Riots That Sparked the Gay Revolution.* New York: St. Martin's Press.

D'Emilio, John. 1983. *Sexual Politics, Sexual Communities: The Making of a Homosexual Minority in the U.S., 1940–1970.* Chicago: University of Chicago Press.

Eisenbach, David. 2006. *Gay Power: An American Revolution.* New York: Carroll & Graf.

Faderman, Lillian, and Stuart Timmons. 2006. *Gay L.A.* New York: Basic Books.

Jay, Karla. 1999. *Tales of the Lavender Menace: A Memoir of Liberation.* New York: Basic Books.

Liz Highleyman

Provincetown

On November 21, 1620, one hundred and two Puritans, arriving for the first time in North America, landed in Provincetown, Massachusetts. While the remote tip of land that would come to be known as Provincetown was annexed in 1630 by the Puritans' Plymouth settlement, it quickly became a lawless port of call for those who could not and would not heed the Puritan way. According to Donald Wood's *Cape Cod—A Guide,* the sand dunes that would come to be known as Provincetown sheltered "a wild, undisciplined and unprincipled crew of traders and fishermen from nearly all parts of Europe. Drinking, gambling and bacchanalian carousals, were continued sometimes for weeks with unrestrained license" (Woods 1973, 86). Continuing a legacy of harboring lifestyles defying societal norms, the twentieth century saw the birth of Provincetown as a flourishing art colony. During this time Charles Hawthorne, a great American master, established an art school in Provincetown. In 1915 the Provincetown Players was established, and it quickly became a mecca for theater. Eugene O'Neill joined the players in 1916.

Today, Provincetown (commonly known as P-Town) is world renowned as a quaint summer resort town with as many as 50,000 visitors on any given summer day (3,431 people report year-round residence according to the 2000 U.S. Census). LGBTQ and straight people come from all over the world to wander the bustling shops and restaurants of Commercial Street (a narrow road that runs 2.5 miles through the town's center, providing priority to strolling pedestrians and cyclists), to visit national seashore beaches of unrivaled beauty amid the Provincelands dunes, to tour art galleries and museums and attend live theater, to board the flourishing fleet of whale-watching vessels that reflect the resurgence of these well-protected species, and to climb to the top of the Pilgrim Monument, which marks the first landing place of the pilgrims and is visible from miles around as it rises 252 feet above the 100-foot-high hill it sits on. Throughout the summer season, Provincetown hosts a number of annual week-long celebrations including a Portuguese Festival complete with the "blessing of the fishing fleet," LGBTQ family week, a lesbian women's week, a gay men's circuit party week, bears' week, and pet appreciation week.

Further Reading

Krahulik, Karen. 2007. *Provincetown: From Pilgrim Landing to Gay Resort.* New York: New York University Press.

Manso, Peter. 2002. *Ptown—Art, Sex, and Money on the Outer Cape.* New York: Scribner.

Woods, Donald. 1973. *Cape Cod—A Guide.* Boston: Little, Brown.

Jeff Walker

Proyecto contra SIDA por Vida

Proyecto contra Sida por Vida was a crucial Latino/Latina HIV/AIDS organization that targeted underserved Latino/Latina pansexual populations in San Francisco. It was founded in 1986 by gay Latino activists and was housed in the largely Latino Mission District of San Francisco at 2973 16th Street. In response to the structural racism of white-dominated AIDS organizations and the heterosexism of mainstream Latino services, Proyecto fulfilled an important role in offering culturally appropriate Spanish/English bilingual prevention, counseling, and other AIDS services to Latinos/Latinas. For example, the organization understood the tendency for first-generation Latino males who sexually penetrate other males to not identify as gay and subsequently targeted the sexual activity rather than the gay identity in bilingual or Spanish prevention campaigns. Transgendered people, gay men, bisexuals, men who sleep with men, lesbians, women, and addicts were among the different Latino groups targeted by the organization, which made important strides in serving transnational immigrant Latinos/Latinas. With limited funding and great community needs, Proyecto found itself cycling through leaders who championed diverse and sometimes conflicting interests. Eventually, mainstream Latino and AIDS agencies began to offer more culturally appropriate services for Latinos/as, like those pioneered by Proyecto. In 2005, the organization evolved into a trans-Latina HIV/AIDS service agency, serving the transsexual Latina/Latino community of San Francisco.

Further Reading

GLAAD People of Color Media Program. Available at: http://www.glaad.org/poc/latina/latin_kit/contacts.php. Accessed July 15, 2008.

Gabriel S. Estrada

psychiatry and homosexuality

For about 150 years, psychiatrists have asked, "What causes homosexuality?" To date, no one knows the answer, nor what causes heterosexuality for that matter. However, by the late nineteenth and early twentieth centuries, scientific theories to explain what causes same-sex attractions began to fall into three broad categories: homosexuality is either (1) a normal variation of human sexuality, (2) a form of psychopathology (mental illness), or (3) an expression of psychological immaturity.

Theories of normal variation regard homosexuality as "natural." A typical normal-variant approach is to compare homosexuality to left-handedness. Most of the scientific theories of normal variation have come out of research done in the field of sexology (see below). Studies that support a normal-variant theory suggest homosexuality has a biological component; this has been popularly interpreted to mean that people are "born gay." The born-gay theory is most favored by the gay and lesbian civil rights movement. Since 1973, American psychiatry and other mental health professions regard homosexuality to be a normal variation of human sexuality.

Theories of pathology are based on three assumptions: (1) adult heterosexuality is the normal, nondiseased state; (2) deviations from conventional gender roles are symptoms of a disease; and (3) some external trauma causes the homosexuality. Depending on the theory, the external event can occur before or after birth and may include exposure to hormones during pregnancy, too much mothering, inadequate fathering, seduction, molestation, or a "decadent" lifestyle. Religious therapists who consider homosexuality a disorder and members of the "ex-gay" movement subscribe to pathologizing theories.

Theories of immaturity regard homosexuality as a normal step in the development of heterosexuality; ideally, it should be a passing phase that eventually is outgrown on the road to sexual adulthood. Theories of immaturity are common to many schools of psychoanalytic thought.

At one time, official pronouncements on the meanings and implications of same-sex behaviors were primarily the province of religion. However, in nineteenth-century Europe, as power shifted from religious to secular authority, homosexuality received increased scrutiny from other fields, such as law, medicine, psychiatry, sexology, and human rights activism. In 1869, Hungarian journalist Károli Mária Kertbeny first coined the terms *homosexual* and *homosexuality*. He argued for the normative view in a political treatise criticizing laws that criminalized male homosexuality.

Richard von Krafft-Ebing, a neurologist, considered homosexuality a "degenerative" disorder. He would adopt Kertbeny's terminology but not his theory of normal variation. Krafft-Ebing's 1886 *Psychopathia Sexualis* viewed unconventional sexual behaviors through the lens of an increasingly popular Darwinian approach: all nonprocreative sexual behaviors were considered psychiatric disorders. In a twist of the born-gay theory, although Krafft-Ebing believed one might be born with a homosexual predisposition, he nevertheless considered such an inclination an inborn disease. *Psychopathia Sexualis* was influential in disseminating to the medical and scientific communities both the term homosexual as well as its author's view that homosexuality was a psychiatric disorder.

Unlike Krafft-Ebing, the prominent British sexologist Havelock Ellis considered homosexuality a normal variation of sexual expression. This was also the position of the German **homophile movement,** led by an openly homosexual psychiatrist, Magnus Hirschfeld. In contrast to both Ellis's and Hirschfeld's theories of normal variation and Krafft-Ebing's theory of pathology, Sigmund Freud, put forward a third kind of theory.

Believing that everyone was born with bisexual tendencies, Freud argued that expressions of homosexuality could be a normal phase of heterosexual development. He argued against homosexuality being a degenerative condition because, among other reasons, it is "found in people whose efficiency is unimpaired, and who are indeed distinguished by specially high intellectual development and ethical culture" (Freud 1953, 139). He further argued that bonds of friendship would be impossible without the sublimated (nonsexual) expressions of normal homosexual instincts. Instead, Freud saw expressions of adult homosexual behavior as arrested psychosexual development. He wrote several papers attributing the homosexuality of specific individuals to their family dynamics. For example, in his 1910 *Leonardo da Vinci and a Memory of His Childhood,* he attributed the artist's homosexuality to prolonged mothering and an absent father. While Freud believed that homosexuality was not an illness, his stress on family dynamics causing something akin to "stunted growth" allows his case histories to be read as theories of pathology.

By the early twentieth century, psychiatrists mostly regarded homosexuality as pathological. After Freud's death in 1939, most psychoanalysts did as well. Neo-Freudian analysts based their views on the work of Sandor Rado, whose theories had a significant impact on psychiatric and psychoanalytic thought in the mid-twentieth century. Rado claimed there was no such thing as either innate bisexuality or normal homosexuality. Heterosexuality was the only biological norm and homosexuality a "phobic" avoidance of the other sex caused by inadequate parenting.

Pathologizing homosexuality was not limited to psychoanalysts or psychiatrists. Endocrinologists, following the discovery of sex hormones, treated male homosexual patients with male hormones to make them more "masculine." Although this increased homosexual desire, it did not make gay men heterosexual. Behavioral therapists, primarily psychologists, developed aversion therapy techniques to "cure" homosexuality: while watching pictures of naked men, male homosexual patients were given either electric shocks or drugs to make them vomit. This was intended to discourage same-sex attractions that behaviorists believed to be a learned behavior. Afterwards, in efforts to encourage heterosexuality, they would have the patients masturbate while watching pictures of nude women.

Efforts to cure homosexuality were mostly unsuccessful. As Freud pessimistically wrote in a 1920 case report, *The Psychogenesis of a Case of Homosexuality in a Woman*, "In general, to undertake to convert a fully developed homosexual into a heterosexual does not offer much more prospect of success than the reverse, except that for good practical reasons the latter is never attempted" (Freud 1920, 151). Even psychoanalysts who considered homosexuality an illness did not report encouraging results. In one of the few scientific studies done by analysts, Irving Bieber and colleagues treated 106 homosexual men. They claimed a 27 percent cure rate with psychoanalysis, although when challenged a decade later to produce some of their cured patients, they were not able to do so. Although early practitioners of aversion therapy also claimed cures, by the 1970s behavioral therapists admitted that few of their patients managed to stay converted for very long.

While psychiatrists, physicians, and psychologists were trying to cure homosexuality, sexology researchers of the mid-twentieth century were studying and trying to make sense of human sexual behavior in the general population. Their work focused on a wider spectrum of individuals that included nonpatient populations. Psychiatrists and other clinicians tended to draw conclusions from a self-selected group (patients seeking treatment for their homosexuality) and wrote up findings about whoever came into their office as case reports. Sexologists, in contrast, went out and recruited large numbers of subjects for their studies.

Most prominent among sexologists' studies were Alfred Kinsey's 1948 *Sexual Behavior in the Human Male* and his 1953 report on *Sexual Behavior in the Human Female*. The Kinsey reports surveyed thousands of people and found homosexuality to be more common in the general population than was generally believed. His now-famous 10 percent statistic (today believed to be closer to 1–4 percent) was sharply at odds with psychiatric views of that time that claimed homosexuality was extremely rare in the general population. In 1951, Ford and Beach published *Patterns of Sexual Behavior*, a study of many cultures and of animal behaviors that confirmed Kinsey's view that homosexuality was more common than psychiatry maintained and that it was found regularly in nature. In 1957, psychologist Evelyn Hooker published a study that showed, again contrary to psychiatric beliefs of the time, that nonpatient homosexual men showed no more signs of psychological disturbances than did nonpatient heterosexual controls.

American psychiatry, influenced at the time by a psychoanalytic theory called ego psychology, mostly ignored this growing body of sexology research. In 1952, the American Psychiatric Association (APA) published its first edition of the *Diagnostic and Statistical Manual* (*DSM-I*) that listed all the conditions psychiatrists considered to be a mental disorder. There, homosexuality was classified as a "socio-pathic personality disturbance" (APA 1952, 38–39). In a 1968 revision (*DSM-II*), homosexuality was classified as a "sexual deviation" (APA 1968, 44).

However, the growing body of scientific research arguing for a normal-variant view of homosexuality would be brought to the attention of the APA in 1970. In the aftermath of the 1969s **Stonewall Riots,** members of the Gay Activists Alliance, believing that psychiatric attitudes about homosexuality were a major contributor to social stigma, disrupted the 1970 meetings of the APA. The protests led APA to organize educational panels at their next two annual meetings. The 1971 panel, entitled "Gay Is Good," featured gay activists Frank Kameny and Barbara Gittings explaining to their psychiatrist audience the stigma caused by the homosexuality diagnosis. At the 1972 meeting they returned, this time joined by **John Fryer,** MD, as Dr. H Anonymous, a "homosexual psychiatrist" who disguised his true identity from the audience and who spoke of the discrimination gay psychiatrists faced in their own profession.

At the same time, APA embarked on an internal process of studying the scientific question of whether homosexuality should remain a psychiatric diagnosis. The Nomenclature Committee, APA's scientific group addressing this issue, reviewed the psychiatric and psychoanalytic literature on the subject. They also reviewed the literature of sexology, a subject not often taught in psychiatric training programs at that time nor familiar to most practicing psychiatrists. Following its scientific study of the issue, the committee concluded that homosexuality was not a mental disorder. Then, the decision was reviewed and approved by several other APA committees and deliberative bodies. Finally, in December 1973, APA's Board of Trustees voted to remove homosexuality from the *DSM*.

This marked the end of the classification of homosexuality per se as an illness. Within two years, other major mental health professional organizations, including the American Psychological Association, the National Association of Social Workers, and the Association for Advancement of Behavior Therapy, endorsed the APA decision.

However, psychiatrists from the psychoanalytic community, objecting to the APA decision, petitioned to have a referendum in which the entire membership voted on the issue. In 1973, the decision to remove homosexuality was upheld by a 58 percent majority of voting members. Shortly afterward, APA issued a groundbreaking position statement supporting civil rights protection for gay people:

> Whereas homosexuality in and of itself implies no impairment in judgment, stability, reliability, or vocational capabilities, therefore, be it resolved that the American Psychiatric Association deplores all public and private discrimination against homosexuals in such areas as employment, housing, public accommodations, and licensing, and declares that no burden of proof of such judgment, capacity, or reliability shall be placed on homosexuals greater than that imposed on any other persons. Further, the APA supports and urges the enactment of civil rights legislation at local, state, and federal levels that would insure homosexual citizens the same protections now guaranteed to others. Further, the APA supports and urges the repeal of all legislation

making criminal offenses of sexual acts performed by consenting adults in private. (APA, "Resolution" 1974: 497)

The 1973 decision, however, did not immediately end psychiatry's pathologizing of homosexuality. For in place of homosexuality's place, the *DSM-II* contained a new diagnosis: Sexual Orientation Disturbance (SOD). This diagnosis considered homosexuality an illness if an individual experiencing same-sex attractions found them distressing and wanted to change. The new diagnosis served the purpose of legitimizing the practice of sexual conversion therapies, even if homosexuality per se was no longer considered an illness. The new diagnosis of SOD also allowed for the unlikely possibility that a person unhappy about a heterosexual orientation could seek treatment to become gay. Reflecting the realities of clinical practice, in 1980, the next edition, *DSM-III,* instead included Ego-Dystonic Homosexuality (EDH). However, it was obvious to psychiatrists more than a decade later that the inclusion first of SOD, and later EDH, had been the result of political compromises and that neither was really a disorder. "Did people of color unhappy about their race have a psychiatric disorder?" critics asked. Did short people unhappy about their height? Ego-Dystonic Homosexuality was subsequently removed from the next revision, *DSM-III-R,* in 1987. In so doing, the APA fully accepted the normal-variant view of homosexuality in a way that had not been possible 14 years earlier.

APA's approach to diagnosis would eventually be emulated by others. In 1992, the World Health Organization (WHO) removed homosexuality from the tenth edition of the *International Classification of Diseases* (*ICD-10*), replacing it with a diagnosis similar to Ego-Dystonic Homosexuality. Countries with national diagnostic systems also followed suit. In 2000, the Chinese Classification of Diseases replaced homosexuality with an EDH diagnosis as well.

In the wake of the 1973 decision, the American Psychiatric Association gradually became more "gay friendly." By the mid-1970s, a group of gay, lesbian, and bisexual APA members were officially recognized as the Caucus of Homosexually Identified Psychiatrists. This group would later become the Caucus of Gay, Lesbian, and Bisexual (GLB) Psychiatrists, joining other minority caucuses such as Black Psychiatrists and Asian American Psychiatrists. The GLB Caucus would eventually go on to form its own organization allied to APA, the **Association of Gay and Lesbian Psychiatrists (AGLP).** In addition to the caucus, by the 1980s APA had an executive-branch Committee on GLB Issues to advise the Board of Trustees.

Over time, APA gradually expanded its positions on gay and lesbian civil rights. In 1990, APA issued a statement opposing "exclusion and dismissal from the armed services on the basis of sexual orientation" ("Homosexuality and the Armed Services Position Statement"). In 1992, APA called on "all international health organizations, psychiatric organizations, and individual psychiatrists in other countries to urge the repeal in their own countries of legislation that penalizes homosexual acts by consenting adults in private" ("Homosexuality"). In 1998, APA issued a statement opposing "any psychiatric treatment, such as 'reparative' or 'conversion' therapy, that is based on the assumption that homosexuality per se is a mental disorder or is based on the a priori assumption that the patient should change his or her homosexual orientation" (APA 1998). In 2000, APA strengthened the statement, recommending that "ethical practitioners refrain from attempts to change individuals' sexual orientation" (APA 2000).

Then in 2000, following Vermont's enactment of civil union laws, APA endorsed "the legal recognition of same sex unions and their associated legal rights, benefits and responsibilities" ("Same Sex Unions"). In 2002, APA called for "initiatives which allow same-sex couples to **adopt** and co-parent children" ("Adoption") and expressed support for "all the associated legal rights, benefits, and responsibilities which arrive from such initiatives." In 2003, APA signed onto an amicus brief for the gay plaintiffs in the U.S. Supreme Court case of *Lawrence and Garner v. Texas* ("Amicus Curiae"). This historic Supreme Court decision abolished discriminatory U.S. **sodomy laws.**

In 2005, after Massachusetts's 2004 legalization of marriage equality, APA issued a statement supporting "the legal recognition of same-sex civil marriage with all rights, benefits and responsibilities conferred by civil marriage," and opposing "restrictions to those same rights, benefits, and responsibilities" ("Support"; Sharfstein 2005).

In 2006, APA created the John Fryer Award for "a public figure who has made significant contributions to LGBT mental health" (Moran 2006). Its first recipients were Frank Kameny and Barbara Gittings, two of the gay activists who 35 years earlier had brought the issue of psychiatric stigmatization of homosexuality to APA's attention.

See also science and medicine of homosexuality (history).

Further Reading

"Adoption." American Psychiatric Association. Available at: http://www.psych.org/Departments/EDU/Library/APAOfficialDocumentsandRelated/PositionStatements/200214.aspx. Accessed July 15, 2008.

American Psychiatric Association. 1952. *Diagnostic and Statistical Manual of Mental Disorders*, 1st ed. Washington, DC: American Psychiatric Association.

American Psychiatric Association. 1968. *Diagnostic and Statistical Manual of Mental Disorders*, 2nd ed. Washington, DC: American Psychiatric Association.

American Psychiatric Association. [December 15, 1973]. "Resolution." Reprinted in *American Journal of Psychiatry* 131 (1974): 497.

American Psychiatric Association. 1998. Position Statement on Psychiatric Treatment and Sexual Orientation. *American Journal of Psychiatry* 156: 1131.

American Psychiatric Association. 2000. Commission on Psychotherapy by Psychiatrists (COPP): Position Statement on Therapies Focused on Attempts to Change Sexual Orientation (Reparative or conversion therapies). *American Journal of Psychiatry* 157: 1719–21. Available at: http://www.psych.org/Departments/EDU/Library/APAOfficialDocumentsandRelated/PositionStatements/200001.aspx. Accessed July 15, 2008.

American Psychiatric Association Committee on Gay, Lesbian, and Bisexual Issues. 1993. Position Statement on Homosexuality. *American Journal of Psychiatry* 150: 686.

"Amicus Curiae." American Psychiatric Association. Available at: http://ww2.psych.org/MainMenu/EducationCareerDevelopment/Library/AmicusCuriae_1.aspx. Accessed July 15, 2008.

Bayer, Ronald. 1981. *Homosexuality and American Psychiatry: The Politics of Diagnosis*. New York: Basic Books.

Bullough, V. 1979. *Homosexuality: A History*. New York: Meridian.

Drescher, J. 1998. *Psychoanalytic Therapy and the Gay Man*. Hillsdale, NJ: The Analytic Press.

Drescher, J., T. S. Stein, and W. Byne. 2005. "Homosexuality, Gay and Lesbian Identities, and Homosexual Behavior." In *Kaplan and Sadock's Comprehensive Textbook of Psychiatry, 8th Edition*, ed. B. Sadock and V. Sadock, 1936–65. Baltimore, MD: Williams and Wilkins.

Freud, S. 1953 [1905]. *Three Essays on the Theory of Sexuality*. Standard Edition of the Complete Psychological Works of Sigmund Freud, vol. 7, 123–246. London: Hogarth Press.

Freud, S. 1920. *The Psychogenesis of a Case of Homosexuality in a Woman*. The Standard Edition of the Complete Psychological Works of Sigmund Freud, vol. 18, 145–75 *(1920–1922): Beyond the Pleasure Principle, Group Psychology and Other Works*. London: Hogarth Press.

"Homosexuality." American Psychiatric Association. Available at: http://www.psych.org/Departments/EDU/Library/APAOfficialDocumentsandRelated/PositionStatements/199216.aspx. Accessed July 15, 2008.

"Homosexuality and the Armed Services Position Statement." American Psychiatric Association. Available at: http://www.psych.org/Departments/EDU/Library/APAOfficialDocumentsandRelated/PositionStatements/199013.aspx. Accessed July 15, 2008.

Lingiardi, V., and J. Drescher, eds. 2003. *The Mental Health Professions and Homosexuality: International Perspectives*. New York: Haworth Press.

Moran, Mark. 2006. "Activists Forced Psychiatrists to Look Behind Closed Door." *Psychiatry News* 41(21): 17. Available at: http://www.pn.psychiatryonline.org/cgi/content/full/41/21/17. Accessed July 15, 2008.

"Psychiatric Treatment and Homosexual Orientation." American Psychiatric Association. Available at: http://www.psych.org/Departments/EDU/Library/APAOfficialDocumentsandRelated/PositionStatements/199820.aspx. Accessed July 15, 2008.

"Same Sex Unions." American Psychiatric Association. Available at: http://www.psych.org/Departments/EDU/Library/APAOfficialDocumentsandRelated/PositionStatements/200003.aspx. Accessed July 15, 2008.

Sharfstein, Steven S. 2005. "Psychiatry and Legal Recognition of Same Sex Marriage." *Psychiatry News* 40 (18): 3. Available at: http://pn.psychiatryonline.org/cgi/content/full/40/18/3. Accessed July 15, 2008.

"Support." American Psychiatric Association. Available at: http://www.psych.org/Departments/EDU/Library/APAOfficialDocumentsandRelated/PositionStatements/200502.aspx. Accessed July 15, 2008.

Jack Drescher

Publishing Triangle

This organization of lesbians and gay men in publishing, founded in 1989, annually presents significant literary awards. The Bill Whitehead Award for Lifetime Achievement, named after the editor-in-chief at Dutton who died of AIDS, has been awarded to **Christopher Bram,** Samuel R. Delany, **Lillian Faderman, Edward Field, Judy Grahn, Doris Grumbach,** Andrew Holleran, Karla Jay, Jonathan Ned Katz, M. E. Kerr, **Audre Lorde,** Armistead Maupin, Michael Nava, Joan Nestle, **James Purdy, John Rechy, Adrienne Rich, Jane Rule,** and Edmund White.

The Judy Grahn Award, recognizing the best nonfiction book of the year affecting lesbian lives, has been awarded to **Alison Bechdel,** *Fun Home*; Tania Katan,

My One-Night Stand with Cancer; Alison Smith, *Name All the Animals*; Lillian Faderman, *Naked in the Promised Land*; **Terry Wolverton,** *Insurgent Muse: Life and Art at the Woman's Building*; Laura L. Doan, *Fashioning Sapphism*; **Amber Hollibaugh,** My *Dangerous Desires*; Hilary Lapsley, *Margaret Mead and Ruth Benedict: The Kinship of Women*; Judith Halberstam, *Female Masculinity*; Margot Peters, *May Sarton: A Biography*; and Bernadette Brooten, *Love between Women*.

The Randy Shilts Award for gay nonfiction has gone to Kenji Yoshino, *Covering*; Martin Moran, *The Tricky Part*; David K. Johnson, *The Lavender Scare: The Cold War Persecution of Gays and Lesbians in the Federal Government*; John D'Emilio, *Lost Prophet: The Life and Times of Bayard Rustin*; Neil Miller, *Sex Crime Panic*; Ricardo J. Brown, *The Evening Crowd at Kirmser's*; Robert Reid-Pharr, *Black Gay Man*; Mark Matousek, *Lost Father*; Eric Brandt, *Dangerous Liaisons: Blacks, Gays and the Struggle for Equality*; John Loughery, *The Other Side of Silence*; David Sedaris, *Naked*; and Anthony Heilbut, *Thomas Mann*.

The Audre Lorde Award for Lesbian Poetry has been awarded to Jennifer Rose, *Hometown for an Hour*; Jane Miller, *A Palace of Pearls*; Maureen Seaton, *Venus Examines Her Breast*; **Daphne Gottlieb,** *Final Girl*; Melanie Braverman, *Red*; Gerry Gomez Pearlberg, *Mr. Bluebird*; and **Marilyn Hacker,** *Squares and Courtyards*. The Thom Gunn Award for Gay Poetry has been awarded to **Justin Chin,** *Gutted*; Richard Siken, *Crush*; **Carl Phillips,** *The Rest of Love*; **Brian Teare,** *The Room Where I Was Born*; Greg Hewett, *Red Suburb*; **Mark Doty,** *Source*; and **Thom Gunn,** *Boss Cupid*.

The Edmund White Award for Debut Fiction has been won by Martin Hyatt, *A Scarecrow's Bible*; and Mack Friedman, *Setting the Lawn on Fire*. The Ferro-Grumley Awards recognize experimental fiction and have been won by Lisa Carey, *Every Visible Thing*; Patricia Grossman, *Brian in Three Seasons*; Stacey D'Erasmo, *A Seahorse Year*; Nina Revoyr, *Southland*; Carol Anshaw, *Lucky in the Corner*; Emma Donoghue, *Slammerkin*; Sarah Waters, *Affinity*; Judy Doenges, *What She Left Me*; Patricia Powell, *The Pagoda*; **Elana Dykewomon,** *Beyond the Pale*; Persimmon Blackbridge, *Sunnybrook*; **Sarah Schulman,** *Rat Bohemia*; Heather Lewis, *House Rules*; Jeanette Winterson, *Written on the Body*; **Dorothy Allison,** *Bastard Out of Carolina*; **Blanche McCrary Boyd,** *The Revolution of Little Girls*; Cherry Muhanji, *Her*; Ruthann Robson, *Eye of the Hurricane*; Christopher Bram, *Exiles in America*; Barry McCrea, *The First Verse*; Adam Berlin, *Belmondo Style*; Trebor Healey, *Through It Came Bright Colors*; Jamie O'Neill, *At Swim Two Boys*; David Ebershoff, *The Rose City*; Edmund White, *The Married Man*; **Paul Russell,** *The Coming Storm*; **Michael Cunningham,** *The Hours*; Colm Toibin, *The Story of the Night*; Andrew Holleran, *The Beauty of Men*; Felice Picano, *Like People in History*; Mark Merlin, *American Studies*; John Berendt, *Midnight in the Garden of Good and Evil* (nonfiction); **Randall Kenan,** *Let the Dead Bury Their Dead*; **Melvin Dixon,** *Vanishing Rooms*; Allen Barnett, *The Body and Its Dangers*; and Dennis Cooper, *Closer*.

The Robert Chesley Award for Lesbian and Gay Playwriting has gone to Eric Bentley, Chris Weikel, Kathleen Warnock, Megan Terry, Michael Kearns, Jorge Ignacio Cortiñas, Rebecca Ranson, Jane Shepard, H. M. Koutoukas, Reverend Alvin Carmines Jr., Christopher Shinn, Shelia Callaghan, Maria Irene Fornes, Jeff Weiss,

Madeleine Olnek, **Chay Yew, Paula Vogel, Robert Patrick,** Susan Miller, Victor Lodato, Lisa Kron, and **Doric Wilson.**

The organization lists, on its Web site, the 100 lesbian and gay novels it considers the best.

Further Reading

Lambda Literary Foundation. Available at: http://www.lambdaliterary.org/. Accessed July 15, 2008.

Publishing Triangle. Available at: http://www.publishingtriangle.org. Accessed July 15, 2008.

John C. Hawley

pulp fiction, gay

Gay pulp fiction refers to a loosely defined series of texts published in the United States from the post–World War II era through the early 1970s. Often frankly erotic, gay pulps are generally characterized by stock, formulaic characters and plots, oft-shoddy writing, cheap production values, and lurid, sexualized cover art. Nevertheless, gay pulp fiction remained one of the few sources of gay literature during the mid-part of the twentieth century and became an important part of gay male subculture during that same era. Advancements in printing technology in the late 1930s gave rise to slim paperback books that could be cheaply produced and quickly and widely distributed. Unlike traditionally published works, which were largely sold in chain and independent bookstores, these paperback novels were circulated by magazine distributors. Usually priced at less than a dollar and often less than 50 cents, the books were displayed and sold on newsstands, at bus stations, in cigar and cigarette shops, and even sometimes through direct mail. Because of their manner of display, the books were given colorful, graphic, and often sexualized covers, to pique the interest of passersby. These covers are often reproduced today as parts of calendars, T-shirts, and other collectibles. Thanks to their content and covers, the books were termed pulp, a reference to both the cheap paper used in the publishing process and the lurid exploits written on that paper.

Because of their inexpensiveness to publish and purchase, pulp works proved enormously successful. Sex became a popular topic of pulps, both fiction and non-fiction, and Alfred Kinsey's 1948 report on human sexuality (a popular pulp book itself) fueled an explosion of curiosity into many facets of American sexual identity. Numerous pulp publishers sprang up all over the country to take advantage of this, and it is no surprise that certain enterprising publishers focused on the underground but very real gay market. Lesbian pulp was especially popular, in no small part because it appealed not only to gay women but also (and even more so) to heterosexual men. Gay male pulp proved less popular for a couple of reasons. Primarily, the target audience—gay men—was much smaller and harder to reach than the audience for lesbian pulp. Also, gay men's fiction began to appear as traditionally published literary novels in the late 1940s, including such texts as

Gore Vidal's *The City and the Pillar* (1948). Gay male authors and readers thus had more traditional outlets for publishing and reading than their lesbian counterparts and so relied less on pulp. Nonetheless, gay pulp fiction became steadily more popular, largely because gay pulp novels became more frankly erotic and were more readily available and numerous than traditionally published texts. To provide some indication of the number of gay pulp titles published, in 2007 the Gay Men's Pulp Fiction collection, housed at Brown University, listed over 4,600 titles, with another 700 on a sought-after list, although the collection included pornographic as well as more traditional pulp titles.

Gay pulp fiction reached its zenith in the later 1950s and 1960s. Greenleaf and Guild Press were the most important pulp publishers of the time, but other companies like Corinth Publications, Brentwood Publishing, and Phenix Publications turned out numerous gay pulp novels as well. Many of these companies also reproduced classic gay novels, some of which had been published only a year or two previously. Titles like **James Baldwin**'s *Giovanni's Room*, **James Purdy**'s *Malcolm*, and *Teleny, or the Reverse of the Medal*, then attributed to Oscar Wilde, were just some of the classic books republished by the pulp industry. Most gay pulps, however, were written originally for the market. Generally speaking, they were relatively short novels (often around 60,000 words) and the standard of writing in them was often considered subpar at best. Titles included works such as *Sir Gay* by Lynton Wright Bent (1965), *Skid Row Sweetie* by Gene North (1968), *The Erection* by Chad Stuart (1972), *Mr. Ballerina* by Ron Marvin (1961), and *Go Down, Aaron* by Chris Davidson (1967).

Most pulp authors published pseudonymously, but several of the authors became well respected in the field, including Chris Davidson, Phil Andros, and Don Holliday, who was best known for a trio of books about *The Man from C.A.M.P.*, a gay spoof of the 1960s television series *The Man from U.N.C.L.E.* Not all gay pulps were written by gay men, and indeed not all were written by men: Blair Niles, a founding member of the Society of Women Geographers; Marijane Meaker, who wrote the famous pulp *Whisper His Sin* (1954) under the name Vin Packer; and Helen Morgan, a pseudonym likely hiding a female author, all authored gay pulps. Most pulp writing was contract work; writers probably made no more than $250 a book and never received royalties, which helped to keep the cover price of the books to a minimum.

Gay pulps have often been criticized for their redundant and recycled plots, which are characterized by abusive power structures and unhappy endings. As critic Michael Bronski has noted, a typical gay pulp plot may go something like this: a young, handsome, naïve youth, usually from a rural part of the country, arrives in New York City (or sometimes San Francisco). He may be eager and unbowed, or he may be anxious and unsure, but, generally speaking, he soon finds himself lost—literally and metaphorically. Fortunately, the young hero stumbles onto a more worldly, knowledgeable male who can initiate him into the wild ways of the city, which usually includes initiation into male-male sex. Our hero must now confront his sexuality, all the while not realizing that his newfound friend or friends are interested in him only for his virginal youth and looks. Or, perhaps, the protagonist's love is genuinely returned, but the intervention of a cruel and homophobic world proves too great an impediment for the young lovers to overcome. Before long, the young hero of the pulp is somehow rejected by the world that so eagerly seduced him, and the young man dies, often at his own hands, a seeming victim of his own desires.

As numerous critics have pointed out, while the above plot is fairly ubiquitous, not all gay pulps followed the same story line, and not all of them featured an unhappy ending. The stereotype that all gay literature of the first 60 years of the twentieth century featured distinctly moribund endings was just that—a stereotype. Many gay pulps deviated wildly from that story line, and happy endings have been present in gay literature since as early as 1933. In fact, the most famous, and one of the best-selling gay pulp novels of all time, *The Song of the Loon,* featured an uplifting and very positive ending for its gay male protagonist.

The Song of the Loon is a pastoral novel set in the American Northwest in the latter half of the nineteenth century. It tells the story of Ephraim MacIver, a frontiersman who, after experiencing a self-destructive, one-sided love affair with a man named Montgomery, goes on a journey to seek the semilegendary Bear-who-drums, the head of the Loon Society, a Native American organization of men who love and desire other men.

Gay Safari, a typical pulp fiction title. Courtesy of the Gay, Lesbian, Bisexual, Transgender Historical Society, San Francisco.

Ephraim's journey is one toward self-acceptance, and along the way he meets Cyrus Wheelwright, a hulking backwoodsman who becomes his lover. Still, Ephraim leaves Cyrus to continue his quest for Bear-who-drums, eventually becoming initiated into the Loon Society before partnering up with Cyrus.

The Song of the Loon was published in 1966 and was followed by two sequels: *Song of Aaron* (1967) and *Listen, the Loon Sings* (1968). The book was also made into a faithful, full-length film in 1970. Though no exact sales records for the series exist, it must have sold tens of thousands of copies, an enormous amount for original gay pulp fiction. Popular for the books' unabashed romanticism and eroticism, the *Loon* series propelled author Amory, a one-time high school English teacher, into a minor gay celebrity, making him the most famous of the novelists whose work was primarily published as gay pulp.

The **Stonewall Riots** of 1969 and the cultural examination of gay life and culture that followed impacted the appeal of gay pulp fiction. As more traditional outlets for gay creative expression grew—not only novels, but theater and eventually even film and television—the demand for gay pulp decreased. Eventually, as the 1970s wore on, the novels turned from gay pulp to wholly gay pornography. Though many critics have noted that gay pulp often included scenes that were "one-handed reading," pornographic novels differed from pulp in that their entire intention was sexual titillation. Pulp novels, for all of their poor writing and erotically charged moments, proved to be something more. For several decades, gay pulp fiction proved to be a reflection of midcentury gay male identity, books where gay men struggled with self-acceptance, self-love, and romance and where, sometimes, those ideals won out in the end. Works like *The Song of the Loon* showed gay men living in pre-Stonewall America the possibilities that perhaps existed, if only on paper, for a fulfilling life as an avowed and, sometimes, even a happy gay man.

Further Reading

Bergman, David. 1999. "The Cultural Work of Sixties Gay Pulp Fiction." In *The Queer Sixties*, ed. Patricia Juliana Smith, 26–41. New York: Routledge.

Bronski, Michael, ed. 2003. *Pulp Friction: Uncovering the Golden Age of Gay Male Pulp*. New York: St. Martin's Griffin.

Gunn, Dewey Wayne. 2005. *The Gay Male Sleuth in Print and Film*. Lanham, MD: Scarecrow Press.

Norman, Tom. 1994. *American Gay Erotic Paperbacks: A Bibliography*. Burbank, CA. Private printing.

Stryker, Susan. 2001. *Queer Pulp: Perverted Passions from the Golden Age of the Paperback*. San Francisco: Chronicle Books.

Michael G. Cornelius

pulp fiction, lesbian

The term *pulp fiction* refers to a type of sensationalistic literature intended for a mass audience, heavily dependent on genre conventions, produced and sold cheaply, and without pretensions to literary merit. Novels and magazines of this type are often called *pulps*. The term *pulp* actually refers to the type of paper on which such works were originally printed: paper produced from wood pulp, with a high acid content, which was cheap but disintegrated rapidly, unlike the expensive, fiber-based paper used for library editions. Although some contemporary writers describe their works as pulps, this article concentrates on novels written during the "golden age" of the 1950s and early 1960s, when the societal and the publishing contexts were vastly different than they are today.

The pulp fiction genre dates back to the middle of the nineteenth century, when new technology made it possible to produce and distribute books and magazines much more cheaply than ever before. In addition, literacy was becoming more common throughout society, creating a mass audience for magazines and books, whose tastes did not demand works of the highest literary merit. The first pulps were published in England and known as "penny dreadfuls," referring both to their price and sensationalistic content. Pulps became very popular in the United States as well and included works in a variety of genres, including westerns, adventure stories, science fiction, romances, and horror: many emphasized the lurid and sensational aspects of their material.

Paperback books were first produced in Germany and England in the 1930s; Pocket Books was the first paperback publisher in the United States. These early paperbacks were usually re-releases of hardcover books, often classics; the genre known as pulp fiction truly began with Fawcett, which began commissioning original material for paperback publication in 1950. Fawcett's paperback originals were more explicitly sexual than earlier paperbacks and explored many previously taboo topics, including drug addiction, juvenile delinquency, and homosexuality. The success of this new type of pulp novel led other publishers to produce similar works, and erotic fiction eventually became the mainstay of the pulp trade. Pulp novels were distributed through the same outlets as pulp magazines, such as drugstores and bus depots. Because these outlets existed in many towns too small to have a bookstore, and because many of the topics covered by pulps were excluded from mainstream books, for many readers pulps provided their first introduction to topics such as lesbianism and homosexuality. In addition, for some readers the somewhat-illicit and "underground" nature of pulp fiction was an appropriate analogue to the furtive and secretive nature of gay and lesbian life during this period, and pulp novels became cult items that were shared among friends long after they had gone out of print.

Pulps are often derided, particularly in academic and literary circles, for their self-evident commercial nature: many were written in haste, are rife with clichés, and rely on the sensational and lurid to attract an audience. To some extent these criticisms are fair: no one would claim that *Beebo Brinker* is the literary equal of *Herzog*. However, pulps deserve attention precisely because they exist outside the world of academic and literary culture; as such, they were able to discuss topics that were taboo in mainstream literature and society and could be written in a style accessible to the least-educated reader. In addition, then as now, works of real quality slipped through the cracks. Against all odds, some lesbian pulp novels are well written and present sensitively the concerns of people whose stories were not otherwise represented. Pulps displaying these qualities, such as the works of **Ann Bannon,** became immediately popular and remained a part of lesbian culture long after their publisher, Fawcett Gold Medal, went out of business. Many classic pulps have been reprinted in modern editions and are enjoyed today by readers not yet born when they were first published, providing evidence of their quality and continuing relevance.

The history of lesbian pulps is different from that of gay male pulps because of the large numbers of heterosexual men who bought lesbian novels. Many lesbian novels were obviously written for this heterosexual male market and were little more than variants on erotic novels that included a lesbian character for purposes of male titillation rather than to explore that character and her world. Even the covers of lesbian pulps (generally not under the control of the author) were usually similar to those of heterosexual erotic novels, featuring large-busted women in suggestive poses; the lesbian aspect of the novel was often indicated by the presence of an older, short-haired woman lurking in the background.

Appreciation of 1950s and 1960s pulps requires that the reader understand the commercial context in which such works were produced and often requires "reading between the lines" to discover the story suggested by the author, but which could not be told explicitly. In those years publishers sometimes dictated plot content in a manner analogous to the Hays Code that governed motion pictures produced in the United States, requiring that lesbian relationships end unhappily and lesbian characters be killed off or otherwise punished; sometimes an improbable marriage was even tacked onto the end of a lesbian story. In part, this **censorship** was necessary to keep a book from being seized as "obscene literature" and placing the publisher in danger of prosecution; in part it was a bow to the prejudices of the majority.

Despite these difficulties, lesbian pulps have been enjoyed by generations of women, and many cite them as a formative influence in coming to understand their own sexuality. The writers discussed below are a small selection of those (see the Further Reading section below for references to many more lesbian pulps) who managed to portray realistic aspects of contemporary lesbian life and to raise issues confronting gay and lesbian people living at that time. In addition, they all wrote works that have been reprinted in modern editions and can be enjoyed today.

LESBIAN PULP FICTION AUTHORS

Tereska Torres (c. 1920–?) drew on her experience serving in Charles de Gaulle's Free French Forces during World War II in her novel *Women's Barracks* (1950), originally written in French but first published in English by Fawcett. *Women's Barracks*, published with a salacious cover and marketed as a novel featuring explicit presentation of lesbian relationships, was phenomenally successful and was the first widely available lesbian novel in America. Torres declined to write a sequel, because her intent had been to write a serious book based on real life during wartime, not an exploitation novel, but *Women's Barracks* inaugurated a series of novels and films exploiting the prurient possibilities of women in barracks, women in prison, women in boarding school, and similar locations. The success of *Women's Barracks* convinced Fawcett to commission Vin Packer to write *Spring Fire*.

Vin Packer (Marijane Meaker; 1927–) was a prolific author who wrote in many genres, under several pseudonyms. She is most famous for *Spring Fire* (1952), whose success convinced Fawcett and other publishers that there was a continuing market for lesbian novels. *Spring Fire* concerns the relationship between two university students, one of whom is bisexual but is concerned with maintaining a façade of respectability, and one who is just discovering her lesbian sexuality. Meaker also published several lesbian novels under the name Ann Aldrich, including *Carol in a Thousand Cities*, *We Walk Alone: Through Lesbos' Lonely Groves*, and *We Two Won't Last*, and a fictionalization of the Parker-Hume murder case, *The Evil Friendship* (1958), under the name Vin Packer.

Ann Bannon (Ann Weldy; 1932–) is probably the best-known writer of lesbian pulps. She published six lesbian pulp novels with Fawcett in the years 1957–1962, before she ceased writing fiction to concentrate on her academic career. From Fawcett's point of view these novels were typical lesbian sensationalist fiction and were marketed as such, but within the lesbian community Bannon's novels were treasured for their sensitive and genuine portrayals of lesbian characters. Naiad

Press reissued five of the novels (excluding *The Marriage*) in 1983, and the same five were reissued by Cleis Press in 2001–2003, with autobiographical forewords written by Bannon.

Bannon's novels portray the relationships over a period of years among two women, Beebo and Laura, and several of their friends. Beebo is a butch lesbian whose early story is told in *Beebo Brinker* (published last but narrating the events that take place first in the story), a Bildungsroman or coming-of-age novel that begins with Beebo's move to Greenwich Village and portrays her growing acceptance of her sexuality and adjustment to life in New York. The other central character is Laura, who discovers in Bannon's first published novel, *Odd Girl Out*, that she is a lesbian. Bannon's second novel, *I Am a Woman*, followed Laura to Greenwich Village, where she and Beebo meet. In *Women in the Shadows*, Laura marries her best friend, Jack, who is gay; their marriage is chronicled in *The Marriage*. *Journey to a Woman* concerns relationships among Laura (still married to Jack), Beebo, and Beth, Laura's first lesbian lover from *Odd Girl Out*. In the Beebo Brinker chronicles, Bannon created a group portrait of some aspects of the gay and lesbian world of the 1950s and 1960s and confronted many issues still relevant today, such as the "lesbian until graduation" phenomenon, the personal costs of either remaining in the **closet** or revealing one's sexual identity, and discrimination within the gay and lesbian community based on age and appearance.

Patricia Highsmith (1921–1995) published her novel *The Price of Salt* (1953) under the pseudonym Claire Morgan. Highsmith, most famous for her novel *Strangers on a Train* (1950) and the series of novels involving the character Thomas Ripley, had been a professional writer for more than 10 years before approaching her publisher with *The Price of Salt*; however, it was initially rejected due to its lesbian content and happy ending. The story of *The Price of Salt* concerns the relationship between a young woman, Therese, and an older married woman, Carol. During a brutal child custody hearing, Carol's husband reveals that he hired a private investigator to collect evidence of Carol's lesbianism. Despite this setback, however, the novel ends with the possibility that Carol and Therese will continue their relationship and find happiness.

Valerie Taylor (Velma Nacella Young; 1913–1997) began writing novels after she divorced her husband in 1953; her first lesbian pulp was *Whisper Their Love* (1957), brought out by Crest Books, a division of Fawcett. It concerns an affair between a teenage girl, Joyce, and an older woman, which ends both abruptly and improbably with Joyce renouncing the relationship in the last three pages and marrying a man. Taylor published two more novels including lesbian themes with Fawcett, *The Girls in 3-B* (1959) and *Stranger on Lesbos* (1960). She also published *A World without Men* (1963), *Unlike Others* (1963), and *Journey to Fulfillment* (1964) with Midwood, a press specializing in soft-core erotica.

Two lesbian novels originally published in the 1930s by Gayle Wilhelm (1908–1991) were re-released as pulps in the 1950s, a tribute to the commercial success enjoyed by lesbian novels at the time. *We Too Are Drifting* concerns the relationships among the lesbian artist Jan, her bisexual female lover Madeline, and the younger women she loves, Victoria, who ultimately chooses to leave Jan to marry the man chosen by her family. *Torchlight to Valhalla*, titled *The Strange Path* in the reprint edition, is a rare lesbian novel with a happy ending: in it, the novelist Morgan ends a relationship with an unsuitable young man and finds love with a teenage girl, Toni.

Further Reading

Forrest, Katherine V., ed. 2005. *Lesbian Pulp Fiction: The Sexually Intrepid World of Lesbian Paperback Novels, 1950–1965*. San Francisco, CA: Cleis Press.

Keller, Yvonne. 1999. "Pulp Politics: Strategies of Vision in Pro-Lesbian Pulp Novels 1955–1965." In *The Queer Sixties*, ed. P. J. Smith, 1–25. New York: Routledge.

Lesbian Pulp Fiction Collection: Introduction. 2006. Duke University Libraries. Available at: http://library.duke.edu/specialcollections/bingham/guides/lesbianpulp/. Accessed July 15, 2008.

Server, Lee. 2002. *Encyclopedia of Pulp Fiction Writers: The Essential Guide to More than 200 Pulp Pioneers and Mass-Market Masters*. New York: Facts on File.

Stryker, Susan. 2001. *Queer Pulp*. San Francisco, CA: Chronicle Books.

Zimet, Jaye. 1999. *Strange Sisters: The Art of Lesbian Pulp Fiction, 1949–1969*. New York: Viking Studio.

Sarah Boslaugh

James Purdy (1923–)

James Purdy is an American novelist, short story writer, poet, and playwright. Author of more than a dozen novels, numerous short story and poetry collections, and plays, Purdy's work has been translated into more than 30 languages. In the United States, however, Purdy's work generally has been better received by other writers (e.g., **Gore Vidal, Tennessee Williams, Edward Albee**) than by critics and the public. This can be attributed in part to Purdy's treatment of homosexuality and in part to his work's idiosyncratic qualities, which make it hard to classify.

Although homosexuality plays a role in Purdy's early novels—such as *64: Dream Palace* (1956), *The Nephew* (1960), and *Cabot Wright Begins* (1964)—it is brought to the fore in *Eustace Chisholm and the Works* (1964), the novel that marks Purdy's arrival as a fully mature writer with a distinctive voice and vision. Set during the late 1930s, *Eustace Chisholm* features the tender yet tragic love between the young and beautiful Amos Ratcliffe and the military-hardened and seemingly heterosexual Daniel Haws. Unable to admit his love for Amos, Daniel reenlists in the army to escape his desire. This attempt at escape, however, leads to the death of both men: Daniel is brutally tortured by a sadistic officer, while Amos is shot by chance. Although the suffering and negative outcome of Amos's and Daniel's relationship have led some critics to misread Purdy's work as a critique of homosexuality, the novel introduces a recurring theme in Purdy's novels: the disastrous consequences that result when a man cannot accept the love of another man.

This love between men, moreover, is depicted as a vital necessity within a fictional oeuvre that features homeless, young male characters abandoned by fathers and set adrift in a world where others are primarily interested in exploiting their innocence. Heterosexual relationships, far from providing solace, are more often depicted by Purdy as the source of a character's demise, either literally, as in *Malcolm* (1959), or figuratively. Love between men, in contrast, when fully embraced, is depicted as spiritually affirming and capable of bringing back to life characters often left half-dead by the brutality and emptiness of American life. In *In a Shallow Grave* (1976), for instance, Garnet Montrose, a horribly disfigured Vietnam veteran, is restored to human form through the love of two men who are able to see beyond his ghastly appearance. Such love, however, is depicted as rare and fleeting, its regenerative powers unrecognized by the larger number of Purdy male characters who are unable to acknowledge their passionate love for other men. Consequently, Purdy's characters are often left hollow, alienated and without any sense of community. Even in *Garments the Living Wear* (1989), which addresses the devastation and desperation produced by AIDS, the characters are depicted as isolated and alone, nomads in a plague-ridden city. Often dark, gothic, grotesque, and surreal, Purdy's fiction stands apart from most of the gay literature of the 1970s and 1980s in a category of its own.

Further Reading

Adams, Stephen. 1976. *James Purdy*. New York: Barnes & Noble.

Chupack, Henry. 1975. *James Purdy*. Boston: Twayne.

Pease, Donald. 1982. "False Starts and Wounded Allegories in the Abandoned House of Fiction of James Purdy." *Twentieth Century Literature* 28: 335–49.

Susan Feldman

Q

Carol Queen

A feminist, writer, sexologist, educator, activist, adult actress, sex worker, and theorist, Carol Queen is most renowned for her work in helping to shape and develop the pro-sex (or **sex-positive**) feminist movement. After receiving a doctorate from the Institute for Advanced Study of Human Sexuality in San Francisco, Queen went on to found GAYouth, one of the first groups for underage gays and lesbians in the nation, as well as the Center for Sex and Culture, which has as its mission "to provide non-judgmental, sex-positive, sexuality education" (http://www.sexand culture.org/). Currently, Queen is co-owner of Good Vibrations, a woman-owned and -operated sex toy and book emporium that seeks to disseminate information about, and products for, sex-positive sexual experiences. In this role, she was featured as an instructor and star in two installments of female-to-male anal sex (i.e., "pegging") videos, called the *Bend over Boyfriend* series. In her role as activist, she has participated in the Lusty Lady Theater, worked to decrease exposure to HIV and disease in sex clubs, fought for better safe-sex outreach programs, and worked tirelessly for quality sex education. As a bisexual activist, she served as grand marshal of San Francisco Pride in 2001. Queen has also written sexually explicit fiction and memoir, essays, commentary, and film reviews and has anthologized several volumes of bisexual erotica. Her most widely known texts, *Real Live Nude Girl: Chronicles of Sex-Positive Culture*, *Pomosexuals: Challenging Assumptions about Gender and Sexuality*, and *Leather Daddy and the Femme*, have been critically acclaimed.

Further Reading

Benderson, Bruce. 1997. "Review of *Real Live Nude Girl.*" *Lambda Book Report* 6 (1): 9.

Carol.Queen Web Site. Available at: http://www.carolqueen.com/pages/queen.htm. Accessed July 19, 2008.

Fogleboch, Holly. 1998. "Review of *PoMoSexuals.*" *Lambda Book Report* 6 (11): 32.

Tsui, Kitty. 1997. "Queers Misbehaving: An Interview with Authors Lawrence Schimel and Carole Queen." *Lambda Book Report* 6 (1): 1.

Breanne Fahs

queer

The term *queer* has been contested and changed over time. It originated as a derogatory term and was later appropriated by **activist** groups. The term originated in the sixteenth century as a synonym for odd or strange. It was also used to refer to individuals of questionable character, but by the early twentieth century, it was used to refer to male homosexual practices. George Chauncey (1994) has demonstrated that masculine gay men employed the term queer as a sexual identity to differentiate themselves from their more effeminate counterparts, commonly called fairies. However, Chauncey clarifies that the distinction between the two terms later collapsed, and queer became the term used to refer to all males who engaged in homosexual practices. Robin Brontsema (2004) indicates that by World War II, the term *gay* replaced queer in common parlance within the LGBT community. The term queer then acquired a negative connotation, and for many years it was used as a pejorative term. That use of the term remained until the 1990s when queer was appropriated by activists to unify the community and gain visibility for political action. Steven Epstein (1994) explains that the appropriation of queer was motivated by the need to organize during the **HIV/AIDS** crisis, but it has been associated with the political organizations **Queer Nation, ACT UP,** and **Out-Rage!** (England). The term was used to refer to both gay males and lesbians and was used to unite fronts for political mobilization. Queer became an inclusive term to account for multiple forms of sexuality. For Epstein the linguistic reclamation of queer became a symbol for a political position that rejected conventional forms of looking at sexuality. However, he recognizes that as an identity marker it also evidences generational differences between those who embrace and those who reject the term. The contemporary use of queer is often seen in general publications as well as publications targeted at the LGBT community, referring to people who are gay, lesbian, **bisexual,** transgender, transsexual, and/or intersexual; however, it can include all forms of sexuality outside of monogamous heterosexual procreative intercourse, including **sadism** and **masochism.** The academic usage of the term queer is influenced by poststructuralism and the work of Judith Butler, Michel Foucault, Teresa de Laurentis, and Eve Kosofsky Sedgwick, among others. The poststructural conceptualization rejects the categorization of sexuality. Thus, an important characteristic of the academic use of queer is that sexuality is viewed as a discursive construct; in fact, multiple sexualities that extend beyond procreative intercourse are recognized. Some critics of the use of queer as an identity marker argue that the term is inseparable from its discriminatory and loaded history. In fact many find the term disrespectful and degrading and refuse to use it as a self-descriptor. The history of the word has provoked reactions from two main groups. First, the use of queer has been difficult for those who cannot conceive calling themselves queer; second, it has also been an impediment for allies of lesbian and gay issues. For these groups, the problem with using the term is that they cannot separate the word from a history of abuse. Its use to include all forms of "deviant" sexuality has also been a site of scrutiny, since some activists prefer terms that do not lump all constituencies together. Others object to the commercialization of queer in popular culture: many argue that queer as used in the media (e.g., *Queer as Folk* or *Queer Eye for the Straight Guy*) refers exclusively to gay males and specific patterns of consumption. In these shows the term is depoliticized and ripped from any social cause, thereby subverting the goals of using queer as an all-inclusive term.

Further Reading

Brontsema, Robin. 2004. "A Queer Revolution: Reconceptualizing the Debate over Linguistic Reclamation." *Colorado Research in Linguistics* 17 (1): 1–17. Available at: http://www.colorado.edu/ling/CRIL/Volume17_Issue1/paper_BRONTSEMA.pdf. Accessed July 19, 2008.

Chauncey, George. 1994. *Gay New York: Gender, Urban Culture, and the Making of the Gay Male World, 1890–1940*. New York: HarperCollins.

Epstein, Steven. 1994. "A Queer Encounter: Sociology and the Study of Sexuality." *Sociological Theory* 12 (2): 195–96.

Jagose, Annamarie. 1996. *Queer Theory: An Introduction*. New York: New York University Press.

Kirsch, Mark. 2000. *Queer Theory and Social Change*. London: Routledge.

Sycamore, Mattilda Bernstein, ed. 2008. *That's Revolting!: Queer Strategies for Resisting Assimilation*. New York: Soft Skull Press.

Yarma Velázquez Vargas

queercore movement

Arising out of the punk-rock music scene and heavily influenced by the spirit of radical political activism, queercore (also referred to as homocore) is a social and cultural movement that first appeared in the mid-1980s and has burgeoned rapidly in the new millennium. The major instruments of its dissemination are 'zines, film, and music, usually produced in a low-budget, do-it-yourself fashion, often all by the same individuals. Queercore's defining characteristics are an anti-assimilationist stance on LGBTQ issues, a rejection of what it sees as the bourgeois agenda of the mainstream gay and lesbian social and political movement, a grounding in anarchist or collectivist values, and a commitment to fighting sexism, racism, and classism.

The 1985 publication of the zine *J.D.s*, a joint venture between Canadians G. B. Jones (an artist and musician who later founded the queercore band Fifth Column) and queer auteur Bruce LaBruce, marked the inception of the queercore movement. Running for eight issues, *J.D.s* stated its commitment to troubling not only the **homophobia** of the punk community but also the accommodationist, consumerist ethos that pervaded the mainstream gay and lesbian movement. Sharing this sentiment were 'zines like Deke Nihilson and Tom Jennings's *Homocore*, Donna Dresch's *Chainsaw*, and *Holy Titclamps* by Larry-bob.

The artistic output of the queercore movement is plentiful and passionate, occurring in a variety of media including music, film, and writing. Several queercore festivals were held during the mid- to late 1990s; the Dirtybird 96 Queercore Festival, held in San Francisco, was one of the first. Additionally, Queereruption, a gathering where "alternative/radical/disenfranchised queers can exchange information, network, organise, inspire and be inspired" (Queeruption Web site), which features queercore performances, has taken place from 1998 to the present in cities worldwide, including New York, Berlin, Sydney, Barcelona, and Tel Aviv.

Further Reading

Ciminelli, David, and Ken Knox. 2005. *HomoCore: The Loud and Raucous Rise of Queer Rock.* New York: Alyson Books.

Queeruption Web site. Available at: http://www.queeruption.org/index.html. Accessed July 19, 2008.

Christianne Anastasia Gadd

queer film festivals

Lesbian and gay film festivals today are seemingly ubiquitous. The festivals stem from the mid-1970s, with **San Francisco** as their mythic place of origin at the height of sexual, women's, and **gay liberation,** nearly a decade after New York City's **Stonewall Riots** and several years before **HIV/AIDS.** During the 1980s film festivals went continental across the United States and Canada but first to larger cities. Now they pepper North America, both in major urban centers as well as in smaller towns. Through the 1990s these festivals quickly went global. The vast majority of European countries have at least one or two, with a few notable exceptions. They also exist in Japan, South Korea, the Philippines, Australia, New Zealand, South Africa, Brazil, and Mexico, among others. Precisely how they manifest themselves in these diverse locations, each with its own constellation of races, ethnicities, socioeconomic classes, and local sexual histories, is difficult to predict.

A number of factors contributed to the formation of lesbian and gay film festivals in the late 1970s. The 1970s sexual liberation movement spawned the gay liberation movement, which joined with lesbians and bisexual women from the women's movement on the common issue of homosexual rights and freedoms. The general post-Stonewall vigor and enthusiasm for standing publicly for gay rights led to more visible practices, which included interest in lesbian and gay representation in popular culture.

On the cultural front, the festivals certainly did not come out of nowhere. There existed and still exist today the formats of screening a film reel accompanied with a lecture and of thematic film series held at a cinematheque, public library, university, community center, or private home, among other places. Perhaps most famously, the New York–based gay **activist** Vito Russo toured in the 1970s and 1980s with a reel of film clips and lectured on the unwritten history of homosexuality in Hollywood films. His early tour and book *Celluloid Closet* (1981) were adapted into the well-known film version in 1995 by the filmmakers Rob Epstein and Jeffrey Friedman. Russo also played an important role in the founding of the media watch group **Gay and Lesbian Alliance against Defamation (GLAAD).** Others likewise toured and presented lesbian and gay films and continue to do so, particularly for special presentations in film festivals and at universities. Similarly, the film series has also been a steady practice in queer film culture. In place of the intense screening of hundreds of films over a week or so, the series takes place over a longer duration, from months to a year. Such series of gay and lesbian films were screened at various institutions in major cities or on university campuses across the continent, from the posh film museum to the functional community center.

In 1976 in San Francisco the first gay film festival was organized by small groups of local filmmakers and activists in order to show one another their work. Typically these filmmakers already knew, or knew of, each other from the local film and gay **bar** scenes. In San Francisco, they met at **Harvey Milk**'s famous camera shop where their films were processed. The shop served as an informal hub of activity for the burgeoning independent gay film scene. The festival screenings were opened up to the public, and many attended. The filmmakers were naturally delighted to discover that their work found an audience beyond the filmmakers themselves. The original organizers, however, quickly passed the festival on to keen film buffs, curators, and programmers, since the filmmakers themselves were more concerned about making films than administrating a festival. The festival, today under the umbrella media organization Frameline, stands as the largest and longest running in the world.

New York City had a gay film festival in the 1980s, followed by MIX Experimental Queer Film Festival and the New Festival of Lesbian and Gay Film. MIX and the New Festival have happily coexisted for over a decade, appealing to quite different tastes in film. MIX is an artists-run festival that seeks to push boundaries in the art of filmmaking and the representation of sexuality, showing, for example, lower-budget do-it-yourself short and independent feature films, while the New Festival appeals to a less specialized, arguably more mainstream sensibility, with, for example, high-production feature films. Similar festivals are now flourishing in Austin, Chicago, Houston, Kansas, Los Angeles, Miami, Milwaukee, and New Orleans, among many other U.S. cities, as well as in the Canadian cities of Toronto, Montreal, and Vancouver.

The lesbian and gay film festivals were not the first or only ones to deal explicitly with sexuality. **Pornographic** films have been with us since the beginning of cinema itself. There were several important erotic film festivals during the 1970s, inspired by the sexual liberation movement; of course, today there are many pornographic film festivals throughout the world. Similarly, women's film festivals already existed throughout North America, and to this day they provide an important associated context for films by lesbians and bisexual and trans women. What the lesbian and gay film festivals contributed to film culture was their heightened emphasis on homosexual desire, its representation in various forms and practices, and its cultural and sociopolitical contexts.

With respect to the selection process such practical questions inevitably arise as "What are the criteria for programming a film in a LGBTQ film festival?" and "What is a queer, gay, or lesbian film?" Some festivals try to involve their prospective audiences in the process through a sort of selection committee that pre-screens and reviews the submitted films. The committee members stem from the local LGBTQ communities; their collective vote and comments help the head programmer decide which films to program in the festival. This style of selection was introduced into festivals in the late 1980s and 1990s to demonstrate a stronger sense of commitment and responsibility to community representation. Other festivals place their confidence in the connoisseurship of their respective programmers to select films and group them into enticing, relevant programs. Generally, the films and videos selected have an explicit LGB or T theme, or appeal to some part of the LGBT communities, for example, **camp** films that might not have any explicit sexual themes. Any borderline cases, such as a film with a queer character in a minor role, are discussed in view of the particular film's overall relevance to the programming of the festival.

The festivals have become embroiled in controversy over the years. Infamously, during the culture wars of the 1980s and 1990s, the LGBTQ festivals, filmmakers, and their films were attacked by conservative politicians because of public funding the received from the National Endowment for the Arts (NEA). The film *Tongues Untied* (1989) by gay African American Marlon Riggs and PBS, which broadcasted it in 1991, became a target of the presidential candidate Pat Buchanan and the American Family Association. Conservatives used Riggs's film and others in their fight against the public funding of LGBTQ films, PBS, and the NEA. For several years such lobbying efforts severely diminished the public funding of art or films and festivals with any theme concerning sexuality.

Lesbian and gay film festivals have gone through a number of name changes over the years that reflect changes in their organization and content. In fact, to discuss these festivals is quite a linguistic challenge. Several distinct phases in their historical development require some attention and reveal the cultural politics of their times. Not only have their names changed, but also the meaning of the words comprising the names. In the 1970s the festivals began as gay film festivals, organized and run mainly by enthusiastic gay white men, independent filmmakers and film buffs alike, with very little lesbian content. As women became more present and vocal within the organization and the audience of the festivals, demands for greater lesbian representation increased. Consequently, the name shifted to "gay and lesbian film festival" and then to "lesbian and gay film festival" to forefront lesbian visibility and the need for more work by and concerning women. Alongside the film festivals were the even-rarer gay video festivals in San Francisco and New York City in the late 1970s. The politics of community access and cable television production opened some festivals to video submissions, which was followed by the ungainly name change to "lesbian and gay film and video festivals." This change brought into the festivals a curious mixture of professional and amateur work; for example, feature films were programmed alongside video art, documentary films alongside amateur short films or videos, and so on. Similarly, the politics of inclusion has continued up to the current "LGBTT film and video festival," which for the sake of brevity is sometimes called a "queer film festival." While these festivals work hard to accommodate each of the sexual identities represented in their titles, specialized festivals also exist for each category as well as for racial and ethnic identities. For instance, there are now lesbian film festivals, bisexual film festivals, trans film festivals, and South Asian queer film festivals, to name a few. Effectively, the name play across almost three decades hints at the sexual and gender politics in and around all these festivals.

The text that is often used as a marker of the breakthrough of lesbian and gay cinema is Ruby Rich's celebrated 1992 article "**New Queer Cinema,**" originally written for the *Village Voice*. Its original aim was to boost the then-upcoming Museum of Modern Art "New Directors Series" that had programmed many of the mentioned films in New York City; but the article's success exceeded its intention and quickly became a rallying cry for a new generation of queer filmmakers, arguably also constituting a new canon of films.

Questions arise now and then regarding the future of lesbian and gay film festivals, namely, whether they have served their purpose and whether new modes of media distribution will supercede the festivals or render them redundant? The purpose of the festivals has broadened over the years. Many of the larger festivals found their plateau of audience members in the mid-1990s. Thus, while the number of festivals has expanded, many have also discovered that a more efficient, modest program of titles would serve their purpose well. Instead of including television shows and highly successful commercial feature films, the tendency now is to aim for tighter programming that speaks to a diversity of issues in the LGBTQ communities, uncovers new voices or voices rarely heard, challenges audiences to rethink issues critically, and develops new audiences, for example, through a touring series of festival films. The purpose of the queer film festival is forever tied to its media and its communities and their pertinent issues; without either, the lesbian and gay film festival would cease to have any meaning or import.

The new digital media have radically opened up video production, postproduction (editing), and distribution (Internet) to the amateur video maker, artist, and activist alike. These new digital means of manipulating audiovisual work on just about any current personal computer have a profoundly democratizing effect. More people have access to the media that would enable them to make and distribute their digital videos than ever before. The enthusiastic film buffs and cinephiles who populate the festivals' administrative posts and audiences are committed to the promise of the new films and videos and their exhibition, as well as to the experience of viewing them in the social context of the festival. Lesbian and gay film festivals address the most current issues of importance to the LGBTQ communities in the real social space of face-to-face interaction. While the new media enable production and distribution, they may augment but cannot supplant the experience of community building that the culture of festivals affords.

Further Reading

Gamson, Joshua. 1996. "The Organizational Shaping of Collective Identity: The Case of Lesbian and Gay Film Festivals in New York." *Sociological Forum* 11: 231–61.

Straayer, Chris, and Thomas Waugh, ed. 2005. "Queer Film and Video Festival Forum, Take One: Curators Speak Out, Moving Image Review." *GLQ: A Journal of Lesbian and Gay Studies* 11 (4): 579–603.

Stryker, Susan. 1996. "A Cinema of One's Own: A Brief History of the San Francisco International Lesbian and Gay Film Festival." In *The Ultimate Guide to Lesbian and Gay Film and Video*, ed. Jenni Olson, 364–70. New York: Serpent's Tail. (The guide has been extended in an online version at PopcornQ, available at: http://www.popcornq.com.)

White, Patricia, ed. 1999. "Queer Publicity: A Dossier on Lesbian and Gay Film Festivals." *GLQ: A Journal of Lesbian and Gay Studies* 5 (1): 79–93.

Ger Zielinski

queer gaze

Queer gaze is a multidimensional phrase filled with different meanings and complex ideas about looking at the world, popular culture, people, and society in a different and queered way. While there are a variety of meanings, two are most commonly associated with the phrase: the first meaning revolves around the idea of "gaydar" and the ways in which gays or lesbians can supposedly tell if someone is a member of the LGBTQ community, normally based on nonverbal mannerisms and physical appearance; the other meaning is centered within a media studies context and refers to the ways in which the meanings embedded in various media artifacts can be altered or queered when that artifact is looked at or understood through the use of a queer gaze or lens. In this scenario, queer meanings are ascribed to the artifact that straight observers might miss.

Performing a queer reading can sometimes result in an interpretation purposefully at odds with the stated intention of the work's creator. Interpreting a media artifact through what is known as a queer gaze requires a significantly more nuanced conception of queerness than is used when simply saying that the presence of an out gay or lesbian character on a sitcom makes it queer. Looking at a cultural artifacts with a queer gaze requires one to go beyond a surface-level understanding, to dig deeper and explore queerness as a complex, and often paradoxical set of social cues and norms often only recognizable to countercultural insiders (in this instance, LGBTQ folks). In this case, queerness is the opposite of normality, and exploring an artifact with a queer gaze involves looking for subtle queer messaging, often through depictions of gender or sexual deviance, as well as the inclusion of comments or gestures that are coded as queer.

There are a number of reasons that would cause someone or a group of people to choose to look at an artifact through a queer lens. Looking with a queer gaze at an artifact that is part of mainstream culture and thus not seen as subversive by the majority of the population can be highly liberating to someone within the queer community, as it allows them to identify with an object of popular culture and see their lives, values, families, friends, and communities represented in a mediated context. This is an experience that many queer folks seldom have, and the act of creating one's own media representations through the appropriation of existing media artifacts has been and continues to be highly popular. Social bonding may occur when LGBTQ people seek in cultural objects evidence of deviance from normativity. In this way, queer folks have been and continue to be able to organize and socialize through the use of inside jokes and understandings based off of a queered understanding of a mainstream popular culture item.

Judy Garland and the queer cultural obsession/fascination with her is itself a perfect example of the queer gaze and its place and power over LGBTQ community. *The Wizard of Oz,* in particular, the song and scenes surrounding the idea of "Somewhere over the Rainbow," have become meshed with queer culture. The queer readings taking place in this particular situation revolve around the idea of the rainbow as a queer symbol of pride and community. Thus, when one looks at the film with a queer gaze, it takes on different dimensions than the wholesome, benign, family entertainment those outside of the community might read it as being. In this instance, the interpretation obtained through the use of a queer gaze has become completely embedded within LGBTQ cultural knowledge.

The other primary component to discussions of the queer gaze revolves around the conception of gaydar, whereby an attempt is made to see gay people, regardless of their sexual orientation or gender identity. The idea of gaydar or the queer gaze is something that scientists have attempted to study, but LGBTQ activists have dismissed it as homophobic stereotyping; nonetheless, it remains a part of American culture both in and out of the LGBTQ community.

Part of common vernacular, the idea of a queer gaze has spawned lines in sitcoms and talk shows and integrated itself into nearly every part of public life. It relies exclusively on what are perceived to be cultural signifiers of queerness, specifically effeminate characteristics of male-bodied individuals, or masculine mannerisms or appearance of someone female-bodied. In this way, instances of gaydar are rooted in stereotypes of how a gay or lesbian person looks or acts and neglect to take into account gays and lesbians who do not fit into these narrow definitions. Furthermore, it fails to account for the fact that gays and lesbians are every bit as diverse in terms of presentation, appearance, mannerisms, and other nonverbal social cues as heterosexuals within our society, and as such it is impossible to make judgments about the perceived sexuality of an individual based on these clues alone.

While queer gaze or gaydar can be and has been used in homophobic and noninclusive ways by members of the straight community, it has also become a major part of queer culture and queer life. The queer gaze is utilized in efforts to build community, to stand in solidarity with others who live lives outside the norms of gender and sexuality. In this way the queer gaze becomes a tool in order to find others like oneself, to recognize members of the queer "family" particularly when in public situations that are not exclusively LGBTQ. Through the use of the direct and unflinching gaze, other queer people become recognizable as queer through culturally coded behaviors. One also thinks, in this context, of the use of the **hanky code** within a queer BDSM/leather culture. The hanky code is a set of different-colored handkerchiefs, where each color corresponds to a sexual act or activity like **fisting** or play **piercing.** The hankies are worn in the back pocket, and which pocket the hanky is worn in can signify such characteristics as whether the person is a top or bottom in various sexual acts. Through insider queer knowledge of the hanky code, individuals can anticipate intimate details of another person's sexual interests, which will fly under the radar of cultural outsiders, specifically members of the straight community who likely will have no idea what the hanky signifies or that it has any significance at all.

Overall, it is clear that the multidimensional conceptions of the queer gaze play an intricate role within queer culture. Specifically, in terms of LGBTQ folks and the media, it shapes the ways in which queer people consume media artifacts and the meanings they attribute to them. Furthermore, the queer gaze can serve as a tool for bringing people together, whether or not the heuristics are tongue-in-cheek.

Further Reading

Gross, Larry. 2002. *Up from Invisibility.* New York: Columbia University Press.

Peele, Thomas. 2007. *Queer Popular Culture: Literature, Media, Film and Television.* New York: Palgrave Macmillian.

Sassafras Lowrey

queer hotlines

Queer hotlines, alternatively called helplines or switchboards, are telephone call-in services for members of the LGBTQ community. Queer youth or adults may voluntarily call published hotline numbers to talk about personal issues and social problems. Individuals who contact a hotline may self-identify but in most cases remain anonymous. Services are free and confidential. Callers generally discuss a wide range of concerns such as sexual orientation or gender identity, **coming out,** coping with prejudice or harassment, drug and **alcohol** use, sexual behaviors, safe-sex practices, HIV/AIDS anxiety, transitioning, and relationship concerns.

Most queer hotlines in the United States began in the 1970s and early 1980s. They started as grassroots efforts launched by local LGBTQ community activists responding to an upswing in violence against queer individuals and the emerging HIV/AIDS epidemic. These hotlines gained popularity as a source of emotional support and reliable information. Over the years, a variety of nonprofit organizations have developed and sponsored hotlines.

Queer hotlines usually are staffed by volunteers or paraprofessionals who have undergone training in active empathic listening skills and been educated about topics pertinent to the queer community. Staff are trained to offer nonjudgmental emotional support, to help a caller problem-solve a situation, and to provide referrals to local agencies, services, and support groups in a caller's community.

Currently the National GLBT Hotline and National Youth Talkline are sponsored by the GLBT National Help Center that has volunteers in New York City and San Francisco. In addition to this national organization, many LGBTQ community centers and local LGBTQ nonprofit agencies sponsor hotlines to offer peer counseling, support, and referral to local resources. With the rise of the Internet, some organizations have begun to sponsor Internet-based communications that are modeled on call-in hotlines and that provide the same sort of assistance and support via electronic communications.

Further Reading

Brigham, R. 2006. "Hotline Aims to Help Queer Youth." *Bay Area Reporter* 12 (9): 2.
VanDeCarr, P. 2004. "A Phone Call Away." *The Advocate* (December 21): 32–33.

John Sauvé

Queer Nation (1990–1992)

Queer Nation was a short-lived but influential direct-action organization founded in New York City by former **ACT UP** activists—including **Michelangelo Signorile** and Alan Klein—who were outraged at the escalation of antigay and -lesbian violence and prejudiced portrayals in entertainment and the media. Queer Nation began on March 20, 1990, when 60 LGBT individuals met at the Gay, Lesbian, Bisexual, and Transgender Community Center in New York's Greenwich Village with the intent of developing a new direct-action organization. Utilizing similar tactics to ACT UP, Queer Nation drew on the urgency of AIDS activists who favored short-term, highly visible, media-oriented actions.

Described by scholars Allan Bérubé and Jeffrey Escoffier (1991) as the first "retro-future/postmodern" activist faction to tackle lesbian, gay, bisexual, and transgender issues, Queer Nation helped significantly increase positive LGBT representation. To illustrate that queers would no longer accept being ghettoized, the group's first action took place at a straight venue, Flutie's Bar, on April 13, 1990. Similar visibility actions became known as "Queer Nights Out."

Although the name Queer Nation had been bandied about since the group's inception, it was not officially adopted until a general meeting on May 17, 1990. Their catchy slogan, "We're Here. We're Queer. Get Used to It," concisely encapsulated the group's political philosophy. Queer Nation emerged onto the national scene after activists at New York's 1990 gay pride parade distributed their manifesto, printed on both sides of a single newspaper-sized newsprint; it bore headlines blaring, "I Hate Straights!" and "Queers Read This!" Within days, Queer Nation chapters popped up in San Francisco, Washington, D.C., and other major cities. After a pipe bomb exploded at a Greenwich Village gay bar, injuring three on April 28, 1990, Queer Nation quickly mobilized 1,000 protesters who filled the streets, carrying banners that proclaimed, "Dykes and Fags Bash Back."

Queer Nation continued to "bash back" against homophobic attitudes and vio-lence with media-attention-grabbing tactics like phone zaps that overloaded offices of antigay politicians with phone calls, kiss-ins and other spirited demonstrations, and memorable chants like "Two, four, six, eight. How do you know your kids are straight?" With their in-your-face actions, Queer Nation irrevocably established that LGBT people had the right to occupy social and cultural space without apology.

Queer Nation chapters were founded in dozens of other cities, from Washington, D.C., to Boise, Idaho. In San Francisco, where Jonathan D. Katz was a cofounder, the group led a successful protest visiting religious fundamentalists who had vowed to "exorcise the demons" from San Francisco's raucous Halloween celebration. An offshoot of the group, the Street Patrol, provided safety patrols of the gay Castro District; it outlived the rest of Queer Nation's San Francisco chapter by a year. Meanwhile, Los Angeles's Queer Nation spearheaded a 1991 demonstration pro-testing California Governor Pete Wilson's veto of gay civil rights legislation. They attracted national headlines when they protested homophobia in Hollywood with an Oscar night action.

Queer Nation was also linked to controversial outings of closeted public figures. Popularized in *Outweek* magazine (of which Signorile was a founding contributor), outing was a way to illustrate that gay people *were* in positions of power and to force those outed individuals (and organizations that employed them) to take a position on issues concerning LGBT people.

Queer Nation is credited for reclaiming the word *queer*—which had previously been a derogatory characterization—although at the time the group's use of the word was considered shocking. Queer Nation not only popularized the term but led to the term queer becoming a critical social and academic concept—expanding gay and lesbian communities into a unified movement inclusive of bisexual and trans-gender people and helping launch the scholarly field of **queer studies.** Queer came to symbolize individuals whose gender identities and sexualities were at odds with social and cultural norms. However, the LGBT community did not universally ac-cept the term, and Queer Nation chapters were laden with discordant views about issues related to race, gender, and class.

With no formal structure or leadership, the anarchistic Queer Nation relied on boisterous, community-wide meetings to set the agendas and plan the actions of its ingeniously christened committees and subgroups (for example, LABIA, or Lesbi-ans and Bisexuals in Action; SHOP, or Suburban Homosexual Outreach Project). Queer Nation faded from existence after President Clinton's election ended the im-mediate threat of the hostile Reagan-Bush era. Major setbacks, including the loss of activist members to burnout and AIDS-related deaths, and the military's "don't ask, don't tell" policy—which suggested that visibility and fund-raising capacity did not translate into political power—eroded both the confidence and influence of activist groups like Queer Nation. Despite its shortcomings, Queer Nation's tac-tics significantly altered perceptions of lesbians and gay men and formed a foun-dation for the contemporary concept of an inclusive gay, lesbian, bisexual, and transgender community. A contemporary New Zealand television program, *Queer Nation*, focuses on LGBT issues and airs regularly.

Further Reading
Bérubé, Allan, and Jeffery Escoffier. 1991. "Queer/Nation." *Out/Look* (Winter): 13–14.
Johansson, Warren, and William A. Percy. 1994. *Outing: Shattering the Conspiracy of Silence.* New York: Harrington Park Press.
Seidman, Steven, ed. 1996. *Queer Theory/Sociology: 20th Century Social Theory.* Malden, MA: Blackwell Publishers.

Jacob Anderson-Minshall

queer skinheads

Generally speaking, within the queer skinhead (queerskin) subculture, there are those who identify as authentic skinheads who happen to be gay or queer and also those who, though they may not identify with any aspects of skinhead cultural or social ideology, fetishize skinheads and skinhead gear, sometimes adopting the skinhead look themselves as a fashion statement and erotic signifier. Although lesbian skinheads also exist, queerskin subculture is male centered.

Skinheads first emerged as a youth subculture in Britain in the late 1960s as a working-class alternative to effeminate middle-class mods. Inspired by the West Indian rude boys, a subculture of streetwise immigrants in working-class British neighborhoods, skinheads adopted a tough, hypermasculine look and West Indian music (ska and reggae). The word *skinhead* is derived from the shaved head adopted by those who identify as skins. The typical skinhead uniform consists of tight-fitting jeans or Sta-Prest trousers; Doc Martens or bovver boots; braces or suspenders; and Fred Perry or Dan Sherman shirts or tight T-shirts. Tattoos have always been popular among skinheads.

During the 1970s, many skinheads in Britain identified strongly with punk music's rebelliousness and working-class, outsider image. As a result, the punk and skinhead subcultures became intertwined. Around this same time, a noticeable number of skinheads joined forces with the racist and **homophobic** National Front in Britain. In the public's mind, skinheads became linked with racist violence. In the United States, some white-power and neo-Nazi youth groups adopted a racist skinhead ideology and look.

Some European and North American skinheads have organized against racist skins, claiming that being a skinhead is incompatible with racism: skinhead ideology is primarily about working-class unity and fighting against forces that oppress working-class people. Nonracist skinheads often point to the rude boys as skinhead precursors, maintaining that racism is tantamount to a denial of authentic skinhead history and culture.

Skinhead subculture migrated to the United States in the late 1970s and early 1980s. Oi!, a high-energy offshoot of punk that aggressively challenged middle-class sensibilities and the commercialization of mainstream punk, gained a following among skinheads. Nicky Crane—a British skinhead whose photo appeared on the album cover of *Strength through Oi!* (a compilation oi! album first released by Decco Records in 1981) and a founding member of the neo-Nazi organization Blood and Honour—came out as gay on British television and denounced his racist and homophobic past as incompatible with his identity as a gay skinhead.

Skinhead subculture offers gay men a working-class, hypermasculine alternative to the iconic middle-class, effeminate aesthete. Queer skinheads were instrumental in the formation of **queercore,** a subculture characterized by hard-core punk music and critiques of heterosexism, representing an alternative to more mainstream gay movements.

Queer **pornography** and **sadomasochism** fetishize queer skinheads. Bruce La-Bruce, founder of the queercore 'zine *J.D.s,* has featured neo-Nazi skinheads in several of his films, including *No Skin Off My Ass* (1991) and *Skin Flick* (1999). Among other things, these films depict homophobic skinheads as objects of queer desire and eroticize fascist violence and aggression.

Further Reading

Bell, David, John Bennie, Julia Cream, and Gill Valentine. 1994. "All Hyped Up and No Place to Go." *Gender, Place and Culture: A Journal of Feminist Geography* 1 (1): 31–47.

Dawson, Ashley. 1999. "Do Doc Martens Have a Special Smell?: Homocore, Skinhead Eroticism, and Queer Agency." In *Reading Rock and Roll: Authenticity, Appropriation, Aesthetics,* ed. Kevin J. H. Dettmar and William Richey, 125–43. New York: Columbia University Press.

Healy, Murray. 1996. *Gay Skins: Class, Masculinity and Queer Appropriation.* London: Cassell.

Marshall, George. 1991. *Spirit of '69: A Skinhead Bible.* Dunoon, Scotland: S. T. Publishing.

Waldner, Lisa K., Lyndsay R. Capeder, and Heather M. Martin. 2006. "Ideology of Gay Racialist Skinheads and Stigma Management Techniques." *Journal of Political and Military Sociology* 34 (1): 165–84.

Krista L. May

queer studies

Queer studies at the university as an area of interest to the LGBTQ community began in the 1990s, particularly in several Californian and East Coast universities, as a revolution against the perception that "traditional" gay and lesbian studies were already part of the established academic landscape. Queer studies should be understood as an academic parallel to **ACT UP** on some level; there was a shock value intended to dispel complacency. Queer studies as an academic domain, initiated by works such as Judith Butler's *Gender Trouble* (1990), Eve Sedgwick's *Epistemology of the Closet* (1990), and the journal *GLQ: A Journal of Lesbian and Gay Studies* (beginning in the early 1990s), attempts to situate its myriad approaches against the backdrops of **essentialism** and self-identification that have been a part of gay and lesbian studies, particularly those politically focused studies aimed at helping gays and lesbians achieve minority status in the United States. Both Butler and Sedgwick take on the definition of terms and the implicit difficulties in traditional binaries: homosexual/heterosexual, health/illness, natural/unnatural.

The rapid development of queer studies, in fact, has led Helene Myers (1997) to speculate that many institutions that do not already have a gay and lesbian studies program as a discrete discipline may likely adopt queer studies as a more inclusive way of examining the challenging triangulation of sex, gender, and sexuality (performance). To aid the deployment and understanding of queer theory and studies, Annamarie Jagose (1996), Nikki Sullivan (2003), and Donald Hall (2003) have provided important works detailing the conflicting histories that underlie the shift from gay and lesbian studies to queer studies, along with, in the case of Hall's book, providing learners new to the field with important critical tools for analysis.

A discussion during a class exercise in a Queer Cultures and Society class at San Francisco State University in San Francisco, 2007. Helping fuel the rise of specialized degree programs are endowments from gay alumni and demands from students who are coming out of the closet at younger ages. AP Photo/Jeff Chiu.

In today's academy, queer studies, powered by various queer theories, attempts to do on a grand cultural scale what Derrida performed on language through the act of deconstruction. In that way, queer studies today is the newest expression of deconstructionism. Just as deconstruction needed semiotics to lend boundaries to its enterprise, so queer studies needs traditional gay and lesbian studies along with fixed notions of gender, race, and ethnicity found in other critical forms to serve as its boundaries. Queer studies domesticates the "high literary theory" of the 1970s and 1980s to the needs of cultural analysis.

FOUNDATIONS

Butler, in *Gender Trouble* (1990), confronts the notion that a word such as *women* refers to a particular identity and thus initiates an important point of departure that queer studies would use. Politics in the gay liberation movement have revolved around a fixed and knowable notion of identity. Butler argues that the notions of women and feminism have not been stable over time. Pushing further apart what sociologists have meant by separating "sex" and "gender," Butler argues that the feminine gender might be applied to a male body and that the masculine might be applied to the female body—a concept that Halberstam explored in *Female Masculinity* (1989). Further, Butler dismisses the notion that feminist politics must be connected to women. The performance or act of the feminine itself constitutes feminism. And the performative *should* be disruptive of norms. There is an implicit challenge left at the end of her book that a new politics separated from identity must develop. In this way, her text would open a venue for queer studies in the next 15 years. The last five years have seen a resurgence of interest in this foundational work.

Since the early work of Butler and Sedgwick, what is clear—and some would argue that clarity is not at all possible nor even desirable—is that queer studies has transformed and enriched the project of gay and lesbian studies by questioning some of the most deeply held conventions about sexual orientation and identity, particularly in terms of a fixed conception of heterosexuality and homosexuality. In theory and practice, queer studies may investigate both same-sex and opposite-sex desire, locating the gaps in identity and performance and at times questioning whether there is any real difference at all in various sexual identities. A scholar's engagement in queer studies, unlike gay and lesbian studies, is less likely to be an indicator of his or her own sexual orientation. In that sense, queer studies assumes a more democratic politics, but scholars have noted that these developments have their own implicit challenges. *Straight with a Twist: Queer Theory and the Subject of Heterosexuality* (2000), a collection of essays edited by Calvin Thomas, takes as its point of departure the notion of "critical queerness" of Butler's *Bodies That Matter* (1993) and argues effectively for the presence of queerness in the assigned category of heterosexuality as studied in film, artistic media, and literature.

An open series of questions remains: What does the word queer mean with respect to gays and lesbians? What does queer mean with respect to gays, lesbians, bisexuals, transgendered, and intersexed people? What does it mean with respect to various aspects of race and gender, including in a postcolonial context? Does queer mean only middle-class gay men? Where do men and women of color fit into the queer frame of reference? Has queer studies forgotten gay and lesbian issues as a political category relative to social justice? All of these questions are important to the expanding field of queer studies.

AREAS OF STUDY

Queer studies has had a growing impact in the fields of sociology and education. Steven Seidman's *Queer Theory/Sociology* (1996) introduced queer theory to a discipline that already held that all gender and sexual categories are social constructions, but he moved the argument forward by challenging the fixed analyses that were still a part of that examination of categories. Stephen Valocchi (2005) has noted sociologists' reluctance to take up Seidman's work, but some changes are occurring that bode well for advances in the future. The world of curriculum studies in education has been very receptive to queer theory. James T. Sears and William Pinar have contributed to a critique of schools and curriculum, with the latter also pursing lines of analysis that connect queerness and race. Dennis Sumara and Brent Davis (1999) argue that school texts by their nature affirm heteronormativity and that, by the inquiry methods of queer theory, these assumptions may be destabilized in the curriculum. These scholars and their studies rely heavily on the work of Foucault and Sedgwick to power their analyses.

To date, literary studies have seen the greatest amount of work employing queer theory within the academy, and perhaps not in the areas where it might be expected. There are myriad queer-theory studies on the literature of Europe and the Americas of both the nineteenth and twentieth centuries, particularly of such authors as Whitman, Dickinson, and Wilde. Perhaps surprisingly, medieval and Renaissance studies have seen some of the most engaging work. Beginning with the assumption that categories of sexuality were constructed socially in the nineteenth century, a queer analysis before that point can aid our understanding of premodern and modern sexualities. Working from the vantage of Segdwick's **"performativity,"** rather than identity categories, has helped scholars to understand the fluidity of sexual expression in light of modes of production and consumption, to use categories that Foucault uses to define European history. Carolyn Dinshaw's *Getting Medieval: Sexualities and Communities, Pre- and Postmodern* (1999) forms a bridge between medieval behaviors that are difficult to define, including some in Chaucer's *Canterbury Tales* and Margery Kempe's *The Book of Margery Kempe*, and postmodern sexualities, and she attempts to write a queer history through close textual analysis. Glenn Burger's *Chaucer's Queer Nation* (2003) shows the medieval poet situated between the medieval and modern worlds and raising questions about the nature of identity and performance. Jonathan Goldberg's *Queering the Renaissance* (1994), a collection of essays, also relies on the less-fixed nature of sexual identities to critique same-sex desire in the historical past. Carla Freccero's *Queer/Early/Modern* (2006), taking on the hegemonic determining of new historicism, argues that queerness—defined in multiple ways throughout her study—has a past and yet, at the same time, has *always already* existed. These represent only a few such studies undertaken on the more distant literary past, yet all affirm that the past is best suited for analyzing the origins of a queerness that is present today. Sexualities do have a history that is now being rewritten by queer studies, with a different set of political assumptions and goals.

The intersection of race and queer studies since 2000 has seen the emergence of a seemingly separate area of queer studies: black queer studies. From papers given by both black studies scholars and queer studies scholars, E. Patrick Johnson and Mae G. Henderson developed a collection entitled *Black Queer Studies: A Critical Anthology* (2005). Essays by scholars such as Dwight A. McBride (author of *Why I Hate Abercrombie & Fitch*, 2005), Rinaldo Walcott, Kara Keeling, Charles I. Nero, and Faedra Carpenter, to name a few, demonstrate historical parallels between the social forces that that brought black studies into existence in the 1960s and 1970s and queer studies in the 1990s. Until that time and to a certain extent even after it—although there have now been significant studies on queer identities in Hispanic and Asian studies—queer studies has suffered from the same problem often noted in the 1990s about masculinity studies: the absence of people of color both as speakers and subjects of analysis in favor of white middle- and upper-class males. Giving queer studies an infusion of nonwhite identities is at the heart of the collection, and its editors have invented the term *quaring* to call attention to this attempt to take a fresh look at the heretofore white expectations of queer studies scholars. Continuing this tradition of exploring areas of intersection between race and queerness is Kathryn Bond Stockton in *Beautiful Bottom, Beautiful Shame: Where "Black" Meets "Queer."* Investigating such phenomena as **"down low"** sexual activity; lynching; male rape; literary works by Toni Morrison, James **Baldwin,** Radclyffe Hall, and Jean Genet; and artistic works by Robert Mapplethorpe, Stockton examines the way in which debasement is enacted, at times even in a **camp** way, and internalized as part of identity. The intersection of black studies and queer studies has a most prophetic future, and it is likely to add a great deal to the academic study of areas of LGBTQ life that have not yet been examined, in large part because race was not originally a concern of queer studies scholars.

CHARTING TODAY AND TOMORROW

So what should happen to gay and lesbian studies today? Thomas Piontek in *Queering Gay and Lesbian Studies* (2006) demonstrates the challenges that lie ahead. His book asserts that the function of traditional gay and lesbian studies has been creating a minority identity and the implicit politics of that action. Labeling this agenda as "modern," he argues for a more "postmodern" approach that rests between—even uneasily—affirming identity and rejecting its institutionalizing limits. Queering gay and lesbian studies would allow this contentious negotiation to continue. In the book, Piontek examines the changing views of **Stonewall,** including its uneasy connection with the **homophile movement,** the struggle between **sex-positive** and sex-negative attitudes on multiple levels in the world of **HIV/AIDS,** the rejection of the sissy boy by the gay movement by allowing the development of Gender Identity Disorder (GID) in *DSM-III*, gender alternatives for men and women, and the omission of sexual practices that blur gender distinctions such as sadomasochism. By no means rejecting gay and lesbian studies, Piontek sees the potential for a more inclusive politics that acknowledges internal tensions.

Considerations of the future of queer studies in the academy center around a discussion dramatized by Lee Edelman and Donald Hall. Edelman's *No Future: Queer Theory and the Death Drive* (2004) could well be the most highly polemical work of queer studies to date. Drawing on the ideas of Lacan and the symbolic, Edelman contends the future is tied to a heteronormative notion of the child. The exaltation of that image then places queerness in the position of the death drive. Through his analysis of texts by Charles Dickens, George Eliot, and Alfred Hitchcock, Edelman argues that there can be "no future" for the queer unless the symbolic other is supplanted. In this way, literature and politics of all stripes have worked toward preserving the place of the child and the further alienation of the queer. In essence, there is no political future. Contrasting with this view is the position of Donald Hall, who in a 2006 article in the *Chronicle of Higher Education* assesses the state of queer studies and its future. Acknowledging that queer studies may be "in the doldrums" to some degree at present, Hall argues that it is essential to return to an implicit politics of resistance, deeply rooted in the work of Butler. Asserting that there is a future, Hall contends that classrooms must provide an opportunity for students to explore their own utopian visions of the future; otherwise, there is no chance of living toward them. Given that the field has some important foundational texts, he argues that students and scholars of queer studies can find new light and energy through a return to those texts. Edelman and Hall have differing views, but there is an intriguing overlap in that both see the present practices as less effective for a variety of reasons.

Queer studies in the academy, which began as a new way to examine the lives, literature, politics, and aesthetics of gays and lesbians, has opened to include bisexual, transgendered, and intersexed people. It has lent a powerful tool for the exploration of race and **class,** and, as illustrated in the work of Robert McRuer in *Crip*

Theory (2006), it can become a metaphor for exploring the contours of the body's heterosexual ableness. Queer theory in its "inclusive" qualities, however, as Sharon Marcus (2005) notes, faces the possibility of seeing every person and every phenomenon as "queer," thereby losing effectiveness as an evaluative source for difference. Whether a new form of deconstruction, an extension of Lacanian analysis, or a further reshaping of New Historicism, queer studies has already had a considerable impact in the academy. What some scholars now contend is that the academy itself must be queered.

Further Reading

Burger, Glenn. 2003. *Chaucer's Queer Nation*. Minneapolis: University of Minnesota Press.

Butler, Judith. 1990. *Gender Trouble*. New York: Routledge.

Butler, Judith. 1993. *Bodies That Matter*. New York: Routledge.

Dinshaw, Carolyn. 1999. *Getting Medieval: Sexualities and Communities, Pre- and Postmodern*. Durham, NC: Duke University Press.

Edelman, Lee. 2004. *No Future: Queer Theory and the Death Drive*. Durham, NC: Duke University Press.

Freccero, Carla. 2006. *Queer/Early/Modern*. Durham, NC: Duke University Press.

Goldberg, Jonathan, ed. 1994. *Queering the Renaissance*. Durham, NC: Duke University Press.

Halberstam, Judith. 1989. *Female Masculinity*. Durham, NC: Duke University Press.

Hall, Donald E. 2003. *Queer Theories*. London: Palgrave.

Hall, Donald E. 2006. "Imagining Queer Studies Out of the Doldrums." *Chronicle of Higher Education* 53(4, suppl.): 58.

Jagose, Annamarie. 1996. *Queer Theory: An Introduction*. New York: New York University Press.

Johnson, E. Patrick, and Mae G. Henderson, ed. 2005. *Black Queer Studies: A Critical Anthology*. Durham, NC: Duke University Press.

Marcus, Sharon. 2005. "Queer Theory for Everyone: A Review Essay." *Signs* 31 (1): 191–220.

McBride, Dwight A. 2005. *Why I Hate Abercrombie & Fitch*. Durham, NC: Duke University Press.

McRuer, Robert. 2006. *Crip Theory: Cultural Signs of Queerness and Disability*. New York: New York University Press.

Myers, Helene. 1997. "To Queer or Not to Queer: That's Not a Question." *College Literature* 24 (1): 171–82.

Pinar, William F. 2004. *What Is Curriculum Theory*. Mahwah, NJ: Lawrence Erlbaum.

Piontek, Thomas. 2006. *Queering Gay and Lesbian Studies*. Urbana: University of Illinois Press.

Sears, James T. 2005. *Gay, Lesbian and Transgender Issues in Education: Programs, Policies and Practice*. New York: Routledge.

Sedgwick, Eve Kosofsky. 1990. *Epistemology of the Closet*. Berkeley: University of California Press.

Seidman, Stephen. 1996. *Queer Theory/Sociology*. Cambridge, UK: Blackwell.

Stockton, Kathryn Bond. 2006. *Beautiful Bottom, Beautiful Shame: Where "Black" Meets "Queer."* Durham, NC: Duke University Press.

Sullivan, Nikki. 2003. *A Critical Introduction to Queer Theory*. New York: New York University Press.

Sumara, Dennis, and Brent Davis. 1999. "Interrupting a Queer Curriculum Theory." *Curriculum Inquiry* 29 (2): 191–208.

Thomas, Calvin, ed. 2000. *Straight with a Twist: Queer Theory and the Subject of Heterosexuality*. Urbana: University of Illinois Press.

Valocchi, Stephen. 2005. "Not Yet Queer Enough: The Lessons of Queer Theory for the Sociologist of Gender and Sexuality." *Gender and Society* 19 (6): 750–70.

Daniel F. Pigg

Queers United against Straight-Acting Homosexuals (QUASH)

QUASH is a queer rights group that protested the 1993 Gay Rights March on Washington by distributing a newsletter criticizing the march for advocating an assimilationist agenda. QUASH claimed that the march downplayed the unique qualities of LGBTQ culture and that march organizers were complicit with a social system of racism, sexism, **classism,** and **homophobia** in order to be accepted into mainstream society.

Targeting "straight-acting" members of the LGBTQ community was intended to reveal and question the commitment to normative gender roles in the queer community. QUASH, along with other radical and anti-assimilationist groups such as **ACT UP** and **Queer Nation,** tapped into a broader movement that sought to challenge all aspects of a political and cultural system believed to be fundamentally broken. Critics of these groups argue that their radical politics prevent them from being able to reform the American political system and that emphasis on the normalcy of the lives of LGBTQ people and their families allows for greater political power and broader social acceptance. Although QUASH did not become a major presence in LGBTQ activism, the group's ideas point to a tension in the queer community over the value of acceptance in a **heteronormative** culture.

Further Reading

Berlant, Lauren, and Elizabeth Freeman. 1992. "Queer Nationality." *Boundary 2*. 19 (1): 149–80.
Gamson, Joshua. 1995. "Must Identity Movements Self-Destruct? A Queer Dilemma." *Social Problems*. 42 (3): 390–407.
Labont, Richard, and Lawrence Schimel, eds. 2007. *First Person Queer: Who We Are (So Far)*. Vancouver, Canada: Arsenal Pulp Press.
Smith, Sharon. 1994. "Mistaken Identity—or Can Identity Politics Liberate the Oppressed?" *International Socialism Journal* 62: 3–50. Available at: http://www.isj.org.uk/?id=311. Accessed July 20, 2008.

Katie Hladky

queer theology and spirituality

It would be a mistake to assume that queer theology and spirituality are done solely from the standpoint of LGBTQ *experience*. In fact, queer theology and spirituality developed in a similar manner to liberation theologies of race, class, and gender that began with the notion of experience as the starting point of theological reflection but progressed into a more self-critical analysis of the available categories in theology and spirituality.

Three clear streams of analysis can be discerned in the development of queer theology and spirituality. There are, first, early examples of "gay and lesbian theology" that emerged as a distinctive voice in constructive theology, which emphasized experience. Early constructive theological voices, largely within the North American and North Atlantic context, accentuated the sense of alienation that gay and lesbian persons experienced at the hands of ecclesial institutional structures. The main target of these voices was the **Roman Catholic** Church and its absolutist views on sexual relations, but mainline **Protestant** denominations, Orthodox Judaism, and fundamentalist churches were also identified as contributing to oppressive practices of exclusion. In so doing, gay and lesbian theologies aligned themselves with political and liberation theologies that argued for theological insights arising in the context of unequal power relations that allowed one party to categorize the other, to define the terms of the discussion, and to decide who might be considered members of a church. The politics and theologies of liberation resisted **homophobia** and **heterosexism,** and **essentialist** forms of sex/gender relations that necessitated ecclesial and sociocultural practices of policing sexual behavior. These theological voices mounted a strong and clear criticism of those institutional and ecclesial practices that provided a rationale for hatred toward persons of policed sexualities. Homophobic practices legitimized by ecclesiastical authorities were shown to be mirrored in the cultural practices of naming homosexual behavior as perverted or pathological dysfunctions. Nevertheless, these initial movements to articulate a queer theology exhibited only a rudimentary comprehension of the essentialist moves undergirding the liberation theology call for inclusion.

Consequently, following closely on the heels of suspicion of all identity-based political movements that performed necessary self-correctives by looking askance at the marginalizing positions conferred on "other" groups by dominant ones, gay and lesbian theology attempted to provide more historical analyses of Christianity and homoerotic relations in the Christian tradition. This move was significant because the historical analyses threw light on the manner in which "experience" was constructed in a matrix shot through with unequal power relations.

John Boswell's *Christianity, Social Tolerance and Homosexuality: Gay People in Western Europe from the Beginning of the Christian Era to the Fourteenth Century* (1980) became a key resource for these newer historical analyses. Boswell argued that homosexual interest and practice were understood as an ordinary part of human erotic behavior in the cities of the Roman Empire. In his view, early Christianity was not necessarily opposed to homosexual behavior, as it was culturally acceptable and "normal." Boswell's thesis, however, was vehemently opposed in a brilliant exposé of his overwhelmingly masculine material in Bernadette Brooten's *Love between Women: Early Christian Responses to Female Homoeroticism* (1996).

Brooten advances not only the historical analyses of female-female romantic and erotic relationships in antiquity; she also complicates the essentialist framing of names such as "gay" and "lesbian," following Judith Butler's 1990 suggestion that all categories of gender and sexual identity are constructed in a power matrix saturated with heterosexist and homophobic thought. Brooten's work also was a major advance on the history of male ideas about lesbians and lesbian behavior. For example, she argues that Paul's condemnation of sexual relations between women reflects more accurately his understanding of gender relations in which men are to be "superordinate and active and women subordinate and passive" (192).

Sexual relations among women were presented in Paul as sullying this "natural order," specifically in Romans 1:18–32. The natural order is the priority of man over woman, which preserves gender polarity and asymmetry. Brooten's forceful argument asserts that Paul's condemnation of **homoeroticism,** particularly female homoeroticism, is in service of gender asymmetry based in female subordination. Brooten's highly acclaimed work underscores a key element that earlier gay and lesbian theologies had overlooked or understated. Sexuality is only one of the many axes of oppression that mark heteronormative claims by ecclesial, social, cultural, and political policing bodies. Analyses that ignored the intersecting nature of these axes of oppression only continued to mark the already-marginalized space accorded them by dominant power.

The third move in LGBTQ theology and spirituality is marked by the impact of the word queer as verb, suggested first by feminist film critic Teresa de Lauretis. Queering as a verb is therefore the logical outcome of the insight proposed by Brooten: if Paul's condemnation of homoeroticism has much more to do with conserving gender asymmetry, then what feminist theory needs to do is "queer the pitch" of patriarchal ecclesial heteronormative claims. Following that call, a number of innovative methodological strategies and interpretive methods attempted to queer feminist constructive theology.

An interesting analysis in this regard is Elizabeth Stuart's book *Religion Is a Queer Thing: A Guide to the Christian Faith for Lesbian, Gay, Bisexual and Transgendered People* (1997), which argued that the debate over homosexuality in the minds of present-day churches has much more to do with "how far heterosexuality can be stretched" (1). The church debates on homosexuality, in other words, have a norming function: it really is about how to construe heterosexuality. Stuart's argument draws from queer theorists such as Michel Foucault, Gayle Rubin, Eve Kosofsky Sedgwick, Judith Butler, and Jeffrey Weeks to assert a social constructionist view of sexuality. In this view, nothing is "natural," including heterosexuality. Given the social constructionist emphasis, she concludes that lesbian and gay people, as well as their opponents in the church, have too easily bought into modern constructions of sexual identity. Consequently, they have cut themselves off from a Christian tradition that is far more "queer" in that it refuses to accept the stability of gender and sexual desire. Thus, Christianity itself is a queer thing.

Baptism is the queerest sacrament here. Baptism demands a questioning of every culturally negotiated identity through which Christians identify themselves and takes these identities up in the processes of redemption. The "taking up" is defined as "parody," that is, "an extended repetition with critical difference" (Stuart 2003, 108). Christianity parodied gender from the beginning, she asserts, pointing to the fluid boundaries between female and male identities, constricted though they were by patriarchy, making fluidity between males to females less possible. Stuart also identifies a major lacuna in the earlier gay and lesbian theologies. Their failure to address the HIV/AIDS epidemic and to devise creative responses to the many suffering, dead, and dying without repeating preexisting theological paradigms and assumptions inaugurates the urgent and ethical moment for queer theology and spirituality.

Stuart chronicles the many contributions of queer theologians who address different dimensions of a queered analysis. There is, for example, Michael Vasey's *Strangers and Friends: A New Exploration of Homosexuality and the Bible* (1995), which presents a genealogical argument to assert that the contemporary Western gay (male) culture is essentially a resistance movement that opposes the construction of masculinity. With Foucault, Vasey attempts to desexualize homosexuality and models it on friendship. Queer theologian Kathy Rudy also adopts a genealogical reflection on gender and homosexuality, focusing on the context of North American industrial urbanization. The creation of urban spaces that allowed people with similar desires to congregate was an outcome of industrialization. Further, for Rudy, the task of thinking about what constitutes "moral sex" in such spaces is critical, for moral sex in her view must be "hospitable" in the sense that it procreates by opening up the boundaries of our homes, institutions, and private spaces to those considered "outsiders." Thus, the private space of "home" becomes the public space of "church," and gender is riven from its status as the only thing that is able to perform "unitive" and procreative acts.

Eugene F. Rogers queers baptismal identity that molds Christians in the shape of Christ. For him, the recovery of marriage (which has nothing to do with procreation) and monasticism are both ways to learn to be hospitable to the stranger. Rogers's theology of sexuality is trinitarian in its emphasis on the trinity as a marriage. No procreative principle is enshrined by such a view of trinitarian marriage because in this view of marriage (which he traces to Richard of St. Victor, Aquinas, and Barth), the purpose of sex is sanctification through mutually inhering relationships.

James Alison, a queer Roman Catholic theologian from Great Britain, argues that gay and lesbian theologies are too reactive. Instead of reacting against the strictures of socially constructed gay and lesbian identities, he suggests that the baptismal identity can relativize or even dissolve the modern constructions of gender identity. As a movement, radical orthodox theologians such as Graham Ward embrace queer theory and emphasize that the premodern Christian tradition itself is queer in the manner that it played out the constructions of the body of Jesus. Here, materiality, gender, and sexual identity are first underscored and then dissolved in the body of Jesus, radically calling into question the undue emphasis on the body by postmodern narratives.

The notion that the Christian tradition is essentially queer in its attitude to identity is mirrored in the work of theologians such as Virginia Ramey Mollenkott, who emphasize that boundaries between socially constructed identities are essentially porous. Mollenkott, who identifies as "somewhat transgendered," argues that queerness in God is evident in the manner that God's incarnation agency disrupts the clear distinction between divine and human, thus providing the model for interrupting social constructions of gender binaries. In this way, the incarnation provides the framework for all disruptive gender-bending activities. Another attempt at radical queering has been performed by Marcella Althaus-Reid's "indecent theology," which points out the failures of liberation theology in excluding sexual and gender codes. Liberation theology, in her analysis, is controlled by the requirement of culturally imposed gender behavior that raises the Virgin Mary as an ideal to discipline and control real women's bodies and behaviors. In other words, sexuality, as the most disciplining heterosexist norm supporting deeply unequal economic structures, bolstered by traditional "vanilla" theology, becomes the occasion for queering everything: God, Mary, Christ, and church. Althaus-Reid's procedure of "theological queering" (2003, 2) interrogates heterosexual experience and thinking that has shaped the field of theology. Queering in her work is intrinsically connected to liberation strategies against the current global capitalist system. She points to the spiritual practices of the many millions of poor in Latin America as evidence for God's "coming out of the closet of Christianity" by making alliances with the religions of "others." Syncretistic formulations of religious identity, in other words, are the result of "queering God."

LGBTQ theologies currently argue, therefore, in the words of Elizabeth Stuart (2003, 115), that the focus be less on sexuality and its socially mandated forms and much more on the God who created infinite variety and diversity in the world. Consequently, relationships and solidarities that emerge in response to multifaceted oppression are evidence of God's original transgression in the incarnation.

Further Reading

Alexander, M. Bennet, and J. Preston. 1996. *We Were Baptized Too: Claiming God's Grace for Lesbians and Gays*. Louisville, KY: Westminster John Knox Press.

Alison, James. 2001. *Faith beyond Resentment: Fragments Catholic and Gay*. London: Darton, Longman and Todd.

Althaus-Reid, M. 2001. *Indecent Theology: Theological Perversions in Sex, Gender and Politics*. London and New York: Routledge.

Althaus-Reid, M. 2003. *The Queer God*. London and New York: Routledge.

Boswell, John. 1980. *Christianity, Social Tolerance and Homosexuality: Gay People in Western Europe from the Beginning of the Christian Era to the Fourteenth Century*. Chicago: Chicago University Press.

Brock, R. N. 1992. *Journeys by Heart: A Christology of Erotic Power*. New York: Crossroad.

Brooten, B. J. 1996. *Love between Women: Early Christian Responses to Female Homoeroticism*. Chicago and London: University of Chicago Press.

Butler, Judith. 1990. *Gender Trouble: Feminism and the Subversion of Identity*. London and New York: Routledge.

Clark, J. M. 1989. *A Place to Start: Toward an Unapologetic Gay Liberation Theology*. Dallas, TX: Monument Press.

Clark, J. M. 1990. *A Defiant Celebration: Theological Ethics and Gay Sexuality*. Garland, TX: Tangelwüld Press.

Clark, J. M. 1993. *Beyond Our Ghettos: Gay Theology in Ecological Perspective*. Cleveland, OH: Pilgrim Press.

Clark, J. M. 1997. *Defying the Darkness: Gay Theology in the Shadows*. Cleveland, OH: Pilgrim Press.

Cleaver, R. 1995. *Know My Name: A Gay Liberation Theology*. Louisville, KY: Westminster John Knox Press.

Cloke, G. 1995. *This Female Man of God: Women and Spiritual Power in the Patristic Age AD 350–450*. London and New York: Routledge.

Comstock, G. D. 1999. *Gay Theology without Apology*. Cleveland, OH: Pilgrim Press.

Comstock, G. D., and S. Henking. 1999. *Que(e)rying Religion: A Critical Anthology*. New York: Continuum.

Congregation for the Doctrine of the Faith. 1986. *Letter to the Bishops of the Catholic Church on the Pastoral Care of Homosexual Persons*. London: Catholic Truth Society.

Foucault, Michel. 1978. *The History of Sexuality*. Vol. 1, *An Introduction*. New York: Random House.

Gilson, A. B. 1995. *Eros Breaking Free: Interpreting Sexual Theo-Ethics*. Cleveland, OH: Pilgrim Press.

Glaser, C. 1990. *Come Home! Reclaiming Spirituality and Community as Gay Men and Lesbians*. San Francisco: Harper and Row.

Glaser, C. 1998. *Coming Out as Sacrament*. Louisville, KY: Westminster/John Knox Press.

Goss, Robert. 1993. *Jesus Acted Up: A Gay and Lesbian Manifesto*. San Francisco: HarperSanFrancisco.

Goss, Robert. 2000. "The Beloved Disciple: A Queer Bereavement Narrative in a Time of AIDS." In *Take Back the Word: A Queer Reading of the Bible*, ed. R. E. Goss and M. West, 206–18. Cleveland, OH: Pilgrim Press.

Hanway, Donald G. 2006. *A Theology of Gay and Lesbian Inclusion: Love Letters to the Church*. Binghamton, NY: Haworth Pastoral Press.

Harrison, V. 1990. "Male and Female in Cappadocian Theology." *Journal of Theological Studies* 41(2): 441–71.

Helminiak, Daniel A. 2006. *Sex and the Sacred: Gay Identity and Spiritual Growth*. Binghamton, NY: Harrington Park Press.

Heyward, C. 1984. *Speaking of Christ: A Lesbian Feminist Voice*. New York: Pilgrim Press.

Hunt, M. E. 1991. *Fierce Tenderness: A Feminist Theology of Friendship*. New York: Crossroad.

Jordan, M. 2000. *The Silence of Sodom: Homosexuality in Modern Catholicism*. Chicago and London: University of Chicago Press.

Kitteredge, C., and Z. Sherwood, eds. 1995. *Equal Rites: Lesbian and Gay Worship, Ceremonies and Celebrations*. Louisville, KY: Westminster John Knox Press.

Lorde, Audre. 1994. "Uses of the Erotic: The Erotic as Power." In *Sexuality and the Sacred: Sources for Theological Reflection*, ed. J. B. Nelson and S. P. Longfellow, 75–79. London: Mowbray.

Macourt, M., ed. 1977. *Towards a Theology of Gay Liberation*. London: SCM Press.

Mollenkott, Virginia R. 1993. *Sensuous Spirituality: Out from Fundamentalism*. New York: Crossroad.

Morrison, M. 1995. *The Grace of Coming Home: Spirituality, Sexuality and the Struggle for Justice*. Cleveland, OH: Pilgrim Press.

Nelson, J. B. 1992. *The Intimate Connection: Male Sexuality, Masculine Spirituality*. London: SPCK Press.

Nicholson, R. 1996. *God in AIDS?* London: SCM Press.

O'Neill, C., and K. Ritter. 1992. *Coming Out Within: Stages of Spiritual Awakening for Lesbians and Gay Men*. San Francisco: HarperSanFrancisco.

Phipps, W. 1996. *The Sexuality of Jesus*. Cleveland, OH: Pilgrim Press.

Rambuss, R. 1998. *Closet Devotions*. Durham, NC, and London: Duke University Press.

Rogers Jr., Eugene F. 2002. *Theology and Sexuality: Classic and Contemporary Readings*. Boston: Wiley-Blackwell.

Rudy, K. 1997. *Sex and the Church: Gender, Homosexuality and the Transformation of Christian Ethics*. Boston: Beacon Press.

Sedgwick, Eve K. 1990. *Epistemology of the Closet*. Berkeley: University of California Press.

Stevenson, K. 1998. *The Mystery of Baptism in the Anglican Tradition*. Norwich: Canterbury Press.

Stuart, E. 1995. *Just Good Friends: Towards a Theology of Lesbian and Gay Relationships*. London: Mowbray.

Stuart, E. 1997. "Sex in Heaven: The Queering of Theological Discourse on Sexuality." In *Sex These Days: Essays on Theology, Sexuality and Society*, ed. in J. Davies and G. Loughlin, 193–204. Sheffield: Sheffield Academic Press.

Stuart, E. 2003. *Gay and Lesbian Theologies: Repetitions with Critical Difference*. Burlington, VT: Ashgate.

Stuart, E., with A. E. Braunston, J. McMahon, and T. Morrison. 1997. *Religion Is a Queer Thing: A Guide to the Christian Faith for Lesbian, Gay, Bisexual and Transgendered People*. London and Herndon: Cassell.

Swidler, A. 1993. *Homosexuality and World Religions*. Valley Forge, PA: Trinity Press International.

Vasey, Michael. 1995. *Strangers and Friends: A New Exploration of Homosexuality and the Bible*. London: Hoddern and Stoughton.

Vernon, M. 1999. "'I Am Not What I Am': Foucault, Christian Asceticism and a 'Way Out' of Sexuality." In *Religion and Culture by Michel Foucault*, ed. J. Carrette, 199–209. Manchester: Manchester University Press.

Ward, Graham. 2005. *Christ and Culture*. Boston: Wiley-Blackwell.

Wilson, N. 1995. *Our Tribe: Queer Folks, God, Jesus and the Bible*. San Francisco: HarperSanFrancisco.

Woodward, J. 1990. *Embracing the Chaos: Theological Responses to AIDS*. London: SPCK Press.

Susan Abraham

queer theory and social science

Queer theory is a strand of philosophical investigation that raises and responds to questions and issues of gender and sexuality, especially those with strong relevance to cultural politics. Accordingly, queer theorists often rely on deconstruction and other poststructuralist approaches, as prompted by the writings of Michel Foucault and Jacques Derrida, to challenge or "problematize" categorizations of sex, gender, and sexuality. Prominent American queer theorists include, among others, Judith Butler, Eve Kosofsky Sedgwick, Judith Halberstam, David Halperin, and Michael Warner, all situated in literary departments around the country. Positioned in such a strong literary tradition, **queer studies** as an interdisciplinary field has often been criticized as too humanities oriented and not social scientific enough. Upon careful reflection, however, the rupture between queer theory and social science seems to have not always been so conspicuous nor entirely consistent. Scholars working in the social sciences—history, sociology, psychology, and anthropology in particular—have helped shape the establishment of queer theory in many important ways. While contemporary queer theorists anchor their earlier discussions in the **essentialist and constructionist positions** and focus their more recent writings on issues of gender and sexual diversity, social scientists have engaged in these endeavors from the very outset.

The essentialist versus social constructivist debate was in part initiated by historians and sociologists, especially those who first voiced their findings that meanings and definitions of gender and sexuality vary across time and society in significant ways. For scholars who think of sexuality from the perspective of essentialism, sexuality represents a biological drive or a natural given. Essentialist historians, including **John Boswell** and Jonathan Ned Katz (particularly when he first published *Gay American History* in 1976), make the implicit assumption that any form of sexual desire is transhistorical and transcultural. According to this line of reasoning, modern typologies of sexuality, regardless of when they are invented, can be applied to people living in different time periods, regions, and cultures. For instance, proponents of essentialism argue that the concept of homosexuality can be associated with the sexual behavior, desire, and even identity of those individuals who lived their lives prior to the coinage of the term in 1869. In contrast, most historians and sociologists today position themselves within the constructivist camp and argue that sexuality is not a biological given but a cultural construct. While essentialists view categories such as gay and straight as universally objective, social constructivists understand them as subjective in the sense that the labeling process itself carries a myriad of specific cultural connotations and social interpretations that are neither universally coherent nor historically identical.

One of the major debates among social constructivists who study the history of homosexuality, for example, is the precise time period in which the concept of "homosexual identity" first emerged. The earliest piece of literature in the social sciences that introduced the social constructivist view of homosexuality appeared in 1968 and was written by a British sociologist and labeling theorist, Mary McIntosh. In her article, McIntosh maintains that the homosexual role first emerged from the burgeoning homosexual transvestite clubs in late seventeenth-century London. McIntosh's hypothesis was later supported by the findings of historian Randolph Trumbach. According to Michel Foucault, sociologist Jeffrey Weeks, and other followers of Foucault, however, the concept of homosexual identity was really solidified in late nineteenth-century medical discourse. Still others, including Marxist-oriented historian John D'Emilio and sociologist Barry Adam, suggest that conceptualization of an identity based on same-sex desire was actually first enabled in the late eighteenth century, when the societal transformation from household economy into industrial capitalism occasioned the expansion of the wage labor sector. Whether the concept of homosexual identity first developed around the turn of the eighteenth century from homosexual transvestite clubs in major cities like London, around the turn of the nineteenth century from the intense social transition of economic structure to industrial capitalism, or around the turn of the twentieth century from the discourse of sexology, all of these social scientists fundamentally agree that homosexuality as a concept of identity is a relatively recent invention in Western societies and not a transhistorical, essentialist category. In reaching this consensus regarding the less codified understanding of sexuality prior to the past three centuries, and providing critical insights regarding the unstable definitions of discrete identity categories across time and space, historians and sociologists have laid the groundwork for the early formulations of queer theorists.

In dealing with issues of gender and sexual diversity, psychologists and other social scientists also participated in building the foundation of queer theory in different ways. In 1956, for example, clinical psychologist Evelyn Hooker at the University of California, Los Angeles, published a report in the *Journal of Psychology* analyzing the social psychology of male homosexuals, portraying them as a victimized minority group. Subsequently, Hooker published a series of two studies, in 1957 and 1958 respectively, that together show how the psychological performances of normal homosexual and heterosexual men did not differ significantly. Situated in the sociopolitical context of her time, Hooker's effort in the 1950s to "normalize" homosexuals through social science represents an attempt to promote sexual diversity when both the **mental health** profession and society at large depicted homosexuals as mentally ill and morally wrong. Building on Alfred Kinsey's earlier studies that employed quantitative social scientific methods and documented the high frequency of homosexual behavior, Hooker eventually collaborated with gay activists to challenge the mental health experts' pathologizing view of homosexuality. After the American Psychiatric Association removed homosexuality from its list of mental disorders in 1973, health care providers began to emphasize helping gay and lesbian clients cope with social stigma instead of converting their sexual orientation. The recent publication of a volume edited by Linda Garnets and Douglas Kimmel, *Psychological Perspectives on Lesbian, Gay, and Bisexual Experiences* (1993; 2002), exemplifies this transformation in the mental health profession. If part of the goals of contemporary queer theorists is to encourage a social environment less hostile to sexual minorities, social scientists like Hooker and Kinsey had already begun doing so prior to the rise of the second-wave feminist movement and the modern **gay liberation movement.**

Historically speaking, an impressive number of research studies conducted in anthropology have also assisted the ways in which queer theory took shape. In the late 1920s and the 1930s, Ruth Benedict and Margaret Mead, students of Franz Boas, provided ethnographical support for the idea that sex roles varied across cultures in their classic texts: Mead's *Coming of Age in Samoa* (1928), *Growing Up in New Guinea* (1930), and *Sex and Temperament in Three Primitive Societies* (1935) and Benedict's *Patterns of Culture* (1934). Around the same time, a number of other cultural anthropologists had begun studying the role of the *berdache*, an individual whose socially sanctioned role was the opposite of his or her sex anatomy, in **Native American** societies. More recent definitive writings on the subject by contemporary anthropologists include Walter William's *Spirit and the Flesh* (1986), Will Roscoes's *The Zuni Man-Woman* (1991), and Sabine Lang's *Men as Women, Women as Men* (1998). Taken together, anthropological studies have a long history of showing the cultural malleability of sex roles and gender conventionalities, a project dear to twenty-first-century queer theorists; sharing a similar enterprise in this respect, both anthropological research and queer theorization aim at creating greater social inclusion of gender and sexual diversity.

Further Reading

Cohen, Cathy J. 1997. "Punks, Bulldaggers, and Welfare Queens: The Radical Potential of Queer Politics?" *GLQ: A Journal of Lesbian and Gay Studies* 3 (4): 437–66.

Garnets, Linda, and Douglas Kimmel. 2002. *Psychological Perspectives on Lesbian, Gay and Bisexual Experiences*, 2nd ed. New York: Columbia University Press.

Hooker, Evelyn. 1956. "A Preliminary Analysis of Group Behavior of Homosexuals." *Journal of Psychology* 42: 217–25.

McIntosh, Mary. 1968. "The Homosexual Role." *Social Problems* 17: 182–92.

Nardi, Peter M., and Beth E. Schneider, eds. 1998. *Social Perspectives in Lesbian and Gay Studies: A Reader.* New York: Routledge.

Seidman, Steven, ed. 1996. *Queer Theory/Sociology.* Cambridge, MA: Blackwell.

Howard Hsueh-Hao Chiang

queer zines

The intersection of punk and gay subcultures has produced decades worth of queer zines, self-published amateur magazines for a queer punk audience. As the modern **gay liberation movement** began in the 1970s after the legendary **Stonewall Riots** in the summer of 1969, punk music permeated youth culture in both England and the United States, often spread through legendary zines like *Sniffin' Glue*. By the late 1980s, with the rise of hard-core music and culture within punk, the terms *homocore* and **queercore** were used to describe the body of gay-themed zines, films, and music that included zines like *Holy Titclamps*, the longest-running English-language queer zine, and bands like Pansy Division and Team Dresch.

The queercore culture was aligned not only with punk dissent against mainstream society, but also against the mainstream gay culture that had evolved. Queercore created a space within punk culture, using many of the same tools and strategies favored by punk and do-it-yourself communities for creating an alternative culture. Also, zines serve a different function than gay newspapers like the *Washington Blade* or magazines like the *Advocate*, because they act more as a social and cultural network for queer punks, a subculture within a subculture, rather than aiming to provide news reports or journalistic stories. An example would be *Androzine*, a long-running anarcho-gay zine published in French. Over 100 issues of queer zines are archived online at the Queer Zine Archive Project, including zines like *Brat Attack, Go Fuck Yourself, boycrazyboy*, and *How to Fuck a Tranny*. Larry-bob, publisher of *Holy Titclamps*, publishes *Queer Zine Explosion*, which has reviewed queer books, zines, and music for over 20 issues. In 1991, SPEW, the first queer punk fanzine convention, was held in Chicago, and its direct descendent is Homo-a-go-go, a music and arts festival held yearly in Olympia, Washington.

Further Reading

Duncombe, Stephen. 1997. *Notes from Underground: Zines and the Politics of Alternative Culture*. New York: Verso.

Gever, Martha. 1993. *Queer Looks*. New York: Routledge.

Peraino, Judith. 2005. *Listening to the Sirens: Musical Technologies of Queer Identity from Homer to Hedwig*. Berkeley: University of California Press.

Raha, Maria. 2004. *Cinderella's Big Score: Women of the Indie and Punk Underground*. San Francisco: Seal Press.

Spencer, Amy. 2005. *DIY: The Rise of Lo-Fi Culture*. New York: Marian Boyars.

Jackie Regales

R

American playwright and screenwriter David Rabe, whose plays feature gay or bisexual characters, garnered early fame and critical acclaim with his trilogy of Vietnam Plays, including *Sticks and Bones* (1971), *The Basic Training of Pavlo Hummel*
(1972), and *Streamers* (1976). Rabe himself considers a fourth play, *The Orphan*
(1973), to be part of his work on Vietnam. Loosely structured on Aeschylus's *Ores-
teia*, *The Orphan* compares the violence of the Charles Manson murders with that of
the Southeast Asian conflict. David Rabe's other notable plays include *In the Boom
Boom Room* (1973), *Goose and Tomtom* (1982), *Hurlyburly* (1984), *Those the River
Keeps* (1991), *A Question of Mercy* (1998), and *The Dog Problem* (2001). Rabe has
also achieved fame as a screenwriter for his screenplays for *I'm Dancing as Fast as
I Can* (1983), *Casualties of War* (1989), and the adaptation of John Grisham's *The
Firm* (1993). He wrote the screenplay for films based on his own plays *Streamers*
(1983), starring Matthew Modine and directed by Robert Altman, and *Hurlyburly*
(1998), starring Sean Penn, Kevin Spacey, Meg Ryan, and Anna Paquin.

Born in Dubuque, Iowa, David William Rabe had a Catholic school education;
his graduate studies at Villanova University were interrupted by his two-year service
in the army, the last 11 months of which were spent in a hospital unit in Vietnam.
After his army service, Rabe returned to Villanova to finish his master's degree in
1968 and later became an assistant professor there.

Several of Rabe's plays feature gay or bisexual characters or themes of sexuality,
including *In the Boom Boom Room*, in which Chrissie, a go-go dancer who suffered
childhood abuse engages in (unhealthy) relationships with both men and women.
Her gay neighbor, Guy, attempts to prevent her downward spiral. *Hurlyburly* focuses on the cocaine-addicted, sexually driven lives of 1980s Hollywood jet-setting
men. *Streamers* explores the potential damages of differences based upon race and

sexuality. Set in an army training camp where soldiers await their deployment to Vietnam, the play opens with the suicide of Martin, a young man afraid of his ability to function in battle. Once the specter of battle performance has been raised, the play introduces the many factors influencing how soldiers anticipate their own failure and that of their peers, often to terrible effect. The bulk of the play features four male leads. Among them are Richie, an openly gay, highly educated and privileged New Yorker, whose willingness to engage in homosexual acts in the soldiers' barracks triggers the play's violent climax, and Carlyle, who, though ostensibly heterosexual, seeks sexual attention from Richie.

Streamers ironically presages the 1992s "don't ask, don't tell" policy concerning homosexual military service members, for Richie's self-proclaimed homosexuality is not believed by the rest of his barracks-mates until after Carlyle kills another soldier in a scuffle over whether or not the boys can have sex in the barracks. Like the boys' service in Vietnam, then, homosexuality remains unconstituted in actions, suspended as some future threat. In this manner, Rabe posits irrational fears about homosexuality (and the service capacity of gay soldiers) as a metaphor for the psychological and physical trauma of an impending crisis and demonstrates that the anticipation of crisis created by war has brutally damaging effects akin to the social ills of discrimination and violence.

David Rabe's many theater awards include two Drama Desk awards, one for Most Promising Playwright for *The Basic Training of Pavlo Hummel* (1971) and the other for Outstanding New Play for *Streamers* (1976). *Sticks and Bones* won the Tony for Best Play in 1971, an award for which David Rabe has been nominated three other times: for *In the Boom Boom Room* (1974), for *Streamers* (1977), and for *Hurlyburly* (1985). Rabe married actress Jill Clayburgh in 1979 and is the father of actress Lily Rabe (born in 1982).

Further Reading

McDonough, Carla J. 1977. "David Rabe: Men under Fire." *Staging Masculinity: Male Identity in Contemporary American Drama*, 103–32. Jefferson, NC: McFarland.
Radavich, David. 1993. "Collapsing Male Myths: Rabe's Tragicomic *Hurlyburly.*" *American Drama*, 3 (1): 1–16.
Zinman, Toby Silverman. 1991. *David Rabe: A Casebook*. New York: Garland.

Jon Robert Adams

Radicalesbians

Among the first radical lesbian feminist groups, the Radicalesbians formed in 1970. The collective produced "The Woman-Identified Woman," an influential manifesto that made important connections between the fear and hatred of lesbians and more general versions of misogyny. Although the group did not last long, both the manifesto and their presentation of it had a significant impact on lesbian feminist politics.

The Radicalesbians formed in a political context of explosive radical political movements among women and gay rights advocates. They were **lesbian feminists** who felt dismissed in their specific concerns as women in the Gay Liberation Front (GLF). Like women in other radical groups, they experienced their concerns as secondary to those of men and, specifically for them, to those of the "larger" gay rights agenda.

Liberal feminist groups who sought access, assimilation, and power for women in public institutions tended to see lesbians as a problem to be handled gingerly. Lesbians were famously referred to as the "lavender menace" by the president of the National Organization for Women (NOW), Betty Friedan. In addition, heterosexual radical feminists were less than receptive to lesbians, as their analysis focused on the relationships between men and women as the primary source of oppression. Early feminist theorizing did not see any necessary connection between feminism and sexual orientation. In fact, those were seen as mutually exclusive concerns. There was hostility among heterosexual radical feminists about "role-playing" **butch–femme** lesbians, whom they saw as crude imitations of traditional male–female relationships. Some radical feminist thinkers also felt that sex itself was a male preoccupation and did not really concern women much. Additionally, many lesbians felt used by curious heterosexual women who wanted to experiment with lesbian sex without any affectional or political commitments. Lesbian feminists thus felt alienated from what might have seemed to be relatively obvious political allies and saw the need to develop an analysis specific to their politics and concerns.

Originally called the Lavender Menace, the group formed first among women from the GLF, including Rita Mae Brown, Lois Hart, Suzanne Levier, Ellen Bedoz, and Arlene Kirsner, and then recruited other radical lesbian feminists, including Ellen Broidy, Sidney Abbott, Barbara Love, Michelle Griffo, Martha Shelley, Cynthia Funk, Jennifer Woodul, and March Hoffman (later Artemis March). They started in early 1970 by attending feminist talks and conferences to actively raise the issue of lesbianism.

The Radicalesbian's spectacular debut took place on May 1, 1970, during the opening night of the NOW-sponsored second annual Congress to Unite Women. They had distributed copies of "The Woman-Identified Woman" on chairs, and as the event was about to open, they cut the lights. In the darkness 17 of them took the stage wearing lavender T-shirts bearing the words "LAVENDER MENACE." Other members of the group were dispersed in the audience as supportive plants, but as it turned out, most of the audience was sympathetic. In fact, Kate Millett, a chair of the New York NOW chapter, set to preside over the meeting, had been forewarned and encouraged the audience to listen to the demonstrators. The action reportedly turned into a two-hour-long conversation about lesbian experience in a heterosexist culture, workshops on lesbian issues were held during the Congress along with an all-women's dance, consciousness-raising groups were planned, and the Congress adopted a four-point pro-lesbian platform advanced by "The Lesbian Menace: Gay Liberation Front Women and Radical Lesbians."

After the Congress, the group changed its name first to Lavender Liberation, then to Radicalesbians, and continued to meet. They were committed to a nonhierarchical structure and consensus on all decisions. This proved difficult and fractious with conflict emerging over de facto leaders and disputes over their separatist stance. They refused to deal with any men or women who were connected to men and/or dominant culture. They came to denounce **Kate Millett,** their one-time ally, as too close to the mainstream. The group disbanded by late 1971 but within two years after that, NOW had incorporated lesbian rights into its agenda.

Certainly, one of the most important things to come out of the group was their manifesto, "The Woman-Identified Woman." This is among the first feminist documents to politicize lesbianism. It had several purposes. A primary goal was to create common ground with straight women for political solidarity. One of the ways they did this was to make explicit the political costs of lesbian-baiting among feminists:

> To have the label applied to people active in women's liberation is just the most recent instance of a long history; older women will recall that not so long ago, any woman who was successful, independent, not orienting her whole life about a man, would hear this word, for a woman to be independent means she can't be a woman—she must be a dyke.... [W]omen and person are contradictory terms. (Schneir 1994, 163)

A related and overlapping purpose was to mollify straight feminists' fears of lesbians and ease some of the tensions within the feminist movement. In fact, according to Jennifer Woodul, they used the term "woman-identified woman" as a way, first, to not use the word "lesbian" so much, which was seen as off-putting to many straight women, and, second, to politicize the identity in a way that made it less about sex and more about political unity with other women. It was a conscious and strategic move away from the common assumption at the time that lesbians were "male-identified." They did this by arguing that lesbians in fact are more "woman-identified" than straight women who create their lives around men. Their point was that lesbianism is an important political choice that involves committing unequivocally to women, something that women who are defined by relationships to men cannot do.

Although the tone was intended to be conciliatory on one hand, it was also clear in its point that heterosexuality is the primary institution that oppresses women:

> We are authentic, legitimate, real to the extent that we are the property of some man whose name we bear. To be a woman who belongs to no man is to be invisible, pathetic, inauthentic, unreal. (Schneir 1994, 166)

They were clear, as well, that lesbianism is the solution primarily because it shows the way out of male identification:

> [I]t must be understood that what is crucial is that women begin disengaging from male-defined response patterns. In the privacy of our own psyches, we must cut those cords to the core. For irrespective of where our love and sexual energies flow, if we are male-identified in our heads, we cannot realize our autonomy as human beings.... It

is very difficult to realize and accept that being "feminine" and being a whole person are irreconcilable. Only women can give each other a new sense of self. That identity we have to develop with reference to ourselves, and not in relation to men. (Schneir 1994, 165, 167)

Although these assertions ultimately led to a dead end of reductionist notions about lesbians and the politically problematic move away from building a mass movement and toward a more insular concern to grow a women-only community, the theoretical contribution of making the connection between gender and sexual oppression is significant. For example, they wrote:

"Dyke" is a different kind of put-down from "faggot," although both imply you are not playing your socially assigned sex role...are not therefore a "real woman" or a "real man." The grudging admiration felt for the tomboy, and the queasiness felt around a sissy boy point to the same thing: the contempt in which women—or those who play the female role—are held. (Schneir 1994, 163)

This framing of the issue as one of the derogation of "the female role" is one of the explicit ways they forged the theoretical link between heterosexuality as a co-ercive institution and misogyny. It is the intellectual and political link that con-nects the gay rights movement and the women's movement.

In viewing this connection as fundamental, the authors refused the patholo-gizing of lesbians. Lesbians are not pitiful creatures, but "the rage of all women condensed to the point of explosion" (Radicalesbians 1970, 1). Still, for the most part, they stay within the parameters of liberal humanist individualism, whereby the lesbian is not so much socially constructed but a thing that already exists and is simply struggling for "authenticity" in a hostile world. On the one hand, this is a politically powerful and intuitively seductive idea, crucial to the development of lesbian feminism. On the other hand, it does lead to an essentialist notion of "the lesbian," which is the political and intellectual limitation that doomed lesbian feminism. It leaves very little room to conceptualize the lesbian as a contradictory, multiply constituted subject, as has become the standard in more current political and theoretical work.

Further Reading

Echols, Alice. 1989. *Daring to Be Bad: Radical Feminism in America 1967–1975*. Minneapolis: University of Minnesota Press.

Jay, Karla. 1999. "Radicalesbians." In *The Encyclopedia of Lesbian and Gay Histories and Cultures*, vol. 1, ed. Bonnie Zimmerman, 635–36. New York: Routledge.

Phelan, Shane. 1989. *Identity Politics: Lesbian Feminism and the Limits of Community*. Philadel-phia: Temple University Press.

Radicalesbians. 1970. "The Woman Identified Woman." Available at: http://scriptorium.lib.duke.edu/wlm/womid/. Accessed July 20, 2008.

Rapp, Linda. "Radicalesbians." In *glbtq: An Encyclopedia of Gay, Lesbian, Bisexual, Transgender and Queer Culture*. Available at: www.glbtq.com/social-sciences/radicalesbians.html. Ac-cessed July 20, 2008.

Schneir, Miriam, ed. 1994. *Feminism in Our Time: The Essential Writings, World War II to the Present*. New York: Vintage.

Jennifer Reed

radical faeries

Radical faeries arose as a social formation in 1979, when urban gay men inspired by gay back-to-the-land counterculturists organized a gathering in rural Arizona to investigate gay spiritual nature. Participants who then claimed radical faerie identity returned to their primarily urban lives across the United States to begin organizing subsequent rural events at rented retreat centers, older gay communes, and lands they purchased. Two major stories circulated at the time to explain their emergent culture. One characterized texts published by early participants, who cited the work of cofounder Harry Hay to frame radical faerie identity, as the culmination of twentieth-century conversations about gay spirituality. Hay traced gay male nature to a shamanic role that he argued appeared in indigenous societies throughout the world and all time, a role that radical faeries awoke in modern gay men by removing them to a rural, natural, and quasi-indigenous life. Hay's proponents argued that radical faeries absorbed earlier back-to-the-land countercultures into a movement to realize gay nature.

Yet the myriad participants in rural gatherings and urban "faerie circles" that sustained community year-round formed a more eclectic culture not defined by conformity to the core organizers' identities. Rural gay communes founded in the early 1970s sustained their regional identities amid new faerie ideologies. The fostering of gendered and sexual play and emotional communication at gatherings drew varied LGBTQ people who mutually sought alternatives to normative gay culture, from self-help and human development practitioners to counterculturist practitioners of **drag,** radical sex, or collectivism. These participants—arguably a majority at rural and urban events—tended to claim faerie identity situationally, if at all; to welcome interested participants regardless of sexual or gender identity; and to know less about Hay's vision, since they encountered the radical faeries more as a subculture for specialized socializing than as a spiritual movement.

Across the differences, however, narrators of both sets of stories mutually invested in resolving dilemmas of sexual subjectivity by appealing to non-Native ways of imagining indigenousness. U.S. back-to-the-land movements historically adopted versions of American Indian identity or culture to resolve their subjective and material experiences of settling stolen land. But prior to adopting back-to-the-land counterculturism, U.S. LGBTQ people already linked to indigeneity through popular stories that framed their sexual difference as a primitive opposition to civilized sexuality. Faerie culture creatively linked all such stories. Radical faeries claimed that their intimacy with indigenousness (evidenced by quasi-anthropological tales of gay shamanism) proved their sexuality was ancient and natural. They then used such stories to mediate their non-Native relation to settlement: by describing gayness as part of American Indian culture, gay settlers could allow their own sexuality to tie them to the land. Joining the radical faeries let non-Natives identify, on *sexual* terms, as more like indigenous people than the settler subjects they otherwise would be.

Further Reading

Hay, Harry. 1996. *Radically Gay: Gay Liberation in the Words of Its Founder.* Ed. Will Roscoe. Boston: Beacon Press.

Morgensen, Scott. (forthcoming). "Arrival at Home: Radical Faerie Configurations of Sexuality and Place." *GLQ: A Journal of Lesbian and Gay Studies* 15 (14).

Povinelli, Elizabeth. 2006. *The Empire of Love: Toward a Theory of Intimacy, Genealogy, and Carnality.* Durham, NC: Duke University Press.

Scott Morgensen

rainbow flag

Any community, in order to be considered as such, needs a symbol to identify itself. This symbol constitutes a space for the community to look for its identity and its particular characteristics. The rainbow flag has been used as a symbol of gay and lesbian pride since the 1970s. It was used as an alternative to the inverted **pink triangle** that had become an international symbol of gay pride and the gay rights movement, although the rainbow flag was used more frequently and soon became more popular. It is a multicolored flag consisting of stripes in the colors of the rainbow. The different colors symbolize diversity in the gay community, and the flag is often used as a symbol of gay pride in gay rights marches. Although it originated in the United States, it is now used around the world.

The rainbow flag was first used to symbolize gay pride and diversity in the San Francisco Gay Freedom Day Parade on June 25, 1978. Designed by the San Francisco artist Gilbert Baker and flown by Justin Fox, the lead singer of Last Blue Film, the flag made reference to the symbols used by hippy and antiracist movements. The original rainbow flag had eight horizontal bands of equal width, each with a different meaning. From the top, they were hot pink for sex, red for life, orange for healing, yellow for the sun, green for serenity, turquoise for art, indigo for harmony, and violet for spirit. In 1979, the stripes for sex (hot pink) and art (turquoise) were eliminated, and blue was substituted for indigo, leaving the

Courtesy of Shutterstock.

now-familiar flag with bands of red, orange, yellow, green, blue, and violet. It is most commonly flown with the red stripe on top, as the colors appear in a natural rainbow.

One of the precedents of the flag seems to lie in the movie *The Wizard of Oz* (1939). In the movie, Dorothy follows a world full of color, led by the rainbow, to escape her black-and-white world, full of boredom, in Kansas. In any case, the rainbow comes to represent the search for a better world carried out by a persecuted minority group. Today the rainbow flag is a feature of gay pride celebrations around the world, and many lesbian and gay men fly it at their homes. Its colorful design has inspired a host of variations, including a seven-striped flag with a black band at the bottom to symbolize the fight against AIDS. Although today the meaning of its colors might have been forgotten, it is still very well received; its success may derive from its positive and optimistic connotations. It has been recognized by the International Congress of Flag Makers. The design is also featured on everything from pins to T-shirts.

There are several unrelated rainbow flags in use today, with the flag of the rainbow family being an obvious example. The rainbow peace flag is especially popular in Italy. There are also other, less well-known rainbow flags as well as other flags of a similar design but with a different purpose, such as the European flag "barcode" style.

Further Reading

Drucker, Peter, ed. 2000. *Different Rainbows*. London: Gay Men's Press.

Hogan, Steve, and Lee Hudson. 1998. *Completely Queer*. New York: Henry Holt.

Katz, Jonathan. 1976. *Gay American History: Lesbians and Gay Men in the U.S.A.* New York: Thomas Y. Crowell.

Sara Munoz

Margaret Randall (1936–)

Writer, photographer, oral historian, and women's rights activist, Margaret Randall was born in New York City. She moved with her family to Albuquerque, New Mexico, when she was 10 years old, then returned to New York as a young adult, before living in Spain and Latin America. After divorcing her first husband, Randall moved to Mexico City with her infant son in 1960. In Mexico, she cofounded and coedited the bilingual poetry magazine *El Corno Emplumado*. She married co-editor Sergio Mondrágon, and the couple had two daughters. They divorced in 1969, and Randall had a third daughter with editor Robert Cohen.

Randall's identification with the Mexican student movement caused the U.S. government to revoke her citizenship, forcing her to go underground. She moved to Cuba with Robert Cohen where they lived with Randall's four children from 1969 to 1980. In Cuba, Randall worked at the Cuban Book Institute and as a writer and freelance journalist. At this time she also began using photography and oral history to document the lives and struggles of Latin American and Vietnamese women. In 1980, Randall moved to Nicaragua with her two youngest daughters to continue her work as an oral historian.

Following her return to the United States, Randall received a deportation order from the Immigration and Naturalization Service. Based on her writings, the U.S. government accused her of being "ill disposed to the good order and happiness of the United States" (Human and Constitutional Rights Web site). She won her immigration case in 1989, and this allowed her to **come out** as a lesbian. Randall has also used her writing to work through her experiences as an incest survivor. In the decade following her return to the United States, Randall taught women's studies and American studies at a number of colleges and universities. She has written over 100 books of nonfiction and poetry.

Further Reading

Cvetkovich, Ann. 2002. "Sexual Trauma/Queer Memory: Incest, Lesbianism, and Therapeutic Culture." In *Incest and the Literary Imagination*, ed. Elizabeth Barnes, 329–57. Gainesville: University Press of Florida.

Human and Constitutional Rights Web Site. Available at: http://www.hrcr.org/ccr/randall.html. Accessed July 20, 2008.

Erica Reichert

rape, sexual assault, and domestic violence laws

In the landmark decision in *Lawrence v. Texas* (2003), the Supreme Court gave LGBTQ citizens a historic civil rights victory. Overturning *Bowers v. Hardwick* (1986), the Court declared that sodomy statutes, which had criminalized anal and oral sex, were unconstitutional. Such statutes had served as the basis for denying LGBTQ persons custody and visitation rights, employment and housing, marriage and civil unions, domestic partner benefits, and freedom of association, and for banning teaching about LGBTQ materials in some public schools. However, the Court did not base its decision on the Equal Protection Clause of the 14th Amendment, which would have defined the sodomy statutes as reducing LGBTQ persons into a "suspect class" that, as such, lacked equal protection of the law. Rather, the Court anchored its holding in the due process clause of the Fifth Amendment, which prohibits government from depriving persons from rights to life, liberty, and property without due process of law. Fifth Amendment rulings have defined the home and intimate personal conduct as having an inviolable, sacred character and protected the autonomous value of individuals by vesting them with the power to share or withhold information. If secrecy can be defined as the information that a group holds or "secrets" within itself to exclude those on the outside from accessing or refuting the secret, then privacy maintains the right of the individual to refuse to "confess" or not to live in terror of surveillance under the secret. However, while providing LGBTQ individuals with the control over personal information that enables both authentic intimate communication and meaningful public communication, the Court left gender and sex under the domain of secretiveness. The decision reinforced the considerable obstacles to coherent speech about sexual crimes, both within and outside the LGBTQ community, and perpetuated the incoherence and capriciousness that characterize legal statutes on rape, sexual assault, and domestic violence.

The emergence in the early 1970s of the antirape and domestic violence movement led, among other things, to the creation of national data banks that compile yearly statistics on reported incidents of child abuse (molestation) as well as rape and sexual assault. Since their inception, the number of reported incidents of child abuse and domestic abuse (now termed *intimate partner violence* [IPV]) has soared; the same trend has occurred in more recent reporting of elder abuse and IPV, although rape and sexual assault have been declining since 1993. Nonetheless, in 2006, there were approximately two million reports of child abuse, and one-third of all women reported having been the victims of rape, domestic abuse, sexual assault, or harassment over their lifetimes. While the anti–sexual abuse movement has brought this national epidemic to the attention of the public and has called for vigorous prosecution of criminal offenders, most believe that chronic underreporting remains a problem. Further, despite the cataclysmic costs of sex- and gender-related crime, the public perceives the problem as intractable. Little has been done toward timely intervention or prevention other than providing persons with lists of "warning signs" of potential abusers; the apathetic fatalism about abuse seems founded in adherence to an idealistic image of **heteronormativity** that prohibits apprehending how it generates sexual violence. Heteronormativity is a term coined by Michael Warner that is rooted in the "sex and gender system" and "compulsory heterosexuality" (concepts formulated by Gayle Rubin and Adrienne Rich, respectively); it has been defined by Cathy J. Cohen (1997) as the practices and institutions that privilege heterosexuality as normative within society and that implicate sexuality in structures of power intertwined with race, class, and gender oppression. Single mothers on welfare and sex workers might be heterosexual but are not heteronormative and, therefore, are not perceived as normal, moral, or meriting state support. However, Jillian Todd Weiss (2001) contends that heteronormativity functions less as a "norm" than a "normative principle" or absolute standard below which people are not permitted to deviate. Enshrined into law, heteronormativity transforms social custom into "gendered natural law." Hence, transgendered persons cannot fight for inclusion directly but must first establish their claim to gender identity as the grounds for their claims on social identity. The epidemic of sex- and gender-related violence emerges from the chances of failing to achieve "right" gender identity. This caste system enshrines heterosexual relations as natural and moral and, most important, grounds the rearing of well-adjusted, secure, and psychologically healthy children to its practice. The "secret" behind this caste system is that in maintaining rigid male and female roles, behaviors, and traits, it constructs "masculinity" as a mode of maintaining power through manipulative, coercive, and controlling behaviors that inflict massive harm on children, women, and LGBTQ persons.

Given the gender-identity caste system of heteronormativity that informs law, public policy, and social custom, not to mention the incoherence of definitions of moral sexual/gender conduct on the one hand and the categories of persons named (or nameable) as victims or perpetrators on the other hand, it comes as no surprise that, in 2007, the United States has no uniform national definition of what constitutes rape, or the relation of rape to the broader categories of sexual assault, sexual molestation, child abuse and incest, and domestic violence. Chaos, redundancy, and oversight pervade statutes pertaining to "statutory" rape and "date" or "acquaintance" rape, the domain of "sexual assault," and the persons and personal relations that can claim protection under "domestic violence" laws. Beneath the proliferating categories of sexual, familial, and domestic crime—spousal rape, date rape, statutory rape, molestation, neglect, stalking, battering, sodomy, serial rape, and trafficking—one suspects not only vast quantities of cruel private behavior but also the disruptions, loneliness, and paranoia generated by the need to guard secrets and maintain the kind of "proper" gender identity that confers legitimacy and, most important, the perception by others that one is the sort of person "qualified" to rear children. Most jurisdictions define rape as sexual intercourse involving penetration of the anus or vagina by a penis, another body part (e.g., fingers), or an object, without the valid consent of one of the parties (oral sex or masturbation are less often mentioned). Consent obtained through force, coercion, or blackmail or judgment impaired by alcohol or drugs, illness, or mental disability, lacks validity. Statutory rape, in turn, refers to sexual relations between an adult and a "minor," whether or not such sex is consensual or coerced. It appears curious that such statutes feel obliged to refer to consent or coercion, as they claim that persons beneath the age of consent (variously defined according to jurisdiction as between 12 and 16 years of age, but sometimes 18) cannot give meaningful consent, although, at the same time, some of these same jurisdictions have younger ages for "marriageability" and criminal liability. The penalties increase depending on the amount of trust and authority vested in the adult in question, and the commentaries now uniformly mention priests, teachers, and coaches. At present, nearly half of all states have narrow statutes that focus on "biological sex" as the defining element of the crime and that specify a male perpetrator and a female victim. Such statutes differ from the now-erased sodomy statutes, which defined oral or anal sex between adults as crimes but also prohibited those forced or coerced into these acts from claiming criminal assault. The point of such whimsical codes appears to be to define "immoral sex" as emanating from persons outside the domestic sphere: the sodomite or, better, pederast, lurking on the corner, and the older male predator hunting for young and vulnerable girls. While reliable research on pedophilia remains, at best, sketchy, it appears striking that few have made the plausible connection between pedophilia and incestuous desires, inasmuch as both are directed at children or young adolescents below the age of consent and, moreover, vulnerable to indoctrination into secret "bonds" with the elder seducer. To further illustrate the moral squalor that defines this legal landscape, ex-familial adults in positions of authority are, at this juncture, under scrutiny. However, their authority appears confined to the nature of their offices and their personal conduct, and not to exercising that authority by vigorously protecting their charges from assault, either by their peers or by members of their biological families. The "open secret" of the rape of boys by adolescent "rape packs" has only recently entered into discussions; these remain perilous "double binds" for the victims. Further, the rape of inmates—particularly younger or more vulnerable ones—has become an accepted part of the penal system. The tolerance or even the approval of the brutalization, rape, and traumatic humiliation of feminized "bottoms" by vicious older "tops" as punishment fitting their crimes speaks volumes. Society bemoans the sexual abuse of children but then permits often quite young men to experience sexual bondage and degradation, and these predators might well see prison as an ideal locale for sating their appetites for raping and, sometimes, killing young men.

Of course, men suffer the same rape trauma as do women, which researchers have recognized as the biphase symptoms of rape trauma syndrome. Survivors can first experience shock, denial, and emotional numbing, and they attempt to disconnect their identities from the "raped person." Feeling tainted, culpable, and disoriented, they have nightmares and flashbacks and sometimes endeavor to protect the perpetrator. Later, the victims endeavor to recreate their prerape identities, and if they do not find the courage to speak out, they can suffer enduring rage, loneliness, distrust, and paranoia. Socialized to consider same-sex sexual acts as demasculinizing, most men perceive the consequences of speaking out—and thus facing ostracism from other men—as far worse than remaining silent, which again suggests that silencing lies at the root of the trauma; the individual is robbed of the right to choose what he communicates or withholds as knowledge about himself to others. The veil surrounding this crime has been lifted with respect to Catholic priests because the aggressors in these cases have less common social lives and are not only associated with homoerotic preference but also viewed as pederasts. Research reveals, however, that male "pack rape" of another man remains the most prevalent form of male-male rape, but the law reduces rape among those below the age of consent to "prankster mischief" and therefore refuses to see how much peer perceptions matter in formulating gender identity. Further, incest or child molestation within the domestic familial realm carries less severe penalties than other forms of rape and remains sheltered by privacy (actually, secrecy) and other factors. The rape of gay men by other gay men in all likelihood remains underreported, in part due to fears of arousing homophobia, in part to fears of betraying other gay men, and in part because forced sexual assault is perceived as one of the perils of being a gay man; often enough rape is included among the childhood or adolescent memories of adult gay, bisexual, and transgendered men.

As for women, the law does not recognize rape of a boy (or man) by a woman except in cases of statutory rape and perceives female-female rape as inconceivable (although it will doubtless soon be recognized that women are as capable of driving the mechanisms of heteronormativity as men, as the incidence of maternal abuse and neglect of children proves). In Kansas, for instance, one woman cannot charge another woman with sexual assault, unless the two are "biologically related," which would transform the charge into incest or non-sex-related domestic abuse. Hence, a mother in Kansas could charge her biological daughter with domestic violence as a subset of elder abuse. However, if the daughter had an intersexed, bisexual, lesbian, or transgendered partner who assaulted the mother, the partner could not be charged with criminal conduct. The partners listed above have no legal existence in Kansas under domestic law, and, as women, they partake in the fiction of their putative "gendered incapacity" to commit felonious assault. An underhanded miscreant could neglect, verbally assault, and reduce the mother to grinding misery and not only escape detection but also use the situation to extort, manipulate, and terrorize her partner.

The enormous range of sexual offenses included in the category of sexual assault has consequences for LGBTQ persons because the law levels differences that ought to matter. Sexual assault includes rape (but not the statutory variety); forced, coerced, or violent assault; inappropriate touching and fondling; and, most revealingly, incest, although the same must, in general, include penetration to count as such. Given that families now regularly include nonbiological members, sexual molestation often replaces incest, which, as such, levels distinctions of age and trust that mattered within statutory rape. What compels attention, moreover, particularly because the incest prohibition is universal among human cultures, while views of intergenerational same-sex (and heterosexual) sexual and romantic relations are culture specific, are the long discussions of incest within "nature" or "the biological realm" that accompany most discussions save feminist ones. LGBTQ persons have often been accused of inappropriate touching or fondling, but the fact remains that the most common—and the most egregious—form of sex- and age-related violence not only visited on LGBTQ persons but also children and women and elderly persons remains their abuse, neglect, rejection, and disowning by their families of origin. The relation of such childhood traumas to the manifold forms of violence and shunning visited on LGBTQ persons beyond the original domestic sphere, violence that culminates its long journey in the alarming prevalence of abuse and manipulation of elderly LGBTQ persons, has not been adequately studied in terms of how it informs IPV among LGBTQ persons. Domestic violence can manifest as physical abuse; pathological jealousy and suspicion; threats and intimidation; destruction of property, reputation, and social connections; blaming and isolation; and gender-based expectations that the abused partner must assume unequal responsibilities for domestic labor, financial support, attentiveness, nurture, and acceptance of degrading behavior. Further, statistics suggest that domestic violence occurs almost as often within LGBTQ couples as heterosexual ones, although caution seems advisable for numerous reasons. Abusive LGBTQ partners can use homo-hatred and homophobia as weapons of control. They can threaten to "out" the partner or use accusations of cowardice, deceitfulness, or internalized homophobia to isolate, imperil, and silence the abused partner. Victims can be told that the homophobic police and judicial system will refuse to believe, protect, or assist them. Lesbians often internalize societal views that women do not abuse other women, that lesbian relationships are idyllic refuges against patriarchal violence, and that only "transgressive" or "inauthentic" lesbians, such as those engaged in sadomasochism, butch–femme role-playing, or transgendered partnerships, become abusive because "real women" are not violent, and women in relationships have equal power. Persons of the same gender do not engage in abuse but rather mutual and consensual "combat." Partners deserve abuse for falling below the standard of "authentic" LGBTQ identities. The partner has "wrong" prior sex and gender relationships or the "wrong" friends, children, or sexual practices and desires. Further, the abusive partner can wield the weapon that the embattled LGBTQ community will ostracize, reject, and blame the partner for claiming domestic violence and therefore not only promoting homophobic censure but also puncturing cherished myths about lesbian egalitarianism and gay male mutuality. Heteronormativity encourages all men, straight and gay, to dominate others to maintain control, to silence and demoralize already socially vulnerable lesbians, and to blame violence in transgendered or bisexual relationships on gender roles and identifications.

Therefore, LGBTQ victims of domestic violence confront double closets and walls of silence, as often the topic remains so taboo, invisible, disowned, or legally unrecognized that the partners do not even recognize the abuse they suffer as "real abuse." Gay men have in particular remained reluctant to acknowledge domestic violence because, like their straight counterparts, they perceive themselves not as helpless "feminine" victims but rather as initiating or controlling aggression. Abuse is often reinterpreted as consensual role-playing—meaning something intrinsically different from the horrid images of forced anal rape or sexual, physical, or psychological abuse often suffered by gay, bisexual, or transgendered men as children, adolescents, or prisoners. In these cases, the abusers often identify themselves and their behaviors with real manhood and their victim with womanhood. If the victim, as an acquaintance or stranger, identifies as or appears to be gay because of falling beneath the standard of heteronormativity, then misogynistic rape fantasies will paint the victim either as secretly willing or as deserving of assault. Although matters have improved somewhat in recent years due to advances in LGBTQ rights and recognition of the prevalence of **hate crimes** against them, the criminal justice system has offered little assistance to LGBTQ victims of rape, sexual assault, or domestic violence. The police and the courts have become less overtly homophobic but remain solidly committed to heterosexism and heterosexist privilege. The police often claim they cannot distinguish the abuser from the victim, refuse to believe that women can assault one another, and see the matter as mutual violence, which either complicates obtaining a restraining order or results in the ordering of a mutual restraining order without reasonable investigation into the facts. Of course, mutual restraining orders offer the abuser another means of control and misrepresent the harm suffered by the victim, who can anticipate that future incidents of abuse, including stalking, threats, blackmail, and destruction of character and reputation, will be treated as mutual aggression. Further, lesbians who seek refuge in shelters often encounter homophobic animus, while shelters for gay and bisexual men, and, of course, transsexuals, remain virtually nonexistent.

Prosecuting domestic violence and other forms of sexual assault and educating the police, the courts, and public policy makers remain important goals. However, the evidence suggesting that battered women feel more comfortable discussing the violence in their lives with friends and family members than with trained professionals holds true for the same human reasons for LGBTQ individuals who, unfortunately, often cannot speak to others about the traumatic facets of their lives as LGBTQ persons, either because their families reject them or adopt polite distance around the topic or because of rejection and ostracism by friends, the LGBTQ community, and other community organizations, such as places of worship and workplaces. LGBTQ persons who do not reside in states with gender-neutral statutes have scant recourse and face multiple risks for reporting such crimes. Pervasive social acceptance of sex- and gender-related violence as unstoppable and covert allegiance to heteronormativity help explain why apathy and inaction have persisted despite the creation of laws that have strengthened responses to domestic violence. Almost half of Americans in a 1996 survey reported that men abused women because of stress or drunkenness rather than a "real" desire to harm them. The perception of domestic violence as an "intimate" private matter between two individuals, the view of rapists as marginal deviants, and the sense that child abuse within families can seldom be successfully halted or prosecuted all reflect the state of affairs caused by heteronormativity, and that can only be successfully challenged by far more vigorous and public discussion of the causes, consequences, and costs of IPV and its intergenerational dynamics. Over three million incidents of IPV occur each year among women and over three million among men. It results in two million injuries and over 1,000 deaths per year. Those who separate from abusive partners remain at risk for violence, and those who have experienced repeated incidents of sex-gender violence face far more serious consequences than those who have experienced isolated incidents. Retraumatization often results in chronic headaches; back pain; gynecological, central nervous system, and gastrointestinal disorders; as well as the sequels of posttraumatic stress disorder, such as depression, suicidal ideation, antisocial behavior, panic, low self-esteem, the inability to trust, and fear of intimacy. The more severe the exposure and the less access to healing through support networks, the more engagement in ill-advised sexual behavior and romantic attachments, abuse of harmful substances, eating disorders, and overuse of health services occurs. The costs of medical services and lowered work productivity are staggering, and IPV often disrupts schooling and causes chronic health problems, unemployment, and impoverishment. Risk factors include repeated exposure to sex- and gender-related violence and oppression, social isolation and marginalization, emotional dependence, belief in strict gender roles or gender myths, the desire to exercise domination and power over others, economic stress, low social capital, communities that perceive IPV with indifference, and the terror of plunging into social isolation.

Feminist theory has begun to correct its once-exclusive focus on sexual crimes committed against women, to acknowledge the specific effects of heterosexism and heteronormativity on LGBTQ persons and, at last, to recognize that the abuse of power accounts more persuasively for these crimes than patriarchal dominance alone. Further, the patterns that emerge through analysis of the construction of the categories of rape, sexual assault, and domestic violence suggest that queer and feminist scholars and activists might not yet have fully captured the foundational mechanisms of homophobic animus. Recently, Cheshire Calhoun has argued persuasively that LGBTQ persons suffer most from their literal displacement from the public and private spheres of civil society; they are recognized neither as legitimate public nor private persons. Recognition of the mechanisms of displacement demands new methodological approaches. According to Calhoun, three things remain most at stake for LGBTQ persons: the liberty to represent their identities in public, the liberty to have a protected private sphere, and the liberty to have equal opportunity to influence future generations. This desire (or fear) that future generations will be influenced has, perhaps, been at the heart of many ancient cultures' acceptance of same-sex relations between older and younger persons and that, conversely, has generated the explosive controversies surrounding the right to marriage, civil union, adoption, and parenting by LGBTQ persons in the United States. For Calhoun, feminist theory has failed to capture the specific concerns of lesbians and claims too much for lesbianism as the sublime embodiment of feminist revolt against patriarchal domination. The laws and public policies on rape, sexual assault, and domestic violence have yet to grapple with the extent to which they appear grounded in an intense biological and cultural narcissism that is determined to bar LGBTQ persons from cultural or biological reproduction and intergenerational continuity. Lesbians are not abstract icons of feminist heroism but rather real and embodied persons who fall in love and act to establish households with particular women, not women as a "class." For the most part, both feminist and lesbian feminist theorists have, like the larger society, penalized and diminished lesbianism. Due to new reproductive technologies, lesbians can now literally give birth to their own families and thus have the liberty to influence and participate in future generations. The advent of the marriage and civil union debate presents the most dramatic contest to the tenet at the heart of heteronormativity: that LGBTQ persons are constitutionally unfit for the duties of parenting or the politically sanctioned relations of parents to children. The prevalence of child molestation and abuse, along with the marginalization of lesbians and the pervasive violence against gay men, as well as children, women, and elders, not to mention the continual rise in incestuous-like compacts of secrecy, coercion, abuse, and denigration within the protected sphere of the family, all appear to argue that heteronormativity has become an intensely private affair that will be played out on the very public stage of family "values," parenting, and reproduction in the years—and decades—to come. Perhaps only an unwavering commitment to speech that replaces the regime of secrecy (which so damages our highly social species) and that not only enables the survival of LGBTQ cultural artifacts and interrupts the death-dealing cycle of heteronormative violence, but also the very grounded creation of children and families by LGBTQ persons can realize an enduringly viable survival past the gender caste system under which most now must manage to survive, if not to flourish.

Further Reading

Calhoun, Cheshire. 2002. *Feminism, the Family, and the Politics of the Closet: Lesbian and Gay Displacement*. Oxford, UK: Oxford University Press.

CAVNET: Communities against Violence. Available at: http://www.cavnet2.org/. Accessed July 20, 2008.

Cohen, Cathy J. 1997. "Punks, Bulldaggers, and Welfare Queen: The Radical Potential of Queer Politics?" *GLQ: A Journal of Lesbian and Gay Studies* 3 (4): 437–66.

Dorais, Michel. 2002. *Don't Tell: The Sexual Abuse of Boys*. Montreal, CA: McGill-Queen's University Press.

Mezey, Gillian, and Michael King. 2000. *Male Victims of Sexual Assault*. Oxford: Oxford University Press.

National Coalition of Anti-Violence Programs. Available at: http://www.ncavp.org/issues/DomesticViolence.aspx. Accessed July 20, 2008.

Scarce, Michael, and William B. Rubenstein. 1997. *Male on Male Rape: The Hidden Toll of Stigma and Shame*. Cambridge, MA: Perseus Press.

Sloan, Lacey M., and Nora S. Gustavvson. 1998. *Violence and Social Injustice against Lesbian, Gay and Bisexual People*. Binghamton, NY: Haworth Press.

Warner, Michael. 1991. "Introduction: Fear of a Queer Planet." *Social Text* 9 (4): 3–17.

Weiss, Jillian Todd. 2001. "The Gender Caste System: Identity, Privacy, and Heteronormativity." *Law and Sexuality* 10: 123–86. Available at: phobos.ramapo.edu/~jweiss/tulane.pdf. Accessed July 20, 2008.

Corinne E. Blackmer

rappers and hip-hop

Gay hip-hop, commonly called homohop, aims to create spaces for gay and lesbian emcees, rappers, and hip-hop artists primarily by using Internet portals and social networking sites such as My Space and independent/self-released recordings for promotion, distribution, and marketing. Gay rappers also use tours and club performances to build audiences and establish name recognition. Due to sexism and **homophobia** in the mainstream rap and hip-hop segments of the music industry, artists who choose to speak directly about their sexuality and gay subject matter in their rhymes are often ignored by the major labels. Documentaries such as *Pick Up the Mic* chronicle the emergence of the homohop movement, profiling artists such as Cazwell, Crasta Yo, the San Francisco trio Deep Dickcollective, Morplay, and Caushun. For performers and audiences, homohop becomes a way to counter dominant constructions of American gay and lesbian culture as white and middle class by appealing to "homothugz," gays and lesbians of color, and working-class audiences. Two of the most visible homohop stars are Augustana, whose work is widely available on the Web and platforms such as Itunes, and God-Des and She, whose debut music video "Love You Better" got significant airplay on Viacom's Logo network in 2006 and who appeared in the finale of the third season of *The L Word*. Homohop artists exhibit media savvy by crafting their own images, developing press kits, and maximizing the effectiveness of the Internet for distribution and promotion.

Further Reading

C-Lee. 2001. "B-boy to Boy Toy: Brooklyn Rapper Caushun Takes Hip-Hop to a Truly Higher Level." *Out* (December): 24.

Galtney, Smith. 1999. "Kim's Turn." *Out* (December): 70.

Walters, Barry. 2000. "Down and Out: Gay Duo Morplay Fight Hip-Hop's Homophobia by Diluting Fear and Injecting Fun." *Out* (October): 48.

Ben Aslinger

Robert Rauschenberg (1925–2008)

Robert Rauschenberg was one of the premier artists of the latter half of the twentieth century. His work is often credited for helping to break abstract expressionism's stronghold on the art world, opening the way for the pop art movement of the 1960s.

Born in Port Arthur, Texas, Rauschenberg served a stint in the navy before going on to study art under the GI Bill at the Kansas City Art Institute and the Académie Julian in Paris. He later enrolled in the legendary Black Mountain College in North Carolina, where he formed relationships with artists such as Cy Twombly, Merce Cunningham, and **John Cage,** with whom he would collaborate in later years. Rauschenberg was briefly married to the painter Susan Weil, and they had a son, but he is most closely identified with American painter **Jasper Johns,** with whom he was artistically and romantically involved from 1954 to 1961. During this time Johns and Rauschenberg both maintained studios in the same dilapidated loft in lower Manhattan, and it was from here that they would each produce many of their best-known works, which are often described as belonging to the "neo-dada" or "proto-pop" style.

Rauschenberg's early work included series of monochromatic white, red, and black paintings and prankish pieces such as *Erased de Kooning* (1953)—literally a drawing by abstract expressionist painter Willem de Kooning that Rauschenberg meticulously erased. Increasingly, he incorporated three dimensional objects into his work, resulting in his signature "combines" of the late 1950s, which blur the line between painting and sculpture. These combines blended elements of traditional painting with assemblages of found objects such as chairs, textiles, cardboard, and, in one of his most famous works (*Monogram*, 1959), a large stuffed goat. In the 1960s Rauschenberg returned to two-dimensional work, creating collages of paint and silk-screened images from newspapers and magazines.

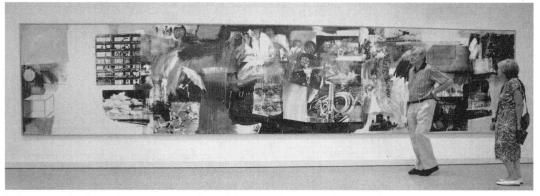

Robert Rauschenberg's *Barge* is seen in the exhibition "The Guggenheim Collection" in the Federal Art and Exhibition Hall in Bonn, Germany, in 2006. AP Photo/Hermann J. Knippertz.

In 1961, Johns and Rauschenberg split up and did not speak to or see one another for more than a decade. After this, Rauschenberg became increasingly involved with performance and modern dance, serving in a variety of roles including set and costume design, choreography, stage lighting, and also as a performer. He was also very influential in other fields including photography, papermaking, and, in particular, printmaking. Largely confined to a wheelchair as a result of a stroke in 2002, Rauschenberg still continued to produce art from his sprawling studio compound in Captiva, Florida. He died on May 13, 2008.

Further Reading

Kotz, Mary Lynn. 2004. *Rauschenberg: Art and Life*. New York: Harry N. Abrams.
Mattison, Robert. 2003. *Robert Rauschenberg: Breaking Boundaries*. New Haven: Yale University Press.

Paul Falzone

John Rechy (1931–)

The youngest son of Guadalupe Flores and Roberto Rechy, John Francisco Rechy—who would become a pioneering American novelist—was born in El Paso, Texas. Rechy's father, a successful musician during his younger years, grew up in Mexico City; his mother was from a working-class family in rural Mexico. Both were immigrants who met and married in El Paso. Rechy's poverty-stricken childhood was for the most part an unhappy one: his father was angry and abusive, his mother fiercely possessive. He sought refuge in literature and movies and at the age of 10 began writing short works of fiction. In 1952, after graduating from Texas Western College, he enlisted in the army. After a two-year stint he returned to El Paso briefly, then moved to New York City to begin graduate studies at Columbia University. But almost immediately after arriving in Manhattan he discovered the world of male **prostitution.** Rechy became a street hustler and sporadically worked as one well into his forties—even after becoming an established novelist and even while employed as an instructor of creative writing at Occidental College in Los Angeles during the 1970s. Rechy, who now teaches in the Professional Writing Program at the University of Southern California, is the author of 13 works of fiction, a few unpublished plays, and dozens of insightful essays on politics and contemporary culture.

Among contemporary American novelists, Rechy is one of the most insistently autobiographical. *City of Night* (1963), his most celebrated work and arguably his magnum opus, chronicles its unnamed narrator's odyssey through the sexual underground. Structurally, it alternates between chapters that focus on the narrator's journey and chapters that present individual portraits of memorable characters he encounters during his exilic wandering; collectively, the various sections of the book offer a sweeping vision of a world that is largely terra incognita for most people. It is a world of lonely misfits and sexual outcasts. The narrator's picaresque journey—his sexual vagabondage—often resembles a Dantesque descent into hell. Having rejected his childhood Catholicism, he frantically seeks a substitute for salvation; yet his quest, which began in El Paso and ends there many months later, remains sadly thwarted. A few mean-spirited reviews aside, the critical reception accorded *City of Night* was favorable, and the novel was a commercial success. Its bold treatment of taboo subjects, intricate narrative architecture, and lyrical prose elicited generous praise from fellow novelists such as **James Baldwin** and **Gore Vidal.**

Since the publication of *City of Night*, Rechy has written a dozen novels, many of them critically acclaimed, but none has achieved the canonical status of his first book. In *Numbers* (1967), the protagonist Johnny Rio compulsively seeks anonymous sexual encounters to reassure himself that he is physically attractive. The novel's elaborate biblical imagery and ironic inversions of Catholic rituals give Rio's quest a quasi-religious fervor and allegorical dimension. *This Day's Death* (1969) is an angry indictment of the statutory oppression of sexual minorities. Rechy's rage against the heterosexual establishment becomes stunningly articulate in *The Sexual Outlaw* (1977); in this text that blurs genre boundaries, Rechy blends autobiography, fiction, journalism, political commentary, and jeremiad to deliver a defiant and devastatingly precise analysis of sexual oppression. Two years later Rechy published *Rushes*. Set in a **leather** bar in an unnamed American city, *Rushes* advances the debatable thesis that **sadomasochistic** sexual practices within gay communities are symptomatic of internalized **homophobia** and self-contempt. In this novel he also critiques the sexism, racism, and **ageism** that he finds to be pervasive in gay enclaves. In *The Coming of the Night* (1998), set in 1981, Rechy offers a compelling and at times humorous portrait of gay promiscuity just before the advent of AIDS.

Since the late 1980s Rechy has widened his thematic territory. Straight women occupy the center stage in works such as *Marilyn's Daughter* (1988), and ethnic concerns are central to *The Miraculous Day of Amalia Gomez* (1991). In *The Life and Adventures of Lyle Clemens* (2003), a fast-paced picaresque novel, the protagonist is a heterosexual male. *Beneath the Skin* (2004) is a superb collection of Rechy's cultural commentaries and political essays written over a period of 40 years. Rechy speaks from the margins of American society, but he expertly uses his radical voice to disrupt and destabilize racist, patriarchal, and heterosexist hegemonies.

Further Reading

Bruce-Novoa, Juan. 2001. "Rechy and Rodriguez: Double Crossing the Public/Private Line." In *Double Crossings/EntreCruzamientos*, ed. Mario Martin Flores and Carlos von Son, 15–34. Fair Haven, NJ: Nuevo Espacio.

Casillo, Charles. 2002. *Outlaw: The Lives and Careers of John Rechy*. Los Angeles: Advocate Books.

Castillo, Debra. 1995. "Interview: John Rechy." *Diacritics* 25 (1): 113–25.

Emmanuel S. Nelson

Lou Reed (1942–)

Born Lewis Alan Reed in Brooklyn, Lou Reed is a critically acclaimed songwriter, singer, guitar player, poet, and photographer. In 1959, he underwent a series of shock treatments to "cure" him of homosexuality. Critics have characterized Reed and his artistic sensibility as **bisexual.**

In 1965, Reed formed the Velvet Underground with John Cale, Sterling Morrison, and Maureen Tucker. **Andy Warhol** became the band's manager. Reed left the band in 1970 for a solo career. Wearing heavy eye makeup and black lipstick, Reed cast himself as glam and gay for *Transformer* (1972), coproduced by David Bowie and Mick Ronson. "Make Up" resonated with the **gay liberation movement:** "Now we're coming out. Out of our closets, out on the streets." *Transformer* also includes "Walk on the Wild Side," a musical homage to Warhol's **transgender** and gay-hustler superstars.

Reed's work took a dark turn with *Berlin* (1973). He remade himself into a streetwise rocker for *Rock 'n' Roll Animal* (1974), and in 1975 he released *Metal Machine Music*. On *Coney Island Baby* (1976), Reed dedicated the album's title song to Rachel, his transgender lover and companion. *New York* (1989) solidified Reed's image as the quintessentially cool New Yorker. In 1990, Reed repartnered with Cale on *Songs for Drella*. *Magic and Loss* (1992) was written after the death of two close friends, Doc Pomus and Rotten Rita. *Ecstasy* (2000), inspired by Reed's long-term relationship with performance artist Laurie Anderson, was released to enthusiastic reviews.

Further Reading

Bockris, Victor. 1994. *Transformer: The Lou Reed Story*. New York: Simon & Schuster.
Roberts, Chris. 2004. *Lou Reed: Walk on the Wild Side: The Stories behind the Songs*. Milwaukee, WI: Hal Leonard.
Witts, Richard. 2006. *The Velvet Underground*. Bloomington: Indiana University Press.

Krista L. May

Paul Reed (1956–2002)

Paul Reed was an American author and essayist who published erotica under the pseudonym Max Exander. Reed, who lost a partner to HIV and was himself HIV positive, frequently wrote about AIDS. *How to Persuade Your Lover to Use a Condom and Why You Should* (1987), which Reed cowrote, is a safe-sex polemic, and *Serenity: Challenging the Fear of AIDS from Despair to Hope* (1987) contains essays resisting fear while facing AIDS. Reed's nonfiction continued with *The Q Journal: A Treatment Diary* (1991), which chronicles his experiences in the Compound Q clinical trials, and with his essay "Early AIDS Fiction" (1993). Reed self-published his journal *The Savage Garden* (1994), which explores sex and spirituality in the age of AIDS.

Reed's first novel, *Facing It* (1984), is often celebrated as the earliest American AIDS novel, for its early focus on the virus and its impact on its protagonist Andy and his partner David. His second novel, *Longing* (1988), is a typical chronicling of the gay exodus to San Francisco, but its existential examination of longing is distinctive. Reed's third novel, *Vertical Intercourse* (2000), explores its unnamed protagonist's experiences with aging and AIDS. These themes are poignantly presented in Reed's last published work, *The Redwood Diary* (2001), which chronicles his life from April 1995 to March 1996. During this year, as Reed turns 40, he withdraws to a California cabin to write. Having written during the emergence of AIDS, Reed pseudonymously explored the erotic possibilities surrounding safer sex in *ManSex* (1985), *LoveSex* (1986), *Safe Stud* (1986), and *Deeds of the Night* (1995). Reed's work has been criticized for stilted, if not pedantic dialogue. What this criticism overlooks is the possibility of a new narrative mode, an AIDS medical realism, which may have found its introduction in Reed's *Facing It*.

Further Reading

Isola, Mark John. "Paul Reed." 2007. GLBTQ Encyclopedia Online. Available at: http://www. glbtq.com/literature/reed_p,4.html. Accessed July 20, 2008.

McGovern, Terrence. 1993. "Paul Reed." In *Contemporary Gay American Novelist: A Bio-Bibliographical Critical Soucebook*, ed. Emmanuel Nelson, 352–58. Westport, CT: Greenwood Press.

Mark John Isola

religion

The tremendous amount of religious diversity makes it impossible to consider the religious reasons behind the acceptance or rejection of queer people by people of all faiths in America. While some religious groups have been more receptive to queer people (for example, Reform Judaism, America **Buddhism,** Unitarian Universalism, the **United Church of Christ,** and neopaganism) than others, there is diversity even within traditions generally considered to be wholly hostile to queer people. Queer-positive groups have developed in **Islam** (Al-Fatiha), **Mormonism** (Affirmation), Orthodox Judaism (GLYDSA), **Roman Catholicism** (Dignity), and evangelical Christianity (Evangelicals Concerned). Though formal institutional positions on homosexuality and gender identity may appear monolithic, Americans' actual religious beliefs do not always conform to the teachings of religious authorities. Indeed, the challenges queer people have presented to religious orthodoxy have resulted in the division of some religious institutions. In 2003, openly gay minister Gene Robinson became a bishop in the **Episcopal Church,** a fact that resulted in an increasingly formalized church schism over the validity of queer ordination. The intensity of religious divisions like those occurring in the Anglican and Episcopal churches is relatively characteristic of the passionate positions held by individuals and institutions on both sides of the debate. However, the continued invisibility of transgender people has resulted in less religious conversation about the specific concerns of the transgender community.

The concern for gender conformity seems to be foremost in religious concerns about queer people, especially in the Abrahamic traditions, which have systems for regulating male and female gender roles. In contrast, many **Native American spiritualities** and religions have a special religious category, the two-spirit, for queer people. Queer people are not outside of the religious system but a critical part of its operations. Of course, many queer Native Americans experience isolation and rejection because of varying interpretations of indigenous religions and the adoption of nonindigenous religions. Smaller American religious groups, like Buddhists, tend toward more positive valuations of queer people, noting that the Buddha left no teaching against homosexuality. Neopagan religious communities in America are almost wholly queer-positive, fostering large constituencies of queer men and women in groups like Dianic **Wicca,** which caters to large numbers of lesbians, and gay-exclusive covens of Faery Witch men.

More important than the teachings of religions about queer people are the consequences, sometimes deadly, for those who feel rejected by their religious community. Their life of secrecy is sometimes accompanied by a parallel life in which queer people live in heterosexual relationships, are socially active against queers, maintain antiqueer religious beliefs, and/or conform to gender expectations. The outing of religious figures like Ted Haggard, who was accused of buying methamphetamines and soliciting sex from a gay prostitute, have shone light on the deep internalization of **homophobia** in the church. The presence of struggling queer people among institutions that actively seek to curb queer rights and religious tolerance continues to be a phenomenon that parallels the high number of queer people who engage in homophobia, violence, and hate because of their own struggles with their identity.

Reparative therapy is one formal way religious people attempt to deal with queers. Most famous of these organizations is Exodus International, an umbrella organization for individuals who claim to be able to cure queer people of gender nonconformity and/or same-sex attractions. Though psychologists practicing reparative therapy are dismissed from the American Psychological Association, a network of psychologists and religious specialists continue to practice reparative therapy because of their religious conviction that homosexuality is a sickness or a sin. Mel White, a former ghostwriter for major leaders of the religious right, including Jerry Falwell and Pat Robertson, struggled for decades to overcome his same-sex attractions. White underwent electroshock treatments and various psychological and reparative therapies but found no escape from his sexual orientation. In 1993, White came out in a sermon when he was installed as dean of the Metropolitan Community Church, the first American Christian church founded specifically on the principle of queer inclusion. In the same year White and his partner founded Soulforce, an organization whose mission is to free lesbian, gay, bisexual, and transgender people from religious bigotry and religious and political oppression.

Political action like that practiced by Soulforce has become increasingly important in queer communities because of the rise in political campaigns intended to limit or preemptively restrict civil rights for queer people. While the political and religious outlook often seems slow moving and bleak, queer-positive religious groups offer a place for religious queer people to affirm their identities in the face of civil discrimination.

See also Clergy; Protestants, evangelical; Protestants, mainline.

Further Reading

Erzen, Tanya. 2006. *Straight to Jesus: Sexual and Christian Conversions in the Ex-Gay Movement.* Los Angeles: University of California Press.

Rogers, Jack. 2006. *Jesus, the Bible, and Homosexuality: Explode the Myths, Heal the Church*. Louisville, KY: Westminster John Knox.

Soulforce: Freedom for Lesbian, Gay, Bisexual and Transgender People. Available at: www.soulforce.org. Accessed July 20, 2008.

White, Mel. 2006. *Religion Gone Bad: The Hidden Dangers of the Christian Right*. New York: Penguin Group.

Katie Hladky

religion and HIV/AIDS

Today, despite the fact that only a few religious organizations allow openly gay and lesbian applicants to take religious orders—and even then often only if they vow to remain celibate—many lesbians and gay men continue to be drawn to the religious life. Unfortunately, most major religions have at one time or another harbored leaders who condemned same-sex eroticism. Some religious people interpret AIDS as a punishment exacted by God for homosexual behavior, and such people have referred to AIDS as a "gay plague." This was an early term that was used to refer to AIDS before there was a reasonable level of medical understanding of the syndrome. It was then seen primarily as affecting gay people, rather than as a syndrome that can be passed on in sexual and nonsexual ways (e.g., blood transfusions) to any person, but particularly to any sexually active person not practicing safe sex, irrespective of sexual orientation. Some representatives of these religions also oppose measures like condom distribution to stop the spread of the disease, instead advocating abstinence as the only completely reliable way to prevent this disease. Some are now promoting an "ABC" message: abstain, be faithful, condomize.

Further Reading

Ellens, J. Harold. 2006. *Sex in the Bible: A New Consideration*. Westport, CT: Praeger Publishers.

Herek, Gregory M., and Beverly Greene, eds. 1995. *AIDS, Identity, and Community: The HIV Epidemic and Lesbians and Gay Men*. Thousand Oaks, CA: Sage Publications.

Stuart, Elizabeth. 1997. *Religion Is a Queer Thing*. Washington, DC: Cassell.

Sara Munoz

religion and politics

Since the 1970s, religion has played a pivotal role in shaping the politics surrounding sex, **sexuality,** and gender in America. By making connections between religious values and citizenship, groups on the right and the left and in the center of the American political and theological spectrums put issues such as **marriage,** adoption, discrimination, and **hate crimes** at the forefront of local, state, and federal politics.

In the late 1970s a backlash against the **feminist** and **gay liberation** movements helped fuel the rise of the Christian right and the fusion of theological conservatism, including Christian fundamentalism, with conservative political activism. Organizations such as Focus on the Family (FOF), founded by psychologist James Dobson in 1977, formed and thrived over the decades on a platform of protecting the American family from the dangers of secularism, feminism, and gay liberation, or the "gay agenda."

While FOF started as a Christian counseling organization and not a political advocacy organization, Dobson and his organization have long been considered a mouthpiece for the Christian right on issues of politics and homosexuality. From its inception FOF has operated on the premise that homosexuality is destructive, not just to the individual but to society as a whole, and has poured extensive financial resources into influencing politicians and voters to ban gay marriage, restrict **adoption** rights, oppose legislation against hate crime and discrimination, and strip school curriculums of tolerance and diversity programs that would include references to LGBTQ persons.

In 2004 Focus on the Family Action Council was launched as the official political arm of Focus on the Family. The online magazine *Citizenlink*, which focuses on "Issues in Policy and Culture," includes a section on "Fighting the Homosexual Agenda." In 2006 FOF took out full-page advertisements in local and national newspapers to sanction politicians who did not support the Federal Marriage Amendment.

In 1992 the organization Colorado for Family Values pushed a state referendum known as Amendment 2, which denied gay, lesbian, and bisexual individuals the right to make discrimination claims against their employers. With the support of FOF and other Christian right organizations including the Christian Coalition, Traditional Values Coalition, and Concerned Women for America, the referendum passed but was judged unconstitutional by the U.S. Supreme Court in 1996.

Other organizations on the Christian right have worked diligently to make homosexuality the focus of local, state, and national political debates. In 1979 televangelist Jerry Falwell founded the Moral Majority with the goal of mobilizing not just fellow fundamentalist Christians but also Protestants, Catholics, Jews, and other conservatives who opposed political advancements of secularists, feminists, and gay rights advocates. The Moral Majority, which claimed to be pro-moral and pro-family, sought to elect officials who shared their vision of making America a nation of "Christian" values once again.

After the Moral Majority dissolved in 1989, Falwell remained in the political spotlight as a major voice within the Christian right. Shortly after the attacks of September 11, 2001, Falwell went on Pat Robertson's television show *The 700 Club* and blamed gays and lesbians, among other groups attempting to secularize America, for God's judgment. Falwell announced on November 14, 2004, the creation of the Moral Majority Coalition. That same year Falwell led the "One Man One Woman" campaign to raise money in support of the Federal Marriage Amendment banning any legal recognition for same-sex couples.

After a failed 1988 presidential bid, Christian media mogul Pat Robertson picked up where the Moral Majority had left off by forming the Christian Coalition, which utilized Robertson's unspent campaign dollars to recruit, train, and mobilize "people of faith" in order to influence local, state, and national elections. One of the effects of this mobilization was the Christian takeover of the Republican Party and the subsequent Republican takeover of Congress in 1994. Instrumental in the takeover was the Christian Coalition's executive director Ralph Reed. Reed, who would later serve behind the scenes of George W. Bush's presidential campaign, lobbied heavily against gay rights legislation. Lobbying efforts of the Christian Coalition and other religious right organizations during this period resulted in legislation such as the military's "don't ask, don't tell" policy and the Defense of Marriage Act (DOMA).

Other organizations with a focus on opposing LGBTQ rights and protections include the Traditional Values Coalition and the Family Research Council. The Traditional Values Coalition (TVC) was founded by Louis P. Sheldon as a lobbying organization based in Washington, D.C., representing the values of conservative Christians. TVC believes that homosexual behavior should be criminalized because it violates Christian doctrine. The organization promotes the idea that homosexuals recruit children and therefore should not be permitted adoption or parental rights. In their efforts to lobby against hate crimes and nondiscrimination legislation, the TVC produced a video entitled *Gay Rights, Special Rights*. The Family Research Council (FRC) is a conservative Christian think-tank and lobbying organization, also based in Washington, D.C., and founded by James Dobson. While legally separate, the FRC shares the same ideology as FOF. In 2005 they hosted a banquet at which Dobson criticized a video aimed at teaching tolerance in public schools and featuring cartoon character SpongeBob SquarePants because it supported gay rights.

In May 1994 many of these organizations were represented during two days of top-secret meetings held at the Glen Eyrie Conference Center in the mountains above Colorado Springs. The focus of the conference was to address the growing threat of the "gay agenda," also referred to as the "militant gay movement." Many goals were sketched out during the conference, including changing the public perception about gay rights and developing a long-term project to convince evangelical pastors to support the antigay movement. Specific political goals included creating voter guides, participating in precinct organization, and cultivating leaders, as well as fund-raising and campaigning for candidates who opposed gay rights legislation.

In that same year the Interfaith Alliance formed to counter the religious political extremism of the Christian Coalition and other religious right organizations through bipartisan national grassroots advocacy. Representing people of faith and goodwill from over 75 religious traditions and belief systems and led by Baptist pastor Welton Gaddy, the Interfaith Alliance has worked to mobilize coalitions of religious and nonreligious groups from the center to the left of the American political and theological spectrums to oppose the Federal Marriage Amendment and support inclusion of sexual orientation in both the Employment Non-Discrimination Act and hate crimes legislation.

Hate crimes legislation catapulted to the forefront of American politics with the killing of University of Wyoming student Matthew Shepard. On the night of

October 6–7, 1998, Shepard was attacked and left to die on a fence post. Many believed Shepard was targeted by his attackers, Russell Henderson and Aaron McKinney, because of his sexual orientation. Laws at the time, however, did not support stiffer sentencing for hate crimes than other crimes. This incident spawned a national debate not just over the need for hate crimes legislation but also about "special rights" being granted to homosexuals.

While some Christian right organizations chose to focus on their opposition to hate crimes legislation, others used the national attention being paid to Shepard's death to denounce gays themselves. Reverend Fred Phelps and supporters from his Kansas Westboro Baptist Church picketed Shepard's funeral with signs stating "God Hates Fags." A Web site of the same name was set up by Phelps's church, depicting Shepard burning in hell.

On November 18, 2003, the Massachusetts Supreme Court ruled in favor of same-sex marriage, setting off heated debate over civil rights for LGBTQ citizens. Those on the religious right, including Protestant, Catholic, Jewish, and Muslim leaders, supported campaigns (including petitions, fund-raisers, and advertising on both the state and federal levels) to pass constitutional amendments defining marriage as between one man and one woman. Many of the campaigns centered on protecting the institution of marriage from "activist judges."

Christian right organizations also mobilized faith leaders, including African American pastors, to stir up opposition. On December 11, 2004, Bishop Eddie Long, leader of New Birth Missionary Baptist Church in Lithonia, Georgia, organized a "Re-Ignite the Legacy" march to mobilize African American Christians against gay marriage. By 2006 more than 20 states had passed marriage protection amendments, leaving Arizona as the only state to defeat such an amendment. Riding this momentum, FRCAction, the political arm of the Family Research Council, sponsored the 2006 Values Voters Summit, which focused on denunciations of gay marriage, activist judges, and the gay agenda.

Gay rights organizations such as the **Human Rights Campaign** have tried to counter the message of the religious right by recruiting progressive members of faith communities to speak on behalf of legislation and offer resources countering the theological claims of the right. Other organizations include Soulforce, which was founded in 1999 by Mel White, former ghostwriter for Jerry Falwell and Pat Robertson. Soulforce is an interfaith organization that confronts conservative churches and organizations such as Focus on the Family through nonviolent civil disobedience.

Further Reading

Cobb, Michael. 2006. *God Hates Fags: The Rhetorics of Religious Violence*. New York: New York University Press.

Jelen, Ted G. 1991. *The Political Mobilization of Religious Beliefs*. Westport, CT: Praeger Publishers.

Pellegrini, Ann, and Janet R. Jakobsen. 2003. *Love the Sin: Sexual Regulation and the Limits of Religious Tolerance*. New York: New York University Press.

White, Mel. 2006. *Religion Gone Bad: The Hidden Dangers of the Christian Right*. New York: Penguin Group.

Andrea Tucker

religious groups and movements, LGBTQ

Before gay liberation and Stonewall, religious communities began working to recognize a historically invisible gay and lesbian population. Today LGBTQ religious groups practically equal the number of religious sects in the United States, ranging from Seventh-Day Adventists to Orthodox Judaism to the Al-Fatiha Foundation (LGBT Muslims). This diverse array of LGBTQ churches, temples, and religious groups can be divided into two categories: (1) those that work for reform from within their own tradition and (2) autonomous groups that form their own congregation or denomination.

Reformist LGBTQ religious movements preserve much of the same worship style and theology as their traditional denominations. Typically, these groups emerged as revitalization efforts from within **mainline** and progressive religious denominations, such as the **United Church of Christ,** Disciples of Christ, Presbyterians (U.S.A.), **Episcopalians,** Society of Friends (Quakers), American Baptists, Reformed Judaism, as well as others. Most of these congregations tend to be very welcoming of openly gay and lesbian people, making a conscious effort not to reject them, but including people of all sexual orientations in the life and ministry of the religious group. In some cases the national denomination or governing body is more conservative than individual congregations, or in other cases individual congregations are more conservative than the national denomination. When individual congregations vary within a denomination, there are denominationally specific labels to identify a church or temple that welcomes LGBTQ persons. One might come across a "More Light" Presbyterian church, an "Open and Affirming" United Church of Christ congregation, or a "Reconciling" Methodist church. The membership makeup of these churches and synagogues varies widely and could primarily be gay and lesbian, LGBT, heterosexual, or a mixture of all types of individuals and families, but such congregations are often linked by their shared commitment to social justice causes. These "welcoming" congregations differ in their activism, visibility, and acknowledgment of sexuality issues. Some might march in gay pride parades or lobby for revised adoption laws, while other congregations avoid activism, focusing instead on worship and liturgical possibilities. Other reform congregations are locked in theological debate with national denominational governmental bodies: the United Methodists and Evangelical Lutheran Churches of America have been rent over the ordination

The Metropolitan Community Church in early days. Courtesy of the Gay, Lesbian, Bisexual, Transgender Historical Society, San Francisco.

of gay and lesbian clergy and the blessings of **same-sex marriages** or commitment ceremonies.

Historically, most churches and synagogues were considered homophobic and oppressive, and during the burgeoning gay liberation movement of the late 1960s, gays and lesbians often rejected religious life and groups. Yet, a number of gay and lesbian religious coalitions formed to address civil rights, education, and advocacy issues pertaining to religious involvement and the needs of gay and lesbian believers. In San Francisco, Reverend Ted McIlvenna of Glide Memorial Methodist Church and the employees of the Glide Foundation counseled gay and lesbian homeless youth who, they discovered, were often homeless after being evicted for acknowledging same-sex desires. Wanting to learn more about sexual identities, McIlvenna worked with the **homophile** organizations **Daughters of Bilitis** and the **Mattachine Society** to initiate dialogue between the gay and lesbian community and clergy in the Bay Area. The ministers quickly learned about the mistreatment, discrimination, and abuse experienced by gay and lesbian people from police, churches, and other facets of society. The group formed the Council on Religion and the Homosexual (CRH) in 1964 and was successful in reducing police brutality against gay and lesbian persons. CRH chapters formed throughout the country with educational and some advocacy goals to initiate dialogue between religious leaders and the gay and lesbian community using the common goal of civil rights.

Eventually, some denominations that allowed opportunities for dialogue also allowed space for reform groups or gay and lesbian caucuses within their tradition. Other reform groups are not formally recognized by their tradition but are nonetheless committed to their religious tradition. Some examples of groups within the larger organizations, with the date of the founding, include Dignity (Roman Catholic, 1969), Unitarian Universalist Association's Office of BLGT Concerns (1970), Gay Friends (Quakers, 1971), American Baptists Concerned (1972), United Church of Christ Coalition for LGBT Concerns (1972), Lutherans Concerned (1974), More Light Presbyterians (1974), Integrity (Episcopal Church, 1974), Evangelicals Concerned (1975), Affirmation (United Methodists, 1976), Brethren/Mennonite Council for Lesbian/Gay Concerns (1976), Affirmation (Church of Jesus Christ of Latter-day Saints, 1979), the World Congress of Gay, Lesbian, Bisexual, and Transgender Jews (1980), Rainbow Wind (Pagan, 1995), and Gay **Buddhist** Fellowship (1999), among others.

Not all LGBTQ religious people have the hope or stamina for reform within their own tradition, so choose or are forced to find and create alternative religious communities. Many conservative Christian denominations and Orthodox branches of Judaism deny membership to openly LGBTQ people, enforce a "don't ask, don't tell" policy, or assume LGBTQ persons are emotionally and spiritually ill victims who can change or "heal" their same-sex desire. Reverend Troy Perry felt such exclusion from his Pentecostal church and thus began the first gay-specific denomination, the Universal Fellowship of Metropolitan Community Churches (MCC), in Los Angeles in 1968. Currently, the MCC has over 40,000 members worldwide, practices an ecumenical worship style, and provides a safe and welcome place to meet the spiritual needs of LGBT Christians. Additionally, more than 30 gay-specific synagogues exist in North America, including Beth Chaim Chadashim in Los Angeles (1972) and South Florida's Congregation Ez Chaim (1974). The Reverend Carl Bean began the Unity Fellowship Church movement in 1982, primarily for gay and lesbian African Americans in the Los Angeles area, which has since grown to be a movement that welcomes all types of people interested in an inclusive message and activism for social change. Reconciling Pentecostals International established a network for Pentecostal ministers and churches in 2000 and helped support nondiscriminating Pentecostal churches such as Potter's House Fellowship in Tampa, Florida.

Both reform and innovative LGBTQ religious movements contribute to the diversity of the American religious landscape, which will continue to be shaped, negotiated, renewed, resisted, and sometimes rejected by individuals and communities.

See also Religion.

Further Reading

Comstock, Gary David. 1996. *Unrepentant, Self-Affirming, Practicing: Lesbian/Bisexual/Gay People within Organized Religion.* New York: Continuum.

Comstock, Gary David, and Susan E. Henking, eds. 1999. *Que(e)rying Religion: A Critical Anthology.* New York: Continuum.

Gearhart, Sally, and William R. Johnson. 1974. *Loving Women/Loving Men: Gay Liberation and the Church.* San Francisco: Glide Publications.

The Lesbian, Gay, Bisexual, and Transgender Religious Archives Network. Available at: http://www.lgbtran.org. Accessed July 20, 2008.

Thumma, Scott, and Edward R. Gray, eds. 2005. *Gay Religion.* Walnut Creek, CA: Altamira Press.

Howell Williams

Guillermo Reyes (1962–)

Having emigrated to the United States from Chile in 1971, Guillermo Reyes is one of the only gay Latino playwrights in the United States creating material focusing on the gay Latino experience. His first professionally produced and published piece is the collection of monologues *Men on the Verge of a His-panic Breakdown*, which premiered in Celebration Theatre in Los Angeles in 1994 and won two Ovation awards. In this play, Reyes depicts the lives of several gay Latinos and Latin American immigrants. Premiering two years later, *Deporting the Divas*, like *Men on the Verge*, also uses **camp** and humor to explore the fluidity of nationality, gender, and sexuality. Taking place on both sides of the San Diego/Tijuana border and tracing the gay love affair of an apparently heterosexual border officer, Reyes insists that audiences recognize the ways sexuality and other aspects of identity are inextricable from each other. Reyes deploys characters that momentarily fit, but ultimately break out of, the **stereotypes** with which they are usually identified.

Further Reading

Cortez, Beatriz. 1999. "Hybrid Identities and the Emergence of Dislocated Consciousness: *Deporting the Divas* by Guillermo Reyes." In *Chicano/Latino Homoerotic Identities*, ed. David William Foster, 131–45. New York: Garland.

Fitch, Melissa A. 2002. "Gender Bending in Latino Theater: Johnny Diego, the His-Panic Zone, and *Deporting the Divas* by Guillermo Reyes." In *Latino/a Popular Culture*, ed. Michelle Habell-Pallán and Mary Romero, 162–73. New York: New York University Press.

Huerta, Jorge. 2000. *Chicano Drama: Performance, Society and Myth*. Cambridge: Cambridge University Press.

Liberty Smith

Adrienne Rich (1929–)

Born in Baltimore, Adrienne Rich is an award-winning American poet and essayist best known for her feminist writings. Rich has received numerous awards, among them the Lannan Lifetime Achievement Award, the Ruth Lilly Poetry Prize, the National Book Award, the Fund for Human Dignity Award of the National Gay Task Force, the Lambda Book Award for lesbian poetry, an Academy of American Poets Fellowship, and a MacArthur Fellowship. Rich was born in a white, middle-class, southern world that greatly influenced her early work. Her father, Arnold Rice Rich, worked as a doctor at Johns Hopkins medical center, while her mother, Helen Jones Rich, gave up a career as a concert pianist and composer to raise her children.

Educated at home by her mother, but under the watchful eye of a demanding father, Rich was drawn toward the study of poetry, which she learned by copying the works of poets like Blake and Yeats over and over again; thus, it is no surprise that her first two collections, *A Change of World* (1953) and *The Diamond Cutters* (1955), showcase her formalist training. Rich went on to graduate from Radcliffe College, and, as is often noted, her career began when W. H. Auden selected her poem "A Change of World" for the Yale Series of Younger Poets Prize in 1951. In 1953, Rich married Alfred H. Conrad, an economist, and gave birth to three sons during the next six years. After separating from Conrad in the 1960s, Rich came out as a lesbian in 1976, and she began to live with **Michelle Cliff,** her life partner, with whom she coedited the lesbian/feminist journal *Sinister-Wisdom* from 1980 to 1984. Since 1984, Rich has lived in California.

Rich's works include more than 17 volumes of poetry and 5 nonfiction books that include her essays, as well as the seminal work *Of Woman Born: Motherhood as Experience and Institution* (1976). Rich's first collection, *A Change of World* (1951), reveals the beginnings of the voice we now associate with her poetry as the traces of confidence, anger, concern with women's positions, and the dangers of language all exist under the seemingly modest surface of poems that, as Auden famously stated, "do not tell fibs." In her prose writing, Rich explains that her style was formed by her schooling in male poetry, and it is not surprising that her first collection contains only three poems, out of forty, that concern women as their primary subject: "Aunt Jennifer's Tigers," "An Unsaid Word," and "Mathilde in Normandy." This formalist, objective poetic voice continues in *The Diamond Cutters* (1955), her second collection, and reviews from this time period categorize Rich's poetry as "sweet," "modest," and "delightful"—all gendered adjectives that downplay her poetic talent.

Many critics view *Snapshots of a Daughter-in-Law*, Rich's third collection, published in 1963, as a pivotal work. The title poem of the collection explores the representations of a number of different women—the southern belle, a housewife, a woman poet, as well as women striving to preserve their fading beauty. Rich places these women in a historical and cultural context as she purposefully adds quotations that reveal the expectations of the society and time periods these various women inhabited. This poem marks Rich's first foray into gendered experience, notable through her first use of the pronoun "she," and stands as an indication of Rich's future women-centered subject matter and concern with women's identities in a patriarchal culture.

After only hesitantly using the pronoun "she" in *Snapshots of a Daughter-in-Law*, Rich moved to confidently using the pronoun "I" in subsequent publications. With *Necessities of Life* (1966), Rich confronts the social construction of woman that trained her to write with a gender-neutral voice. Her reinterpretations of women's lives launched her fully on a feminist career, concerned with how women's identities are constructed by the cultures of North America. This collection was followed by *Leaflets* in 1969, which suggests that the poet believes language is the key to understanding identity, gender, and sexuality. Rich then shifted from the androgynous voice of *Diving into the Wreck* (1973) to a radical, lesbian-identified voice in *The Dream of a Common Language* (1977), which calls for a community based on the power of women rather than traditional patriarchal power.

The Dream of a Common Language also contains the "Twenty-One Love Poems" sequence, which provides a sharp break from Rich's previous work. Through these poems, Rich openly chooses lesbianism and women-identified communities. Motivated by the women's movement of the 1970s and her own feelings of desire for relationships with women, Rich's poetry confronts compulsory heterosexuality—the belief that the culture socializes people toward heterosexual relationships—and argues for a lesbian continuum. It is important to note that the term lesbian continuum means much more than simply describing Rich's sexual orientation. According to Rich, in her well-known essay "Compulsory Heterosexuality and Lesbian Existence," written in 1980, the term includes the range of women's experiences, including women's meaningful friendships.

From the early 1980s on, Rich's work becomes more politically charged as she articulates the cultural traditions and personal relationships within the United States that have influenced her understanding of self-identity. For example, *An Atlas of the Difficult World* (1991) examines North American culture and the poet's identity during the time of the first Persian Gulf War, while *Dark Fields of the Republic* (1995) asks readers to revision North America, to reconstruct the history of North America in an effort to accept personal and public responsibility for the oppressions and injustices riddled throughout history. In recent years, Rich's poems continue to interrogate American politics and culture as seen in *Midnight Salvage* (1999) and *The School among the Ruins* (2004); both collections acknowledge the power of language to inscribe meaning, to create and revise history, to foster or dismantle democracy. Throughout her later writings, Rich illustrates the need to understand one's identity and position in North America as individuals in one's local community and as citizens in the world.

Further Reading

Gelpi, Albert, and Barbara C. Gelpi, eds. 1993. *Adrienne Rich's Poetry and Prose: Poems, Prose, Reviews and Criticism*. New York: W. W. Norton.

Keyes, Claire. 1986. *The Aesthetic of Power: The Poetry of Adrienne Rich*. Athens: University of Georgia Press.

McGuirk, Kevin. 1993. "Philoctetes Radicalized: 'Twenty-One Love Poems' and the Lyric Career of Adrienne Rich." *Contemporary Literature* 34 (1): 61–87.

Stimpson, Catherine. 1985. "Adrienne Rich and Lesbian/Feminist Poetry." *Parnassus* 12 (2)–13 (1): 249–68.

Jeannette E. Riley

rights of association and assembly

The First Amendment declares that "Congress shall make no law…abridging the freedom of speech, or of the press, or the right of the people peaceably to assemble.…" These freedoms have been understood since at least the late 1950s to include a freedom of association allowing groups to organize for political and social purposes. For advocates of gay legal and social equality there has been no more reliable and important constitutional text than the First Amendment. The freedoms it guarantees have protected gay cultural and political institutions from state regulation designed to impose a contrary vision of the good life. Gay organizations, clubs, bars, journals, newspapers, radio programs, television shows—all these could be swept away in the absence of a strong First Amendment.

The First Amendment sheltered gays from some state regulation even when most of the country thought they were not just immoral but also sick and dangerous. In an era of almost unrelenting hostility, Yale law professor William Eskridge has written, "the right to associate was an appealing normative argument in both the political and judicial arenas" (1999, 114). The shelter afforded by this right allowed gays to organize for the purpose of accumulating and applying political power, a precondition for the effective exercise of other important liberties. For gay America, it truly is the First Amendment. It took a while to get to that point, however. Even as state authorities from the 1920s through 1960s harassed dissident political and civil rights organizations, they did the same to nascent gay associations.

The experience of the earliest known gay rights organization in the United States illustrates the destructive consequences of state intrusion into gay association. In 1924, a small group of gay men in Chicago decided to organize an association that would work for gay civil rights. "One of our greatest handicaps was the knowledge that homosexuals don't organize," wrote a leader of the group, Henry Gerber, almost four decades later. "Being thoroughly cowed, they seldom get together" (Katz 1992, 389). The key to overcoming inequality, in the eyes of the earliest organizers of the gay civil rights movement, was to form groups devoted to that goal. It was, in short, to form expressive associations.

Within months, authorities learned of the organization's existence. They quickly ordered the arrest of its leaders for disorderly conduct. The police, without a warrant but with a newspaper reporter in tow, arrested Gerber in his home at 2 A.M. They seized his typewriter, the literature of the society, his personal diaries, and his bookkeeping accounts. One of the organization's leaders pled guilty to the disorderly conduct charge. Gerber, who had also been threatened with a bogus federal obscenity charge, hired a lawyer. The disorderly conduct charge against Gerber was dismissed because of the warrantless search, and no obscenity charge was filed. However, he was promptly fired from his job at the post office for "conduct unbecoming a postal worker" (Katz 1992, 393). Although his attorney offered to sue to get the job back, Gerber "had no more money for fees and took no action" (Katz 1992, 393). The litigation had financially ruined him. The whole episode doomed the Society for Human Rights. It would be a quarter of a century before gays would again form an association explicitly dedicated to advancing their civil rights.

Two fledgling gay rights groups, the **Mattachine Society** (mostly men) and the **Daughters of Bilitis** (DOB) (women), formed in the 1950s. The Federal Bureau of Investigation (FBI) closely monitored their activities, beginning an internal security investigation of Mattachine in 1953 and of DOB in 1959. Neither group, of course, represented a credible internal security threat. "Nonetheless," William Eskridge (1999, 75) writes, "FBI agents infiltrated both organizations, archived their declarations and publications, reported their meetings and activities, recruited informants, compiled lists of members whom they could identify, and speculated on the organizations' influence and future activities." Agents interviewed the staff of the Mattachine's publication *One* and notified their employers. Group members resorted to using pseudonyms to protect their identity. Similar monitoring and harassment of gay groups by state and federal authorities occurred throughout the country. Police harassment and spying on gay organizations continued into the 1970s.

State intrusion on gay expressive association took many forms. Congress tried to revoke the Washington, D.C., Mattachine Society's license as an educational group on the ground that government should not support association by people whose acts were ungodly and illegal. The Internal Revenue Service initially refused to grant tax-exempt status to groups that "promoted" homosexuality. States like Ohio, New York, and Florida (which barred recognition of "organized homosexuality") disallowed the articles of incorporation of gay rights groups on public policy grounds. Gay bars were routinely raided and shut down as places of immoral congregation.

As the Supreme Court ruled in favor of stronger protection for the freedom of association in the late 1950s, gay political organizations, bars, and other groups benefited. For example, courts overturned many state decisions to deny corporate status to gay groups, often on freedom of association grounds. The associational freedom shielding a group's membership list from government officials was extended to gay groups. When public university administrators attempted in the 1970s and 1980s to deny school recognition and funding to gay student groups, their decisions were almost invariably reversed by courts applying the freedom of association precedents that had protected black civil rights organizations from state harassment.

The reasoning in one especially influential freedom of association decision, *Gay Students Organization of University of New Hampshire v. Bonner*, stands out: "The [Gay Student Organization's] efforts to organize the homosexual minority, 'educate' the public as to its plight, and obtain for it better treatment from individuals and from the government thus represent but another example of the associational activity unequivocally singled out for protection in the very 'core' of association cases decided by the Supreme Court...." (502 F.2d 652, 660 [1st Cir. 1974]). The decision in *Bonner* placed gays solidly inside the emerging First Amendment tradition protecting the freedom of association.

Even First Amendment freedom claims that started out by protecting organizations hostile to gay equality have been applied by courts to protect gays as well. In *Rosenberger v. Rector and Visitors of University of Virginia*, the Supreme Court held that a public university could not refuse to give funds from a student activities fee to a controversial Christian student newspaper espousing antigay views. Superficially a defeat for the interests of gays, *Rosenberger* was soon applied by a federal court to reverse the decision of another public university to deny funding to a gay student group. Congress passed the Equal Access Act of 1984 at the urging of social conservatives who wanted religious student groups to be able to meet on public school grounds. Since then the very same law, along with associational freedom claims, has been used by gay student groups to secure access to public facilities.

Not surprisingly, gay political organizations, bars, and other institutions have flourished since recognition of the freedom of association in the late 1950s. For example, by 1981, 80 percent of all public colleges had recognized gay student groups. The Gay, Lesbian, and Straight Education Network estimates there are now 700 gay-straight student alliances in high schools, few of which would exist without strong protection for associational liberty. The rise of gay equality and public visibility coincided—not coincidentally, however—with the rise of vigorous protection for First Amendment freedom, especially the freedom of association.

The freedom of association is not a one-way street. It protects the freedom of antigay groups to control their membership and their message just as much as it protects the freedom of gay rights groups. In 1991, the Supreme Court unanimously decided in *GLIB v. Hurley* that an Irish group could exclude a gay Irish contingent from its annual St. Patrick's Day parade in Boston.

In 2000, the Supreme Court held in *Boy Scouts v. Dale* that the freedom of association allows the Boy Scouts of America to exclude an openly gay scoutmaster. The Boy Scouts maintained that the presence of an openly gay scoutmaster was contrary to the group's teaching that a scout should strive to be "morally straight" and "clean." James Dale, who had been an Eagle Scout as a youth, sued based on a state law that forbade large groups like the Boy Scouts from discriminating on the basis of sexual orientation. The Supreme Court concluded that the Boy Scouts were an expressive association organized to instill what they regard as proper moral values in boys. These moral values would be compromised by the presence of an openly gay scoutmaster, held the Court. Additionally, the Court noted that a group's control over its own membership is critical to achieving its purposes. Thus, the Boy Scouts could not be required to admit Dale.

The *Hurley* and *Dale* decisions were denounced by many gay rights groups, which called them victories for intolerance and **homophobia.** Others, however, noted that it would set a dangerous precedent to allow the government to decide who a group must admit to its membership or parade. The freedom that allows an Irish group to exclude a gay contingent, for example, would allow religious fundamentalists to be excluded from an annual gay pride parade.

Further Reading

Carpenter, Dale. 2001. "Freedom of Expressive Association and Anti-Discrimination Law After *Dale*: A Tripartite Approach." *Minnesota Law Review* 85 (6): 1515–17.

Eskridge, William. 1999. *Gaylaw: Challenging the Apartheid of the Closet.* Cambridge, MA: Harvard University Press.

Katz, Jonathan Ned. 1992. *Gay American History: Lesbians and Gay Men in the U.S.A.* New York: Meridian.

Dale Carpenter

Jerome Robbins (1918–1998)

Jerome Robbins (né Rabinowitz) was born in New York City to Russian-Polish-Jewish immigrants who fled Russia to escape the pogroms. Always encouraged by his mother to participate in the arts, young Robbins played violin, composed his own music for the piano, wrote poetry and stories, and made puppets. His sister Sonja was raised to be the family dancer, with Jerome's dancing—an activity his parents found odd for a boy—initially limited to summer camp performances or fooling around with Sonja. He began taking modern dance classes in 1935. After beginning coursework in chemistry at New York University at the request of his parents, financial difficulties landed Robbins in his father's corset factory. Sonja helped her brother escape the factory by arranging an audition with Gluck Sandor, who urged the young dancer to train in ballet, a suggestion he heeded—despite his less-than-passionate feelings about this dance form.

In 1938, Robbins landed a spot in the chorus of the Broadway musical *Great Lady*. After its short run, he took work dancing and choreographing at Camp Tamiment in the Poconos. *Straw Hat Revue* (1939), a show comprised of dances and sketches from the summer performances, made its way to Broadway with Imogene Coca and Danny Kaye. Despite his extensive creative contribution, Robbins received no credit for his choreography, which led to his future stringent policies regarding rights and billing. Robbins's career took a turn with his next Broadway flop, *Keep off the Grass* (1940), when he crossed paths with renowned choreographer George Balanchine and headed into the first major phase of his career in ballet.

In 1940 Robbins successfully auditioned for the new Ballet Theatre, an organization presenting a combination of classical and innovative ballet. With 40 dollars a week, a steady dance gig, and the possibility of choreographing some of his own work for the company, he was set. Robbins stayed with Ballet Theatre until 1949, rising to the role of soloist by 1941. He originated such roles as Hermes in *Helen of Troy* (1942)—a comic performance that Agnes deMille claimed upstaged the prima ballerina—and Benvolio in *Romeo and Juliet* (1943). His continued work with Ballet Theatre ultimately led to Robbins's major break as a choreographer: in 1944, the company found itself with an unexpected hole in its schedule and offered the young choreographer the space for a one-act ballet. His one act, *Fancy Free,* stretched the bounds of traditional ballet to embrace movements more closely associated with vernacular dance and images specifically tied to the American experience. Based on a painting of three sailors on leave—*The Fleet Is In* by Paul Cadmus—*Fancy Free* integrated traditional narrative and ballet. Robbins received rave reviews upon the show's debut. Less than a year later, Betty Comden and Adolph Green wrote the book and lyrics for *On the Town,* the Broadway translation of *Fancy Free,* providing Robbins his first glimpse of success as a Broadway choreographer.

Over the following years, Robbins shifted back and forth between Broadway and ballet, choreographing successful shows like *High Button Shoes* (1947), for which he won the Tony for choreography, the autobiographical *Look Ma I'm Dancin'* (1948), and *The King and I* (1951). Simultaneously, he choreographed at the Ballet Theatre and Balanchine's New York City Ballet shows such as *Summer Day* (1947), *The Guests* (1949), and *Jones Beach* (1950, with Balanchine). Robbins was able to merge the two forms most successfully—and perhaps memorably—in his 1957 Tony Award–winning choreography for *West Side Story*. He saw the show as fulfilling his desire to integrate ballet, theatrical narrative, and opera more fully. The show also enabled him to delve into more emotional subject matter—startling critics with a death at the end—and allowed for further combination of traditional dance with everyday movement. Robbins soon headed to Hollywood to codirect the film version of *West Side Story* (1960). After he conceived of the famous opening aerial shot of New York City and choreographed "Cool," the production company fired Robbins from the project. He shared the 1961 Oscar for Best Direction of a Motion Picture with codirector Robert Wise and accepted an honorary Oscar for Brilliant Achievements in Art of Choreography in Film. After this bitter brush with Hollywood, however, he swore off motion pictures and California.

Despite his break with the movies, Robbins continued to thrive at ballet as well as musical and "legitimate" theater. In 1963 he directed Bertolt Brecht's *Mother Courage* and the dark comedy *Oh Dad, Poor Dad, Mama's Hung You in the Closet and I'm Feeling So Sad.* The 1964 musical *Fiddler on the Roof* brought dual Tony Awards for direction and choreography for Robbins. The project allowed him to integrate his Jewish heritage as he worked to distance the piece from standard dance numbers and create a show around natural movements and celebrations of the Jewish tradition. In 1966 a grant from the National Endowment for the Arts allowed him to open the American Theatre Lab, an experimental dance lab. In the 1970s and 1980s, while largely eschewing the theater, Robbins choreographed over 40 original ballets, mainly with the New York City Ballet (of which he was ultimately co-balletmaster until he stepped down in 1990). He choreographed and directed his final Broadway show, *Jerome Robbins Broadway*, in 1989, and through that showcase of his most famous numbers he preserved his work for future generations.

Alongside decades of professional success, Robbins endured public and private tribulations as he found both his sexuality and politics fodder for scrutiny. In 1953 Robbins appeared in front of the House Un-American Activities Committee (HUAC) for his participation in the Communist-affiliated Theatrical Transient Group. With a possible threat of his sexuality being revealed if he did not cooperate, he ultimately named names (but managed to evade a crippling blow to his career). As a male dancer maturing in the highly **homophobic** 1930s, 1940s, and 1950s, Robbins struggled with conflicting desires to live up to his family's traditional expectations and to raise a family and his burgeoning sexual ambivalence. He was linked romantically with dancer Buzz Miller and Hollywood idol Montgomery Clift, as well as engaged to dancer Nora Kaye and intimately linked with longtime friend Christine Conrad. His personal struggles emerged in his work as early as the ballet piece *Facsimile* (1944), featuring three lonely individuals—two men and a woman. As the men struggle for the woman's attention, they nearly kiss each other. Ironically, *Facsimile* was performed by Robbins, Kaye, and Johnny Kriza (rumored to have attracted the affections of the choreographer). Robbins's unfinished *Poppa Piece* was to be a penultimate rumination on his strained relationship with his father, HUAC trials, and sexual experiences. The choreographer ultimately found the piece too painful to complete.

Robbins left a lasting impression on the worlds of ballet and musical theater and brought the two closer together. His perfectionism and respect for his craft led to increased acknowledgment of the choreographer's role, as Robbins fought to retain the rights to his Broadway choreography and to receive recognized billing. Robbins helped shape the coming decades of musical theater by providing Bob Fosse with his first big break choreographing *The Pajama Game* (1954) and later *Bells Are Ringing* (1956). His legacy also includes charitable acts through the Jerome Robbins Foundation. Founded in 1958 to honor his mother, the organization sought to give financial support to activities in dance and theater. As the creative communities suffered through the AIDS crisis, Robbins directed additional foundation funds toward AIDS organizations. In 1964 he turned his checkbook toward preserving dance performances by donating a half a percent of his residuals from *Fiddler on the Roof* to create the Lena Robbins Dance Film Archive (now the Jerome Robbins Archive of the Recorded Moving Image) at the New York Public Library. He would succumb to a stroke on July 29, 1998, only two months after mounting *Les Noces* for the New York City Ballet's 50th-anniversary season.

Further Reading

Conrad, Christine. 2000. *Jerome Robbins: That Broadway Man*. London: Booth-Clibborn Editions.

Jowitt, Deborah. 2004. *Jerome Robbins: His Life, His Theatre, His Dance*. New York: Simon and Schuster.

Lawrence, Greg. 2001. *Dance with Demons: The Life of Jerome Robbins*. New York: G. P. Putnam's Sons.

Vaill, Amanda. 2006. *Somewhere: The Life of Jerome Robbins*. New York: Broadway Books.

Kelly Kessler

Aleida Rodríguez (1953–)

Aleida Rodríguez was born in Cuba and at age nine was one of 15,000 Cuban children brought to the United States for temporary adoptive living after Fidel Castro came to power. In 1967 her Cuban parents emigrated to Los Angeles, and she rejoined them. She attended classes at the Boston Conservatory of Music, at California State University in Los Angeles, and at the University of California, Los Angeles, and founded Books of a Feather, a woman-run press, in Los Angeles. *Garden of Exile* appeared in 1999; it was selected by the *San Francisco Chronicle* as one of the best books of 2000 and won several literary awards.

Further Reading

Costa, Maria Dolores, ed. 2003. *Latina Lesbian Writers and Artists*. New York: Harrington Park Press.

John C. Hawley

Richard Rodríguez (1944–)

Born in San Francisco, Richard Rodríguez was the third of four children in a working-**class** Mexican immigrant family. The seasonal rhythms of field labor in California's Central Valley became part of Rodríguez's imaginative landscape when the family moved to Sacramento. Identifying as mestizo, Catholic, and queer, Rodríguez embodies paradoxes that make his material challenging to classify. His probing, lyric, and often-controversial essays have established him as one of America's most distinguished public intellectuals. In his memoir titled *Hunger of Memory* (1982), Rodríguez performed what he now calls the optimistic Protestant act of affirming his individual identity. He describes working intensely to translate his private ambitions within American culture by speaking English, performing diligently in school, and studying classic literature of the West. Although the focus on literacy as a key to autonomy placed Rodríguez in the company of writers such as Frederick Douglass, **James Baldwin,** and Ralph Ellison, some academics and Chicano activists criticized Rodríguez for speaking against bilingual education and quota-style affirmative action in this book.

In two subsequent essay collections, *Days of Obligation* (1992) and *Brown: The Last Discovery of America* (2002), Rodríguez examines shifts of ethnic, religious, and cultural identity on an international scale. He weaves reflections about faith, art, and sexuality into a vast historical and political scope, connecting the peoples of Mexico, America, and Europe. Exploring dilemmas of his own existence inside cultural borderlands, Rodríguez locates creative and erotic power in what he calls "browning," as traditions and races overlap, merge, and change, losing their idealized purity. He embraces this phenomenon as an alternative to intellectual polarities that too glibly divide self from other.

Rodríguez completed degrees at Stanford, Columbia (where he also attended Union Theological Seminary), and Berkeley. As a Fulbright scholar, he studied at London's Warburg Institute. Despite prestigious offers, Rodríguez has refused university professorships because of his frustrations with political correctness. He eventually returned to his birthplace, San Francisco, where he now lives and writes. His essays appear regularly on *The News Hour with Jim Lehrer* on PBS.

Further Reading

Elie, Paul. 2004. "A Fugitive Catholicism: The Work of Richard Rodríguez, Dave Eggers and Czeslaw Milosz." *Commonweal* 131 (19): 35–40.

Romero, Rolando J. 2004. "Richard Rodriguez (1944–)." In *Latino and Latina Writers, I: Introductory Essays, Chicano and Chicana Authors*, ed. Alan West-Durán, 455–74. New York: Scribner's.

Torres, Hector A. 2003. "'I Don't Think I Exist': Interview with Richard Rodríguez." *MELUS: The Journal of the Society for the Study of the Multi-Ethnic Literature of the United States* 28 (2):164–202.

Jo Scott-Coe

Roman Catholicism

In approaching this broad topic of investigation, it is crucial to note that *homosexuality* itself as a term referring to a psychological condition that grounds a psychological, personal, and sexual identity did not enter into common usage until the late nineteenth century. Prior to the development of psychological theories purporting to account for and map the terrains of human sexuality, and establishing sexuality in theories of a psychological person, Catholic moral and theological discourse focused primarily on sexual acts performed by human moral agents without advertence to psychological or biological factors bearing on the development of **sexualities** or sexual identities. It is necessary to read both the history of Catholic treatment of same-gender sex and current debates over Catholic teaching on the matter in light of this crucial fact.

PREMODERN APPROACHES

It is not easy to generalize about the early church's approach to same-sex relations since there is little advertence to it in the early literature. Instead, it is instructive to understand the array of views about sexuality and the body that stretched from the subapostolic church, influenced by the writings of Paul of Tarsus, to the developments that attended the gradual Hellenization of Christianity in the second and third centuries (Brown 1988). The popular interpretation of the Pauline spirit-flesh dualism also led to suspicion of the body (even though this is not what Paul intended by use of that metaphor). Through this entire period, early Christianity worked within a tension between social obligations toward marriage (still a civil and family institution and not yet a sacrament) and the ideal of sexual renunciation. Early Christian rationales for marriage varied from marriage serving as a defense against desire, to toleration of it as a school of wisdom, to the assumption by the second and third centuries that marriage was indeed the norm for young men and women. Still, undergirding this development in attitudes toward marriage was the sense that sexual urges, particularly among young men, even more than among young women, were potentially dangerous, unleashing uncontrollable forces. The sheer power of sexual urges was to be countered by a disciplined aspiration toward continence, order, and a cultivation of the spiritual senses. By the fifth century, sexual renunciation in the form of consecrated states of continence or celibacy had become a widespread practice among Christians. (Its adoption as a canonical discipline for the clergy was to emerge later.)

During this period, Christian theology did not dwell on the morality or immorality of same-sex relations. It was assumed that such acts lay outside the field of sanctioned sex in which Christians could participate. In an era prior to a modern critical understanding of scripture, Paul's injunctions against same-sex activity (particularly in Romans) and other passages of scripture apparently condemning such activity were taken for granted: such acts lay outside the pale of a Christian worldview. Two important points need to be made in this regard. First, the texts condemning same-sex activity to be found in the Hebrew Scriptures (Old Testament) and the writings of Paul are focusing on sexual acts and are not referring to what would later be understood as a homosexual condition or the relations that might flow from a committed same-gender relationship. This focus on acts would pervade Christian thinking about sexuality (and, later on, homosexuality) in a significant way. Second, even though such acts lay outside the sanctioned range of possibility for Christians, early Christians may have observed a degree of toleration toward non-Christians who did engage in such practices (**Boswell** 2005). In addition, some scholars contend that there is some evidence that certain same-sex unions received official sanction in some places (Boswell 2005), although this interpretation of events is contested by various historians. There can also be little doubt that male participants in same-sex acts were viewed with suspicion, especially the passive partners.

This focus on acts, however, was to undergo a gradual shift from a term descriptive of types of acts into a substantive category of sin and, finally, to the attribution of a particular identity to those who engaged in such sinful acts. In *The Invention of Sodomy in Christian Theology*, theologian Mark Jordan describes the shift of interpretation of Genesis 19, the story of the city of Sodom, from one of divine retribution for refusal of hospitality into a story exclusively about sex among men. This hermeneutical shift corresponded to a gradual shift of the ancient notion of *luxuria* (connoting self-indulgence and self-gratification) into a sexual sin. In the fourteenth century, Peter Damian, writing at a time of some concern over the sexual activity of clerics who had taken vows of celibacy, linked this category of sin to the forces of the libido, describing a "sodomitic vice" that included masturbation, mutual masturbation, and other same-sex acts. Appealing to reason and natural law, Damian described sodomy as a sin against the order of creation itself—a sin that cannot be repented of and is deserving of death.

It was a short move from the establishment of the theological category of sodomy as a set of sinful sexual acts to the description of the sexual actors as sinful sodomites. While this was not tantamount to a modern sense of a self-claimed identity (e.g., as a homosexual or a gay person), it nevertheless gave objective status to this class of sinner. The objectification of same-sex acts as a particular kind of sin, and indeed of the actors as particularly named sinners, resulted in the inclusion in confessors' manuals (the penitentials) of advice about how the confessor could best deal with the sodomites who might confess their sin. Ironically, for some theologians, masturbation was viewed as a more serious sin than sodomy, as it involved the spilling of seed intended for procreation. Damian's theological developments paved the way for such theologians as Thomas Aquinas to view sodomy as a sin against nature.

THE NATURAL LAW TRADITION

Strongly informing the Catholic approach to homosexuality in modern times has been the natural law tradition within Catholic philosophical theology. Natural law tradition has an enormously rich and complex history. In its classical formulation, it is influenced by the Stoic notion that "nature" denotes the order of the universe and that reason (*logos*) is the key to understanding that order. The order of nature rests on principles of causality and finality (teleology) with a view toward how all the parts of nature conspire together toward a universal harmony. In Aristotle, and later in Roman philosophy (Cicero), this order is seen to be properly reflected in society and human institutions: there is a morally legitimate moral order within which human beings function. Within such a view, Roman society viewed marriage as a constitutive part of the natural order of society, and Roman citizens had an obligation to enter into marriage in order to produce new Roman citizens and to contribute to the general order of society. This emphasis on social order was reflected in the writings of Augustine of Hippo, who saw the ends of persons as fulfilled in and through a constellation of Christian virtues, ascertainable on the basis of revelation (scripture and tradition), reason, and human experience. The stress in this tradition is on the building of virtue.

The medieval period, however, saw a shift from a natural social teleology to a supernatural teleology reached through the eternal laws inscribed in human nature, where the human person is understood as an individually embodied being of a rational nature. This led to a focus not on general teleology but to a more particular finality, how various faculties of embodied nature, when used in accordance with reason, might lead toward the created ends of those faculties. Thus, Thomas Aquinas would argue that reason tells us that human nature has three basic inclinations: to keep ourselves in existence, to procreate and to educate offspring, and to worship

God. Use of bodies, or parts thereof, that might not lead to these ends could not be understood as rationally working in accord with the laws of nature. The most defined form of this approach was a physicalism or biologism, which tended to reduce human nature to objective biological parts, so that particular physical acts, such as masturbation, could be viewed as contrary to natural law because the organ involved is not being used for its created end, procreation. In general, this later part of the tradition of natural law has strongly informed Catholic understanding of human sexuality up to the present time. Homosexuality was simply assumed alongside other extramarital sex acts to be contrary to nature and certainly intrinsically evil. But there were developments in the understanding of human sexuality, even within this tradition. While in *Casti Connubii* (1931), Pope Pius XI focused on procreation as the end of marriage, the famous birth control encyclical, *Humanae Vitae* (1968), of Pope Paul VI developed the openings made by his predecessors toward viewing the ends of marriage not only as procreative but unitive.

CURRENT CHURCH TEACHING

The vectors set by Damian and medieval theology, reinforced by a narrower reading of natural law, obtained in Catholic theology and teaching until the late twentieth century. Several developments led to a new appraisal of the church's position and its adequacy. Three stand out: (1) developments in the theology of marriage, (2) developments in the medical and psychological understandings of human sexuality, and (3) massive social changes surrounding sexual identity and practices.

Developments in the Catholic understanding of marriage had subtle ripple effects in understanding human sexuality. Preeminent among these was the theological development in *Humanae Vitae* mentioned above, that the ends of marriage are not only procreation but the unity of the marriage partners themselves in sacramental marriage. This approach acknowledged the possibility that not every sexual act issues in conception and that, indeed, couples could arrange (through nonartificial means) to engage in sexual acts with an explicit intention to avoid conception. There thus entered into the consciousness of Catholic moral reasoning the admission that sexual union involved dimensions that could be conducive to ends other than procreation. Sexuality itself was now subtly separated out from a singular focus on its natural procreative end.

These developments in Catholic moral theology were occurring as psychological and medical understandings of human sexuality were themselves developing. Freud's psychological theories gave rise to a range of theories about the origin of same-sex attraction, and therefore about the moral and ethical status of homosexuality, not as a description of sexual acts and actors, but as a psychological condition. Although this condition was heavily "medicalized" in its interpretation and "treatment" in the first half of the twentieth century, the assumption of an identity as a homosexual person, later as a gay, lesbian, or transgendered person, was developing at the same time. By the second half of the twentieth century, early Freudian categories had generally been abandoned for an eclectic understanding of human sexuality, as had the medicalization of homosexuality and its interpretation as a pathology.

This, in turn, corresponded with the emergence of openness about sexuality in general and a gradual toleration of homosexual persons as people who assumed an identity as such. While the etiology of homosexuality continued to be debated (Was it the result of genetic determination, genetic predisposition mixed with volitional factors, or purely an act of freedom?), the fact of the existence of homosexual persons and their lives became more visible and, in some quarters, accepted. The so-called sexual revolution of the 1960s and 1970s in particular posed a challenge to traditional Catholic approaches to homosexuality, which up to then could presume upon the consensus that homosexual acts are sins to be avoided.

In light of these developments, a series of major teachings on human sexuality and/or homosexuality emerged that aimed to clarify the church's position. The foundational Catholic position on homosexuality was established in *Homosexualitatis problema* (1986) (the English title is "Letter to the Bishops of the Catholic Church on the Pastoral Care of Homosexual Persons"). This document followed an earlier document, *Persona humana* (1976), that had taught that a homosexual inclination (same-sex attraction) is not a sin, although homosexual acts are intrinsically disordered. Still, the 1986 document expressed concern that an "overly benign" interpretation of homosexuality had been given from certain readings of the earlier document. Therefore, *Homosexualitatis problema* went further: "Although the particular inclination of the homosexual person is not a sin, it is a more or less strong tendency ordered toward an intrinsic moral evil; and thus the inclination itself must be seen as an objective disorder" (*Homosexualitatis problema* Web site). The document clearly states the practical implication for homosexuals of this teaching: "Therefore special concern and pastoral attention should be directed toward those who have this condition, lest they be led to believe that the living out of this orientation in homosexual activity is a morally acceptable option. It is not" (*Homosexualitatis problema* Web site).

The teaching wishes to state that the attraction of one person for another of the same gender is not in itself a sin but, if acted upon, would be objectively sinful. The inclination of one person toward another of the same gender is therefore, in itself, objectively disordered, that is, not in keeping with the normal order of nature, because, if acted upon, it can only lead to sin, an intrinsic evil, and not toward a good. The teaching does not wish to imply that the homosexual person himself or herself is somehow disordered but only that their condition is itself objectively disordered. It is important to note that this teaching therefore does not focus only on sex acts, as older moral theology had done, even in the theology of Peter Damian; this teaching focuses on the inclination itself of one person toward another of the same gender: this inclination is the fundamental problem, even if it is not in itself sinful. The person in possession of this objective disorder is the object of pastoral concern, precisely because of the disorder. The essential parts of this teaching were later enshrined in the *Catechism of the Catholic Church* (1994).

This teaching reflects a mixture of older Catholic theological principles rooted in theories of natural law, which focuses on objective reality and makes moral determinations about that objective reality, and a certain quasi-psychological understanding of homosexual inclinations, similar to those found in the older Freudian schools, which sees them not only as nonnormative but as essentially pathological. This synthesis is captured in the language of "objective disorder." Critics of this approach have argued that, despite the intentions of the teaching, it can be read as casting homosexual persons themselves, not only their inclination, into the category of the objectively disordered and, even more, suggesting that they are therefore themselves intrinsically ordered toward evil by virtue of that condition. While this is not the intention of the teaching, the critique has forced further study of the basic assumptions about homosexuality that the teaching implies. The writings of theologians such as James Alison and Mark Jordan, and ethicists such as James Keenan, Stephen Pope, and Margaret Farley, present some of the more compelling theological analyses of this teaching or its implications.

LATER DEVELOPMENTS

Catholicism as an institution continues to struggle with how to incorporate developments in the understanding of human sexuality, including homosexuality, into a religion that is defined not only by church teaching but by actual communities of faith. Five modern developments bear mention: (1) efforts by homosexual Catholics themselves to establish communities of faith and to work for inclusion in the regular life of the church, (2) the effects of the AIDS epidemic on Catholic approaches to homosexuality, (3) the crisis over sexuality within the Catholic clergy, (4) efforts by U.S. bishops and some other bishops' conferences to address homosexuality within the parameters of cultures that have found ways of accommodating the reality of homosexuality within social life, and (5) the effects of the movement toward same-sex marriage and broadened understandings of family.

The gay Catholic organization DignityUSA is perhaps the best-known effort by homosexual Catholics to establish a presence within the institutional church and to provide a place where they might participate fully in the sacramental life of the church. Founded in 1969, Dignity also advocates for the legal rights of gay, lesbian, bisexual, and transgendered people, including Catholics. This advocacy function, together with the perception that Dignity did not uphold church teaching, led to the banning of Dignity from Catholic properties, beginning in 1986. Today, the vast majority of Dignity chapters meet in Protestant churches or other venues. A number of other ministries and movements emerged during this period, including New Ways Ministry, founded by Sister Jeanne Grammick and Father Patrick Nugent in 1978. Sister Grammick and Father Nugent were removed from their ministry under Vatican pressure, but the organization continues under lay leadership, and a number of other advocacy groups have sprung from it, including several led by parents of gay and lesbian Catholics. In the wake of the Vatican action against Dignity, a small number of Catholic dioceses inaugurated ministries to gay and lesbian Catholics.

The emergence of AIDS on the world scene in 1982 was another factor that brought to the fore the reality of sexually active gay Catholics, apparently including some members of the clergy, within the church itself. This led to multiple responses by the church, notably a concerted effort on the part of Catholic dioceses and charitable institutions to provide spiritual, social, and medical services to people with AIDS. One result of this involvement was the establishment of the National Catholic AIDS Network in 1989, which links various Catholic agencies and individuals involved in ministry to persons with AIDS and which in recent years has turned its attention to the burgeoning AIDS problem outside the United States. The presence of AIDS within the church, including among clergy, forced a recognition within the public rhetoric of the church of the reality of Catholic homosexuals and more open and frank discussions of church teaching on homosexuality and the prevention of HIV infection.

Correlative with these developments in the church and in wider society, evidence gradually emerged that a statistically significant number of Catholic priests were of homosexual orientation and that some of them were sexually active, or at least had been to some degree, however limited. Part of the evidence came with a number of priests succumbing to AIDS, apparently acquired through sexual transmission. There were also a number of cases of priests who had been involved in pedophilia, the sexual abuse of children, and particularly ephebophilia, the sexual abuse of boys. In fact, the majority of these cases involved the sexual abuse of boys. While ephebophilia is not endemic to homosexual orientation, an objectively determinable form of same-sex behavior was nevertheless involved in these cases. Unlike the homosexuality described even in church teaching, these were pathological sex acts, deriving in many cases from proven emotional or mental pathology. Nevertheless, the crisis had a chilling effect within some sectors of the priesthood and in the larger life of the church. In 2006 the Vatican Congregation for Education issued a document banning men of homosexual orientation from seminaries.

In the face of a greater awareness of homosexuality as a reality among families and in broader social life, some bishops' conferences have attempted to provide more pastoral approaches to addressing the challenges that homosexual Catholics face within the church itself. Two documents from the U.S. bishops are noteworthy: "Always Our Children" (1997) and, more recently, "Ministry to Persons with a Homosexual Inclination: Guidelines for Pastoral Care" (2006), which provide directives for the baptism of the children of homosexual couples in Catholic churches and also counsels parishes to be welcoming of gay couples. Both documents also reiterate the teaching of the church found in the *Catechism of the Catholic Church*, which is a distillation of the 1986 document, *Homosexualitatis problema*.

Related to this latter document is the fact that some Catholic churches in the United States and other Western cultures now include among their parishioners open, committed gay and lesbian couples, many of whom have **adopted** children. Some of these people are among those in the United States and elsewhere who advocate marriage for homosexual couples. While the chances are nonexistent that the Catholic Church will change its teachings on Christian marriage so as to include homosexual unions, the fact that homosexuals are marrying in some countries or states or are living in long-term committed relationships, and for life, has forced an expansion of the church's understanding of homosexuality from a category of sinful conduct to a social reality that cannot be ignored. This massive social shift becomes evident in the Church itself when such couples present children for baptism and education in Catholic schools. Where this change in understanding of homosexuality will lead cannot be predicted. How the Catholic Church itself might lead societies in the future on questions related to it is equally unpredictable.

See also Protestants, evangelical; Protestants, mainline.

Further Reading

Boswell, John. 2005. *Christianity, Social Tolerance, and Homosexuality: Gay People in Western Europe from the Beginning of the Christian Era to the Fourteenth Century.* Chicago: University of Chicago Press.

Brown, Peter. 1988. *The Body and Society: Men, Women and Sexual Renunciation in Early Christianity* (Part 1). New York: Columbia University Press.

Catechism of the Catholic Church. 2003. New York: Doubleday.

Farley, Margaret. 2006. *Just Love: A Framework for Christian Sexual Ethics.* New York: Continuum.

Homosexualitatis Problema. Available (in English) at: http://www.vatican.va/roman_curia/con gregations/cfaith/documents/rc_con_cfaith_doc_19861001_homosexual-persons_en.html. Accessed July 20, 2008.

John Paul II. 1997. *The Theology of the Body: Human Love in the Divine Plan* (portions). New York: Pauline Books & Media.

Jordan, Mark. 1998. *The Invention of Sodomy in Christian Theology.* Chicago: University of Chicago Press.

Stevenson, Thomas B. 2006. *Sons of the Church: The Witnessing of Gay Catholic Men.* Binghamton, NY: Harrington Park Press.

Paul G. Crowley

Ned Rorem (1923–)

Ned Rorem is an American composer and memoirist. Rorem was born in Richmond, Indiana, and reared as a Quaker. He attended the American Conservatory, Northwestern University, the Curtis Institute, and the Juilliard School and studied privately with Leo Sowerby, **Aaron Copland,** and **Virgil Thomson.** His many awards include Fulbright and Guggenheim fellowships, a Pulitzer Prize (1976) for his orchestral suite *Air Music,* and France's *Ordre des Arts et des Lettres* (2004). The Atlanta Symphony Orchestra won a Grammy Award for Best Orchestral Recording in 1989 for a collection of Rorem's music. He has taught at the University of Buffalo, the University of Utah, and the Curtis Institute. Several of his composition students have launched successful careers; the best known is opera composer Daron Hagen.

Like **Paul Bowles,** Rorem achieved distinction as both writer and composer. Expatriate life from 1949 to 1958 provided the grist for his wittily readable *Paris Diary* (1966), which offered an indiscreet glimpse into gay circles among the talented and famous in cosmopolite society. His later diaries *New York Diary* (1967), *An Absolute Gift* (1978), *The Nantucket Diary* (1987), *Knowing When to Stop* (1994), and *Facing the Night: A Diary and Musical Writings* (2005), as well as two published volumes of correspondence, have undoubtedly contributed to the public's curiosity about his music. Rorem's writings about music, collected in anthologies such as *Music from the Inside Out* (1967), *Music and People* (1968), *Setting the Tone* (1983), and *Settling the Score* (1988), are treasured for their acerbic and candid evaluations of his contemporaries' music. He has frequently disagreed with the evolution of a semiofficial canon of twentieth-century candidates for the standard repertory and is an inexhaustible critic of the system that lavishly rewards famous performers, leaving the composers who write music for them in comparative neglect.

Rorem's earliest successes and fame were generated by his songs, but as his career progressed he composed numerous longer works. Rorem's orchestral works include *Pilgrims* (1958), *Air Music* (1976), and *String Symphony* (1985). His Symphony No. 3, premiered by **Leonard Bernstein** and the New York Philharmonic at Carnegie Hall in April 1959, is the most performed of his large-scale orchestral works. Notable conductors who have programmed his works include Leopold Stokowski, Dmitri Mitropoulos, Eugene Ormandy, Maurice Abravanel, Kurt Masur, Zubin Mehta, and André Previn. Rorem has written concertos for piano, flute, organ, and English horn, a "mallet concerto" for percussionist Evelyn Glennie, a double concerto for violin and cello, and an unpublished harpsichord concerto. His chamber works include three piano sonatas, five string quartets, and numerous pieces for flute, cello, or guitar, solo or in various combinations.

Rorem has written several short operas and two full-length ones. The most recent, *Our Town* (2006), with a libretto by Sandy McClatchy based on the play by Thornton Wilder, is the most successful. The others include *A Childhood Miracle* (1951); *The Robbers* (1956), with a libretto by the composer, revised by **Marc Blitzstein;** *Bertha* (1968); *Three Sisters Who Are Not Sisters* (1968), a setting of a text by Gertrude Stein; and *Fables,* a short opera written in 1970, based on poems of La Fontaine in Marianne Moore's translations. An opera based on Strindberg's play *Miss Julie,* written in 1965, has been revived with success after a substantial revision in 1978. A new opera based on the comic strip *Little Nemo* has been commissioned by the Sarasota Youth Orchestra for the 2009 season.

By common consent Rorem's lasting fame will likely rest on his compositions for voice: the operas, numerous choral works, and over 300 songs, which include settings of texts by Paul Goodman, Janet Flanner, **Elizabeth Bishop,** W. H. Auden, Frank O'Hara, Thom Gunn, and Walt Whitman. He won extensive critical notice and praise for the song cycle "Poems of Love and the Rain" (1962/1963), in which nine poems are each set twice, to contrasting music. The 1994 song cycle "Evidence of Things Not Seen," one of his most-performed recent works, was followed in 2002 by "Another Sleep," a memorial to his long-term companion Jim Holmes, who died of AIDS in 1999. Rorem has long been identified as the foremost living composer of the art song, and his catalog in this genre is his surest enduring legacy. Singers Phyllis Curtin, Gianna d'Angelo, Donald Gramm, Leontyne Price, and Susan Graham have championed and recorded his songs. Described in one of the standard Grove dictionaries as "lean and firmly elegant," Rorem's music, while modern, has consistently avoided avant-garde fads and gimmicks.

Further Reading

Hubbs, Nadine. 2004. *The Queer Composition of America's Sound: Gay Modernists, American Music and National Identity*. Berkeley: University of California Press.

Christopher H. Walker

Paul Rudnick (1957–)

Piscataway, New Jersey, native Paul Rudnick—screenwriter, novelist, and prolific dramatist—claims an interest in celebrating absurdity. His comedies *Poor Little Lambs* and *Cosmetic Surgery* received mixed reviews. However, his third play, *I Hate Hamlet* (1991), solidified his steady and popular theater career. *Hamlet* centers on television actor Andrew Rally, cautiously accepting training for the role of Hamlet from deceased Shakespearean actor John Barrymore, whose ghost is channeled during a séance. This play's successor, the revolutionary and award-winning *Jeffrey* (1992), presents a young, gay, promiscuous Jeffrey who, terrified by the rampant AIDS epidemic, chooses to abstain from sex but falls in love with HIV-infected Steve. Following the success of *Jeffrey*, Rudnick penned the farce *The Naked Eye* (1996), set at a Mapplethorpe exhibit, and the one-act *Mr. Charles, Currently of Palm Beach* (1998), featuring the flamboyant host of a cable access program. Rudnick returned that same year with *The Most Fabulous Story Ever Told*, a biblical twist presenting gay couple Adam and Steve and their lesbian friends Jane and Mabel. In 2004, Rudnick transgressed historical lines in *Valhalla*, which brings together the stories of Ludwig of Bavaria, the mad king of the 1880s, and James Avery, a 1940s Texas teenager, by means of the opera *Lohengrin*. Rudnick continues to live and write in New York City.

Further Reading

Clum, John. 1994. *Acting Gay: Homosexuality in Modern Drama*. Rev. ed. New York: Columbia University Press.

"Paul Rudnick." 1996. *American Repertory Theater*. May 1, 1996. Available at: http://www.amrep.org/people/rudnick.html. Accessed July 20, 2008.

Román, David. 1998. *Acts of Intervention: Performance, Gay Culture, and AIDS*. Bloomington: Indiana University Press.

John Pruitt

Muriel Rukeyser (1913–1980)

Muriel Rukeyser was a prolific writer and political activist. Her work sought to integrate the public and the private while shattering the silence surrounding common themes of women's experience. Rukeyser grew up in an upwardly mobile

Jewish family in New York City. She attended elite private schools and Vassar and Columbia until her father's financial troubles forced her to leave college. Rukeyser's family eventually disinherited her. She was married for two months, after which her marriage was annulled. She later raised a son as a single mother, never publicly revealing the father's identity. Although bisexual, Rukeyser never explicitly spoke or wrote about her sexual relationships with women.

Rukeyser was fascinated by science and technology. She also had a strong sense of history and of her role in it. She was drawn to Communism and other political movements of the Left, although she refused to follow any party line. Rukeyser's political independence drew attacks from critics on the Right and the Left. In 1933, Rukeyser was arrested in Alabama while reporting on the famous Scottsboro trial. As a journalist, she also traveled to Spain at the beginning of the Spanish Civil War and investigated the Gauley Bridge, West Virginia, silicon-mining disaster. She traveled to North Vietnam in 1972 on a peace mission with fellow writer Denise Levertov. In 1972, she held a silent protest vigil outside South Korean poet Kim Chi-Ha's prison cell.

Rukeyser received the Yale Younger Poets Prize at the age of 21 for her first book of poetry, *Theory of Flight* (1935). In 1967, she was elected to the National Institute of Arts and Letters. Rukeyser published 18 volumes of poetry, 3 biographies, a series of lectures, a novel, numerous translations, children's books, and plays. She taught at Vassar, Sarah Lawrence College, and the California Labor School. She also worked in theater and film and as a consultant for the Exploratorium, a San Francisco arts and science museum. In the 1960s and 1970s, Rukeyser served as the president of PEN's American Center. Kenneth Rexroth called Rukeyser "the best poet of her exact generation." She had a profound influence on many subsequent women writers, including Anne Sexton and **Adrienne Rich.**

Further Reading

Herzog, Anne F., and Janet E. Kaufman, eds. 1999. *"How Shall We Tell Each Other of the Poet?"*: *The Life and Writing of Muriel Rukeyser*. New York: St. Martin's Press.

Kertesz, Louise. 1980. *The Poetic Vision of Muriel Rukeyser*. Baton Rouge: Louisiana State University Press.

Erica Reichert

Jane Rule (1931–2007)

Novelist, short-story writer, and essayist Jane Rule was born in Plainfield, New Jersey, graduated from Mills College, briefly attended University College, London, and Stanford University, and taught English and biology in Massachusetts before moving to Vancouver, Canada, in 1956. She lectured at the University of British Columbia from 1959 to 1972 and began to write full-time in 1974. Rule received awards including the Terasen Lifetime Achievement Award for Outstanding Literary Career in British Columbia (1996); the Canadian Institute Award for the Blind Book of the Year for *After the Fire* (1991); the U.S. Gay Academic Union Literature Award (1978); the Canadian Authors Association Best Story of the Year Award

(1978); and the Canadian Authors Association Best Novel of the Year Award for *The Young in One Another's Arms* (1978).

Rule's first and best-known novel, *Desert of the Heart* (1964), gave lesbians a different kind of fiction, leading away from the stereotypes of many previous novels. The story is about Evelyn, a professional who came to Reno awaiting a divorce, and Ann, who is younger and free-spirited. This led to the film *Desert Hearts* (1986). The novel and movie are considered classics among the lesbian community.

Rule confronts the silence and lies in lesbian writings in positive ways. She offers a uniquely optimistic view not often found in such themed texts. While Rule's material often relates to lesbian relationships, she goes beyond and weaves in many other life issues, including different types of loss. *Memory Board*'s (1987) Constance suffers from short-term memory issues, *After the Fire*'s (1989) characters learn to live united and independently after separations, and *Against the Season*'s (1971) Amelia deals with the loss of her sister. Other subject matter revolves around families, finding oneself sexually or otherwise, and a variety of women's issues. *The Young in One Another's Arms* (1977) is a multifaceted novel set at the end of the Vietnam War, combining issues of race, gender, sexuality, and politics.

Rule has also published short story collections such as *Theme for Diverse Instruments: Stories* (1975), *Outlander* (1981), and *Inland Passage* (1985) and nonfiction including *Lesbian Images* (1975) and *Hot-Eyed Moderate* (1985). In *Lesbian Images* she discusses her own sexuality and the history of lesbianism.

Detained at Customs: Jane Rule Testifies at the Little Sister's Trial (1995) deals with testimony in the Supreme Court of British Columbia on behalf of Little Sister's Book and Art Emporium on October 24, 1994, during a constitutional challenge to the Canada customs' practice of seizing materials destined specifically for a gay and lesbian bookstore, and "A Tribute to Literary Mothers" is a strongly worded article discussing the challenges women were and are up against when it comes to writing. Even with all that Rule has expressed about these many avenues of life and lesbianism, she is often overlooked by lesbian theorists for not being political enough. She died in November 2007 of liver cancer.

Further Reading

Breen, Margaret Soenser. 1997. "Narrative Inversion: The Biblical Heritage of *The Well of Loneliness* and *Desert of the Heart*." In *Reclaiming the Sacred: The Bible in Gay and Lesbian Culture*, ed. Raymond-Jean Frontain, 187–206. Binghamton, NY: Haworth.

Schuster, Marilyn R. 1999. *Passionate Communities: Reading Lesbian Resistance in Jane Rule's Fiction*. New York: New York University Press.

Sheridan, Susan. 1998. "Jane Rule's Sexual Politics." *Canadian Literature* 159: 14–35.

Cynthia Keiken

Michael Rumaker (1932–)

Michael Rumaker has produced fiction, poetry, and memoirs that illustrate both the difficulties and joys of being gay in the United States in the second half of the twentieth century. His early short stories, published as *Gringos and Other Stories*

(1967; new edition, 1991), depicted various outsiders in search of identity. A novel, *The Butterfly* (1962), dealt with life in a mental hospital and the narrator's efforts to achieve sanity. Beginning in the 1960s, Rumaker published poetry in which he developed a celebratory style to accompany the hard realism of his fiction; these poems are now collected in *Pizza: Selected Poems* (2005), which features his best-known poem "The Fairies Are Dancing All Over the World." In the 1970s, Rumaker began to write directly about gay life in the fictional *A Day and a Night at the Baths* (1979) and *My First Satyrnalia* (1981) and the memoir *Robert Duncan in San Francisco* (1996). The first two celebrate a developing gay culture while also illustrating its frustrations and dangers. The third depicts gay life in San Francisco in the 1950s. Rumaker spent the 1980s writing a long novel, *Pagan Days* (1999), in the voice of an eight-year-old child, delineating an emerging gay sensibility. In the thriller *To Kill a Cardinal* (1991), various sexual outsiders conspire to demonstrate against the Catholic Church in New York City. Finally, his 2003 memoir of his student days at the experimental Black Mountain College, *Black Mountain Days*, among much else vividly depicts the joys and confusions of a young man discovering his gay identity.

Further Reading

Beam, Jeffery. 2002. "A Portrait of the Artist as a Young Pagan." *North Carolina Literary Review* 11: 172–74.

Beam, Jeffery. 2003. Review of *Black Mountain Days*. *The Independent Weekly* (October 15).

Butterick, George. 1983. "Michael Rumaker." In *The Beats: Literary Bohemians in Postwar America*, ed. Ann Charters, 465–72. Detroit: Gale Research.

Smith, Leverett T., Jr. 1999. *Eroticizing the Nation: Michael Rumaker's Fiction*. Black Mountain College Dossiers, No. 6. Asheville, NC: Black Mountain College Museum and Arts Center.

Young, Ian. 1995. *The Stonewall Experiment: A Gay Psychohistory*. New York: Cassell.

Leverett T. Smith

Kate Rushin (1951–)

Author of the poetry collection *The Black Back-Ups* (1993), poet Kate Rushin creates down-to-earth "people poetry," marrying free verse and oral presentation in her own conversational yet forceful narrative style. Influenced by Langston Hughes, Gwendolyn Brooks, and Nikki Giovanni, Rushin's work captures the stories of African American women, offering readers a chance to participate in the lives and speech of ordinary people. Rushin captures recognizable black female voices and experiences, portraying ways African American women are disempowered. Her poems that are centered on specifically lesbian themes always place black lesbians within the context of the larger African American community.

Rushin's "The Bridge Poem," which opens the collection *This Bridge Called My Back: Writings by Radical Women of Color* (1981), has received the most attention, although not expressly written for that anthology. Exposing the broken hopes many had for the feminist movement, the poem, and the author's refusal to be relegated to the position of "bridge" between the largely white movement and other African Americans, expresses the anger many women of color have felt toward the larger political and social movements that have marginalized them.

Donna Kate Rushin was born in Syracuse, New York, and grew up in Camden and Lawnside, New Jersey. She received a BA in communications and theater from Oberlin College and an MFA in creative writing from Brown University. In 1988, she became the first African American woman to receive the Grolier Poetry Prize, and she is also recipient of the Rose Low Rome Memorial Poetry Prize and the 1989 Amelia Earhart Award from the Greater Boston Lesbian/Gay Political Alliance. She has been poet in residence at South Boston High School and was Connecticut Poetry Circuit Poet in 1997. A frequent speaker and reader on college campuses and workshop leader, Rushin is director of the Center of African American Studies at Wesleyan University, where she is also visiting writer in the African American Studies Program and adjunct lecturer in English.

Further Reading

Hammonds, Evelynn M. 1993. "Kate Rushin." In *Contemporary Lesbian Writers of the United States: A Critical Sourcebook*, ed. Sandra Pollack and Denise D. Knight, 476–79. Westport, CT: Greenwood Press.

Reginald Harris

Joanna Russ (1937–)

Joanna Russ is an American science fiction writer, feminist literary critic, and essayist. Author of seven novels, three short story collections, and several nonfiction essay collections, Russ is among the first explicitly feminist science fiction writers of the 1970s to use the genre to challenge both literary and social conventions about women and female sexuality and to create new myths featuring active female characters. Best known for the novel *The Female Man* (1974), Russ uses parallel universes to explore how different social arrangements between the sexes reshape the life of the same woman. Jeannine, who comes from an alternative earth with even more restrictive gender roles, is the most oppressed of the four, while Janet is the most liberated, coming from an alternative future earth, Whileaway, which has survived eight centuries without the existence of men. While Russ challenges the patriarchal assumption that men are necessary for women's sexuality or survival through this lesbian utopian society, in "When It Changed," a short story for which Russ won a Nebula Award in 1972, she explores this same lesbian society now facing the arrival of men. Russ's other science fiction novels include *And Chaos Died* (1970), *We Who Are About to . . .* (1977), and *The Two of Them* (1978). Russ's only novel to depart from the science fiction genre is *On Strike against God* (1980), a lesbian **coming-out** story exploring the relationship between a university professor and graduate student that has been included on the **Publishing Triangle**'s list of the 100 Greatest Gay Novels. In her nonfiction collections, such as *How to Suppress*

Women's Writing (1983) and *To Write Like a Woman* (1995), Russ addresses the limits imposed on women writers by both literary tradition and social expectations, the work of other women writers, as well as the aesthetics of science fiction.

Further Reading

Cortiel, Jeanne. 1999. *Demand My Writing: Joanna Russ, Feminism, Science Fiction*. Science Fiction Texts and Studies. Liverpool: Liverpool University Press.

Delany, Samuel R. 1985. "Orders of Chaos: The Science Fiction of Joanna Russ." In *Women Worldwalkers: New Dimensions of Science Fiction and Fantasy*, ed. Jane B. Weedman, 95–123. Lubbock: Texas Tech Press.

Susan Feldman

Paul Russell (1956–)

Paul Russell is the author of five novels; one nonfiction book, *The Gay 100: A Ranking of the Most Influential Gay Men and Lesbians, Past and Present*; and several **short stories.** Russell was born in Memphis, Tennessee, and earned a BA in English from Oberlin College in 1978 and both an MA in English and an MFA in creative writing from Cornell University in 1982. In 1983 he completed a dissertation on Vladimir Nabokov and received a PhD in English from Cornell. Since 1983, he has taught English at Vassar College, pioneering a course on lesbian and gay literature.

Russell's evocative work centers around contemporary gay life and, in particular, intergenerational gay male relationships. His first novel, *The Salt Point*, which takes place in 1980s Poughkeepsie, is about the complications of friendship that occur when Anatole, a gay hairdresser, and Lydia, his straight friend, fall in love with the same 18-year-old boy. *Boys of Life*, his next novel, is narrated by Tony Blair, a 16-year-old living in a Kentucky trailer park before he is discovered and brought to the East Village by an avant-garde filmmaker to star in his sexually graphic films. *Sea of Tranquillity* is Russell's most ambitious work in terms of scope and setting: set in various places in the United States, Turkey, Africa, and the moon, the narration shifts between four points of view, highlighting issues of family relations and AIDS. In *The Coming Storm*, set in an all-boys prep school in upstate New York, Russell explores pedophilia and the complications of a relationship between a teacher and a teenage student. His most recent novel, *War against the Animals*, explores issues of class and tensions that exist between gay and straight citizens in a town in the state of New York.

Further Reading

Canning, Richard. 2003. *Hear Us Out: Conversations with Gay Novelists*. New York: Columbia University Press.

Bryan Kim-Butler

Ryan White CARE Act

The Ryan White Comprehensive AIDS Resources Emergency (CARE) Act is the largest federally funded program created to provide **HIV/AIDS**-related medical, psychological, and social services. Named after the deceased teenage AIDS activist Ryan White (1971–1990), the program provides services for those who do not qualify for Medicare, Medicaid, or other insurance coverage for HIV/AIDS. For example, in 2006, 17 percent of federal HIV/AIDS monies went to Ryan White, or $2.1 billion, in order to serve over half a million HIV/AIDS clients, while 51 percent of federal AIDS expenditures went to Medicaid and 26 percent to Medicare. AIDS activists helped to legislate the Ryan White CARE Act in 1990. Since then, the continuously funded CARE Act evolved to decrease AIDS fatalities and to target a changing demographic of patients, who shifted from U.S. gay white male identifiers to increasing numbers of heterosexuals, women, people of color, drug addicts, and international clients.

See also youth and youth groups.

Further Reading
HIV/AIDSPrograms. Available at: http://hab.hrsa.gov/. Accessed July 20, 2008.

Gabriel S. Estrada

S

sadomasochism, sadists, masochists, and BDSM

Sadomasochism (frequently abbreviated as S/M, SM, or S&M) is part of one of the least understood subcultures in American society, comprised of individuals of all genders and sexual orientations who are interested in the consensual exchange of pain and power. The term *sadomasochism* is a compound of *sadism* and *masochism* and was coined in the psychoanalytic tradition. Although literature provides evidence that the relationship between pain and sexuality is ancient and pervasive in Western culture, the interest in classification and mental processes in nineteenth-century Europe led to theories that divided ways of thinking about sex into normal and abnormal ones. What had previously been known only as particular sexual acts, such as flagellation or humiliation, became a sign of a degenerate character. German psychiatrist Richard von Krafft-Ebing's *Psychopathia Sexualis* (1886) popularized the use of sadism and masochism as terms for the desire for sexualized pain. Krafft-Ebing created a suggestive link to mental disorder when he drew these names from two men obsessed with violence and sexuality, the Marquis Donatien Alphonse François de Sade, who wrote of nonconsensual, graphically violent, and often pedophiliac group encounters, and Leopold von Sacher-Masoch, who wrote of men overcome by the torments of cruel noblewomen dressed in furs. Early psychiatrists like Krafft-Ebing and Sigmund Freud believed elements of biological dysfunction and even mental disorder were present in patients who exhibited the desire to inflict or receive pain, and they based their theories about sadomasochism on these patients. Often, gender/sex stereotypes, such as heterosexuality and the inherent submissiveness of women, were foundational assumptions for these theories. Sadism and masochism were considered conditions primarily suffered by men.

Many practicing sadists and masochists find psychoanalytic approaches to sadism and masochism incomplete, or even flawed, because of their pathological focus and outdated assumptions. The current edition of the *Diagnostic and Statistical Manual of Mental Disorders* (*DSM-IV TR*), a standard reference book for psychiatric professionals, calls fantasies and behaviors related to sexual sadism and masochism paraphilias, meaning sexual desires or acts that deviate from the norm and cause distress or interfere with a subject's activities. Classifying "the norm," however, has proven problematic for psychiatry, as normalization reflects cultural biases, and a diagnosis as a sexual deviant suggests that one's sexual tastes can be treated as a condition and "cured." For example, homosexuality was considered a paraphilia until 1980, when controversy pressured the revisers of the third edition of the *DSM* to change the diagnostic criteria. Similarly, the classification of sexual sadism and masochism as paraphilias has created controversy among individuals who resist the idea that acts and fantasies of sexualized pain should be treated as a disorder. Moreover, the very names sadist and masochist irrevocably link those who enjoy sexualized pain with the authors Sade and Sacher-Masoch. Their notoriety has helped to create **stereotypes** of the sadist as a dangerous criminal compelled to rape and mutilate and of the masochist as a man enslaved by powerful women in fetish attire. Many sadists and masochists are actively involved in increasing awareness of the wide range of practices and diverse population interested in S/M.

Sadists and masochists interested in connecting with others with similar fantasies or practices are able to do so by locating their local S/M community. Many American cities have regular meetings called "munches," discussion groups, and parties for like-minded adults. These groups often have a presence on the Internet via Web sites or discussion lists. Many, but not all, sadists and masochists consider themselves part of a subculture in America called kink or BDSM, an acronym that stands for "bondage, discipline, sadism, and masochism," with the "D" and "S" also signifying "dominance and submission." In the BDSM subculture, consensuality, trust, and safety are stressed. The acronyms SSC (safe, sane, and consensual) and RACK (risk-aware consensual kink) are frequently used as guidelines for how S/M should be approached within the subculture. BDSM activities take place in semipublic or private "dungeons" across the nation, where equipment and props for role-playing are available, and social areas encourage communal gathering. Euphemisms such as *play*, *play space*, and *toys* describe the activities, places, and implements used for S/M, suggesting that for the participants, the undertakings are pleasurable and fun, even if they are also intense and fear inspiring.

BDSM interactions generally take place within the following rubric: two individuals will decide who will be the "top," or mutually agreed-upon person in charge of the "scene," or particular activity negotiated, and who will be the "bottom," or the person who follows the top's lead during the scene. Individuals are encouraged to self-identify as one of several roles involving the way pain and power are exchanged between partners. Some people enjoy being exclusively a top or a bottom; many people switch roles. Many strive to maintain power dynamics for longer than a single scene, extending the roles of master/mistress and slave, for example, into relationship dynamics.

After the top and bottom roles are determined, individual tastes dictate the style of the encounter. Three major areas are usually addressed: (1) whether there will be physical sensation play and the level of intensity; (2) whether there will be power exchange, or dominance/submission (D/s), in which the top and bottom may adopt roles of master/mistress and slave or other authority figure dynamics; and (3) in what way, if any, sexual intimacy will be undertaken. BDSM is practiced by people of all sexual orientations, and a top and bottom may choose to engage in cross-orientation play. If fetishes, particular fantasies, or role-play interest the participants, these can be integrated into the three areas. To ensure that no harm is being done to the bottom, who may want to cry or fight back during the scene, the bottom may have a "safe word," or a word that is distinct from other words and signals the top to stop play.

Within the BDSM nomenclature, sadists and masochists refer to those interested in sensation play, or the giving or receiving of physical pain (e.g., through whipping, spanking, caning, cutting) and acts such as humiliation or deprivation. Quite unlike the Marquis de Sade, sadists who enjoy inflicting consensual pain or emotional torment have willing "victims" in their masochist partners. Not all sadists and masochists are interested in power exchange with dominant and submissive roles for the top and bottom. Some receive sexual gratification from the sensation of physical pain alone. Those interested in D/s may not be at all interested in giving or receiving pain. With such a variety of interests and experiences, it is difficult to assess why sadists and masochists are drawn to BDSM. Interviews and articles written by S/M practitioners repeatedly refer to experiencing a deep, transformative pleasure that creates a release of adrenalin and/or endorphin high. No convincing studies have been done that conclusively link childhood trauma with an adult interest in sexualized pain.

The history of S/M in many ways mirrors and complements that of homosexuality in America. Police raids on bars and clubs, censorship and prosecutions for mailing materials related to S/M, widespread disapproval of the so-called deviancy of sexualized pain, plus the fear of legal trouble mandated secrecy and led to reluctance to have a public presence for many years. Freud and his followers dominated publishing about S/M in the first few decades of the twentieth century. Beginning in the late 1940s, the options for both reading about and meeting people involved in S/M began to increase. Irving Klaw published female bondage photographs, most famously of Bettie Page, and other photographers published gay physique photographs with bondage touches. John Willie's fetish magazine *Bizarre*, which featured women bound and gagged, ran from 1946 to 1959. In 1945, the Canadian magazine *Justice Weekly* began publication; although ostensibly reporting on punishment, it also ran highly coded personal ads for S/M encounters. In 1949, Alfred Kinsey filmed gay male S/M sexual intercourse for his research, and his findings were among the first that showed nonpathological perspectives on sexualized pain.

The earliest organizers of S/M publications, events, and associations were urban gay men, mainly centered in New York, San Francisco, Los Angeles, and Chicago. In the 1950s, the association with **leather** developed, and the term *leather man* became a code word for a subculture interested in gay S/M. Marlon Brando's portrayal of a biker in *The Wild One* (1953) and James Dean's friend Sal Mineo in *Rebel without a Cause* (1955) created a demand for leather jackets nationwide, but the rebellious, hypermasculine figures cut by the Brando and Dean characters created new icons for homosexual men attracted to strength and power. In 1954, the Satyrs Motorcycle Club, the first gay motorcycle club, was formed in Los Angeles; many others followed. The first American leather **gay bars** opened in the early 1950s. A subtle system of postures, clothing arrangement, and body gestures indicated to the initiated which men were interested in topping or bottoming and were looking for partners. A strict and thorough mentor and training system was developed for teaching new tops how to safely practice S/M within many of these communities. During the 1950s and 1960s, police raids in San Francisco gay clubs affected the leather bars, causing several to close, but more opened in their wake, including The Tool Box, which featured Chuck Arnett's mural of muscular men in leather jackets that appeared in a famous article on gay America in *Life* magazine in 1964. The BDSM subculture's association with leather is a legacy of this era; the term leather culture is used to describe the lifestyle, and supporters wave a leather pride flag at parades, even though many of the people wearing leather today have never mounted a motorcycle.

The easing of American obscenity laws in the late 1960s led to wider distribution of fetish material through the mail. S/M newsletters and fiction proliferated, and artists like Etienne and Tom of Finland, who specialized in drawings of stylized muscle-bound leathermen in various bondage poses, became more readily available. Gay S/M films began to be produced and distributed. In 1971, New York City's Eulenspiegel Society (for all sexual orientations) and the Chicago Hellfire Club (for gay men), the first organizations dedicated to S/M, were founded. San Francisco's Society of Janus followed in 1974. All of these organizations are still functioning.

During the 1960s and 1970s, the act of **fisting,** or handballing, became popular in some circles of gay men, and clubs and bars began to cater to this trend. After-hours parties at the Mineshaft in New York (which opened in 1976) and weekly fisting parties at the Catacombs in San Francisco (1975) ushered in a new style of S/M, slick with Crisco and less strictly codified than what became known as the "Old Guard." Cynthia Slater, a San Franciscan **bisexual** who founded the S/M association Society of Janus for all sexual orientations in 1974, was lovers with the owner of the Catacombs, Steve McEachern, and began attending the all-male fisting parties at the Catacombs. With some resistance, pansexuality, or the mixing of all sexual orientations, was thereby introduced to S/M public events for the first time. Slater began bringing female friends to the club, and eventually, the Catacombs began holding parties for lesbians and mixed groups. One of these friends was the author and activist Pat (now Patrick) Califia, a female-to-male transsexual and former leather dyke, whose book on practicing lesbian S/M and other writings on lesbian leather culture and sexuality are widely read in the community.

The first lesbian feminist S/M support group was Samois in San Francisco, named after the estate owned by the tight-lacing dominatrix who trains O in the S/M classic *The Story of* O (the first English translation appeared in 1965). Samois existed from 1978 to 1983 and published pamphlets that demystified aspects of lesbian S/M and also an anthology of stories and technique pieces, *Coming to Power: Writing and Graphics on Lesbian S/M*, in 1981. The group was a significant opponent of the antipornography campaign in the **sex wars of the 1980s,** arguing that feminism could be compatible with S/M, both in pornography and relationships.

In the 1990s, the growing popularity of the Internet opened doors to more people interested in S/M, and the usenet group alt.sex.bondage was founded for discussions related to bondage, D/s, and S/M. By the end of the decade, more Web sites, chat groups, and discussion threads were being hosted; these are now heavily frequented resources for social networking and personals. Although many local groups and online communities endeavor to be inclusive and open to different styles of BDSM, in-fighting and factionalism persist, and gender stereotypes, especially concerning **transgendered** people, continue to play a significant role in S/M culture.

The BDSM community conducts outreach and education in many American cities. The National Coalition of Sexual Freedom tracks raids, prosecutions, and discrimination against people engaged in consensual, adult, sexual practices, including S/M. The Gay Male S/M Activists (GMSMA) and the Lesbian Sex Mafia in New York are two of the leading S/M organizations for gay men and women, respectively. Chicago's Leather Archives and Museum, incorporated in 1991, holds a collection of artifacts and documents related to American S/M. The Kinsey Institute in Bloomington, Indiana, also has a significant number of S/M-related materials.

Further Reading

Califia, Pat[rick]. 1994. *Public Sex: The Culture of Radical Sex*. Pittsburgh: Cleis Press.

Cooper, Dennis. 2005. *The Sluts*. Cambridge, MA: Da Capo.

Kleinplatz, Peggy J., and Charles Moser, eds. 2006. *Sadomasochism: Powerful Pleasures*. Binghamton, NY: Haworth.

Noyes, John K. 1997. *The Mastery of Submission: Inventions of Masochism*. Ithaca, NY: Cornell University Press.

Thompson, Mark, ed. 2001. *Leatherfolk: Radical Sex, People, Politics, and Practice*. Los Angeles: Daedalus Publishing. (Orig. pub. 1991.)

Townsend, Larry. 2000. *The Leatherman's Handbook*. 6th ed. Beverly Hills, CA: L. T. Publications. (Orig. pub. 1972.)

Wiseman, Jay. 2001. *SM 101: A Realistic Introduction*. 2nd ed. Emeryville, CA: Greenery Press.

Jennifer Burns Levin

Assotto Saint (Yves François Lubin) (1957–1994)

Haitian poet, playwright, and performer, as well as founder of Galiens Press, Assotto Saint was an important figure in the explosion of black gay male expression in the late 1980s and early 1990s. Born Yves François Lubin, he assumed his pen name in 1980—*Assotto* is the name of a drum used in the voodoo religion; *Saint* alludes to the Haitian liberation leader Toussaint L'Ouverture.

Assotto Saint's life and work mixed the personal and the political. His poems and performance pieces combined elements of history and ritual to comment on contemporary issues, often using religious imagery forming a composite of mysticism, eroticism, gender-bending, outrage, and outrageousness. An outspoken writer on AIDS and its impact on the lives of black gay men, the majority of his work appeared after he was diagnosed as HIV positive. Saint sought to give the black community a sense of the contributions of its gay members and to replace racism and **homophobia** with new myths and families of black writers.

Inspired by the feminist Kitchen Table Press, Saint founded Galiens (a word formed by combining *gay* and *aliens*) Press to publish his own work (*Stations,* 1989; *Wishing for Wings,* 1994) and the work of others in the anthologies *The Road before Us: 100 Gay Black Poets* (1991) and *Here to Dare: 10 Gay Black Poets* (1992). Much of his work is collected in *Spells of a Voodoo Doll: The Poems, Fiction, Essays and Plays of Assotto Saint* (published by Richard Kasak Books in 1996).

Saint studied medicine at Queens College, danced with the Martha Graham Company, and participated in the gay black writers collective Other Countries. His partner was the Swedish Jan Holmgren (1939–1993). He received the James Baldwin Award from the Black Gay and Lesbian Leadership Forum in 1990 and the 1991 Lambda Literary Award for Gay Men's Poetry for *The Road before Us.* Saint interrupted the funeral of fellow Other Countries Collective member Donald Woods to speak out against the repression of the late writer's sexuality at the event; the act forms the core of **Thomas Glave**'s short story "The Final Inning."

Further Reading

Glave, Thomas. 2000. *Whose Song?: And Other Stories.* San Francisco: City Lights Press.

Steward, Douglas. 2003. "Assotto Saint (Yves François Lubin)." In *Contemporary Gay American Poets and Playwrights: An A–Z Guide,* ed. Emmanuel S. Nelson, 383–87. Westport, CT: Greenwood Press.

Reginald Harris

same-sex marriage. *See* marriage, same-sex, and domestic partnerships

San Francisco

San Francisco has been the "homosexual capital of the world" since at least 1964, when *Life* magazine gave that title to the city. Ironically, the recognition, very much unwanted by civic leaders, came during a period of intense harassment of lesbians and gays by local and state government agencies. Within 10 years, however, individuals, organizations, and events would come together to create a true gay and lesbian community.

San Francisco's gay men especially had experienced increasing harassment since World War II, but police persecution intensified during the mayoral campaign of 1959, when the city's so-called leniency toward homosexuals emerged as the election's central issue. Gays were an easy target. They had no political influence, no cultural institutions, few businesses to meet their needs except **bars**—where they could not legally gather—and little sense of community beyond circles of friends. Even with the national homophile organizations such as the **Mattachine Society** and the **Daughters of Bilitis** headquartered in San Francisco, they seemed powerless to fight the government discrimination against them.

A month after the election, the California Supreme Court, settling a long-fought case, affirmed the right of

Female impersonators at Finocchio's, a famous San Francisco club featuring female impersonators, which closed in 1999 after a 63-year history. Courtesy of the Gay, Lesbian, Bisexual, Transgender Historical Society, San Francisco.

homosexuals to go to bars, as long as they did not engage in illegal sexual activities on the premises, which could cause the establishment's liquor license to be revoked. The decision motivated one local bar owner to inform the city's district attorney that for the previous two years he had been forced to pay off members of the police department to stay in business. Dubbed the "gayola" scandal by local newspapers, an investigation led others to come forward and resulted in numerous indictments for corruption. During the trial that followed, however, the defense put homosexuality on trial, suggesting that homosexuals were unreliable witnesses (Agee 2006). All the defendants were acquitted.

The election and the "gayola" scandal had three important results. First, for almost two years, the public read about homosexuality in its daily newspapers; no doubt few minds were changed, but the subject, previously hidden, now was openly discussed. Second, the police intensified their harassment of gays. (Using entrapment to circumvent the court's decision, raids of homosexual bars reached a peak in 1961 with the arrest of 89 men and 14 women at the Tay-Bush Inn. One judge, branding San Francisco a "Parisian pansy's paradise," threatened harsh punishments for any homosexuals brought before him.) Third, the attacks caused some gays and others to step forward to defend their civil rights through political action.

The city's institutional discrimination and persecution prompted José Sarria, a performer at the famed Black Cat Café, to become the first openly gay man to run for office in San Francisco in 1961. He had difficulty finding 25 people willing to sign his nominating petition—their names would become part of a public record— but almost 7,000 voted for him in the privacy of the polling booth, which showed the possibility of a gay voting bloc for the first time. The same year, Sarria and Guy

A participant on the way to the Beaux Arts Ball in 1970. In early 1965 bar owners united to form the Tavern Guild of San Francisco and to put on San Francisco's first large, public drag ball, the Beaux Arts Ball. Courtesy of the Gay, Lesbian, Bisexual, Transgender Historical Society, San Francisco.

Strait founded the League for Civil Education (LCE) to develop a political voice for gays in the city. Its *LCE News*, published weekly, was San Francisco's first gay newspaper. The organization disbanded in 1964.

The ongoing harassment of their businesses and their customers prompted some of the city's bar owners to form the Tavern Guild in 1962, the first lesbian and gay business association in the United States. Unlike many cities, most bars in San Francisco were locally owned and operated, which gave their proprietors an incentive to organize against government persecution. The Guild quickly developed ways to help protect its members, their employees, and patrons from harassment. It published and distributed a free brochure that explained what to do if arrested by the police, retained legal assistance for anyone arrested near a gay bar, and raised money for homophile organizations.

Among its many activities, the Tavern Guild sponsored both an annual picnic and an annual Beaux Arts Ball, first held in 1963. Two years later, when José Sarria was crowned Queen of the Ball, he responded that because he already was a queen, he should be an empress instead. He took the name "Her Royal Majesty, Jose I, Empress of San Francisco, the Widow Norton," honoring local nineteenth-century merchant and self-proclaimed first emperor of the United States, Norton I. Now an international organization, the imperial court system raises money for many charities.

The discrimination against gays in San Francisco led several prominent local clergy to created the Council on Religion and the Homosexual (CRH) in 1964, to promote better understanding between mainstream churches and the city's homophile groups. As a fund-raiser, the council sponsored a costume ball on New Year's Day, 1965, at California Hall. Even with all permits secured, some 50 uniformed and plainclothes police showed up, photographed everyone entering the building, and arrested anyone who protested their intimidation tactics. The next day, the ministers held a news conference denouncing the police for "deliberate harassment and bad faith" (Society of Individual Rights Web site). When local media also condemned the police action, the department temporarily halted its raids on gay bars—which finally ended in 1971—and appointed a member of the police-community relations board to serve as a liaison to the gay community.

Also founded in 1964, the Society for Individual Rights (SIR) soon became America's largest homophile organization. Recognizing the need for gays to have a political voice, it began sponsoring candidate nights in 1965. To create a place for social gatherings and events in addition to the bars, it also opened a community center for gays in 1966, the first in the nation, which helped foster a feeling of community that until then was only vaguely present among gays.

Maud's Study, the world's longest-surviving lesbian bar, opened in the Haight district in 1966. The same year, Compton's Cafeteria in the Tenderloin became a battleground between gays and police when the latter tried to evict a group of noisy customers, many who were drag queens. One officer received a cup of coffee in his face; the rest were routed by flying dishes, trays, and flatware. Not only was it a bumpy night, it was the first time gays forcibly resisted their oppression in the United States (presaging the more noted **Stonewall** resistance in New York).

By the mid-1960s, San Francisco was developing several districts with establishments specifically for gays; bars and clubs for women, never numerous, were outnumbered by those for men by perhaps 3 to 100. The city's first leather bar, the Why Not?, opened in the Tenderloin in 1961. The Tool Box, the first leather bar located south of Market, opened at 4th Street and Harrison in 1962. By the time FeBe's opened its doors in 1966, Folsom Street was well on its way to becoming leather's "miracle mile." When the Boot Camp opened in 1971, the news appeared in Herb Caen's *San Francisco Chronicle* column. In only 10 years, San Francisco had gone from having no leather bars at all to being home to a world-famous leather community.

By the early 1970s, Polk Street on the western edge of the Tenderloin—also known as Polk Strasse and the Valley of the Queens—had become the city's first "gay downtown," with numerous businesses catering to lesbians and gays. The first establishments had been bars and clubs, but as the neighborhood became a gay enclave, they soon were joined by bookstores, gift shops, clothiers, florists, coffee shops, hotels, and others that opened specifically for a gay clientele.

The community staged its first **pride parade** down Polk Street on Saturday, June 27, 1970, when 30 or so "hair fairies" marched from Aquatic Park to City Hall, where they rallied for "Christopher Street Liberation Day." Sunday's "gay-in," held at Speedway Meadows in Golden Gate Park, attracted considerably more participants. No organized pride celebration took place in 1971, but some 3,000 people participated in the 1972 parade, also down Polk Street, and the number grew every year. When the route changed to Market Street in 1976, the parade attracted more than 200,000 participants and onlookers. It is now the largest such event in the nation and the largest parade in the city.

From the beginning the parade was open to everyone who wished to participate. Dykes on Bikes (now the Women's Motorcycle Contingent Dykes on Bikes) began with a small contingent of women riders in the 1976 parade; it now continues a long-established tradition of inaugurating the procession each year. The San Francisco Gay Freedom Day Marching Band and Twirling Corps (now the San Francisco Gay/Lesbian Gay Freedom Band) debuted at the 1978 parade, the first musical organization in the world to include lesbian or gay in its name. The **rainbow flag,** designed by Gilbert Baker, appeared for the first time in the parade the same year.

The Castro was once a worker's neighborhood known as Eureka Valley. Its Victorian houses spared not only by the Great Earthquake and Fire of 1906 but also by urban renewal in the 1950s and 1960s, underwent dramatic change after World War II as the old residents moved to the suburbs and a new generation, including many lesbians and gays, moved in. By the mid-1970s, it had become a truly gay

Harvey Milk (lower right) talking to supporters in his 1977 run for San Francisco's Board of Supervisors. Courtesy of the Gay, Lesbian, Bisexual, Transgender Historical Society, San Francisco.

San Francisco neighborhood, where it was possible to live, work, shop, and socialize without ever interacting with straight people. Many saw the neighborhood as narrow and not welcoming to women and minorities, but it showed what was possible when people were let alone to build a community.

Among its many other visible achievements, the community created and exported the "Castro Clone" look, which became extremely popular: tennis shoes or boots, snug 501s, T-shirt, hooded jogging jacket (affectionately known as a *fag wrap*), short hair, and moustache. When some men began dying their jeans black, Levi Strauss started manufacturing them in that color, creating a mainstream style.

Harvey Milk organized the first Castro Street Fair in 1974 to show the Eureka Valley Merchants Association, then refusing to cooperate with the neighborhood's gay businessmen and women, the extent of the gay community. From the beginning, the fair included local organizations sharing information, artisans selling merchandise, and participants simply spending time in the sunshine. It has become a major celebration of community pride, attended by individuals and families from all over the Bay Area.

The first attempt to change the legal restrictions against gays in California came in 1968, when San Francisco Assemblyman Willie Brown introduced AB-743 to legalize sex between consenting adults. Assemblyman John Burton, also from San Francisco, cosponsored the bill. After a long struggle, the bill to repeal the antisodomy law passed in 1975. When the state senate deadlocked on the legislation, Senate Majority Leader George Moscone locked the chamber doors until Lieutenant Governor Mervyn Dymally could return to cast the tie-breaking vote. Governor Jerry Brown signed the bill soon afterward. Moscone was elected San Francisco's mayor in 1976.

A growing community with a growing awareness of its cultural contributions to the arts held the world's first gay film festival in 1977. Now known as the San Francisco International LGBT Film Festival—the longest-running and largest LGBT arts event in North America—it has been joined by the Black GLBT Film Festival and the South Asian LGBT International Film Festival. Theatre Rhinoceros was founded in 1977 not only to commission, foster, and present work by lesbian and gay artists but to explore and document the depth and breadth of queer experience. One of the best-known and most successful gay **theater companies** in the world, it has presented everything from *Twelfth Night* to *Boys in the Band* to *Drag Queens from Outer Space*.

After two unsuccessful bids, Harvey Milk, by then the "mayor of Castro Street," won election to the San Francisco Board of Supervisors on November 8, 1977, the city's first openly gay elected official. He soon made a difference in human rights, introducing legislation that barred the city from doing business with contractors and organizations that discriminated against lesbians and gays. Mayor Moscone quickly signed the new ordinance.

On November 27, 1978, barely a year after Supervisor Milk's election, he and Mayor Moscone were assassinated in their City Hall offices by Dan White, a former supervisor. That evening, a candlelight march of 30,000 mourners retraced the walk Milk took from the Castro to the Civic Center on his first day in office. The San Francisco Gay Men's **Chorus,** the first men's chorus to have the word gay in its name, began that night on the steps of City Hall, singing to comfort the grieving. On May 21, 1979, Dan White was found guilty only of two counts of voluntary manslaughter. That evening, members of the community protested at City Hall, breaking windows and burning police cars. Later, police retaliated, smashing up the Elephant Walk bar at 18th and Castro.

By the beginning of the 1980s, San Francisco's gays and lesbians had established the social, cultural, religious, and service institutions—dance troupes, newspapers, choirs, magazines, theater companies, film festivals, churches and synagogues, **bookstores,** gift stores, restaurants, and clubs—that form the institutional core of a community and contribute to the enrichment and joy of daily life. They had organized against discrimination and fought back against political attacks. If they had not yet achieved equal rights, at least they had achieved political strength and vitality. They had even developed a fourth queer neighborhood, centered along what became known as the Valencia Corridor, that focused primarily on the needs of lesbians and bisexual women.

No one knows when what became known as HIV (human immunodeficiency virus) first infected San Franciscans, but in mid-1981 rumors of a "gay cancer" began circulating in the community. In December 1981, Bobbi Campbell (also known as Sister Florence Nightmare, RN of the Sisters of Perpetual Indulgence) became the city's first resident to disclose publicly that he was a person with AIDS. As "AIDS poster boy" he appeared on the cover of *Newsweek;* helped found the Kaposi's Sarcoma Research and Education Foundation with Marcus Conant, MD, Cleve Jones, and others; and with Dan Turner, organized People with AIDS San Francisco, the first organization of, for, and by people with the disease. Campbell, Bobby Reynolds, and Gary Walsh organized San Francisco's first AIDS Candlelight March, which took place on May 2, 1983. It marked the first time persons with AIDS (PWAs) marched behind a banner proclaiming what was to become the motto of the PWA

The Patio Café, a favorite San Francisco gathering place specifically for LBGTQ patrons. Courtesy of the Gay, Lesbian, Bisexual, Transgender Historical Society, San Francisco.

self-empowerment movement: "FIGHTING FOR OUR LIVES." Lesbians and gays from all backgrounds began to create the services AIDS victims needed when no private charities or public agencies were willing to help. The San Francisco Model, as the programs became known, provided a safety net of mostly private organizations and volunteers to help with the vital daily needs of people with AIDS: food, shelter, quality of life, counseling, testing, legal assistance, and education. Among many groups providing care and support, the AIDS Emergency Fund began in 1982 to help pay basic living costs such as rent, utility bills, and medical expenses for poverty-level San Franciscans with HIV or AIDS and to help clients avoid eviction or the shutting off of utilities, improve the quality of their lives, and maintain stable housing. Project Open Hand, founded by Ruth Brinker in 1985, provided meals, when no other social service agency did so, to those who had become too weak or too impoverished to feed themselves.

Impatient with government response to the AIDS epidemic, several organizations formed to bring attention to the egregious disregard. The ARC/AIDS Vigil began on October 27, 1985, at the United Nations Plaza in San Francisco's Civic Center to publicize the connections between poverty, homelessness, and HIV. Members of the group also distributed health information and held marches, protests, and rallies to spotlight the need for help for people with ARC (AIDS-related complex) and AIDS and the slow or nonexistent response of government. Cleve Jones established the **Names Project AIDS Memorial Quilt** to remember those who had died of the disease. With panels from every state and dozens of countries, the quilt is now the largest community art project in the world. In 1989, the quilt was nominated for a Nobel Peace Prize.

Remarkably, in the face of the epidemic, gay and lesbian San Franciscans also continued their fight to gain the "certain unalienable rights." Tom Waddell, a former Olympian, established the Gay Olympic Games to celebrate the accomplishments of lesbian and gay athletes. The U.S. Olympic Committee objected to the use of Olympic in the organization's name and forced Waddell to delete it, although it allows frog, pancake, math, and urology olympics, among others. The first two meets were held in San Francisco in 1982 and 1986. They have been held in different major cities around the world every four years since.

The first Folsom Street Fair was held in 1984. More than simply a joyous celebration, it was organized by a group of community and housing activists to show that there was a viable neighborhood South of Market (SoMa), one that was increasingly being threatened by urban redevelopment. The dominance of the leather community in the area turned the fair into the world's largest leather event, even after urban renewal vanquished the residents. A second, smaller SoMa street fair for the leather community, Up Your Alley, started in 1985.

In 1988, a group of San Franciscans decided to create a living tribute in Golden Gate Park to those lost to AIDS. Five years after work on the site began in 1991, Congress passed the National AIDS Memorial Grove Act, officially designating the park's historic DeLaveaga Dell as the nation's first AIDS memorial. Unlike most national memorials, however, it is not listed on the National Register of Historic Places.

San Francisco established its domestic partnership registry through a referendum passed in 1990. On February 14, 1991, the day it became available, more than 275 lesbian and gay couples registered at City Hall, and domestic partner benefits became available to city and county employees. In 1997, companies having contracts with the city were required to offer the same benefits to unmarried domestic partners as to married employees.

San Francisco hosted its first Dyke March in 1992. Now attracting more than 50,000 women, it is the largest lesbian celebration in the world. Their stated objectives, as of 1999, were the following: "We fight for freedom, for power, for sisterhood, for love, for control of our bodies, for self defense, for dignity, for human rights, for our children, for joy, for liberation, for sex, for equality, for justice, for our lives, for all women forever!" (Queer Arts Festival 1999 Web site).

The James C. Hormel Gay and Lesbian Center, opened in the city's new main library in 1996, was the first center in a public library in the United States dedicated to collecting, preserving, and studying lesbian, gay, bisexual, and transgender culture and achievement. The next year, San Francisco philanthropist Hormel himself made history when he became the first openly gay American to be nominated for an ambassadorship.

The San Francisco Lesbian Gay Bisexual Transgender Community Center opened in March 2002. The first center in the United States built from the ground up and among the largest in the world, it provides a broad range of legal, wellness, social, educational, and cultural programs and services to benefit LGBTQ people throughout their lives.

On February 12, 2005, stating that "Today a barrier to true justice has been removed" (CNN Web site), newly inaugurated mayor Gavin Newsom authorized **same-sex marriages** in San Francisco. Some believed that a presidential election year was not the right time to challenge discrimination, but others argued that there is never a wrong moment to demand equality. The first license issued and the first marriage performed were for pioneer **activists** Phyllis Lyon and Del Martin. Although they had by then been a couple for more than 50 years—an anniversary seldom reached in any relationship—no government had previously recognized the validity of their union. Before the California Supreme Court ordered San Francisco officials to cease issuing the licenses on March 11, 2004, more than 4,000 same-sex couples had applied for them.

Whatever the future, lesbian and gay San Franciscans are rightfully proud of the communities they have built, the successes they have achieved, and the contributions they have made to the culture, politics, and progress of the city, all intrinsically and integrally woven into the fabric of place and people that is San Francisco.

Further Reading

Agee, Christopher. 2006. "Gayola: Police Professionalization and the Politics of San Francisco's Gay Bars, 1950–1968." *Journal of the History of Sexuality* 15 (3): 462–89.

Boyd, Nan Alamilla. 2005. *Wide Open Town*. Berkeley: University of California Press.

Clendinen, Dudley, and Adam Nagourney. 1999. *Out for Good*. New York: Touchstone.

CNN. "San Francisco Weds Gay Couples." Available at: http://www.cnn.com/2004/LAW/02/12/gay.marriage.california.ap/. Accessed July 16, 2008.

Higgs, David, ed. 1999. *Queer Sites*. London: Routledge.

Lipsky, William. 2006. *Gay and Lesbian San Francisco*. Charleston, SC: Arcadia.

Queer Arts Festival 1999 Web site. Available at: http://www.queerculturalcenter.org/QccPdfs/NQAF99.pdf. Accessed July 16, 2008.

Society of Individual Rights (SIR). Available at: http://www.shapingsf.org/ezine/gay/files/sirights.html. Accessed July 15, 2008.

Stryker, Susan, and Jim Van Buskirk. 1996. *Gay by the Bay*. San Francisco: Chronicle Books.

Bill Lipsky

San Francisco Bay Area Poets

The poets Robin Blaser, James Broughton, Robert Duncan, Thom Gunn, Jack Spicer, Allen Ginsberg, and John Weiners, also known as San Francisco Bay Area Poets, are connected by association and by location. The Bay Area may claim all of these poets as influenced by the culture of San Francisco and its environs, especially in the 1950s and 1960s, when many of these men were in the formative stage of their creativity.

No specific poetic genre may claim the works of all of these figures, and several defy branding with the name of any poetic movement. The factors of generation, physical location, sexual reference, and community created a fraternity of creative alliance that may be labeled the Bay Area Poets. The intersection of inspiration and culture that occurred in San Francisco at the midpoint of the twentieth century profoundly affected the writing and practices of all these poets.

Allen Ginsberg in front of City Lights Bookstore, San Francisco. Photo by Robert Pruzan, courtesy of the Gay, Lesbian, Bisexual, Transgender Historical Society, San Francisco.

Born in Newark, New Jersey, Allen Ginsberg (1926–1997) grew up in Paterson. His father, Louis, was a poet and high school teacher, and his mother, Naomi, was an active member of the Communist Party. Ginsberg's childhood was influenced greatly by his mother, and he was moved to write one of his most famous poems after her death. "Kaddish for Naomi Ginsberg (1894–1964)" would become a chronicle of his mother's life, but it is also highly autobiographical.

Ginsberg attended Columbia University where he contributed to the *Columbia Review* and the *Jester* and also won the Woodberry Poetry Prize. At Columbia, Ginsberg's fate took another turn when he met the artist Lucien Carr; through Carr he was introduced to those who would form the nexus of the future beat movement: Jack Kerouac, **William S. Burroughs,** John Clellon Holmes, and Neil Cassady. It was also at Columbia, in 1946, that Ginsberg would **come out.** In high school, Ginsberg had discovered Walt Whitman; a correspondence with William Carlos Williams also proved to be highly influential. From Williams, he would learn the tactics of modernism and to write in the voice of the common man. Through his close friendship with Chogyam Trungpa Rimpoche, Ginsberg would eventually embrace Tibetan Buddhism. In 1954, Ginsberg would follow Jack Kerouac to the West Coast and the Bay Area. He was introduced to the poetry scene by the poet Kenneth Rexroth and Gary Snyder. That same year in San Francisco, Ginsberg met Peter Orlovsky, who would become his lover and lifelong companion.

A major event for West Coast poetry at this time was the occasion known as "Six Poets at the Six Gallery," which took place on October 7, 1955. At this reading Ginsberg would debut his poem "Howl" to much acclaim; this incident is considered the launch of beat poetry. An anthem for a generation of poets, *Howl* was first published by City Lights Press and subsequently banned for obscenity. Allen Ginsberg would go on to become one of America's most famous poets. An icon of popular culture, as well as a celebrated writer, Ginsberg publicly protested the Vietnam War, championed gay rights as an openly gay public figure, and celebrated human sexuality in his work. During the 1960s he befriended such major figures as Timothy Leary and Bob Dylan. In the 1970s, he was elected to the Academy of Arts and Letters and became a lecturer at New York's City College. In 1976, Ginsberg and the poet Anne Waldman were asked by Trungpa to create a writing school at the Naropa Institute in Boulder, Colorado, that was named the Jack Kerouac School of Disembodied Poetics. Ginsberg would continue to lecture there until his death.

The poet Robert Duncan (1919–1988) was born in Oakland, California. In part, the circumstances of his upbringing have contributed to his mystique and mythos. When his biological mother died, Edwin and Minnehaha Symmes, devoted theosophists, adopted him. Thus, Duncan grew up with knowledge of the occult, which would later affect his poetic methods. He attended the University of California at Berkeley for two years and then moved to New York City. There, he became a member of the downtown arts scene and associated with literary figures such as Henry Miller, Anais Nin, and Kenneth Patchen, whom he would publish in his magazine, the *Experimental Review*.

Duncan taught at Black Mountain College and was influenced by Charles Olson's method of "open composition," in which a poem is composed thematically, yet is also open to associations invoked during the process of creation. Duncan returned to San Francisco in 1945 and became an associate of Kenneth Rexroth. He returned to the University of California at Berkeley at this time to study medieval and Renaissance literature. Duncan was openly homosexual and came out in the mid-1940s. This highly controversial announcement caused his work to be withdrawn from the *Kenyon Review*. In 1944, *Poetics* published his essay, "The Homosexual in Society," which discusses the plight of the homosexual in modern culture. Duncan is also known for his anti-Vietnam War stance and antiwar poetry of that time, including the collection *Bending the Bow* (1968). In 1951, he met the artist Jess Collins, with whom he lived until death. Robert Duncan is best known for his books *The Opening of the Field* (1960), *Groundwork*

Robert Duncan, 1985. Photo by Robert Pruzan, courtesy of the Gay, Lesbian, Bisexual, Transgender Historical Society, San Francisco.

I and II (1984, 1988), and *Fictive Certainties* (1979), a collection of essays. In 1984, Duncan won the National Poetry Award.

A friend and associate of Robert Duncan, the poet Jack Spicer (1925–1965) was born in Hollywood and in 1945 moved north to Berkeley to attend the University of California. Upon arrival, he sought out other poets and formed a strong bond with Duncan and with Robin Blaser. Duncan, especially, persuaded Spicer to openly embrace his homosexuality, and the two shared a deep interest in the occult. Even though the beat poetry scene surrounded them, both Duncan and Spicer were set apart from it by a more intellectual approach to the act of creation. Spicer, Duncan, and Blaser were also known for educating younger poets about the idea of a "queer genealogy," an artistic legacy handed down from homosexual writers such as Rimbaud and Lorca.

At Berkeley, Spicer studied Anglo-Saxon and Old Norse to prepare for a career in linguistics. In part from this background, he would develop his form and theory of poetics. After refusing to sign a loyalty oath to the United States in 1950, Spicer lost his teaching assistantship and subsequently left the Bay Area. He lived for a while in Boston, while Robin Blazer was working there, and became acquainted with the poet John Weiners.

Around this time, Spicer developed his ideology of poetry as "dictation" from another source. He likened the poet to a radio that received transmissions from an "invisible world." He viewed words as "furniture" that could be moved about and believed the mind of the poet was like an empty room. It is obvious that Spicer's knowledge of linguistics contributed to this theory. Spicer's book *After Lorca* (1957) was written during this period. Spicer returned to San Francisco that year and taught at San Francisco State College and was the center of the Spicer Circle, an openly gay group of poets.

Robin Blaser was born in Denver and raised in rural Idaho, but like other Bay Area poets he came west to the University of California at Berkeley for his education. After graduation, he relocated and worked as a librarian at Harvard University. During this period, he was associated with the San Francisco Renaissance poets. In 1966, Blaser mover to Vancouver to teach English at Simon Fraser University. His major work is *The Holy Forest*. Blazer is also well known for his work as a literary critic.

Another poet associated with the Bay Area scene is John Weiners (1934–2002). Born in Massachusetts, Weiners attended Boston High School and Boston College. In 1958, he moved to San Francisco and was an active member of the San Francisco Renaissance for a two-year period. In 1958, *Hotel Wentley Poems* was published. It portrays an urban landscape of homosexual love, drugs, madness, and despair. After returning from the West Coast to Boston in

Poet and filmmaker James Broughton and William Burroughs. Photo by Robert Pruzan, courtesy of the Gay, Lesbian, Bisexual, Transgender Historical Society, San Francisco.

1960, Weiners was institutionalized; he was committed again in 1969 and from this experience wrote *Asylum Poems*. Between these two periods, Weiners studied in the graduate program at the State University of New York, Buffalo, where he worked as a teaching assistant under Charles Olson and became a friend and compatriot of the poet Robert Creeley. After 1971, Weiners moved back to Boston, where he would live out his life as a poet while battling his various demons.

James Broughton (1913–1999) is also considered a Bay Area poet, as well as a queer experimental filmmaker and practitioner of a Dionysian lifestyle he termed "big joy." He began his career in the 1940s with the films *The Potted Psalm* (1946) and *Mother's Day* (1948). Like his contemporary Allen Ginsberg, Broughton claimed to have poetic visions, his first at age three. He was born in Modesto, California, and for a time attended Stanford University. His celebration of the human body in both poetry and film is key to his legacy, and he is considered by many critics to be an heir to the artistic sensibilities of Walt Whitman. Broughton is considered an integral member of the San Francisco Renaissance and was a member of the **radical faeries.**

Broughton was married to Susanna Hart, with whom he created an intellectual community, but in 1974 he met Canadian filmmaker Joel Singer, with whom he shared the rest of his life. Together, they created the short avant-garde film, *The Gardener of Eden* (1981), and others. In his lifetime, Broughton produced 23 films and 23 books. His film *The Pleasure Garden* (1953) won an award at the Cannes Film Festival.

The poet Thom Gunn (1929–2004) was born in Kent, England, but died in his adopted home of San Francisco. Gunn was a member of the Movement, a poetry movement that eschewed performance poetry and the neoromantic climate of the 1950s. These poets embraced form and content. Although Gunn's poetry was formal, his content was nontraditional in that it dealt with homosexuality and the AIDS epidemic.

Gunn attended Trinity College, Cambridge, and the year after his graduation he published *Fighting Terms* (1954) to much acclaim. He received a fellowship to Stanford University, where he studied with Yvor Winters; over the next two decades, Gunn would begin to write more openly about his homosexuality. His most important work is considered to be *The Man with Night Sweats* (1992), a memorial to those close to him who died of AIDS. Gunn received the Lenore Marshall Poetry Prize for this book. Gunn is also known for his collection of essays, *The Occasions of Poetry* (1982). His honors include an Arts Council of Great Britain Award, a Rockefeller Prize, and fellowships from the Guggenheim and the MacArthur foundations. In 1994, his *Collected Poems* was published.

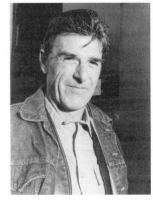

Thom Gunn. Photo by Robert Pruzan, courtesy of the Gay, Lesbian, Bisexual, Transgender Historical Society, San Francisco.

Further Reading

Ellingham, Lewis, and Kevin Killman. 1998. *Poet Be Like God: Jack Spicer and the San Francisco Renaissance*. Hanover, NH: University of New England Press.

Nancy McGuire Roche

Sapphire (1950–)

Recipient of a BFA from the Davis Center for the Performing Arts and an MFA from Brooklyn College, poet, novelist, and short story writer Sapphire (Ramona Lofton) was born in Fort Ord, California, and has worked as a performance artist, social worker, and educator. In 1987, she published her first poetry collection, *Meditations on the Rainbow*. Dedicated to silenced queer women, *Meditations* explores the impact that racism and **homophobia** have had on the lives of lesbian and bisexual African American women and calls for greater empowerment and visibility for queer women within the African American community. Sapphire's next work, *American Dreams* (1994), is a fierce and often painful collection of poetry and prose, which uses visceral, vivid language to explore the violence and oppression experienced by African American women and men in America's homophobic, racist, and **classist** society. *American Dreams* includes numerous poems about the author's experiences of childhood sexual abuse, as well as the controversial poem "Wild Thing," narrated from the perspective of a young male rapist. In 1996, Sapphire published her first novel, the critically acclaimed *Push*, which tells the story of Precious Jones, an HIV-positive incest survivor who finds healing from her troubled past through reading and writing poetry. Sapphire's 1999 poetry collection *Black Wings and Blind Angels* includes her "Gorillas in the Mist" cycle, which explores the prevalence of police brutality against African American men, poems about her healing from childhood sexual abuse, her relationship with her abusive parents, and the evolution of her sexual identity. Having previously identified as a lesbian, in *Black Wings and Blind Angels*, Sapphire rejects this label, writing poems about her desire for, and relationships with, men. In both her poetry and prose, Sapphire offers brutally honest, and often painfully personal, reflections on race, sexuality, and violence in American society.

Further Reading

Fran, Gordon. 2000. "Breaking Karma: A Conversation with Sapphire." *Poets and Writers* (January–February): 24–31.

Mackel, Kimberly M. 2001. "Sapphire and Scholinski: Women's Voices Resisting Rape in Contemporary United States Literature and Culture." PhD diss., Appalachian State University.

Holly M. Kent

May Sarton (1912–)

May Sarton, born in Belgium, came to the United States in 1916, where she produced over 50 works, including novels, poetry volumes, journals, memoirs, and children's books before her death in 1995. Sarton was already a published poet before she was 18 but turned her energies to pursuing a career in the theater. Her theatrical aspirations thwarted by the Great Depression, Sarton returned to writing and soon published two collections of poetry as well as her first novel, *The Single Hound*. Throughout her life, Sarton considered herself first a poet and expressed great regret that her poetry never received the same acclaim as her other works. Although Sarton's letters and memoirs attest to her commitment to her poetry, her journals and memoirs brought her the greatest acclaim and audience. *Plant Dreaming Deep* (1968) and *Journal of a Solitude* (1973) seemed to hit a chord with readers, particularly women, as both works detailed Sarton's struggle to establish a life as a woman living alone and pursuing her own interests. Arriving at a time when feminism was making special headway into the academic and social worlds, the books were quickly adopted as feminist works. Later journals continued to explore similar themes over Sarton's life course. *Recovering: A Journal* detailed Sarton's recovery from a mastectomy and a failed relationship, while *After the Stroke, Endgame, Encore*, and *At Eighty-Two* all dealt with the vicissitudes of an aging and solitary female artist at work despite a number of health issues and setbacks, including a 1990 stroke, several bouts with depression, and a number of conflicts with friends and fans. Sarton eschewed being labeled a lesbian writer, asserting her desire to reach a universal audience, but much of her work explores lesbian relationships to some degree. Sarton's own romantic attachments figure in her journals and memoirs. References to possible liaisons with such luminaries as Eva Le Gallienne appear in many of Sarton's works, and Sarton does explore her long-term relationship with Judy Matlack, most especially the great loss Sarton felt when Matlack died in 1982. Two of Sarton's novels in particular address gay and lesbian issues. *Mrs. Stevens Hears the Mermaids Singing* (1965; in 2004 a film version appeared under the same name) is often hailed as Sarton's acknowledgment of her own lesbianism and relates the events of a single day in the life of a renowned poet who counsels a young male poet friend dealing with his own sexuality and then faces the piercing questions of a literary magazine interview. *The Education of Harriet Hatfield* (1989) is the story of a woman who, after losing her female partner of several decades, opens a woman's bookstore, which is the object of vandalism and which eventually leads to the outing of the main character in the local newspaper. In these novels, as well as in the journals and memoirs, Sarton seemed to speak to the experience of readers who sought lives outside of the usual boundaries.

Further Reading

Fulk, Mark. 2001. *Understanding May Sarton*. Columbia: University of South Carolina Press.

Milton W. Wendland

Frederic Allen Sawyer (1957–)

San Francisco playwright and director, Frederic Allen Sawyer Jr. began his career collaborating with John Karr, developing new works at Theatre Rhinoceros, the nation's oldest gay theater. From there, the pair moved on to the ArtFull Circle

Theatre, where they staged drag musical adaptations of Hollywood movies. Working with Mark Sargent and Paul Anelli, Sawyer wrote *Christmas with the Crawfords*, which became a perennial favorite. From his experience working with drag performers, Sawyer was inspired to find ways to expand the genre. He wrote the plays *Women's Prison Christmas* (with Sargent) and *Whatever Happened to Sister George*. These productions had all the over-the-top costumes and camp of his drag shows but were performed by all-women casts.

In the mid-1990s Sawyer formed his own acting company, the Hot Pants Homo Players. The company had great success with Sawyer's trilogy, *Hot Pants Homo*, *Senator Swish*, and *Lavender Lockeroom*. Each of these plays used a 1960s pulp novel as a starting point. As was required at the time, these novels all had unhappy endings in which the characters had to renounce their homosexuality or end up in a sad, lonely existence, but not so in Sawyer's version. In what he calls his "pornographic after-school specials" a pro-gay message is always hidden within the campy comedy, but, most importantly, his protagonists never find happiness until they completely accept their homosexuality. In contrast, Sawyer's *Gross Indulgences: The Trials of Liberace* showed how tragic a life in the closet could be.

Further Reading

"San Francisco Professional Queer Theater: Theatre Rhinoceros." Available at: http://www.therhino.org/history.html. Accessed April 30, 2007.

Jim Van Buskirk

Sarah Schulman (1958–)

A second-generation immigrant from a European Jewish family, playwright, novelist, and nonfiction writer, Sarah Schulman was born in New York City. She lives on Manhattan's Lower East Side, where much of her writing finds its setting. Her work has been awarded the American Library Association Book Award and the Stonewall Book Award, and she has received three New York Foundation for the Arts Fiction Fellowships. Her novels include *Shimmer* (1998), *Rat Bohemia* (1995), *Empathy* (1992), *People in Trouble* (1990), *After Delores* (1988), *Girls, Visions and Everything* (1986), and *The Sophie Horowitz Story* (1984). Schulman established herself in her earliest novels as a postmodern "queer" writer unafraid to confront political issues unapologetically and oftentimes against the trends of political correctness. Her novels often superimpose the fragmentation and alienation of a multifaceted contemporary life onto more traditional forms such as romance, mystery, or the picaresque through several postmodern techniques such as the use of nonlinear narrative, magical realism, and self-conscious irony. She is concerned with presenting and exploring the multiplicity and fluidity of urban identity, inclusive of and across variations of race, **class,** sexuality, and gender, as well as confronting the political implications of such an identity. Schulman has been a political activist involved in and coordinating such organizations as ACT UP Oral History Project and the **Lesbian Avengers.** Her novel *People in Trouble* has controversially been named as the original behind the award-winning musical *Rent.* In her nonfiction *STAGE-STRUCK: Theater, AIDS, and the Marketing of Gay America* (1998), Schulman addresses this controversy in addition to giving her comments on the presentation of homosexuals and homosexual issues for consumption by mass audiences.

Further Reading

Bachmann, Monica. 2008. "'My Place in Judaism': Geography, Ethnicity and Sexuality on Sarah Schulman's Lower East Side." *Shofar* 26 (2): 81.

Kulp, Denise. 1986. "Sarah Schulman: 'On the Road to....'" *off our backs* 16 (11).

Munt, Sally R. 1992. "What Does It Mean to Sing 'Somewhere over the Rainbow...' and Release Balloons?: Postmodernism and the Fiction of Sarah Schulman." *New Lesbian Criticism: Literary and Cultural Readings*, ed. Sally R. Munt, 33–49. New York: Columbia University Press.

Brandy T. Wilson

science fiction, fantasy, and horror

Critics often argue for a distinction between mimetic and fantastic literature, and within the fantastic for a subdivision into three modes or genres: science fiction, fantasy, and horror. Definitions of these fields are controversial, but as a rough approximation it can be said that science fiction works take place in worlds that are extrapolated from the writer's present by some means—that is, in worlds that are arguably possible. Fantasy works take place in worlds that are not arguably possible, most commonly because of the presence of some kind of magic.

Science fiction, as it emerged in the pulp magazines of the 1920s and 1930s in the United States, was subject to two contradictory tugs on its depictions of gender and sexuality. The first was the extent to which speculation freed its authors from contemporary constraints on how humans relate to each other. The second was an undeniable tendency toward social conservatism, for instance, toward the presumption that science and discovery would always be undertaken by men. (Justine Larbalestier [2002] reprints 1938–1939 correspondence from the teenage Isaac Asimov to the magazine *Astounding* decrying the presence of women—"swooning dames"—in science fiction at all.)

In these circumstances, exceptions to the conservatism of science fiction are rare but notable. Theodore Sturgeon (1918–1985) was perhaps the most persistent explorer of ideas about gender and sexuality. In "The World Well Lost" (1953), he describes Earth's reception of aliens exiled from their own culture because of their homosexuality, and in *Venus Plus X* (1960), he depicts a future utopia in which gender has been superceded, intercut with scenes from contemporary life showing—as the book argues—the ways in which traditional gender roles were being eroded. Sturgeon was not a lone example, though: Robert A. Heinlein (1907–1988), arguably the dominant figure of science fiction's "golden age," wrote "All You Zombies" (1959), a story in which, through time travel and a sex change, a young man is tricked into becoming his own father and mother. Its effect is, thus, solipsistic: its title defines how the protagonist feels about the rest of the human race.

The emergence of LGBTQ themes as subjects in the mainstream of these genres is inextricably linked with two other phenomena: (1) the rise of feminism in the genres between the mid-1960s and the end of the 1970s and (2) the "new wave" of experimentation in style and content heralded by Michael Moorcock's editorship (1964–1969) of the magazine *New Worlds* and Harlan Ellison's taboo-breaking anthologies *Dangerous Visions* (1967) and *Again, Dangerous Visions* (1972). Five authors are particularly emblematic of these changes: Samuel R. Delany (1942–), Thomas M. Disch (1940–2008), Ursula K. Le Guin (1929–), Joanna Russ (1937–), and James Tiptree Jr. (real name Alice B. Sheldon, 1915–1987).

Of these authors, Delany's career has been particularly wide-ranging. A black prodigy from Harlem, he began publishing at the age of 20 with conventional but colorful novels such as *The Jewels of Aptor* (1962). His work became denser and more ambitious over the following years and began reworking mythological materials; this phase came to a climax with *Nova* (1968). His protagonists became increasingly sexually ambiguous, but this aspect of his work only came to the forefront with *Dhalgren* (1975), a huge book depicting the arrival of the mysterious Kid in the weirdly dislocated near-future city of Bellona. The Kid's exploits—sexual and otherwise—are the core of the book and are rendered with almost autobiographical specificity. *Dhalgren* became a best-seller and for some remains a definitive rendering in fiction of the urban American experience in the 1960s. Delany's next novel, *Triton* (1976), was subtitled "An Ambiguous Heterotopia" and followed its male protagonist through a series of societies offering him a range of sexual possibilities, including that of becoming a woman. Delany's next major work was the four-volume Return to Nevèrÿon sequence, which used the trappings of heroic fantasy to examine some of Delany's growing concerns with society's relationship to the erotic, including the trappings of sadomasochism. The third volume, *Flight from Nevèrÿon* (1985), is particularly notable for containing "The Tale of Plagues and Carnivals," written in 1984, which offered parallels between the onset of a sexually transmitted disease in Delany's fantasy world and the arrival of AIDS in New York in the early 1980s. After another science fiction novel, *Stars in My Pocket like Grains of Sand* (1984), which foregrounded a gay relationship and was the first half of a never-completed diptych, Delany largely abandoned publishing fiction and turned his energy to other activities—largely within the context of academia. He has long been one of the most insightful critics of the fantastic and arguably the leading one from a queer perspective: his critical works include *The Jewel-Hinged Jaw: Notes on the Language of Science Fiction* (1977), *Starboard Wine: More Notes on the Language of Science Fiction* (1984), and *Longer Views: Extended Essays* (1996). He has also written a number of autobiographical works such as *The Motion of Light in Water: Sex and Science Fiction Writing in the East Village 1957–65* (1988), an important document on gay life in that period.

One of Delany's critical works is *The American Shore* (1978), a book-length study of "Angouleme," a short story by a gay near-contemporary, Thomas M. Disch. Disch emerged in the field as a writer of mordant and literate stories in the mid-1960s. He is best known within science fiction for a trio of novels that are often considered among the best the field has produced. *Camp Concentration* (1968) is a formidably dense story of artificial intelligence enhancement, without much LGBTQ content. *334* (1972), which includes the short story "Angouleme," is a depiction of a grimly realistic near-future New York, encompassing a range of perspectives from its disenfranchised subcultures—including gay people. *On Wings of Song* (1979) can be read without much difficulty as a fantastic rendering of the experience of growing up gay. Daniel Weinreb, raised in the conservative Midwest, discovers the hidden powers of song and flight and, through them, the lure of the big city. Disch has also written outside the genre—for instance, as a prolific poet and as theater critic for *The Nation*—but his major recent work is a sequence of horror novels set in a "meta-Minneapolis," beginning with *The Businessman: A Tale of Terror* (1984).

Ursula K. Le Guin had been publishing science fiction since the early 1960s but came fully to prominence with *The Left Hand of Darkness* (1969), a novel set within a larger "future history" sequence known as the Hainish books. *The Left Hand of Darkness* is set on a planet called Gethen, or Winter, and follows the progress of a Genly Ai, a human envoy attempting to establish better diplomatic relations with the Gethenian natives. He is soon befriended by Estraven, a Gethenian noble, and comes up against the immutable fact of Gethenian biology. Although Gethenians appear broadly human, they are neuter most of the time and only occasionally experience "kemmer," a period during which they are sexualized as either female or male. Genly falls in love with the (female) Estraven during a long and ultimately tragic journey across the planet's icy wilderness. Widely admired for its evocation of an alien culture—Le Guin's father, the anthropologist Alfred Kroeber, was an acknowledged influence on her—*The Left Hand of Darkness* is surely science fiction's best-known work addressing transgender issues. Le Guin has written prolifically since, often dealing with issues of gender and sexuality, and has also been an active critic. Perhaps her most prominent contribution in that area was coediting with Brian Attebery *The Norton Book of Science Fiction: North American Science Fiction, 1960–1990* (1993), a book presenting a canon skewed by design (some critics felt, excessively) to the presentation of perspectives on gender that had otherwise been excluded from science fiction.

Joanna Russ has an importance for feminist thought that extends far beyond science fiction, for instance, through books such as *How to Suppress Women's Writing* (1983). But her career in the field—from roughly 1960 to a public retirement in the late 1980s—produced a body of work that did more than any other to open up wider perspectives on gender and sexuality. "When It Changed" (1972), a short story set on an all-female utopia called Whileaway, was (as Larbalestier argues) "the first text in this period in which the case for heterosexuality has to be put at all" (Larbalestier 2002, 90). A novel, *The Female Man* (1975), offers Whileaway as one of a range of possibilities open to women, all available to be thought about and argued with.

James Tiptree Jr. was the pseudonym of Alice B. Sheldon, who led perhaps the most extraordinary life of any science fiction writer. She spent significant periods as a child traveling through Africa with her explorer parents; briefly married an alco-holic poet; served in U.S. Army photo intelligence in World War II; married Hunt-ingdon Sheldon, one of the leading lights of the newly formed Central Intelligence Agency; completed a PhD in experimental psychology; began submitting science fiction stories to magazines around her 50th birthday; and, in 1987, with both her husband and herself in poor health, shot him and then herself. She worked most effectively at shorter lengths, and the best of her stories are collected in *Her Smoke Rose Up Forever* (1990). As John Clute argues in the introduction to that volume, they tend to end in conflations of sex and death. "Houston, Houston, Do You Read," for instance, subjects the idea of an all-female utopia (1976) to even more detailed scrutiny than "When It Changed" had. "And I Awoke and Found Me Here on the Cold Hill's Side" (1972) searchingly examines the drive to have sex with the Other, an idea explored at much greater length in "A Momentary Taste of Being" (1975). Elsewhere in her work, such as the late novel *Brightness Falls from the Air* (1985), she takes for granted that homo- and heterosexual relationships can coexist in society and explores some of the implications.

After the pioneering work of these writers, it could be argued that LGBTQ themes were, if not normalized within the fantastic, then certainly legitimized to an extent they had not been before. It therefore becomes more difficult to select landmarks in the field, but a few can be suggested. An award was established from 1991 in the name of James Tiptree to honor work that expands or explores read-ers' understanding of gender. The Lambda Literary Award, instituted from 1988, is given to works in the fantastic, among other fields, and an annual convention, Wiscon, dedicated to exploring issues of gender and sexuality, celebrated its 30th meeting in 2006. (See, respectively, www.tiptree.org, www.lambdaliterary.org, and www.wiscon.info.)

Horror literature since the 1970s has been dominated by the work of Stephen King, but a number of other authors have emerged, some treating LGBTQ themes as their central concern. Clive Barker (1952–), British-born but long-term resident in the United States, is ecumenical in his treatment of sexuality. His early story "In the Hills, the Cities" (1984) treats the tensions in its central gay relationship matter-of-factly, while later works such as *The Great and Secret Show* (1989) and *Sacrament* (1996) encompass, among other things, the impact of AIDS. The works of Anne Rice (1941–), most famously *Interview with the Vampire* (1977), reimag-ine the old tropes of horror literature, with a distinctly erotic (and queer) slant. Poppy Z. Brite (1967–) is both a horror writer and a regional one, deeply attached to southern settings, particularly to New Orleans. Novels such as *Drawing Blood* (1993) depict gay relationships very directly while also playing with traditional tropes such as the haunted house. Michael Blumlein (1948–), a practicing physi-cian based in San Francisco, has produced some of the most striking fiction to date dealing with issues of gender mutability. "The Brains of Rats" (1986) and X, Y (1993) transform the chilly tone of medical reportage into a curiously humanistic exploration of the fragility of identity.

In the field of fantasy, one preeminent name is Marion Zimmer Bradley (1930–1999), who throughout her prolific career wrote about homosexual and bisexual characters. Her most famous sequence, the Darkover books, beginning with *The Planet Savers* (1962), presents a range of narratives, as it were, for making non-heterosexual characters part of wider families and communities. Ellen Kushner (1955–) is well known for *Swordspoint* (1987), a novel that complicates a dynastic fantasy setting with a gay relationship. Another prominent figure is Lawrence Schimel (1971–), who has produced both collections such as *The Drag Queen of Elfland* (1997) and anthologies such as *Things Invisible to See: Gay and Lesbian Tales of Magic Realism* (1998).

In science fiction, successors to the arguments begun by Russ's feminist utopias include *Woman on the Edge of Time* (1976) by Marge Piercy (1936–) and, in a rather different vein, *Walk to the End of the World* (1974) by Suzy McKee Charnas (1939–). The latter is a harrowing work depicting a misogynist dystopia where homosexual men rule and oppress the women necessary for the continuation of the species; in subsequent volumes reconciliations are reached with a necessary degree of difficulty. Octavia E. Butler (1947–2006) was, for most of her career, an almost unique example of an African American woman working in the field. Although she said that she was not a lesbian, many of her works, such as the alien pregnancy story "Bloodchild" (1984) and the Xenogenesis sequence, beginning with *Dawn* (1987), are amenable to a queer reading. Maureen McHugh (1959–) made a striking debut with *China Mountain Zhang* (1992), depicting a Chinese-dominated near-future and her gay protagonist's attempts to make sense of his life in a world where homosexuality is punishable by death. Melissa Scott (1960–) has written prolifically, depicting characters who are gay, lesbian, and transgendered; perhaps her best-known work is *Trouble and Her Friends* (1995), winner of a Lambda Literary Award. Nicola Griffith (1960–) has created one of the most interesting careers in science fiction, beginning with her novel *Ammonite* (1993) and its intriguing depiction of an alien planet's lesbian culture; she has also served as editor of Bending the Landscape, an anthology series of gay and lesbian fantastic work. Perhaps the most prominent contemporary writer of LGBTQ science fiction is Geoff Ryman (1951–), born in Canada, raised in Los Angeles, and residing in London for several decades. Ryman's work has ranged widely across genres, but includes a science-fictional treatment of Cambodian history, *The Unconquered Country* (1986); a lesbian love story set in a radically transformed London, *The Child Garden* (1988); and the story of the last village in the world to join the Internet, *Air* (2004), which features an unusual treatment of pregnancy. His fantasies include *The Warrior Who Carried Life* (1985), which begins with a woman transforming herself into a man, and *Lust* (2001), a meditation on gay life and love set in contemporary London.

If this entry has concentrated on written work rather than that in other media, this reflects to some extent the constraints on depictions of sexuality in mainstream film and television. There are exceptions, of course, most notably Joss Whedon's *Buffy the Vampire Slayer* (television, 1997–2003). But fans of media science fiction have found their own ways of queering straight texts, most obviously through fan fiction and slash fiction. The subgenre of "Kirk-Spocking" derived from the original 1960s *Star Trek* may be the earliest example of this, but slash fiction can now be found on the Internet taking almost any fantastic television series or franchise as its starting point—as well as many nonfantastic ones. Once again, queering the fantastic has become a quasi-underground activity. But the achievement of the last few decades means that it is not only underground.

Further Reading

Curlovich, John Michael, Michael Rowe, and David Thomas Lord. 2006. *Triptych of Terror: Three Chilling Tales by the Masters of Gay Horror*. New York: Alyson Books.

Delany, Samuel R. 1996. *Longer Views: Extended Essays*. Hanover and London: Wesleyan University Press.

Delany, Samuel R. 2001. *Times Square Red, Times Square Blue*. New York: New York University Press.

Larbalestier, J. 2002. *The Battle of the Sexes in Science Fiction*. Middletown, CT: Wesleyan University Press.

Le Guin, Ursula K., and B. Attebery, eds. 1993. *The Norton Book of Science Fiction: North American Science Fiction 1960–1990*. New York and London: Norton.

Phillips, J. 2006. *James Tiptree, Jr.: The Double Life of Alice B. Sheldon*. New York: St Martin's Press.

Russ, Joanna. 1995. *To Write Like a Woman: Essays in Feminism and Science Fiction*. Bloomington and Indianapolis: Indiana University Press.

Graham Sleight

science and medicine of homosexuality (history)

The term *homosexuality* was first coined in 1869 by the German-Hungarian nobleman and writer Karl Maria Kertbeny after using the term in private correspondence with Karl Henrich Ulrichs. Considered by many as the first homosexual **activist,** Ulrichs invented the term *Urnings* to designate men with same-sex erotic desire. In his writings, Ulrichs theorized that an Urning was neither a true male nor a true female but constituted a third sex, a "half-man" who possessed characteristics and the soul of the opposite sex. This notion of "sexual inversion" reflected what the German physician Karl Westphal had called "contrary sexual feeling" in an 1869 German psychiatric journal article. By 1886, when Richard von Krafft-Ebing published his magnum opus *Psychopathia Sexualis*, sexual pathology had emerged as a new field over which psychiatrists and other medical professionals held the most authority. In his influential study, Krafft-Ebing described homosexuality as a form of diseased neurotic degeneracy. According to this perspective, the homosexual body was a sign of evolutionary regression: since homosexual traits blurred the distinction between masculinity and femininity, homosexual individuals exhibited an unfavorable anatomical and psychological hermaphroditism that resembled the lower end of the evolutionary scale.

Toward the end of the nineteenth century, in part under Krafft-Ebing's influence, scientists, doctors, and self-appointed experts in Europe, followed by the ones in the United States, began to produce numerous volumes and an extensive literature on the subject of homosexuality. In Europe, monographs exclusively devoted to the subject that were published in the 1890s include Albert Moll's *Perversion of the Sex Instinct* (1891), Albert von Schrenck-Notzing's *Therapeutic Suggestions in Pathological Manifestations of the Sexual Sense* (1892), Julien Chevalier's *An Illness of the Personality: Sexual Inversion* (1893), Edward Carpenter's *Homogenic Love and Its Place in a Free Society* (1894), Magnus Hirschfeld's *Sappho and Socrates* (1896), Marc-Andre Raffalovich's *Uranianism and Unisexuality: A Study on the Different Manifestations of the Sexual Instinct* (1896), and Havelock Ellis's *Sexual Inversion* (1897).

Across the Atlantic, physicians' reports of homosexuality first appeared in American medical journals in the early 1880s. For this group of doctors who claimed to have "discovered" the first cases of homosexuality in the United States, natural and normal sexuality followed the middle-class Victorian ideal of social order, according to which women were thought to be chaste and passive and men dominant and protective. Because homosexuality affronted this class-based Victorian ideal, most American doctors who wrote about homosexuality around the turn of the twentieth century viewed the existence of homosexuality as evidence for a degenerating social order. By the 1910s, not only had American medical writers increasingly adopted Krafft-Ebing's degeneration explanation of homosexuality, but also Freudian psychoanalysis had begun to transform American psychiatric thinking. Following their European counterparts in conceptualizing homosexuality in both degeneration and psychogenic frameworks, medical experts in the United States emphasized that homosexuality was more prevalent among working-class individuals who had less control over their sexual desires than "normal" middle-class people. This class-based interpretation reinforced American physicians' assumption that sexual perversion was closely related to primitive lust.

The first empirically based social scientific study of homosexuality in America was probably undertaken by lesbian researcher Mildred Berryman, who conducted interviews with a sample of 25 self-identified homosexual women (including herself) and 8 homosexual men living in Salt Lake City in the 1920s and 1930s. This project was to have been Berryman's honor's thesis at Westminster College in Salt Lake City, but she stopped working on her unpublished and unfinished manuscript "The Psychological Phenomena of the Homosexual" in 1938 after 20 years of research. Most of the interviewees expressed concerns about revealing their sexual orientation to the public, so it was not until five years after Berryman's death in 1977 that historians Vern Bullough and Bonnie Bullough published their analysis of the empirical data that she had collected 40 years before.

Apart from Berryman's study, American sex scientists under the influence of Freud after the Great War began to view sex as more complicated than a simple form of expression between lovers. Whereas the popular discourse in the 1920s strongly promoted "marital hygiene" and introduced the concept of heterosexual "companionate marriage" as the ideal form of intimacy, the scientific sex researchers of the era regarded homosexual practice—especially lesbianism—with a much greater level of tolerance. In Katherine Bement Davis's pioneer study *Factors in the Sex Lives of Twenty-Two Hundred Women* (1929), for example, same-sex erotic experience was found to be fairly common in the lives of normal women, both married and unmarried. Around the same time, gynecologist Robert Latou Dickinson voiced his firm belief that doctors should concern themselves with assisting women to achieve sexual happiness. Collaborating with psychologist Lura Beam, Dickinson published *A Thousand Marriages* (1931) and *The Single Woman* (1934) based on his gynecological experiences since the 1890s. In addition to promoting sex education for the American public, the writings of Davis and Dickinson also expressed the idea that sexual desire and activity, whether procreative or nonprocreative, were important to the happiness of American women and men. Instead of understanding homosexual desires as merely pathological, sex researchers in the 1920s interpreted homosexuality simply as a variation of normal sexuality.

The best-known scientific and medical study of homosexuality in the 1930s was conducted by the Committee for the Study of Sex Variants (CSSV), established by Dickinson in 1935 in **New York City.** Under the supervision of psychiatrist George Henry, the CSSV was the first government-funded large-scale project exclusively devoted to the study of homosexuality in the United States. The CSSV included prominent experts in the biological sciences, social sciences, and medicine. CSSV members, including Dickinson, used a combination of methods to study sex variants (their term for homosexuals), such as extensive physical examinations, nude photography, X-ray studies, and tracings of genitals and nipples. A majority of the research done by the group culminated in George Henry's *Sex Variants: A Study of Homosexual Patterns* (1941), which featured, most notably, case studies of 40 lesbians and 40 homosexual men.

The formation of the CSSV was linked to a lesbian activist, Helen Reitman, who was the lover of anarchist Emma Goldman from 1908 to 1918 and who later changed her name to Jan Gay in 1927. Before Gay contacted Dickinson, she visited Magnus Hirschfeld's Institute for Sexual Science in Berlin in the 1920s and learned from him techniques for conducting sexuality surveys. After reading about Gay's work, and with some initial financial support from self-identified homosexuals, Dickinson quickly turned to the National Committee on Maternal Health for more funding in order to establish the CSSV. Gay was most instrumental in establishing the CSSV since she recruited most, if not all, of the homosexual volunteer participants whom were studied. In addition to the efforts of people like Ulrichs and Hirschfeld in Europe, Gay's involvement in the CSSV provides a historical example showing how scientific and medical studies of homosexuality were, from the very outset, not merely an "elite" type of discourse that developed without the influence of self-identified homosexuals.

Seven years after the publication of *Sex Variants*, Alfred Kinsey and his research colleagues published their groundbreaking volume *Sexual Behavior in the Human Male* (1948), which documented the high frequency of homosexual behavior in American society. The second Kinsey report, *Sexual Behavior in the Human Female*, followed five years later in 1953. Among the critics of Kinsey's work at the time, in addition to those sociologists and statisticians who were concerned with the quantitative and sampling methods employed, the most vociferous ones were psychiatrists. American psychiatrists, who were already involved in screening military inductees for homosexuality during World Wwar II and had gained increasing cultural authority ever since, argued that Kinsey's studies failed to capture the dynamic and developmental nature of human sexuality. Prominent figures in the profession, such as Sandor Rado, Edmund Bergler, and Irving Bieber, rigidly viewed homosexuality as a developed phobia of the opposite sex: they construed homosexuality as a mental disease that could be and should be cured through psychotherapy.

Nevertheless, according to many historians' interpretations, what Kinsey's research group provided for the emerging **homophile movement** in the postwar era was precisely a piece of scientific evidence that the homosexual community could use to challenge **mental health** practitioners' pathologizing view of homosexuality. As a result of this process, gay activists from the 1960s to the early 1970s—situated within a sociopolitical context in which the feminist, student, and civil rights movements all reached their high point—galvanized a powerful force that pushed mental health experts to reconsider the psychopathological status of homosexuality. The American Psychiatric Association's (APA) decision to remove homosexuality from its list of mental disorders in 1973 exemplifies one of the key accomplishments of the modern **gay liberation movement,** the beginning of which, for many, was marked by the **Stonewall Riots** of 1969.

In reworking medical opinions about gender and sexuality, the gay liberation movement had successfully transformed American society into a social environment that was more tolerant of homosexuality by the end of the 1970s. Meanwhile, however, a new conservative political coalition rooted in right-wing Christian fundamentalism also gained momentum, slowly generating backlashes to the kinds of social activism characteristic of the 1960s cultural revolution. The situation for gays and lesbians changed drastically in the 1980s when the biomedical community confronted a disease unprecedented in nature—the acquired immune deficiency syndrome (AIDS). In July 1981, doctors published the first report of this "rare cancer" in 41 homosexual men in New York and California. By the end of the decade, AIDS had been diagnosed in over 147,000 individuals and had killed 80 percent of them.

Because the disease was first discovered in homosexual patients, the media in the 1980s often associated AIDS exclusively with homosexuality and depicted it as the "gay plague," which was initially thought to be harmless to heterosexuals by both physicians and the American public. Facing enormous pressure nationwide stemming from the new epidemic, many members of the gay community started to blame promiscuity among urban gay men. One of the most influential public figures that advocated this view was **Larry Kramer,** who in 1987 helped found the AIDS Coalition to Unleash Power (**ACT UP**), a direct-action organization that forced governmental agencies; scientific, medical, and pharmaceutical experts; and the general public to prioritize AIDS research and treatment. Under the influence of groups like ACT UP, AIDS service and charity associations eventually drew a broad range of support from straight people, thus building a friendlier, less **homophobic** American environment by the end of the 1990s.

In the closing decades of the twentieth century, the growing visibility of gay men and lesbians in the public sphere was accompanied by their increasing presence in health care professions, which greatly assisted in reducing homophobia and heterosexism in the health care system itself. Even after the 1973 landmark APA decision to depathologize homosexuality, certain members of the mental health community never stopped voicing the possibility of treating homosexuals through "reparative" therapy (see **psychiatry and homosexuality**). In 1992, psychoanalyst Charles Socarides established the National Association for Research and Therapy of Homosexuality (NARTH), whose recent president is Joseph Nicolosi. In two books that he published in the early 1990s, Nicolosi insisted that he had successfully converted several male homosexuals through reparative therapy. At the beginning of the twenty-first century, however, organizations like NARTH are regarded as having very little professional value, because the American Psychological Association in 1997, followed by the American Psychiatric Association in 1998, formally opposed sexual orientation conversion therapies. Most mental health professionals today acknowledge the implicit homophobic assumption made by proponents of this kind of therapy. The increasing number of self-identified gay and lesbian individuals working as health care providers has caused various health professions to place new affirmative emphases on helping sexual minorities cope with social stigma, rather than fixing their sexual orientation.

Since the coining of the term homosexuality in 1869, its etiological causes continue to puzzle the American imagination even to the present day. In the late nineteenth century, most neurologists and psychiatrists adopted Krafft-Ebing's degeneration theory in explaining homosexuality, while other sexologists like Ulrichs and Hirschfeld contended that homosexuality represented nothing but a harmless natural variation within the entire human population. Freudian psychoanalytic theory increasingly permeated the way American psychiatrists understood homosexuality over the course of the first half of the twentieth century. Therefore, by the mid-twentieth century, when Kinsey's research group published large-scale studies of sexual behavior that employed social science–oriented methods, their definition of normality came into direct conflict with the clinical concept of normality that anchored the psychiatric framework of psychosexual development.

Advancements in neuroscience and molecular biotechnology in the second half of the twentieth century enabled gay scientists to reconfirm the "normality" of homosexuality by presenting evidence of its biological causes. Neuroscientist Simon LeVay courageously published his famous article "A Difference in Hypothalamic Structure between Homosexual and Heterosexual Men" in the prestigious journal *Science* in 1991, claiming to have discovered a fundamental difference in neuroanatomical structure between straight and gay men. He subsequently authored the book *The Sexual Brain* (1993) to advance his argument that gay men have brains similar to women's brains. Meanwhile, geneticist Dean Hamer and his research associates investigated the relationship between genes and sexual orientation and published their findings in 1993, also in *Science*. The first part of their study traced the family trees of gay men, looking for patterns in the relationships between gay men and their relatives; the second part of their study identified a genetic marker of homosexuality on a small region of the X chromosome, Xq28, which some people interpreted as evidence of "gay genes."

Both studies were severely criticized on numerous grounds within and without the scientific profession and also drew fire from both inside and outside the gay and lesbian community. For the scientific circle, LeVay's and Hamer's works presented several methodological flaws, and the failure of subsequent attempts by other scientists to replicate their results only increased the suspicion concerning the validity of their findings. For the gay and lesbian community, even if LeVay's and Hamer's scientific findings convincingly demonstrated that sexual orientation is biologically determined at birth (it logically follows that there is nothing "unnatural" about homosexuality), such findings might also have dangerous and unethical repercussions, such as abortion or genetic engineering of gay fetuses.

Interestingly, LeVay's idea of a cross-gendered brain significantly resembled the theory of "sexual inversion" articulated by late nineteenth-century European sexologists, while Hamer's attempts to identify biological markers of homosexuality coincided with the effort of those like Hirschfeld who persistently maintained that homosexuality was a congenital predisposition and thus a benign variation. In addition, the first part of Hamer's study, which mapped the maternal transmission of male homosexuality, strongly echoed the way Krafft-Ebing and his followers attributed homosexuality to hereditary factors in his degeneration framework. Connected as it is to the search for the etiology of homosexuality, the role of contemporary biomedical science as a powerful instrument of either oppression or emancipation continues to loom over the LGBTQ community.

Further Reading

Bayer, Ronald. 1981. *Homosexuality and American Psychiatry: The Politics of Diagnosis*. New York: Basic Books.

LeVay, Simon. 1996. *Queer Science: The Use and Abuse of Research into Homosexuality*. Cambridge, MA: MIT Press.

Minton, Henry L. 2002. *Departing from Deviance: A History of Homosexual Rights and Emancipatory Science in America*. Chicago: University of Chicago Press.

Rosario, Vernon. 2002. *Homosexuality and Science: A Guide to the Debates*. Santa Barbara, CA: ABC-CLIO.

Terry, Jennifer. 1999. *An American Obsession: Science, Medicine, and Homosexuality in Modern Society*. Chicago: University of Chicago Press.

Howard Hsueh-Hao Chiang

David Sedaris (1956–)

Born in Binghamton, New York, but raised in Raleigh, North Carolina, humorist David Sedaris is described by *Publishers Weekly* as "Garrison Keillor's evil twin." He graduated from the Art Institute in Chicago but decided he was not much of an artist. In fact, when he was discovered for his writing abilities, he was working as a house cleaner in New York. He is compared to Augusten Burroughs for his ability to transform the mundane into comic and often touching or revelatory events. Sedaris is the author of best-selling story and essay collections, including *Barrel Fever* (1994), *Naked* (1997), *Holidays on Ice* (1997), *Me Talk Pretty One Day* (2000), *Dress Your Family in Corduroy and Denim* (2004), *Children Playing before a Statue of Hercules* (short stories by others, edited by Sedaris) (2005), and *When You Are Engulfed in Flames* (2008). He is also noted for his appearances on Ira Glass's show on National Public Radio, where he first gained fame for his *SantaLand Diaries* and a notorious description of his crush on one of the other elves in Santa's entourage at Macy's. He regularly writes for the *New Yorker*. He has written some plays with his comic actress sister, Amy (of *Strangers with Candy* fame). David Sedaris has won a **Publishing Triangle** Award and a Thurber Prize for American humor. He was designated by *Time* magazine as Humorist of the Year (2001) and has been nominated for two Grammy awards. He does not drive nor use the Internet or a cell phone. He told an interviewer that he thinks autobiography is "the last place you would look for truth" (Knight 2007, 80), and he has sometimes been accused of blurring the line between truth and fiction in his essays. He finds it odd that there are gay sections in bookstores, as if the sexual orientation defines the writer. Sedaris now spends more time in France and England than in the United States. He recently wrote a story about a leech that lives in the asshole of a hippopotamus: as he observes, everyone has an eye for different things.

Further Reading

Knight, Lania. 2007. "A Conversation with David Sedaris." *The Missouri Review* 30 (1): 72–89. Available at: http://muse.jhu.edu/journals/missouri_review/v030/30.1knight.html. Accessed May 3, 2008.

John C. Hawley

George Segal (1927–2000)

George Segal was an American artist, usually identified with the pop art movement, who was best known for his figurative sculptures and public monuments. Born in the Bronx to Eastern European Jewish immigrants, Segal spent most of his life in South Brunswick, New Jersey, where he worked on his family's poultry farm and later taught art.

In the early 1960s, Segal discovered what would become his signature style when one of his students brought him some plaster-impregnated gauze strips of the kind used to make casts for broken bones. He began using the gauze to make full-body plaster casts of human subjects, placing them amid environmental assemblages made from found objects to create life-sized tableaux. The ghostly figures, usually left white but occasionally painted, were generally engaged in mundane, everyday situations. Segal described the overarching theme of his work as "the presence of man in his daily life."

In the 1970s Segal began casting figures in bronze and went on to create a number of outdoor memorials and monuments. Though heterosexual, Segal was commissioned in 1979 to create a public memorial commemorating the Stonewall Rebellion to be placed in Greenwich Village's Sheridan Park near the site of the original Stonewall Inn. The sculpture that resulted, *Gay Liberation*, was the first piece of public art to deal with the struggles of LGBTQ people. It portrayed two same-sex couples—a pair of standing males and two females seated on a park bench. Rendered in Segal's distinctive all-white patina, one of the men lays his hand on his partner's shoulder while one of the seated women tenderly touches her partner's thigh. Despite the understated tone of the work, local controversy prevented the memorial from being installed, and it was not until 1992 that it was finally permanently placed there.

Further Reading

Hunter, Sam. 1989. *George Segal.* New York: Rizzoli.

Segal, George. 2003. *George Segal: Bronze.* New York: Mitchell-Innes & Nash.

Tuchman, Phyllis. 1983. *George Segal.* New York: Abbeville Press.

Paul Falzone

The sculpture "Portrait of Sidney Janis with Mondrian Painting," was part of an exhibit featuring works of artist George Segal at the Hirshhorn Museum in 1998. The sculpture, created in 1967, is a plaster cast of a renowned art dealer displaying an actual Mondrian painting. Segal wrapped live models with plaster soaked bandages to create the figures. AP Photo/Wilfredo Lee.

Hubert Selby (1928–2004)

Hubert Selby was a novelist chiefly known for his groundbreaking and controversial *Last Exit to Brooklyn.* His other published works include the novels *The Room, The Demon, Requiem for a Dream, The Willow Tree,* and *Waiting Period* and a collection of short fiction, *Song of the Silent Snow. Last Exit to Brooklyn,* first published by Grove Press in 1964, is the work that deals most directly with LGBTQ issues, specifically in its portrayal of the characters of Georgette, a young transsexual, and Harry Black, a union leader who is deeply in the **closet.** Selby's portrayal of these characters is complex and nuanced, at once sympathetic and unflinching, which has led to some controversy, as has the novel as a whole; it was the subject of a 1967 **obscenity** trial in Great Britain.

Neither Georgette nor Harry Black is a particularly admirable character—Georgette is unstable, Harry is incompetent and virtually irredeemable—and the book has been criticized for what are seen as negative portrayals. However, it has also been noted that these characters' behavior is not pathological but environmental: they behave the way they do not as a result of their sexual orientation but as a result of their status as societal outcasts. This naturalistic approach to transsexual and homosexual characters places *Last Exit to Brooklyn* at odds with other works of its time, which often depicted sexual orientation as a pathology and LGBTQ characters as pitiable and ineffectual.

Further Reading

Sorrentino, Gilbert. 1981. "The Art of Hubert Selby." *The Review of Contemporary Fiction* 1 (2): 335–46.

Vorda, Allan. "Examining the Disease: An Interview with Hubert Selby, Jr." *Literary Review* 35 (2): 288–302.

Wertime, Richard A. 1974. "Psychic Vengeance in *Last Exit to Brooklyn.*" *Literature and Psychology* 24: 153–66.

Will Curl

serosorting

Serosorting describes the process by which men who have sex with men (MSM) make decisions about sexual behavior based on the knowledge or perception that a partner has the same HIV serostatus that they have. Specifically, serosorting describes decisions about (a) whether or not to have sex with a given partner or (b) which sex acts one might engage in, especially whether or not to engage in high-risk behaviors like unprotected anal intercourse, given that both participants are HIV-negative or HIV-positive (i.e., seroconcordant). Serosorting is at work when, for example, an HIV-positive man has unprotected anal intercourse with another HIV-positive man; both enjoy the physical sensation of **barebacking** and simultaneously negate the risk of spreading HIV to a previously uninfected person. These behaviors still hold important health risks including the spread of sexually transmitted infections (STI) or HIV superinfection (infection with a different strain of HIV). Using the Internet to meet sex partners may facilitate discussions of HIV status. Public health officials are reluctant to endorse serosorting as an HIV risk reduction strategy because of the possibility that individuals are unaware of their true HIV status (i.e., believe themselves to be HIV-negative but became infected after their last HIV test) and because it encourages suspicion and divisiveness in the LGBTQ community. In the scientific literature, studies have shown trends in sex-partner selection of MSM toward seroconcordant partnerships. This is especially true for HIV-positive MSM, who may also use serosorting to avoid rejection or stigmatization by potential HIV-negative partners.

Further Reading

Parsons, J. T., Joseph Severino, Jose Nanin, Joseph C. Punzalan, Kirk von Sternberg, Whitney Missildine, and David Frost. 2006. "Positive, Negative, Unknown: Serosorting and Assumptions of HIV Status among HIV Positive Men Who Have Sex with Men." *AIDS Education and Prevention* 18 (2): 139–49.

David W. Pantalone

Servicemembers Legal Defense Network (SLDN)

Founded by Michelle M. Benecke and C. Dixon Osburn in the wake of the "don't ask, don't tell" debate of the Clinton administration, the Servicemembers Legal Defense Network (SLDN) works to end legal discrimination against U.S. military personnel who are—or are suspected of being—gay or lesbian. Since its inception in 1993, SLDN has become a formidable political and legal advocate for military people who are gay, lesbian, bisexual, transgender, or HIV-positive. By 2007, SLDN boasted an operating budget of $3 million, 17 full-time staff members, and dozens of dedicated board members, including an advisory board packed with high-ranking veterans from the ranks of the enlisted as well as the officer corps.

Benecke, who served as coexecutive director of SLDN with Osburn through 2000 (Osburn stayed on as sole executive director until April 2007), was commissioned as an officer through Army ROTC and served in air defense artillery. Because of the army's policy against homosexuality, she left the service—and a full scholarship—to attend Harvard Law School. After graduating, Benecke joined forces with Osburn, a graduate of the Georgetown Law Center, to focus on the problems facing military personnel under the "don't ask, don't tell" policy. The policy itself was a compromise forged in the aftermath of a 1992 campaign promise by candidate Bill Clinton, who vowed to end the ban on homosexuals serving in the military. Once in office, President Clinton's plan met resistance from Congress and the Pentagon.

After congressional hearings, a Pentagon task force, and input from military sociologists, Congress passed the "don't ask, don't tell" statute. Crafted to permit homosexuals to serve under certain conditions, the policy failed to stop the harassment and discharge of suspected gay men and lesbians and created new problems of its own. In fact, discharges soared, complaints mounted, and academic criticism of the policy's unfounded assumptions and arbitrary implementation ensued.

SLDN provided legal assistance to thousands of servicemembers facing administrative and criminal sanctions under the awkward new policy. In addition to building its own cadre of military-legal experts, SLDN galvanized the support of hundreds of pro bono attorneys to represent individuals being investigated or threatened

In this March 26, 2007, photo, Andrew Chapin of New York City, takes part in a rally on Capitol Hill in Washington, supporting legislative efforts to repeal the military's "don't ask, don't tell" policy regarding LGBTQ soldiers. AP Photo/Susan Walsh.

with discharge. It waged an effective public relations battle to keep attention focused on the plight of harassed and silenced LGBTQ people in uniform, using tragedies like the gay-bashing murders of Allen Schindler (killed in 1992 onboard a navy ship) and Barry Winchell (killed in 1999 at Fort Campbell, Kentucky) to publicize the injustice of the policy. SLDN's decade of annual reports (1995 to 2004) became gold mines of information for legal scholars and others interested in understanding the policy's impact. SLDN's Web site (www.sldn.org) linked users to government reports, press releases, and stories of servicemembers who suffered under the policy.

After the terrorist attacks of September 11, 2001, SLDN tracked and publicized the plummeting rate of gay-related discharges, pointing out that as the military's need for qualified personnel increased, discharges for alleged homosexuality decreased. SLDN capitalized on the new popularity of arguments about military necessity to increase the pressure to repeal the "don't ask, don't tell" statute. Rising social acceptance of homosexuality and advances in legal protections for gays and lesbians led to enough support for lifting the ban that, in February 2007, Representative Martin Meehan (D-MA), with more than 100 cosponsors, reintroduced a law that would repeal the "don't ask, don't tell" statute and replace it with a law that banned discrimination in the military based on sexual orientation. SLDN also continued to fight for change in the courts by arguing that "don't ask, don't tell" violates the U.S. Constitution. Yet in March 2007, Marine Corps General Peter Pace, the chairman of the Joint Chiefs of Staff, likened homosexuality to adultery and called it immoral in remarks made during an interview with the *Chicago Tribune*. Antigay attitudes clearly remain, at high levels, even if progress is being made in some quarters toward allowing open LGBTQ individuals in the military.

Further Reading

Belkin, Aaron, and Geoffrey Bateman, eds. 2003. *Don't Ask, Don't Tell: Exploring the Debates on the Gay Ban in the U.S. Military.* Boulder, CO: Lynne Rienner Publishers.
Wolff, Tobias Barrington. 2004. "Political Representation and Accountability under Don't Ask, Don't Tell." *Iowa Law Review* 89: 1633.

Elizabeth L. Hillman

Services and Advocacy for GLBT Elders (SAGE)

The oldest and largest agency dedicated to providing services to LGBT seniors, SAGE was founded in 1978 in New York City by volunteers serving a pilot group of 14 clients who were homebound. Today the organization employs a professional staff offering a wide array of clinical services, social activities, and cultural and educational programs to over 3,000 members, volunteers, and clients each month.

In 1978, SAGE had a mission to offer services to the most vulnerable members of the underserved community of elder gays and lesbians in New York City, providing friendly visiting, telephone reassurance, and shopping assistance. Within the first year, the organization expanded its outreach to include social activities by introducing a monthly social event, and participation grew substantially. In the early 1980s, under the organization's second executive director, Ken Dawson, SAGE's mission was further expanded and refined to incorporate an activist, self-help approach for lesbian and gay elders, with the aim of promoting independence and building community, as well as fighting the combined impact of **ageism** and **homophobia.**

SAGE currently offers dozens of social, cultural, and educational opportunities to LGBT seniors each month, from discussion groups and art or music workshops to monthly parties and events. Over the years, SAGE has greatly enhanced the clinical services provided to clients by offering case management, individual and group counseling, assistance with benefits, and support to caregivers. All services, overseen by a staff of professional social workers, are targeted to the particular issues faced by LGBTs as they age.

In 2004, SAGE changed its name from Senior Action in a Gay Environment to Services and Advocacy for GLBT Elders, emphasizing the organization's service and advocacy components, as well as its inclusiveness of all members of the community. In its nearly 30 years of operation, SAGE has adapted existing service models and developed unique paradigms to meet the particular needs of LGBT seniors. In 1984, SAGE opened the first drop-in center in the country specifically targeted to lesbian and gay seniors. In 1989, SAGE established the first program focusing on AIDS in older adults, providing an important service in a field largely concentrated on the treatment of younger people. This will take on new meaning in coming years: the AIDS Community Research Initiative of America projected in 2006 that within the next decade "the majority of HIV-infected New Yorkers will be over 50" (Matthews 2007, 2). In 1998, SAGE sponsored a National Conference on Aging in the Gay and Lesbian Community, the first conference to gather researchers, service providers, and activists from across the country to confer on LGBT aging issues.

In recent years, SAGE adapted the concept of a naturally occurring retirement community (NORC) to create a new model called a NORC of affinity, or a community of LGBT seniors in one neighborhood or geographical location who gather on the basis of their shared LGBT identity to access services. SAGE's Harlem program, which has been funded by the city of New York as a NORC of affinity, expands the organization's outreach and continues its work to build communities of elders empowered to advocate on their own behalf to meet the needs of aging LGBT people.

Further Reading

Gross, Jane. 2008. "AIDS Patients Face Downside of Living Longer." *New York Times* online (January 6). Accessed January 6, 2008.

Kling, Elizabeth, and Douglas Kimmel. 2006. "SAGE: New York City's Pioneer Organization for LGBT Elders." In *Lesbian, Gay, Bisexual, and Transgender Aging: Research and Clinical Perspectives*, ed. Douglas Kimmel, Tara Rose, and Steven David, 265–76. New York: Columbia University Press.

Matthews, Karen. 2007. "Agency Offers AIDS Education to Elderly." Associated Press online (July 25). Available at: http://www.washingtonpost.com/wp-dyn/content/article/2007/07/25/AR2007072501574.html. Accessed July 16, 2008.

Beth Kling

sex over cyberspace

Men's Associated Exchange (MAX) has been, for several decades, a popular fraternal organization in San Francisco where gay men can meet and socialize. Each month, MAX stages 10 to 15 social events and activities that draw from 25 to 400 members and guests. These range from potluck dinners and cultural events to international trips and personal development seminars. But in recent years less formal or traditional means of socializing have been gaining popularity.

Communications technology and **queer** sexuality are ineradicably linked, as almost every advance in telecommunications has inspired a matching form of nonnormative, mediated erotic activity. In her influential "Cyborg Manifesto" (1984/1991), feminist Donna J. Haraway makes the ominous observation that some machines seem more alive than the people who use them—an insight that eerily anticipated the concerns and controversies that have arisen since millions of Americans began taking their sex lives online in the mid-1990s. From phone sex and cybersex to online hook-ups and "showing off" on webcam, telephones and computers have become *the* **sex toys** of the digital age. Infusing sexuality and (hyper)textuality, the World Wide Web (WWW) has fostered a profusion of online queer communities and LGBTQ-themed Web sites, newsgroups, discussion boards, and chat rooms. Whether used for hooking up or **community-based organizing,** there is something for everyone in "cyburbia." The Web has made the Internet "user friendly"; queers in cyberspace have made the Web queer-friendly.

Phone sex and cybersex are high-tech variations of the same practice—long-distance mutual masturbation; because autoeroticism is considered a nonreproductive sexual practice, phone sex and cybersex are queer by default. Furthermore, because no physical contact occurs, both are methods of **safe sex** enjoyed by millions of Americans all across the LGBTQ spectrum.

Alexander Graham Bell invented the telephone in 1876, and people have been "talking each other off" ever since. Phone sex commonly takes place between people at a distance from each other. In this queer combination of aural sex and autoeroticism, partners generally masturbate themselves while describing what they *would* be doing to each other if they were together. Moreover, the advent of three-way and conference-calling capabilities has enabled opportunities for group phone sex, as well.

When the U.S. government dissolved the monopoly that phone companies held on prerecorded message services in the 1980s, the phone sex industry proliferated into a billion-dollar enterprise. For a fee, people could dial a 900-number and listen to xxx-rated recordings. Soon 900-numbers changed to 800-numbers, and prerecorded fantasies were replaced by live phone sex operators. Decades later, phone sex and sex work continue to go hand-in-hand.

The recent ubiquity of cellular phones has further queered phone sex in other ways. Many cell phones come equipped with digital cameras, enabling the transmission of pictures and videos—including sexual content. The XTC Mobile company actually specializes in beaming **pornography** directly into its customers' cell phones. No longer tied specifically to the home, mobile technology has translated phone sex into a form of public sex. Moreover, through the lingo of "Textspeak," text messaging has provided a new language for queer sexualities, allowing people to express feelings and desires they may be too inhibited to say out loud. Phone sex has been around for over a century, and because its possibilities are limited only by contemporary technologies, it will continue to change with each innovation—as it has since the arrival of the Net and the Web.

Though often conflated, the Internet and the World Wide Web are actually separate entities. The Internet is the largest group of computer *networks* in the world. While its origins date back to the Industrial Revolution, most histories of the Net chart its development from a select group of interconnected computer networks employed by the U.S. Defense Department during the Cold War, to a white-collar tool for academic research in the 1980s and 1990s, to the present-day mass public appeal of the Web. Collectively, the Net and the Web constitute "cyberspace." Often evoked as a synonym for the Internet itself, the term *cyberspace*—initially coined by William Gibson in his science fiction novel *Neuromancer* (1982)—is the virtual universe created by interconnected computer systems. From its inception, the Web was meant to be a collaborative arena of knowledge sharing, and it is in precisely this spirit that many LGBTQ individuals and groups have made cyberspace a haven for queer living. By the late 1990s, telephone lines and computer terminals across America had literally hooked up and generated a hybrid form of queer sexuality—cybersex.

Simply stated, cybersex is eroticism that takes place in cyberspace—and its blurring of the boundaries between masturbation and autoeroticism, solo sex and coitus, intercourse and group sex, private and public sex, voyeurism and exhibitionism, make it incontrovertibly queer. Technically, the category includes the use of Internet pornography during solo masturbation ("one-handed Web surfing"); however, its most common denotation is simulated sexual activity between two (or more) individuals that is mediated via computer technology, whether through e-mail, with an instant messaging (IM) program, or in a chat room.

Though the *cyber* in cybersex is the most immediate facet of its nonnormativity, in practice, this cyberqueerness tends to vary by the degree of computer mediation involved. For example, cybersex carried out over email is not radically different from exchanging lusty letters through the "snail mail" system—the recipient merely opens an email instead of an envelope. The ready availability of pornography on the Web plays a key role here. Instead of a personalized erotic fantasy, one could send pornographic pictures and/or video clips taken from Web sites, could offer the uniform resource locator (URL) address of a free porn site, or could enclose a password to a site that requires paid memberships—in effect, trading passwords and porn much like sexual favors. While the swapping of erotic emails can happen within the context of a preexisting—perhaps even long-distance—relationship, this need not be the case. Both the trafficking in Internet pornography and the exchange of xxx-emails are quite similar to their counterparts outside of cyberspace, the major difference being the electronically mediated source of interaction and arousal.

The cyberworld of online hook-ups, however, takes cybersex to an even queerer level. Though a sexy letter sent via email will probably achieve its (cyber)sexual effect much more quickly than it would if mailed the old-fashioned way, the essence of its eroticism is still largely that of solitary masturbation and delayed gratification. By contrast, real-time communication possibilities like chatting online create more instantaneously interactive cybersexual encounters.

Cybersex is mutual masturbation in which partners use computers to relay lines of sexually explicit text back and forth. Like phone sex, participants typically describe what they would be doing together in real life. Though usually practiced one-on-one, conferencing and multiuser domains (MUDs) like chat rooms enable cyber group sex and orgies. While committed couples may engage in cybersex when apart, hooking up online with a complete stranger is more common.

An online hook-up is a casual cybersexual encounter. While some Web sites such as Craigslist (www.craigslist.org) and location-specific chat rooms are designed for using the Web to locate a partner for a real-life hook-up (which raises issues of **promiscuity,** safe sex, sexual assault, and **sexually transmitted infections**), many others are devoted to online hook-ups that transpire strictly in cyberspace. In this way, hooking up online has reinvented the art of **"cruising"** by enabling public-like sex in the private sphere. At the click of a mouse people can search for cybersex in LGBTQ-themed Web sites, chat rooms, newsgroups, and communities rather than in **bars, bathhouses and sex clubs,** public parks, adult novelty shops, and interstate highway restrooms—without leaving home.

Computers are the defining medium of cybersex, but additional devices like webcams and microphones create even more layers of mediation. A webcam is a relatively inexpensive video camera that enables live videoconferencing among Internet users. While some consider "camming" to be a kind of **performance art,** others see it simply as a way in which anyone can act like an amateur porn star. Most instant messengers allow users to display a picture of themselves—or of a customized "avatar"—while they are chatting; however, with webcams, chatters can view each other "live." Sex on camming brings cybersex into the realms of voyeurism (pleasure in watching) and exhibitionism (pleasure in showing off). Webcams make abbreviations like NIFOC (nude in front of the computer) and NIFOK (naked in front of the keyboard) obsolete—anyone watching will know what one's state of (un)dress is. Cammers control who can or cannot watch their broadcasts, usually by forcing prospective spectators to ask for permission before viewing. For some cammers, though, regulating the audience actually means letting everyone and anyone (including, possibly, minors) enjoy the show; a webcam broadcast available to all viewers is called an *open cam*. Though a cammer may be aroused by racking up as many viewers as possible, she/he may still wish to engage in a one-on-one cybersex chat with another cammer. This form of cybersex is called *cam-to-cam* (c2c, cam2cam) and allows partners to watch each other masturbate, reserving their imaginations for the fantasy scenarios they (may or may not) chat about.

If visual stimulus is not enough (or is not even desired), people can cruise for partners interested in "fone" (phone sex) or "cam and fone." Moreover, many IM programs allow people to place free computer-to-computer calls and to "voice chat" with each other using microphones, speakers, and headphones. This form of phone sex is called *mic to mic* and can be practiced in conjunction with webcamming (mic and cam) or on its own. While some cammers enjoy dominance and submission dynamics, enlisting an audience to tell them "what to do," others might offer an open cam on the condition that viewers *do not* send them messages. Some cammers elect not to appear on their own cams at all, offering "porn cams" showing free videos instead; some put on live sex shows with others. Like phone sex, cybersex has also proved profitable as a mode of sex work, as many Internet porn sites enable customers to chat with and even c2c (cam-to-cam, webcam chat) with **pornography stars.**

Now that wireless technology allows people to access the Web from their cell phones, Netspeak and Textspeak combine as people typing at their computers can communicate with others who are texting on their cells, and vice versa. This array of computers, cams, mics, and phones can provide near-infinite permutations of queer cyberpleasure. As recent **films** like the romantic drama *On_Line* (2002) and the erotic thriller *Open Cam* (2005) suggest, cybersex and webcamming are becoming more mainstream threads in the fabric of queer culture, both on- and offline.

Real-life hook-ups tend to be one-night stands—and even if they lead to subsequent "booty calls," they rarely result in long-term relationships. Although most online hook-ups follow this same model, there are significant exceptions. The expressed purpose of IM programs and Web sites like Myspace (www.myspace.com) and Facebook (www.facebook.org) is to help people not only keep in touch with friends they already have but also meet new people—often from different parts of the world. A hot cybersexual hook-up, then, may well encourage partners to add each other to their contact or "buddy" lists for future sessions. Like Web surfing in general, searching for cybersex can be an extraordinarily time-consuming endeavor—building a list of partners and potential partners can greatly reduce the time it might take to find someone compatible. Of course, repeat cybersexual encounters may either promote greater intimacy (possibly leading to a long-distance relationship) or incite the sharing of too much information (TMI) and ruin the fantasy altogether.

The key feature of cyberculture is anonymity. Anyone can be anything online, and the impact of the Web on **identity and identity politics** has been tremendous. Virtual queer communities have provided millions of Americans with the acceptance they often cannot find in real life. Incidents of individuals **coming out** online while remaining in the **closet** offline have become increasingly prevalent.

Ironically, however, the promise of anonymity—which is quintessential to the Internet's appeal—is one that it cannot always keep. Like any culture, cyberculture has its own formal and informal mores and conventions, or "Netiquette." The understood rule of communicating online is to treat others as one would treat them in person. To ensure amicability, many chat rooms not only have rules and other terms of use with which chatters must agree to comply but are also supervised by moderators who enforce those rules. Numerous Web sites use content filters and account verification measures to prevent minors from accessing "adult" content and to protect them from potential sexual predators. More formally, the modus operandi of communication undergirding the Net is called Internet protocol, and, by extension, every computer has a unique Internet protocol address (IP address). This set of four numbers separated by periods (e.g., 11.10.98.76) functions, like an electronic thumbprint, to identify that computer's connection to the network via an Internet service provider (ISP). Most chat rooms and IM programs are not secure, and many record users' IP Addresses. Hacking, identity theft, and even cyberterrorism are all causes for concern. Because instant messengers and chat rooms use people's IP addresses to link their computers, finding out someone's IP address can be easy. Once that number is obtained, the person behind the computer screen can be located through the ISP—which has resulted in a rapid increase in John Doe lawsuits.

Organizations claiming to have been wronged by someone's online activities initiate these legal proceedings to find the culprit. One such lawsuit gained national attention in 1998 when the U.S. Navy, in violation of its own "don't ask, don't tell" policy, convinced America Online (AOL) to breach its privacy policy by exposing the identity of Timothy McVeigh (no relation to the Oklahoma City bomber), a naval officer who, in an online profile, had described his marital status as "gay." Although a judge ruled in favor of McVeigh, the experience ruined his 17-year military career and forced him into early retirement. In many ways, the Web has made the world even smaller, and surfers being caught in compromising situations by people who recognize them is always a possibility. Thus, complete anonymity in cyberspace is a dangerous illusion (many otherwise uninhibited webcammers never show their faces for precisely this reason), to which end McVeigh's **outing** serves as a convenient cautionary tale.

Anonymity and responsibility are two sides of the same coin: just because cybersex might take place via a wireless connection does not mean that there are no strings attached. An open cam and open mind are not always synonymous, and **stereotypes** skew interactions online just as they do offline. Moreover, not all LGBTQ resources on the Web are equally welcoming, and it can be a completely disillusioning experience to log on and find the same vicious **ageism,** racism, misogyny, **sissyphobia and femiphobia,** and even **homophobia** among queers in cyberspace that one might find anywhere else. The personal is still political, and cybersex and cybersexism are often too easily commingled.

In the late 1980s, cultural critic Douglas Crimp promulgated condom use as one way to "have promiscuity in an epidemic"; in the twenty-first century, cybersex is another. However, although some couples see cybersex as a way to enrich their relationships and buffer the emotional demands of **monogamy,** the prevalence of infidelity online raises difficult questions about queer **ethics.** Does phone sex with a third party constitute adultery—or does cybersex? Is masturbating on an open cam in a chat room cheating? If no physical contact is involved, can either phone sex or cybersex be considered real sex at all? These are just some of the questions facing LGBTQ America today.

Despite—and because of—the real dangers of offline discrimination, oppression, and violence, the Web remains an indispensable tool for community-based organizing and "e-activism." Many nationally renowned LGBTQ groups have Web sites: **ACT UP** (http://www.actupny.org), **Gay and Lesbian Advocates and Defenders (GLAD)** (http://www.glad.org), the **Gay and Lesbian Alliance against Defamation (GLAAD)** (http://www.glaad.org), the **National Gay and Lesbian Task Force** (NGLTF) (http://www.thetaskforce.org), the **National Transgender Advocacy Coalition (NTAC)** (http://ntac.org), and **Parents, Families, and Friends of Lesbians and Gays (PFLAG)** (http://www.pflag.com), to name just a few. Though most of these organizations are headquartered on the East and West Coasts, the Web has helped make these groups accessible to people from anywhere in the nation. From e-mailing congressional representatives to circulating e-petitions, e-activism has revolutionized how people fight for LGBTQ rights, collectively and individually. More personally, LGBTQ individuals can express their views in newsgroups, chat rooms, and discussion boards—and, of course, in the ever-more-popular mode of online communication, the "Weblog," or "blog," which enables people to publish daily commentaries about their lives that can then be viewed by any Web surfer. In these ways, queers all across the country can connect with each other, pooling resources and sharing experiences. For someone living in the rural **Midwest,** small-town America, or other areas where LGBTQ people are said to be nonexistent, the basic reassurance that there *are* other like-minded queers out there—not just in cyberspace but in the real world—can be a lifeline; it is this opportunity for genuine connection that makes the Web so special.

Howard Rheingold wrote the book on virtual communities in the early 1990s; however, whether cruising for c2c action or lobbying for LGBTQ rights, the activities of cyberqueers have rewritten the narrative of what belonging to a community might mean. While Haraway's harrowing vision of mechanical activity and human inertia remains an important comment on the digital age, responsible queers in cyberspace will continue to make the Web a user-friendly means of exploring queer sexualities and organizing virtual communities.

Beyond the realm of LGBTQ politics, many other Web resources exist. PlanetOut Inc. (http://www.planetoutinc.com) is the self-described "leading global media and entertainment company exclusively serving the lesbian, gay, bisexual and transgender (LGBT) community," and its "digital media brands" include Gay.com, PlanetOut.com, Advocate.com, Out.com, OutTraveler.com, and HIVPlusMag.com (see: http://www.planetoutinc.com/company). For a more academic perspective on queer culture, David Gauntlett's Theory.org site (http://www.theory.org.uk) is a good place to begin.

Further Reading

Campbell, John Edward. 2004. *Getting It on Online: Cyberspace, Gay Male Sexuality, and Embodied Identity*. Haworth Gay and Lesbian Studies. New York: Haworth Press.

Crimp, Douglas. 1988. "How to Have Promiscuity in an Epidemic." *AIDS: Cultural Analysis/ Cultural Activism*, 237–71. Cambridge, MA: MIT Press.

Gunter, Barrie. 2002. *Media Sex: What Are the Issues?* London: Lawrence Erlbaum Associates.

Lane, Frederick S., III. 2000. *Obscene Profits: The Entrepreneurs of Pornography in the Cyber Age*. London: Routledge.

Ray, Audacia. 2007. *Naked on the Internet: Hookups, Downloads, and Cashing In on Internet Sexploration*. Emeryville, CA: Seal Press.

Rheingold, Howard. 1993/2000. *The Virtual Community: Homesteading on the Electronic Frontier*. Repr. Cambridge, MA: MIT Press.

Wakeford, Nina. 2002. "New Technologies and 'Cyber-Queer' Research." In *Handbook of Lesbian and Gay Studies*, ed. Diane Richardson and Stephen Seidman, 115–44. London: Sage.

Christopher Lozensky

sex-positive movement

Sex positivity is a movement both within and outside of LGBTQ culture, dedicated to open celebration of the multiplicity of and variation in sexual desires and behavior. This movement arose largely in response to what its adherents see as the "antisex" politics of 1970s and 1980s feminism, particularly Andrea Dworkin's antipornography activism. In response to Dworkin's and others' large-scale attempts to criminalize pornography, adherents of the sex-positive movement have argued that sexual behavior is a matter of free speech and that female agency depends on women's right to desire as we please. In "Thinking Sex," a foundational essay for sex positivity, Gayle Rubin also argues that the "moral panics" that have ensued over sexual behaviors are a fundamentally conservative effort to create prejudicial social hierarchies based on exclusionary and regressive moral systems.

Some manifestations of the sex-positive movement in the United States include COYOTE ("call off your old tired ethics"), an advocacy organization for sex workers; sex toy stores such as Good Vibrations and Babes in Toyland, which are geared toward education about sexual practices, especially for women; pornography made by and for lesbians, such as the works by Fatale Media and Pink and White Productions; performances and publications by sex-positive activists Carol Queen, Annie Sprinkle, and Susie Bright; the Lusty Lady, a worker-owned, cooperative, unionized strip club in San Francisco; the lesbian sex magazine *On Our Backs*; and finally, the efflorescence of BDSM culture among gay men and lesbians nationwide.

Critics of sex-positive culture and thought include the camp of antipornography feminists in response to whom the movement arose, who argue that historically sex has been used to oppress rather than to empower women. A less polemical, but possibly more trenchant critical opposition might be seen to emerge from historians of sexuality influenced by the French philosopher Michel Foucault, for whom seemingly rebellious sexual expression can actually enmesh people all the more in the power relations by which we are judged and hierarchized in terms of sexuality. In response to these objections, proponents of sex positivity claim that the proliferation of sexual practices and efforts to decriminalize all consensual sexual behavior can only help produce a culture free of the subjugation of nonnormative genders or sexualities.

Further Reading

Boston Women's Health Book Collective. 2005. *Our Bodies Ourselves*. New York: Touchstone.

Cornell, Drucilla, ed. 2000. *Feminism and Pornography*. New York: Oxford University Press.

Foucault, Michel. 1978. *The History of Sexuality*. Vol. 1, *An Introduction*. Trans. Robert Hurley. New York: Vintage Books.

Queen, Carol. 1997. *Real Live Nude Girl: Chronicles of Sex-Positive Culture*. Pittsburgh, PA: Cleis Press.

Rubin, Gayle. 1984. "Thinking Sex: Notes for a Radical Theory of the Politics of Sexuality." In *Pleasure and Danger: Exploring Female Sexuality*, ed. Carole S. Vance, 3–44. Boston: Routledge & Kegan Paul.

Amy Jamgochian

sex toys

Sex toys are objects and devices that are used for creating human sexual pleasure. In several states the use of sex toys is regulated or illegal. There are numerous types of sex toys ranging from feathers and handcuffs to vibrators, dildos, and strap-ons. Sex items can be used externally or internally or as a prop, and they may be used as part of BDSM play (e.g., sex swings). Some sex toys, especially penetrative toys, are made to have a fleshlike feel; these are often made from silicone, cyberskin, jelly, or latex rubber. They are common additions to sexual stimulation regardless of how a person identifies his/her sexual orientation. Some women who have sex with women believe that using penetration toys, such as strap-ons and dildos, conflicts with their sexual identity. Others view these devices as play items that do not reflect their sexual orientation. Sex toys should be used under adult consent of all participants involved in the sexual act. When sex toys are used, proper sanitary use is recommended because if not properly maintained and cleaned their use can spread some infections. Items made of silicone, a nonporous product, are easier to keep clean. Condoms may be placed over dildos to help prevent disease transmission.

Further Reading

Lotney, Karlyn. 2000. *The Ultimate Guide to Strap-On Sex: A Complete Resource for Women and Men*. San Francisco, CA: Cleis Press.

Venning, Rachel, and Claire Cavanah. 2003. *Sex Toys 101: A Playfully Uninhibited Guide*. New York: Fireside Books.

Helen Smith

sexual harassment law and policy

Sexually explicit remarks, demands for sex in exchange for benefits, and sexually aggressive behavior have long been common in workplaces, schools, and other domains. Few thought these actions were impermissible, even a decade after Title 7 of the Civil Rights Act of 1964, the first federal law prohibiting sex discrimination in employment, took effect. Instead, women, who were most commonly the targets of sexual harassment, especially at work, were often told that sexually hostile behavior was simply part of the employment package.

Beginning in 1979, popular understandings of sexual harassment began to shift. Feminist legal theorist Catharine MacKinnon published a pathbreaking book, *The Sexual Harassment of Working Women,* in which she argued that sexual harassment in the workplace harms women not only because the harassment causes discomfort and, at times, physical and psychological injuries but also because the harassment interferes with their ability to succeed in the workplace. MacKinnon and other theorists explained that sexually oriented behavior in the workplace creates inequality by leaving vulnerable workers in fear of sexual coercion and by demeaning workers as sexual objects, thereby limiting their opportunities. Simply put, the argument maintained that sexual patter and conduct in the workplace, rather than being an unpleasant fact of life for its targets, amount to discrimination based on sex.

The theorists identified two broad categories of harassment based on countless descriptions, mostly from women, of experiences at work and in school. The first, called *quid pro quo,* refers to demands for sex in exchange for some kind of advantage, which could include hiring or promotion, a better grade, or special privileges. The other, called *hostile environment,* describes a situation in which the sexualization of the workplace, classroom, or other setting makes it difficult or impossible for those being harassed to work or learn successfully.

Women began to take these theories to court, and, in 1986, the U.S. Supreme Court ruled that unwelcome sexual advances at work constitute unlawful discrimination based on sex. In that case, called *Meritor Savings Bank v. Vinson,* the bank had argued that even if a bank teller faced repeated sexual advances by her supervisor, she did not have a legal claim for sexual harassment because she had not lost her job or suffered other economic harm. The Court agreed with the teller, however, concluding that the abusive work environment violated Title 7's ban on sex discrimination.

In 1993, the Supreme Court took another step toward broadening the types of sexual behavior in the workplace that could be found to violate the federal sex discrimination law. In a case called *Harris v. Forklift Systems, Inc.,* the Court found that sexually demeaning remarks, even without overt demands for sexual relations, can create a discriminatory and abusive work environment that impedes an employee's ability to succeed at work. The Court also said, however, that an employee who filed a sexual harassment lawsuit would have to show that the sexual comments or other behaviors were not "merely offensive" but rather were "severe or pervasive."

Over the years, the Supreme Court and other courts have continued to shape the law of sexual harassment in both workplace and school settings. While courts have been willing to grant legal remedies to individuals who can show they have been subjected to extremely severe sexual harassment, they frequently find that explicit sexual conduct is not severe enough to amount to unlawful harassment. As a result of the very high standard for proving sexual harassment claims, many employees and students continue to experience sexual harassment in the workplace without an effective remedy at their disposal.

One additional important development in the law came in 1998, in a case called *Oncale v. Sundowner Offshore Services, Inc.*, when the Supreme Court decided that same-sex sexual harassment violated the federal sex discrimination law. In that case, a man who worked as a roustabout on an oil rig was repeatedly physically assaulted in a sexualized way and threatened with rape by his coworkers. The Court held that so long as an individual could prove that the attacks were "because of sex" rather than merely being workplace horseplay or other non–sex-specific behavior, a sexual harassment claim could be made.

Some debate remains after the *Oncale* case about how someone targeted for sexual harassment by a person of the same sex can prove that the harassment was "because of sex" rather than for some other reason. The Supreme Court had said that the victim would have to show that he or she faced conditions that coworkers of a different sex would not have experienced. Many critics and some lower courts have observed that this approach leaves individuals free to harass others sexually so long as they aim their harassment equally at men and women. The Court also made clear that the harassment did not have to be motivated by sexual desire, so that, in the case of same-sex harassment, the targeted individual would not have to prove that the harasser was gay or lesbian to prevail in his or her claim. Notwithstanding this point, gay rights advocates have noted that a portion of sexual harassment lawsuits filed against lesbians and gay men are triggered not by actual harassment but instead by the litigant's discomfort with openly lesbian or gay coworkers.

In the years since *Oncale* was decided, some federal and state courts have begun to interpret sexual harassment law to cover sexualized harassment of individuals who do not conform to sex role stereotypes. In these cases, lesbians, gay men, and transgender individuals who have been targeted with severe hostility at work have succeeded in showing that the harassment they suffered should be considered sex discrimination. For example, a gay man prevailed in his sexual harassment claim after showing that he had faced a constant stream of sexist comments and vulgar name-calling from his coworkers during his four years as a waiter. The coworkers called him by female pronouns and mocked his feminine mannerisms. These constant verbal attacks, which reflected the coworkers' view that the waiter was not sufficiently manly, created a hostile environment rife with sex discrimination, according to the court.

Other courts, by contrast, have determined that hostile remarks and acts targeted at gay and transgender individuals for their failure to conform to sex role stereotypes do not amount to sex discrimination. These courts have found that even physical assaults against these individuals in the workplace are not discrimination "because of sex" but rather discrimination because of sexual orientation or gender identity, which they conclude is not covered by the sex discrimination law.

The law regarding sexual harassment in educational settings has not developed as extensively as the workplace law, but there are many similarities between the two. It is possible for a student to prevail on a sexual harassment claim by showing that sexualized comments or advances were so severe or pervasive that he or she was not able to learn or study in a meaningful way. In addition, since the mid-1990s, a number of gay and lesbian students have succeeded in lawsuits against schools that failed to protect them from antigay harassment and attacks. These lawsuits are somewhat different from traditional sexual harassment suits in that they typically focus not just on the harassing acts themselves but also on the school's failure to provide equal protection against harassment to gay or non–gender-conforming students. As in the workplace, the threshold for proving sexual harassment is quite high, and even sexually oriented name-calling and bullying are often not sufficient to prevail in a sexual harassment lawsuit. Also, as in the workplace, a student must report the harassment to the proper authority if the school, rather than only the harasser, is to be held liable for a violation of law.

In addition to the federal law on sexual harassment, many states have developed their own sexual harassment jurisprudence based on state sex discrimination laws. In some states, courts have reacted to the very high federal threshold for proving sexual harassment by developing a demanding, but less difficult, standard for showing, under their own state's law, that harassment has occurred. Many employers and schools also have their own sexual harassment policies. These policies often require that employees undergo training and that workers and students be informed about what to do if they experience sexual harassment.

As sexual harassment law and policy have developed, conflicts have arisen over how sexual harassment should be defined and whether and how severely it should be punished. Some believe that the courts have made it so difficult to prove sexual harassment that the law has been rendered ineffective, or at least far less effective than it might be. These individuals point to the continuation of sexual harassment in the workplace and in school settings in ways that obstruct the working and learning environment. They contend that stronger laws are essential to send harassers and their employers or schools the message that their conduct has consequences. Others believe that sexual harassment law has gone too far. These individuals argue that employers and educators have become so concerned about sexual harassment lawsuits that they have inappropriately censored reasonable speech and activity in the workplace. The law will likely continue to evolve as popular understandings of the causes and effects of sexual harassment change over time. Advocates who believe the law is too restrictive will also continue to press for their views to be adopted, as will advocates who believe the law needs to be strengthened if it is truly to be effective.

Further Reading

Gregory, Raymond F. 2004. *Unwelcome and Unlawful: Sexual Harassment in the American Workplace*. New York: Cornell University Press.

MacKinnon, Catharine A. 1979. *Sexual Harassment of Working Women: A Case of Sex Discrimination*. New Havent, CT: Yale University Press.

MacKinnon, Catharine A., and Reva B. Siegel, eds. 2003. *Directions in Sexual Harassment Law*. New Havent, CT: Yale University Press.

Suzanne B. Goldberg

sexualities

The concept of sexuality differs from the concepts of sex and gender in that the definitions of the latter two do not directly involve an erotic dimension. Whereas *sex* usually refers to various biological characteristics, such as chromosomes, genes, genitals, hormones, and other physical markers, *gender* typically refers to its psychosocial display, such as masculinity, femininity, and the common behaviors associated with them, including those culturally grouped under the categories of maleness, femaleness, manhood, and womanhood. *Sexuality*, a nineteenth-century neologism, is a concept that usually refers to the different aspects and manifestations of an individual's erotic urges, inclinations, and fantasies. Besides its psychosubjective component, sexuality also denotes a behavioral-morphological component that is physically visible and a sociological component that holds some significance on the population level.

The current entry situates sexuality in relation to the evolving meanings of sex and gender in a historical framework, with a particular emphasis on the relationship between expertise knowledge and social experience. The period since the mid-nineteenth century witnessed a dramatic transformation in which the concepts of sex, gender, and sexuality gradually became more distinct and less intertwined, often reflecting the dominant trends in scientific and medical discourses. However, around the turn of the twenty-first century, a group of scholars, commonly known as queer theorists, began to call into question once again the distinctions between sex, gender, and sexuality, as well as the scientific and medical claims about their significance.

According to the intellectual historian Thomas Laqueur, prior to the eighteenth century, the "one-sex model" dominated scientific thinking and understandings of sex in Western civilization. According to this model, male and female differed in degrees based on a single-sexed body and were not separated into two distinct kinds of species. Medical experts showed that male and female reproductive anatomies highly resembled one another and attributed the different versions of the single-sexed body to at least two genders, men and women. The boundaries between male and female were shaped through ideologies of gender hierarchy, not rooted in medical and scientific observations of physical differences.

Then, the Enlightenment movement of the eighteenth century generated a shift in the Western understanding of the human body from the one-sex model to a two-sex model. After this transition, people no longer perceived the female organ as a lesser form of the male's or, by implication, woman as a "lesser man." Male and female bodies were now understood to be opposites, serving as the biological basis upon which meanings of gender could be socially inscribed; men and women became two distinct types of species that occupied different realms of social life, performed unique social and cultural duties, and behaved with separate sets of manners. Gender, as it was conceived after the Enlightenment, changed from being the definition of sex to the socialization of sex.

Medical and scientific authorities, along with those who depended on them, ceased to emphasize the importance of female pleasure and orgasm around the same time that the female body came to be understood as the incommensurable opposite of the male's. So as female orgasm "disappeared" between the seventeenth and the nineteenth centuries, in historian Nancy Cott's interpretation of the Victorian sexual ideology, women's feelings were relegated to a place of "passionlessness," characterized by a lack of sexual appetite, motivation, and aggressiveness. According to Cott (1978:221), "the ideology of passionlessness was [first] tied to the rise of evangelical religion between the 1790s and the 1830s," and it was later prescribed as the sexual norm for women by physicians in "a second wave, so to speak, beginning at mid-century." Therefore, by the time the nineteenth century entered its second half, the fortification of the two-sex model, as it was linked to the erasure of female sexual pleasure, gradually emerged as an exclusive task that simultaneously reflected and reinforced the medical establishment's authoritative power in understanding sex and sexuality.

This historical development of an ever-clearer demarcation of the two sexes supports the influential observation made by Michel Foucault and his followers, who have argued that the concept of sexuality, strictly speaking, emerged precisely from the late nineteenth-century discourse of sexual science. According to the historian and philosopher of science Arnold Davidson (2001), prior to the second half of the nineteenth century, medical authorities theorized about people's sex using an "anatomical style of reasoning," by which reproductive anatomy exhausted the cultural interpretation of an individual's sexual character. But starting in the latter half of the century, medical experts began to speak of people's sex using a "psychiatric style of reasoning," by which psychological inclinations came to play a decisive role in the social significance of one's sexual character. Precisely around this time, the early discourse of sexology, by consolidating a possible conception of *sexuality*, also consolidated the two-sex model that mediates the modern conceptual relation between sex and gender.

Although the two-sex model had prevailed in both scientific and popular thinking since the late nineteenth century, the 1920s cultivated the roots that allowed a variation of the one-sex model to return to being in vogue and led to the research studies on sexual difference during the 1930s. In fact, earlier sexologists, most notably Havelock Ellis, Sigmund Freud, and Magnus Hirschfeld, hinted at a theory of human bisexuality that viewed men as possessing female traits and women as having male traits. Back then, however, they lacked concrete scientific findings to support such a theory. Throughout the 1920s and 1930s, scientists from various disciplines, including endocrinology and cultural anthropology, provided ample evidence to support the theory of human bisexuality. In endocrinology, Dr. Clifford A. Wright, a physician at the Los Angeles County General Hospital, wrote many articles on hormonal research and homosexuality that situated men and women on a continuum, based on the startling findings of other biochemists that both men and women have both female and male hormones. According to Wright, "All individuals are part male and part female, or bisexual, and this fact is substantiated by hormone assays in the urine. The urine of the normal man or woman shows the presence of hormones of both the male and female types.... In the normal male, the male hormone predominates; in the normal female, the female hormone predominates" (1938, 449).

Similarly, the cultural anthropologists Ruth Benedict and Margaret Mead provided ethnographical support for the idea that sex roles varied across culture in their classic texts: Mead's *Coming of Age in Samoa* (1928), *Growing Up in New Guinea* (1930), and *Sex and Temperament in Three Primitive Societies* (1935), and Benedict's *Patterns of Culture* (1934). Based on her fieldwork at Arapesh, Mundugumor, and Tchambuli, Mead remarked that "the temperaments which we regard as native to one sex might instead be mere variations of human temperament, to which the members of either or both sexes may, with more or less success in the case of different individuals, be educated to approximate" (1935, xl). Around the same time, a number of other anthropologists had begun studying the role of the *berdache,* an individual whose socially sanctioned role was the opposite of his or her sex anatomy, in Native American societies. Taking this evidence together, scientists in the 1930s posited a model of sexual fluidity that portrayed the differences between men and women only as degrees on a continuum, which resonated with the one-sex model that Laqueur identified in the pre-Enlightenment period.

However, even though scientists' situating of men and women on a continuum may appear to represent the resurgence of the one-sex model in the 1930s, one critical difference existed between the two. For pre-Enlightenment physicians, socialization of the sexes was the definition of sex itself, and "men" and "women" represented merely two versions of the single-sexed body. In the early twentieth century, however, a paradigm shift characterized scientific and medical understandings of the human body, namely, the introduction of a chemical model of sex and the body through the emergence of sex endocrinology. According to Nelly Oudshoorn, after the concept of hormones was coined in 1905, the new science of "sex endocrinology established its material authority by transforming the theoretical concept of sex hormones into material realities: chemical substances with a sex of their own" (1994, 43). The "seat" of masculinity and femininity, alongside the "essence" of maleness and femaleness, "came to be located not in an organ but in chemical substances: the sex hormone" (Oudshoorn 1994, 8). As a result of this new enterprise that involved laboratory scientists, clinicians, and pharmaceutical entrepreneurs, scientific and medical conceptualizations of men and women did not only remain in the framework of a continuum, but more importantly hypostatized the idea that biological men and women were fundamentally different.

By the mid-twentieth century, the theory of universal bisexuality began to play an important role in the popular understandings of sex and gender, as exemplified in the way it surfaced in the medical debate over the proper treatment of transsexualism. On the one hand, some medical experts, mostly in Europe, used the theory of human bisexuality to legitimate the administration of sex-transformation surgery on transsexuals. For instance, Harry Benjamin, the main endocrinologist and physician of Christine Jorgensen, the first American male-to-female transsexual to undergo sex-reassignment surgery abroad in Denmark, justified Jorgensen's sex-change surgery based on the idea that transsexuals were simply extreme versions of a universal bisexual condition. Adopting this type of argument, other individuals who felt a strong drive to become members of the opposite sex began to seek professional surgical intervention in the 1940s and 1950s to change their own physical sex.

On the other hand, most American medical professionals, in particular, psychiatrists and psychoanalysts, rejected the view of universal human bisexuality arguing that identifications and behaviors that did not conform to the rigid opposition of the two sexes were the result of troubled early childhood experiences. In refuting the biological model of bisexuality that situated sex on a continuum, this group of experts advocated the necessity of psychotherapeutic intervention for those individuals with behaviors and identifications that did not follow the conventional sexual norm. They disapproved of medical intervention in the form of sex-change surgery as the ideal method for treating transsexuals. Implicitly, these psychologists and psychiatrists relied on the rigid notion of opposite sexes to see various forms of atypical sexual identification as a psychological, not physical, problem.

Meanwhile, the conceptual distinction between gender and sex first appeared in the medical literature, reflecting the ascending cultural authority of the mental health profession over the course of the twentieth century. In an article published in 1955, the medical psychologist John Money at Johns Hopkins University used the phrase *gender role* for "all those things that a person says or does to disclose himself or herself as having the status of boy or man, girl or woman" and *gender* to refer to "outlook, demeanor, and orientation" (254, 258). In 1964, building on Money's vocabulary, the psychoanalyst Robert Stoller, working with his colleague Ralph Greenson at the University of California, Los Angeles, medical school, coined the concept of *gender identity* to indicate more directly one's core sense of self as "being a member of a particular sex" (Greenson 1964, 217). In fact, they further differentiated gender identity from *sexual identity*, which encompasses one's sexual desire and erotic drive, thus distinguishing gender from sexuality (Stoller 1964). Whereas notions of sex, gender, and sexuality were undistinguishable in the nineteenth century, the language of psychoanalysis now provided medical and scientific authorities sufficient working definitions for setting them apart, as well as allowing the lay public to articulate a sense of self with respect to these definitions.

Yet, whereas psychoanalytic theories of sexuality had dominated both the medical debate over transsexuality and the conceptual distinction between sex and gender, a third aspect of the mid-twentieth-century epistemic turning point in the history of sexuality indicates an exact opposite trend. The publication of the two Kinsey reports on male and female sexual behavior in 1948 and 1953, respectively, denotes a significant revolution in the cultural conceptualization of sexuality. In both volumes, by providing statistical findings of the prevalence of homosexual behavior in American society, Kinsey explicitly challenged the mental health profession's description of homosexuality as a psychological illness. While many psychoanalysts and psychiatrists dismissed Kinsey's statistics outright by arguing that the numbers do not reflect the unconscious and dynamic nature of sexual experience, Kinsey insisted that his measurement of sexual behavior was more "scientific," given that it was based on a broad sample of the entire American population. According to Kinsey, it is more appropriate to speak of only sexual behavior rather than sexual identity in any scientific "assessment" of human sexuality. The clashing conceptions of sexual normality between Kinsey's sociological approach and the psychiatric experts' clinical perspective around the mid-twentieth century, therefore, reflected the declining influence of psychoanalysis in the American mental health profession.

The political climate in the United States since the mid-twentieth century has fostered an increasingly critical perspective on scientific claims about sex, gender, and sexuality. The rise of the second-wave feminist movement and the modern gay and lesbian movement in the 1960s and 1970s allowed many women and sexual minorities to rework the existing normative frameworks of gender and sexual behavior. As a famous example, due to the combined effort of gay and lesbian activists, notable clinical psychologists like Evelyn Hooker, and other psychiatrists such as Judd Marmo, the American Psychiatric Association finally removed homosexuality from its list of mental disorders in 1973.

Subsequently, a strand of philosophical and literary criticism called queer theory has emerged since the 1980s. Because its advocates concern themselves primarily with challenging and "problematizing" the dominant discourses and categorizations of sex, gender, and sexuality, their earlier writings sparked the influential debate between the biological **essentialist and social constructionist positions.** For scholars who think of sexuality from the perspective of essentialism, sexuality represents a biological drive or a natural given. Essentialist historians, such as **John Boswell,** make the implicit assumption that any form of sexual desire is transhistorical and transcultural. According to this line of reasoning, modern typologies of sexuality, regardless of when they are invented, can be applied to people living in different time periods, regions, and cultures. For instance, proponents of essentialism argue that the concept of homosexuality can be associated with the sexual behavior, desire, and even identity of those individuals who lived their lives prior to the coinage of the term in 1869.

In contrast, most queer theorists position themselves within the constructivist camp and argue that sexuality is not a biological given but a cultural construct. While essentialists view categories such as "gay" and "straight" as universally objective, social constructivists understand them as subjective in the sense that the labeling process itself carries a myriad of specific cultural connotations and social interpretations that are neither universally coherent nor historically identical. Others such as Judith Butler have also championed the notion that sex is always already gender, and vice versa, challenging any claims about the distinction between sex and gender. Moreover, what "bisexuality" meant more than half a century ago in the scientific theory of universal bisexuality differs significantly from what it means today as part of the modern LGBTQ political lexicon. Therefore, in addition to issues of labeling and identification, constructivists emphasize that each of the multiple sexualities that exist today has followed a different historical trajectory, in which its acquired social meaning and cultural significance has evolved over time in its own unique way.

Further Reading

Boswell, John. 1990. "Revolutions, Universals, and Sexual Categories." In *Hidden from History: Reclaiming the Gay and Lesbian Past*, ed. Martin Duberman, Martha Vicinus, and George Chauncey Jr., 17–36. New York: Meridian.

Butler, Judith. 1990. *Gender Trouble: Feminism and the Subversion of Identity*. New York: Routledge.

Cott, Nancy. 1978. "Passionlessness: An Interpretation of Victorian Sexual Ideology, 1790–1850." *Signs: Journal of Women in Culture and Society* 4: 219–36.

Davidson, Arnold. 2001. *The Emergence of Sexuality: Historical Epistemology and the Formation of Concepts*. Cambridge, MA: Harvard University Press.

Foucault, Michel. 1978. *The History of Sexuality*. Vol. 1, *An Introduction*, trans. Robert Hurley. New York: Vintage Books. (French edition 1976.)

Greenson, Ralph R. 1964. "On Homosexuality and Gender Identity." *International Journal of Psycho-Analysis* 45: 217–19.

Laqueur, Thomas. 1990. *Making Sex: Body and Gender from the Greeks to Freud*. Cambridge, MA: Harvard University Press.

Mead, Margaret. 1935. *Sex and Temperament in Three Primitive Societies*. New York: Morrow.

Money, John. 1955. "Hermaphroditism, Gender, and Precocity in Hyperadrenocorticism." *Bulletin of the Johns Hopkins Hospital* 96: 253–64.

Oudshoorn, Nelly. 1994. *Beyond the Natural Body: An Archeology of Sex Hormones*. New York and London: Routledge.

Stoller, Robert J. 1964. "A Contribution to the Study of Gender Identity." *International Journal of Psycho-Analysis* 45: 220–26.

Wilkerson, William S. 2007. *Ambiguity and Sexuality: A Theory of Sexual Identity*. New York: Palgrave Macmillan.

Wright, Clifford. 1938. "Further Studies of Endocrine Aspects of Homosexuality." *Medical Record* 147: 449–52.

Howard Hsueh-Hao Chiang

sexually transmitted infections

Sexually transmitted infection (STI) is a term used to describe any illness that is predominately spread through sexual activity. These illnesses can be viral, bacterial, fungal, or parasitical and can infect anyone regardless of race, sexual orientation, or gender. Although many illnesses can be spread via sexual activity, most other illnesses are not predominately spread sexually. For an infection to be labeled an STI, it needs to be spread mainly through sexual activity. The Centers for Disease Control and Prevention (CDC) estimate that 19 million cases of STIs occur each year in the United States. STIs are also sometimes called sexually transmitted diseases (STDs). STI has become the more prevalent term as someone may be infected with a virus or bacteria but not have immediate disease.

STIs such as herpes or genital warts are spread through direct skin-to-skin contact, but many other STIs are transmitted easily through the mucous membranes of two or more people involved in sexual contact. Mucous membranes are different from other types of skin in that they absorb and/or secrete fluids; they can therefore also absorb and/or secrete various pathogens. Many STIs are excreted from the body in fluids that are present in the mucous membranes. Mucous membranes are an extension of the skin that lines body cavities, including the vulva, the foreskin, the glans of the penis, the lips, and the lining of the mouth. In someone who is circumcised, the glans of the penis is a dry mucous membrane similar to the lips, whereas an uncircumcised person has a moist glans. STIs are transmitted from an infected person to an uninfected person or people during sexual activity. All sexual behavior that involves contact with another person or their bodily fluids has some potential risk for the transmission of STIs. Studies have proven that the more sexually active a person is, the more likely that person is to become infected with and to spread an STI. Individuals such as sex workers are more likely to become infected with an STI due to the variety of sexual contacts they are involved with regularly.

Regular STI testing rates among women who have sex with women (WSW) are much lower than testing rates among gay or heterosexual men or bisexual or heterosexual women. This rate is correlated to the perception in the lesbian community that STI risk is negligible among WSW. However, studies have shown that this belief of negligible risk is incorrect in certain respects. Herpes, trichomoniasis, human papillomavirus (HPV), bacterial vaginosis (BV), chlamydia, and pelvic inflammatory disease (PID) are STIs that are regularly seen in WSW populations. STI testing among self-identified gay men has historically been higher than for the rest of the population, due to the HIV epidemic. Men who have sex with men (MSM) are also at risk for STIs other than HIV and have a higher incidence of many STIs than heterosexual men.

BACTERIAL STIS

Syphilis is an STI caused by a spirochete bacterium, *Treponema pallidum*. Spriochete bacteria are so named because of the spiral appearance of the long cells. Another common spirochete bacteria is Lyme disease. Ten days to three months after infection with the syphilis bacteria, a sore or "chancre" will appear at the site of infection. It will have hard edges and generally will not be painful. If left untreated, the chancre will disappear and six to eight weeks later, the secondary stage begins with flulike symptoms, swollen glands, and rashes (including red rashes on the palms of the hands). It can be accompanied by sores that appear flat and gray. Contact with the highly contagious sores or rashes is the most common cause of infection with syphilis. These symptoms will disappear in time on their own, but tertiary syphilis will manifest itself, causing slow destruction of the nervous system, liver, heart, and other organs. Syphilis is treated successfully with a course of antibiotics, generally penicillin. Some antibiotic-resistant cases have made multiple drug treatments necessary. Because syphilis is spread through sores, transmission can occur during any variety or combination of heterosexual or homosexual activity. At present, there is an epidemic of syphilis among gay men in many U.S. cities. Also, syphilis is harder to treat and has an accelerated course when present in HIV-infected patients. The CDC recommends at least annual screening for syphilis among sexually active gay and bisexual men.

Gonorrhea is caused by the bacteria *Neisseria gonorrhoeae*. Visible symptoms generally appear 2–14 days after infection. Most common symptoms involve a pus-like discharge from either the penis or the vagina. This leads to one of the slang names for the disease, the drip. Some studies indicate up to 60 percent of infected women do not have outwardly visible signs of infection. Other symptoms in all people can include difficulty in urination. Infection in the anal regions can cause a rectal discharge, and infections in the throat or mouth will cause a sore throat or no symptoms at all. The disease can spread in women to the uterus or fallopian tubes, leading to PID. PID is an infection and inflammation of the upper genital tract of women that causes scarring, infertility, and other serious complications. Gonorrhea also will cause inflammation and infection of the cervix. In men, the disease can go unnoticed and may cause swollen testicles and/or a reddened and inflamed penis, again bringing infertility. Untreated gonorrhea infections can spread to other areas of the body, including joints and the brain. Gonorrhea is also treated successfully with a course of antibiotics—most often ceftriaxone, since penicillin-resistant strains of gonorrhea are relatively common. Seventy-five percent of all cases of gonorrhea in the United States occur in people between the ages of 15 and 29. At present, there is an epidemic of gonorrhea among gay men in many U.S. cities. The CDC recommends at least annual screening for gonorrhea among sexually active gay and bisexual men.

About four million cases of chlamydia occur each year in the United States. It can cause disease in both the eyes and sexual organs. Half of all men and nearly three-quarters of women will not display any symptoms when infected. It is easily cured if caught in time but if not can cause serious complications. Symptoms can include vaginal bleeding, painful urination, abdominal pain, fever, and painful sexual intercourse in women. In men, symptoms can include fever, discharge from the penis, swollen testicles, and painful urination, but it is usually asymptomatic. If left untreated, chlamydia can cause infertility in men and women, as well as Reiter's syndrome, an unusual arthritis that appears in 15,000 young men annually. Chlamydia leads to PID in thousands of women annually. Treatment is usually with oral antibiotics. Women under 25 who are sexually active (gay or straight) should be screened annually for chlamydia infection.

A particularly invasive strain of chlamydia known as *Lymphogranuloma venereum* (LGV) is relatively common in Africa and parts of Asia. Since 2004, LGV has appeared in MSM populations in the Netherlands, the United Kingdom, and, more recently, New York City. Infection, if symptoms occur, will cause a sore at the site of infection a few days afterwards, which will heal on its own. Approximately six months after primary infection, if treatment has not occurred, the lymph glands (in particular those in the groin area) will swell, often causing painful nodes, with drainage occurring through the skin. Initial infection in the anal or esophageal areas will cause lymph glands in those areas to swell and drain. Painful cysts around the vagina will occur in infected women at this point, in addition to the same lymph symptoms. These sores will eventually heal if left untreated. Tertiary LGV can lead to blocked lymph systems, causing elephantiasis of the genitalia in men and women or blocked rectums, if the main infection was in that region of the body. Treatment in the first or second stage involves antibiotics and, if necessary, drainage of the blocked lymph nodes. Treatment is generally successful if caught early in the infection.

Chancroid presents as open sores on the genitals of infected people. It is caused by the bacteria *Haemophilus ducreyi*. Infections are typically seen in developing countries rather than the Western world. Men will have ulcers appear on the penis, testicles, or perianal region. In women, ulcers will appear on the vagina, labia, or perianal area also. If untreated, chancroid can lead to swollen lymph nodes in the groin area, causing extreme pain and drainage through the skin. Uncircumcised men are three times more likely to become infected than circumcised men. Chancroid increases the risk of the spread of HIV due to the open sores created by the infection. Antibiotics are used to treat the disease successfully.

Bacterial vaginosis is currently poorly understood. It is caused by a disruption of the normal flora of the vagina that can cause discharge as well as an unpleasant odor. It can cause complications during pregnancy and birth. BV has been linked to PID and endometriosis through analysis of the diseased tissue. Although BV has been linked to sexual intercourse or a change in sexual partners, there is no clear indication that it is a bacterium spread through sexual activity. Treatment of BV with antibiotics improves symptoms and reduces the chances of further or later complications.

VIRAL STIS

Human immunodeficiency virus, or HIV, which is the virus that causes AIDS, is transmitted by unprotected sexual activity between two people, one of whom has the virus. For an extensive description of HIV and its treatment, see **HIV/AIDS, medical history.**

There are eight human herpes viruses (HHV) that can be spread through sexual activities, although most are predominantly spread through nonsexual contact. Several of the viruses in this family are so widespread that 95 percent of humans have been exposed to them by the time they reach middle age. Herpes simplex virus 1 (HSV1) causes open sores known as cold sores, night fevers, or fever blisters in and around the mouth two to three days after infection. Approximately 50 percent of adults have been exposed to this virus. HSV2 causes similar watery, painful blisters in the genital region of the body. Both HSV1 and 2 are highly contagious during the blister stage and can be transmitted by skin-to-skin contact. Both viruses cause outbreaks several times over the first year and can slowly decrease in intensity and frequency over time (but may not). Rarely, some people will not show signs of initial infection. It is possible to pass the virus when sores are not present because the virus is shed from the body through the skin. Treatment with antiviral medications decreases both the intensity of outbreaks of HSV2 and the amount of virus that is produced, thereby lessening the chance of passing the virus to sexual partners. Condoms can also lessen the chance of passing of HSV2 to sexual partners. More women are infected with HSV2 than men because of the increased amount of mucosal tissue in the vaginal area. Recent studies indicate 11 percent of men and 23 percent of women in the United States carry HSV2.

HHV8 is the virus that causes Kaposi's sarcoma, a once-rare cancer of the skin that was generally seen in older men of African or Mediterranean origin but became prevalent in people infected with HIV during the 1980s. HHV8 is the first virus to be implicated in causing cancer. In the United States it is passed predominantly through sex. Approximately 2 percent of the general population in the United States have been exposed to the virus, but close to 60 percent of gay men have the virus in their body. It is generally an asymptomatic virus until a person's immune system is compromised. Other viruses in the HHV family are predominantly spread through daily activities and can cause many types of infection, including chicken pox and mononucleosis.

Human papillomavirus (HPV) causes human warts. It is believed that nearly every human has been exposed to at least one subtype of HPV. Approximately 30 varieties of the virus can be transmitted sexually, and studies have shown that nearly 75 percent of women will be exposed to one of these viruses during their lifetime. Most varieties of HPV that are spread sexually do not cause any symptoms, though several cause typical wartlike growths singly or in clusters. These growths occur in and around the exposure site, including on the penis, around the anus, in and around the vulva and vagina, on the cervix, and even in the larynx and throat. The body's immune system generally clears HPV in a matter of months, and the warts will disappear. Some warts however, will need to be removed surgically or through chemical treatment. This is often the case with warts that occur inside the vagina, on the cervix, or in the anal canal. HPV can be passed through simple skin-to-skin contact without any outward sign of infection necessary. Certain types of HPV can lead to cervical and vulvar/vaginal cancers in women, penile cancer in men, and anal or head/neck cancers in women and men. The incidence of cancers due to HPV rises dramatically in HIV-infected people. Simple PAP smears can detect these varieties of HPV in both men and women. A vaccine has been developed that will prevent exposure to certain types of HPV, though not to all of the varieties that can cause cancer, and it is being recommended to young women for prevention of HPV. Ongoing studies are exploring the vaccine's effectiveness in men.

Hepatitis simply means inflammation of the liver. Several viruses can cause hepatitis. The hepatitis A virus (HAV) is spread through exposure to fecal matter, either through food products or sexual activity. People who engage in "rimming" (properly called analingus) may put themselves at greater risk for hepatitis A. Hepatitis A is a short-term illness that does not develop into a chronic problem as other forms of hepatitis do. Once people recover, they can no longer pass the virus to others. It can last from a week to six months and is rarely fatal. Symptoms of any hepatitis infection can be swelling of the liver, vomiting, jaundice (a yellowing of the skin and eyes), fever, fatigue, and a darkening of the urine. Vaccination against hepatitis A is usually successful in preventing the illness in those exposed to the virus and is recommended for all gay men and for those traveling outside of the United States.

Hepatitis C is the most common chronic bloodborne illness in the United States. Hepatitis C virus (HCV) is spread mainly through blood-to-blood contact such as found in injection drug use. It can be spread sexually and is more easily contracted if someone is infected with HIV. HIV infection makes the course of hepatitis C more rapid, which can lead to liver failure (cirrhosis) and even liver cancer. Treatments for hepatitis C are available.

Hepatitis B virus (HBV) is spread through blood and sexual contact. It takes much less effort to transmit hepatitis B than to transmit HIV because the amount of virus in the blood or genital fluids is much greater. HBV cannot be spread through food, drink, or casual contact. Hepatitis B is often asymptomatic in its initial infection, though it can cause symptoms similar to those of hepatitis A. Hepatitis B can also change from an acute disease, one of limited time, to a chronic disease, one of a long-standing nature. Some people will never clear the virus during the acute phase and will go on to become chronic carriers of HBV, as well as having chronic inflammation of the liver. In 15–25 percent of chronic HBV infections, the person will go on to develop cirrhosis and/or liver cancer. HIV infection accelerates and worsens the course of hepatitis B infection. Hepatitis B can be prevented through a vaccine that involves a series of three shots over six months. HIV-infected people may not have a full response to the HBV vaccine. Several treatments now exist for chronic hepatitis B. One is an injection drug, alpha interferon, and the others are antiviral pills that can be taken to reduce the viral load, thus reducing stress on the liver and lessening the chance of spreading the virus to others. Treatment with alpha interferon can in some instances spur someone with chronic HBV to recover and no longer have the chronic infection. Current oral antiviral treatment does not cure HBV but simply reduces the intensity of the illness over time. Other hepatitis viruses include D, E, and G.

PARASITES

Crabs or pubic lice are small creatures one to three millimeters in size that live on the pubic hair follicles. Their body structure is such that they cannot live in regular hair, and they are therefore different than head or body lice. The adult louse can live up to a day away from a human and therefore can be acquired from bedding or clothing that is shared. Contrary to urban myths, pubic lice cannot be acquired from using public toilet seats as lice cannot grasp the smooth surface with their legs and fall off such surfaces quickly. The main symptom of pubic lice is itching of the area of infestation. Lice feed on human blood, and the itching results from their bites. The female louse lays her eggs on human hair. They appear as tiny white beads, called nits. Treatment is with an insecticide shampoo and careful removal of all nits through either shaving the hair from the region or combing with a small-tooth comb. Failure to remove all of the nits will lead to reinfestation as the eggs hatch.

Scabies is another small mite that can be passed through sexual activity. This is the common mode of transmission in adults, though children acquire scabies most often through simple person-to-person contact. The microscopic mite that causes scabies burrows into human skin and lays eggs that hatch into larvae in 3 to 10 days. Scratching and an allergic reaction to the mites give rise to the rash-like symptoms generally seen four to six weeks after initial infestation. As with lice, thorough cleaning of clothing and bedding is necessary to remove the mites from the home, and insecticide shampoo is used to kill the mites. People on immunosuppressive drugs or with HIV may not develop a proper immune response to scabies, leading to large sections of crusty and scaly skin called Norwegian scabies. A different course of medication in addition to the shampoo will be necessary in such cases.

PROTOZOAL STIS

Trichomoniasis, also called ping-pong disease or trich, is caused by the protozoan *Trichomona vaginalis.* It causes a smelly yellow or green discharge from the vagina in women and from the urethra in men. It is possible to be infected and show no symptoms, particularly in men. It is called ping-pong disease because it is often difficult to eliminate the problem unless both partners are treated. Trichomoniasis has been associated with an increased risk of HIV transmission as well as an increased chance of low birth weight in children born to mothers who were infected during pregnancy. It can easily be passed between WSW as well as between men and women in sexual activity. It can, however, be treated easily with antibiotics, as long as both partners are treated.

Further Reading

"Can Women Give Other Women STDs? Yes." *Public Health, Seattle and King County.* Available at: http://www.metrokc.gov/health/glbt/lbstd.htm. Accessed July 16, 2008.

"Lesbians, Bisexual Women and Safe Sex." *Avert.org.* Available at: http://www.avert.org/lesbian safesex.htm. Accessed July 16, 2008.

"Pelvic Inflammatory Disease: NIAID Factsheet." Available at: http://www.wrongdiagnosis.com/artic/pelvic_inflammatory_disease_niaid_fact_sheet_niaid.htm. Accessed July 16, 2008.

"Safer Sex and STD Prevention for Lesbian and Bi Women: LGBThealth channel." Available at: http://www.lgbthealthchannel.com/stdwsw/index.shtml. Accessed July 16, 2008.

"Sexually Transmitted Diseases Treatment Guidelines, 2006." *Morbidity and Mortality Weekly Report.* August 4, 2006. Available at: http://www.cdc.gov/mmwr/PDF/rr/rr5511.pdf. Accessed July 16, 2008.

Sowadsky, Rick. "Health Concerns for Gay Men." *The Body.* Available at: http://www.thebody.com/sowadsky/gaymen.html. Accessed July 16, 2008.

Steve Stratton

sex wars of the 1980s

The sex wars or lesbian sex wars were a time of intense political and cultural debate surrounding contentious sexual issues including **pornography, sadomasochism** (S/M), **butch–femme** relationships, and the use of sex toys. Feminist activism of the 1970s problematized forms of sexuality that were seen as heteropatriarchal, and so sexual practices seen as oppressive or male-identified came under fire in feminist and lesbian communities. Others then sought to undermine what they saw as feminist hegemonic control over sexuality, championing various sexual practices. The American dimension of the sex wars is widely acknowledged to have begun during the conference The Scholar and the Feminist IX, held at Barnard College in New York on April 24, 1982. This conference sparked an ongoing feud between lesbian feminists and sex radicals that continued through the 1980s and into the 1990s.

Lesbians played an active and important role in the evolution of the feminist movement, and yet some elements of the feminist movement rejected lesbian feminist activists, fearing that all feminists would be perceived to be lesbians. Lesbian feminists objected to this treatment, asserting not only that should the women's liberation movement include lesbians and take lesbian issues seriously but also that this was essential to the movement's success. In 1970 a group known as the **Radicalesbians** was formed to protest the **homophobia** of various straight feminists and feminist organizations; their "lavender menace" action at the Second Congress to Unite Women is generally considered to be the beginning of the lesbian feminist movement. The Radicalesbians' manifesto, "The Woman-Identified Woman" (1970), proclaimed that patriarchal society forced women into the subservient role of sex objects and that this could also be the case in women's relationships with one another.

These sorts of ideas led radical lesbian feminists to reject sexual practices that were deemed to be male-identified in their rendering of women as sexual objects. This label came to be applied to a wide range of sexual activities and identities including pornography, sadomasochism, the use of dildos, and butch–femme relationships. Some groups and individuals even saw vaginal penetration or one lover lying on top of the other as replicating heterosexual colonization of women's bodies or enacting power dynamics in a relationship. Many lesbians came to see these political prohibitions against certain forms of sexual expression as restrictive and questioned whether it was indeed a useful feminist cause to repress women's sexuality and cause them to feel shame about their desires, considering that women's repression and shame about sex have always been a feature of heteropatriarchal society. The utilization of sex toys and experimentation with new sexual practices thus came to be seen by many within lesbian communities as a transgressive and political gesture.

The issue most commonly associated with the sex wars is pornography. In this issue, the lesbian sex wars were part of a dialogue about pornography within the larger feminist community. Writers and activists like Andrea Dworkin and Catherine MacKinnon had denounced pornography, seeing it not only as oppressive to women but as a stimulus for rape. Many lesbians, including those who later became prominent sex radicals, took part in antipornography campaigns and guerrilla actions against stores that stocked materials deemed harmful to women.

In a spirit of rebellion against what was seen as the dominant feminist order, many lesbians began producing lesbian erotica and pornography, arguing not only that the lesbian framework removed oppressive patriarchal elements but also that it was necessary and empowering for lesbians to explore their sexualities through such outlets. Magazines like *Bad Attitude* (1984–1987) and *On Our Backs* (1984–1995, 1998–2006)—whose title played on the name of the popular feminist journal *Off Our Backs*—were key in encouraging lesbian sexual expression through disseminating lesbian erotic images and stories and had a clear focus on promoting lesbian S/M and butch–femme cultures. Tensions between lesbian feminists and sex radicals were raised further when antipornography ordinances campaigned for by feminists were used specifically to discriminate against queer publications.

The return of butch–femme cultures into fashion in the 1990s, and the subsequent media attention this received, was also a result of the sex wars. Many North American lesbians of the 1950s identified as butch or femme, and butch–femme culture was a prominent aspect of lesbian culture, particularly among working-class lesbians and in lesbian **bars.** Discussion of the lesbian butch–femme culture of this era can be found in such sources as **Leslie Feinberg**'s *Stone Butch Blues* and the work of Joan Nestle. An important part of feminist thought is the critique of rigid gender roles. Therefore, lesbian feminists viewed butch–femme communities with suspicion and considered them to be replicating heteropatriarchal models and roles. Lesbian feminists called on butches and femmes to reject these identities in the name of feminist sisterhood. Femmes were seen as straight women forcing lesbians into the male role that, it was considered, butches took. While some, swept up in the excitement of the feminist movement, indeed did reject these identities, many lesbians began to view this as another form of control over their lives and as a rejection of their lesbian heritage and identities. As a result, the late 1980s and early 1990s saw a reclamation and resurgence of butch and femme identities, though the forms these took were often more flexible than those of the 1950s.

Sadomasochism was perhaps the most contentious issue during the sex wars, and the term came to be utilized as a negative umbrella term for other controversial practices. Lesbian practitioners of S/M were growing in numbers throughout the 1970s, and groups such as Samois (1978–1983) and Lesbian Sex Mafia (1981–) increased the public profile of lesbian S/M, which made them obvious targets of lesbian feminist activists who objected to what they saw as violence against women. Samois was a San Francisco–based lesbian BDSM (bondage, discipline, and sadomasochism) group founded by Pat Califia and Gayle Rubin. The group asserted that S/M was not inconsistent with feminism and promoted the safe and consensual practice of S/M through publications and events. Samois's publication of the well-known anthology *Coming to Power: Writings and Graphics on Lesbian S/M* (1981) was a milestone defense of lesbian S/M; it served as one of the key ideological texts of the sex wars. The later group, the New York–based Lesbian Sex Mafia (1981–) was less explicitly an S/M group. Cofounder **Dorothy Allison** writes that this group attempted to act as a consciousness-raising group around sex, though still concentrating on attracting members interested in S/M, butch–femme, and other taboo sexualities (Vance 1984).

The intersection of female and male S/M cultures, together with the rejection of lesbian separatist ideas that men were the enemy, was part of the myriad forces that brought lesbians back into alliance with gay men, establishing the greater fluidity associated with the queer 1990s. While some contend that in these new, neoconservative times the sex wars' lessons about sexual diversity have been lost, there is no doubt that the sex wars of the 1980s have had an enormous impact on contemporary lesbian sexualities and cultures. Lesbian magazines, films, and sexual cultures of today reflect the extent to which the **sex-positive** values promoted during the sex wars have permeated contemporary lesbian culture.

Further Reading

Duggan, Lisa, and Nan Hunter. 1995. *Sex Wars: Sexual Dissent and Political Culture*. New York and London: Routledge.

Healey, Emma. 1996. *Lesbian Sex Wars*. London: Virago.

Radicalesbians. 1970. "The Woman-Identified Woman." Pittsburgh: Know, Inc. Reprinted online by Duke University's Special Collections Library. Available at: http://scriptorium.lib.duke.edu/wlm/womid/. Accessed July 16, 2008.

Vance, Carole S., ed. 1984. *Pleasure and Danger: Exploring Female Sexuality*. Boston: Routledge and Kegan Paul.

Wilton, Tamsin. 1996. *Finger-Licking Good: The Ins and Outs of Lesbian Sex*. London and New York: Cassell.

Rebecca Beirne

Barbara Seyda

Barbara Seyda is a freelance photographer who focuses her skills on LGBTQ causes as well as on the lives of the poor and oppressed. She earned an MFA from Rutgers in painting. After college, while living in the New York area, she was a photojournalist for *Outweek*. Eventually, she and her partner, Diana Herrera, moved to the Southwest. There, one Thanksgiving, surrounded by lesbians and their children, Seyda and Herrera decided that lesbian mothers and their children needed to be documented. Seyda approached *Mothering* magazine but was rejected, after having been given the initial go-ahead. After getting rejections from all of the mainstream media, they were able to raise enough money to do the project on their own. In 1998, *Women in Love: Portraits of Lesbian Mothers and Their Families* was published to much critical acclaim, eventually earning Seyda and Herrera a Lambda Literary Award. Seyda's next project was *Nomads of a Desert City* in 2001, which focused on the homeless of Tucson, Arizona. Her most recent project is as the editor of *People around Us*, published in 2006; it depicts, in their own words, the plight of low-wage earners in Tucson. Published by the Southwest Center for Economic Integrity, Seyda's latest work is only available locally in Tucson from the center and the local women's bookstore Antigone. Seyda has freelanced for many publications including *Essence, British Elle, Sojourner,* and *New Mexico Magazine*. She continues to live in Tucson working on her photography and using her skills to highlight the plight of the oppressed and underrepresented.

Further Reading

Seyda, Barbara. 1995. "Massacre of the Dreamers: An Interview with Ana Castillo." *Sojourner* 20 (9): 16–17.

Seyda, Barbara. 1996. "Divine Testimonies: Sydne Mahone and the Crossroads Theatre Company." *TDR: The Drama Review: A Journal of Performance Studies* 40 (1): 119–40.

Katherine J. J. Pionke

Reginald Shepherd (1963–2008)

A prolific African American poet, editor, critic, and educator, Reginald Shepherd is the author of five books of poetry, all published by the University of Pittsburgh Press: *Some Are Drowning* (1994), *Angel, Interrupted* (1996), *Wrong* (1999), *Otherhood* (2003), and *Fata Morgana* (2007). His work combines references to classical mythology and Western canonical literature with modern concerns over issues of loss, identity, and race. Influenced by the work of T. S. Eliot, W. B. Yeats, Wallace Stevens, and **Hart Crane,** Shepherd's often-complex lyrical work can be intentionally opaque, reflecting his desire for the reader to engage consciously with each word of his poems. In his sometimes-controversial essays, such as "On Not Being White" (in Beam 1986/2007) and "Coloring outside the Lines" (published in *Callaloo*, 1999), Shepherd has tackled such topics as the complexity of interracial gay male relationships. Much of Shepherd's work often reflects feelings of alienation and the peripatetic nature of his own life and upbringing.

Born in New York City and raised by his mother in a housing project in the Bronx, Shepherd attended three schools and was tutored at home for a year prior to his mother's death 10 days before his 15th birthday. He left New York to be raised by his aunt's family in Macon, Georgia, before attending Bennington College. He earned a BA from Bennington in 1998 and MFAs in creative writing from both Brown (in 1991) and the University of Iowa (in 1993). He has taught at Northern Illinois University and Cornell and currently lives with his partner in Pensacola, Florida.

Shepherd's awards and honors include a "Discovery"/The Nation Award (1993), the Associated Writing Programs' Award Series in Poetry (for *Some Are Drowning*, 1994), the George Kent Prize (1994), a National Endowment for the Arts Creative Writing Fellowship (1995), an Illinois Arts Council Poetry Fellowship (1998), and a Pushcart Prize (1999). Shepherd's poetry has appeared in the 1995, 1996, 2000, and 2002 editions of *Best American Poetry*. He is editor of *The Iowa Anthology of New American Poetries*.

Further Reading

Beam, Joseph, ed. 1986/2007. *In the Life: A Black Gay Anthology*. Boston: Alyson Publications. Repr., Washington, DC: Redbone Press.

Boxwell, David A. 2003. "Reginald Shepherd." In *Contemporary Gay American Poets and Playwrights: An A–Z Guide*, ed. Emmanuel S. Nelson, 398–405. Westport, CT: Greenwood Press.

Hennessy, Christopher. 2005. *Outside the Lines: Talking with Contemporary Gay Poets*. Ann Arbor: University of Michigan Press.

Shepherd, Reginald. 1999. "Coloring outside the Lines: An Essay at Definition." *Callaloo* 22 (1): 134–40.

Shepherd, Reginald, ed. 2004. *The Iowa Anthology of New American Poetries*. Iowa City: University of Iowa Press.

Shepherd, Reginald 2008. *Reginald Shepherd's Blog*. Available at: http://reginaldshepherd.blogspot. com. Accessed July 16, 2008.

Reginald Harris

Martin Sherman (1938–)

Martin Sherman, best known for *Bent* (1979), was born in Philadelphia and currently resides in London. Early in his career, Sherman experimented with short plays such as the murder mystery *Cracks* (1975), the gay comedy *Passing By* (1975), and *Things Went Badly in Westphalia* (1970), which explores a postapocalyptic United States where oppressed groups undergo torture and slavery. Such plays led to Sherman's best-known work, which begins the morning of the "Night of the Long Knives" in 1934 Berlin. The play centers around Max, a gay German Jew trapped in a Nazi prison camp, alongside Horst, who teaches Max that love and spiritual fulfillment are essential to survival in defiance of subjugation and tyranny. Sherman's extensive dramatic oeuvre also includes a translation of Luigi Pirandello's play *Cosi è (se vi pare)* as *Absolutely! (Perhaps)* (2003), a dramatic adaptation of Forster's novel *A Passage to India* (2002), and *Rose* (1999), a dramatic monologue narrating twentieth-century Jewish life. Sherman's interest in Judaism continued in plays such as *Messiah* (1982), in which hysterical Jews nearly annihilated by Cossacks convince themselves that Sabbatai Sevi will deliver them to redemption. His full-length plays also include *When She Danced* (1990), a comedy about modern dance legend Isadora Duncan; *A Madhouse in Goa* (1989), in which a writer deals with the realities of Chernobyl's radioactive cloud and terrorist activity on a Greek island; and *Some Sunny Day* (1996), in which an alien vacations in Cairo during World War II, where spies and murder run rampant.

Further Reading

Clum, John M. 2000. *Still Acting Gay: Male Homosexuality in Modern Drama*. New York: St. Martin's.

Shewey, Don. 2000. "Martin Sherman: Dramatizing a Century of Jewish Memories." *New York Times* (April 9).

John Pruitt

Susan Sherman (1939–)

Born in Philadelphia, Susan Sherman was raised in Los Angeles by her stepfather, a Russian Jewish immigrant, and her American Jewish mother. She achieved her BA in English and philosophy at the University of California in Berkeley in

1961. During this time she discovered an inner connection with three key elements that would forever influence her life and career: poetry, jazz, and political involvement. She documents her life in *America's Child: A Woman's Journey through the Radical Sixties* (Clausen, 2007).

In 1967, she received her MA in philosophy from Hunter College in New York. Sherman flourished there and became routinely involved in the domain of poetry. Rather amazingly, nine of her works were produced off Broadway and she became the poetry editor and theater critic for the *Village Voice*. Sherman's endeavors took her around the world, but one of the more powerful influences in her life and career resulted from her decision to attend a cultural conference in Havana, Cuba, in 1968. She returned to Cuba the following year for a lengthy sojourn.

Sherman is a well-known frontline advocate for the women's movement, gay and lesbian rights, antiapartheid and antiracism efforts, and the evolution of the Central American peace faction. Her tireless efforts toward political resolution in these strongholds are reflected in her poetry and writing for which she has received numerous awards and recognition. Her distinctions include the 1986 editor award from the New York State Council on the Arts, her appointment to the Maryland State Council on the Arts Poetry Panel (1990–1991), and the Delaware State Council on the Arts Poetry and Non-Fiction Panels (1989–1990).

Throughout her work Sherman articulates sensual and cultural identity in the evolution of life. Her books include *The Color of the Heart,* a collective work of prose, poetry, and essays from 1959 through 1990; *With Anger/With Love* reflects her political connection and the natural progression of change, both personal and universal.

Further Reading

Bernikow, Louise. 1976. "Out of the Bell Jar." *New Times* (October 29): 46–54.

Clausen, Jan. 2007. "America's Child: A Woman's Journey Through the Radical Sixties." *Lambda Book Report* 15 (3): 15.

Reyna, Bessy. 1991. Interview with Susan Sherman. *Curbstone Ink* 1.

Vicki Lynn White

Randy Shilts (1951–1994)

Born in Davenport, Iowa, and raised in a conservative Methodist family, Randy Shilts became a national correspondent for the *San Francisco Chronicle* in 1981. He was the first openly gay journalist hired by a major metropolitan newspaper.

While still in high school, several years before **coming out,** Shilts founded a local chapter of Young Americans for Freedom. At the University of Oregon, he became a leader in the local branch of the Gay People's Alliance and graduated at the top of his class. Early incidents of social **activism** foreshadowed Shilts's tenacious documentation of renaissance and tragedy in **San Francisco** gay life in the late 1970s and 1980s. Not only did he persuade *Chronicle* editors to move his stories about gay political struggles and early cases of gay-related immuno-deficiency diseases (GRID) to the front of the newspaper, but he also amassed his reports into three massive epics of the period: *The Mayor of Castro Street: The Life and Times of Harvey Milk* (1982), *And the Band Played On: Politics, People and the AIDS Epidemic* (1987), and *Conduct Unbecoming: Gays and Lesbians in the U.S. Military* (1993).

While Shilts's books have been criticized by some for their use of composite or renamed characters, reconstructed dialogue, and nontraditional structure, such techniques legitimately place Shilts in the company of a previous generation of New Journalists, including Tom Wolfe, Norman Mailer, and **Truman Capote.** By employing dramatic narrative techniques to express meticulous research, Shilts put a human face on subjects that might have otherwise remained marginal: the election and subsequent assassination of gay politicians, the beginning years of the AIDS epidemic, and discrimination against gays in the U.S. armed forces.

Randy Shilts (right) and friend. Photograph by Marie Ueda, courtesy of the Gay, Lesbian, Bisexual, Transgender Historical Society, San Francisco.

While reaching a wider readership, Shilts recognized the controversial nature of his approach. In the Author's Note for his Milk biography, he acknowledged, "This book will not please ideologues looking for a political tract. Conversely, some may complain that it is sympathetic to the gay point of view" (1982, xiv). Indeed, schizophrenic responses to Shilts's work continued to haunt him throughout his short but intense publishing career.

In *Mayor of Castro Street*, one of the first gay political profiles, Shilts traced the path of Harvey Milk's brief but energetic ascendancy in San Francisco politics. Milk become a more radical presence for **gay rights** in the late 1970s, only after leaving behind the East Coast, Goldwater Republican conservatism of his younger years. Shilts describes how, in a moment of hope and progress, San Francisco Mayor George Moscone appointed Milk to the role of city supervisor. Both Moscone and Milk were shot dead by Dan White, who had formerly held the position. Shilts documents White's trial, with its verdict of voluntary manslaughter and prison sentence of seven years and eight months. He also details the subsequent riots surging from the Castro District of San Francisco toward City Hall. Shilts concludes with appendices including Milk's notes, speeches, and other documents: artifacts of a living legacy rather than simple martyrdom.

By far Shilts's best-known and most provocative work is *And the Band Played On*, which was translated into seven languages and ultimately made into an HBO docudrama. While it scrutinized the slow pace with which the Centers for Disease Control, the government, and even some gay organizations came to terms with AIDS, the book was also controversial for its unfavorable characterization of sexual practices such as **fisting** and rimming, as well as its open criticism of **bathhouse** culture and promiscuity. Shilts did not disclose his own status as HIV-positive until a year before his death.

Shilts's final opus, *Conduct Unbecoming*, sought to place American military witch hunts against gays and lesbians within an historical perspective. Because of declining health, Shilts had to dictate the closing pages. The book appeared the same year Bill Clinton issued his "don't ask, don't tell" compromise for members of the armed forces, and Shilts died before he could hear Clinton and other politicians publicly criticize the policy as ineffective.

Shilts received many awards during his lifetime, including Outstanding Author from the American Society of Journalists and Authors (1988) and a Lifetime Achievement Award from the National Lesbian and Gay Journalists Association (1993). Cleve Jones, founder of the **Names Project,** has called Shilts a hero for his commitment to literary witness.

Further Reading

Brodsley, Laurel. 1992. "Defoe's *The Journal of the Plague Year:* A Model for Stories of Plagues." In *AIDS: The Literary Response*, ed. Emmanuel S. Nelson, 11–22. New York: Twayne.

Dawes, James. 1995. "Narrating Disease: Aids, Consent, and the Ethics of Representation." *Social Text* 43: 27–44.

Shilts, Randy. 1982. *The Mayor of Castro Street: The Life and Times of Harvey Milk.* New York: St. Martin's Press.

Wachter, Robert M. 1991. *The Fragile Coalition: Scientists, Activists and AIDS.* New York: St. Martin's Press.

Jo Scott-Coe

Ann Allen Shockley (1927–)

A prolific author, Ann Allen Shockley is a successful archivist, literary critic, and fiction writer. Born in Louisville, Kentucky, she began her writing career with the *Louisville Defender,* where she addressed topics ranging from bored housewives to the black lesbian feminist group Salsa Soul Sisters. As a newspaper columnist and librarian at Fisk University, Shockley's work has been some of the first to improve access to the oeuvres of countless black writers like Anna Cooper, Claude Brown, and Pauline Elizabeth Hopkins who likely would have otherwise gone unnoticed. In Shockley's work, she is ever-aware of the politics of publishing, that is, the way that ideologies of gender, race, class, and sexuality play out among publishing houses, literary journals, critics, and bookstores to influence which texts are made accessible. Through her archival studies, Shockley has indeed achieved her stated goal of according African American women writers their due place beside their male cohort.

In the late 1970s and 1980s, Shockley dedicated much of her scholarship to black lesbian writers, her most famous article being "The Black Lesbian in American Literature: An Overview," anthologized in *Home Girls: A Black Feminist Anthology* (1982). In this piece, she examines why black lesbians have been anomalous in American literature (religious constraints, black nationalism, **homophobia** in the women's movement) and discusses the available representations of black lesbians.

Shockley's contribution to contemporary American lesbian and gay culture emerges in her fiction as much as in her scholarship. Upon the publication of Shockley's *Loving Her* (1974), Jewelle Gomez acknowledged that black lesbians were for the first time able to recognize themselves in the pages of a novel. Reprinted in 1997, *Loving Her* is now Shockley's most renowned work, known as the first novel to deal openly with an interracial lesbian relationship—an especially bold move given that it was conceptualized at the height of black nationalism and its emphasis on racial unity. Her volume of short stories *The Black and White of It* (1980) investigates themes like homophobia in some black communities as well as racism and sexism that affect the lives of African American lesbians. Shockley's 1982 novel *Say Jesus and Come to Me* again approaches gay oppression, this time in the black church. Here, a strong critique of middle-class values comes through more clearly than the underlying class resentment in *Loving Her*. Shockley's unflinchingly **lesbian feminist** writing earned her the 1990 OUTlook Award honoring her groundbreaking contribution to lesbian and gay writing.

Recently, Shockley went on to pen *Celebrating Hotchclaw* (2005), which follows similar themes to her previous work, this time amid the backdrop of a southern black college and its efforts to stay afloat in spite of financial scarcity. Following her earlier interest in documenting and challenging antiqueer ideas in African American subcultures, she attends to the politics of transgenderism and passing. Shockley continues to publish critical essays and short stories in journals like the *African American Review* and *Sinister Wisdom*.

Further Reading

Dandridge, Rita B. 1987. *Ann Allen Shockley: An Annotated Primary and Secondary Bibliography.* Westport, CT: Greenwood Press.

Mimi Iimuro Van Ausdall

short stories

The short story has been readily adopted by contemporary LGBTQ authors as a flexible and powerful form with which to represent an increasingly wide range of voices, concerns, and experiences. In particular, the racial and ethnic diversity of current LGBTQ short story authors promotes ever more nuanced acts of creative expression, cultural identification, and cross-cultural understanding. Further, the length of short stories, typically between 1,000 and 7,500 words, allows for publication in a rich mix of venues, including single-author short story collections, national literary and LGBTQ-oriented journals, and community-based newsletters and magazines. Gay and lesbian authors have been able to achieve wide-scale recognition through the growing practice of publishing LGBTQ short story anthologies, including works such as *Lavender Mansions: 40 Contemporary Lesbian and Gay Short Stories* (1994), *Afrekete: An Anthology of Black Lesbian Writing* (1995), and the long-running *Women on Women* and *Men on Men* series. These compilations demonstrate the increasing awareness of and cultural capital attached to collective LGBTQ identities. The sometimes striking differences within and between such collections simultaneously point to the divisions that run through and help to define various LGBTQ communities. Presented here are 25 of the most well-known and representative contemporary LGBTQ short story authors.

The conventions of short fiction, which include single settings, simple or distilled plotlines, a limited number of characters, epiphanic moments, central crises that are often not fully resolved, and ambiguous moral lessons, can lend themselves in unique ways to representations of gay and lesbian experiences, the epiphanic moment being a foremost example. The startling moment of recognition, understanding, or disclosure that typifies the short story in general has particular salience for LGBTQ short narratives in which epiphany is structured by a character's revelation of his or her LGBTQ identity, an act known as **coming out.** Such a revelation can not only provide the central moment of crisis in a story but, moreover, sometimes indicate a complete rupture of past and future for the LGBTQ character who comes out. Thus, in Sandy Boucher's "The Day My Father Kicked Me Out," published in *The Notebooks of Leni Clare and Other Short Stories* (1982), the rejection of the lesbian narrator by her parents opens an unbridgeable emotional and geographic space between them. In contrast, the full outcome and repercussions of the epiphanic coming out are often left necessarily unexplored in LGBTQ short stories. For example, **Ann Allen Shockley,** known for her groundbreaking representations of black lesbians, portrays in "Family Reunion" (1996) a mother living in the Deep South who is struggling to accept her lesbian daughter who has returned after a long exile. That difficult homecoming, eased by an aunt's own coming out and interpreted through the lens of social justice efforts in the civil rights era, reconnects mother and daughter but does so with clear markers of how difficult the work of reforging family bonds can be after coming out. Equally revelatory are moments in which characters discover unknown or unexpected LGBTQ friends, relatives, and communities. In Richard Hall's "Country People," collected in *Fidelities* (1992), a college instructor of gay literature realizes he has been teaching a community of kindred spirits—literally ghosts—dramatizing the importance of knowing and sharing LGBTQ history, of keeping the past alive through stories. Similarly, but in a different cultural context, Jewelle Gomez, in the title story to her 1998 collection *Don't Explain*, emphasizes the importance to Letty, a black lesbian waitress in 1959, of being invited to a party comprised, to her surprise, entirely of other black lesbians.

As these stories suggest, the search for and celebration of community has been a major theme in LGBTQ short stories. One of the most celebrated LGBTQ short story authors, Allen Barnett, writes a classic tale of gay men summering on New York's Fire Island even as their numbers are diminished by the AIDS epidemic. "The Times as It Knows Us" (1990) raises painful and poignant questions about what a community owes to its members, arguing, ultimately, for a more expansive sense of humanity. Similarly, Beth Brant's title story "Food and Spirits" (1990), informed by her Mohawk heritage, imagines an expanded community created through the open-hearted, open-minded tradition of sharing food. However, other

LGBTQ authors recognize that "community" is an ever-contested term for people with minority social and sexual identities. The Latina lesbian community of Terri de la Peña's 1991 story "Mujeres Morenas" appears vibrant in its differences, standing in stark contrast to the earlier feminist lesbian community of Shockley's 1979 story "A Meeting of the Sapphic Daughters," fractured as that assembly is by racism expressed between black and white women. Such tales remind readers that collective LGBTQ identities offer the potential for safety but also for risk.

Indeed, a range of risks and vulnerabilities are exposed by LGBTQ short stories. Gil Cuadros's "Unprotected," collected in *City of God* (1994), explores the psychology of an HIV-infected Latino man fatalistically drawn to potentially dangerous sexual encounters. Concerned with the difficulties of lesbian embodiment, Patricia Roth Schwartz's "Bodies," originally published in the renowned feminist literary journal *Sojourner,* offers a wide-ranging critique of the ways the female body is undermined by impossible standards of "fitness," the effects of age, and the inevitability of death. Although a phrase associated with gay male safe-sex educational efforts, when adapted by Ruthann Robson, "Kissing Doesn't Kill" (1991) becomes a powerfully ironic commentary on the physical and emotional threats to lesbians in times of homophobic political crisis at both local and national levels. While threats to gay men and women thus often diverge, risks of the body also make for interesting parallels between them, as in Barnett's titular story "The Body and Its Dangers" (1990). In that story, the cancer of the lesbian narrator represents only the most urgent of assaults on the body, others of which include misogyny, pregnancy, sex, abortion, and, for the gay man's body, AIDS. A similar gender parallel arises in "Zigzagger," the title story of Manuel Muñoz's 2003 collection, when the author draws a parallel between a Chicana mother, wise to the dangers of forbidden desire, and her teenage son, similarly seduced by the touch of a handsome stranger.

As "Zigzaggers" attests, the difficulties of youth are central to many contemporary LGBTQ short stories. Like Muñoz, John Keene refuses to oversimplify portraits of LGBTQ people coming of age. In "My Son, My Heart, My Life" (1996), Keene offers a complex depiction of a 13-year-old adolescent clearly attuned to the erotic possibilities, both treacherous and at times intriguing, that exist between children and adults. Jacqueline Woodson, in both "Tuesday, August Third" (1994) and "What Has Been Done to Me" (1996), laments the ways African American children, both gay and straight, are lost to drugs, sexual molestation, war, and suicide. Woodson thus reveals the complexity of the struggle to move out of one's painful history, specifically, out of the hollow childhood structured simultaneously by racism, misogyny, and **homophobia.** Stories such as Woodson's are significant in that they take up the work of remembering and recording the often-forgotten or untold stories of LGBTQ youth. Joan Nestle, an outspoken figure in the struggle to create powerful and positive representations of lesbians, engages in the politics of remembering in a story of unfulfilled adolescent desire, "Liberties Not Taken," written for her 1987 collection, *A Restricted Country.* The missed lesbian encounter that catalyzes the narrative prompts a reflection on the necessity of lesbian role models and the difficulty of maturing without a lover's touch, a touch that is made impossible not only by cultural prohibitions on homosexuality but also by the sexist appropriation of young women's bodies by older men. Robson also takes up the case of the absent lesbian role model in "pas de deux," the story of a vanished ballet instructor and her star pupil's long and ultimately successful search to locate her, if not literally then metaphorically, everywhere.

One of the most consistent themes in recent gay and lesbian short fiction is that of the family drama. Such narratives portray moments when familial bonds are tested, broken, strengthened, or renewed. Often they reveal the dangers that families pose to LGBTQ members, as in Hall's "The Jilting of Tim Weatherall," which recounts the resentment of a gay son dying from AIDS whose Texas family has rejected him, and Jess Wells's "Aqua" (1987), which portrays lesbians, daughters living in the shadows of unhappy mothers. The astonishing capacity of a family to turn violently against one of its own, especially when she is considered to be sexually "deviant," powerfully reverberates through the finale of Cuadros's Mexican American family drama, "Indulgences" (1994).

But as contemporary LGBTQ short stories portray families divided by homophobia, they just as often reveal family bonds to be resilient, if tenuous. The politics of familial separation ground Beth Brant's "A Long Story" (1995), a dual narrative of two grieving mothers—one an American Indian in 1890, the other a divorced mother in a lesbian relationship in 1978—whose children are forcibly removed from them by the government and the court system, respectively. Brant's story is at once painful and empowering, however, as lesbian union becomes a foundation of strength and courage for coping with loss. Similarly, both Melanie Kaye/Kantrowitz and Patricia Roth Schwartz place grown children within family genealogies of love and pain in "Jewish Food, Jewish Children" (1990) and "The Names of the Moons of Mars" (1989), focusing on the difficulty of relating to one's parents as an adult child.

Schwartz simultaneously maintains a focus on the economic straits of women who are divorced from their husbands and struggling to regain a sense of financial and emotional security in a patriarchal system that dramatically disempowers the divorced lesbian and mother, as suggested by her suffocating title "Underwater Women" (1989). Indeed, contemporary LGBTQ authors have been especially attuned to issues of **class** and the ways that socioeconomic structures support homophobic and heterocentrist interests. Sandy Boucher, in "Charm School" (1982), portrays a young female employee disempowered both economically and sexually by her abusive male employer. The story ends ambiguously, with the reader unsure whether the protagonist ultimately learns to counteract the ways men can use sex as a tool of power. In "Learning to See," the opening story of *Eye of a Hurricane* (1989), Robson turns the lens of class back onto the white female narrator, exposing the social realism of the narrator's photography as an exploitative act of cultural tourism. Class- and race-based exploitation takes on an erotic valence in Muñoz's tale of sexually vulnerable Mexican American boys who are both desired for and silenced by their brown skin in "Everything the White Boy Told You."

Unquestionably, a central concern of LGBTQ short story authors has been to offer insight into the complex ways desire circulates through and becomes meaningful in relation to the raced and ethnically identified body. Muñoz thus deals with the intersection of desire and Chicano identity. In "Campo," one boy's ability to speak both Spanish and English allows him, ambiguously, to lay claim to an immigrant boy who cannot communicate with the white townspeople who are suspicious of his presence. Both allure and mistrust charge the linguistic and erotic divide between the boys. Also interested in portraying characters struggling to reconcile multiple subject positions, Lev Raphael focuses on gay male Jewish identity in several collections including *Dancing on Tisha B'Av* (1990) and *Secret Anniversaries of the Heart* (2006). Although in "Shouts of Joy" he depicts a joint spiritual and sexual revelation for his gay Jewish protagonist, Raphael elsewhere offers darker portraits of gay men, often writers, trying to cope with their painful family history of being Jewish after the Holocaust, as in "The Life You Have" and the politically engaged "Secret Anniversaries of the Heart." The difficulty of speaking or writing in a coherent voice, one that would unify one's sexual, racial, and cultural identities, is taken up by Richard Hall in "The Language Animal" (1992), a story loosely based on the life of African American writer and social critic **James Baldwin.** The protagonist confronts the problem of writing the truth in the face of overlapping pressures to be the kind of black man that white America wants, to be both black and gay, and to be himself. The truth, he finds, can be found only by embracing his many selves, his multiple identities that are blended and complicated but never unified.

As suggested in the works of Raphael and Hall, the act of writing is often foregrounded in LGBTQ short stories. Writing about writing, or metatexuality, serves the special interests of LGBTQ authors who, reacting against the long history of suppression and silence that has made LGBTQ lives invisible, not only redress the problem of the blank page but also thematize and promote writing as a politically engaged act within their stories. Lesléa Newman, perhaps most widely known for her children's book titled *Heather Has Two Mommies* (1989), emphasizes the importance of recording one's history of loss and survival in the title story to her 1988 collection, *A Letter to Harvey Milk*, by intertwining stories of gay and Jewish responses to subjugation and murder. Newman also raises the craft-oriented issue of point of view by adopting the subject position of an elderly heterosexual Jewish man in the story. In doing so, she implicitly argues that the act of storytelling can be a vicarious experience, an exercise in giving voice to histories not directly our own but in need of telling. Other LGBTQ short story authors also find value in writing from diverse subject positions, crossing borders of race, sexuality, and generation, for instance. Brian Leung, in his award-winning collection of stories entitled *World Famous Love Acts* (2004), thus incorporates elements from his Asian American heritage in stories such as "Six Ways to Jump Off a Bridge" and "White Hand," but in "Executing Dexter" he takes the point of view of a young African American boy. Like Newman, Leung writes from various gay and straight points of view; the category of the LGBTQ short story thus cannot be delimited in terms of gay or lesbian content. It is more appropriate to understand these stories as informed, but not bounded, by the experiences of their LGBTQ authors.

Nevertheless, one of the dominant features of many LGBTQ short stories is an author's attempt to translate personal experience into fiction so as to redress the underrepresentation of minorities and people of color within LGBTQ literature. Leung thus joins authors such as Lola Lai Jong in bringing stories of LGBTQ Asian Americans to light. Already mentioned are the efforts of Gil Cuadros, Terri de la Peña, and Manuel Muñoz to represent the lives of Latino/Latina and Chicano/Chicana peoples. Achy Obejas and Mariana Romo-Carmona can be added to this list. Obejas's collection, humorously titled *We Came All the Way from Cuba So You Could Dress Like This?* (1994), records the story of a family's immigration from Cuba to the United States and the regrets that accompany such a border-crossing. Beth Brant has been largely responsible for bringing the stories of American Indian culture to the printed page, both in her collections and in her edited volume *A Gathering of Spirit* (1984, 1988). The stories of Melanie Kaye/Kantrowotz, Lesléa Newman, and Lev Raphael thread Jewish and LGBTQ identities together, just as Jewelle Gomez, Ann Allen Shockley, John Keene, and Jacqueline Woodson depict minority sexual identities woven into the African American community.

The strength of many contemporary LGBTQ short stories lies not in the relative "newness" of their effort to recover suppressed or invisible lives but, rather, in their capacity to extend and reshape long-standing literary traditions. While Gomez, for example, reconstructs the intriguing and complicated sexual life of black women in New York City in "White Flower," another story entitled "Houston" (which continues the work of her 1991 novel, *The Gilda Stories*) participates in the **science fiction and fantasy** genres, mixing lesbian desire with mystical impulses in a futuristic vampire story. In Gomez's reimagining of that story, however, the vampire named Gilda draws blood without killing, allowing for a more nuanced tale of unrecognized alliances and populations at risk. Lawrence Schimel also adopts the fantasy genre in the title story to his 1997 collection, *The Drag Queen of Elfland*, enabling him to effectively translate typically straight archetypical characters into gay ones. Likewise, in the hands of Ruthann Robson the traditional murder mystery receives a lesbian valence in "The Death of the Subject." Jacqueline de Angelis, in "Joshuas in the City with a Future" (1995), adopts the aesthetic style of naturalism in order to set the petty minutiae of relationship struggles against the grand scope of a threatening natural environment; while Mariana Romo-Carmona's "Death of Rabbits" does not address specifically gay and lesbian concerns, as a tale of magical realism it effectively demonstrates the range of literary genres LGBTQ authors are working in today.

Reflecting the concerns of LGBTQ people striving to form romantic relationships, LGBTQ short stories are often intimately framed by matters of the heart. At times these stories suggest that love is universal, as some have argued that Annie Proulx's famous "Brokeback Mountain" does, and at times they dramatize the particularities and differences that set LGBTQ intimacies apart. While both Melanie Kaye/Kantrowitz and Achy Obejas portray the unraveling of lesbian love, the former sets "The Printer" (1990) in the context of a broader world where lesbian relationships happen to exist while the latter sets "Wrecks" (1994) in the microcosmic world of an unstable lesbian relationship. Oftentimes, LGBTQ short stories depict complicated relationships that straddle straight and gay worlds, as when they portray marriages of convenience. Sandy Boucher's "Humming" (1986), while it foregrounds the difficulties of a female protagonist who is married to a man while maintaining a relationship with a younger woman, also offers a vision of lesbian sex as a sacred act, thereby reimagining the possibilities for how women might arrange their lives in fulfilling ways.

Indeed, many LGBTQ authors foreground the importance of sex and the erotic in LGBTQ lives. Joan Nestle perhaps best represents the effort to depict LGBTQ sexuality in straightforward, unabashed, and unstigmatized ways. In stories such as "My Woman Poppa" and "Woman of Muscle, Woman of Bone," both published in *A Fragile Union* (1998), Nestle candidly explores the complexities of gender performance in **butch–femme** sex roles, the mysteries of the lesbian body, and woman/woman sexual power and control. Better known for her poetry and political activism, Eileen Myles, in her short story collections *Bread and Water* (1987) and *1969* (1989), offers overtly sexual portraits of "hard-living" urban lesbians. In *His Tongue* (2001), Schimel offers a less positive commentary on the ways sex trumps relationships in urban gay men's lives, as in "Past Tense." "The Story of Eau," however, depicts a more integrated picture of sex and love, suggesting that the two can operate in mutually revelatory ways.

Further Reading

McKinley, Catherine E., and L. Joyce DeLaney, eds. 1995. *Afrekete: An Anthology of Black Lesbian Writing*. New York: Anchor Books.

Nestle, Joan, and Naomi Holoch, eds. 1996. *Women on Women 3: A New Anthology of American Lesbian Short Fiction*. New York: Plume.

Pollack, Sandra, and Denise D. Knight, eds. 1993. *Contemporary Lesbian Writers of the United States: A Bio-Bibliographical Critical Sourcebook*. Westport, CT: Greenwood Press.

Zahava, Irene, ed. 1994. *Lavender Mansions: 40 Contemporary Lesbian and Gay Short Stories*. Boulder, CO: Westview Press.

Matthew Brim

Aaron Shurin (1947–)

Aaron Shurin is a gay poet and writer, born in Manhattan, whose childhood transplanted him to Texas and then Los Angeles. As an undergraduate at Berkeley in 1969, Shurin studied under Denise Levertov who influenced him poetically and in social activism. Following graduation he moved to Boston, where he was active within the Boston Gay Liberation Front, which founded *Fag Rag* magazine; in this atmosphere, Shurin cofounded Good Gay Poets in 1972, one of the country's first gay men's publishing collectives.

After his move to San Francisco in 1974, Shurin engaged in homosexual activist politics and in his own style of self-reflexive gay poetics. Throughout the 1980s,

Aaron Shurin (1947–)

Aaron Shurin (right) with Thom Gunn. Photo by Robert Pruzan, courtesy of the Gay, Lesbian, Bisexual, Transgender Historical Society, San Francisco.

Shurin's poetry ventured from line breaks and other conventional forms of lyricism in favor of the prose poem. Influenced by the **San Francisco Bay Area Poets** like Robert Duncan, for whom he worked as archivist from 1980 to 1982, Shurin brought together sexuality and textuality in his work, attempting to unite feminist, gay activist, and poetic concerns with form, language, and meaning. In collections such as *The Graces* (1983) and *A's Dream* (1989), the structure allows him freedom to focus on issues of homosexual identity, sexuality, and gender while also simultaneously exploring issues of language and self-representation. Syntactical ruptures typify Shurin's past and present attempts to explore the interrelation between sexuality—particularly of gay men—and textuality, thus placing Shurin's work in an important overlapping space between language and desire. Additionally, Shurin's evocations of Walt Whitman, Allen Ginsberg, Marcel Proust, and Jean Genet speak to and from a canon of homosexual identity and desire, at the same time insisting on newer representations.

While *The Graces* and *A's Dream* could not ignore the AIDS crisis of the 1980s, especially as Shurin's poetry continued to depict the reality of desire and sex between men, his work *Unbound: A Book of AIDS* (1997) placed the illness front and center. As a collection of writing—prose poems, elegiac essays, and a performance piece—from the 1980s and the 1990s, *Unbound* addresses AIDS by remembering the dead while interrogating AIDS linguistically and historically, seeking meanings from personal, poetic, and physical bodies.

Shurin's most recent poetry collection, *Involuntary Lyrics* (2005), marks a return to line breaks after 15 years of prose poetry. Shurin's cue for matching the lines' end words comes from the correspondingly numbered sonnets of Shakespeare; he thus continues to interrogate poetically the sexual and textual spaces between personal, social, and cultural concerns. Shurin's *The Paradise of Forms: Selected Poems* was named one of the best books of 1999 by *Publisher's Weekly*, and he has received awards including the Gerbode Poetry Award and a National Endowment for the Arts fellowship. Since 1999, he has been codirector of the MFA in Writing program at the University of San Francisco. *King of Shadows* (City Lights Books, 2008) is a collection of essays dealing with his life in San Francisco in the 1960s, and his relationsip with Denise Levertov and Robert Duncan.

Further Reading

Esch, Deborah. 2002. "What History Teaches: Aaron Shurin's *Unbound: A Book of AIDS*." In *Lost in the Archives,* ed. Rebecca Comay, 511–19. Toronto: Alphabet City.

Shepherd, Reginald. 2003. "Aaron Shurin." In *Contemporary Gay American Poets and Playwrights: An A-to-Z Guide*, ed. Emmanuel S. Nelson, 412–20. Westport, CT: Greenwood Press.

Kristian T. Kahn

Michelangelo Signorile (1960–)

Journalist, activist, writer, and radio presenter, Michelangelo Signorile was raised in a blue-collar Italian family in Brooklyn and Staten Island. He studied journalism at Syracuse University and, after coming out and returning to New York in the 1980s, worked as an entertainment publicist. In the late 1980s he became heavily involved in gay politics and AIDS activism. He was a cofounder of **Queer Nation** and from 1988 ran the media committee of **ACT UP**, after a much-publicized zap (a sudden energetic public "event") against Cardinal Ratzinger protesting the future pope's proclamation of the "intrinsic evil" of homosexuality. In 1989, with Gabrielle Rotello, Signorile launched *OutWeek*, the short-lived but influential New York–based magazine at the center of the controversy over "outing." One of the political practice's original and most vocal instigators, Signorile exposed in the pages of *OutWeek* the gay or lesbian orientation of several senior figures in politics or the media and film industries, such as the record label owner David Geffen and the publisher Malcolm Forbes (who was outed posthumously), who stood accused of failing to use their position to challenge **homophobic** policies and products. Also targeted were **closeted** individuals who were seen to be hypocritically celebrating heterosexuality, such as the gossip columnist Liz Smith. Signorile later produced a book-length critique of the closet, *Queer in America*, published in 1993.

Signorile attracted considerable criticism for his radical tactics, which were compared to **McCarthyism** and deemed insensitive to the personal and professional consequences faced by individuals whose sexuality had been exposed. In 1991, the journalist **Andrew Sullivan** began a column hostile to Signorile's tactics in *The New Statesman* in reaction to the outing of his friend Pete Williams, a Pentagon spokesperson. The exchange marked the beginning of an ongoing public feud between the two men (the most notable clash being Signorile's exposure in 2001 of Sullivan's unsafe sexual practices, despite the latter's public admonishments of gay men for their sexual abandonment). However, Signorile has argued that agendas and policy have shifted as a direct consequence of his campaigns, with, for instance, the status of gays in the military becoming a live issue after Williams's outing. Furthermore, he claims, outing has increasingly become an unremarkable aspect of the political landscape, with many former critics of the practice—Sullivan included—now favoring it as a political strategy.

Signorile's *Life Outside*, published in 1997, represents a shift away from examining homophobia and the closet and focuses instead on the excesses and narrowness of urban gay subculture, which is excoriated for its heavy **drug** consumption, reckless promiscuity, and insecurity-breeding obsession with body image. In turn, it celebrates the apparently growing number of gay men who have chosen more mainstream lifestyles in suburbs, small towns, and rural areas. In spite of his otherwise progressive politics, both Paul Robinson and Michael Warner have argued that Signorile's attack on gay promiscuity marks him as a "sexual conservative," a label Signorile rejects.

Signorile's recent journalism and activism, including his role as radio talk show host on Sirius Out Q, continue to challenge sexual hypocrisy and battle homophobia in America. Recent concerns include sexual abuse in the Catholic Church, the experiences of gays in the armed services, and gay and lesbian support for the Republican Party.

Further Reading

Robinson, Paul. 2005. *Queer Wars: The New Gay Right and Its Critics*. Chicago: University of Chicago Press.

Martin Dines

sissyphobia and femiphobia

Sissyphobia and femiphobia are terms used to refer to fear and resentment of effeminate gay men. In American queer male culture, a divide is perceived to exist between gay and bisexual men who "act straight," a phrase that refers to the man's ability to conform to male gender stereotypes and **pass** as straight, and men who "act gay," meaning that they are perceived as having feminine traits. Though disgust over effeminacy extends beyond gender and sexual orientation, the phenomenon is typically associated with gay and straight men who express discomfort with other men who act outside of their gender role. It is typical to hear these men express ambivalence or acceptance toward queer men who are masculine, while expressing hostility and disgust about queer men who are not normatively masculine. Traits often associated with male effeminacy are lisping, a swishing walk, and limp wrist actions. On both sides of the divide some have argued that sissyphobia and femiphobia are responses to the relatively large percentage of queer men who have some traits perceived to be feminine.

Critics of sissyphobia and femiphobia argue that at the heart of the phenomenon lie negative stereotypes about the value of women and femininity, as well as a desire for queer people to assimilate into the broader society. These individuals argue that **homophobia** is based on concerns about the maintenance of gender roles. Homophobia erupts because LGBTQ people challenge the gender binary. Since gender is supposed to dictate sexual desire, the very nature of LGBTQ identity defies gender dictates. That femiphobia and sissyphobia exist in both straight and LGBTQ culture indicates the pervasive nature of homophobia in America.

The pervasive nature of sissyphobia and femiphobia is particularly evident in queer male dating culture. Dating profiles, both online and in print, often express men's desire for a masculine partner requesting that "no femmes" respond to their profile. In response, men manifest the desirability of masculinity by listing "straight-acting" as a positive trait they possess. The valuation of masculinity in the queer community has resulted in pressure on and marginalization of gay, bisexual, and transgendered men who are not "properly" masculine.

LGBTQ and heterosexual concern over the maintenance of gender binaries also helps us to understand the marginalization of **transgendered** individuals within the queer community. Transgendered people are often maligned and devalued for their gender nonconformity. Some critics argue that the transgender community is actually the only unity in the queer community: by either physically manifesting gender transgression, or by defying gender through same-sex sexual attractions, all queer people transgress gender stereotypes.

The valuation of masculine men over feminine men, however, is not a monolithic phenomenon. **Drag** culture has allowed a space in the queer community for men to be revered for their femininity and their appropriation of female costume and actions. Drag queens not only are important as entertainers in queer club culture but also have a political and activist legacy that extends from their central role in pride parades to the African American drag queens who led the **Stonewall Riots** in 1969.

Further Reading

Bailey, J. Michael. 2003. *The Man Who Would Be Queen.* Washington, DC: Joseph Henry Press.

Bergling, Tim. 2001. *Sissyphobia, Gay Men and Effeminate Behavior.* Binghamton, NY: Harrington Park Press.

Ducat, Stephen J. 2004. *The Wimp Factor: Gender Gaps, Holy Wars, and the Politics of Anxious Masculinity.* Boston, MA: Beacon Press.

Katie Hladky

Sisters of Perpetual Indulgence

One of the most distinctive and controversial organizations formed by the gay and lesbian community of the United States made its debut during Easter weekend in 1979, when three men went out onto the streets of San Francisco in full nun's habits (originally borrowed from a convent in Cedar Rapids, Iowa, supposedly for a production of *The Sound of Music*); further recruiting for the new group took place at the International Faerie Gathering in the fall of that year. The new order was formally named in 1980 as the Sisters of Perpetual Indulgence, with their habits and characteristic whiteface makeup forming a sharp break with the then-dominant socially narrow clone image adopted by many gay men. The group immediately began addressing matters of concern to the gay community in the areas of political activism, human rights, and religious intolerance. This last concern has been a particularly consistent target of their wide range of demonstrations, protests, and active and innovative street theater and their avowed aim of opposing actions that create shame and stigmatic guilt: they regard organized religion as conveying these negative feelings in its position on homosexuality and its impact on the personal, spiritual, and psychological development of LGBTQ people. The spiritual content of the order is an amalgamation of tenets drawn from many belief systems and traditions, ranging from Buddhism and Hinduism to orthodox Catholicism and

The Sisters of Perpetual Indulgence. Courtesy of the Gay, Lesbian, Bisexual, Transgender Historical Society, San Francisco.

the contemporary vision-seeking practices of the **radical faerie** communities, with an emphasis on rejecting the idea of sin as a relevant spiritual concept. The Sisters' public appearances in San Francisco have ranged from participating in the March 1980 Three Mile Island Protest (performing their "Rosary in Time of Nuclear Peril" that included a pom-pom routine) and a demonstration at the University of San Francisco against the censure of a gay student organization, to a full-scale exorcism held in Union Square during the 1987 visit of the pope. By choosing for themselves deliberately humorous and provocative names such as Sister Holly Lewya and Sister There's No Place Like Rome (combining elements of formal clerical tradition and popular culture with references drawn from gay camp), the members (who have expanded from the original gay male core to include lesbian, bisexual, and heterosexual people of both genders) directly challenged the entrenched hierarchy of organized religion through taking back its language. By 2006, the Sisters had established autonomous chapters across the United States and in Scotland, Switzerland, Australia, Colombia, Uruguay, France, the United Kingdom, and Germany.

Although the Sisters' fund-raising efforts have benefited many small organizations and service providers, with over $500,000 gathered and distributed since 1979 to groups promoting diversity and tolerance, they are perhaps best known for their activities related to the AIDS pandemic. They produced the first pamphlet on safe-sex practices for people with AIDS, *Play Fair,* in 1982, the same year that astrologer Jack Fertig (also known as Sister Boom Boom) ran for the San Francisco City Council on the "Nun of the Above" ticket, garnering over 23,000 votes. This incident led to the passage of a city ordinance requiring all candidates for office to use their real names. In 1983, the Sisters organized the city's first AIDS Candlelight Vigil, and in 1991 one member created the STOP the Violence Campaign to counter the rise in street crimes in San Francisco, including hate crimes, with safe spaces marked by window placards. This was followed in 1995 by a benefit for the Women and Cancer Walk. The Sisters were represented as well in the **Names Project AIDS Memorial Quilt** display in 1987 on the Mall in Washington, D.C., with panels memorializing more than 30 members who had succumbed to AIDS. The various houses of the Sisters have taken diverse approaches to the problem of AIDS in their local communities, with some emphasizing outreach while others stress intervention and prevention through the distribution of condoms and other prophylactics. An updated and gender-inclusive edition of *Play Fair* was published in 1999, and in the aftermath of the 9/11 attacks the Sisters organized and led a candlelight vigil through the Castro district in memory of the LGBTQ lives lost.

Basing their ministry on claiming the combination of humor and sexuality that lies within the spiritual experience, the Sisters have brought an opportunity for LGBTQ individuals to redefine both the range of possible options for expressing their alternative identity and their relationship to religious experience. Typical of the membership, purpose, and tongue-in-cheek spirit of this organization is Sr. Phyllis Stein the Fragrant, who is described as having joined the Order in May 1994, and having taken vows of full profession in April 1995. Records indicate that "since that time, she has been the Mistress of Sistory (Archivist) and has spent tireless hours hunting down and digging up as much dirt about this Order of 21st Century Nuns as possible. Originally founded as an Order of gay male nuns, the Sisters are now comprised of gay, lesbian, bisexual, heterosexual and transgendered men and women" (http://www.queerculturalcenter.org/QccPdfs/NQAF99.pdf).

Further Reading

Haggerty, George, ed. 2000. *Gay Male Histories and Cultures: An Encyclopedia.* New York: Garland.

Queer Arts Festival 1999 Web site. Available at: http://www.queerculturalcenter.org/QccPdfs/NQAF99.pdf. Accessed July 16, 2008.

Thompson, Mark. 1981. "Not Wholly Nunsense from the Sisters of Perpetual Indulgence: Getting in the Habit to Give Up Guilt." *Advocate* 311 (February 19): T11–13.

Robert Ridinger

Gwendolyn Ann Smith (1967–)

Gwen Smith is a **transgender** activist, writer, and graphic designer. In 1998, Smith founded Remembering Our Dead, a Web site to memorialize people who have died as a result of gender-based hatred and prejudice. The site also documents and disseminates information about antitransgender murders, which occur at a rate of about one per month. Smith has documented that this rate has remained stable for over a decade and claims that antitransgender violence has not received significant media attention or recognition outside of transgender communities.

The Internet memorial prompted the founding of Annual Transgender Day of Remembrance, which is recognized every November 20. Originating with a candlelight vigil in San Francisco in 1999, Day of Remembrance is currently commemorated by transgendered communities internationally.

Joan Snyder (1940–)

Writing is an important component of Smith's activism. From 2000 through 2006, Smith wrote "Transmissions," a biweekly newspaper column published regularly in *Baltimore Gay Life, Bay Area Reporter* (San Francisco, California), *Between the Lines* (Michigan), and *Philadelphia Gay News,* and intermittently in various other LGBT community publications across the United States. Smith is also a regular guest lecturer at colleges and universities.

See also hate crime law and policy.

Further Reading

Ellis, Alan, and Liz Highleyman. 2002. "Transgender and Intersex Studies." In *The Harvey Milk Institute Guide to Lesbian, Gay, Bisexual, Transgender, and Queer Internet Research,* ed. Alan Ellis, Liz Highleyman, Kevin Schaub, Melissa White, and Ronni Sanlo, 61–70. Haworth Gay and Lesbian Studies. New York: Harrington Park Press.

Andy Inkster

Joan Snyder (1940–)

Born in Highland Park, New Jersey, Joan Snyder is an American abstract painter and mixed-media artist. After receiving an MFA from Rutgers University in 1966, Snyder earned early acclaim for her stroke paintings, which emphasized the nature of the paint and the actual brushstroke itself. Her later works include abstract landscapes, "beanfields," and ponds. Critics considered her take on abstract expressionism both bold and uniquely sensitive, and it was often written that she "feminized" her medium. Snyder was one of the first women artists who openly identified as a feminist and whose feminism has been seen influencing her art, both in style and in subject; her famous work *Women in Camps* (1988) is one prime example; in it, Snyder, through a dearth of color and plaintive but harrowing expression, depicts female victims of the Holocaust. Snyder's work is known for reflecting both the social issues of the day and personal struggles: her piece *Journey of the Souls* (1993) reflects the AIDS crisis, while the piece *The Cherry Tree* (1993) was inspired by the death of her father. Critics have even seen Snyder's lesbian identity in her works, especially in the piece *Heart On* (1975), a mixed-media painting depicting a grid of earthy colors and evocative imagery. Today, Snyder's work hangs in some of the finest museums in the country, including the Museum of Fine Arts in Boston, the National Museum of Women in the Arts in Washington, D.C., and the Museum of Modern Art in New York. Her work has been seen as having an important impact on American abstract expressionism, both in contemporizing and in feminizing it.

Further Reading

Henry, Gerrit. 1986. "Joan Snyder: True Grit." *Art in America* 74 (2): 96–101.

Michael G. Cornelius

Society for Lesbian and Gay Philosophy

The late John Pugh of John Carroll University founded the Society for Lesbian and Gay Philosophy in 1988 in order to address philosophical and professional concerns. Initially cochaired by John Pugh and Claudia Card, the Society was officially recognized by the American Philosophical Association (APA) in 1990. As a professional organization, the Society encourages philosophical inquiry about sexuality and sexual identity in ethics, metaphysics, history, and epistemology, while spanning both analytic and continental traditions. To accomplish this, the Society sponsors programs and organizes conference sessions and meetings at the APA's Eastern, Central, and Pacific Division conferences.

The Society for Lesbian and Gay Philosophy publishes the "Newsletter on Philosophy and Lesbian, Gay, Bisexual, and Transgender Issues" through the APA semiannually. Additionally, the Society addresses professional development concerns for LGBT persons in academia (such as hiring and tenure practices, publishing, etc.) through professional networks and efforts to institutionalize lesbian and gay studies in academic curricula.

Further Reading

Card, Claudia. 1995. *Lesbian Choices*. New York: Columbia University Press.

National Consortium of Directors of LGBT Resources in Higher Education. 2007. "LGBT Studies Resources: Professional Caucuses/Organizations." Consortium of Higher Education LGBT Resource Professionals. December. Available at: http://www.lgbtcampus.org/resources/lgbt_studies.html#professional. Accessed July 16, 2008.

Kelly Hudgins Ball

sodomy

Originating in the eleventh century, the word *sodomy* was coined by Saint Peter Damian to replace the earlier term *sin of Sodom* (Sodom and Gomorrah being those cities in the Bible that were destroyed by God for their unredeemable moral depravity). There is textual support in Christian and Jewish scripture for the belief that the sins of Sodom were not sexual in nature. In the book of Ezekiel, God speaks through the prophet, saying, "Behold, this was the iniquity of thy sister Sodom, pride, fulness of bread, and abundance of idleness was in her and in her daughters, neither did she strengthen the hand of the poor and needy. And they were haughty, and committed abomination before me: therefore I took them away as I saw good" (16:49–50, King James Version). According to recent critiques by some liberal Christians, the sins of Sodom were related more to violation of hospitality laws rather than sexual sins. In the King James version of the Bible, the term sodomy is used to translate a heterogeneous group of original-language terms, thus linking the passages where these terms are found to the biblical account of Sodom and to "sodomy" as currently understood in ways that may not have been intended by the authors of the original texts.

Canonical authors have stated that the main sin of sodomites was homosexuality. Sodomy therefore is the name of a sin that for many past centuries represented what today is called homosexuality. However, homosexuality and sodomy represent different realities. Sodomy is a religious and legal term covering a wide range of usually noncoital sexual activities. Michel Foucault calls sodomy "that utterly confused category" (1978, 31) because the term, which dates back to the Middle Ages, has been used to describe so many kinds of sexual behavior, including incest and sex between "man and beast." Depending on the time period and jurisdiction, courts have most commonly judged sodomy to mean (1) anal intercourse between two men, (2) all male-male sexual activities, (3) all male-male and female-female sexual activities, and (4) any sexual activity other than vaginal coitus.

The British term *buggery* is very closely related to sodomy in concept, and the terms are often used interchangeably in law and popular speech in the United Kingdom. In the various criminal codes of the United States, the term sodomy has generally been replaced by "deviant sexual intercourse," which is precisely defined by statute. The remaining criminal interest is largely confined to acts where the victim did not or could not legally consent.

Sodomy laws can be found around the world. As of 2006, consensual homosexual acts between adults are illegal in about 80 of the 192 countries of the world; in 42 of these, only male-male sex is outlawed (ILGA World Legal Survey). This number has been declining since the second half of the twentieth century. From the earliest times in the United States, sodomy (variously defined) was prohibited, although some historians feel that early sodomy laws were mainly used to address issues of nonconsensual behavior or public behavior. Eighteenth- and nineteenth-century judges often editorialized about the act of sodomy as they handed down their rulings. "That most detestable sin," the "horrid act," "the horrible crime," "that which is unfit to be named among Christians" characterized some of the colorful language used by British and American jurists when punishing sodomites. Indeed, emphasis is usually on the notion that the act of anal intercourse is so abominable and offensive "to God almighty" that the term sodomy (literally, that which occurred in Sodom) is the only appropriate way of designating the activity. In other words, when reference was made to "an unspeakable act" having occurred, it was clear that the act in question was none other than anal intercourse. Some say, however, that the sin of Sodom accurately referred not to anal sex but rather to the agglomeration of *all* the unholy activities said to have occurred in Sodom and that it is thus inaccurate to imply a one-to-one relationship. Historians also note that not until the 1970s did sodomy laws concern homosexual acts exclusively.

Sodomy laws in the United States, primarily intended to outlaw gay sex, were historically pervasive but were invalidated by the 2003 U.S. Supreme Court decision *Lawrence v. Texas*. On June 26, 2003, the Court in a 6–3 decision struck down the Texas same-sex sodomy law, ruling that private sexual conduct is protected by the liberty rights implicit in the due process clause of the U.S. Constitution. This decision invalidated all state sodomy laws insofar as they applied to noncommercial conduct in private between consenting civilian adults and overruled an earlier ruling from 1986 in which Georgia's sodomy law had been upheld (*Bowers v. Hardwick*).

Before that 2003 ruling, 27 states, the District of Columbia, and 4 territories had already repealed their sodomy laws by legislative action; 9 states had had them overturned or invalidated by state court action; 4 states still had same-sex laws; and 10 states, Puerto Rico, and the U.S. military had laws applying to all regardless of gender. Prior to 1962, sodomy was a felony in every state, punishable by a lengthy term of imprisonment. Over the years, many of the states that did not repeal their sodomy laws had enacted legislation reducing the penalty. Immediately prior to the *Lawrence* decision in 2003, the penalty for violating a sodomy law varied very widely from one jurisdiction to the next among those states retaining their sodomy laws. The harshest penalties were in the state of Idaho, where sodomy could theoretically earn a life sentence. Michigan followed, with a maximum penalty of 15 years imprisonment.

In most U.S. states, prior to 2003, the laws were no longer enforced or were very selectively enforced. The continued presence of these rarely enforced laws on the statute books, however, was often cited as justification for discrimination against gay men and lesbians. However, *Lawrence v. Texas* has not changed the Uniform Code of Military Justice Article that bans all servicemen and -women from engaging in sodomy. The U.S. Armed Forces Code (section 28-319) defines the offense thus: "Any person subject to this chapter who engages in unnatural carnal copulation with another person of the same or opposite sex or with an animal is guilty of sodomy. Penetration, however slight, is sufficient to complete the offense" (Find Law Cases and Codes Web site).

Further Reading
Andersen, Ellen Ann. 2005. *Out of the Closets and into the Courts: Legal Opportunity Structure and Gay Rights Litigation*. Ann Arbor: University of Michigan Press.
Dynes, Wayne R., and Stephen Donaldson, eds. 1992. *History of Homosexuality in Europe and America*. New York and London: Garland Publishing.
Find Law Cases and Codes. Available at: http://caselaw.lp.findlaw.com/scripts/getcase.pl?court=ne&vol=sc/072000/99-1102&invol=1. Accessed July 16, 2008.
Foucault, Michel. 1978. *The History of Sexuality: An Introduction*. New York: Vintage.
Goldberg, Jonathan. 1992. *Sodometries: Renaissance Texts, Modern Sexualities*. Stanford, CA: Stanford University Press.
ILGA World Legal Survey. Available at: http://www.ilga.org/statehomophobia/LGBcriminal laws-Daniel_Ottoson.pdf. Accessed July 16, 2008.
Jordan, Mark D. 1997. *The Invention of Sodomy in Christian Theology*. Chicago: University of Chicago Press.
Kuefler, Mathew, ed. 2006. *The Boswell Thesis: Essays on Christianity, Social Tolerance, and Homosexuality*. Chicago: University of Chicago Press.

Sara Munoz

sodomy laws

For more than 500 years, criminal laws were the primary means by which society regulated same-sex sexuality. These laws not only directly prohibited certain specific sexual activities, but also provided a legal basis for regulating lesbian, gay, and bisexual life in general (prohibiting relationships, restricting custody and child visitation rights, and justifying exclusion from certain jobs, for instance). One example of this phenomenon is that the mere existence of sodomy laws made lesbians seeking to become attorneys unindicted felons, which legally justified their exclusion from law school, or, if they had graduated from law school, precluded their admission to the bar. In fact, gay men and lesbians were often excluded from any profession requiring a state license (dentist, pharmacist, social worker, or cosmetologist, among many others). Child custody, visitation, or adoption were proscribed, since an open lesbian or gay man was presumed to engage in felonious activity, even in the absence of an arrest or conviction.

In *Lawrence v. Texas* (2003), the U.S. Supreme Court declared unconstitutional laws making it a crime for two persons to engage in "certain intimate sexual conduct." In doing so, the Court set aside not only its own 17-year-old decision of *Bowers v. Hardwick* (1986), but also the entire structure on which **homophobic** executive, legislative, and judicial bodies had justified discrimination against the LGBTQ community and denied legal protections to its everyday relationships.

Sodomy laws can no longer prohibit LGBTQ activities in bedrooms and can also no longer be used to justify legal schemes that have historically been used to deny LGBTQ people employment opportunities, visitation or custody of children, or choices as to whom they can leave estates when they die. What remains to be decided is whether the abolition of sodomy laws will eventually lead to the recognition of LGBTQ rights to decide whether (and with whom) to enter into marriage. It is clear, however, that even discussing about same-sex marriage would never have been possible as a practical matter until sodomy laws were abolished.

Buggery and *sodomy* are legally synonymous in most instances, with the former term having been used in England, whereas the latter came to be used more commonly in the United States. Buggery was made criminal by the English Reformation Parliament of 1533 during the reign of Henry VIII. Until Henry split from the **Roman Catholic** Church, a specific criminal law enacted by the state had been unnecessary, since sexual offenses were tried in ecclesiastical courts. The initial definition of buggery was "an unnatural sexual act against the will of God and man" (Buggery Act of 1513). English courts interpreting the phrase decided that it prohibited only **anal** copulation (both between two men and between a man and a woman). The punishment for buggery in England was hanging, a penalty not changed until 1861, when it was reduced to 10 years in prison. By contrast, the word sodomy is biblical in origin (Leviticus). The original English law used buggery to contrast with the prior religious prohibition. The first colonial statutes regulating the same activity were passed during the Puritan period, however, and use of the term sodomy was deliberately intended to make the point that the acts were violations of both man's law and God's.

As the North American colonies became states, different terms were used to criminalize similar actions. The three phrases primarily used in the United States were "sodomy," "crime against nature," and "deviate sexual intercourse." Until the last half of the twentieth century, no state's laws used explicit language to describe what was illegal. It would have been quite simple for a state to say, for instance, that anal intercourse was illegal, but none did so.

In general, courts have held that the Constitution requires that criminal statutes must be explicit enough to place the ordinary citizen on notice as to what was prohibited by the criminal law. If it fails to do so, the statute is unconstitutionally vague. Sodomy laws were an inexplicable exception to this rule, however. State courts were left to decide for themselves both what actions were prohibited and how those actions could be punished. Not surprisingly, the rules varied widely from state to state, with sometimes bizarre results.

The buggery statutes prohibited anal but not **oral** intercourse, as mentioned above. Lesbian sexual activity did not entail anal intercourse and so was legal in England. In the United States, several state courts traced their state's prohibitions back to the buggery statutes and similarly found that lesbian sexual acts were not prohibited. Even as to sexual activity between men, courts in some states sometimes found different acts brought dramatically different penalties. Anal intercourse might be punished by up to 20 years in prison (in those states that recognized the buggery law's anal/oral intercourse distinction), while oral intercourse might only be punishable by the relatively minor sanctions provided for such crimes as lewd and lascivious behavior.

By 1961, all 50 states had some version of a sodomy law on their books. Most prohibited both oral and anal intercourse. Depending on the state, however, the statute might apply to either consensual or nonconsensual behavior (or both). Many states prohibited these activities even between husband and wife. Not a single statute, however, applied only to same-sex sexual activities. Penalties were extremely severe. Some states enacted sexual psychopath laws that permitted indefinite sentences until "cure." Aside from these statutes, maximum imprisonment ranged from 3 years to life, with 10 years the most commonly authorized maximum (17 states) and 20 years the next most frequent (9 states).

Twenty years later, fewer than half the states had sodomy laws in force. Most of the states had legislatively repealed their statutes. The first to do so was Illinois in 1961; no other state followed until Connecticut did so in 1971. Cases arose in the context of defenses to criminal charges, as well as in civil test cases. A handful of statutes were overturned by judicial decisions, but reasons given for the decisions were inconsistent. Most judicial challenges were unsuccessful. Furthermore, it seemed clear that legislative reform had ground to a halt and that sodomy laws still existing would remain on the books for the foreseeable future.

Attorneys for the **American Civil Liberties Union (ACLU)** and **Lambda Legal Defense and Education Fund (LLDEF)** began meeting in the fall of 1982 to devise strategies to eradicate the remaining sodomy statutes. A number of things were clear to those professional civil rights litigators. First, the state-by-state legislative reform movement had pretty much run its course by 1982. Second, state court challenges had been successful in only a handful of cases, and the decisions in those cases were often limited to their particular factual circumstances. Third, abolition of the remaining sodomy laws was essential for the gay and lesbian rights movement to progress. Fourth, the most viable way for the remaining laws to be struck from the books would be a decision by the U.S. Supreme Court after litigation through the federal court system.

A Supreme Court strategy also presented major problems, however. Ronald Reagan had been president for only two years, but it seemed probable that he would soon be able to make one or more appointments to the U.S. Supreme Court. Furthermore, Reagan's appointed justices would probably be considerably less liberal than the justices they would replace. In 1982, the window of opportunity for a successful Supreme Court challenge to the remaining sodomy laws was rapidly closing. The ACLU and LLDEF attorneys had to decide whether to get directly involved with sodomy law challenges or to allow them to proceed on their own. Cases were proceeding regardless, so it seemed clear that the heavy artillery of the nation's foremost civil rights litigators should be brought to bear. Of the cases working their way through the federal court system, two seemed to present especially compelling fact situations. LLDEF and the ACLU got involved with both.

Baker v. Wade arose in Texas as an affirmative challenge to a statute prohibiting only homosexual sodomy. At the time of the filing of the suit in 1979, Donald Baker was 35 and a former Dallas schoolteacher who had received a master's degree from Southern Methodist University. He had never been arrested or convicted of any criminal offense. But he expressed his intent to continue to participate in conduct that was prohibited by the Texas criminal statute. Because of his reasonable fear of prosecution if caught, the federal district court found he had standing to challenge the statute. On August 17, 1982, the federal district court found the statute unconstitutionally violated Baker's right to privacy. Furthermore, the equal protection clause condemned a state statute that prohibited homosexual sodomy but not heterosexual sodomy, without any rational basis for distinguishing between the two.

The other case, then entitled *Hardwick v. Bowers*, involved the claim of Michael Hardwick, who in 1982 had been arrested in his bedroom for committing sodomy (oral sex) with another adult man. After the charges were dropped in state court, Hardwick brought a federal court challenge similar to that in the *Baker* case, although the Georgia statute in question prohibited sodomy between persons of the same or opposite sexes, including married couples. Unlike in the *Baker* case, the federal district court dismissed the challenge.

Hardwick had been thrown out on a technicality rather than after a full trial (as in *Baker*). Because of that fact, it moved more quickly through the federal court system, "quickly" being a relative term in constitutional litigation. The Court of Appeals for the Eleventh Circuit reinstated the case in 1985. The state of Georgia applied to the U.S. Supreme Court for review, which was granted. By that time,

Baker had been reversed by the Court of Appeals for the Fifth Circuit and was also headed to the Supreme Court. Action on that case was stayed, pending the decision in *Bowers*. The Court's decision in *Bowers v. Hardwick* was issued on June 30, 1986. As has often been the case in the last 30 years, the Court was deeply divided, with five of the nine justices misstating the issue as whether homosexuals have a fundamental constitutional right to engage in sodomy.

Justice White wrote the majority opinion. He found that neither the First Amendment (i.e., rights to associate and organize) nor the right to privacy in matters of procreation gave gay men and lesbians a constitutional right to engage in sodomy, despite the fact that the conduct had occurred in the privacy of Hardwick's home. Prior decisions had upheld individuals' rights to possess pornography in their own home on privacy grounds and had overturned restrictions on unmarried couples' rights to use contraceptive devices in private. According to White, the claim that states cannot regulate private sexual conduct between consenting adults was "at best, facetious." Chief Justice Burger joined Justice White's opinion but filed a concurring opinion, gratuitously adding his own personal view that to hold otherwise "would be to cast aside millennia of moral teaching."

The four justices in the minority (Blackmun, Brennan, Marshall, and Stevens) disagreed with the majority in strong terms. The dissent by Blackmun caustically noted that the case was no more about "a fundamental right to engage in homosexual sodomy" than the previous privacy cases has been about a fundamental right to watch obscene movies. Instead, according to the minority, the case was about "the most comprehensive of rights and the right most valued by civilized men," namely, "the right to be left alone." After an extended discussion of various constitutional principles, Justice Blackmun made the following prescient statement:

> I can only hope that here, too, the Court soon will reconsider its analysis and conclude that depriving individuals of the right to choose for themselves how to conduct their intimate relationships poses a far greater threat to the values most deeply rooted in our Nation's history than tolerance of nonconformity could ever do. Because I think the Court today betrays those values, I dissent.

Seventeen years later (a blink of an eye in constitutional terms), seven of the nine justices who had participated in the *Bowers* decision had been replaced, and Justice Blackmun's dissent became the law of the land in *Lawrence v. Texas* (2003). Only Chief Justice Rehnquist and Justice O'Connor participated in both cases. Justice O'Connor filed a concurring opinion in *Lawrence*, stating that she would not overrule *Bowers* but would find that the Texas statute violated equal protection under the laws because it outlawed only homosexual activity.

Justice Kennedy wrote the Court's opinion for himself and four others. With O'Connor's concurrence, six of the nine justices voted to overturn the Texas sodomy law, while Chief Justice Rehnquist and Justices Scalia and Thomas dissented. Because O'Connor's concurrence did not affect the outcome, the majority opinion overturned all remaining sodomy laws throughout the United States. Justice

Kennedy and the majority thoroughly eviscerated the rationale of *Bowers* and argued that gay men and women have the right to engage in private conduct without government intervention. The laws in question, according to Kennedy, touch on the most private human conduct, sexual behavior, and in the most private of places, the home. They sought to control a personal relationship that, whether or not entitled to formal recognition in the law, is within the liberty of persons to choose without being punished as criminals. The liberty protected by the Constitution allows gay men and lesbians to choose to enter into relationships in the confines of their homes and their own private lives and retain their dignity as free persons. That "liberty" is protected by due process. Kennedy made clear the Court's decision: "*Bowers* was not correct when it was decided, is not correct today, and is hereby overruled."

As a result of *Lawrence*, private sodomy (whether oral or anal) between consenting adults is no longer illegal in any state of the Union, although cases involving the military are more complicated and are still not resolved. Servicemembers committing consensual sodomy in private are considered to violate the Uniform Code of Military Justice and may be prosecuted for doing so (Article 125). Punishment may include confinement for five years, dishonorable discharge, and forfeiture of all pay and allowances.

Despite the overturning of sodomy laws, local authorities and prosecutors still have several statutes they can use to prosecute sexual acts in situations that are not totally private (on secluded beaches or in rest areas, for instance). Among these are the offenses of "disorderly conduct" and "lewd and lascivious behavior." Unlike sodomy statutes, these offenses are generally misdemeanors (depending on the law of the jurisdiction) and seldom involve jail sentences. People arrested for such behavior are often those most vulnerable to harassment by police officers, and they will sometimes plead guilty to avoid getting negative publicity. A priest or a married man, for instance, who seeks sexual release with another man at a rest stop is not likely to challenge the facts underlying his arrest and may well plead guilty, thinking the matter can then be put behind him. Such a plea, however, can lead to disqualification for a number of jobs and, in some states, can become the basis for a later finding that the person is a sex offender, leading to his having to register with local police. Any arrest for a sexually related offense is potentially serious, and a person accused of such an offense is well advised to seek legal counsel.

Further Reading

Bowers v. Hardwick, 478 U.S. 186 (1986).

Buggery Act of 1513. Available at: http://en.wikipedia.org/wiki/Buggery_Act_1533. Accessed July 16, 2008.

Irons, Peter. 1988. "What Are You Doing in My Bedroom?" In *The Courage of Their Convictions: Sixteen American Who Fought Their Way to the Supreme Court*, 392–403. New York: Penguin.

Jeffries, John C., Jr. 1994. *Justice Lewis F. Powell, Jr.* New York: Fordham University Press.

Lawrence v. Texas, 539 U.S. 558 (2003).

Thomas, Kendall. 1992. "Beyond the Privacy Principle." *Columbia Law Review* 92 (6): 1431–1516.

Jim Kellogg

South Asian Lesbian and Gay Association (SALGA)

The South Asian Lesbian and Gay Association (SALGA) has been providing support, organizing cultural events, and promoting visibility for the South Asian LGBT community since the early 1990s. SALGA is perhaps best known for fighting for the right to march in the annual India Day Parade in New York City: parade organizers had carefully policed community boundaries and sought to exclude those it deemed as outside the nation, in this case those who were seen as alien because of their sexuality. SALGA has continued petitioning for inclusion and has protested on the sidelines of the parade. SALGA's activism became transnational when controversy arose over Indian screenings of Deepa Mehta's film *Fire*, and they protested in solidarity with the newly formed New Delhi–based Campaign for Lesbian Rights. As these events make clear, SALGA is part of a larger community of South Asian diasporic organizations—both virtual and actual—that includes *Trikone*, the oldest South Asian gay and lesbian organization, the DesiQ conference, and the Canadian *Khush*.

Further Reading

Eng, David L., and Alice Y. Hom, eds. 1998. *Q & A: Queer in Asian America*. Philadelphia: Temple University Press.

Gopinath, Gayatri. 2005. *Impossible Desires: Queer Diasporas and South Asian Public Culture*. Durham, NC: Duke University Press.

Parmar, Pratibha. 1991. *Khush*. Women Make Movies.

Ratti, Rakesh. 1993. *A Lotus of Another Color: An Unfolding of the South Asian Gay and Lesbian Experience*. Boston: Alyson Publications.

Alexandra Barron

southern United States

Queer history in the southern United States has taken on a distinct flavor owing to this region's unique religious and racial history. The rise of conservative Christianity in the South has fostered similarly conservative attitudes toward expressions of gender and sexuality that deviate from biblical norms. As a result, the South's major metropolitan centers, Atlanta and Houston, have played important roles in the development of its queer communities and civil rights movements. These cities provide homes to two prominent gay publications, the *Southern Voice* and *Houston Voice*, and a variety of political organizations, such as Georgia Equality. In June 1971, the Georgia Gay Liberation Front (GGLF) organized the first Gay Pride March down Atlanta's main thoroughfare, Peachtree Street, to Piedmont Park. On June 11, 1978, when Anita Bryant, who had founded her "Save Our Children" campaign a year earlier in Dade County, Florida, was slated to address the Southern Baptist Convention at the Georgia World Congress Center, Atlanta Pride was temporarily moved to that date in response to her presence.

While evangelical and fundamentalist Christian communities were generally active in leading and sustaining antigay campaigns, it is also true that churches and church-related activities have served as clandestine meeting spaces for gay and lesbian people. This is true particularly in rural communities, where churches have often served as the primary, or potentially only, social outlets for gay and lesbians to meet other gay and lesbian individuals. Today, more liberal, gay-affirming churches have been established, in part due to the centrality of church life for many gay, lesbian, bisexual, and transgender persons. Reverend Troy Perry, for example, founded the first Metropolitan Community Church in Los Angeles, California, partly because of his experiences growing up as an evangelical Christian in Florida and, later, in Georgia.

Southern cities have become home to prospering black and Latino gay and lesbian communities. For some LGBTQ people of color, particularly those persons who must remain "on the **down low**" due to real or perceived nonacceptance of their sexuality within their own racial or ethnic communities, churches and church-related activities retain a central position in social life. At the same time, there are also more venues in which to be "out" with regard to LGBTQ sexualities. Mainstream festivals such as Gay Pride and New Orleans's Southern Decadence, which began in 1972, serve as spaces in which the significance of racial differences may be lessened, in favor of LGBTQ unity, or heightened, due to the underrepresentation of queer people of color. Alternatively, Black Gay Pride celebrations have become well established in cities like Atlanta, Nashville, and Dallas.

One of the most notable events in southern, as well as national, gay history is the 1986 Supreme Court decision handed down in *Bowers v. Hardwick* (478 U.S. 186), which upheld Georgia's **sodomy laws.** This ruling was overturned by the Georgia Supreme Court in the 1998 case *Powell v. State of Georgia* (270 Ga. 327). A more sweeping victory over sodomy laws came with the 2003 Supreme Court case *Lawrence v. Texas* (539 U.S. 558) in which the Court ruled that sodomy laws violated a person's right to due process under the 14th Amendment.

Further Reading

Howard, John. 1999. *Men Like That: A Southern Queer History.* Chicago: University of Chicago Press.

Small Town Gay Bar. 2005. Dir. Malcolm Ingram. Red Envelope Entertainment. Film.

Russell Cambron

Dean Spade (1977–)

Dean Spade, a lawyer and **activist** in the **transgender** and **queer** community, grew up in a rural community in Albemarle County, Virginia. Spade graduated from Barnard College prior to attending the University of California, Los Angeles

(UCLA), and currently serves as a law teaching fellow jointly hosted by Harvard University and the UCLA Law School. He was the first person to teach a seminar on transgender law at Harvard Law School. Spade's writing has been published in *That's Revolting! Queer Strategies for Resisting Assimilation* (2004), *The Transgender Reader* (2006), and *Without a Net: The Female Experience of Growing Up Working Class* (2004).

In 2002 Spade founded the Sylvia Rivera Law Project (SRLP), a nonprofit organization that advocates for the rights of low-income persons and people of color who are transgender, intersex, and gender nonconforming. Spade ran SRLP for four years before stepping down to let the organization run as a collective.

Widely published in a variety of contexts and featured in the documentaries *Toilet Training, Boy I Am,* and *Cruel and Unusual,* Spade seeks to challenge narratives about transpeople that medicalize, pathologize, and objectify them, and he fights to ensure that people are free to determine their own gender identity and express it without fear of retribution. He focuses on populations in prisons, shelters, foster care, and other institutions, with an emphasis on economic justice that challenges a mainstream LGBT movement that prioritizes marriage and inheritance rights over affordable housing and universal health care.

Further Reading

Spade, Dean, and Sel Wahng. 2004. "Transecting the Academy." GLQ 10 (2): 240–53.
Winnubst, Shannon. 2006. *Queering Freedom*. Bloomington: Indiana University Press.

Alexandra Barron and Steve Stratton

Tom Spanbauer (1946–)

Pulitzer-nominated author Tom Spanbauer has written four novels, *Faraway Places, The Man Who Fell in Love with the Moon, In the City of Shy Hunters,* and *Now Is the Hour.* Spanbauer studied writing under legendary *Esquire* editor and novelist Gordon Lish at Columbia University. His first novel, *Faraway Places* (1993), deals with a teenager coping with his own emerging sexuality in addition to the fallout of a murder he witnessed. The novel highlights many themes that reoccur in Spanbauer's fiction, including religion, family, sexuality, and isolation. *The Man Who Fell in Love with the Moon,* Spanbauer's second effort, has been warmly received by fans and critics alike for its coming-of-age story about a young bisexual Native American boy. The book further expounds on some of Spanbauer's recurring themes, including how gender, sexuality, individuality, community, and family get refigured in groups outside of the cultural mainstream.

In many interviews, Spanbauer has called his third novel, *In the City of Shy Hunters* (2001), "the book that almost killed him" because of its very personal, emotional story. Set in New York in the early 1980s, the book deals with the AIDS crisis and its effects on American homosexual communities. The novel follows its protagonist and his burgeoning sexuality throughout this devastating period of gay history. Spanbauer himself, as an openly gay author and activist, had seen the effects of AIDS directly for many years before he was diagnosed with the disease in 1996.

Now Is the Hour (2006), Spanbauer's latest release, returns to familiar themes of family, community, and sexuality as readers follow the protagonist on his physical and spiritual journey from his small-town home in Wyoming to San Francisco in the 1960s.

In addition to his novels, Spanbauer is also the founder of the "Dangerous Writing" workshop in Portland, Oregon, which has been the training ground for other writers such as **Chuck Palahniuk,** Monica Drake, Gregg Kleiner, Ken Foster, and many more.

Further Reading

Camper, Cathy. 2006. "Interview with Tom Spanbauer." *Lambda Book Report* (Summer): 4–5.

Jeffrey A. Sartain

sports

Sports play an enormous role in U.S. culture, and many people find enjoyment as athletes, recreational participants, and fans. For LGBTQ-identified individuals, however, sports frequently fail to provide a welcoming environment because of **homophobia** and heterosexism. One notable exception is the Gay Games, the sports and cultural festival that welcomes LGBTQ participants and fans every four years. The first Gay Games took place in **San Francisco** in 1982 and consisted of a week of sporting and cultural events for 1,300 athletes. In 2006, Chicago hosted the Games for 12,000 athletes in 30 sports and received extensive public and financial support.

Participants in the second Gay Games in 1986. Courtesy of the Gay, Lesbian, Bisexual, Transgender Historical Society, San Francisco.

The Gay Games' founder, Tom Waddell, envisioned a sporting climate that embraced and deliberately applied the spirit of the Olympic Games by emphasizing participation, inclusion, and giving one's personal best. These core values made the Gay Games open and inviting to both LGBTQ-identified athletes and their allies, to competitive and recreational athletes, and to athletes from the United States and around the world. As a heptathlete in the 1968 Olympics, Waddell possessed firsthand knowledge of sports' potential to serve as an agent of social change, and he applied this knowledge to his work with the Gay Games. Other goals of the Gay Games are to break down **stereotypes** surrounding gay men and lesbians in sport, as well as to establish connections with the mainstream sporting community.

These goals also come to fruition in another LGBTQ-oriented sporting event, the Outgames. The first Outgames, held in Montréal in the summer of 2006, opened with an international conference on LGBTQ human rights and ended with a sporting and cultural festival. The 35 sporting events rivaled the offerings of the Gay Games as 16,000 people from 120 countries participated. The Outgames differ from the Gay Games in their effort to focus on global LGBTQ human rights issues and their emphasis on including athletes and teams from developing nations. Although events like the Gay Games and the Outgames signify progress and many would agree that the climate for LGBTQ athletes within mainstream culture has improved, LGBTQ-identified participants still face hurdles in the sporting world.

Tom Waddell, MD, founder of the Gay Games. Courtesy of the Gay, Lesbian, Bisexual, Transgender Historical Society, San Francisco.

The reception of individual LGBTQ athletes typically depends on the gender of the athlete, the particular sport within which the athlete competes, the level at which the athlete competes, and the larger historical and sociocultural context. Women's sports, for instance, include a history of scrutiny directed at the gender and sexual identity of female participants. Societal norms requiring women to maintain femininity as mothers and caregivers have been seen as directly opposite to the "masculine" characteristics necessitated by many sports, such as power, strength, and speed. Women displaying masculine characteristics within their sports have been labeled as lesbians, whether they identify as such or not, in order to diminish their accomplishments and to protect the male sport space.

In order to deflect the stereotype that all female athletes are lesbians, a hostile environment exists for lesbians in most sports and lesbians are discouraged from being open with their sexual identities. For example, when Alissa Wykes, a member of the Philadelphia Liberty Belles, came out as a lesbian in *Sports Illustrated for Women*, the chief executive officer of the Independent Women's Football League publicly scolded Wykes for doing so, echoing a prevailing sentiment that Wykes's announcement would not only bring negative attention to the league but perhaps cause a loss of fans and potential sponsors. Additionally, when Diane Whipple, two-time member of the U.S. Women's World Cup Lacrosse team and lacrosse coach at St. Mary's College was killed by an attacking dog, her partner needed the help of the National Center for Lesbian Rights in order to sue and receive damages for a wrongful death claim.

Two female athletes in particular have been instrumental in breaking through societal norms and taking a stand for female athletes, both straight and gay. Billie Jean King and Martina Navratilova both are noted for their excellence on the tennis court, each winning a multitude of singles and doubles grand slam championships, including 20 Wimbledon championships each. King is perhaps best known, however, as a gender-equity advocate. King has fought for equal pay for women in professional tennis and for equal opportunities for girls and women to participate in sports through the Women's Sports Foundation, which she founded in 1974. Her victory over Bobby Riggs in the Battle of the Sexes tennis match was a cornerstone event of the 1970s feminist movement. In 2006, the United States Tennis Association's National Tennis Center in Flushing Meadows-Corona Park was rededicated as the USTA Billie Jean King National Tennis Center; it is the largest sports facility in the world to be named after a woman.

Navratilova, a native of the former Czechoslovakia, came out as bisexual early in her career due to concerns over how an open lesbian identity would impact her efforts to obtain U.S. citizenship. Although she would later come to identify as lesbian, Navratilova's relative openness about her sexuality cost her potential sponsorships and became the subject of media scrutiny and attention, especially in regard to her on-the-court rivalry with Chris Evert. Navratilova's muscular physical presence, Czechoslovakian heritage, and identity as a lesbian were continually pitted against Evert's femininity, all-American looks, and heterosexuality. Nevertheless, Navratilova continued to play tennis and recently retired as the Women's Tennis Association's oldest player ever at age 49. Today, her sexuality is no longer the controversial issue that it was in her early days, and she regularly uses her celebrity to speak on the issue of LGBTQ rights.

Ramona Gatto, Patty Sheehan, Diana Nyad, and Missy Giove have also had successful careers as out athletes. Ramona Gatto is a nine-time International Kickboxing Federation champion and is active with her daughter in the gay community in northern California. Patty Sheehan now plays on the Women's Senior Golf Tour and has been inducted into the Ladies Professional Golf Association (LPGA) Hall of Fame. Diana Nyad is best known for her charismatic and insightful work on television and radio, in print, and as a public speaker. In 1979, her name was first in print when she swam from the Bahamas to Florida (102.5 miles), setting a long-distance swimming record. Missy "the Missle" Giove recently retired from full-time mountain bike racing but left her mark by pushing the sport and her competitors with her aggressive downhill style and her openness about her lesbian identity.

Voted the Greatest Female Athlete of the First Half of the Twentieth Century by the Associated Press, Babe Didrikson Zaharias's athletic accomplishments are too numerous to list. Olympic medals in track and field in 1932 and basketball championships with her Amateur Athletic Union teams are only a few. Although Susan E. Cayleff, one of Zaharias's biographers, speculates that she was involved in a lesbian relationship later in her life, her outstanding performances in track and field, basketball, tennis, and eventually as one of the founding members of the LPGA are the reasons she will always be regarded as such an accomplished athlete. Zaharias was before her time in that she actively sought compensation for her athletic accomplishments and desired to make a living from her talent and the entertainment that she provided audiences.

Another facet of lesbians' participation in sports of late has been sponsorships motivated by sexual identity. Both Sheryl Swoopes, three-time Women's National Basketball Association (WNBA) Most Valuable Player, and Rosie Jones, LPGA player for 24 years, are now sponsored by Olivia Cruises and Resorts. Both athletes came out in conjunction with their announcements that they would be sponsored by Olivia, which caters to lesbian couples. Swoopes's announcement also garnered attention due to other reasons: she is the first African American professional team sport athlete to come out publicly, and she did so while still a mainstay in her field.

Working on the academic and social justice side of studies of LGBTQ sports, Pat Griffin has contributed greatly to the growing body of knowledge concerning the historical and

A gay baseball team, the Kokpits. Courtesy of the Gay, Lesbian, Bisexual, Transgender Historical Society, San Francisco.

lived experiences of LGBTQ-identified athletes. Her influential book *Strong Women, Deep Closets: Lesbians and Homophobia in Sport* (1998) is a comprehensive history of lesbians' participation in sports and the social climate that shaped their experiences. As a recognized expert on LGBTQ topics in sports, she has created many educational resources on the topic, continues to speak widely, and is the current director of the It Takes a Team! Education Campaign for LGBTQ Issues in Sport, offered through the Women's Sports Foundation. A former college coach and athlete, Griffin has also been a participant in the Gay Games.

Not surprisingly, transsexual athletes face great difficulty navigating the gender-segregated world of sport. Renee Richards became the first transsexual athlete to participate in professional sports in 1977 when the Supreme Court of New York ruled in *Richards vs. United States Tennis Association* (93 Misc. 2d 713) that Richards had to be allowed to compete on the women's tennis tour. Richards's career as a professional women's tennis player did not last long; after only a few years, she moved on to coaching Navratilova. Richards's time as a player on the women's circuit proves noteworthy as it occurred when gender testing still existed as a component of women's sports. Dating back to the 1968 Olympic Games in Mexico City, gender testing originally endeavored to uncover male athletes masquerading and attempting to compete as women in women's events. Gender testing took on various forms including the inspection of women's unclothed bodies, pelvic examinations, and chromosomal screening, assessed via a buccal smear/cheek scrape. The history of these tests, which were not conducted on male athletes, marks women's muscular, athletic, and achieving bodies as suspect. In 1999, gender testing was finally eliminated, and in 2004 the International Olympic Committee adopted policies allowing transsexuals to participate in the Olympic Games.

For male athletes, instead of being seen as a site where their heterosexuality is compromised, sporting participation provides a forum wherein they can confirm and affirm their heterosexuality. Contrary to the situation in women's sports, the historical connection of sports with masculinity creates great difficulty for male athletes who identify as gay or bisexual. In early 2007 basketball player Tim Hardaway met with great criticism for publicly announcing his hatred of homosexuals and expressing displeasure at sharing a locker room with them. This prompted the cancellation of one of Hardaway's endorsement contracts and denunciation by fellow basketball player John Amaechi, who had just published *Man in the Middle*, in which he came out. Chauncey Billups, Shaquille O'Neal, Steve Nash, Charles Barkley, and others pointed out that times had changed, that they knew gay players existed, and that it had really become something of a nonissue. Still, athletes in sports in which strength and power are emphasized tend to be seen as more "male" and subsequently heterosexual than those in individual sports and/or those sports deemed more graceful and artistic, such as figure skating.

Professional football players David Kopay, Roy Simmons, and Esera Tuaolo all enjoyed varying degrees of athletic success while competing as **closeted** gay men in the National Football League (NFL). Kopay, the eldest of the three men, **came out** in 1975, three years after retiring from professional football. His decision to go public about his gay identity in a *Washington Star* newspaper series on homosexuality in sports made an important inroad for gay men in sports. Although *The David Kopay Story* (1977) made the *New York Times* best-seller list, it would be a number of years before another NFL player, Simmons, felt able to come out publicly. Simmons, a college star at Georgia Tech and an NFL offensive lineman from 1979 to 1984, came out publicly on the *Phil Donahue Show* in 1992 after years of struggle with drug and alcohol abuse. Ten years after Simmons's admission, Tuaolo, who played nine years in the NFL, came out in a 2002 *Real Sports* episode. For Tuaolo, a Samoan who was raised on the Hawaiian Islands, coming out provided him with opportunities to advocate on behalf of gay families, survivors of sexual assault, and LGBTQ persons inside and outside of sport. Additionally, Ed Gallagher, who played football for the University of Pittsburgh from 1977 to 1979, became disabled when he attempted suicide as a way to cope with his struggle with his sexual identity. He eventually became a gay and disability advocate speaking to organizations and hosting a cable talk show that, in part, addressed the issues of homosexuality and disability.

Although Kopay, Simmons, and Tuaolo garnered much attention due to their status as high-profile football players, a number of other gay male athletes made their mark in individual sports. Swimmers Bruce Hayes, a 1984 Olympic gold medalist, and Alex Kostich, an All-American at Stanford University, continue to compete in Masters swimming events. In equestrian events, gay athletes Jim Graham and Robert Dover found their sexuality to be a nonissue. Graham met success both as a member of the U.S. equestrian team and as a clinician working with horses. Dover, the 1994 United States Olympic Committee's Male Equestrian of the Year, was a five-time captain of the U.S. equestrian team and has competed in six Olympic competitions. In 1996, Dover and others established the Equestrian

AIDS Foundation (now the Equestrian Aid Foundation) to help equestrians living with HIV/AIDS. Greg Louganis, a medalist in diving at the 1976, 1984, and 1988 Olympics, came out publicly at the 1994 Gay Games. His 1995 autobiography, *Breaking the Surface*, in which he revealed his HIV-positive status, became a made-for-television movie.

Two other men, Rudy Galindo and John Curry, successfully competed in the sport of figure skating. Galindo placed first in the 1996 U.S. National Championships and turned professional shortly thereafter. Curry won the gold medal at the 1976 Winter Olympics and is widely recognized for adding ballet and artistic moves to men's figure skating. In tennis, 1920s athlete Bill Tilden and former Santa Clara University Coach Sean Burns (1993–2002) weathered concerns about their sexual preference to varying degrees. Tilden helped to build the popularity of tennis via an increased attention to technique but faced tough times off the court, spending time in jail for having sex with a minor. After Burns retired in 2002, he began a coaching business and speaks on the topic of sexual diversity.

The increasing visibility of LGBTQ athletes, coaches, and administrators forces society to acknowledge that LGBTQ athletes participate in all sports and at all levels. Several national organizations and Web sites also work to ensure that sports are a safe place for LGBTQ persons by providing resources and services. The Gay and Lesbian Athletes Association (GLAA), a registered charitable organization in Canada and the United States, aims to create an atmosphere where athletes can compete without concerns about sexual orientation. GLAA organizes a peer mentoring program for gay and lesbian athletes and, in addition to other educational resources, provides an action guide for athletes, coaches, athletic administrators, and parents. The mission of the Web site Outsports.com is to build the most informative and entertaining gay sports community. The Web site contains a mixture of breaking news, commentary, member profiles, photo galleries, and discussion boards to celebrate the participation of LGBTQ athletes and their fans.

Further Reading

A Brief History of the Gay Games. Available at: http://thecastro.net/gaygames/gaygamehist. html. Accessed July 22, 2008.

Anderson, E. 2005. *In the Game: Gay Athletes and the Cult of Masculinity.* Albany: State University of New York Press.

Bean, Billy. 2003. *Going the Other Way: Lessons from a Life in and out of Major-League Baseball.* New York: Marlowe and Company.

Cahn, S. K. 1994. *Coming on Strong: Gender and Sexuality in Twentieth-Century Women's Sport.* New York: Free Press.

Griffin, P. 1998. *Strong Women, Deep Closets: Lesbians and Homophobia in Sport.* Champaign, IL: Human Kinetics.

Magic Johnson Foundation. Available at: www.joeant.com/DIR/info/get/7610/19472. Accessed July 16, 2008.

Pronger, B. 1990. *The Arena of Masculinity: Sports, Homosexuality, and the Meaning of Sex.* New York: St. Martin's Press.

Woog, D. 1998. *Jocks: True Stories of America's Gay Male Athletes.* Los Angeles: Alyson Books.

Megan Chawansky and Claire Williams

Matthew Stadler (1959–)

Matthew Stadler, born in Seattle, is the author of the engrossing novel *Landscape: Memory* (1990), a love story between two high school boys at the beginning of the twentieth century, at times harrowing and at times endearing. Stadler has received various fellowships and awards and has written for as well as edited a number of publications. Most of Stadler's male narrators are very keen on 15-year-old boys and the little hollow above their sternum. *The Dissolution of Nicholas Dee* (1993), a very metafictional novel, should be read in its "writer's cut" 2000 edition, complete with **Michael Cunningham**'s exquisite introduction. *The Sex Offender* (1994) is an intriguing *exercice de style*. Hypercontrolled narrative twists abound, as well as shades of Franz Kafka, Aldous Huxley, George Orwell, and, of course, Anthony Burgess, whose *Clockwork Orange* mechanics are reworked to tremendous effect. A **drag queen** appears in the story, more central to the plot than one might initially suppose, but she is not the principal sex offender. *Allan Stein* (1999) is a postmodern masterpiece. Less of a "university novel" than *The Dissolution of Nicholas Dee*, it chronicles the French masquerades of rogue teacher "Matthew" (but the name is used much as Dennis Cooper uses "Dennis" for his narrators) who is embarked on the trail of Gertrude Stein's nephew—an Allan Stein who has more to do with erotic literary fantasy than historical reality—at the same time as he is falling for yet another 15-year-old boy and pondering the meaning of identity between the lines. As a main character, Matthew is less swayed by events than his predecessors. *Allan Stein* echoes some of the best Vladimir Nabokov material and at times even hints at Marguerite Duras. Like all of Stadler's fiction, it is often extremely comic.

Further Reading

Bergman, David. 1999. "You Can Lead a Boy to Culture." *Lambda Book Report: A Review of Contemporary Gay and Lesbian Literature* 7 (6): 7–9.

Canning, Richard. 2004. "Matthew Stadler." In *Hear Us Out: Conversations with Gay Novelists*, 259–92. New York: Columbia University Press.

Georges-Claude Guilbert

stereotypes

Stereotypes are, in their most general sense, concepts or labels used to describe members of particular groups. LGBTQ culture is rife with stereotypes: from self-proclaimed identifications such as **"bear"** and "boi" to cultural associations like "men with lisps" or "women in comfortable shoes," LGBTQ stereotypes present subcategories and myths within the more general groupings of homosexuality. Stereotypes are often associated with prejudicial and uninformed judgment; by generalizing about groups, such a view suggests, we make unfair assumptions and lose sight of individual particularities. For instance, believing every lesbian must be either "butch" or "femme" might impose expectations of male or female gender identifications onto women who do not necessarily experience or understand their sexuality or gender in this way, at the same time as this attribution might prevent one from perceiving other possible modes of sexual identification in another person. Some argue, however, that stereotypes are useful means for categorizing and understanding ourselves and others. From this standpoint, in the example of butch and femme, such labels could be seen as indispensable categories that allow for a range of legible experience and visible cultural existence for lesbians, making use of supposedly heterosexual gender designations while simultaneously subverting them. Yet in contemporary American LGBTQ culture, stereotypes are a more complex phenomenon than such pro or con positions can express. Through stereotypes both the history of homosexuality and structures of LGBTQ identities and identifications can be understood, as well as some of the intricacies of different stances in sexual politics.

A stereotypical view of gay men. Photo by Marie Ueda, courtesy of the Gay, Lesbian, Bisexual, Transgender Historical Society, San Francisco.

ETYMOLOGY

The word *stereotype* stems from the Greek words *stereos,* meaning "solid," and *tupos,* which means an impression made by a blow or strike. The term was first coined in English in 1798 to name a printing technique in which a plate is made from the mold of composed type and then used for reproduction of printed material. In the 1920s stereotype came to be used more figuratively to describe the process by which persons might be similarly "typecast." Numerous aspects of this etymology are useful for understanding the workings of LGBTQ stereotypes. First, the Greek roots of the word—meaning the mark made by a solid blow—evoke not only the tool that might effect such force but the more malleable surface on which this strike effectively falls, as well as, finally, the potential concreteness of the resulting product. More specifically, in the context of LGBTQ culture this etymology suggests that human groups might be pliable, susceptible to different designations and arrangements, but that such labeling is an imposition of power and can produce a certain hardness of meaning, an ostensible truth-value or naturalness in place of previous contingency. An example of this might be the stereotype of gay men as effeminate: some sexological theories of the late 1800s postulated that homosexuality was caused by "gender inversion," that is, it was an effect of mismatched gender identity, resulting in, for instance, men who felt like and acted like women. Certainly, with the variety of gender presentations in Western culture, such a claim was sure to find its confirmation in numbers of persons whose gender identifications were as divergent from the norm as their sexual behaviors. But once such confirmation occurred, very soon effeminacy in men came to be read as an irrefutable index of male homosexuality, seemingly written as it was on the level of the body. Any gestures, facial characteristics, movements, or modes of dress in men that were coded as feminine could thus immediately be read together as symptoms of inversion. Coming as this interpretive strategy did with the stamp of the medical establishment, such a stereotype easily gained force as an institutionally ratified certainty about homosexuality rather than the statistical coincidence of factors from which it emerged. Thus the stereotype of the limp wrist in gay men was born, out of a pseudoscientific hypothesis and into a pathological symptom.

The origin of the English word stereotype in industrialized print culture is also significant: the process of stereotyping allowed for the generation of limitless copies, in the twofold process of typesetting and mold-making that obscured the original. The "original" in question was moreover a *text*, separate from its author. Thus, the association of stereotypes about people with a mechanized printing process suggests both the difficulty in ascribing an origin to stereotypes and the potential result of the mass production of copies. This is probably instanced most perfectly with the stereotype "clone," which signifies a specific culture of masculine gay men. Gathering together under its rubric a number of signs, such as the "clone uniform" of jeans and T-shirts, as well as the mustaches worn by so-called clones particularly in the 1980s and 1990s, clone as an identity marker might seem in fact to be an act of resistance to the stereotype of gay male effeminacy. The macho clone thereby becomes part of an infinitely reproducible mass of masculine men. Gender identifications appear to be easily and defiantly legible to the antigay world around them; in fact, the individual has joined a tribe and put on an identity like a costume.

Yet insofar as it allows for infinite reproducibility, the stereotype also allows for the overlooking of other possible differences between individuals in order to fit them into one category. Once the stereotype exists, individual examples of it proliferate: easily found and easily reproduced. The gay subculture thereby formed similarly loses its basis in any ostensibly originary source—masculinity in this case—and is an infinitely iterable form. Grouping together a number of people by such signs can lead to minimization of their idiosyncrasies and the reduction of persons to a set of superficialities. Finally, with widespread use of the term, the conflation of male same-sex practices with this particular look and style allows for a truth-effect, such that proof of masculine gay identity might in some circumstances involve brandishing such arbitrary and origin-less markers as the clone uniform. The result would be a paradoxical situation at the level of etymology: the only way to achieve the "solid strike" of "true" homosexuality would seem in this case to involve becoming a copy, accepting the impersonal identity of typecasting.

STEREOTYPES AND THE HISTORY OF SEXUALITY

The account of the history of sexuality most commonly referred to by contemporary **queer theory** and history suggests that LGBTQ **identity** is not so much a truth of self but rather a recent invention, only somewhat older than the term stereotype. The French philosopher Michel Foucault famously claimed in the first volume of

The History of Sexuality that before the late 1800s, the homosexual did not exist. By this, Foucault explains, he means that until the late nineteenth century, homosexuality was understood as an act, not an identity. That is, same-sex romantic and sexual acts were not used as organizing categories for groups of persons. Identities did not coalesce around sexual behavior, desires, or associations as they so often do now; what is now considered stereotypically LGBTQ behavior certainly occurred but was not attached, as it has been since the late nineteenth century, to sexually organized and identified groups. The new order of sexual identification was born, according to Foucault, out of the proliferation of discourses that aimed to regulate sex more closely, including Christian confession and psychoanalytic therapy. Both of these trained subjects in Western culture to excoriate themselves for the secrets of their souls, thus producing individuals who regulate their own sexual practices just as authorities would wish them to. New taxonomies emerged for the description of sexual selfhood in these contexts, such as "androphile," "calamite," "catamite," "ganymede," "invert," "masturbator," "tribade," "urning," "pederast," "sapphism," and "sodomite." Among these, and overtaking them in the end, was "homosexual," the first known use of which occurred in the 1892 English translation of Richard von Krafft-Ebing's *Psychopathia Sexualis.* At the same time as words were coined and identities created, a cultural imperative for individuals to locate the truth of their sexuality emerged. Thus, rather than stereotypes emerging from the church or medical establishment and being imposed on persons, the beings for whom the establishments coined such terms actively embraced such designations, accepting and redoubling their proliferation.

SPECIFIC STEREOTYPES

Although Foucault posits a historical division between acts and identities, LGBTQ stereotypes suggest that both sexual acts and sexual identities hold concurrent significance in contemporary understandings of how sexuality works. While a good number of LGBTQ stereotypes in contemporary America focus on the identity of the individual, others seem to have more to do with the identity of the individual's object of desire, and still others with the *act* desired. With this in mind, one way of categorizing LGBTQ stereotypes is into three different types: subjects of desire, objects of desire, and aims of desire.

Subjects of desire refers to the LGBTQ person in question. Stereotypes about subjects of desire are ubiquitous: Castro clone (a clone specifically to be found in **San Francisco**'s Castro neighborhood), twink (a smooth or hairless young gay man on the club circuit), Chelsea boy (a twink in the Chelsea area of **New York City**), on the **down low** (African American men who lead heterosexual lives in the open and have sex with men on the side), sissy (an effeminate male), **bear** (a hairy, usually large gay man), seal (a hairless bear), otter (a hairless and/or thin bear), wolf (an aggressive otter), cub (a younger or smaller bear), mommy-obsessed, woman-hater, man-hater, bulldagger (a usually older masculine lesbian), **lipstick lesbian** (a feminine lesbian who is attracted to other feminine lesbians), **granola lesbian** (a lesbian who is concerned about the environment and natural health), aggressive (a subculture of generally very masculine African American lesbians in

New York City), sports dyke (an athletic lesbian), bridge and tunnel (lesbians who live in the suburbs and visit the city for entertainment), boi (a young, smooth, masculine lesbian), high femme (a very feminine lesbian), stud (a butch lesbian of color), baby dyke (a young, urban lesbian), and so on.

Object of desire refers to the individuals whom the LGBTQ person in question desires. Such stereotypes include chub chaser (someone who is attracted to larger lovers), tranny chaser (someone who is attracted to transsexual folk), troll (an older gay man who unsuccessfully tries to seduce younger men), chicken hawk (an older man who likes young men), rice queen (a man who likes Asian men), bean queen (a man who desires Hispanic men), African queen (a man who desires black men), potato queen (an Asian man who desires white men), heeb queen (a man who desires Jewish men), size queen (a man for whom penis size is important), sticky (an Asian man who desires other Asian men), and mashed potato (a white man who only desires other white men).

Finally, some LGBTQ stereotypes focus more on sexual activity (or inactivity) than on the identities or identifications of its practitioners. Certainly, the detachment of desire-oriented stereotypes from their actors means that they are not confined to LGBTQ culture, but the following stereotypes are common to LGBTQ culture: top (a person who takes the dominant role in sex), bottom (a person who takes the submissive role in sex), pillow queen (a person who receives pleasure in sex without reciprocating), power bottom (a person who dominates sexually through submission), **lesbian bed-death syndrome** (the myth that lesbians in particular stop having sex with each other after extended coupledom), **trade** (a young male prostitute), player (someone who flirts and/or has **promiscuous** sex with many partners), stone butch (a very masculine lesbian who does not want to be touched sexually), **polyamory** (**non-monogamy** as a celebrated lifestyle), sadist (someone who likes to wield sexual power and/or inflict pain in sexual situations), and masochist (someone who likes to play out sexual submission and/or receive pain).

The attempt here to subcategorize LGBTQ stereotypes into subjects, objects, or desires falls prey to at least one of the same criticisms as stereotypes: that it ignores other important distinctions between stereotypes. For instance, the stereotypes listed above, which are some of the most typical LGBTQ stereotypes in contemporary circulation, could also easily be split into subsets of **class**, race, age, and gender. Unsurprisingly, there is a great deal of overlap between sexual categories and the other classifications used to organize people in Western culture. Alternately, one might wish to divide LGBTQ stereotypes into either derogations or self-identifications: groups alternately of hatred of the other or love and pride for oneself. This might be an attractive scheme except that different sides disagree fiercely about which stereotypes constitute insult and which constitute affirmation, and about which stereotypes emerged from external sources and which strike their bearers as motivated by internal verities. *Queer* might be the prime example of this problem. Originally a term of slander that suggested same-sex relations were abnormal and therefore morally wrong, the term is now touted by many as a mode of radical revaluation of values by which we can acknowledge and celebrate difference, not as abnormality, but as a new and beneficial option. Crucially, neither view is right or wrong; rather, debates about the term illustrate the difficulty of categorizing specific LGBTQ stereotypes as "positive" or "negative," self-motivated or other-enforced. While the division of stereotypes into identities and acts is as arbitrary as other classifications, it illustrates that LGBTQ stereotypes may have more of a hold on contemporary subjects than merely in matters of personal identity, as they also concern desires and acts.

ANALYSIS

Such issues tend to shape debates about the value of stereotypes in the LGBTQ context, which this entry will conclude by discussing more specifically. Much of the tension around the practice of stereotyping has to do with what this article has discussed as the "truth-effect" of stereotypes. That is, although stereotypical categories and generalizations about LGBTQ folk may be born in specific cultures out of convenience or myths, these stereotypes have a tendency to calcify into seeming facts or truths about humanity in the universal sense. Not only have such calcifications resulted in a set of derogatory beliefs about LGBTQ communities, but they also produce a situation in which self-identifications are limited by the stereotypical terms that culture has deemed to be "true." Thus, a person wishing to proclaim affiliation with the LGBTQ community has limited options about which terms he or she might take on; those wishing to denounce sexual affiliation altogether face exclusion as well as fierce social constraint and pressure to conform. Moreover, any self-association with a stereotype necessarily partakes of what Foucault understands as self-discipline: by pointing to a category as the truth of our identity, we are acceding to the regime of sexuality that deems that selves are at base sexual selves and to the regime of politics that organizes persons by their capacity to further heterosexual destinies.

Yet according to the theories of identity of philosophers such as Judith Butler and Denise Riley, stereotypes may shed some of their disciplinary capacity in situations in which they are riven from claims of truth or naturalness. When stereotypes no longer necessarily stand for essential, inborn features of the people they describe but are rather taken to be the copies of copies that the etymology of stereotype suggests they are, then we may be able to mobilize them strategically without being as bound by their limitations or by the idea that they are unmovable truths. We might thus retain the political value of at least temporarily identifying with a group, without being totalizingly bound to the category. For example, Butler has famously argued that drag can operate as a "subversion of identity" because when men impersonate women, the truth of gender is undermined, revealing only a set of stereotypes that any human might inhabit or take on (see **performativity**). While this theory by no means suggest that stereotypes are mantles that we can don and throw off at will, the shift in value systems that philosopher Friedrich Nietzsche called "revaluation of values" is shown to be possible through such subversion, once the truth-value of stereotypes is called into question.

Further Reading

Butler, Judith. 1989. *Gender Trouble: Feminism and the Subversion of Identity*. New York: Routledge.

Foucault, Michel. 1978. *The History of Sexuality*. Vol. 1, *An Introduction*. Trans. Robert Hurley. New York: Vintage Books.

Susan Stinson (1960–)

Nietzsche, Friedrich. 1989. *On the Genealogy of Morals*. Trans. Walter Kauffmann. New York: Vintage Books.

Riley, Denise. 2000. *The Words of Selves: Identification, Solidarity, Irony*. Stanford, CA: Stanford University Press.

Sedgwick, Eve Kosofsky. 1990. *Epistemology of the Closet*. Berkeley: University of California Press.

Amy Jamgochian

Susan Stinson (1960–)

Susan Stinson, born in Amarillo, Texas, is an award-winning novelist, poet, and activist in the **fat acceptance** movement. Her works center on the lives of fat lesbians, exploring desire, love, belonging, creativity, identity, and loss. Her novels and poetry challenge the ways in which the fat body is a consistent Western metaphor for ugliness, laziness, and psychological problems; instead, Stinson creates fat lesbian characters who are beautiful, complex, and resilient.

Stinson's best-known novel, *Venus of Chalk* (2004), was a Lambda Literary Award finalist and was named one of the top 10 lesbian novels of the year by the Publishing Triangle. *Venus* tells the story of Carline, who leaves behind a secure job and relationship to take a bus trip to visit her aunt in Chalk, Texas. Along the way, Carline explores her conflicting feelings about her fleshy body, her desire for love, and her awakening about her aunt's grief and erotic life. Stinson's other works include *Martha Moody* (1995), a love story between two fat women in an imaginary Western town; *Fat Girl Dances with Rocks* (1994), a coming-of-age story about a fat teenager who struggles with her awakening desires and her confusion over the activism of local nursing home patients; and *Belly Songs: In Celebration of Fat Women* (1993), a collection of poetry. Stinson makes us see the beauty and pain in that which has often been overlooked or undervalued, from the shimmering quality of the curtains Carline makes in *Venus* to the richness of the butter that Amanda Linger forms into round, glistening balls in *Martha Moody* to the searing humiliation of a fat girl at a Sunday school gym game in her poem "The Line."

Stinson resides outside Northampton, Massachusetts, where she can be seen riding on a trike, her transportation of choice. She is working on a new novel, *Spider in a Tree*, about the eighteenth-century theologian Jonathan Edwards. *Spider* explores the roots of the body hatred that Stinson challenges in her fiction and in her activism.

Further Reading

Cooper, Charlotte. "Interview with Susan Stinson." Available at: http://www.charlottecooper.net/docs/fat/susanstinson.htm. Accessed February 22, 2008.

Stinson, Susan. Homepage. Available at: http://susanstinson.net. Accessed July 16, 2008.

Amy Farrell

Kathryn Bond Stockton (1958–)

"Sometimes a signifier is just a signifier," Kathryn Bond Stockton would say about her tattoo that reads "tattoo" on her forearm. Her theories about the liveliness of signs with various intricate connections to queerness are why Stockton continues to receive praise within queer theory communities. Signs or markings—like the black diamond Stockton sports in the back of her hair—and the various signifiers they contain are integral to Stockton's scholarship. This scholarship points to moments in her past—divinity school; racially diverse schooling in Bloomfield, Connecticut; and a recognition of her retroactively birthed queer childhood. Stockton's first book, *God between Their Lips*, explores desires between women from a theological point of view. This book complicates the signifier lesbian by viewing it through the double prism of her master of divinity from Yale University and doctoral work on literature at Brown University. Stockton continued her contributions to queer theory with her second book, *Beautiful Bottom, Beautiful Shame*, which demonstrates Stockton's interest in shame, here at the switchpoint between black and queer. The Lambda Literary Awards recognized this book's contributions to queer scholarship, nominating Stockton as a finalist for their LGBT award. Stockton's third book, *The Queer Child, or Growing Sideways in the Twentieth Century*, births queerness through the child that has typically remained invisible throughout history.

Further Reading

Williams, Troy. 2006. "Queer Gnosis." Available at: http://www.fugosushi.com/_nqt/. Accessed October 8, 2007.

Kristopher L. Cannon

Stonewall Riots

The Stonewall Riots began at a gay bar named Stonewall Inn, located at 53 Christopher Street, just off Sheridan Square in Greenwich Village, New York City, on June 27, 1969. Police raided the bar and attempted to arrest patrons and cart them to jail, a common practice in those days—but on this occasion the patrons resisted. The five days of rioting that ensued are commonly considered as marking the beginning of the contemporary gay and lesbian political movement. For more than three decades, the Stonewall Riots, arguably the most emblematic event in American gay and lesbian history, have been memorialized with annual gay **pride parades and festivals** in the month of June throughout the United States and around the world; for many, the term *Stonewall* itself has become synonymous with the struggle for gay rights.

In the 1960s, tolerance of homosexuals in **New York City** was severely limited, and the New York City police had systematically closed all gay bars by revoking their licenses. The only remaining gay bars at the time were largely run by the mafia, who paid off the local police so that they would turn a blind eye to what were basically illegal operations. In this climate the patrons of gay bars were accustomed to police harassment and routine raids, and it is commonly assumed that a failure to pay off the police led to the raid on the Stonewall Inn. The usual reaction to a police raid was cowering. This time, however, the clientele of the Stonewall Inn and the crowd that gathered outside the bar fought back against the police. Patrons of the bar and other protesters threw bottles and cobblestones at the police and tactical patrol force reinforcements and even used an uprooted parking meter to ram the door when the officers retreated into the tavern to regroup. As it happened, this was also the day that Judy Garland, the tragic actress, singer, and gay male icon was buried in New York City—an event that, some claim, may have in part precipitated the riots.

In spite of the Stonewall Riots' indisputable status as an important and enduring symbol in gay history and gay politics, the precise meaning of Stonewall remains contested even today. One source of disagreement has been the claim that the Stonewall Riots constitute the beginning of gay and lesbian activism in the United States. Starting in the early 1980s, historians pointed out that the definition of Stonewall as an absolute beginning trivializes—or altogether ignores—gay and lesbian organizing and community building in other parts of the country and in previous decades. In fact, the political efforts of gay men and lesbians were spearheaded by a generation of **activists** in the 1950s and 1960s in the **homophile movement,** comprised of such organizations as the **Mattachine Society** and the **Daughters of Bilitis.** In the late 1960s, gay activists looked down on homophile organizations such as Mattachine for being assimilationist, frequently seeing it as the gay movement's equivalent of the National Association for the Advancement of Colored People at a time when groups like the Black Panther party inspired young radicals. Consequently, gay activists portrayed the discord between the two groups as a generational conflict between the old homophile organizations and the younger group of gay radicals, and they used Stonewall as a symbol of the gay liberation movement's militancy. When gays organized in the wake of Stonewall by establishing the Gay Liberation Front (GLF), they capitalized on the implausible fact that, for once, cops, not gays, had been defeated and forced to retreat, and they coined the phrase "gay power" to describe a novel force to be reckoned with. For the new generation of gay liberationists the Stonewall Riots symbolized a point of rupture, a radical break with the past that suggested that a qualitative difference between the time periods on either side of the divide—before and after Stonewall. Nonetheless, according to several historical accounts, homophile organizers and gay activists, in spite of their differences, *did* work side-by-side in organizations such as the GLF in the months and years following the riots.

Ironically, radicalism did not remain the dominant tendency of the post-Stonewall movement for long. Only six months after Stonewall, on December 21, 1969, 19 people meeting in a Greenwich Village apartment created a platform for those who disagreed with the GLF's philosophy and tactics by constituting a new organization, the Gay Activists Alliance (GAA). Whereas the GLF considered the fate of gay people in the context of a broader "revolutionary" movement, the GAA was exclusively dedicated to securing basic rights for homosexuals by working within the system, rather than trying to transform it. Both organizations sought greater rights: the GLF would be more confrontational in seeking them, and the GAA would be more accomodational.

Under the sign Stonewall, then, gay and lesbian activists joined a larger movement for social change—"the Movement," as it liked to call itself—and so found a legitimacy that they had not had before. This transformation of Stonewall led to the hegemony of rights-oriented gay activists, for whom liberation meant simply extending the legacy of American freedoms to homosexuals in a pluralistic society. Originally conceived as a catalyst for a radical political change, Stonewall eventually became the central trope of a mainstream gay culture. **Gay rights** activists were—and are—characterized by a highly pronounced respect for the middle-class sensibilities of mainstream America. Lesbians, people of color, and the so-called fringe elements of the gay community such as **drag queens** and **leathermen** were no longer considered ideal poster children for a movement intent on assimilating into mainstream culture by convincing the white, heterosexual, male powers that be that "we are just like you"—except for that one minor difference that eventually came to be known as sexual orientation. Paradoxically, while today's gay movement traces its origins to the radicalism of the Stonewall generation, what seems to have endured is a peculiar sense of respectability, which clearly is more reminiscent of the homophile movement that preceded it.

Another dispute arose about the question of who was actually at the Stonewall Inn on that fateful night in June 1969. In the decade following the riots, Stonewall was represented as a rebellion of white men. Only in the mid-1980s did gay historians begin to challenge the traditional representation of the events at the Stonewall Inn as an all-male, all-white revolt. According to more recent accounts, gay men *and* lesbians fought back in 1969, and many of them were of color, and many were drag queens. While the participation of several Puerto Rican drag queens in the riots has been incorporated into the lore of Stonewall, albeit reluctantly, the lesbian presence at Stonewall remains contested. According to some accounts, the arrest of a cross-dressed lesbian (and her violent resistance) was *the* incident precipitating the riots, while other accounts firmly deny that a lesbian was even present in the bar. The changing iconography of Stonewall thus reflects the gay movement's historical difficulty in acknowledging the ways that race complicates sexual identity and the difference that gender makes. The erasure is twofold. First, there is the effacement of gender and race in accounts of the riots that do not mention the presence of Puerto Ricans, drag queens, and lesbians among the patrons at the Stonewall Inn during the first night of the riots. On a symbolic level, celebrating Stonewall as the "birth" of the (white) gay (men's) movement eclipses the history of those who came to gay liberation via the black civil rights struggle, who, as it were, proclaimed that "black is beautiful" before they realized that "gay is good." Second, the exclusive focus on Stonewall erases female specificity by discounting the experience of lesbians who trace their own origins back to the women's movement or **lesbian feminism** rather than to Stonewall.

Poststructuralist and queer theorists and critics argue that we need to abandon the quest for an objective, reliable, and definitive historical narrative of what happened at Stonewall. Accepting the twin notions that any historical representation is necessarily partial and that Stonewall has no settled, definitive meaning, they argue, allows us to write race, gender, and class into accounts of the riots in order to enable a future politics that includes people of color, women, and those fringe elements of the community symbolized by the figure of the drag queen. In other words, these critics hope that a greater number of queer fictions of the past will allow us to challenge the notion of a unitary gay community with a single shared history, to acknowledge the diversity that exists among queer people, and to proliferate the number of approaches to the project of LGBTQ liberation.

Further Reading

Bravmann, Scott. 1997. *Queer Fictions of the Past: History, Culture, and Difference*. Cambridge, UK: Cambridge University Press.

Carter, David. 2004. *Stonewall: The Riots That Sparked the Gay Revolution*. New York: St. Martin's Press.

D'Emilio, John. 1983. *Sexual Politics, Sexual Communities: The Making of a Homosexual Minority in the United States, 1940–1970*. Chicago: University of Chicago Press.

Duberman, Martin. 1993. *Stonewall*. New York: Dutton.

Piontek, Thomas. 2006. "Forget Stonewall: Making Gay History Perfectly Queer." In *Queering Gay and Lesbian Studies*, 7–29. Urbana and Chicago: University of Illinois.

Thomas Piontek

Jonathan Strong (1944–)

Jonathan Strong was born in Winnetka, Illinois, and attended Harvard University, where he received his degree in 1969. Strong's works include *A Circle around Her* (2000), *The Haunts of His Youth* (1999, a revised and expanded edition of his 1969 *Tike, and Five Stories*), *The Old World* (1997), *Offspring* (1995), *Companion Pieces* (1993), *An Untold Tale* (1993), *Secret Words* (1992), *Elsewhere* (1985), and *Ourselves* (1972). Strong has made a point throughout his career of establishing the difference between being construed as a "gay writer" as opposed to a writer who happens to be gay. His goal is to be characterized as the latter, eschewing the former as too constrictive and marginalizing. Strong's work often centers on the family unit in modern society and the ways that personal desires and beliefs are navigated in the public arena. Strong's work has been commended by critics like Marianne DeKoven for its formal innovation and focus on character. Originally viewed by critics as a writer speaking for the 1960s (and therefore outmoded), Strong has received increased praise from reviewers over the last decade. In *A Circle around Her*, Strong's most recent work, themes of family life and homosexuality are interwoven in an exploration of the life of Mary Lanaghan, a divorcee approaching midlife. In a quite matter-of-fact manner (as in all his work), Strong includes gay characters who are admirable and intelligent and whose sexuality is not the primary focus or difficulty in the novel. Strong is currently a professor of creative writing at Tufts University.

Further Reading

Bamber, Linda. 1986. "Made in Somerville." *Boston Review* 11 (6): 15.
DeKoven, Marianne. 1985. "Later and Elsewhere." *Partisan Review* 53: 315–18.
Gooch, Brad. 1986. "Surrogates." *The Nation* (March 8): 280–81.

J. G. Adair

suburbs

In the United States, more people live in suburbs than in urban and rural areas combined. Despite the pervasiveness of suburban living, the suburbs are not typically regarded as the most comfortable residential spaces for gays and lesbians. While the situation has been changing in recent years, the uneasy fit between gays and suburbs can be traced to the early development of suburban life.

During the late 1800s, when suburban growth began in the United States, Catherine Beecher and other writers promoted the importance of traditional gender roles performed within the nuclear family, arguing that the detached, suburban home was the ideal setting for such a lifestyle. During both suburban boom periods of the twentieth century (the 1920s and the postwar 1940s and 1950s), the family was a driving force behind people's decision to locate in the suburbs. In both eras, developers and advertisers promoted suburbia as an escape from the overcrowding, dirt, and disease of the city and as a safe place to raise a family. During the postwar boom, the government worked with developers and financiers to make sure that suburban houses were built and sold to returning soldiers and their young families.

The suburban focus on traditional nuclear families did not attract many singles or same-sex couples. Additionally, the lack of acceptance of homosexuality led most openly gay men and women to choose the relative anonymity of city life over the community-oriented life of suburbia. As gay populations in cities grew, **gay bars,** clubs, **bookstores,** and social networks developed in these areas. The suburbs' lack of such gay infrastructures further diminished their appeal to gay and lesbian residents.

In recent years, however, the number of gays and lesbians living in the suburbs has steadily increased as a result of a number of factors. Rising prices in urban real estate have made it difficult for many gays to buy homes in the traditionally gay urban ghettoes, forcing them to look elsewhere for affordable property. Increases in the number of gay/lesbian-parented families have also drawn more gays and lesbians to the suburbs. They move for many of the same reasons families have always moved to the suburbs—larger yards, safer streets, and better schools. Some see the move to the suburbs as part of a larger political movement. For gays striving for mainstream acceptance based on the mantra "we're just like you," suburban life can be a way of underscoring one's averageness.

Andrew Sullivan (1963–)

In response to the rising number of gay residents, some communities are seeing the development of a previously absent gay infrastructure. Social and support networks like Out in the Suburbs (Chicago) and the Dulles Triangles (Washington, D.C.) help connect gay suburbanites as gay bars, bookstores, and other establishments around the country are moving beyond the bounds of large cities. Some real estate agents specifically target LGBTQ families as potential suburban home buyers, further increasing the number of suburban gays. Although more gays still live in cities than in suburbs, the balance between the two is much more even than it once was.

See also ghettoes, gay.

Further Reading

Brekhus, Wayne H. 2003. *Peacocks, Chameleons, Centaurs: Gay Suburbia and the Grammar of Social Identity*. Chicago: University of Chicago Press.

Lynch, Frederick R. 1991. "Nonghetto Gays: An Ethnography of Suburban Homosexuals." In *Gay Culture in America: Essays from the Field*, ed. Gilbert Herdt, 165–201. Boston: Beacon Press.

David Coon

Andrew Sullivan (1963–)

A journalist and writer born in South Godstone, England, to a middle-class family, Andrew Sullivan graduated from Oxford University with a degree in modern languages and modern history, and in 1989 received a PhD from Harvard for his thesis on the conservative political theorist Michael Oakeshott. In 1991 Sullivan became the youngest-ever editor-in-chief appointed for *The New Republic*. Under his stewardship, the magazine moved in a conservative direction while simultaneously publishing material focusing on gay issues, including articles by the lesbian libertarian academic Camille Paglia and Sullivan's own essays on gay rights—most notably "The Politics of Homosexuality" in May 1993, which was later developed into his first book, *Virtually Normal* (1995). Since the early 1990s, Sullivan has consistently prioritized the case in favor of gay marriage. Sullivan's justifications are principally conservative: state-sanctioned marriage, he argues, would sustain the kind of self-respect and emotional stability that gay subculture is seemingly not able to provide, offering gay men in particular an alternative to the sexually promiscuous lifestyle that has apparently turned heterosexuals against them. By reducing **homophobia** and rendering gays and lesbians "virtually normal,"

Andrew Sullivan speaks at the annual convention of the Log Cabin Republicans at the Wyndham Palm Springs Hotel, 2004, in Palm Springs, California. AP Photo/Nam Y. Huh.

gay marriage promotes social cohesion by further integrating gays and lesbians into mainstream society. However, Sullivan has also argued contrarily that gay men are constitutionally more inclined toward promiscuity than heterosexuals and that marriage between two men may well accommodate an understanding of the need for extramarital sex.

In the mid-1990s Sullivan disclosed that he had recently become HIV-positive, shortly afterwards writing the controversial essay "When Plagues End," published in the *New York Times Magazine* and reprinted in *Love Undetectable* (1998). Sullivan argued that developments in the treatment of the HIV virus had reached the extent that HIV-infected individuals found themselves living with a manageable, rather than a fatal illness and that the climate of fear that had overtaken gay subculture in the previous decade had come to an end. Sullivan's account has been widely condemned for being overly optimistic about the effects of combination therapy and for encouraging a new wave of irresponsible sexual behavior (though Sullivan argues that the experience of AIDS provoked a heightened sense of responsibility and camaraderie among gay men). Sullivan was embroiled in even more controversy in 2001 when he was accused of hypocrisy after the *Village Voice* editor Michael Musto and journalist **Michelangelo Signorile** alleged that he had been soliciting unsafe sex on a gay sex Web site, after being publicly critical of gay promiscuity.

Sullivan lectures widely and writes regularly for numerous publications, including *Time*, *The Times* (in London), and salon.com. His "Daily Dish" is also one of the most popular political blogs on the Internet. Topics that continue to arouse Sullivan's interest include homophobia in the **Roman Catholic** Church, to which he belongs; misdirection of the American war effort in Iraq; and environmental and fiscal policy. Several of these topics find expression in his recent critique of the Bush administration, *The Conservative Soul* (2006).

Further Reading

Harper, Phillip Brian. 1997. "Gay Male Identities, Personal Privacy, and Relations of Public Exchange: Notes on Directions for Queer Critique." *Social Text* 52–53: 5–29.

Sullivan, Andrew. "The Daily Dish." Available at: http://time.blogs.com/daily_dish/. Accessed July 16, 2008.

Warner, Michael. 1999. *The Trouble with Normal: Sex, Politics, and the Ethics of Queer Life*. Cambridge, MA: Harvard University Press.

Martin Dines

Conrad Susa (1935–)

Conrad Susa is an American composer best known for choral and operatic works. Susa studied at Carnegie Institute of Technology and at Juilliard, where his teachers included Vincent Persichetti and William Bergsma. Early work composing music for prominent theater companies including the Old Globe Theatre in San Diego and the American Shakespeare Festival in Stratford, Connecticut, led to numerous commissions to write scores for documentary films and television productions. Of his five operas (to date), *Transformations* (1973), based on nine poems from a book by Anne Sexton, and *Dangerous Liaisons* (1994), based on the novel by Choderlos de Laclos, have been the most successful. His song sequence *Carols and Lullabies from the Southwest* (1992) is rapidly gaining a place in the standard repertory for the Christmas season. Susa has written numerous choral works commissioned by gay and lesbian **choruses** in New York, Seattle, San Francisco, Boston, Minneapolis, and San Diego, including *Chanticleer's Carol* (1982), *The Cricket Sings* (1985), and *Dirge from Cymbeline* (1991). Critics have widely praised the brilliant orchestration typical of his large-scale pieces and the effective eclecticism of his settings of theatrical works. Susa's prizes and awards include a George Gershwin Memorial Scholarship, two Ford Foundation Fellowships, a Gretchaninoff Prize, and grants from the National Endowment for the Arts. He is a member of the composition department at the San Francisco Conservatory, which he has chaired since 2000.

Further Reading

Sadie, Stanley, ed. 2001. *The New Grove Dictionary of Music and Musicians*. 2nd ed. London: Macmillan Press.

Christopher H. Walker

May Swenson (1913–1989)

May Swenson approached her poetic subjects—nature, animals, and, more obliquely, desire—with a seductive playfulness and lack of pretense. Her work as a poet and translator (of Swedish poet Tomas Tranströmer) garnered the prestigious Bollingen Prize for Poetry, as well as Guggenheim and MacArthur fellowships. Yet Swenson remains an underrated writer; many fine poems from her 12 published volumes are inaccessible and out of print.

Born in a Swedish Mormon family in Utah, Swenson attended Utah State University, emerging with a BA in 1939. Soon after, she moved to New York City, where she held a variety of jobs, often writing poems at her typewriter during lulls in office work. She became an editor at the vanguard New Directions press but left New York City to concentrate full-time on her writing. With her partner Rozanne Knudson, Swenson eventually settled in Delaware.

Swenson was aloof from much of the era's literary politics, though she did become friends with the prominent poet **Elizabeth Bishop.** After their meeting at the writers' colony Yaddo in 1950, they carried on a lifelong correspondence, and Swenson would finally elegize Bishop in her 1979 poem "In the Bodies of Words." In their poetry, both Swenson and Bishop refract their identity through animal surrogates.

Like Bishop, Swenson abjured the feminist political affiliations that empowered a poet like **Adrienne Rich.** While Swenson does not overtly mention her sexuality in her work, in her poems about nature a palpably queer eroticism emerges, especially in "Swimmers" and "At First, at Last," in which the waves of the sea become indistinguishable from waves of sexual pleasure.

Further Reading

Arditi, Neil. 2002. "'In the Bodies of Words': The Swenson-Bishop Conversation." *Parnassus: Poetry in Review* 26 (2): 77–93.

Felstiner, John. 2007. "'Why Is Your Mouth All Green?': Something Alive in May Swenson." *American Poetry Review* 36 (4): 19–21.

Christopher Schmidt

Sylvester (1947–1988)

Born Sylvester James, gay African American singer Sylvester is often called the first male diva of disco, the personification of the gay and black origins of disco, although ballads and slow covers comprise the bulk of his recorded material. Raised in Los Angeles in a family that included legendary jazz singer Julia Morgan, Sylvester grew up singing in local churches, but the community waffled between celebrating his voice and puzzling over his behavior and dress, which were decidedly feminine. Stifled by this scene, Sylvester moved to San Francisco in 1970, where he soon joined the Cockettes, a flamboyant musical troupe, and quickly made a name for himself. He released his first album with Hot Band in 1973 (*Scratch My Flower*, complete with a scratch-n-sniff gardenia in tribute to the late Billie Holiday), but it was not until he hired Martha Washington and Izora Rhodes, two gospel singers dubbed "Two Tons o' Fun" (later to become the Weather Girls), that Sylvester's unique style blossomed, earning him great popularity, first in the United Kingdom and Europe and then in the United States. His biggest break came with *Step II*, the 1978 album featuring the song for which he is probably best known, "You Make Me Feel (Mighty Real)," a song that topped both R&B and pop charts and that was later one of the first songs inducted into the Dance Music Hall of Fame. Fans reacted strongly to Sylvester's soaring falsetto vocals and to the sexual innuendo of the lyrics and melody. The hit was quickly followed by "Dance (Disco Heat)" and 1982s "Do You Wanna Funk." Sylvester's success, though, came at the apex of the disco era and his success throughout the waning years of disco is attributable in part to his early song "You Make Me Feel (Mighty Real)," a collaboration with Patrick Cowley, whose synthesized sounds melded well with Sylvester's vocal range and helped ensure Sylvester's continued popularity. Although his music garnered critical and popular acclaim, Sylvester was equally (if not more) well known for his feminine-androgynous appearance and dress. While early reviews of Sylvester's live performances are a mix of praise for the music and unease with Sylvester the performer, Sylvester himself seemed to have no problem with self-understanding. In concert and in life, Sylvester adopted a style that fit his spirit, paying homage to idols like Bessie Smith, Patti LaBelle (who was a close friend), and other

Sylvester (1947–1988)

Sylvester in 1980. Photo by Robert Pruzan, courtesy of the Gay, Lesbian, Bisexual, Transgender Historical Society, San Francisco.

strong female performers yet without reducing himself to a **stereotype.** In the clone-filled Castro district of San Francisco, where he lived for the last 15 years of his life, Sylvester stood out by crossing identification boundaries. Not a **drag** queen, not a transvestite, he proclaimed himself, simply, "Sylvester." It is this unapologetic "Sylvester-ness" that partly explains his appeal, especially as the AIDS epidemic made pariahs and outcasts of the gay community. While battling AIDS himself, Sylvester made one of his last public appearances in a San Francisco gay pride parade. Sylvester died of complications from AIDS. Sylvester's music can still be heard at dance clubs, and the effects of his refusal to be anyone but himself paved the way for and influenced other performers, from RuPaul to Bette Midler.

Further Reading

Diebold, David. 1988. *Tribal Rites: San Francisco's Dance Music Phenomenon 1977–1988*. Northridge, CA: Time Warp Publishing.

Gamson, Joshua. 2005. *The Fabulous Sylvester: The Legend, the Music, the Seventies in San Francisco*. New York: Henry Holt.

Lawrence, Tim. 2006. "'I Want to See All My Friends at Once': Arthur Russell and the Queering of Gay Disco." *Journal of Popular Music Studies* 18 (2): 144–66.

Shapiro, Peter. 2005. *Turn the Beat Around: The Secret History of Disco*. New York: Faber and Faber.

Milton W. Wendland

T

Joel Tan (1968–)

Joel Barraquiel Tan, born in Manila, is a playwright, poet, editor, and **activist.** Tan attended the University of California at Berkeley, where he received his BA in ethnic studies, and Antioch University, where he received an MFA in creative writing. Since the late 1980s, Tan has also done considerable work in the field of HIV/AIDS education, cofounding the Asian Pacific AIDS Intervention Team in Los Angeles.

Tan's first volume of poetry, *Monster,* was published in 2002 and was followed by *Type O-Negative* in 2006, which also served as his MFA thesis at Antioch University. His poetry is characterized by a blunt sense of humor, vivid imagery, and frank, sharp language, and as a result his work has won a number of awards, including the *Spoon River Poetry Review* Editor's Prize. He has also edited the anthologies *Inside Him—Gay Erotic Fiction* and *Best Gay Asian Erotica,* and his essays and short fiction have been widely published and anthologized.

Tan's 2002 play *The Cure,* coauthored with **Ginu Kamani,** deals with some of the cultural and historical aspects of AIDS. Set in the early 1990s, the play specifically takes a critical view of the industry that grew up around caring for victims of the disease. Making heavy use of South Asian cultural and spiritual motifs, the play is reminiscent of the work of **Harry Kondoleon** in its use of humor and vivid staging.

Further Reading

Le, Viet. 2004/2005. "Monster." *Amerasia Journal* 30 (3): 116–18.

Lo, Mun-Hou. 2000. "Double Jeopardy; Or, What's Eating You?" *GLQ: A Journal of Lesbian and Gay Studies* 6 (4): 609–29.

Will Curl

Tristan Taormino (1971–)

Niece of Thomas Pynchon and Phi Beta Kappa graduate of Wellesley, Tristan Taormino is an award-winning author, editor, and columnist, who is best known as a sex educator. She received her bachelor's degree in 1993 in American studies at Wesleyan University in Middleton, Connecticut. Her work has been featured in over 200 publications including the *New York Times*, *Men's Health*, and *Playboy*. Her celebrated book, *The Ultimate Guide to Anal Sex for Women* (1997), won a Firecracker Book Award and was Amazon.com's #1 best-seller in women's sex instruction in 1998. She is an editor for the Lambda Award–winning anthology *Best Lesbian Erotica* and has collaborated with many authors within this oeuvre, including **Patrick Califia.** In 1999, Taormino collaborated with Evil Angel Productions and made a film version of *The Ultimate Guide to Anal Sex for Women*, which received mixed reviews from feminist/queer audiences. Currently, she has her own adult film production company, Smart Ass Productions. Despite the mixed reactions to her work by the queer community, Taormino was named one of *Out* magazine's 100 Gay Success Stories and one of the *Advocate*'s Best and Brightest Gay and Lesbian People under Thirty in the late 1990s.

Mary Shearman

Cecil Taylor (1929–)

Cecil Taylor became one of the earliest and most celebrated contributors to the genre of music known as free jazz that emerged in the late 1950s. Whereas the bebop jazz movement that was in vogue during the late 1940s and early 1950s (led by Charlie Parker and Dizzy Gillespie) primarily consisted of a series of solo improvisations upon complex chord changes, Taylor's music was a radical departure from this previous style in its emphasis on the rhythmic structures forged by the band as a whole. While this approach may sound chaotic to those who hear it for the first time, in fact, Taylor's music is primarily the result of very intricate and careful composition. In this respect, many critics have commented on the similarities between Taylor and avant-garde classical composers such as **John Cage** and Karlheinz Stockhausen. As a pianist, Taylor is one of the great living virtuosi and is known for his distinctly rhythmic approach and for the nearly incomparable level of passion and intensity that he brings to his challenging compositions. Taylor has played with many of the greatest jazz musicians, including Mary Lou Williams, Max Roach, John Coltrane, and Archie Shepp. His many honors include being invited to play at the White House in 1979, a fellowship from the MacArthur Foundation, and a fellowship from the Guggenheim Foundation. He is openly gay.

Further Reading
Gill, John. 1995. *Queer Noises: Male and Female Homosexuality in Twentieth Century Music.* Minneapolis. University of Minnesota Press

Marc Lombardo

Paul Taylor (1930–)

Born in Allegheny County, Pennsylvania, Paul Taylor is the only son of Elizabeth Rose Pendleton and Dr. Paul Bellville Taylor, an academic. Shortly after Paul was born, his parents divorced. This was his mother's second marriage, and Paul had three stepbrothers and stepsisters from his mother's first marriage. As Taylor was the youngest, he was often shuttled between friends and family and, later, sent off to summer camp. He rarely saw his mother, whom he adored, and his father was almost nonexistent in his young life. He was a lonely child, which greatly influenced his early dances. Taylor's grades were average for the most part, but he truly excelled in athletics. He attended Syracuse University from 1950 to 1953 on a swimming scholarship, but by his last year, he knew that he wanted to dance. He was able to attend several dance workshops and eventually was accepted into the then-new dance program at Juilliard.

Living in **New York City,** Taylor studied with many famous dancers, including Merce Cunningham, George Balanchine, and Martha Graham, all of whom he eventually worked for as a dancer. Though Taylor, at 22, was older than most of the other dancers, he still caught the eye of his mentors with his unusual fluidity of movement, even with his 6'3" frame. Balanchine was so impressed with Taylor's ballet skills that after the first production of *Episodes* in 1959, he asked Taylor to join his company. Taylor refused because, although he enjoyed ballet, he wanted to do modern dance. After working for Merce Cunningham for two years, he became a dancer for Martha Graham's company and stayed with her for years. Although Taylor had formed the Paul Taylor Dance Company in 1954, it was not until 10 years later that he stopped dancing for other people's companies and danced solely for himself. While he was working for Graham, Taylor started experimenting with choreography and put on his own productions in-between shows with Graham. The most notorious of these shows was *Seven New Dances* (1957), for which, famously, dance critic Louis Horst left his review completely blank and signed his name at the bottom of it. This was the beginning of Taylor's love/hate relationship with the critics, but this particular production, and its review by Horst, also made him well known.

Taylor's most famous work is *Aureole* (1962). Critics proclaimed it as a visual expression of what dancers felt when they danced, full of life and joy. It has been performed by many dance and ballet companies worldwide and continues to be his most popular dance. With *Aureole* many people felt that Taylor went from being a superb dancer to a rising star as a choreographer. His company traveled more extensively than many other companies, but as a result they were on the brink of financial ruin more than once. Somehow, the company has managed to survive through the good times and the bad.

In 1974, Taylor ended his dancing career and focused solely on choreography. The years shortly after his retirement were crucial for his company as they proved that the company could survive without Taylor actually dancing. The official reason Taylor gave up dancing was illness, but it was in fact due to a combination of factors: dancing is certainly brutal on the body; he was addicted to dexamyl, a combination amphetamine and barbiturate antidepressant drug popular in the 1950s and 1960s; and his health was also deteriorating because of untreated hepatitis (Taylor 1999, 355–56).

In 1987, at the age of 57, Taylor published his autobiography, *Private Domain*. It was hailed by literary critics as a superb work and was entirely written by Taylor himself with no assistance from a ghostwriter. It is a tell-all book that revolves around his dancing career and his early home life, though he says very little about his sexuality or partners. He does, however, mention that he consistently sublimated his sexuality in favor of dancing, and he implies a great deal of sexual confusion, which he ultimately resolves by saying, "As to preferred partners, with men.... It was like faulty electronics, like two positive terminals that can't close a circuit.... And when I was with a woman...I tended to look for familiar traits in her that might make me feel more comfortable with our differences. I guess most times I preferred whomever I wasn't with" (Taylor 1999, 319).

With the death of Taylor's protégé, Christopher Gillis, of AIDS in 1993, the future leadership of the Paul Taylor Dance Company remains uncertain. Paul Taylor continues to choreograph for his company and started a junior company, Taylor 2, in 1992. He continues to be a leader in dance and has been awarded numerous high-profile awards throughout his career including a Guggenheim Fellowship, an Emmy, a Kennedy Center Honor Award, and a National Medal of Arts. He lives in New York City.

Further Reading

Paul Taylor: Dancemaker. 1998. Dir. Matthew Diamond. Docurama. DVD.

Stanley, Richard, and Mary Jo Stanley. 2004. *Paul Taylor Dance Company: The First Fifty Years.* New York City: Paul Taylor Dance Company.

Taylor, Paul. 1999. *Private Domain.* Pittsburgh: University of Pittsburgh Press.

Katherine J. J. Pionke

Richard Tayson (1962–)

American poet Richard Tayson won the 1997 Wick Poetry Prize for his first book of poetry, *The Apprentice of Fever*. In 1998, he coauthored *Look Up for Yes* with Julia Tavalaro, a book of prose that was a best-seller in Germany. *The World Underneath* is his second book of poems.

Tayson's poems have been published in numerous journals and magazines, including *Paris Review*, *Bloom*, *Hanging Loose*, *Art and Understanding*, *The Gay and Lesbian Review-Worldwide*, *Prairie Schooner*, and the *James White Review*, among others. His work has been awarded a 2003 New York Foundation for the Arts Fellowship, the 2004 Edward Taylor Award, the 2004 Edward Stanley Award, and a Pushcart Prize, among others.

Apprentice of Fever is composed of poems told with wit and passion about a man living with AIDS. Tayson's work often explores *esho funi*, the Buddhist concept of the oneness between self and the environment.

Tayson is also a strong voice in examining LGBTQ poetry. His work in the *Gay and Lesbian Review-Worldwide* explores a brief history of lesbian and gay poetry and its vital exploration of "the other," and his essay on Walt Whitman's "Live-Oak, with Moss" was published in the prestigious *Virginia Quarterly*. Tayson is currently a fellow at the City University of New York's Graduate Center.

Further Reading

Tayson, Richard. 2005. "Manly Love: Whitman, Ginsberg, Monette." *Gay and Lesbian Review Worldwide* 12 (5): 23–26.

Tom Smith

Brian Teare (1974–)

Brian Teare's prize-winning first book of poems, *The Room Where I Was Born*, received a great deal of acclaim. Drawing self-consciously on his Southern background, even including a poem called "Set for a Southern Gothic," the book explores how the telling of memories and the choice of language reshape experience, conjuring up material too volatile to handle directly, while holding it at that distance in which it becomes transformed into art. A brother picking the locks to rape his younger brother; a boy getting paid for sex by men who both desire and despise him, who love him and hate themselves, buying an imaginary innocence made possible only by guilt: Fairy tales serve to frame the pain, vivid and livid as a bruise that will not heal, and make it beautiful. The knife still cuts, but the wound is turned into story, the once-upon-a-time with which these poems begin and end.

The book's last section modulates toward a more affirmative view of sex between men. "—of a Sleeping Man, and a Second Man Awake" celebrates the fleeting contentment of two men sharing a bed, one watching the other sleep. In the book's closing sequence, "Toward Lost Letters," the speaker seeks to recreate the gay life of a long-dead relative, or even to create a gay life that relative never got to lead: "I write out loud your sexed and crowded mouth." Writing is used not just to record but to remake the world.

Further Reading

Williams, Susan Settlemyre. 2004. "Review of *The Room Where I Was Born*." *Blackbird Archive* 3 (2). Available at: http://www.blackbird.vcu.edu/v3n2/nonfiction/williams_ss/teare.htm. Accessed July 20, 2008.

Reginald Shepherd

tearooms

An infrequently used term today, tearooms are public toilets where men have sex with men. Some facilities develop a reputation for being "cruisy" (see **cruising**), particularly near highways and in public parks. During much of the twentieth century in America, an "out" homosexual identity was professionally impossible, and commercial businesses such as **bars** that catered to homosexuals faced legal action and closure, factors contributing to tearooms becoming common meeting places for casual sex. Tearoom activity originated in the late 1800s in urban areas, spread to suburban areas in the 1950s, and has been in decline since **gay liberation.** Contemporary locations change due to undercover vice operations by police squads, leading to the occasional celebrity arrest and public **outing,** such as of singer George Michael in 1998.

Sociologist Laud Humphreys's 1968 doctoral dissertation *Tearoom Trade,* published as a book in 1970, was a landmark in identifying subgroups and blurred identities including sexually frustrated heterosexual males, out gay males, **closeted** gay males, and closeted **bisexual** males. His research was controversial for legal and ethical reasons: he observed conduct that was criminal, and he identified participants through motor vehicle records, collecting detailed confidential biographical data in subsequent interviews. Later Humphreys came out as a gay man, faced investigation by the Federal Bureau of Investigation, and disclosed that he had been a participant-observer. His data dispelled the myth that such men are sexual predators victimizing straight teenagers, showing that teenagers were shunned in tearooms, and even feared, as they sometimes physically assaulted men who approached them for sex.

Further Reading

Galliher, John F., Wayne H. Brekhus, and David P. Keys. 2004. *Laud Humphreys: Prophet of Homosexuality and Sociology.* Madison: University of Wisconsin Press.

Marcus C. Tye

television shows

Like cinema, television has historically been reluctant to include positive portrayals of LGBTQ characters. Television's need to broadcast programs that appeal to the masses, including conservative elements, has meant that gay characters have been fairly invisible on television until recent times. When queer characters did appear on television during its early years, this was generally in the form of one-off characters in an issue-based episode, and, even then, queer characters were frequently presented in a negative light.

Notable one-off appearances of gay characters in American television drama during the 1960s and 1970s generally took place on shows with a medical focus, in keeping with general society's medicalized perception of homosexuality as a disease or disorder. Examples include *The Eleventh Hour*'s portrayal of a potentially lesbian character seeking psychiatric help (1963), or two episodes of *Marcus Welby, M.D.*, the first of which showed the eponymous doctor treating a married gay male alcoholic (1973), while the second presented a boy molested by his male teacher (1974). Both of these story lines were protested by gay activists (Tropiano 2002). Another common way to represent gay characters was in the context of criminal activity. A particularly salacious episode of *Police Woman*, for example, depicted a group of lesbians killing the residents of a retirement home (1974). For further discussion of early queer images on television see Capsuto (2000), Gross (2001), and Tropiano (2002). To counter these types of representations, various LGBTQ groups campaigned during the 1970s for more accurate and inclusive representation of queer characters on television (examples of such groups include the Gay Media Project, the Gay Media Coalition, and Lesbian Feminist Liberation, Inc.). Such groups also often acted as advisors to early public affairs broadcasts on gay issues.

Over the years, various telemovies focusing on gay issues have presented gays and lesbians in a more positive light, albeit often a victimized one. These have included *That Certain Summer* (1972), about a teenager with a gay father; *A Question of Love* (1978), about a lesbian fighting for custody of her children; *An Early Frost* (1985), focusing on a gay male lawyer with AIDS; and *Serving in Silence: The Margarethe Cammermeyer Story* (1995), a biopic about a lesbian in the U.S. military, as well as the more recent *Common Ground* (2000) and *If These Walls Could Talk 2* (2000).

As society became more accepting of gays and lesbians due to the gay rights movement and Stonewall rebellion, slightly more gay characters crept onto television during the 1980s and 1990s. While the last 20 years have seen a great increase in the number and quality of representations of LGBTQ people on television, some argue that these representations are not indicative of progress, given their limited or stereotypical nature. An example of such a program is *Heartbeat* (1988–1989), the first prime-time U.S. television program to include a regularly appearing lesbian character in a series, nurse Marilyn McGrath (Gail Strickland) who worked in a women's health clinic. While this portrayal was not an overtly negative one, several critics have commented on its overly desexualized nature. More overt depictions of gay sexuality of the period, such as the *thirtysomething* (1987–1991) scene, which depicted two men talking in bed together, prompted the withdrawal of numerous advertisers from the program.

The first woman-to-woman kiss on television occurred in 1991, when **bisexual** lawyer C. J. Lamb (Amanda Donohoe) kissed a heterosexual female colleague in *L.A. Law* (1986–1994). During the 1990s, many popular television programs engaged in sensationalized "lesbian" kisses to boost ratings, particularly during sweeps week. These instances were heavily and lasciviously promoted, and they generally included at least one straight participant who would confirm her heterosexuality by the end of the episode. These lesbian sweeps kisses stand in stark contrast to the desexualized manner in which lesbian characters were usually presented during the period.

The PBS miniseries *Tales of the City* (1993), adapted from the books by Armistead Maupin, was remarkable and groundbreaking in the variety of queer characters represented. Gay male character Michael "Mouse" Tolliver (Marcus D'Amico) is a far cry from either a self-loathing homosexual or a bed-hopping hedonist, and his story lines in this series and its follow-up seasons center on his search for romantic love and his attempts to come out to his conservative parents. There are also various bisexual characters, including Mouse's friend Mona Ramsay (Chloe Webb) and the sinister Beauchamp Day (Thomas Gibson). Their enigmatic landlady, and the universal mother of the series, Anna Madrigal (Olympia Dukakis), is revealed at the end to be a transsexual woman. This character constitutes one of the few sympathetic portrayals of transsexual women on television to this day, as transsexual women generally appear on television as plot devices that are often played for laughs (as seen in *Ally McBeal* or *Dark Angel,* for example).

During the 1990s, examples of gay representation increased. The ABC situation comedy *Roseanne* (1988–1997) portrayed bisexual character Nancy (Sandra Bernhard); a gay male character Leon (Martin Mull), who married his partner Scott (Fred Willard) onscreen in 1995; and Roseanne's mother Bev (Estelle Parsons), who came out during the final season. The first woman-woman kiss where neither participant was straight on U.S. television took place between lesbian character Rhonda (Lisa Edelstein) and her girlfriend on *Relativity* (1996–1997) in 1997. Matt Fielding (Doug Savant) on the popular series *Melrose Place* (1992–1999) gained much attention for being a likable gay character, though he lacked a romantic life, in direct contrast to his bed-hopping heterosexual cocharacters, and Fox refused to air his only onscreen kiss.

Ellen (ABC). "The Puppy Episode," April 30, 1997. Shown from left: Ellen DeGeneres, Laura Dern. In this final episode of the series Ellen came out as a lesbian and kissed Dern. ABC/Photofest. © ABC.

Aside from Leon's on *Roseanne,* gay marriages on television during the 1990s included the 1994 wedding of innkeepers Ron (Doug Ballard) and Erick (Don McManus) on *Northern Exposure* (1990–1995), which was criticized for not including a kiss between the couple after they exchanged their vows, and a 1995 wedding on *Friends* between minor character Carol (Jane Sibbett), who is the ex-wife of major character Ross (David Schwimmer), and her partner Susan (Jessica Hecht).

The situation comedy *Ellen* (1994–1998) was undoubtedly the best-publicized instance of a coming-out story on national television. Ellen

DeGeneres, a well-known comedian and the star of the show, alluded to her own and her characters' coming out long before its occurrence, building anticipation of the event. DeGeneres herself came out on the cover of *Time* on April 14, 1997, while her character Ellen came out during "The Puppy Episode" on April 30, 1997. The religious right reacted extremely negatively to this episode; some conservative advertisers ceased sponsoring the show, and even the producers of the show became nervous about its gay content. *Ellen* survived only one more season, amid claims from some quarters that the show became too gay after "The Puppy Episode."

The next notable situation comedy with a gay central character was the highly popular *Will & Grace* (1998–2006), which centered on the relationship between gay lawyer Will Truman (Eric McCormack) and his straight female best friend, interior designer Grace Adler (Debra Messing). Although this mainstreamed representation of gay men was certainly a breakthrough, by utilizing the formula of gay man/straight woman popularized by 1990s film, the producers managed to avoid that which had perhaps led to *Ellen*'s demise—too clear a focus on gay life and relationships. The series has been criticized not only for being depoliticized but also for its desexualized depiction of gay men, as during its run the show's attempts at portraying gay male sexuality, or even relationships, were extremely limited.

In the cult hit *Buffy the Vampire Slayer* (1997–2003), teenage witch Willow (Alyson Hannigan) fell in love with fellow witch Tara (Amber Benson) during the year 2000. While their relationship was presented in a nonsensationalized manner, their sexual contact was mainly limited to allegorical magic-as-sex, and Tara was murdered in 2002 immediately after the characters were presented at their most visibly sexual, which prompted Willow to attempt to destroy the world. In the final season (on new network UPN), Willow confirmed her sexuality through a relationship with female vampire slayer Kennedy (Iyari Limon) and finally had an onscreen sex scene.

In contrast to *Will & Grace* and *Buffy*, cable network Showtime's *Queer As Folk* (2000–2005) did not hesitate to present sexualized gay images. The U.S. *Queer As Folk*, produced by Ron Cowen, Daniel Lipman, and Tony Jonas, was an adaptation of the eponymous British series created by Russel T. Davies. *Queer As Folk* was remarkable in U.S. queer television history not only for its willingness to show queer characters as fully sexual beings, but for its presentation of a queer community relating to one another, instead of framing LGBTQ characters in relation to the straight world. It centered on a group of five

Queer as Folk Season finale, 2004. Shown: Michelle Clunie as Melanie, Thea Gill as Lindsay. Courtesy of Showtime/Photofest. © Showtime Photographer: L. Pief Weyman/Photofest.

gay male friends: Brian (Gale Harold), a gay Cassanova; Michael (Hal Sparks), his best friend and comic book aficionado; **camp** Emmett (Peter Paige); accountant Ted (Scott Lowell); and Brian's 17-year-old on-again, off-again lover Justin (Randy Harrison). Other characters included two lesbians, Melanie (Michelle Clunie) and Lindsay (Thea Gill), who had a child using Brian's sperm. Their story lines on the series were generally secondary to both the gay male characters and Michael's straight but queer-identified mother Debbie. Over the course of the five seasons, many queer issues were addressed on this series, including coming out, assimilation, queer parenting, and HIV.

In light of the success of *Queer As Folk*, Showtime reconnected with producer Ilene Chaiken regarding a television show she had previously pitched to them revolving around a group of lesbians. Initially entitled *Earthlings*, the drama series was renamed *The L Word* and began screening in 2004. It centers on the lives and relationships of a group of lesbian and bisexual women in Los Angeles. The main characters are Jenny Schecter (Mia Kirshner), a writer who spends the first season struggling to come to terms with her sexuality; Bette Porter (Jennifer Beals), a lesbian art museum director; Bette's partner Tina (Laurel Holloman), who spends the first season attempting to become pregnant, the second being pregnant, and the third attempting to locate a male partner; bisexual journalist Alice, played by the only out lesbian actress among the primary cast members (Leisha Hailey); Dana (Erin Daniels), a closeted tennis player who later comes out before dying of cancer; and Shane (Katherine Moenning), a melancholic lesbian lothario. The series was criticized from the outset for being unrepresentative and for appealing to a straight male audience through its feminine actresses and provocative marketing campaigns. Despite such factors, the series has built a substantial fan base among lesbian communities, some of whom have created Internet-based communities and fan fiction revolving around the series. Despite poor ratings during the second season, the third season showed improved ratings, and *The L Word* has been renewed by Showtime for up to five seasons.

It is not only on drama series and sitcoms, however, that queers have become more visible. Bravo's enormously successful *Queer Eye for the Straight Guy* (2003–) is perhaps the series most clearly associated with bringing gay images onto the television screens of mainstream America. The series features five gay men who make over straight men's wardrobes (Carson Kressley), grooming (Kyan Douglas), homes (Thom Filicia), food (Ted Allen), and interpersonal relationships/"culture" (Jai Rodriguez). Some have argued that the show is overly focused on consumerism, presents stereotypes of gay men, and forever traps them into an "enabler" role for straight

The L Word has generally been well received by the lesbian community. Shown: Mia Kirshner as Jenny and Karina Lombard as Marina. Courtesy of Showtime/Photofest © Showtime 2003.

relationships. However, while the show focuses on heterosexual rather than homosexual relationships, the gay men are not entirely desexualized; indeed, much of the humor of the show is achieved by Carson making the straight guys uncomfortable by rendering them the subjects of his queer, desiring gaze. More remarkably, in this series the queer characters hold power, while the hapless heterosexuals look to them for guidance. During the 2006 season, the series featured the makeover of a transsexual man, undermining dominant notions of what constitutes a straight man. The show prompted British and Australian spin-offs, as well as the series *Queer Eye for the Straight Girl* (2005), which included a lesbian "lifestyle advisor," Honey Labrador.

Gay people have also appeared as contestants on various reality shows—in some cases their gayness formed part of the drama of the series, and in others it went unremarked. MTV's *Real World* (1992–) was one of the earliest programs to feature gay contestants, while the first season of *Survivor* was won by gay nudist Richard Hatch; *Survivor* went on to include other queer contestants. Other reality shows that have featured queer contestants include *Big Brother* (2000–), *Project Runway* (2004–), *Top Chef* (2006–), *Rockstar: Supernova* (2006–), and *Work Out* (2006–). A queer aesthetic is quite central to Tyra Banks's series *America's Next Top Model* (2003–), from the genderqueer judge and coach Miss Jay to Tyra's exhortations that she learned how to "walk" from **drag** queens. The series has also featured a number of bisexual and lesbian contestants, most notably Kim Stoltz, whose female masculinity came under fire throughout the series. Fox Chicago's *Experiment: Gay and Straight* (2002) formed a drama precisely about homophobia by getting a group of gay people to live with a group of straight people.

While Ellen's sitcom may not have fared well, her talk show *Ellen: The Ellen DeGeneres Show* (2003–) has become very popular, winning three consecutive Daytime Emmy Awards for Best Talk Show. This could in part be accounted for by her retreat from her much-publicized 1997 coming out. On *Ellen: The Ellen DeGeneres Show*, DeGeneres's sexuality remains at the level of an open secret—she avoids discussing her partner or even the sexuality and relationships of her gay guests. Rosie O'Donnell, who waited to come out until after her talk show *The Rosie O'Donnell Show* (1996–2002) concluded, became a host on *The View* (ABC, 1997–) in 2005, making her the second out lesbian on a daytime talk show. Unlike DeGeneres, O'Donnell has been open about her sexuality on the show and has utilized her role as a platform to discuss gay issues, particularly gay marriage.

While queerness once was relegated to an "adult" issue, queer characters have in recent years also gradually become visible on television series aimed primarily at teen audiences. Notable examples from the 1990s included acclaimed evening teen-drama *My So-Called Life* (1994–1995), which featured gay teenager Rickie Vasquez (Wilson Cruz), and teen character Jack from the prime-time series *Dawson's Creek* (WB, 1998–2003), who started exploring his sexuality in 1999. The increase in gay and bisexual story lines on teen shows in the late 1990s prompted protests from right-wing Christian activists who demanded a "homosexual content" label be added to the already-existing advisory codes for language, violence, and so on. While numbers of gay teen story lines and characters increased during the 1990s, the biggest rise in visibility has occurred since 2000. *Tree Hill* (2003–)

has portrayed a young bisexual woman, Anna (Daniella Alonso), among its recurring characters, while prime-time teen soap *The O.C.* (2003–) saw one of its major female characters engage in a short-lived relationship with a bisexual girl. Teen gay characters have also been appearing on daytime soap operas such as *All My Children* (1970–), *General Hospital* (1963–), and *As the World Turns* (1956–). *South of Nowhere* (2005–), broadcast on **youth**-oriented cable channel The N, has been a remarkable example of queer teen representation on television, in that its queer story line is central to the ongoing narrative. The series has been a ratings success, and the relationship between teenage main characters Spencer (Gabrielle Christian) and Ashley (Mandy Musgrave) has spawned a significant fan following.

Negative and limited characterizations of queer characters still exist, and American television is still a long way from truly incorporating complex and honest queer characters into its regular programming. Murderous lesbians are still seen on crime dramas, bisexual characters are still frequently characterized as oversexed or villainous, and gay male characters still cannot show as much onscreen affection on network television as their heterosexual or even lesbian counterparts. Substantial progress has, however, been made over time in the quantity and quality of gay, lesbian, and bisexual characters on television. Much less progress has been made in terms of the representation of **transgender** or **intersex** characters, or the representation of queer characters of color or working-class queers. The majority of queer representations on television have been of white, affluent gays and lesbians with fairly normative gender presentations.

Notable exceptions to queer television characters' overwhelming whiteness include the African American Carter Heywood (Michael Boatman), who works for the New York City mayor on *Spin City* (1996–2002), and Keith, an African American police officer in *Six Feet Under* (2001–2005) who is the partner of one of the primary (white) characters. Female exceptions include Original Cindy from *Dark Angel* (2000–2002) and Latina characters Anna (*One Tree Hill*) and Carmen (*The L Word*). The biracial Bette in *The L Word*, however, is the closest that television has come to portraying a queer character of color in a lead role.

In *Nip/Tuck* (2003–), a drama about two plastic surgeons that includes a secondary lesbian character, an overtly negative transgendered character was recently introduced. Ava Moore (Famke Janssen), characterized by producers as the villain of the series's second season, was a transsexual character who underwent sexual reassignment in order to make the straight object of her affection love her. Even overtly queer programs like *Queer As Folk* or *The L Word* have made little effort to include positive representations of transgender characters. The closest *Queer As Folk* came to representing the transgendered community was the ongoing bit-part of Kiki the transsexual waitress, whose largest presence in the series was as the butt of jokes, occasionally as a drag queen, and, infrequently, as a voiceless transsexual character in order to prove a political point. *The L Word*, in contrast, did make some attempt at portraying transgender/transsexual characters in the form of Ivan and Moira/Max. These characters, however, were a long way from constituting positive or affirming images of transgendered men—with characterizations ranging from duplicity to aggression bordering on violence. The character of Max in particular appeared to be deliberately included by the producers of *The L Word* in order to make a rather reactionary point about the growing number of female-to-male transsexuals in the lesbian community.

An exception to these limited or negative portrayals was the Sundance Channel's *Transgeneration* (2005), an eight-part documentary that followed four transgendered college students as they underwent transition. Other, more mainstream depictions of transgender experiences included Lifetime's telemovie *A Girl Like Me: The Gwen Araujo Story* (2006), based on the murder of real-life transsexual teenager Gwen Araujo, which played the role of introducing mainstream America to the concept of transsexuality, asserting a message of tolerance and acceptance of difference. Daytime soap *All My Children* is also slated to include a male-to-female transsexual in a story line beginning in late 2006. The show's writers have worked with **Gay and Lesbian Alliance Against Defamation** and transgender consultants in creating the character Zarf (Jeffrey Carlson).

Intersex characters have been even more invisible, generally appearing only on medical programs. Recent examples include an intersex teenage model, the medical mystery of the week on *House* (2004–), who uses sex to manipulate people, even her own father, and is subject to open scorn and ridicule once her intersexuality is discovered. *Grey's Anatomy* (2005–) took a more sensitive approach, depicting Bex (Becca Gardner), a depressed teenager who takes too many birth control pills in an effort to spark her breast growth, frustrated at being different from her peers. While the parents do not react well to the news that their child is intersex, refusing to tell her and demanding sexual reassignment surgery without Bex's knowledge or consent, ongoing doctor character George (T. R. Knight) insists on the patient's right to know the truth and asserts that any choice of gender assignment must be up to Bex.

There is a tendency to take note of queer television only in terms of mass-market examples. It is important to acknowledge the ongoing work done by community and public broadcasters. *In the Life* (1992–), for example, is a television newsmagazine dedicated to LGBTQ issues and culture and is now broadcast on multiple public television stations nationwide. Another example is *Dyke TV* (1993–), an explicitly political community television production that initially screened only in New York but is now broadcast on over 100 public access cable channels. The Internet has become an important resource in terms of distributing these productions and other queer television programs, making them available to a wider audience than was possible previously.

Recent years have seen the advent of gay cable networks such as Logo, Here!, and Q. While problematic in terms of access and the potential for ghettoization, the presence of such networks provides a crucial forum for the production and screening of queer television content. As their intended audience is primarily LGBTQ, shows produced by such networks do not have to alter programming in order to cater to the mainstream, thus opening up new possibilities for the representation of queer characters on television.

Further Reading

Beirne, Rebecca, ed. 2007. *Televising Queer Women: A Reader.* New York: Palgrave Macmillan.

Capsuto, Steven. 2000. *Alternate Channels: The Uncensored Story of Gay and Lesbian Images on Radio and Television.* New York: Ballantine Books.

Gross, Larry. 2001. *Up from Invisibility: Lesbians, Gay Men, and the Media in America*. New York and Chichester: Columbia University Press.

Keller, James R., and Leslie Stratyner, eds. 2006. *The New Queer Aesthetic on Television: Essays on Recent Programming*. Jefferson, NC: McFarland.

Tropiano, Stephen. 2002. *The Prime Time Closet: A History of Gays and Lesbians on TV*. New York: Applause Theatre and Cinema Books.

Rebecca Beirne

theater companies

Theater since its inception has always attracted the queer community. Historical records clearly document that the earliest performers were **drag** troupes. A common thread that unites all queer troupes or companies is a desire to see themselves reflected in the mirror that is being held up to nature; in the process a new aesthetic is created. This aesthetic can be seen when reviewing the influences of the companies listed below.

CAFFE CINO (1958–1968)

Founded by Joseph Cino, the New York–based Caffe Cino stands out among LGBTQ experimental and mainstream theater companies because of its contributions to off-off-Broadway and for being a trailblazer for gay theater. Unable to pursue his first career choice as a dancer because of his short height and stout physique, Cino started his company as a means to express himself. From the inception he knew the importance of developing new talent. In the early stages of its development, the eight-foot by eight-foot flexible stage of the Caffe Cino helped foster such artists as **Lanford Wilson,** Sam Shepard, Bernadette Peters, Harvey Keitel, Neil Flanagan, and John Guare.

The Caffe's uniqueness was in part due to its **camp** performance aesthetic. The aesthetic sprang out of Joseph Cino's distinctive management style, as well as a strong gay presence. The Caffe's mission was the opposite of the "mainstream subculture" that was political and conformist because the Caffe was birthed by creating and supporting works that were considered bohemian and nonpolitical. Money was always an issue at Caffe Cino. As a result Cino did not pay his playwrights, actors, or directors but offered performers carte blanche in the interpretation of their works, thereby becoming a haven for gay artists and those on the fringes. This freedom naturally led to Caffe Cino's deconstruction of gender and an irreverent depiction of traditional gender roles that came to be known as "genderfuck."

There can be no doubt that the inconsistent reviews, Cino's unique management style, and the types of plays produced all played a role in the financial woes of Caffe Cino. However, another major factor that was a significant ordeal for all the coffeehouse theaters like Caffe Cino, was the "coffeehouse wars." A mixture of the political and criminal, the coffeehouse wars kept small, struggling companies like Caffe Cino in debt. After Cino's death, Caffe Cino was eventually forced out of business because the new directors refused to pay bribes to the police officers and administrators who were orchestrating the "wars."

CHARLES LUDLAM AND THE RIDICULOUS THEATRICAL COMPANY (1967–1987)

Charles Ludlam founded the Ridiculous Theatrical Company in large part as a reaction to the literal representations on the American stage that were present even in the world of camp, such as in the Caffe Cino. Coming of age in the mid-1960s, the Ridiculous Theatrical Company had no official manifesto but eventually was able to make a significant mark due to its unique aesthetic, often referred to simply as the Ridiculous. It has been defined as a style that is both camp and extremely self-conscious by nature. However, most definitions of the Ridiculous aesthetic go further and discuss its use of genderfuck, mixing of genres, political and social undercurrents, and a (re)visioning of popular American entertainments.

Sometimes referred to as a scavenger because of the way he picked through various genres to create his work, Ludlam made the reprocessing of culture a mainstay of the Ridiculous aesthetic. Through the freedom gained from excavating Euro-American culture, Ludlam had the power to endow the subjects he covered in his plays with admiration or contempt. Perhaps the most popular theatrical form recycled by the Ridiculous Theatrical Company was that of opera. For example, Ludlam's play *Galas* was a tribute to the opera diva Maria Callas. While only three of his plays were explicitly connected to opera, the hallmark of extravagance and posturing can be seen throughout his production aesthetic.

In the late stages of his career Ludlam began to incorporate children's theater into his work in an effort to bolster a new generation of freethinkers. While working on his play *The Artificial Jungle* Ludlam died from complications of AIDS on May 28, 1987. While the company did continue on for a time after Ludlam's death, his passing marked the end of a 20-year era.

THEATRE RHINOCEROS (1977–PRESENT)

Still in existence, Theatre Rhinoceros bills itself as the world's oldest continuously producing professional queer theater. Much like Ludlam and the Ridiculous Theatrical Company, Theatre Rhinoceros utilizes a conglomeration of styles and representations in its work. However, unlike Ludlam the theater is not restricted by any given style and moves freely from traditional to camp. Founded in San Francisco in August 1977 by the late Allan B. Estes Jr., Rhinoceros's first production, *The West Street Gang*, was staged in a **leather bar** and was so successful that it provided the momentum for a move to their first home in the Goodman Building, where they resided from 1977 until 1984. Since then the theater's mission has been to develop new works and to serve as a reflection of the queer community. Theatre Rhinoceros produced works by New York writers that included **Doric Wilson,** Robert Patrick, Lanford Wilson, **Terrence McNally,** and **Harvey Fierstein** (including the pre-Broadway one-acts *The International Stud* and *Fugue in a Nursery* that became part of his 1983 Tony Award–winning play *A Torch Song Trilogy*). The works of lesbian writers such as Pat Bond, **Jane Chambers,** and Adele Prandini have also been produced. In 1981 Theatre Rhinoceros moved to its present location in the Mission District's historic Redstone Building.

After Estes's death (1984), Theatre Rhinoceros premiered *The AIDS Show: Artists Involved with Death and Survival*, a work coauthored by 20 San Francisco Bay Area artists. Theatre Rhinoceros lists this play as the first work by any theater company in the nation to deal with the AIDS epidemic. The show ran for two years, touring the United States, and was the subject of a 1987 PBS documentary directed by Academy Award winners Rob Epstein and Peter Adair.

While the death of a founder would close most companies, Theatre Rhinoceros continued under the artistic direction of Kristine Gannon until 1987. Continuing its exploration of the impact of AIDS on the gay community, Theatre Rhinoceros produced several new plays, including Doug Holsclaw's *Life of the Party* and *The Baddest of Boys*, Leland Moss's *Quisbies*, and Robert Pitman's *Passing*. Theatre Rhinoceros redefined its boundaries of diversity by staging an African American production of Eve Powell's *Going to Seed*, **Cherríe Moraga**'s *Giving Up the Ghost*, and a historic interracial production of **Mart Crowley**'s *The Boys in the Band*. Artistic director Adele Prandini (1990–1999) solidified Theatre Rhinoceros's reputation for diversity and artistic quality with works by **Chay Yew, Guillermo Reyes,** Wayne Corbitt, Sara Felder, the Five Lesbian Brothers, and Split Britches. As artistic director, Doug Holsclaw (1999–2003) brought to fruition new works by Marga Gomez, Latin Hustle, John Fisher, **F. Allen Sawyer,** and Guillermo Reyes. Holsclaw's most noteworthy accomplishment was negotiating a contract with Actor's Equity Association, making Theatre Rhinoceros the first gay theater company to employ actors under a professional seasonal agreement.

Artistic director John Fisher (2002 to present) has steered the company to critical acclaim with works by Erika Lopez, G. B. Shaw, **Martin Sherman,** Nicky Silver, and **Tennessee Williams.** In 2005 Theatre Rhinoceros and the American Conservatory Theatre coproduced the U.S. premiere of Michel Marc Bouchard's *Lilies*. Founder Allan Estes's original vision of developing and producing works of theater that explore both the ordinary and extraordinary aspects of queer community still continues today at the very active Theatre Rhinoceros.

SPLIT BRITCHES (1981–PRESENT)

With a lesbian feminist aesthetic, Peggy Shaw, Lois Weaver, and Deb Margolin are the cofounders of Split Britches. According to Laurie Stone, "Split Britches [are exploring] butch-femme stylistics and, in every piece, women's rage, desire, poverty, hope and love. Their performances are sites of clarity, inspiration and community" (Split Britches Web site). For the last two decades Split Britches has been leading the way in inventive lesbian performance.

In 1980, Weaver began to develop a performance centering around her family history. Together with Shaw, Weaver created the characters of her aunts who had lived in the Blue Ridge Mountains of Virginia. They named the piece *Split Britches*, after the fact that the pants the women wore in the fields had splits, which allowed them to urinate while working. Deb Margolin joined Split Britches after Weaver and Shaw's performance of the piece at the first Women's One World Festival in

New York. Most major anthologies on lesbian/feminist/women's theaters include at least one article on Split Britches, and they have a significant following from feminist academics and lesbians. Together, Shaw, Weaver, and Margolin composed and performed *Split Britches* (1981), *Beauty and the Beast* (1982), *Upwardly Mobile Home* (1984), *Little Women* (1988), and *Lesbians Who Kill* (1992).

The company has received numerous honors collectively and individually. In 1985 Split Britches was awarded the *Villager* Award for Best Ensemble. The collaborative ensemble of Split Britches and Bloolips earned the ensemble the Obie for Belle Reprieve in 1991. The national organization of Women in Theater has repeatedly showcased the work of Split Britches and organized panel discussions around their innovations. Sue Ellen Case summarizes their importance in the development of modern-day lesbian performance: "the troupe created a unique 'postmodern' style that served to embed feminist and lesbian issues of the times, economic debates, national agendas, personal relationships, and sex-radical role playing in spectacular and humorous deconstructions of canonical texts, vaudeville shtick, cabaret forms, lip-synching satire, lyrical love scenes, and dark, frightening explorations of class and gender violence" (Drag! Web site).

Other notable LGBTQ theater companies include the Other Side of the Stage, the Stonewall Theatre, the Gliens, the Meridian Gay Theatre (all of New York); Diversity (Houston); the Lionheart (Chicago); the Lavendar Cellar (Minneapolis); the Red Dyke Theatre (Atlanta); Lesbian-Feminist Collective (Pittsburgh); and WOW Café (New York).

Further Reading

Brockett, Oscar, and David Ball. 2007. *The Essential Theatre*. Belmont, CA: Wadsworth.

Drag! Web site. Available at: http://www.nyu.edu/classes/jeffreys/GayandLesbianPerformance/ suellentrop/splitbritches.html. Accessed July 20, 2008.

Marranca, Bonnie, and Gautarn Dasgupta. 1998. *Theatre of the Ridiculous*. Rev. exp. ed. Baltimore, MD: Johns Hopkins Press. QLBTQ Encyclopedia. Available at: http://www.glbtq.com/. Accessed July 20, 2008.

Roemer, Rick. 1998. *Charles Ludlam and the Ridiculous Theatrical Company: Critical Analyses of 29 Plays*. Jefferson, NC: MacFarland.

San Francisco Queer Theatre: Theatre Rhinoceros. Available at: www.therhino.org. Accessed July 20, 2008.

Solomon, Alisa, and Framji Minwalla. 2002. *The Queerest Art. Essays on Lesbian and Gay Theatre*. New York: New York University Press.

Split Britches Web site. Available at: http://www.splitbritches.com/. Accessed July 20, 2008.

Stone, Wendall C. 2005. *Caffe Cino: The Birthplace of Off-Off-Broadway*. Carbondale: Southern Illinois University Press.

Cleo House Jr.

theater and performance

In recent decades, theater and performance in the United States have provided both a haven of community and an effective means of political **activism** for LGBTQ Americans; however, American theater has also been a source of **homophobic** representations and practices. The first characters who clearly expressed same-sex desire, albeit doomed to villainy, despair, or death, appeared on the American stage as early as the 1920s; soon after, New York State passed a law barring plays that depicted what was considered sexual deviancy. While female impersonators thrived in Broadway follies and vaudeville, actors who donned **drag** as male characters who expressed desire for other men in a 1928 Mae West play, *Pleasure Man*, were arrested. Several of the most influential and acclaimed **playwrights** of the twentieth century—**Tennessee Williams, William Inge, Edward Albee,** and **Lorraine Hansberry**—were forced to stay on the threshold of the **closet,** out to their immediate circles but guarding against their sexual orientation becoming public. The 1960s advent of off-off-Broadway theaters like Caffé Cino and La MaMa, and the subsequent women's and **gay liberation** movements, paved the way for out performers and representations in companies and performance spaces such as Medusa's Revenge, WOW Café, the Ridiculous Theater Company, and Split Britches. Gay men and lesbians, such as directors Anne Bogart, George C. Wolfe, Michael Greif, and actress Cherry Jones, to name a few, have become influential, award-winning artists on Broadway and in regional theater. While positive depictions in mainstream theater abound today, much of the most vibrant and efficacious work still occurs in local LGBTQ communities, small **theater companies,** and performance venues. But artists and venues still face homophobia, loss of funding, and even threats of violence when producing openly LGBTQ work.

The **HIV/AIDS** epidemic devastated U.S. theater and performance, claiming the lives of many of the most active artists, but reactions to this unfathomable loss and to the local and federal governments' slow response to the crisis fueled new genres of both theater and activism. Playwrights like **Larry Kramer, Paula Vogel,** and **Tony Kushner** and **performance artists** like Tim Miller, among others, created (often-autobiographical) work that explores the lives of people with AIDS in order to engage, educate, memorialize, mourn, and inspire. Though some artists may resist certain of their works being categorized as AIDS theater, others embrace the distinction. Many performing artists turned to activism via groups like **ACT UP,** which has often incorporated bold theatrical techniques into its demonstrations for AIDS awareness, research, and equal access to treatment.

Throughout world history, theater has been associated with unorthodox genders and sexualities. Many performing artists, theorists, and scholars consider the defining methods and goals of theater as aligning with the common ground occupied by the various gender and sexual identities that make up the LGBTQ acronym. The development of **queer theory** in academia in the 1990s helped articulate one explanation for this affinity: Theater, for many practitioners and scholars, suits queerness because it can expose what Judith Butler theorizes as the **performativity** of identity. The practice of a performer of one identity taking on a different identity reveals **essentialism** to be an illusion and casts doubt on the naturalness of identity—gender, sexual, racial, or otherwise. Many LGBTQ performers find acting on the stage familiar because they feel as if they have spent most of their offstage lives acting in order to pass as straight, or at least to avoid homophobic harassment. At the same time, the majority of roles in mainstream theater are still cast within a narrow range of gender attributes, to which many lesbians and gay men cannot, or will not, conform. Also, many successful practitioners resist being ghettoized into doing work that relates only to their LGBTQ identity.

The diversity of experience has led to questioning whether LGBTQ theater and performance can indeed be grouped together. Some see the term queer theater as encompassing multiple perspectives, from performance art to **drag** shows, from community productions to mainstream plays, as well as queer readings of straight plays, and potentially even describing work by non-LGBTQ artists. Some, however, find that the terms queer, gay, or even gay and lesbian theater privilege the experiences of white and upper-middle-class artists and do not represent the unique goals and aesthetics of artists belonging to both LGBTQ and Chicana/o, African American, Asian American, immigrant, or working-class communities. Yet for other scholars and practitioners, queer is a position taken out of a vital need for community building and political resistance through theater and performance.

Further Reading

Bernstein, Robin, ed. 2006. *Cast Out: Queer Lives in the Theater*. Ann Arbor: University of Michigan Press.

Curtin, Kaier. 1987. *We Can Always Call Them Bulgarians: The Emergence of Lesbians and Gay Men on the American Stage*. Boston: Alyson Publications.

On the Purple Circuit. Available at: www.buddybuddy.com/pc.html. Accessed July 14, 2008.

Savran, David. 2003. *A Queer Sort of Materialism: Recontextualizing American Theater*. Ann Arbor: University of Michigan Press.

Sinfield, Alan. 1999. *Out on Stage: Lesbian and Gay Theatre in the Twentieth Century*. New Haven, CT: Yale University Press.

Soloman, Alisa, and Framji Minwalla, ed. 2002. *The Queerest Art: Essays on Lesbian and Gay Theater*. New York: New York University Press.

Catherine Burriss

theology, ethical

Ethical theology, and the synonymous moral theology and Christian ethics, essentially incorporates power, reason, and experience within the ongoing dialogue between entrenched divine-command traditions and historical consciousness. According to theologian Charles Curran (2005), who was hounded out of Catholic University in Washington, D.C., "induction replaces deduction.... Instead of striving for absolute certainty, we realize we only need reasonable probability for action" (Maceoin 1992).

The use of divine-command mandates in determining the ethical Christian position on homosexuality is prominent in many religious traditions. This activity demonstrates the difficulties and diversity of the interpretation of biblical texts. In the Old Testament, the specific condemnation of unnatural sexual behaviors is hardly unambiguous. If we examine the biblical account of Sodom and Gomorrah, and of the Levite's Concubine, in Judges, unnatural sexual behavior is not mutual homosexual intercourse between consenting adults, but homosexual rape. In the

New Testament, Jesus makes no statements about homosexuality. Rather, it is Paul of Tarsus whose letters to the Romans and Corinthians, and 1 Timothy (1:9–11), condemn unnatural acts between two women and between two men as damnable and perverted.

The scholarship of today's progressive theologians reevaluates and challenges the "juridical model of the [**Roman Catholic**] church's teaching authority...in which too much power is concentrated" (Maceoin 1999). The same is true of the major **Protestant** denominations—Baptist, Episcopal, Lutheran, Methodist, and Presbyterian—all of which profess to have unassailable, biblical authority with which to adjudge consensual homosexual acts. Yet, the Roman Catholic church and at least five Protestant traditions have reached a critical juncture on issues such as the ordination of gay and lesbian clergy, the appointment of homosexuals in positions of authority, and **same-sex marriages,** especially when local perspectives are at odds with national denominations. Exceptions are the Metropolitan Community Churches (MCC) and most Unitarian Universalist communities, which wholeheartedly accept and support same-sex couples and homosexual clergy. In other words, according to Edward C. Vacek, divine-command ethics is humanistically inadequate, even though it is the standard-bearer of popular Christian discourse.

Divine-command authority enforces the belief that homosexuality is immoral and against natural law. However, this is being replaced by deliberate and conscious reevaluations of ethical theological theories. In other words, ethical theories, based on mutual love, now perceive that the fulfillment of human nature is the goal of ethical action.

The natural-law approach thus stresses God's role as the creator of a natural order, which is inherently good and which is naturally suitable to a love relationship with God. From this perspective, the attractiveness of union with the divine motivates ethical theology. This position motivates reaching out to and embracing LGBTQ communities and relationships, including same-sex unions, the ordination of gay and lesbian clergy, and the inclusion of lesbians and gays in church communities.

Further Reading

Maceoin, Gary. 1992. "The Catholic Moral Tradition Today: A Synthesis." *National Catholic Reporter* 35 (32): 12. Available at: http://findarticles.com/p/articles/mi m1141/is 32 35/ ai_55052234. Accessed July 20, 2008.

Vacek, Edward Collins. 1996. "Divine-Command, Natural-Law, and Mutual-Love Ethics." *Theological Studies* 57(4): 633–54. Available at: http://www.dearey.alivewww.co.uk/HCE2004/ DivineCommand.htm. Accessed July 20, 2008.

Merry Gangemi

Michael Tilson Thomas (1944–)

The grandson of prominent performers in the Yiddish theater, Michael Tilson Thomas has made history as the first openly gay conductor to achieve professional success without hiding or disguising his sexual orientation. After completing musical training at the University of Southern California, where he studied with composer and conductor Ingolf Dahl and pianist John Crown, Thomas served as an assistant at the Wagner Festival in Bayreuth in 1966 and won the Koussevitsky Prize in 1968. Thomas began his professional life as the youngest assistant conductor the Boston Symphony had ever appointed, breaking into national prominence in October 1969 when he filled in for the ailing William Steinberg.

Thomas's rise through the world of international symphonic music included positions in Buffalo, Los Angeles, and London before his appointment as music director of the San Francisco Symphony in 1995, which welcomed him with a piece by openly gay Bay Area composer **Lou Harrison,** entitled "A Parade for M. T. T." His tenure in this last capacity has been marked by his stimulating and charismatic leadership that has resulted in increased popular support for the orchestra and by his commissioning of works from Harrison and other gay composers or works that take as their subject matter some aspect of gay and lesbian culture or history. Examples of this aspect of Thomas's career range from the founding of the American Mavericks music festival in San Francisco in June 2000 to the premiere of **David Del Tredici**'s 2001 orchestral song cycle *Gay Life*, formed of six songs based on the works of Thom Gunn, **Paul Monette,** and Allen Ginsberg. Other contemporary composers whose innovative work Thomas has chosen to highlight include Lukas Foss, Earle Brown, Steve Reich, and Meredith Monk, from whom he commissioned her first orchestral piece, *Possible Sky*, which premiered in Miami in 2003.

In addition to conducting, Thomas has also worked as a composer in his own right, with two of his pieces, *We Two Boys Together Clinging* and *Three Poems by Walt Whitman,* drawing inspiration from Walt Whitman's poetry. His creative accomplishments were recognized in 2005 when he was voted Artist of the Year by the readers of *Gramophone* magazine.

Further Reading

Rosenberg, Deena, and Bernard Rosenberg, eds. 1979. "Michael Tilson Thomas." In *The Music Makers*, 186–202. New York: Columbia University Press.
Seckerson, Edward. 1994. *Michael Tilson Thomas, viva voce: Conversations with Edward Seckerson.* London and Boston: Faber and Faber.

Robert Ridinger

Virgil Thomson (1896–1989)

Virgil (Garnett) Thomson was born in Kansas City and died in New York City. Long considered one of the great American composers of the first half of the twentieth century, Thomson received an extensive number of awards and honorary degrees, including the Pulitzer Prize in 1949 for the film score to *Louisiana Story,* the only time this award has been given to a film score. Thomson also wrote extensively on music, as the leading music critic of the *New York Herald Tribune* for 14 years and in a variety of books, including *The State of Music* (1938), *American Music since 1910* (1971), and his autobiography, *Virgil Thomson* (1966). Thomson remains best known for the scores he provided to Pare Lorentz's films *The Plow That Broke the Plains* (1936) and *The River* (1937) and his three operas, two with libretti by Gertrude Stein (*Four Saints in Three Acts* [1928] and *The Mother of Us All* [1946]), the third to a text by gay playwright Jack Larson (*Lord Byron*, 1969).

Despite the "queer" content of Thomson's operas, and the fact that he moved in a circle of predominantly queer (or bisexual) men and women, Thomson remained conflicted about his sexuality throughout his life. While his contemporary **Aaron Copland** seems to have been at ease with himself, Thomson told his biographer Anthony Tommasini, "I didn't want to be queer! No, no!" (1999, 69). Despite a series of involvements with other men throughout his life, including a long-term open relationship with painter Maurice Grosser (who provided the stage scenario for *Four Saints*), Thomson did everything he could to disguise his sexuality, including heavily editing his correspondence when it was published and demanding that friends make no mention of sexuality in reference to him. His concerns about staying closeted may have been tied to the night of March 14, 1942, when police raided a "gay bordello" in Manhattan and Thomson was arrested. Bailed out by his publisher from the *Tribune*, he then watched while the career of a leading Democratic senator was destroyed by widely published rumors that he had been a frequent guest at the same bordello. On all matters other than his sexuality, however, Thomson was distinctly opinionated and completely uninhibited about sharing his opinions with everybody else, whether they wanted to hear them or not. On the one hand, he could be incredibly politic and ingratiating ("He could charm the birds out of the trees" according to **Ned Rorem** [Tommasini 1999, 149]) and on the other hand, Maurice Grosser noted that Thomson could be "an intellectual and emotional bully" (Tommasini 1997, 48).

Thomson's two operas with Gertrude Stein set a standard for experimental music theater that was not equaled until the operas of Philip Glass in the late 1970s. *Four Saints*, in particular, helped to launch the notion of a "modern" approach to opera, by exploding just about every convention of the form. Directed by John Houseman, with choreography by Frederick Ashton and set design by the eccentric Florine Stettheimer, the opera featured an entirely African American cast. The premiere of this work was the highlight of the social and artistic season in 1934. Everyone who was anyone headed to Hartford for the premiere. Leading figures of the dance, music, and theater communities attended, including Buckminster Fuller, who arrived in his "dymaxion car." Stettheimer's set, made primarily out of cellophane and lit with bright, un-gelled light, was dazzlingly colorful. The production was such a success that the entire ensemble was then moved to a theater on Broadway, where the work ran for an unprecedented six weeks. Thomson's collaboration with Stein was not without difficulties, beyond the nonlinearity of her text and the challenges it posed for staging. While the collaboration initially went well, in 1931 the two had an argument that resulted in Stein cutting off all contact with Thomson for the next three years, until their opera was actually in production. Even then, she used a lawyer to communicate with Thomson about royalty issues. When Thomson returned to Paris in the late 1930s, he seldom visited Stein. Only after World War II, when he received a commission for a new opera from Columbia University, did he broach the idea of another collaboration. By this time, she was already ill with the cancer that was to take her life in 1946. The libretto of *The Mother of Us All*, about the life of suffragette Susan B. Anthony, was her last work. It would also become Thomson's most successful piece. First presented at Columbia University in 1947, Thomson noted late in life that he had received royalties for some 1,000 productions of this opera. In particular, the American Bicentennial in 1976, which also marked Thomson's 80th birthday, led to numerous productions across the country, including one designed by artist **Robert Indiana** that was recorded and broadcast on public television. *The Mother of Us All* remains the more "comprehensible" of the two Stein-Thomson collaborations.

In the years following World War II, and well into the 1970s, Thomson managed to draw around himself a set of bright gay artists, writers, and musicians. Some of them actually worked for him and received support from him for their efforts, notably composer Ned Rorem, who worked as a copyist for Thomson, which allowed Rorem to live in New York without parental support. **Gore Vidal** was also part of Thomson's circle in the 1960s, and Thomson was present on Fire Island the day in 1966 that poet Frank O'Hara was hit by a dune buggy and subsequently died of internal injuries.

Thomson's third opera, *Lord Byron*, is in many ways his most linear, having the semblance of a plot, thanks to the libretto by Jack Larson. Originally commissioned by the Metropolitan Opera in New York, after a full run-through of the work (semi-staged with singers from the Met as a gala sponsored by the Met's board), Rudolph Bing got cold feet about the work and decided that he did not want to produce it. Another three years of revision and work went into the piece before it was finally presented by the American Opera Center at the Juilliard School in 1972. Larson, who put some 10 years into the project, found the experience of working with Thomson to be daunting. Thomson's needs as a composer were often extremely specific, down to the rhyme scheme and rhythmic cadence of the text that he wanted. The work has typically met with mixed critical response, but the same could be said for many of Thomson's compositions. It remains to be seen whether Thomson's most lasting contribution to American music will be through his compositions, which have always met with divided critical responses, or through his writings about music, which have always been recognized as being of the highest caliber.

Further Reading

Kostelanetz, Richard. 2002. *Virgil Thomson: A Reader: Selected Writings, 1924–1984*. New York: Routledge.

Thomson, Virgil. 1984. *A Virgil Thomson Reader*. New York: Plume.

Tommasini, Anthony. 1997. *Virgil Thomson: Composer on the Aisle*. New York: W. W. Norton.

Jeff Abell

throw shade

A subcultural idiom popularized by the 1990 Jennie Livingston documentary *Paris Is Burning, throwing shade* refers not to an umbrageous conventional meaning but to the processes of a publicly performed dissimulation that aims either to protect oneself from ridicule or to verbally or psychologically attack others in a haughty or derogatory manner. As early as the 1980s, commentators located this new use of shade in the **ballroom** and vogue culture of New York City's ethnic working-class community, particularly among gender and sexual nonconformists.

Further Reading

Becquer, Marcos, and Jose Gatti. 1991. "Elements of Vogue." *Third Text* 16/17: 65–82.

Butler, Judith. 1993. "Gender Is Burning: Questions of Appropriation and Subversion." In *Bodies That Matter: On the Discursive Limits of "Sex,"* 121–40. New York: Routledge.

Paris Is Burning. 1990. Dir. Jennie Livingston. Perf. Anji Xtravaganza, Shari Headley, André Christian, Carmen and Brooke, Danny Xtravaganza. (DVD. Miramax, 2005.)

Ross, Andrew. 1994. "Tribalism in Effect." In *On Fashion*, ed. Shari Benstock and Suzanne Ferriss, 284–300. New Brunswick, NJ: Rutgers University Press.

Joel C. Adams

James Tinney (1942–1988)

Dr. James S. Tinney was a pastor, professor, and journalist and one of the leading authorities on Black Pentecostalism. Born in Kansas City, Missouri, Tinney preached from the age of 14, becoming an ordained minister at 18. During the 1960s he was pastor of churches in Missouri and Arkansas and the assistant editor of *Kansas City Call*. In the early 1970s Tinney completed graduate education in journalism at Howard University while working as the editor of the *Washington Afro-American* newspaper. In 1976 Tinney became an assistant professor of journalism at Howard University and established the first academic journal on Black Pentecostalism, *Spirit: A Journal of Issues Incident in Black Pentecostalism*. In 1979, Tinney came out publicly at the Third World Lesbian and Gay Conference and was subsequently excommunicated from the Temple Church of God in Christ. Tinney was instrumental in opening up a dialogue between Pentecostalism and homosexuality and founding the Pentecostal Coalition for Human Rights in 1980. In 1982, Tinney established a nondenominational church, Faith Temple, which had a large black gay and lesbian congregation. Tinney was politically active until his death from AIDS-related illnesses, organizing a number of conferences and publishing in a variety of books, journals, and newspapers.

Further Reading

Tinney, James S. 1986. "Why a Black Gay Church?" In *In the Life: A Black Gay Anthology*, ed. Joseph Beam, 70–86. Boston, Alyson Publications.

Douglas Field

Nancy Toder (1948–)

Nancy Toder was born in New York City, where she attended the Bronx High School of Science. She majored in psychology at the State University of New York in Buffalo and earned a PhD in psychology from the University of California, Los

Angeles; she completed psychoanalytic training at the Newport Psychoanalytic Institute. Toder works in California as a psychologist focusing on lesbian issues. As a psychologist, Toder has not only contributed professionally to **Lesbian Psychologies,** but she has also reached a wider audience through her contribution to Betty Berzon's *Positively Gay.*

Toder's greatest single contribution to lesbian culture, however, has been her only novel, *Choices.* In part one, college roommates Sandy and Jenny become best friends and eventually become sexually involved. Jenny struggles with internalized **homophobia** and insists on dating men to keep their relationship in the **closet.** This ends with their college graduation, after which Jenny insists that their sexual relationship must end. Part two occurs 10 years later; both women are psychologists and run into each other at a professional convention. Sandy is personally and professionally out as a lesbian and is in a committed lesbian relationship, and Jenny is in a heterosexual marriage. Both struggle to sort out their own lesbian cultural identities as they face their past relationship together and the choices they have made. Jenny is unsure of the meaning of her prior relationship with Sandy; Sandy is unsure of the meaning of her continued attraction to Jenny. By interrogating the ways in which lesbians' choices are limited by cultural, psychological, and political realities, *Choices* is consistent with assumptions that positive literary representations contribute to the possibility of more positive choices for lesbian identity and relationships.

Further Reading

MacPike, Loralee. 1993. "Nancy Toder." In *Contemporary Lesbian Writers of the United States,* ed. Sandra Pollack and Denise D. Knight, 540–43. Westport, CT: Greenwood Press.

Toder, Nancy. 2001. "Lesbian Couples: Special Issues." In *Positively Gay: New Approaches to Gay and Lesbian Life,* ed. Betty Berzon, 41–55. Berkeley, CA: Celestial Arts.

Zimmerman, Bonnie. 1990. *The Safe Sea of Women: Lesbian Fiction 1969–1989.* Boston: Beacon Press.

Danielle M. DeMuth

tourism, cruises, and resorts

The earliest documented examples of what we would today refer to as gay and lesbian tourism can be traced to the Victorian period, when homosexual men from northern Europe embarked on tours of the Mediterranean region, including Italy and Greece. These wealthy and educated men traveled under the guise of seeing historical sites and great works of art and architecture, but their true goal was often to find the companionship of young men. Some women may have also traveled as a way of escaping the strict sexual norms of home, but this was much less common, due to social restrictions that generally prevented women from traveling without male companions. This kind of travel was reserved for the wealthy, as they were the only ones who could afford such excursions. During the twentieth century, however, advances in transportation and communication made leisure travel increasingly available to middle- and working-class individuals. As more LGBTQ people acquired the means to travel, they needed information about where to go to meet others like them, which led to the development of a variety of printed gay travel guides.

The first widely distributed gay travel guides appeared in the 1960s. Most notable among these was *Bob Damron's Address Book,* commonly referred to as *Damron's.* The book's creator, Bob Damron, was a gay bar owner and avid traveler from San Francisco. First published in 1964, the pocket-sized book initially offered a listing of names and addresses of over 750 gay and lesbian establishments, mostly in the nation's largest cities. Subsequent issues of the book became more detailed and professional, expanding beyond a few large cities to reach all parts of the country. Now boasting over 12,000 listings and published in two versions (one for men and one for women), *Damron's* continues to be a valuable resource for gay and lesbian travelers.

Arriving at the end of the 1960s was *Spartacus International Gay Guide.* As *Damron's* became the dominant guide to the United States, *Spartacus* became the dominant international guide. Like *Damron's*, *Spartacus* offered a basic listing of names and addresses of gay-owned and gay-friendly establishments, adding overviews of individual countries' laws and social mores as they applied to LGBTQ individuals.

While *Damron's* and *Spartacus* grew and thrived over the years and continue to be available, many of the other early publications had much shorter life spans. Guides like *The Lavender Baedeker, The Grey Guide, The International Guild Guide, Directory 43, Barfly,* and *World Report Travel Guide* contributed to the dissemination of information about gay establishments, but none of them found the long-lasting success of *Damron's* and *Spartacus*. While these guides generally included listings for both gay men and lesbians, they tended to focus on information for men. *Gaia's Guide* and *The Girls Guide*, both appearing in the 1970s, offered information specifically for lesbian travelers.

Regardless of their gender focus, these early guides all had a few characteristics in common. They were very simple, offering basic lists of establishments, sometimes including a coding or ranking system, but offering little detailed information. They were also limited to **bars,** clubs, **bookstores,** and other gay- and lesbian-oriented establishments. These guides were not intended to help gay and lesbian travelers plan entire vacations. Rather, they represented a network of homosexuals sharing information with one another, allowing each other to find safe spaces and meet other homosexuals when traveling away from home. Eventually, the underground nature of this communication changed, as the publishers of mainstream travel guides began offering editions aimed specifically at gays and lesbians. In the 1980s, both Fodor's and Frommer's published guides for gay tourists. Unlike the basic names-and-addresses approach of most gay guides, these books offered more detailed information about hotels, attractions, museums, and anything else that would likely interest LGBTQ tourists.

In addition to the surviving gay guides and travel books from mainstream publishers, today's gay and lesbian travelers can read about various destinations in a number of magazines and online newsletters. *Passport* is the most popular gay and lesbian travel magazine, covering both international and domestic travel. The magazine offers regular columns about international events and festivals, helpful hints and advice, and issues pertaining specifically to gay and lesbian business travelers. *The Out Traveler,* from the publishers of the glossy gay monthly *Out,* also provides information about domestic and international destinations, along with tips for saving money, interacting with locals, and negotiating travel logistics. *Out and About, Gay Travel News,* and *QT Magazine* all offer online magazines/newsletters about travel and tourist destinations, with links to various hotels, travel agents, and tourist attractions.

Although gays and lesbians travel to all parts of the country and the world, a handful of cities and resort areas have consistently attracted large numbers of gay and lesbian tourists. In general, large cities tend to attract more gay tourists and residents than other areas. In the early to mid-1900s, as suburbs began to grow up around major cities, large populations moved away from the urban cores. This created vacancies in urban areas, and these vacancies were filled not only by racial and ethnic minorities and those of lower socioeconomic status but also by gays and lesbians, who created their

A demonstrator dressed as a blue angel takes part in the annual gay pride parade in Paris in this June 29, 2002, photo. Paris tourism officials want to give new meaning to the term "Gay Paree" by selling Paris as a leading destination for LGBTQ travelers. AP Photo/ Jacques Brinon.

own spaces of safety and acceptance. Some of these urban neighborhoods became particularly well known among gays and lesbians, attracting both permanent residents and visitors who wanted a taste of life in a more tolerant environment.

In particular, West Hollywood in **Los Angeles,** Greenwich Village in **New York City,** and the Castro in **San Francisco** became known as gay havens, attracting large numbers of gay and lesbian tourists to the cities of which they are a part. More recently, the gay gentrification of Miami's run-down South Beach neighborhood has turned it from a hotbed of **homophobia** (thanks to Anita Bryant's well-publicized efforts to repeal the surrounding county's gay rights ordinance in the late 1970s) to a gay mecca, attracting both residents and tourists.

A number of beach resorts have also become favorites among gays and lesbians, drawing crowds during peak vacation times and maintaining significant gay and lesbian populations year-round. **Provincetown,** Massachusetts, a beachfront community located at the tip of Cape Cod, is the largest gay and lesbian resort in the country. The town was initially a summer resort populated largely by artists and playwrights, many of whom were gay, thus establishing a tradition of openness and acceptance in the community. The town promotes itself as a welcoming environment for alternative families, offers same-sex marriage packages, and hosts dozens of gay- and lesbian-themed events throughout the year. It is a particular favorite among lesbian travelers, due to the large year-round lesbian population and the many women-owned restaurants, clubs, and bed and breakfasts. Each October, the town hosts Women's Week, which regularly draws over 5,000 visitors

Russian River, California, 1980, a popular gay tourism spot. Courtesy of the Gay, Lesbian, Bisexual, Transgender Historical Society, San Francisco.

and features concerts, comedians, a golf tournament, and a prom, among other activities.

Key West, Florida, has also made a name for itself, drawing gay and lesbian tourists to its tropical climate year-round. The island features a well-established community of gay-owned businesses, organized and promoted by the Key West Business Guild, which functions as a gay-oriented chamber of commerce. Although the island features events, guesthouses, and activities for both men and women, Key West has primarily been a gay men's resort. The exception to this is the week of the annual Womenfest, which features women-only activities, including snorkeling and fishing trips.

Like Key West, Palm Springs, California, attracts a predominantly gay male crowd. Drawn to the beautiful Southern California climate, visitors are treated to numerous restaurants, clubs, spas, and clothing-optional hotels. For one week during the spring, the tourist population is dominated by lesbians, as women from around the country enjoy the festivities surrounding the LPGA Dinah Shore Golf Tournament. Beyond the tournament itself, visitors take part in dance parties, pool parties, and celebrity entertainment in a lesbian-friendly surrounding.

Fire Island, New York, located just off Long Island, is a popular resort for New York City residents looking to escape the city. The island includes two gay communities, each with its own characteristics and population, in terms of both residents and visitors. Cherry Grove is inhabited by approximately equal numbers of gays and lesbians, while The Pines is predominantly gay male. The Pines has developed a reputation for attracting young, fit, image-conscious gays, while Cherry Grove attracts a more varied crowd, including older gays and lesbians and families. Other beach resorts on the Atlantic attracting large numbers of gay visitors include Rehoboth Beach in Delaware and Ft. Lauderdale in Florida.

Many gay and lesbian travelers choose to build their vacations around organized gay and lesbian tours and cruises. The earliest tours of this kind appeared in the 1960s, when ONE, Incorporated, a San Francisco–based homophile organization, put together tours of Europe, the Mediterranean, and the Caribbean. These early trips were open to members only and were promoted solely within the organization. Hanns Ebensten, recognized by many as the inventor of gay travel, was the first to organize trips that were aimed at the entire gay public. Going beyond the standard beach vacations, Ebensten's company organized tours to such exotic locations as the Amazon River and the Galapagos Islands.

The current market is dominated by three tour organizers: RSVP, Atlantis, and Olivia. RSVP Vacations and Atlantis Events offer packages for both gays and lesbians, while Olivia focuses on women only. RSVP began offering gay cruises in the mid-1980s and currently offers a variety of vacation types, including large ships, small ships, riverboats, and land tours in all parts of the world. Atlantis, started in the early 1990s, bills itself as the largest company in the world dedicated to gay and lesbian vacations. Like RSVP, Atlantis books entire cruise ships and resorts to create a unique, gay-friendly environment away from the heteronormative world.

Olivia Cruises and Resorts began in 1990 as an offshoot of a women's music collective that had been founded in the early 1970s. Founder Judy Dlugacz saw a market for women-only vacations, and Olivia Cruises was born. Drawing on the inspiration that drove the music collective, Olivia currently aims to offer packages that celebrate the lives of lesbians, their friends, and their families, offering empowerment and visibility to all women.

A more recent addition to the cruise industry is R Family Cruises, which gained attention in part because of its celebrity cofounder Rosie O'Donnell, who started the company with her partner Kelli and former Atlantis executive Gregg Kaminsky. R Family is dedicated to providing vacations for gays and lesbians who want to travel with their families. The result is a passenger list composed of different generations of gays and straights, creating a gay-friendly travel atmosphere.

Bringing together all of the tour companies, resorts, and destinations is the International Gay and Lesbian Travel Association (IGLTA). Founded in 1983 and boasting more than 1,000 travel professionals as members, the IGLTA coordinates airlines, hotels, resorts, travel agents, car rental agencies, and more to provide gay and lesbian travelers with information about gay-owned and gay-friendly services and destinations. Because IGLTA is affiliated with many mainstream, straight-owned companies, it acts as a bridge between gay tourists and the mainstream travel industry. In part because of the efforts of IGLTA, and in part because of the increased visibility of the LGBTQ market in general, companies and destinations not previously associated with gays and lesbians have recently begun to openly court them as consumers. Hotels, airlines, and rental agencies regularly run ads in periodicals like the *Advocate*, and cities like Washington, D.C., and Philadelphia prominently feature appeals to gays and lesbians in their marketing campaigns. This seems to reflect an acknowledgment of gays as consumers more than an acceptance of homosexuality in general, as evidenced by the fact that gay cruise ships are sometimes turned away from ports or picketed by hostile locals, and urban gay neighborhoods continue

Drinks are laid out by Hornblower Cruises for visitors to a special wedding pavilion at the Lesbian Gay Bisexual Transgender Pride Business Expo in San Francisco, June 2008. The ruling by the California Supreme Court to legalize gay marriage in the state could give a boost to California's sputtering economy. Thousands of same-sex couples from across the nation may begin to converge on the state for wedding ceremonies after the decision, which took effect on June 16, 2008. AP Photo/Eric Risberg.

to be primary targets of homophobic violence. Despite these problems, in just a few decades gay and lesbian tourism has been transformed from an underground network of individuals sharing bits of travel information to a multibillion-dollar global industry.

Further Reading

Archer, Jesse. 2007. *You Can Run: Gay, Glam, and Gritty Travels in South America*. Binghamton, NY: Haworth.

Clift, Stephen, Michael Luongo, and Carry Callister, eds. 2002. *Gay Tourism: Culture, Identity and Sex*. London: Continuum.

Clift, Stephen, and Simon Carter, eds. 2002. *Tourism and Sex: Culture, Commerce, and Coercion*. London: Pinter.

Waitt, Gordon, and Kevin Markwell. 2006. *Gay Tourism: Culture and Context*. New York: Haworth Hospitality Press.

David Coon

trade

The term *trade* has had numerous meanings since its inception in the late eighteenth century as a term describing male partners of female prostitutes. In the nineteenth century the term migrated to the gay community and referred to the male customer of a "fairy" prostitute, but by 1910 the term referred to any straight man who engaged in sexual activities with gay men. The term became more specific as it came to describe a sexual partner who was "normal," or a "real man" in terms of dominant notions of masculinity in the prewar era. Set in opposition to fairies, trade were aggressively masculine, ideally sailors or soldiers, and generally considered straight even though open to sexual advances by effeminate queers. Because of the dominance of effeminacy in defining gayness, trade could participate in sexual activities without being labeled gay, assuming they maintained a masculine and dominant role. Those who maintain a hypermasculinity are sometimes referred to as *rough trade*.

More recently, trade has referred to reputedly heterosexual men who work as prostitutes in the gay-identified male community, thus allying trade with sex for monetary exchange. Trade can refer to either straight-identified men who trade sex for money or those who have sex with effeminate men for pleasure. Essential to the definition in either case is an assumption of nonreciprocal sexual relations. The relationship marks a disjunction between sexual identity (gay or straight) and sexual acts, in that engaging in sexual activity with men does not necessarily lead to the assumption of a gay identity.

Further Reading

Arobateau, Red Jordan. 1996. *Rough Trade*. New York: Rosebud.

Chauncy, George. 1995. *Gay New York: Gender, Urban Culture, and the Making of the Gay Male World, 1890–1940*. New York: Basic Books.

Delany, Samuel. 2001. *Times Square Red, Times Square Blue*. New York: New York University Press.
Humphreys, Laud. 1975. *Tearoom Trade: Impersonal Sex in Public Places*. Hawthorne, NY: Aldine.

Kate Drabinski

transgender

Although *transgender* has sometimes been used to describe or imply a sexuality, in fact it more technically describes, as Susan Stryker puts it, "people who move away from the gender they were assigned at birth" (2008, 1). This move may simply involve wearing the clothes, or taking on the manners of, the opposite sex, as the clothes and manners are dictated by a particular era, in which case this is more accurately described as transvesting. **Drag** can be implicated in this understanding of the term, but a cross-dressing man like Virginia Prince and her Society of the Second Self (**Tri-Ess**) propagated transvestism as an activity of heterosexual men—thus not implicating one's sexuality. With Christine Jorgensen's emergence onto the public scene in the early 1950s, though, the actual surgical transformation from one gender to another became the more typical understanding of the term transgender. Jorgensen had been a man in the army for a year before going to Denmark for the operation that was, at the time, illegal in the United States.

Stryker's succinct summary is helpful: "one's gender identity," she writes, "could perhaps best be described as how one feels about being referred to by a particular pronoun" (2008, 13). Some choose to invent new pronouns to more accurately reflect new realities, thus, *ze, hir, s/he*, and so on. In today's parlance, those who were born as females but who live as males (whether with or without surgery) are called *transmen*, and those born as males who now live as women (again, with or without surgery) are called *transwomen*.

The gay and lesbian liberation movements are indebted to the early and pivotal roles played by transvestites and transgendered individuals who fought against discrimination by police and restaurateurs at Cooper's Donuts in Los Angeles in 1959, Dewey's coffeehouse in Philadelphia in 1965, and Compton's Cafeteria in San Francisco in 1966, and in the Stonewall Riots in Greenwich Village in 1969. But the history of the movements largely parted company during the **identity politics** that relied on an **essentialist** reading of the biological basis for homosexuality, and then the delisting of homosexuality as a mental illness. As Stryker notes, during this period the transgender community had apparently more in common with the reproductive freedom movement that sought legal and safe access to medical treatment. The women's movement still struggles with the notion of postoperative transwomen as "real" women, sometimes excluding them from women-only events.

Among the significant individuals who played important roles in the slow progress being made in the United States on the issues involved in the meaning and legal rights of the transgendered was Reed Erickson, who helped fund institutes at major American universities exploring the expanding possibilities made possible by modern medicine. Harry Benjamin was the first medical authority on the topic in the United States. Lou Sullivan was an early organizer, as was Sylvia Rivera. **Leslie Feinberg** is, perhaps, the most prominent spokesperson for the transgendered today.

Further Reading

Boylan, Jennifer Finney. 2003. *She's Not There: A Life in Two Genders.* New York: Broadway Books.

Eskridge, William. 1997. *Gaylaw: Challenging the Apartheid of the Closet.* Cambridge: Harvard University Press.

Hirschfeld, Magnus. 1991 [1910]. *Transvestites: The Erotic Drive to Cross-Dress.* Prometheus.

Mollenkott, Virginia Ramey. 2007. *Omnigender: A Trans-Religious Approach.* Pilgrim Press.

Stone, Sandy. 1993. "The 'Empire' Strikes Back: A Posttranssexual Manifesto." Available at: http://www.ucm.es/info/rqtr/biblioteca/Transexualidad/trans%20manifesto.pdf. Accessed July 21, 2008.

Stryker, Susan. 2008. *Transgender History.* San Francisco: Seal Press.

Valentine, David. 2007. *Imagining Transgender: An Ethnography of a Category.* Durham, NC: Duke University Press.

John C. Hawley

transgender health

Since the first documented transsexual surgery, performed in Germany in 1930, transgender health care has evolved substantially but has also been a subject of significant debate, particularly between the nontransgender medical professionals who have developed health protocols and the transgender individuals on whom such protocols have a direct impact. While there have been a few sensational cases of transgender surgeries performed in Europe, all on male-to-female spectrum individuals, surgeons have been performing surgeries and refining techniques in the United States for the last 30 years with increasingly positive results.

Current standards have arisen from the work of Dr. Harry Benjamin, an endocrinologist who was among the first doctors to publish work on the treatment of transgender people with medical rather than psychiatric intervention. His theories, especially his assertion that some transgender individuals would benefit more from hormone therapy and/or other medical treatments, persist to this day in the eponymous Harry Benjamin International Gender Dysphoria Association (HBIGDA) Standards of Care. This document, now in its sixth revision, details a regimen of psychotherapy, hormone replacement therapy, and surgery for transgender persons. Earlier versions were strongly criticized for being dependent on heterosexual outcomes and/or gender normativity as well as excessive "gatekeeping" (the measure of the amount of power in the hands of doctors to decide whether a person is eligible to transition).

Typically, transgender people will do some combination of hormone replacement therapy (HRT) and sex-reassignment surgery (SRS; also called gender confirmation surgery, or GCS), in that order. For female-to-male spectrum transpeople, hormone therapy is a regimen of testosterone, injected or applied in a topical gel. Testosterone therapy often produces a substantial masculinizing effect, including facial hair, masculinized body shape, male pattern baldness, lowered voice, enlarged clitoris, and cessation of menstrual periods. In male-to-female spectrum transpeople, the effects of HRT (injected or oral estrogen, sometimes interspersed with short courses of progesterone) are somewhat feminizing—softer skin, less body and facial hair, breast growth, redistribution of body fat to the hips and buttocks, softening of jawline, and cessation of hair loss.

Male-to-female spectrum transpeople are much more likely to have genital SRS, often called "bottom surgery," in large part because the procedures for vaginoplasty and labiaplasty (creating a vagina and outer labia) are better developed than phalloplasty (creating a penis). An alternative female-to-male spectrum genital surgery, metoidioplasty, releases the hormone-enlarged clitoris so that it more closely approximates a typical penis; it is much more popular as it is less expensive and less invasive, with a much lower risk of loss of sexual sensation. Female-to-male spectrum "top surgery," the removal of both breasts and reshaping of the chest into a more normatively male shape, is conversely a much more popular surgery than the male-to-female spectrum equivalent, breast augmentation, in part because the breast growth brought on by estrogen in men.

It is important to note that not all transgender people who live their lives in their expressed gender choose medical intervention. For some the costs are prohibitive, whereas others have health issues or ideological disagreements with the surgical process. Unfortunately, because surgery is required in all states in the United States to change the sex markers of government documents, transgender medical intervention is not always entirely at the discretion of the individual. For other transgender individuals, medical intervention comes as a substantial relief of their sense that their bodies do not match their expressed gender, and they begin HRT or have SRS as soon as is feasible for them.

Historically, transgender people have been required to be under the care of an HBIGDA-certified therapist or psychiatrist before beginning medical transition. Proponents of this regimen claim that this helps incipient transgender people to clarify what life issues are related to their gender and which ones will best be managed by other methods, whereas those critical of the process claim that this regimen selects for certain kinds of people, mostly those who conform to a white middle-class version of gender normativity in the expressed gender of the transperson. There is also significant debate about the concept of Gender Identity Disorder (GID) as a medical and/or psychiatric condition. Classifying transgender people as "suffering from a medical disorder" is helpful in accessing services for those who choose medical transition, and it often prompts sympathy and understanding from nontransgender people. Some theorists argue, however, that the problem is not with the transperson but with a gendered society, and the discussion rages on.

While no medical research has been done into what has been termed *transsexual regret*—that is, people who socially or medically transition and then wish they had not—there are several well-known cases of doctors re-sexing infants due to atypical genitalia which seem to conclude that gender is innate to a person and not a function of upbringing.

There are several classes of risk involved with transgender medical transition. Female-to-male spectrum transgender individuals taking testosterone have been known to experience liver damage and are believed by many doctors, though no peer-reviewed studies have yet been completed, to be at greater risk for heart disease and stroke. Male-to-female spectrum HRT often contributes to a loss of muscle mass and bone density, believed by some physicians to compromise length of life. Across the transgender spectrum, unused gonads (ovaries and/or testicles) are often prophylactically removed to prevent potential cancerous growth. SRS also carries significant potential risk, not only general surgical risks (aversion to anesthesia, infection) but also loss of nipple sensation (both female-to-male and male-to-female spectrum surgeries), loss of genital sensation (again in both communities), and urinary tract issues (especially when the urinary tract has been rerouted, cases of catastrophic failure have been reported). Nevertheless, transgender people who opt for surgery almost universally report that the rewards outweigh the risks and that their lives are improved even if there are complications because they feel more comfortable with themselves and better able to negotiate the world with bodies that more closely match their expressed genders.

Further Reading

"Transgender Health." Available at: http://www.metrokc.gov/health/glbt/transgender.htm. Accessed February 22, 2008.

"Transgender Health Action Coalition." Available at: http://www.critpath.org/thac. Accessed February 22, 2008.

S. Bear Bergman

transgender life stories

The term *transgender* is one whose definition is more complex than it seems, focusing on the essential point of existence as an individual who rejects a gender assignment based on body configuration in favor of a wider range of options than simply male or female, selecting an outer presentation that truly mirrors a deeply felt emotional reality. Transgender people may choose to identify as heterosexuals, gay or lesbian, bisexuals, or pansexual, or even to refuse any specific label and simply be human.

While the early homosexual activist Karl Heinrich Ulrichs had referred to gay men as having "female souls in male bodies" in the late nineteenth century, this concept was not widely adopted by sex researchers prior to World War II. Prior to the development of successful surgical techniques in Scandinavia in the 1930s that allowed individuals to alter their biological gender of birth (often accompanied by intensive hormone therapies), the concept of physically altering one's identity as male or female belonged to the realm of mythology and legend. These operations laid the foundations for the movement of these people's stories out of purely clinical contexts and into a more accessible format for a wider public. These techniques were often applied to persons diagnosed with a condition termed *gender dysphoria*, defined as the feeling of being male or female but trapped in a physical body not representative of their self.

The genre of biographical and autobiographical writings dealing with the life experiences of transgender and transsexual individuals can be said to have begun in Western European literature with the publication in 1931 in Denmark of *Fra mand til kvinde* (*From Man to Woman*), the story of Lili Elbe and her former life as the painter Einar Wegener; a German translation followed in

Lou Sullivan, an HIV-infected, gay-identified transman, began the first support group that eventually turned into FTM International, the leading national organization for social support for transmen. Photo by Marie Ueda, courtesy of the Gay, Lesbian, Bisexual, Transgender Historical Society, San Francisco.

1932. Translations into English appeared in London and New York in 1933 under the title *Man into Woman: An Authentic Record of a Change of Sex*. Other national literatures ranging from Canada, the United Kingdom, and France to Russia and Australia also have similar accounts, mainly published since the 1980s. One aspect of the subject that makes historical research into its emergence and development somewhat problematic is the shifting meaning assigned to the term transgender, which has at times been applied to subjects such as transvestism as well as transsexual identities, the current set of meanings not stabilizing in general usage in the social sciences until the early 1980s.

In the United States, this species of book made its debut with the publication of Christine Jorgensen's account of her transition from male to female in 1967. The next 40 years would see the gradual crystallization of the transgender sexual community as a focus and constituency within sexual activism and the concomitant rise in demand for (and acceptability of) accounts of the lives of the women and men who determined to resolve their questions of identity by adopting a changed gender identity, whether by modes of speech and dress or through transformative surgery. The majority of English-language works would appear from American publishers, although in some cases the stories of U.S. citizens appeared in print from publishing houses in the United Kingdom and Canada and were never reprinted within the borders of their home nation. This may be due in part to the hidden nature of the subject (unfamiliar to manuscript editors outside the fields of medicine and psychiatry) and the reluctance of transgender persons to reveal this aspect of themselves to anyone beyond a personally trusted circle. There are also cases in which a biological gender body form was damaged through accident and the individual was raised to identify with the other gender in dress and behaviors, but then was moved to reclaim the birth gender in later life, as in the case of John Colapinto, who related his experiences in *As Nature Made Him: The Boy Who Was Raised as a Girl* (2000). A further complication in tracking the history of this genre is the fact that many of the older autobiographical accounts may exist only as parts of medical case files and are thus inaccessible to the general reader.

The genre is marked by several characteristics. A review of titles indicates that the majority of these works are accounts of transitions from male to female gender identity, following the pattern set by the initial Jorgensen book. Female-to-male (FTM) transgender changes are less represented, the one major collection being Holly Devor's 1997 work *FTM: Female-to-Male Transsexuals in Society*. Only three anthologies of personal accounts have been published in English to date: *Finding the Real Me: True Tales of Sex and Gender Diversity* in 2003, *From the Inside Out: Radical Gender Transformation, FTM and Beyond* in 2004, and *Sexual Metamorphosis: An Anthology of Transsexual Memoirs* in 2005. It has even been the subject of doctoral research, as in "Transitional Matters: The Body Narratives of Transsexual Autobiography," a dissertation by Jay Prosser accepted at the City University of New York in 1996, and "Trans/acting Truths: Narrating Transgender in Theory and Practice," presented in 2005 by Dorthe Troeften to the University of Minnesota. The personal account has also been the subject of comparative research in women's studies, for example, in Tracy Lee's 2001 article "Trans(Re)Lations—Lesbian and Female to Male Transsexual Accounts of Identity."

In the extant nonfiction literature on the trans community, consideration is often given to the role that autobiographical and biographical writings can and have played in the discussions of the definition and maintenance of gender. Examples of this are *Invisible Lives: The Erasure of Transsexual and Transgendered People* by Viviane K. Namaste (2000) and *Self-Made Men: Identity and Embodiment among Transsexual Men* by Henry Rubin (2003). An unusual combination of personal written and visual expression is seen in the widely discussed volume *Body Alchemy: Transsexual Portraits*, created by Loren Cameron (1996), which presents groups of high-quality photographs accompanied by reflections. Individual stories also form the framework of evidence presented by activists working for more equitable treatment of transgender and transsexual people in American society, mirroring the books of personal accounts of gays and lesbians that appeared in the first wave of gay liberation in the 1970s. The most recent discussion of this newly vocal liberation effort is Deborah Rudacille's *The Riddle of Gender: Science, Activism and Transgender Rights* (2005).

American actress and transsexual performer Candis Cayne attends the 39th Annual LGBT Pride Parade along Fifth Avenue in Manhattan, June 29, 2008, in New York. Photo by: Curtis Means/NBC NewsWire via AP Images.

Transgender biography and autobiography have also appeared as fiction, both from mainstream writers such as Virginia Woolf (whose 1928 work *Orlando* features a main character whose gender identity shifts over time) and writers creating out of an LGBT cultural context, the latter clustered in the late twentieth and early twenty-first centuries. Recent works of this nature include **Leslie Feinberg**'s *Stone Butch Blues* (1993), which was awarded both the Lambda Literary Award and the Stonewall Book Award for Literature in 1994; Christopher Bohjalian's *Trans-Sister Radio: A Novel* (2000); and the story collection *Transgender Erotica: Trans Figures* (2006).

The rise of the Internet has also provided the transgender community with a new venue for the sharing of information on everything from surgical techniques to the pitfalls of learning the myriad behavioral and cultural acts and clues expected of each biological gender. The open anonymity provided by the online environment has led to a proliferation of sites where personal experiences can be shared and questions posed out of them. Sites vary from the home pages of individuals and their online diaries to a collection of accounts posted as part of a support group at a **Midwestern** university. This faceless accessibility has both assisted and complicated the efforts of those activists who work for a better existence for transgender folk through the sharing of individual lives.

Further Reading

Betz, Phyllis M. 2000. "Transsexualism/Transgenderism: Autobiography." In *Reader's Guide to Lesbian and Gay Studies*, ed. Timothy F. Murphy, 585–86. Chicago: Fitzroy Dearborn.

Boylan, Jennifer Finney. 2008. *I'm Looking Through You: Growing Up Haunted: A Memoir*. New York: Broadway.

Califia-Rice, Patrick. 1997. "Contemporary Transsexual Autobiography." In *Sex Changes: The Politics of Transgenderism*, 163–95. San Francisco: Cleis.

Califia-Rice, Patrick. 1997. "Transsexual Autobiography: The First Wave." In *Sex Changes: The Politics of Transgenderism*, 11–51. San Francisco: Cleis.

James, Andrea, Web site. Available at: http://www.andreajames.com. Accessed December 19, 2007.

Kane-Demaios, J. Ari., and Vern L. Bullough. 2006. *Crossing Sexual Boundaries: Transgender Journeys, Uncharted Paths*. Amherst, NY: Prometheus Books.

Kennedy, Pagan. 2007. *The First Man-Made Man: The Story of Two Sex Changes, One Love Affair, and a Twentieth-Century Revolution*. London: Bloomsbury.

Lev, Arlene Istar. 2004. *Transgender Emergence: Therapeutic Guidelines for Working with Gender-Variant People and Their Families*. Binghamton, NY: Haworth.

Red without Blue. 2007. Dir. Brooke Sebold and Benita Sills. Sundance Channel.

Robert Ridinger

Transgender Nation

Founded in 1992 as an offshoot of the San Francisco chapter of **Queer Nation,** Transgender Nation was part of the burgeoning movement for transgender rights. The same year also saw the publication of **Leslie Feinberg**'s pamphlet "Transgender Liberation: A Movement Whose Time Has Come," one of the first documents to use *transgender* as an inclusive political term for all gender-variant people who struggled with political oppression. Transgender Nation sought to bring transgender issues to the forefront of the **gay liberation movement.**

Queer Nation was inspired by the confrontational and creative direct-action techniques pioneered in the 1980s and 1990s by **ACT UP.** Both groups eschewed political lobbying in favor of public protests at major national institutions, like the National Institutes of Health. Queer Nation fought to eliminate **homophobia** by increasing the visibility of gays and lesbians in the public eye, often resulting in the classic "We're here, we're queer, get used to it!" cheer. Transgender Nation's public protests spanned from 1993, at the American Psychiatric Association's annual meeting, where they decried the pathologization of transgenderism, to 1995, when Transgender Nation successfully lobbied the Freedom Day Parade in San Francisco to include transgender in its title. Shortly thereafter, the group disbanded. Some activists went on to form the **Transsexual Menace,** and others, like the group's founders, went on to other careers in activism. Susan Stryker, PhD, has worked as the executive director of the GLBT Historical Society in San Francisco, and Jessica Xavier is an epidemiologist and member of the National Coalition for LGBT Health.

Further Reading

Currah, Paisley, Richard M. Juang, and Shannon Price Minter, eds. 2006. *Transgender Rights*. Minneapolis: University of Minnesota Press.

D'Emilio, John, William B. Turner, and Urvashi Vaid, eds. 1992. *Creating Change: Sexuality, Public Policy, and Civil Rights*. New York: Stonewall Inn Editions.

Stryker, Susan, and Stephen Whittle, ed. 2006. *The Transgender Studies Reader*. New York: Routledge.

Jackie Regales

transgender rights

This broad concept refers to legal, social, political, and economic equality and justice for transgender citizens without regard to their gender identity or expression. U.S. transgender advocates face issues somewhat different from other civil rights movements. The concept has not yet achieved as much acceptance as other U.S. civil rights movements. At the same time, however, transgender legal rights have increased dramatically since the beginning of the twenty-first century.

One area of strong focus for transgender advocates is the inclusion of "gender identity and expression" in statutes prohibiting discrimination. Such statutes usually include prohibitions on discrimination in public contracts, public accommodations (e.g., theaters and restaurants), housing, and credit and lending transactions. At the time of this writing, however, there is no U.S. federal statute specifically prohibiting discrimination based on gender identity, though advocates have succeeded in passing such laws in nine states and almost 100 cities and counties, as discussed below.

There is some disagreement among advocates as to whether proposed legislation protecting "sexual orientation" should also include "gender identity and expression." Those who say no argue that the categories are conceptually distinct, that it will be easier to pass a law based on sexual orientation alone, that laws based on gender identity will be easier to pass once discrimination on the basis of sexual orientation is prohibited, and that it is unfair to ask gays and lesbians to wait for rights until transgender people are sufficiently accepted by U.S. society at some future point. Others argue, to the contrary, that sexual orientation and gender identity discrimination are twin concepts that should be part of a single LGBT movement, that it is easier to educate the public at one time and to pass one law rather than two, and that it is unfair to ask transgender people to take a backseat to gay and lesbian interests. A sign of the coming of age of the transgender rights movement is the fact that, although the proposed federal Employment Non-Discrimination Act has been introduced a number of times in the U.S. Congress with protection only for sexual orientation, a number of prominent gay and lesbian advocacy organizations have said they will not support the bill unless it is reintroduced with language prohibiting gender-identity discrimination.

Transgender advocates are also currently working on addressing U.S. laws that interfere with transgender people's ability to obtain corrected government documentation in accord with their gender identity. Some states and federal agencies do not permit changing government identification records to reflect a gender different from the sex assigned at birth. Others require expensive sex-reassignment surgery (also known as gender-confirmation surgery) in order to do so, although most U.S. public health benefits systems, as well as private insurers, refuse to cover such surgery on the grounds that it is not "medically necessary." Even when a change is made, courts and government agencies often refuse to honor it. For purposes of marriage, for example, several recent rulings by state courts have held that transgender people are considered to be their original birth sex, even after sex-reassignment surgery.

The surgical requirement is a particularly contentious element of transgender rights. Many transgender advocates consider it problematic because it recognizes transgender identity only when accompanied by surgical sex reassignment. This creates a classic catch-22 situation, because the psychiatric approval required to perform such surgery will not be given unless the transsexual person has lived and worked in the role of the opposite gender for a substantial period of time, usually at least one year. Thus, a transgender person who wishes to obtain sex-reassignment surgery must live for a substantial period of time with government identification that discloses their transgender status, subjecting them to further prejudice and discrimination. In addition, the surgery requirement is problematic because transgender identity is a nontraditional form of gender identity, which is a concept that refers to psychological, behavioral, and social identity as male or female, and therefore does not imply a change in physical sexual characteristics. Thus, the surgical requirement springs from a basic misunderstanding of transgender identity. Sex-reassignment surgery is expensive, subject to medical risks, and not always desirable. It is often ineffective, particularly for female-to-male transsexuals, many of whom choose not to have phalloplasty because of the notoriously poor results. By requiring surgical intervention before recognition of a change in gender identity, these jurisdictions are perpetuating the idea that only anatomical sex is "real" and that mere "gender identity" is not entitled to legal recognition. The inconsistent requirements for different government agencies results in a confusing welter of identification methods for different government agencies, resulting in inconsistent gender markers on such documents as birth certificates, driver's licenses, health insurance cards, and passports.

The surgical requirement for recognizing gender identity has led to other problems. Some courts have held that laws prohibiting discrimination on the basis of gender identity do not permit transgender persons to use the opposite-sex bathroom. While some correctional facilities will place transgender prisoners according to their gender identity, most require placement of male-to-female transgender prisoners in male prisons, which can be physically dangerous, or else in "protective custody" (solitary confinement), which can cause serious mental disability, unless they have had sex-reassignment surgery. Most correctional facilities will also not permit transgender prisoners to receive cross-sex hormone treatments or sex-reassignment surgery, even if paid for from private funds. Some homeless shelters, including those in San Francisco, New York, and Washington, D.C., will admit homeless transgender people to shelters according to their gender identity; most will not. In contrast, those in favor of a surgical requirement feel that, although one's gender identity may be different from one's sex, transgender persons without sex reassignment are not really of the opposite sex, and their introduction into sex-segregated spaces, such as bathrooms and prisons, will pose risks to the safety and comfort of those who are female-bodied.

Transgender advocates also work to change laws that currently fail to protect transgender people from social discrimination. Many U.S. laws prohibiting social discrimination do not protect transgender people. The Americans with Disabilities Act, for example, which protects people with disabilities, specifically notes that it will not cover transgender people on the basis of a diagnosis of Gender Identity Disorder. (It should be noted that some transgender advocates are working to eliminate this diagnosis on the grounds that transgender identity is not a disorder.) The Civil Rights Act of 1964, which prohibits sex discrimination in employment, among other things, has been interpreted by the federal courts to exclude discrimination based on gender identity or expression. The federal hate crimes law, which provides for tracking statistics on bias crimes, does not track crimes based on gender identity, although violence directed against transgender people because of their transgender identity regularly occurs. Parents who transition from one gender to another are subject to state court rulings denying custody and visitation rights to avoid supposed psychological harm to the children.

The transgender rights movement is beginning to achieve many of its goals. Many jurisdictions now permit transgender persons to obtain government identification with changed gender markers and have laws prohibiting discrimination based on gender identity in employment, housing, credit, and public accommodations. One major federal court, the Sixth Circuit Court of Appeals (covering Michigan, Kentucky, Ohio, and Tennessee), as well as a number of lower federal courts, have recently ruled that the Civil Rights Act's prohibition on sex discrimination does apply to gender identity. The placement of transgender persons by gender identity without a surgical requirement has occurred successfully in sex-segregated facilities, such as correctional facilities, homeless shelters, and college dormitories, in some areas of the country.

Many organizations are involved in advancing transgender rights. Some of the most prominent that are specifically devoted to transgender civil rights include GenderPAC, the Sylvia Rivera Law Project (SRLP), and the National Center for Transgender Equality (NCTE). These organizations inhabit a range of organizational identities. GenderPAC is specifically devoted to ensuring that "classrooms, communities and workplaces are safe for everyone to learn, grow and succeed—whether or not they meet expectations for masculinity and femininity" (GenderPAC Web site). Its main method is educative and community oriented, rather than explicitly political or legal, and focuses on "gender" more generally, as opposed to an explicit focus on only transgender issues. By contrast, the mission of the SRLP, named in memory of transgender advocate Sylvia Rivera, is focused more on providing legal services to marginalized transgender people to help them overcome government discrimination, such as obtaining correct government identification, obtaining access to essential services such as medical care, substance abuse treatment, public benefits, public restrooms, and homeless shelters. It is also involved in high-impact litigation that will provide legal precedents helpful in these areas. NCTE, on the other hand, is specifically dedicated to political action on the federal level in Washington, monitoring federal activity and communicating this activity to transgender advocates around the country, providing congressional education, and acting as a clearinghouse for transgender advocates.

An indication of the rapidity of the increase in transgender rights is the rapid increase in city and county ordinances prohibiting discrimination on the basis of gender identity or expression. Ordinances were nonexistent prior to 1975, when Minneapolis was the first city to adopt an ordinance protecting gender identity. By 1997, there were 17 ordinances in existence. The rate of enactment accelerated dramatically in 2002, when the enactment of city and county ordinances increased by over 40 percent from the year before, from 39 to 55, which more than tripled the number of ordinances that existed in 1997. There are, at the time of this writing, 86 cities and counties with ordinances explicitly prohibiting transgender discrimination, as well as nine states. This showing, however, lags behind protections for sexual orientation, which at the time of this writing exist in over 300 cities and counties and 26 states.

The increase in company policies is similarly dramatic. The first company policy proclaiming equal employment opportunity based on gender identity was adopted in 1997 by Lucent Technologies. The rate of adoption accelerated dramatically in 2001, when the adoption of company policies increased by over 100 percent from the year before, from 12 to 25. Currently, 435 employers have policies prohibiting gender identity discrimination (up from 25 in 2001), including 118 Fortune 500 companies and 75 colleges and universities. This showing also lags behind protections for sexual orientation, which at the time of this writing are offered by over 3,000 employers, including 435 Fortune 500 companies and 562 colleges and universities.

In addition to the efforts of those organizations devoted solely to transgender advocacy, gay and lesbian organizations, which have a much larger fund of expertise, resources, and credibility, have adopted the issue of transgender rights as a part of their LGBT rights mission. For example, the Human Rights Campaign has successfully used its Corporate Equality Index, a rating system designed to show corporate diversity leadership in regard to LGBT employees, to raise consciousness about transgender issues in major corporations. The **National Gay and Lesbian Task Force** has also contributed its expertise in political lobbying to transgender advocates across the nation, assisting them in creating proposed legislation and planning lobbying campaigns. This alliance between transgender advocacy organizations and LGBT advocacy organizations has greatly contributed to the rapid increase of transgender rights.

While transgender rights have made great strides, there still remains much discrimination against transgender people. Some legal theorists warn that "rights talk" can disguise rampant discrimination because there often is a disconnect between laws on the books and the law in action.

Further Reading

ACLU: Library of Congress Can Be Sued. Available at: http://www.aclu.org/lgbt/transgender/32896prs20071128.html. Accessed July 21, 2008.

Currah, Paisley, Richard M. Juang, and Shannon Price Minter. 2006. *Transgender Rights*. Minneapolis: University of Minnesota Press.

GenderPAC. Available at: http://www.gpac.org/gpac/2005AnnualReport.pdf. Accessed July 21, 2008.

Sharpe, Andrew. 2002. *Transgender Jurisprudence*. London: Cavendish.

Whittle, Stephen. 2002. *Respect and Equality: Transsexual and Transgender Rights*. Portland: Cavendish.

Jillian T. Weiss

transgender studies

Transgender studies is a nascent, multidisciplinary body of scholarship and activism that, at its core, challenges the naturalness of binary sex categories (male and female), their associated genders (masculine and feminine), and the social, legal, medical, and political systems erected around those distinctions. As a field of knowledge, it claims as objects of study and political struggle the phenomena of transsexuality and **cross-dressing,** transgender **identities** and practices, certain aspects of **intersexuality** and homosexuality, and global and historical incidences of gender diversity. It is both an examination of such phenomena and a critique of the larger social and political systems that produce, define, and regulate gendered identities and practices.

TERMINOLOGY

The term transgender itself incites disagreements over its correct use, meaning, and history. It is most commonly described as an umbrella term for anyone whose gender identity or expression differs from conventional notions of male and female. This almost always includes transsexuals (individuals whose core gender identity does not match the biological sex assigned to them at birth, some of whom seek medical sex-reassignment therapy or surgery), though some feel that transsexuality is a medical condition and transgender is a distinct social category. Transgender also encompasses individuals who may not alter their social gender through medical or surgical means; examples include cross-dressers (those who dress in clothing associated with the other gender), feminine men and masculine women, **drag** kings and drag queens (those who cross-dress for the sake of **performance**), bigender (those who move between masculine to feminine presentation, depending on context), and two-spirit individuals (a third gender category present in many Native American and indigenous Canadian groups), androgynes, genderqueers (people who identity as neither male nor female, or sometimes as both), and many other nonnormative permutations of gender diversity. There is also some debate over the inclusion of intersex individuals (people whose sex chromosomes, genitalia, or secondary sex characteristics fall outside medically established norms for male and female bodies), as some intersex activists adamantly resist the identity transgender.

Transgender identifies one's core gender identity and/or behavior, which can be distinct from individual sexual orientation. Where sexual orientation concerns the object of one's sexual desire or attraction, gender identity delineates the individual subjective sense of "being" male or female (or neither or both or something else entirely). Transgender subjects complicate this distinction, both because they defy the social idea that there are only two discrete gender identities and because transgender persons do not fit neatly into sexual orientation classifications that also rely on dichotomous sex/gender categories. Some individuals see transgender as a discrete identity category; others see it as more of a political term, whose purpose is mainly to unite a diverse set of gender-variant identities and practices.

Many trace the term transgender to its earliest use by Virginia Prince in 1969. In the 1970s, as sex-reassignment surgeries became more widely available, some used it to signify a cross-gender identity without a desire to undergo surgical sex reassignment. In the 1980s, the term took on a more common social use, uniting different groups of gender-variant people. It gained political meaning in the 1990s, as activists mobilized a coalition of gender-variant individuals to challenge the validity of the gender binary, to pursue legal rights, and to build social support. The 1990s also marked the entry of transgender topics into mainstream media, academia, and law. A parliamentary discussion group in London initiated use of *trans* as a stand-alone term in 1998, with the express intent of maximizing its inclusiveness when crafting legislation. Most recently, global advocates for gender rights have introduced transgender into international human rights discourse as a way to signal the persistent violence and discrimination faced by radically diverse communities of people who deviate from gender norms across many different cultural contexts. Its use today combines all of these and continues to evolve.

FOUNDATIONS

As with many revolutionary movements in academia, transgender studies and transgender **activism** have always been linked. It is no coincidence that trans topics began to emerge in classrooms at the same time they became a cultural and media obsession in the 1990s. Likewise, transgender topics provoked equal fascination in disciplines ranging from the humanities and literature to the social sciences, medicine, the hard sciences, bioethics, and others. Building on the work of previous academic movements in feminist and **gender studies,** lesbian and gay studies and **queer theory,** and poststructuralist and postmodern discourses, transgender subjects provide a veritable buffet of case studies that theorists could use to buttress claims about the social construction of gender and gender inequality in many areas of our social world. Scholars trace a long history, particularly in the medical literature, of discussions of gender variance, dating back to the nineteenth century. The transgender studies canon reaches back into that history of medical, psychological, and sexological literature on gender variance to recover a narrative of the ways in which transgender people (or, perhaps more accurately, their predecessors) were classified and treated.

THE RISE OF MEDICAL AUTHORITY

Doctors "discovered" gender-deviant and homosexual phenomena somewhere toward the close of the nineteenth century. Psychiatrist Richard Von Krafft-Ebing's 1877 sexological classic, *Psychopathia Sexualis*, his attempt at a taxonomy of human sexual impulses, considered homosexuality itself to be a form of gender inversion (meaning, for example, that homosexual men were actually "more like" women). Though he had multiple labels for different forms of gender deviance, his term *metamorphosis sexualis paranoica* described what we might today consider transsexuality, a strong identification as the "opposite" gender, which he considered to be a form of psychosis. German sexologist, Magnus Hirschfeld, followed shortly thereafter with a book-length study on transvestism, subtitled "the erotic desire to cross-dress." Once labeled "the most dangerous Jew" (Elgass 1999) by Adolf Hitler, Hirschfeld, a gay Jewish socialist and advocate for homosexual and gender rights, was the author of the first textbook on sexology and founder of a major research institute. In 1933, the Nazis publicly burned his research library, closed his institute, and banned the continuation of his research. He died in exile in France two years later.

Transsexuality emerged as a medical category worthy of study in its own regard in the 1950s, spurred in large part by an outburst of publicity on photographer and ex-GI Christine Jorgensen's sex-change surgery in Denmark. Endocrinologist Dr. Harry Benjamin, considered by many a pioneer of transgender medicine, worked closely with noted sexologist Alfred Kinsey and others who considered transsexuality a form of sexual identity, and he initiated a campaign for the recognition of transsexuality as a distinct medical category. He envisioned gender disorders on a continuum, which allowed him to distinguish transsexuality from transvestism and homosexuality. His 1966 book, *The Transsexual Phenomenon*, published in the same year the first sex-reassignment surgery was performed in the United States, remains the definitive work on the topic. His was the first published effort to create a systematic way of thinking about how the sexed body, gender identity, and sexual desire interrelate in trans phenomena. In it, Benjamin ties the incidence of transsexualism to a combination of psychological, constitutional, and hormonal influences. Because of the complexity of these causal factors, he says, medical intervention (hormones and/or surgery) is the only way to alleviate the psychological distress transsexual individuals suffer.

Around the same time, psychologist and sexologist Dr. John Money, working out of the Johns Hopkins University Medical Center, developed the ideas of "gender role" and "gender identity" to describe aspects of individual consciousness. He argued that these elements of an individual psyche were learned, and thus they could be altered. Money is perhaps most well known for his treatment of David Reimer, a typical male infant, who lost his penis as the result of a botched circumcision. Money convinced the frantic parents to raise Reimer as a little girl. Known publicly as the "John/Joan case," Money published articles on his "successful" reassignment of the child, as proof of the social nature of gender identity. During the next decade, a network of endocrinologists and surgeons began treating an influx of transsexual people. Benjamin and Money remained at the forefront of the field, eventually joining forces to create the first version of the Standards of Care, ethical guidelines for the treatment of transsexualism. In 1992, however, Professor Milton Diamond revealed that David Reimer, at the age of 15, refused further association with Money and, when finally informed by his parents about the history of his medical reassignment, retransitioned to a male gender role and sought surgical reconstruction.

ACTIVIST BEGINNINGS

In many ways, medicine's "discovery" of transsexualism provided the opportunity for groups of people who shared common feelings and desires to coalesce around a static identity category. In the late 1960s, medicine dominated much of the little public discourse on transgender topics. Networks of transsexual people emerged, sharing information on doctors and medical procedures. Susan Stryker, in a series of writings and a film on the history of transgender activism, traces the eruption in San Francisco of a wellspring of collective mobilization around transsexual and cross-dressers' rights to a 1966 riot by transgender street prostitutes protesting police harassment in the tenderloin district's popular all-night restaurant, Compton's Cafeteria. After that, trans activists in San Francisco worked with the Harry Benjamin Institute (named for the noted expert on transsexuality discussed above) and others to create the first city-sponsored networks of support for transsexuals, including access to health care and hormones, as well as federally funded job-training programs. A few national transgender-specific organizations formed in other areas during this time, funding research into transsexuality and opportunities for collaboration among medical professionals willing to treat transpeople. Chief among them, the Erickson Educational Foundation, started by wealthy transman Reed Erickson, distributed money and helped to develop further the standards for treatment of transsexual people.

Stryker also notes that by the end of the 1960s, transgender activism and gay activism became increasingly linked. Transgender people played a large public role in sparking the famous **Stonewall Riots** in 1969 in New York City. Transgender activism in New York was born in this era. Pioneers like Sylvia Rivera, an early member of the Gay Liberation Front and Gay Activists Alliance and a participant in the Stonewall Riots, along with her collaborator Marsha P. Johnson, founded Street Transvestite Action Revolutionaries (STAR) in 1970.

The early 1970s marked an important tipping point for transgender politics and activism on both coasts. While groups sprang up addressing community outreach needs as well as political activism, competing discourses of gender and sexuality, sparked in large part by the burgeoning women's rights movement, began to paint transsexuals as a dangerous capitulation to patriarchy and male domination. On the one hand, there was an incredible proliferation of transgender organizing: In New York alone, there existed STAR, the Queens Liberation Front (for hetero-sexual transvestites), Transsexuals and Transvestites (TAT), Transsexuals Anony-mous, and the Labyrinth Foundation Counseling Service (geared specifically to meet the needs of female-to-male transpeople). In San Francisco, activists started the Transvestite/Transsexual Action Organization (TAO), and prominent queer-identified transsexuals occupied high-level positions in major gay groups like the Gay Liberation Front's Los Angeles chapter and even the famed lesbian organiza-tion, the **Daughters of Bilitis.**

Yet, while the 1970s marked a time of increased presence and visibility of trans-gender organizing, tension mounted within feminist and gay/lesbian groups over the place of transgender people and issues. Transgender people were indeed reaping the benefits of the previous decade of activism, as a handful of places across the United States began to allow transsexuals to change the gender designations on state-issued identity documents. The first local civil rights protections for trans-gender people passed city legislatures as well. At the same time, this growing vis-ibility provoked anxiety within some feminist and gay/lesbian communities. New political ideologies of gender created by feminist and civil rights movements cast transsexuals as defenders of a rigid gender scheme, charging them with a false con-sciousness that leads them to reproduce patriarchal gender distinctions.

Feminist ethicist Janice Raymond levied the most oft-cited and reviled (by transgender scholars) critique of transsexuality in her 1977 Book, *The Transsexual Empire*. Raymond positioned transsexuals as the most visible symbol of a disturbed gender system. In her estimation, rather than working to overturn the gender sys-tem as a whole, transmen and transwomen internalized and attempted to embody outdated stereotypes of masculinity and femininity. Echoing sentiments that ex-isted on the fringes of grassroots feminist communities for nearly a decade, Ray-mond charged transsexual men (female-to-male transsexuals, or FTMs) with being traitors to their sex and transwomen (male-to-female transsexuals, or MTFs) with using their "male" privilege to usurp women's bodies and spaces. She critiqued the male-dominated medical industry for forming transwomen into men's notions of appropriate femininity. Raymond's text is rife with false information, including her assertion that gender-reassignment surgeries were developed and perfected in Nazi death camps, and her paranoid claim that the existence of these surgeries is itself proof of a vast conspiracy by male surgeons to create a population of "artificial women" (the "transsexual empire" her title prophesizes). Yet, though Raymond herself is universally vilified within transgender communities, her work in particular provided the impetus for transpeople to begin theorizing their own lives and to reject the characterizations of their identities provided by both medical and political communities.

A different set of tensions arose around transgender participation in the lesbian and gay movement. As LGB communities gained visibility and acceptance, fears surfaced that the inclusion of visible transpeople might compromise the tenuous acceptance lesbians and gays had begun to achieve. For assimilationist lesbians and gays who sought acceptance and an acknowledgement that, but for their sexual orientation, they were "just like" heterosexuals, transgender people's outward expression of gender deviance threatened to confirm some of the most pernicious stereotypes of homosexuals. Further, while many lesbian and gay activists hailed the removal in 1976 of homosexuality from the *Diagnostic and Statistical Manual of Psychiatric Disorders (DSM)* as a major moment of victory for sexual rights, few noticed that only a few years later, in 1981, the next edition of the *DSM* included a new diagnostic category, Gender Identity Disorder (GID). While a handful of LGB scholars noted that GID diagnoses targeted and pathologized the outward appearance of homosexuality, often itself a form of gender deviance, little effort was made by LGB activists to reject this diagnosis's implementation.

The 1980s brought many seismic shifts in transgender communities. For one, this new diagnostic classification aided the consolidation of medical ideas of transsexuality as a pathology. The AIDS epidemic also ravaged transgender communities, particularly low-income transpeople of color involved in street prostitution and drug subcultures. It also marked the emergence of the first organized networks of FTM transpeople. In San Francisco, Lou Sullivan, an HIV-infected, gay-identified transman began the first support group, which eventually turned into FTM International (FTMI), the leading national organization working on issues of social support for transmen. When Sullivan died from complications related to AIDS in 1991, Jamison Green took over FTMI and remains one of the most visible voices in transgender politics today.

The political response to the AIDS crisis united sexual minority communities across lines of identity, as well as of race, **class,** and national origin. Ultimately, transgender activists were able to contextualize their struggles within broader movements for racial, economic, and social justice and to build multi-issue movement support. In 1992, Leslie Feinberg published hir [sic] influential pamphlet, "Transgender Liberation: A Movement Whose Time Has Come," the first political manifesto of sorts on transgender rights. Trans activists began to adopt the confrontational, performative, and edgy style of protest used by queer groups like **ACT UP** (AIDS Coalition to Unleash Power) and **Queer Nation.** The new politics of queer liberation provided a space for transgender people within sexual minority comities less fraught than their association with lesbian and gay politics in the 1970s and early 1980s had been. In 1993, a group called **Transgender Nation** brought trans politics to local and national attention by appearing at the American Psychiatric Association's annual conference in San Francisco to protest the pathologization of their identities. In the wake of that action, other groups formed across the country that utilized those confrontational types of political displays. In 1993, Riki Wilchins founded **Transsexual Menace** in New York City, most known for organizing a response to the "womyn-only" policy of the Michigan Womyn's Music Festival. They also organized a response to the 1993 murder of Nebraska transman Brandon Teena, whose life and death inspired the 2000 film *Boys Don't Cry*. Today, Wilchins heads GenderPAC, an organization that has sponsored an annual lobby day for transpeople in Washington, D.C., since 1993. As a result of these political efforts and many others, today more than nine states and 86 other jurisdictions have specific legislation protecting citizens from discrimination of the basis of gender identity and expression.

INTERSEXUALITY

Though disagreements persist over whether intersex issues and identities belong under the framework of transgenderism, most transgender studies courses and the sole anthology of transgender studies literature include intersex topics. In the late 1980s and early 1990s, a generation of intersex adults treated under 1950s and 1960s medical protocol (which encouraged and, in many cases, unilaterally imposed surgical "correction" of intersex genitalia in infants) began to voice their outrage at the nonconsensual mutilation of their bodies. Both Alice Dreger and Anne Fausto-Sterling challenged not only the process of standardization to which intersex infants' genitals are subjected by medical authorities, but also revealed a complex network of understandings of gender and sexuality that undergird that standardization. Even today, standard medical practice deems genitals that cannot perform procreative heterosexual intercourse "inadequate" or "abnormal," and doctors suggest surgical intervention in infants and young children to alleviate the potential social stigma associated with atypical gender presentation. Sociologist Suzanne Kessler interviewed medical specialists in pediatric intersexuality and found that the presence or absence of a "viable penis" was the ultimate indicator of sex in infants.

As the transgender movement gained strength and visibility, younger generations of intersex activists emerged who demanded an end to the surgical sex reassignment of intersex infants, and nationwide support networks are being forged to help parents cope with and understand the complicated and oftentimes painful choices they must make about their children's care. In 1993, Cheryl Chase, an intersex activist, founded the Intersex Society of North America (ISNA), the first intersex advocacy group to link intersex issues to larger queer and transgender struggles for self-determination. Working with both queer and trans activists, ISNA began to develop new ways of understanding intersexuality, championing the rights of intersex children and adults to acknowledge their own personal agency, to resist medicalization of their conditions and bodies, to educate the public on intersex issues, and to seek appropriate and sensitive medical care. ISNA has been instrumental in developing a radical new medical protocol, which advocates assigning intersex infants as either boys or girls, depending on which gender category would most likely be chosen by an adult with their particular form of intersexuality, without performing any corrective surgeries. The central concern of such a protocol is that while intersex individuals must realistically live in a gendered society, they should nonetheless be given total control over the medical management of their bodies, reserving all decisions about physical alteration of their bodies until they reach the age of maturity and have a full understanding of their options.

GENDER THEORIES

It is difficult to know where precisely to begin a history of transgender theory, but its foundations range from feminist thought to mainstream social science. Feminist theorist Gayle Rubin first introduced the idea of a sex/gender system in her canonical 1975 article, "The Traffic in Women: Notes on the Political Economy of Sex." In it, she traces the oppression of women to the structure of kinship systems that require a division of the sexes (defined biologically) and that organize gender (our social roles) according to those divisions, thus further necessitating compulsory heterosexuality for their maintenance. Perhaps most revolutionary, Rubin suggests that women are not merely oppressed by virtue of being women, but by having to be *like* women or men at all. She proposes as an alternative not the elimination of men but a radical form of **androgyny.**

As feminist theory began to challenge the notion of essential gender, the social sciences seemed to "discover" trans phenomena in the 1960s and 1970s. The first of such studies, Howard Garfinkel's 1967 chapter on the "achievement" of social gender by an intersex subject, Agnes, introduced the idea that gender is not a static feature of an individual psyche but is continuously managed and produced by individuals in the social world. (Ironically, after its initial publication, Garfinkel learned that Agnes produced far more of her gender than even he knew. Agnes was, in fact, not intersex at all but instead a "typical" biological male who desired to live as a woman.)

In his work, Garfinkel relied on the idea that a fundamental distinction exists between biological sex, based on the body (which he takes to be immutable), and social gender, which individuals manage within a social context. This idea, much like Rubin's notions of the sex/gender system, made up the bedrock of much feminist social science for several decades. For example, sociologists Candace West and Don H. Zimmerman theorized gender as socially prescribed actions or behaviors based on biological sex categories, regulated both in informal social contact and formal law. But in 1978, Suzanne J. Kessler and Wendy McKenna revised Garfinkel's initial analysis to conclude that both our ideas of biological sex itself and the dichotomous gender system built on that assumed distinction are accomplishments of culture and social interactions. In fact, they conclude, our bodies themselves, the ways we identify and define types and parts, are social ideas. This idea, that biological "truths" are themselves social constructions, lies at the heart of much writing by transgender studies theorists.

Non-trans theorists historically used transgender phenomena to buttress the argument that gender is socially constructed. Increasingly, however, some transgender studies scholars are questioning whether these deeply held identities and beliefs about the self could be entirely social phenomena. Though psychologists have offered various explanations for transgender phenomena, they have mainly been the result of studies with poor methodologies. Likewise, the few studies that attempt to differentiate the biology of the brains of transgender and nontransgender people are so flawed that they have little, if any, value as proof. As with debates on the origins of homosexuality, little scholarly consensus exists on why some individuals have trans identities and others do not.

TRANSGENDER THEORY

Some of the earliest work written from the perspective of transgender subjects themselves came in the form of autobiographical accounts. Christine Jorgensen, who became widely known as the first person in the United States to undergo sex-reassignment surgery, published her autobiography in 1967. Many more followed. Transsexual tennis star Renee Richards detailed her successful lawsuit against the United States Tennis Association to allow her to compete in the Women's Open in her 1986 book *Second Serve*. Charlotte Von Mahlsdorf, an East German museum preservationist, detailed her life among an East German homosexual community living in fear of Nazi and then Communist persecution. Her autobiography, which she eventually turned into a stage play, *I Am My Own Wife*, came out in 1992. Perhaps most significantly, Kate Bornstein's 1994 classic, *Gender Outlaw: On Men, Women and the Rest of Us*, part life history and part manifesto, is credited by many as a catalyst for political mobilization around gender issues on college campuses across the country.

Transgender studies theory, soon proliferating both within and outside of the academy, marks a decisive shift away from understanding and cataloguing the permutations of gender diversity towards more wide-ranging critiques of the medical regulation of gendered identities and behaviors by doctors themselves. Many trace the beginning of a coherent transgender-specific body of academic theory to the 1991 publication of Sandy Stone's article, "The Empire Strikes Back: A Posttranssexual Manifesto." Stone critiqued the medical model of transsexuality outlined above, which takes it as its fundamental task to assist "qualified" transsexuals in embodying their reassigned gender, erasing their histories, and fully assimilating into "normal" society. She urges transpeople to break their complicity with a model that requires silence about their pretransition histories and to create a "counter-discourse" by producing multiple and diverse accounts of the lived reality of trans experience, by trans authors themselves. Stone directly challenged feminist critiques that considered transsexuality to be a form of false consciousness or a patriarchal attempt by men to usurp women's unique power.

Transgender theorists continue to answer the call to merge transgender practice and feminist politics in many different ways. Trans theorists argue that Raymond's theory insists that only biological females can or should be "women," thus essentializing gender to biological sex in a way feminists themselves reject. Feminists and transpeople alike also caution against her oversimplifications of what women are and who can have access to a feminist identity. Newer theory introduces the idea of "transfeminism," or a stance from which transwomen can operate that assumes their liberation to be intrinsically connected to the social position of all women. Emi Koyama's 1991 "Transfeminist Manifesto" introduces the idea that transfeminism supplements, without supplanting, the work women have done for decades around examining the privileging of dominant identities and the silencing of minority women, patterns of gender-based violence, sexual self-determination, body consciousness, health, and reproductive choice. It connects the lived experiences of transgender people, who suffer extreme forms of all kinds of gender-based regulation and violence, to larger constructs of gender oppression that operate on all people.

All that said, transgender theorists find themselves accountable to the same sorts of critiques that women of color levy at feminists: the notion that gender is not the sole indicator of identity relevant to one's political position, the unspoken racism that permeates discussions of rights and identity when they center solely around the voices of white, (relatively) privileged activists. Even today, transgender theory as a whole is vulnerable to such critiques, as it tends to be dominated by white voices and based out of and funded by universities and institutions, while transgender people themselves represent a multitude of racial and ethnic groups and suffer disproportionate rates of homelessness and economic marginalization.

Critiques of the medical model of transsexuality rapidly progressed beyond the call to live openly as transpeople. As feminist and gay scholars have done for decades, transgender theorists call attention to the way medical models of transsexuality, by virtue of their existence, reinforce the notion that there are, in fact, "normal" or "normative" male and female bodies. Biologist Anne Fausto-Sterling identifies scientific claims about the "realness" of sex as opposed to constructed notions of gender and culture as a false dichotomy. She argues that, in fact, there is a complex interaction between the biological and the social/political and that scientific notions like "sex" are both literally and ideologically constructed. While this may seem identical to some feminist critiques of biological essentialism levied much earlier, often directed against transsexual people themselves, transgender studies theory uses such critiques in an attempt to dismantle medical authority over transpeople's bodies and to encourage models of bodily self-determination.

Transgender legal scholars identify a host of challenges transpeople face in negotiating some of the most basic aspects of the law. Transgender people are protected from discrimination in only a handful of state and municipal statutes. Vast and conflicting bodies of state law determine who can change their gender designation on government identity documents. Transgender people may find the validity of their marriages or their parenting rights subject to challenge in the courts. Beyond outlining the formidable challenges transpeople face in courts and legislatures throughout the country, transgender studies scholars question the foundational, unspoken assumption that the state has a legitimate interest in regulating the individual gendered identities and behaviors of its citizens.

Beyond critiquing the role of medical and legal institutions in regulating transgender people's identities and social participation, transgender studies engages in many of the same debates that lesbian and gay scholars faced in the 1980s and 1990s. Is gender identity essential and biologically based, or is it socially constructed? Does the answer to that question really matter? In a patriarchal society where access to sex-reassignment technologies is zealously guarded by the medical establishment, are transsexual people who seek medical intervention to bring their physical bodies in line with their psychological selves capitulating to outmoded standards of maleness or femaleness? What role should the medical establishment have in coaching parents of intersex infants about options for gender-related surgeries and/or psychiatric care? Should doctors even be labeling infants intersex, or are intersex conditions merely benign forms of human variation?

At its core, transgender theory rejects medical models that frame transgender identities and practices as mental disorders. It seeks to shift the focus away from transgender subjectivities as instances of pathology, toward forming an expert knowledge of "gender defenders," Kate Bornstein's term of art for those people and institutions that seek to enforce a rigid gender regime. Transgender studies offers a unique opportunity for students and readers to address their own gendered subjectivities by reading accounts of transgender subjectivities, exploring the historical evolution of theories of sex and gender, or engaging in complex discussions of the social structures that regulate and produce our ideas of gender.

GLOBALIZATION

As transgender issues and identities emerge in academia, increasing numbers of scholars, particularly anthropologists, have scoured the globe to find incidences of gender diversity in other cultures. Books exploring the Brazilian *Travesti*, Thai *Kathoey* (or ladyboys), Indian *Hijiras*, Samoa's *F'afafine*, Tonga's *Fakaleiti*, Mexican *Muxe*, Native American *two-spirit* people, and the place of "third-gender" categories in the history of Islam, Arabic cultures, and traditional African customs challenge the idea that gender diversity is a modern Western phenomenon. At the same time, indigenous activists as well as Western scholars caution against using third-gender categories as evidence for a universal transgender presence or identity. While academics engage in these discussions about meaning and labels, gender-variant people all over the world suffer severe social, economic, and bodily violence as a consequence of their gendered identities and behaviors. International human rights activists around the globe are just beginning to acknowledge the existence of a particular type of gender-based violence that is experienced by members of any given social order who transgress gender norms. Thus, a new generation of gender revolutionaries, one that traverses geographical space and cultural context, is emerging to challenge ideas of gender on a global scale.

Further Reading

Elgass, Jane R. 1999. "Hirschfeld Exhibit." *The University Record* (September 7). Available at: http://www.ur.umich.edu/9900/Sep07_99/13.htm. Accessed July 21, 2008.

Hirschfeld, Magnus. 2003. *Transvestites: The Erotic Drive to Cross Dress*. Amherst, NH: Prometheus Books.

Meyerowitz, Joanne. 2002. *How Sex Changed: A History of Transsexuality in the United States.* Cambridge: Harvard University Press.

Stryker, Susan, and Stephen Whittle, eds. 2006. *The Transgender Studies Reader.* New York: Routledge.

Tey Meadow

Transsexual Menace

Transsexual Menace is a direct-action, education, and outreach group directly modeled on **Queer Nation** and **ACT UP.** It is also the name of a 1996 documentary by Rosa von Praunheim, a transgendered Latvian filmmaker. Founded in 1995 by Riki Ann Wilchins and Denise Norris in response to the perceived slighting of transgendered individuals during celebrations of the 25th anniversary of the **Stonewall Riots** in New York City, the organization is part of a growing movement for **transgender rights.** In 1994 and 1995, Transsexual Menace helped raise funds for Camp Trans, a protest outside the Michigan Womyn's Music Fest, and also protested outside the festival in later years. Transsexual Menace also protested at the annual conventions for the American Psychiatric Association, demanding that the association remove Gender Identity Disorder (GID) from its list of mental illnesses. By 1996, 46 chapters of the Menace existed nationwide, and its members were sporting T-shirts with the distinctive logo in bloody red letters.

Chapters of the Menace exist in cities all over the United States and Canada, including long-running chapters in Toronto and southern California. Many have worked with the **Intersex** Society of North America on protests and other projects, and chapters have organized vigils nationwide after slayings of transsexuals, most notably outside the courtroom where Brandon Teena's killer was tried. In 2004, Ethan St. Pierre of the **National Transgender Advocacy Coalition** revived a Washington, D.C., chapter with Gwen Smith, who runs the online Menace discussion group, in order to protest the **Human Rights Campaign (HRC)** during a Unity Rally for Transgender Rights, urging the HRC to support transgender-inclusive federal legislation on hate crimes and discrimination. Original founder Riki Ann Wilchins later founded and directed GenderPAC, a public advocacy coalition to end discrimination and violence caused by gender-based stereotypes.

Further Reading
Nestle, Joan, Riki Wilchins, and Clare Howell, eds. 2002. *GenderQueer: Voices from Beyond the Sexual Binary.* New York: Alyson Books.

Wilchins, Riki. 1997. *Read My Lips: Sexual Subversion and the End of Gender.* Ann Arbor, MI: Firebrand Books.

Wilchins, Riki. 2004. *Queer Theory, Gender Theory: An Instant Primer.* New York: Alyson Books.

Jackie Regales

transvestism. *See* cross-dressing and transvestism

trick

Trick is a term used within the gay community to describe a person involved in a sexual encounter of two or more people over an extremely short period of time. Trick evolved from the culture of **prostitution** where *turning tricks* meant to engage in sexual activities; it came to refer to the sexual act without the monetary exchange. *To trick*, therefore, means to engage in a casual sexual encounter. A trick meeting typically lasts a matter of minutes or no longer than one night, although the parties in question may interact with each other on more than one occasion. Trick was a popular term between the 1970s and 1990s, but it has lately evolved into the phrase *no strings attached*. The term also reached a high status in culture when it was used as the title for the 1999 comedy *Trick*; the film focused on a young gay man who falls in love with a go-go dancer he had planned to trick with in one night.

Further Reading

Queer as Folk. 2000–2005. Russell T. Davis, series creator. Showtime Networks, Inc.
Richardson, Niall. 2003. "Queer Masculinity: The Representation of John Paul Pitoc's Body in *Trick*." *Paragraph: A Journal of Modern Critical Theory* 26 (1–2): 232–44.

James Francis Jr.

Tri-Ess Society (The Society of the Second Self)

Tri-Ess is an educational, social, and support group for heterosexual cross-dressers and their spouses, partners, and families in the United States. Tri-Ess also provides outreach to educators and professionals about issues related to cross-dressing. The organization articulates the view that cross-dressing should not be a matter of shame or secrecy and that each human being has the right to a full expression of masculine and feminine personality traits. For Tri-Ess, cross-dressing is an activity that can lead to the integration of masculine and feminine characteristics and the achievement of psychic fulfillment through this gendered "wholeness." Additionally, Tri-Ess members who cross-dress and who may even wish to be taken for female in public still consider themselves male in a biological sense or ascribe to a fundamentally male gender **identity.** They distinguish themselves from male-to-female transsexuals, who may think of themselves as female in identity and who may or may not seek surgical intervention to remedy any perceived discrepancies between body and identity.

The society's origins can be traced to the Los Angeles–based activism of Virginia Prince (born Charles) in the late 1950s. Prince, herself a cross-dresser, began the first comprehensive magazines for cross-dressers in 1959 (*Transvestia, Femme Mirror, and Clipsheet*) and organized a Hose and Heels Club for Los Angeles–area cross-dressers. Both the magazines and Hose and Heels worked to provide social and networking opportunities for cross-dressers and to promote their self-acceptance through positive reinforcement and cross-dressing "how-to" workshops. In the mid-1960s, Prince rechristened the club the Foundation for Personal Expression (FPE), or Phi Pi Epsilon, using the equivalent Greek letters to suggest an organization akin to the all-female sorority. These sororal vestiges persist within Tri-Ess to the present day. Auxiliary chapters of FPE soon opened in New York and Chicago. After publishing her first book, *The Transvestite and His Wife,* and going on a European media tour, Prince returned to find increased interest in FPE in the United States. Around the same time, activist Carol Beecroft left the Los Angeles chapter of FPE to form the Mamselle Sorority, a competing organization for cross-dressers. In 1976, FPE and Mamselle merged to form Tri-Ess, the Society for the Second Self, with the title of the new organization signaling the "woman within": the personality that heterosexual cross-dressers seek to find via cross-dressing.

During the 1980s, Tri-Ess enjoyed steady growth, with new chapters forming across the country. A 1987 appearance on *Donahue* (one of the earliest extended treatments of cross-dressing by the national mass media) featured Tri-Ess chapter members and brought national attention to cross-dressing and to Tri-Ess, resulting in a massive increase in membership and inquiries regarding the organization.

In the late 1980s Tri-Ess began to create publications and programming for the spouses and partners of cross-dressers, admitting that these genetic women are often unwittingly concerned with transgender issues through their relationships with cross-dressers. In fact, Tri-Ess members who are partners of cross-dressers have become some of the most outspoken protestors of psychological analyses of cross-dressing that hold wives and mothers of cross-dressers partially culpable for the behavior. In such views, cross-dressing is considered a pathology or a paraphilia, and the wife or mother is seen as codependent or subconsciously encouraging the cross-dressing (Stoller 1967). Therapists like Peggy Rudd, herself the wife of a cross-dresser and a member of Tri-Ess, have countered such claims through work that articulates how cross-dressing may be a healthy form of expression and part of a successful heterosexual relationship.

When the Tri-Ess Board of Directors instated the wives and partners of cross-dressers as equal members of Tri-Ess in 1988, much of the trans community outside of the organization was outraged. This reaction signals, to some extent, the marginalized position of heterosexual cross-dressers within the trans movement and the varying degrees to which cross-dressers and their partners have claimed allegiance to the "trans" identity category. Nevertheless, the organization has continued to strengthen ties to the trans community and was one of several trans organizations to sign the International Bill of Gender Rights in 1995.

Since the admission of genetic women to Tri-Ess, the organization has focused more explicitly on relationship issues and the effects of cross-dressing on existing family and romantic relationships. As a part of this work, Tri-Ess formed an annual Spouses' and Partners' International Conference for Education (SPICE), specifically aimed at improving the relationships between cross-dressers and their female partners. Tri-Ess's stated position is that the needs of the cross-dresser are neither more nor less important than the needs of other family members. More recently, Tri-Ess has begun to expand its family support department to include greater outreach to the parents and children of cross-dressers, signaling an area of future growth for the organization.

Tri-Ess is known for several publications. *The Femme Mirror* is a quarterly magazine featuring **coming-out** stories, cross-dressing tips, and community news. *The Sweetheart Connection* is a quarterly newsletter prepared for wives and partners of cross-dressers. The Tri-Ess directory and its accompanying pen pal program support cross-dressers who live in remote areas or areas of the country not served by a chapter of the organization. *Holiday en Femme* is the annual Tri-Ess convention for cross-dressers and their partners, featuring cross-dressing workshops and on-site vendors who serve the cross-dressing community. SPICE is Tri-Ess's annual non–cross-dressed event, directed more toward spousal relations and geared more explicitly to wives and partners of cross-dressers.

Currently, Tri-Ess has approximately 30 chapters in the United States and is a member of the World Congress of Transgender Organizations as well as of the International Foundation for Gender Education (IFGE).

Further Reading

Bloom, Amy. 2002. *Normal: Transsexual CEO's, Cross-Dressing Cops, and Hermaphrodites with Attitude*. New York: Random House.

Bullough, Vern. 1993. *Cross-Dressing, Sex, and Gender*. Philadelphia: University of Pennsylvania Press.

Garber, Marjorie. 1992. *Vested Interests: Cross-Dressing and Cultural Anxiety*. New York: Routledge.

Rudd, Peggy J. 1988. *My Husband Wears My Clothes: Cross-Dressing from the Perspective of the Wife*. Katy, TX: PM Publishers.

Society for the Second Self, Inc., Web site. Available at: http://www.tri-ess.org. Accessed July 21, 2008.

Stoller, Robert. 1967. "Tranvestite's Women." *American Journal of Psychiatrity* 124: 333–39.

Suthrell, Charlotte A. 2004. *Unzipping Gender: Sex, Crossdressing, and Culture*. New York: Berg.

Brad Houston Lane

Trikone

In 1986, Trikone, the first registered nonprofit organization specifically for lesbian, gay, **bisexual,** and **transgendered** people of South Asian ancestry, was created in San Francisco; it would go on to become the oldest continuing group of its kind in the world. Defining South Asia as the area encompassed by the nations of Bhutan, Afghanistan, Tibet, India, Nepal, Bangladesh, Sri Lanka, Pakistan, the Maldives, and Myanmar (Burma), founder Arvind Kumar adopted the Sanskrit word for triangle as a name to affirm the dignity of LGBT individuals' sexual identities and their existence within their home cultures. The group sponsors social events and is involved in political activities, and since January 1986 Trikone has issued a newsletter that became a quarterly award-winning magazine in 1993.

The culmination of Trikone's efforts to make an LGBT identity a visible part of the South Asian reality of the Bay Area came in June 1995, when "Pride Utsav," the first international conference for South Asian queer-identified people ever held on the West Coast, took place at the University of San Francisco's Mission Center. Inspired by earlier similar meetings in New York City and Toronto in 1993 and 1994, it was keynoted by Urvashi Vaid, the former executive director of the **National Gay and Lesbian Task Force.**

A second conference, DesiQ2000, took as its theme "Unfolding Visions," and Trikone celebrated its 20th anniversary with DesiQ2006, held in San Francisco on June 21–24.

Further Reading
Roy, Sandip. 1996. "In the Beginning: An Interview with *Trikone* Founder Arvind Kumar." *Trikone* (Tenth-Anniversary Issue): 8.

Robert Ridinger

David Trinidad (1953–)

Poet David Trinidad was born in Los Angeles. A student of both confessional poetry (Anne Sexton and Sylvia Plath are touchstones) and the so-called **New York School,** Trinidad has the twin graces of meriting serious intellectual attention while writing accessible, plainspoken, almost transparent poems. His first book, *Pavane,* is anomalous in its metaphorical approach, presenting stories of queer dissolution via ancient Greek archetypes. In subsequent volumes, *Monday, Monday* and *Hand over Heart: Poems 1981–1988,* the poet develops his signature direct style. Trinidad's breakthrough, *Answer Song,* a finalist for the 1994 Lambda Literary Award for Poetry, is noted for its frankness in depicting queer desire and the poet's struggles to find equilibrium in his long-term relationship with literary agent Ira Silverberg. But Trinidad's great subject is pop culture: the blandishments and toxic raptures that Barbie and *Valley of the Dolls* offer the gay men who identify with such artifacts. *Answer Song* contains a number of memorable meditations on this theme: strangely compelling found poems ("The Ten Best Episodes of *The Patty Duke Show*") set the stage for the disturbing essay–poem ("The Shower Scene in *Psycho*") that crowns the volume. In *Plasticville,* a finalist for the Lenore Marshall Poetry Prize and the Lambda Award, Trinidad extends his treatment of pop cultural detritus. Employing traditional verse forms like the sonnet and villanelle, Trinidad takes a more critical, less autobiographical approach to his subject. Trinidad's follow-up, *Phoebe 2002: An Essay in Verse,* is an impressive 650-page **camp** collaboration with poets Jeffery Conway and Lynn Crosbie that rhapsodizes over the classic movie *All About Eve. Phoebe 2002* grows more playful in its second half, including gossipy digressions on the backbiting politics of the poetry world are interwoven with camp fantasias starring Joan Crawford and Bette Davis. Unpretentious, unsentimental, unflinching: like his mentor James Schuyler, Trinidad's strengths and singularity grow more apparent with each new volume.

Further Reading

Hennessy, Christopher. 2005. *Outside the Lines: Talking with Contemporary Gay Poets*. Ann Arbor: University of Michigan Press.

Marranca, Richard, and Vasiliki Koros. 1999. "Pop Culture and Poetry: An Interview with David Trinidad." *Literary Review: An International Journal of Contemporary Writing* 42 (2): 323–32.

Schuyler, James. 2004. *Just the Thing: Selected Letters of James Schuyler: 1951–1991*. Ed. William Corbett. New York: Turtle Point Press.

Christopher Schmidt

Kitty Tsui (1952–)

Kitty Tsui (pronounced "Sway") was born in Kowloon, Hong Kong. According to Tsui, her maternal grandmother, Kwan Ying Lin, was a famous Chinese operatic star who toured America in the 1920s and 1930s, and it was she who raised Tsui (in Hong Kong) during early childhood until the age of five (Kitty Tsui Web site).

At 15 years of age, Tsui emigrated with her family to San Francisco, California. Memories of life with her family emerge from a cold darkness: "At mealtime, [I remember] silence. No conversation or laughter. Just the sound of soup spoons and chopsticks against the rice bowls" (Allen 1990, 49). Another childhood memory: "In Hong Kong when I was growing up I heard all around me mothers shouting in exasperation at their children: 'Dead Girl, no use, you dead.' Hearing myself called dead girl so many times I was sure I was a dead girl, meaningless, useless, worthless. In addition to this, I was always told what I couldn't do, what I couldn't say, what I couldn't be. I could dream but I could never be" (50).

Tsui left home at 16 and worked as kitchen help in order to achieve her degree in creative writing in 1975 from San Francisco State University. Early on, she struggled with alcohol, drugs, and rejection. At 21 years of age she revealed that, like her grandmother, she too was lesbian. Tsui's spirit flourishes today as a result of her grandmother's enduring love.

A gold-medal winner (in physique competition) in the 1990 Gay Olympic Games II, Tsui is a prolific writer with an uncanny ability to capture emotion and startling reality. Her work appears predominantly in anthologies and journals.

Further Reading

Allen, Jeffner. 1990. *Lesbian Philosophies and Cultures*. Albany: State University of New York Press.

Kitty Tsui. Available at: http://eths.sfsu.edu/aas214s2005-2/group3/Michelle.htm. Accessed July 22, 2008.

Vicki Lynn White

Tommy Tune (1939–)

This six-foot, six-inch Texan started **dancing** in Wichita Falls at a very young age. After attending the University of Texas, Thomas James Tune headed to **New York,** where he established a career that would forever support his dance habit and revitalize Broadway style. A decade after being plucked from the chorus for a role in Michael Bennett's *Seesaw* (1974), Tune emerged as Broadway's new triple threat—dancer, choreographer, and director. His trademark of showbiz razzmatazz and high-energy tap dancing brought a classical energy to a Broadway overcome by the 1980s British invasion. With nine Tony Awards, Tune is the first artist to win back-to-back director/choreographer awards (*Grand Hotel* [1990] and *Will Rogers Follies* [1991]) and Tonys in four different categories (Best Featured Actor in a Musical for *Seesaw,* Best Choreography for *A Day in Hollywood/A Night in the Ukraine* [1980] and *My One and Only* [1983], Best Direction of a Musical for *Nine* [1982], and Best Actor in a Musical for *My One and Only*). Simultaneous to enjoying mainstream success, Tune challenged social norms regarding gender and sexuality, originating Broadway's first substantial gay role in a musical comedy *(Seesaw),* refusing to omit his partner from his 1974 Tony celebration, and directing gender-bending, Obie-winning plays *The Club* (1976) and *Cloud Nine* (1981). While not publicly **coming out** until 1997, Tune was one of the earliest celebrities to lend money and influence to AIDS causes and to use his artistic power—through *Grand Hotel*'s dying bookkeeper's exuberant Charleston number—to depict the human spirit related to the AIDS crisis.

Further Reading

Gerard, Jeremy. "Keep on Dancin'." *Vanity Fair* (May 1991): 152–55.

Lassell, Michael. 1991. "Tommy Towers over Broadway." *Dance Magazine* (November): 36–40.

Tune, Tommy. 1997. *Footnotes: A Memoir*. New York: Simon and Schuster.

Kelly Kessler

U

Luz María Umpierre-Herrera (1947–)

Luz María Umpierre-Herrera is a Puerto Rican poet and critic who received a doctorate from Bryn Mawr and has taught at Rutgers University and Bates College. Hers was a trailblazing Puerto Rican presence at Bryn Mawr, where she experienced a certain **class** consciousness. She experienced something of the same, it appears, at Rutgers, although it may also have been a subtle instance of **homophobia.** Before transferring to Bryn Mawr, however, Umpierre-Herrera almost completed a law degree at the Universidad Católica de Pónce in Puerto Rico. This came in handy, no doubt, in her various battles in academia. In 1989 she moved to Western Kentucky University as professor and chair of the Modern Languages and Intercultural Studies Department. In 1990 she received a Lifetime Achievement Award from the Coalition of Lesbian and Gay Organizations in New Jersey and the following year became head of the Spanish Department at the State University of New York at Brockport.

Umpierre-Herrera is most noted for *The Margarita Poems* (1987). Her poetry collections prior to this clearly express her anguish as a member of one minority (Puerto Rican), but with this volume her lesbian identity comes distinctly to the fore. This has sometimes rankled the Hispanic community of male scholars.

Further Reading
Foster, David William. 2000. "Erótica lesbiana: Unos ejemplos de la poesía de latinas." *Antípodas: Journal of Hispanic and Galician Studies* 11–12: 159–69.

Luis, William. 1997. "María C(h)ristina Speaks: Latina Identity and the Poetic Dialogue between Sandra María Esteves and Luz María Umpierre." *Hispanic Journal* 18 (1): 137–49.

Martínez, Elena M. 1996. "Lesbian Themes in Luz María Umpierre's *The Margarita Poems. . . . And Other Misfortunes." *Confluencia: Revista Hispánica de Cultura y Literatura* 12 (1): 66–82.

Rivera, Carmen S. *Kissing the Mango Tree: Puerto Rican Women Rewriting American Literature*. Arte Publico Press.

John C. Hawley

United Church of Christ (UCC)

The United Church of Christ (UCC), a Christian denomination, was founded in 1957 through a union of Protestant denominations with the purpose of creating a diverse, yet unified, liberal denomination that lived out the ecumenical movement in mid-twentieth-century American religious culture. UCC churches came to life in the tumultuous social milieu of the 1960s and 1970s, and many of them were involved in ecumenical, peace, justice, and human rights movements. Human sexuality became a topic included in larger justice and human rights movements of the UCC.

In San Francisco in 1964 the UCC helped initiate and finance the Council on Religion and the Homosexual, an organized dialogue between the religious and gay communities. But Bill Johnson's application for ordination from his regional UCC conference ignited an 18-month debate about sexuality and ministry at the autonomous local level and at the national level of the UCC. Johnson was ordained by his conference in summer 1972, and the UCC Council for Church and Ministry formed the Committee on Human Sexuality and Ordination in 1973. The General Synod (national delegate body of the UCC) released statements supporting civil and human rights for gay and lesbian persons in the mid-1970s, and in 1985 the National Synod urged UCC congregations to be open and affirming of all sexual orientations. Today, the UCC Coalition for Lesbian, Gay, Bisexual, and Transgender Concerns is formally supported by the UCC—one of a few progressive denominations that welcome openly gay and lesbian clergy, members, and leaders.

Further Reading

Comstock, Gary David. 1996. *Unrepentant, Self-Affirming, Practicing: Lesbian/Bisexual/Gay People within Organized Religion*. New York: Continuum.

Gearhart, Sally, and William R. Johnson. 1974. *Loving Women/Loving Men: Gay Liberation and the Church*. San Francisco: Glide Publications.

Howell Williams

V

Gore Vidal (1925–)

Although best known as a novelist and political figure, Gore Vidal is also a prolific essayist, critic, and dramatist. In fact, Vidal wrote in a letter to Edith Sitwell that playwriting did not appeal to him. In 1955, playwright George Axelrod expressed interest in producing a Broadway version of Vidal's television play *Visit to a Small Planet,* a comedy about an alien who attempts to begin a war on earth. Harold Franklin of the William Morris Agency approached Vidal and closed the deal with the agreement that Cyril Ritchard would star and direct. After extensively revising the film script, the play opened in Boston to a sold-out theater, but critics and audiences were uncomfortable with the comedy's satire and antimilitarism. But that changed when the actors reinterpreted their characters; at the 1957 premier in New York, the play received congratulatory reviews as a comedy.

Vidal's next television play also appeared on stage. Agreeing to write one for Fred Coe, producer of NBC's *Playwrights '56,* in May 1956 Vidal penned *Honor,* about a wealthy Southerner forced to decide whether to allow Yankee troops into his mansion. Vidal expanded this antiwar play into the full-length drama *March to the Sea.* Because of other obligations, he was forced to table *March,* but the piece finally played at Hyde Park Playhouse in August 1960 before less-than-satisfied audiences. Director and producer David Samples agreed to run the play for a second week, but attendance dropped significantly.

In the meantime, in 1959 Vidal vacationed in **Provincetown,** where he thought through another political play. On his return, he wrote the first draft of *The Best Man,* a satire on political blackmail (a presidential candidate is accused of experimenting with homosexuality). Rehearsals began in the fall with producer Roger Stevens, and the play opened at the Morosco Theater on March 31, 1960, to unanimous applause. After reviewers received the play similarly on Broadway—well-known reviewers Brooks Atkinson and Walter Kerr spoke the loudest—the show ran for 520 performances.

Following the success of *The Best Man*, Vidal, itching to write a new play, capitalized on his admiration for Swiss playwright Friedrich Dürrenmatt and adapted Dürrenmatt's play *Romulus* for an American audience. An antiwar comedy fusing Roman history with American politics, *Romulus* (1962) received less-than-favorable reviews. Directed by Joe Anthony and starring Cyril Ritchard, the play closed at New York's Music Box theater after 69 performances. In retrospect, understanding that Dürrenmatt's original had failed in Europe, Vidal blamed the failure on the repetitive plot and on his choice of Ritchard as the lead.

While on a trip to Greece that same year, Vidal envisioned the idea for his next play, *Drawing Room Comedy*. Despite Vidal's excitement over this work, the play remains unperformed and unpublished, although it nearly reached the stage in 1964. David Merrick committed to producing the play, but he ultimately argued that Broadway audiences would refrain from attending a performance depicting a man dying of a coronary thrombosis. Attempts in London and Berlin failed as well.

Following the completion of his successful novel *Myra Breckinridge* in 1967, Vidal again approached the stage with his new play *Weekend*. A dramatization of contemporary Washington politics, the play satirizes political morality and ambition as Senator Charles MacGruder is faced with his son's engagement to an African American. The play especially attacks Lyndon Johnson's administration; in fact, Johnson's daughter Lynda Bird fled the Washington premier in disgust. Washington and New York critics were not enthusiastic, and the play closed after 22 performances.

Negative reviews certainly failed to quash Vidal's love of political satires. *An Evening with Richard Nixon* (1972), consisting of actual and invented speeches by Nixon, Gloria Steinem, Nikita Khrushchev, Lyndon Johnson, George Washington, and a host of others, attacked Nixon's policies but closed after 13 performances.

Further Reading

Kaplan, Fred. 1999. *Gore Vidal: A Biography*. New York: Doubleday.

White, Ray Lewis. 1992. "Vidal as Playwright: In Gentlest Heresy." *Gore Vidal: Writer against the Grain*, ed. Jay Parini, 120–36. New York: Columbia University Press.

John Pruitt

Village People

A novelty band assembled in the late 1970s at the height of the disco era, the Village People are regarded as masters of self-parody and often remembered more for their eye-catching costumes than their musical talent. While attending a costume party at a gay disco in New York's Greenwich Village, French producer Jacques Morali came up with the idea of putting together a group of masculine singers and dancers who represented various gay fantasy figures and icons of the Tom of Finland variety. The resulting band's original members were Alex Briley (the soldier), David "Scar" Hodo (the construction worker), Glenn Hughes (the **leather**-clad biker), Randy Jones (the cowboy), Felipe Rose (the Indian), and Victor Willis (the policeman, who was the lead singer).

The Village People got noticed in the United States with the release of their song "Macho Man" in 1987. The group's first major U.S. hit, however, was the single "Y.M.C.A." (from the album *Cruisin'*), which spent more than a year on the charts; its success was followed quickly by the group's next major hit, "In the Navy" (from the album *Go West*), in the spring of 1979. That fall, lead singer Willis left the group, just days before the Village People began shooting their ill-fated feature film *Can't Stop the Music* (costarring Steve Guttenberg and Bruce Jenner), a major box-office flop.

The Village People in their 1979 movie, *Can't Stop the Music*. Shown (left to right) top row: Randy Jones, Victor Willis, Alex Briley; (bottom row): David Hodo, Felipe Rose, Glenn Hughes. Courtesy of Can't Stop Productions Inc./Photofest. © 1979 Can't Stop Productions.

In the early 1980s, as disco fell into disfavor, the Village People attempted to move in another musical direction with the release of the album *Renaissance*. With its nondisco style and the band members' new look, the album did not catch on with fans. The group disbanded in 1986 to allow its members to pursue solo projects but then reunited two years later to resume touring, which has continued to the present day. The group's mastermind, Jacques Morali, died in December 1991 of AIDS-related causes, and its original leatherman-biker, Glenn Hughes, died in March 2001 of lung cancer. In the early twenty-first century, three original members (Briley, Hodo, and Rose) and three replacements (Eric Anzalone as the biker, Jeff Olson as the cowboy, and Ray Simpson as the policeman and the band's lead singer) continued to perform and tour together.

Having been named after New York City's **gay ghetto** of Greenwich Village, the Village People are noteworthy for helping to define a pop era with a queer twist. Many fans over the years have wrongly assumed that all members of the band (past or present) are gay. Early on, the band's members were accused of profiting from promoting derogatory gay **stereotypes,** but they argued that the image of six masculine men was not offensive, whereas the image of six screaming queens might be.

Further Reading

Edwards, Victoria. 2006. "All Ages Rock with Village People." *The News-Sentinel* (July 17): D1.
Murphy, Kerrie. 2001. "Moving with the Times." *The Australian* (May 10): M22.
Romesburg, Don. 2002. "De-gaying the Village People." *The Advocate* (May 14): 24.
"The Village People." 1996. *People* (June 17): 60.
Wilson-Smith, Anthony. 2000. "A Straight Road to Gay Stardom." *Maclean's* (April 24): 9.

Kylo-Patrick R. Hart

Chea Villanueva (1952–)

Chea Villanueva was born in Philadelphia and is the author of powerful, controversial fiction and poetry focusing on the experiences of lesbians of color in working-class communities. Her work has been anthologized in a wide variety of collections, including *Making Waves: An Anthology of Writing by and about Asian American Women, Riding Desire: An Anthology of Erotic Writing,* and *The Persistent Desire: A Femme-Butch Anthology.* Exploring the lives of African American, Asian American, and Latina lesbians, Villanueva gives voice to (all-too-often) silenced members of the lesbian community, fearlessly exploring how race and class shape women's experiences in the world and their relationships with one another. Strongly and often explicitly erotic, Villanueva's literary work considers women's efforts to claim sexual autonomy and pleasure in a grim, violent, and homophobic world. In addition to their frank explorations of sexuality and butch identity, Villanueva's works are also profoundly engaged with questions of women's **economic** exploitation, examining the struggles of working-class women in the United States and Latin America. In 1987, Villanueva published *The Things I Never Told You,* a collection of erotic love poetry. She followed this work with two interconnected novels, *Girlfriends* (1987) and *The Chinagirls* (1991), works of fiction told in the form of letters between African American and Asian American female characters, considering questions of sexuality, community, and racial identity. In 1995, Villanueva published *Jessie's Song and Other Stories,* a collection of stark, raw stories exploring poor women's struggles for survival in the face of violence, oppression, and **homophobia.** Villanueva's 1997 *Bulletproof Butches* offered a harsh, bluntly honest examination of queer women's lives within the American prison system. Throughout her work, Villanueva remains uncompromising in her desire to explore the complexities of female sexuality and the impact that homophobia, racism, and classism have on women's lives.

Further Reading

Aguilar-San Juan, Karin. 1993. "Landmarks in Literature by Asian-American Lesbians." *Signs* 18 (4): 936–43.

Wong, Sau-ling C., and Jeffrey J. Santa Ana. 1999. "Gender and Sexuality in Asian American Literature." *Signs* 25 (11): 171–226.

Holly M. Kent

Norah Vincent (196?–)

Norah Vincent is a self-described "libertarian conservative" and freelance journalist. In addition to writing for a variety of periodicals, Vincent was also a senior fellow at the Foundation for the Defense of Democracies, a conservative think tank. She is perhaps best known for her book *Self-Made Man.* Even though she was an out lesbian, she wanted to explore what it felt like to be a man. She did not see herself as transgender or a cross-dresser, but one Halloween night in New York, she dressed up as a man so well that men on the street acknowledged her as if she was part of a club. That prompted her to take an 18-month sabbatical leave from her stint as a columnist at the *Los Angeles Times* and live full-time as a man known as Ned Vincent. She learned how to perfect her appearance and to **pass,** right down to her facial stubble that became so undetectable as a forgery, along with voice lessons to learn male vocal subtleties. She also incorporated a false penis to give her pants heft and realism. With each situation that explored male intimacy, she made a series of startling observations about the stereotypes of men, many of which have some truth in them. She described how women in singles bars were often in the habit of deflating men interested in them, so she could not blame straight men for feeling the way they did about women in general. She found that men, while not seeming as loquacious as women, did truly communicate with each other—perhaps more than women, and often to the point. She joined a bowling league, tried out for sales job interviews, visited strip clubs, and spent time in an all-male monastery. Vincent had always thought that men lived a life of entitlement, but it was not quite so. She discovered that men—gay or straight—have to make many sacrifices that women do not. In fact, in her view, women may have unintentionally contributed to some of the sexual inequity in society.

After the ordeal as Ned was over, Vincent was happy to incorporate "the swagger, the self-confidence, the entitlement" that she exhibited as a man but was much happier to return to her feminine qualities—even qualities that she had not seen in herself before being Ned, such as a fuller range of emotions than men are allowed to express in Western society. She concluded that as Ned, she damaged her own psyche as much as anyone else's: through these experiences she had deceived so many people with whom she made lasting friendships as Ned, yet she had grown from these experiences, even while vowing never to impersonate someone else again.

Further Reading

Green, Jamison. 2004. *Becoming a Visible Man*. Memphis, TN: Vanderbilt University Press.

Khosla, Dhillon. 2006. *Both Sides Now: One Man's Journey through Womanhood*. New York: Tarcher.

Valerio, Max Wolf. 2006. *The Testosterone Files: My Hormonal and Social Transformation from Female to Male*. San Francisco: Seal Press.

Raymond Luczak and Louis M. Miranda

Violet Quill, The

The Violet Quill was a group of writers who were also intimate friends: Edmund White, Andrew Holleran, Felice Picano, Robert Ferro, Michael Grumley, Christopher Cox, and George Whitmore. These seven writers met to discuss their in-process writing eight times from March 1980 to March 1981. Although they did not articulate or adhere to a unified literary theory, they shared a common sexuality and a mutual concern for the craft of writing—particularly as it held the potential to express the individual and subcultural concerns of the gay male. In this way, the group shared a common literary ethos. Although the subject matter of homosexuality was not new to literature, the attention it was beginning to receive from mainstream publishers was a new phenomenon. The relative freedom these writers experienced to narrate and publish the subjects and subjectivities of their subculture, however, did not coincide with an equal cultural advancement regarding the acceptance of homosexuality. In "Edmund White and the Violet Quill Club," Picano goes so far as to characterize the club as a "fortress" that buttressed the writers against a culture and publishing establishment that had largely rejected gay literature and, of course, gay people. If nothing else, the Violet Quill provided a space for these seven authors to experience acceptance when the larger cultural response ranged from tolerance to intolerance.

Even if the Violet Quill's writings had lacked literary merit (the vast majority of them readily show merit), the cultural context surrounding the group imbues its literature with significance. Accordingly, the group's writings incite interest on a literary, biographical, sociological, political, and historical basis. The context to explain the breadth and depth of this interest can be found in the period between the 1969 **Stonewall Riots** and the 1981 emergence of the AIDS epidemic—the dozen years that Violet Quill scholar and poet **David Bergman** (2004) refers to as a darkly golden time. Bergman's adjectival juxtaposition stems from the heady days of liberation following Stonewall and the subsequent era of the epidemic that followed. Accordingly, the group's early writings gesture toward a gay male writing that escapes the nugatory strictures of the **closet** while simultaneously predating the existential decimation of the AIDS epidemic. Specifically, these early writings indicate how the gay literary project might have been textured had the HIV virus not had such a devastating impact on gay literature, much less gay writers. In his essay "Out of the Closet, onto the Bookshelf," Edmund White considers the loss of gay literature after the emergence of AIDS to be incalculable. Although such considerations are speculative, the existential history of the Violet Quill suggests White's assessment has merit. By 1990, Michael Grumley, Robert Ferro, Christopher Cox, and George Whitmore had died from AIDS-related complications, and of the remaining three group members, Edmund White is HIV-positive. A third point of context that greatly informs the consideration of the Violet Quill is the migration pattern of gay men from rural to urban America throughout the 1970s and the consequential development of the gay urban neighborhood. From **San Francisco** to **New York City,** which serves as a primary geography for the Violet Quill, the development of a visible and viable gay urban subculture created new opportunities for the actualization of the gay individual and the formation of a gay subculture. In addition to the development of the "gay ghetto," an attendant growth was seen in gay resort destinations, and Long Island's Fire Island figures as an important vacation geography for the group. Although these points of context do not reveal or inform every aspect of the Violet Quill's written work, this context is often referred to in their writing, and in some degree held them together as a group.

The cultural context surrounding the Violet Quill fostered more than this one group of writers, and the Violet Quill is perhaps more productively understood as an element of a larger literary zeitgeist. Although novels dealing with gay themes had been published over the prior decades, most notably **Christopher Isherwood**'s *A Single Man* (1964), 1978 figures as a prolific year for the gay novel. During this year and the early part of the next, five gay novels were published by mainstream publishing houses. All five novels were best sellers upon their release, and all five have since become touchstones for what is considered post-Stonewall literature. Three of these novels were written by Violet Quill members: Andrew Holleran's *Dancer from the Dance*, Felice Picano's *The Lure*, and Edmund White's *Nocturnes for the King of Naples*. The remaining two novels were written by authors not directly associated with the group: **Larry Kramer**'s *Faggots* and Armistead Maupin's *Tales of the City*. These two novels have had as large an impact, if not larger, than the vast majority of the Violet Quill's writings, and both of them point to the existence of gay writers and writing beyond this one group.

This larger contextual consideration calibrates the understanding of the Violet Quill as a cultural phenomenon that might yet come to be understood as a renaissance in gay American male literature. As such, the Violet Quill may well be properly understood as a component part of a larger literary movement. This point of critical clarification rectifies a misreading of the Violet Quill writers, for they have been criticized for perpetuating, if not producing, a monolithic representation of homosexuality. This criticism is spurious at best. The writings of the Violet Quill frequently contain self-reflexive moments that characterize them as little more than an individual, if not an idiosyncratic, experience of gayness. Considering the Violet Quill as part of a larger literary and cultural phenomenon spares the group the reductive burden of representing the totality of post-Stonewall literature, much less gay literature, yet allows its particular literary continuities and discontinuities to be considered according to the emergence of multicultural American literature. The critical insight offered by multicultural literature, which establishes and explores the diversity of modern North American culture, holds the potential to explicate the Violet Quill in the context of a larger literary movement, thereby avoiding needlessly separatist or "ghettoized" interpretations. Perhaps, the plurality that George Stambolian, founder of the "Men on Men" series, posited as the driving force behind American literature establishes the most productive lens through which to view the writings of the Violet Quill. This understanding holds the potential to rehabilitate the Quill's much-maligned reputation.

Despite the presence of some scholarly efforts, the critical reception surrounding the Violet Quill has yet to be fully established, much less understood. As of this writing, only two book-length projects have been devoted to recording and exploring the Quill's writings: Bergman's *The Violet Quill Reader: The Emergence of Gay Writing after Stonewall* (1994) and his *The Violet Hour: The Violet Quill and the Making of Gay Culture* (2004). These two works and a handful of articles initiate a yet to be fully explored critical project that has at times been derailed by negative criticism. Ironically, for a group of gay writers who largely gathered together to avoid hostile, apathetic, perplexed, or otherwise nugatory responses from nongay readers, their most harsh criticism has come from other gay men. Critiques of the Violet Quill have come from contemporaneous gay writers like Larry Kramer and **Ethan Mordden** and next-generation gay writers like Bruce Bawer and **David Leavitt.** Collectively, the focus of this criticism ranges from simple yet complicated differences in aesthetics and politics to reductive, if not willful, misinterpretations of the Quill's work. Explanations for the spate of negative criticism have ranged from its being the result of publishing envy to something more sinister like internalized **homophobia.** However, a more productive consideration may stem from the Violet Quill's ambivalence toward literary realism. Despite rejecting the strictures of realism, a difficult narrative mode for gay writers under a heteronormative culture, the Violet Quill writers often wrote with an autobiographical impulse. The result destabilized the line between fact and fiction and produced a fictional hybrid, which Edmund White has cautiously termed "auto-fiction." This narrative evolution may have developed faster than its reader, especially since the Quill crafted its new narrative form while simultaneously developing, if not creating, a reading community for gay literature.

The negative critical reception surrounding the Violet Quill merits rehearsing because it minimizes, if not overlooks, the role these seven writers played in popularizing gay fiction. From the news presses to the publishing houses, the members of the Violet Quill worked to foster gay literature and its reading community. These efforts are summarily recorded in Picano's essay "On the Real Violet Quill," and the archives evidence this claim. Picano himself went so far as to establish a gay publishing house. SeaHorse Press, which opened in 1977 and closed in 1991, published a wide array of authors, including the legendary historian **Martin Duberman** and then up-and-coming West Coast narrative novelist Dennis Cooper. Picano also collaborated with other gay presses to form the publishing alliance of the Gay Presses of New York. In addition to directly supporting the publication of gay books, the Violet Quill supported their reception by popularizing gay literature. Through the conduits of both the gay and mainstream media, the Quill members worked toward this goal with reviews, articles, and interviews. Additionally, several of the club's members have taught and lectured about gay literature. Holleran and White have both written about and taught courses on gay writing, and Ferro offered a powerful contribution in the last year of his life with his lecture "Gay Literature Today." Although they were by no means alone in these efforts, the Violet Quill writers frequently pushed beyond the inherent narcissism that stems from the publishing pen to contribute to the larger project of gay literature. This perspective is too often overlooked in hasty debates surrounding the presence or absence of sex and beauty in gay writing.

The Quill's three surviving members remain committed to the larger gay literary project at the beginning of the twenty-first century. In 2001, *Loss within Loss: Artists in the Age of AIDS* was released. This collection of essays dedicated to the remembrance of the writings of those lost to AIDS was edited by White, and Picano contributed an essay on Ferro to the project. In addition, as late as 2006, while touring for his latest work *Grief: A Novel,* Holleran has been known to preface his readings with observations regarding the productive persistence of the gay bookstore and its reading community. Between charges of prurience and puritanical readings, the Violet Quill's critical reception has often been vitiated by articles such as Dennis Altman's 1980 "A Moveable Brunch: The Fag-Lit Mafia." Altman's cheeky title has come to summarily represent a nugatory trend in the critical reception of the Violet Quill, and this response has at times eclipsed the individual writers.

The understanding of the Violet Quill begins with the writings read during their meetings. In two articles rehearsing the group's history, Picano catalogued the works that were shared during the group's eight readings. This catalog claims that excerpts read aloud from then in-progress writings include White's *A Boy's Own Story*, Holleran's *Nights in Aruba*, Ferro's *The Family of Max Desir*, Grumley's *A World of Men* and *Life Drawing*, Cox's *A Key West Companion*, Picano's *Slashed to Ribbons in Defense of Love* and *Ambidextrous*, and several short stories by Whitmore. A cursory review of the publications from this period suggests Whitmore may have been working on the story "Scrabble," or perhaps his nonfiction article "New Frontiers of SM." Picano's memory of the readings is confirmed by White, who includes a similar list in his recounting of the club in his aforementioned essay titled "Out of the Closet, onto the Bookshelf." All three surviving members substantiate the rumors surrounding the sweet delicacies that were served between the evening's readings. The readings were followed by discussion, and this dialogue formed the heart of the group.

Although the readings were reported to be complicated by the typical writer's concerns about literary pickpocketing and competition, they also supplied a supportive venue that was otherwise lacking in which to consider the literary issues surrounding the narration of gay concerns and content. In their reflections on the meetings, Picano and White delineated the larger cultural conditions surrounding the group's unique position. Picano asserts they were alone in the contemporaneous pursuit of an openly gay literature. White confirms the solidarity behind this feeling when he writes about his 1983 return to the United States, during which he realized the devastation of AIDS for his literary peers, describing it as a loss of cultural cohorts. Picano's assertion, coupled with White's characterization, holds the potential to explain the group's feelings of isolation. This potential may well rest in the understanding of their particular chronological context.

During the 1969 Stonewall Riots, all seven members of the Violet Quill were in their twenties. White, the oldest member, was 29, and Cox, the youngest member, was only 20. On a side note, both of these men were present at the riots. As young adults developing into the bloom of adulthood during a revolutionary time for homosexuals in America, these seven men were faced with empowering options that were generally not available to gays before Stonewall. Consequently, all seven members acted, if not literally moved, to become a part of the gay urban subculture of Manhattan. As such, they were able to frame a life around their sexual identity; something that was virtually unheard of in the decades preceding Stonewall. If the Stonewall Riots did not directly transform anything, the subsequent political action and social formations surrounding gay pride changed everything regarding the psychic, social, and geographic opportunities facing young gay men and women in America during the 1970s. This forms a significant generational difference between the Violet Quill writers and the older gay authors who, having matured into adulthood before Stonewall, reflected the closet culture of the 1950s more than street culture of 1970s gay liberation. Moreover, by the time of the Violet Quill meetings, most of the club's members were in their thirties with White just turning 40. These men lived the prime years of their adulthood in the relative freedom of the post-Stonewall decade.

As members of a recently empowered minority, this group of men, who also experienced the relative privilege of their sex and class positions, turned to literature to express the excitement and concerns of their personal and subcultural moment. This impulse mimics the historic efforts of other oppressed minority groups in America as they fought for equality, for example African Americans, Jewish Americans, and women. By virtue of its chronological position, the Violet Quill sought a clarity and openness for the presence of homosexuality in literature that the previous generation had spent a lifetime veiling with codes and sublimations. This formed an important generational difference between the Violet Quill and older gay authors. Picano's assessment was correct. Generational and aesthetic differences left the Quill isolated, as they explored a new way of writing gay literature. The work read during the Violet Quill's meetings was a part of this new literary flourishing.

However, a rigorous consideration of the Violet Quill extends beyond the scope of the writings shared during eight meetings in the early 1980s, for as Bergman notes in his introduction to his book-length study of the group, these seven writers had some degree of group consciousness prior to their first meeting. Moreover, this consciousness extended beyond the group's final 1981 meeting. Indeed, White speaks of leaving the group as late as 1983, when he moved to France. Picano acknowledges the group disbanded with the illnesses and subsequent deaths of four of its members; conversely, he also asserts that something of the Violet Quill consciousness persisted after the deaths of Ferro, Grumley, Cox, and Whitmore. As late as 1997, Picano asserts that the three surviving members of the club—White, Holleran, and himself—continue to share and sometimes read in-progress work to one another before publication. Picano's characterization of these later encounters as more productive than the original group readings suggests the longevity of the Violet Quill.

Further Reading

Bergman, David, ed. 1994. *The Violet Quill Reader: The Emergence of Gay Writing after Stonewall.* New York: St. Martin's Press.

Bergman, David. 2004. *The Violet Hour: The Violet Quill and the Making of Gay Culture.* New York: Columbia University Press.

Picano, Felice. 1997. "On the *Real* Violet Quill Club." In *Queer Representations: Reading Lives, Reading Cultures,* ed. Martin Duberman, 311–18. New York: New York University Press.

White, Edmund. 1995. "Out of the Closet, onto the Bookshelf." In *The Burning Library: Essays,* ed. David Bergman, 275–83. New York: Vintage Press.

Mark John Isola

Paula Vogel (1951–)

Born in Washington, D.C., Paula Vogel is an award-winning playwright, professor of English at Brown University, and fellow of the American Academy of Arts and Sciences. In 2004, she married her longtime partner, Anne Fausto-Sterling, a professor of molecular biology, cell biology, and biochemistry at Brown. While a minority of her characters are lesbian or gay, Vogel's plays disrupt orthodoxies of gender and sexuality, often critically engaging with canonical texts and interweaving sexual, familial, and national politics. *Baltimore Waltz* (1992), Vogel's first play to garner major attention, memorializes the playwright's brother Carl, who died of AIDS in 1988. A surreal, guilt- and mourning-induced fantasy in which the narrator Anna inverts reality so that she is stricken with "acquired toilet disease" (ATD) rather than her brother Carl being diagnosed with AIDS, *Baltimore Waltz* won the Obie Award for Best Play in 1992 for its deft combination of humor and pathos. *How I Learned to Drive* (1997) made the rare transition from a not-for-profit production to a commercial off-Broadway run, winning the 1998 Pulitzer Prize for Drama. This mainstream success came despite the play's unusual approach to the subject of sexual abuse and incest, making the pedophilic Uncle Peck an object of desire and sympathy for the audience and for his victim, the central character and narrator, L'il Bit. Other plays include *Desdemona, A Play about a Handkerchief* (1979), *The Oldest Profession* (1981), *Hot 'N Throbbing* (1994), *The Mineola Twins* (1996), and *The Long Christmas Ride Home* (2004).

Further Reading

Bigsby, Christopher. 1999. *Contemporary American Playwrights*. Cambridge: Cambridge University Press.

Savran, David. 2003. *A Queer Sort of Materialism: Recontextualizing American Theater*. Ann Arbor: University of Michigan Press.

Catherine Burriss

W

Rufus Wainwright

Rufus Wainwright, a piano-based singer-songwriter and son of folk singers Loudon Wainwright III and Kate McGarrigle, grew up performing in the McGarrigle Sisters and Family with his mother Kate, sister Martha, and aunt Anna. After touring the Montreal club circuit, he was noticed by producer Pierre Marchand, and Wainwright's 1998 self-titled debut was released by DreamWorks Records. Wainwright's other albums include *Poses* (2001) and *Want One* (2003) and *Want Two* (2004). His music has been featured in television and film soundtracks such as *Queer as Folk*, *The L Word*, and *Brokeback Mountain*. Wainwright's lyrics are known for their allusions to opera, literature, and mass media, with examples ranging from "Art Teacher," in which the song's narrator, a woman who married well but never got over her teenage crush, describes the sculptural works that inspired her as a teen, to "Grey Gardens," which includes references to Thomas Mann's *Death in Venice*. Songs such as "14th Street," "Vibrate," and "Oh What a World" express the exuberance of new romance, the pain of a broken heart, rejection, and the trendiness of homosexuality in 1990s mass media. Songs such as "Gay Messiah" mark Wainwright's overt politicization of his lyrics, with this song in particular functioning as a retort to religious conservatives, casting the Messiah as a tube-sock clad reincarnation of 1970s gay porn performers. His stylistic blend of rock, pop, and cabaret styles has earned him accolades from both *Rolling Stone* and the gay press.

Further Reading
Hornby, Nick. 2003. *Songbook*. New York: Riverhead Trade.
Schwartz, Deb. 1999. "The Rufus On Fire." *Out* (January): 66.

Ben Aslinger

Andy Warhol (1928–1987)

Born Andrew Warhola in Pittsburgh, Pennsylvania, Andy Warhol was one of the most influential artists of the twentieth century. The youngest of seven sons of Andrij (Andrew) and Ulja (Julia) Warhola, working-class immigrants from Miková in Austria-Hungary (now northeast Slovakia), Warhol enrolled at the Carnegie Institute of Technology in Pittsburgh in 1945, where he studied commercial art. After graduation, he began a career as a commercial artist in New York City. Warhol achieved some measure of success as a commercial artist, and his drawings for I. Miller shoes were particularly popular. *Glamour* magazine used his drawing of girls climbing a ladder to illustrate "Success Is a Job in New York," citing "Andy Warhol" as the article's illustrator. Thus, Andrew Warhola became Andy Warhol.

By the late 1950s, the pop art movement was beginning to make an impact in the United States. Warhol painted images he found in magazine advertisements, dripping and splattering the paintings to distinguish them from the clean-lined illustrations of commercial art. He also painted pictures of comic book frames depicting cartoon characters Little Nancy, Popeye, and Dick Tracy.

The year 1960 marked a turning point in Warhol's career when he painted a picture of a Coca-Cola bottle with clean lines. In 1962, the Fergus Gallery in Los Angeles exhibited 32 Warhol paintings of Campbell's soup cans. Warhol used silk screening to transfer images onto canvases. His silk-screened canvases often repeated rows of the same image, including Coke bottles, dollar bills, soup cans, and portraits of celebrities like Marilyn Monroe and Elvis Presley. He created the *Disaster* series, silk-screened paintings based on crime-scene photos he obtained from tabloid publications, including images of car crashes and electric chairs.

Warhol hired Gerard Malanga in 1963 to assist him with the silk-screening process. This marked the beginning of Warhol's establishment of his studio as a factory—a place where people came together to create and produce works of art, often aided by mechanized processes—rather than as a space for the solitary artist. Warhol and Malanga also constructed, in an assembly-line fashion, a series of plywood grocery box sculptures for Brillo pads, Del Monte peaches, and Kellogg's cornflakes.

Warhol directed films of subjects engaged in everyday activities, including John Giorno sleeping for six hours (*Sleep*, 1963) and **Robert Indiana** eating a mushroom (*Eat*, 1963). He also made *Blow Job* (1964), a film showing only the face of Tom Baker as he received oral sex. In many of these early Warhol films, the camera angle is fixed. The intensity of the filmmaker's gaze upon his subjects helped to create the image of Warhol as a voyeuristic observer.

Andy Warhol in 1966, a scene from *Andy Warhol: A Documentary Film*, 2006 (PBS). Directed by Ric Burns. © PBS Photographer: Gretchen Berg/Photofest.

Billy Linich (also known as Billy Name) designed Warhol's studio, known as the Factory, to be all silver. Several of Name's friends from New York City's underground became fixtures there, including the Sugar Plum Fairy, Rotten Rita, and Ondine. Many of these people were gay or bisexual, and Warhol was attracted to their theatricality, open-minded approaches to sexuality, drug use, and identities as outsiders. The Factory also attracted people like high-society rebel Brigid Berlin (also known as Brigid Polk). Later in the 1960s, transvestite cabaret singer and actor Jackie Curtis, transgender actresses Candy Darling and Holly Woodlawn, and bisexual hustler and actor Joe Dallesandro starred in Warhol's films. Edie Sedgwick—the star of Warhol's most commercially successful film of this period, *Chelsea Girls* (1966)—was one of the most famous Factory superstars.

In 1966, Warhol persuaded the Velvet Underground, fronted by singer and guitar player **Lou Reed,** to take on Nico as a singer and become part of the Exploding Plastic Inevitable, a multimedia performance event that incorporated music, film, and dance. Warhol also produced *The Velvet Underground and Nico* (1967) and designed the album's cover art, a banana that could be peeled.

On June 3, 1968, Valerie Solanas shot Warhol at the Factory. Warhol was not expected to survive; in fact, he was pronounced clinically dead at one point. He survived, but the shooting severely weakened him; he had to wear a corset for the rest of his life to support his abdomen, and his chest was riddled with scars from doctors' cutting open his chest to massage his heart. Radical feminist Solanas had appeared in Warhol's *I, a Man* (1967). She was a survivor of childhood sexual abuse, a prostitute, and a playwright, and she was often homeless and suffered from extreme paranoia. She was the only member of the Society for Cutting Up Men (SCUM) and author of *SCUM Manifesto*. When Warhol told Solanas he had lost a copy of a script she had given to him, she became convinced that he was out to profit from her work without giving her the credit or money she deserved. Solanas was sentenced to three years in prison. After being released, she spent the rest of her life on the streets and in and out of mental institutions and died in San Francisco in 1988.

After the shooting, Warhol relinquished his role as director to Paul Morrissey, the associate director of some of Warhol's earlier films. Although Warhol would continue to produce films—including *Trash* (1969), *Heat* (1970), and *Flesh for Frankenstein* (also called *Andy Warhol's Frankenstein*, 1973)—Morrissey usually directed. During the 1970s, Warhol Enterprises was very profitable. Warhol was commissioned to paint portraits of celebrities and socialites, including **Truman Capote,** Bianca Jagger, and Liza Minnelli. He also completed a series of paintings of Chairman Mao. In 1969, he started an underground magazine, which by 1973 had been transformed into *Interview*, with Warhol and Fred Hughes as the magazine's directors and Bob Colacello as its chief editor. *Interview* featured celebrity interviews (sometimes conducted by Warhol), and its correspondents covered fashion, art, music, movies, nightlife, and Warhol's life and work.

During the early to mid-1980s, Warhol championed the work of several young artists. Warhol and **Jean-Michel Basquiat** collaborated on a series of paintings. Warhol's final completed works included paintings based on Leonardo da Vinci's

Last Supper. Warhol died on February 22, 1987, while in the hospital recovering from routine gallbladder surgery.

Further Reading

Andy Warhol Museum. 2004. *Andy Warhol, 365 Takes: The Andy Warhol Museum Collection.* New York: H. N. Abrams.

Bockris, Victor. 2003. *Warhol: The Biography.* 2nd ed. New York: Da Capo Press.

Doyle, Jennifer, Jonathan Flatley, and José Esteban Muñoz, eds. 1996. *Pop Out: Queer Warhol.* Durham, NC: Duke University Press.

Koestenbaum, Wayne. 2001. *Andy Warhol.* Penguin Lives. New York: Viking.

Warhol, Andy. 1989. *The Andy Warhol Diaries.* Ed. Pat Hackett. New York: Warner Books.

Krista L. May

water sports

Water sports is the common term given to a sexual fetish involving human urine; the act is also known as giving golden showers. The proper term for water sports is *urolagnia* (also *urophilia*). The act is not specific to the gay community, but it has been largely associated with some homosexual sex practices. Water sports is typically not a solo activity; it is usually enacted by one of the participants urinating on the self, someone urinating on another person, or a third party watching the act of urination for sexual gratification. Another common element of water sports features the drinking of urine, either one person consuming another's urine or consumption of one's own in a couple or group setting. Within the queer leather scene it has also been linked as a sexual humiliation act to those who engage in BDSM. Water sports has been deemed fairly harmless as a sexual activity. Health risks for the practice are generally low, barring the presence of disease or infectious bacteria. Like other sexual fetishes, it plays a role in the production of some **pornographic films.**

Further Reading

Bean, Joseph W. 1994. *Leathersex: A Guide for the Curious Outsider and the Serious Player.* San Francisco: Daedalus Publishing.

Bean, Joseph W. 2004. *Soaked! The Watersports Handbook for Men.* Las Vegas: Nazca Plains Corporation.

James Francis Jr.

Peter Weltner (1942–)

Peter Weltner was born in North Carolina and is currently a professor at San Francisco State University. Weltner earned his PhD in English literature in 1969 from Indiana University. Working primarily as a scholar and critic during the first years of his career, Weltner did not begin any creative ventures until roughly 1976. At that time Weltner began to write short stories and novels in fairly rapid succession but chose not to seek publication for any of his work until the late 1980s. *Beachside Entries/Specific Ghosts*, a collection of stories, appeared in 1989 and was followed in 1991 by his first novel, *Identity and Difference*. Focusing on two unrelated stories, *Identity and Difference* tells the stories of Preston and Darryl. Preston, a self-absorbed, upper-class gay man, spends most of his time obsessing about the intricacies of his relationship with Jim, while Darryl, a lower-middle-class adolescent, struggles to come to terms with his older brother's suicide. Although presented in tandem, the stories never connect; rather, they present, in two different styles, the lives of two men struggling to accept and understand their own sexuality. In the end, Preston is presented as the less mature and well adjusted of the two characters, offering an interesting perspective on the nature of self-acceptance, particularly in terms of sexuality. In complex ways, Weltner capably draws parallels between the two stories without ever explicitly uniting them. Weltner published a collection of three short novels in 1991 called *In a Time of Combat for the Angel* and was the recipient of the O. Henry Award twice.

Further Reading

Stambolian, George. 1990. "Searching for Sensibilities." *The Advocate* (October 23): 74–76.
Tushinski, James. 1990. "Late Bloomer: Peter Weltner Blossoms after Ten-Year 'Apprenticeship.'" *Bay Area Reporter* (December 13): 29.

J. G. Adair

Tim'm T. West (1972–)

Tim'm West grew up in Taylor, Arkansas, in a religious evangelical family. Following his graduation from Taylor High School, West pursued a BA in women's studies and philosophy at Duke University, an MA in liberal studies and philosophy from the New School, and an MA from Stanford University in modern thought and literature.

West describes himself as "Black, queer, feminist, poz, and working class" (West Web site). Also known as "25 percenter," Tim'm West is best known as a performance artist, educator, and author. In 1999, West cofounded the hip-hop group Deep Dickollective along with fellow artists Juba Kalamka and Phillip Atiba Goff.

Currently based in Atlanta, Georgia, West is the author of three books including *Red Dirt Revival: A Poetic Memoir in 6 Breaths*, which was followed by his musical release, *Songs from Red Dirt*. West's work has been presented in various publications and anthologies, while his books have been published by the press he founded, Red Dirt Publishing. While his earlier works were explicitly autobiographical, in his more recent works, West has turned to the hip-hop scene more broadly. In *Blakkboy Blue(s)*, West strives to locate himself as a hip-hop artist, while simultaneously providing a critical analysis of the tensions and the politics of the hip-hop scene.

Further Reading

Deepdickollective.com. Available at: http://profile.myspace.com/index.cfm?fuseaction=user. viewprofile&friendid=40396924. Accessed July 15, 2008.

Green, Keith. 2005. "One-on-One with Tim'm West: Tim'm West Journeys into Self-Love—for All." *The Body: The Complete HIV/AIDS Resource*. July/August. Available at: http://www. thebody.com/content/art1162.html. Accessed July 15, 2008.

Tim'm T. West Web site. Available at: http://www.reddirt.biz/pages/timm.html. Accessed July 15, 2008.

West, Tim'm. 2002. *Red Dirt Revival: A Poetic Memoir in 6 Breaths*. Atlanta: Red Dirt Publishing.

West, Tim'm. 2004. *Songs from Red Dirt*. Compact disc. Cellular Records.

West, Tim'm. 2004. *BARE: Notes from a Porchdweller*. Atlanta: Red Dirt Publishing.

West, Tim'm. 2007. *Blakkboy Blue(s)*. Atlanta, GA: Red Dirt Publishing; Brooklyn, NY: Family Ties Records.

West, Tim'm. 2007. *Flirting*. Atlanta, GA: Red Dirt Publishing.

Andy Inkster

West Coast New Narrative Movement, The

This is a term first used by **Steve Abbott** to describe a group of **San Francisco**–based writers who, from the late 1970s to the present day, have been associated with a certain type of innovative writing. A literary movement involves writers producing texts that share certain attributes as well as differences. While Robert Glück (1947–) notes that in the past he was reluctant to promote the idea of a literary school, but he now concedes that there is indeed such a thing as New Narrative (Glück 2005).

Glück (2005) indeed craved the community that the very "straight male" "L = A = N = G = U = A = G = E poets" (influenced by Gertrude Stein and Louis Zukofsky) made for themselves, along with the notion that language generates meaning. Writers would both comment on and appropriate ideas from one another's work, and San Francisco thus became as much a literary city as a center of gay life. Glück and **Bruce Boone** were interested in the work of Dennis Cooper (1953–), and indeed of Kathy Acker, which produced friendships with them, once Cooper had moved from his longtime home of **New York City.** Glück also became friends with Denise Kastan, who lived with Kathy Acker in a downstairs flat. In 1976 Glück volunteered for the nonprofit bookstore Small Press Traffic, of which he soon became codirector, and between 1977 and 1985 he held writing workshops and a small reading group; in 1981 the Left/Write Conference was held at the Noe Valley Ministry, bringing together writers with different aesthetic positions (Glück 2005). Many New Narrative writers began writing poetry but ended up working on short stories and novels.

Glück was constantly reading literary theory. He aimed to produce a literature that was, to a degree, authentic, and, drawing on Roland Barthes and Walter Benjamin, his novels and short stories focus on distorted **autobiography** in a lyrical manner, highlighting deep personal emotion. Glück bases narratives around his life, writes in the first person, and incorporates his name (Bob) and the names of friends (Bruce Boone, Denise Kastan, and Kathy Acker) into his work, risking making the self vulnerable. This is evident in *Elements of a Coffee Service* (1982), *Jack the Modernist* (1985), and *Denny Smith* (2003). In *Jack the Modernist*, the narrator further becomes merged with the author through chapter titles written in this first-person voice. For *Margery Kempe* (1994), Glück has chosen a real-life fifteenth-century figure, believed by some to have written the first autobiography, and here the narrator Bob parallels her fictionalized story with his own. As Glück (2005) reveals, autobiography also consists of making evident the private nature of daydreams and nightdreams (as in *Jack the Modernist*).

Glück further explores how the gay individual exists in relation to the body. For Glück, transgressive writing is that which articulates the present and is therefore not necessarily about sex; nevertheless, transgressive sexual content is an important feature of his work. Gay sexual acts are described in such detail that the reader is able to visualize what is transpiring. His work therefore enters the arena of **por-nography,** seen as a low form presented in magazines, on videos, and on the Internet. Indeed, the transgressive sexual content of New Narrative can be an attraction in itself, rather than a way of moving a storyline forward. Such content is present in *Elements of a Coffee Service* (narratives from which appeared in porn magazines), *Jack the Modernist* (where the narrator refers to sex as pornography and details its effect on his senses), *Margery Kempe* (where the narrator's lust for "L" and their sexual activity parallels Margery's spiritual and, here, sexual devotion to Jesus), and *Denny Smith*. Even when not describing sex, Glück includes sexual puns.

Glück's work also concerns the way in which the gay individual exists in rela-tion to a larger community. He sees the community, consisting of types, as telling itself its story (Glück 2005). Glück draws on Walter Benjamin's notion of mixing high and low forms and not only includes case history in his work but also legiti-mizes the place of gossip, considered a low oral vernacular form, in literature. Here gossip is not spread maliciously but rather involves an intimacy between those doing the gossiping and, as with the subway graffiti, common experiences. Gos-sip prevents important aspects of the community's life from being silenced. These ideas are explicitly stated in his short story "When Bruce Was 36" from *Elements of a Coffee Service*. In *Elements of a Coffee Service*, gossip takes place over coffee and through letter writing, and in *Jack the Modernist*, as in *Margery Kempe*, over the telephone.

The style of *Jack the Modernist* emphasizes the notion of gossip about sexual activity. The prose takes the form of a dramatic script during Bob's telephone con-versations with Denise and Bruce, the latter of whom is told in detail about Bob's excursion to the **bathhouse** and his sexual encounters there, an important aspect of gay culture (as mentioned in "When Bruce Was 36"). Since the style of the prose is akin to a dramatic script, the sense provided is of an everyday conversation taking place. The idea that New Narrative writers formed a "circle" is hence important since the conversation in the narrative mirrors the decade-long conversation that Glück reveals he had with Boone (Glück 2005).

Additionally, Glück presents a model of authorship and readership that is one of gossiper and receiver. For example, there are layers within *Jack the Modernist*. The narrator explicitly speaks of his love affair with Jack as a story told with intimate safety from him to us, thereby framing the text. A later move turns the reader into an eavesdropper on the telephone conversation between Bob and Bruce. At the end of the novel, the narrator reflects on a face-to-face conversation with Bruce and adopts a colloquial manner, making the reader feel part of an ongoing conversation. According to Glück (2005), the writer's exposing himself leaves not only his life open to judgment but also the reader's, since he is part of this community.

But for Glück, drawing on V. N. Voloshinov, the individual and the community are to be read in relation to a larger sociohistorical context (Glück 2005). For Glück, influenced by Georges Bataille, sex is a form of excess expenditure, where the self sheds its social identities, but this is temporary. In addition to exploring the way in which gay men can (to a degree) be connected by being part of a community, Glück explores the very modernist notion of disjunction: the gay individual is divided from wider society and sees himself as fragmented. Indebted to Barthes, Glück uses the "fragment" to illustrate this (Glück 2005), as can be seen in *Jack the Modernist*. Postmodernist references to popular culture are also included, showing how the media interpellate viewers in an Althusserian way as a type of subject, but the narrator makes alternative close readings of the texts that challenge the dominant ideology providing him with pleasures (Frangos, "Ruining the Fun").

In another postmodernist fashion, Glück was interested in metatextuality, commenting on the purposes of writing. Glück (2005) writes that a story can keep a running commentary on itself from the present. Therefore, he lays bare the illusion of writing, again drawing on Barthes. His writing (partly) channels the world, with its continuities and disjunctions, into words, an idea that is explicitly raised in *Jack the Modernist*. The notion that life is a fiction (which, as suggested in *Narrativity*, is partly politically invented) and that these experiences are communicated in a book is also explicitly asserted in *Margery Kempe*.

While Dennis Cooper has stated that no one quite knew what New Narrative was, he has often been grouped with the New Narrative writers: his novels display distorted autobiography and a transgressive pornographic concern with the body and the way in which it influences the mind of the gay male (Lucas 2001). Cooper's early teenage poetry dealt with scandalous subjects, but he is best known for his later books: *Closer* (1989), *Frisk* (1991), *Try* (1994), *Guide* (1997), and *Period* (1999). Cooper's life saw the merging of sex with violence: at age 11, a boy he had a crush on split Cooper's head open with an axe and at age 12 Cooper hiked to a spot in the mountains behind his house where three boys had been raped and killed (Lucas 2001). Drawing on this, some of his novels feature the punk-like quality of aggression and serial killers of young boys. This earned Cooper a reputation as a "dark" writer, but Cooper is more interested in the idea of men taking apart their objects of desire to understand the fascination that they hold (Laurence 1995). His books also concern his working out of his feelings for schoolmate and later lover, the 27-year-old George Miles (Lucas 2001).

Another West Coast writer is Armistead Maupin (1944–), whose serialized *Tales of the City,* centering around a San Francisco community against the social backdrop of the 1970s and 1980s (for example, the AIDS crisis), invites parallels between his work and that of Charles Dickens. Maupin's more recent novel *The Night Listener* (2001) contains some traits associated with New Narrative, the most prominent being distorted autobiography presented in an emotional fashion; the intimate communication between characters over the telephone; and a comment on the act of writing fiction. Like Maupin, Gabriel Noone, the protagonist of *The Night Listener,* is a fabulist who has spent years plundering his life for fiction: Noone is the author of the radio show *Noone at Night* and has presented first-person tales for his listeners, but his long-term lover Jess, who is HIV-positive, has moved out, leaving Noone without inspiration. Similarly, based on an incident from Maupin's own life where he seemingly made friends over the telephone with an AIDS-stricken teenager (Anthony Godby Johnson, who had written a book *Rock and a Hard Place: One Boy's Triumphant Story* [1993] detailing years of child abuse), Gabriel Noone is sent the autobiography *The Blacking Factory,* by an HIV-positive boy Pete, a victim of years of sexual and physical abuse. Noone bonds with Pete over the radio and on the telephone, able to open up to him until he begins to suspect that Pete does not exist and is being "played" by the woman claiming to be his foster mother, a suspicion also held of Johnson.

Further Reading

Abbott, Steve. 1985. "Notes on Boundaries, New Narrative." *Soup: New Critical Perspectives,* 4, ed. Bruce Boone, 81. San Francisco: Soup.

Frangos, M. "Ruining the Fun: History and Desire in Robert Glück's *Jack the Modernist.*" Available at: http://www.uweb.ucsb.edu/~mfrangos/gluck/gluck.html. Accessed July 15, 2008.

Glück, Robert. 2005. "Long Note on New Narrative." *Narrativity* 1. Available at: http://www.sfsu.edu/~newlit/narrativity/issue_one/gluck.html. Accessed July 15, 2008. (Repr. in *Biting the Error: Writers Explore Narrative,* ed. M. Burger, R. Glück, C. Roy, and G. Scott, 25–34. Toronto: Coach House Books.)

Laurence, Alexander. 1995. "Interview with Dennis Cooper." Available at: http://www.altx.com/int2/dennis.cooper.html. Accessed July 15, 2008. In *The Write Stuff: Interviews.* Available at: http://www.altx.com/interviews/. Accessed July 15, 2008.

Lucas, Stephen. 2001. "American Psycho: An Interview with Dennis Cooper." *3:AmMagazine.* Available at: http://www.3ammagazine.com/litarchives/nov2001/cooper_interview.html. Accessed July 15, 2008.

Maupin, Armistead. 2007. *Michael Tolliver Lives.* San Francisco: HarperCollins.

Andrew O'Day

Marvin K. White

Born and raised in Oakland, California, Marvin K. White is a poet, performer, artist, and community arts organizer. He is the author of two books of poetry—*last rights,* which was named a finalist for the American Library Association Stonewall

Award for Literature in 2000, and *nothin' ugly fly*. Both titles were also nominated for Lambda Literary Awards. His work has been published in several anthologies, including *My Brothers Keeper*; *Sojourner: Writing in the Age of AIDS*; *Bum Rush the Page*; and *Think Again*. White's performance play *For Colored Boys Who Have Considered S-Curls When the Hot Comb Was Enuf*, which explores being gay in the black community and being black in the gay community, has been performed in several cities. He has also edited publications including *If We Have to Take Tomorrow* for national HIV/AIDS organizations.

White was a member of the PomoAfroHomos, a critically acclaimed theater and performance troupe that Brian Freeman, another member, described as being comprised of "the love children of **James Baldwin** and **Sylvester**" (Owen Keehnen interview). The group toured internationally performing their work from 1990 to 1995. White also founded the Black Gay Letters and Arts Movement (B/GLAM) in 1999, an organization that acts to present, preserve, and promote black gay artistic expressions. He often runs seminars on writing and performance for youth at schools, clubs, shelters, and LGBTQ youth centers. He currently holds a fellowship in the national African American poetry organization "Cave Canem."

Further Reading

Keehnen, Owen. (n.d.). "The Pomo Afro Homos Return." Available at: http://www.queercultural center.org/Pages/Keehnen/PAHomos.html. Accessed July 15, 2008.

Marvin K. White Web site. Available at: http://www.marvinkwhite.com/. Accessed July 15, 2008.

Steve Stratton

whiteness studies

During the 1990s, scholars of race in the United States formed a subfield that sought to explain racial power by tracing the social construction of whiteness. In their work, *whiteness* invoked the following: a dominant racial status against which others are known and judged; identities or groups claiming that status and its authority; and an array of powerful narratives, or discourses, that invest its authority throughout social life. Scholars including David Roediger, Cheryl Harris, George Lipsitz, and Toni Morrison critically evaluated whiteness in U.S. politics, economics, and culture by revealing how it structured class relations, property, citizenship, and nationalism. While some scholars of whiteness attended to gender or sexuality, most concentrated on race and class in the United States to such an extent that LGBTQ topics remained peripheral to their major claims. But in the 1990s, LGBTQ politics and **queer studies** already sustained unique and long-standing critical conversations about whiteness, which by theorizing the interdependence of race and sexuality promised to deepen and transform whiteness studies.

Critical theories of race arose in late twentieth-century U.S. LGBTQ politics in the wake of critiques of racism by LGBTQ activists of color and antiracist responses by white LGBTQ activists. In the 1970s, activists of color engaged gay liberation, lesbian feminist, and gay and lesbian civil rights projects by marking how they privileged the leadership, cultural values, and political goals of white participants. Lesbians and gays of color created autonomous organizing that linked to but remained distinct from sexual minority formations, as well as from the racial, economic, and national justice movements that they engaged with critiques of heterosexism. In groups like the **Combahee River Collective** or the Latina/Latino organization **Gay Latino Alliance (GALA)** that was documented by Horacio Roque Ramirez, lesbians and gays of color engaged theories in women-of-color feminism to argue that race, class, nationality, gender, and sexuality arise simultaneously in their and in all people's lives. Holding single-issue organizing accountable to challenging multiple forms of power, they critiqued whiteness in sexual minority politics and inspired self-reflection by white lesbians and gays. An early example, **Minnie Bruce Pratt**'s autobiographical essay "Identity: Skin Blood Heart" (1981), examined white privilege in both the U.S. South of Pratt's upbringing and the lesbian politics she later joined. Such critique was echoed in Allan Bérubé's essay "How Gay Stays White and What Kind of White It Stays" (1997), which detailed how white gay activists appealed to whiteness to gain federal approval in the "gays in the military" debates, while Bérubé and other white gay men responded by challenging whiteness in their own politics and lives. Critics today, including Lisa Duggan, continue to evaluate whiteness among sexual minorities as a sign of "homonormativity," whenever LGBTQ people appeal for rights through institutions and values that uphold whiteness and marginalize LGBTQ people of color. Thus, during three decades activist scholars have critiqued the grounding of LGBTQ politics in white racial status and narratives justifying it, in order to foster a multi-issue, antiracist politics of sexuality that centers the interests of LGBTQ people of color. Their work clearly shows that whiteness arises interdependently with sexuality and gender, which suggests that whiteness will not be known before being studied in relation to multiple forms of power.

Following Michel Foucault, queer studies scholars argued that sexuality in modern societies is produced as a discourse, when scientific institutions (schools, clinics, prisons) define and regulate its meaning and practice. When scholars considered how sexuality and race form simultaneously, they immediately marked both as products of colonial discourse, or narratives of cultural difference that justify and mobilize European colonization and its descendant societies. Colonial discourse arises from theories of cultural evolution, which suggest that Europeans' racial superiority led them to attain modern civilization, while colonized people's racial inferiority trapped them in primitive stages of development, a situation justifying European intervention to impose civilized life. Colonial narratives grounded European power in stories of civilized sexuality, one based on marriage, reproduction, and strong sex differences, which then associated the primitivity of colonized people with dangerous and indiscriminate sexualities that blurred the lines between male and female. Queer studies scholars including Nayan Shah and Roderick Ferguson have shown how whiteness became established in the nineteenth-century United States as people of color were assigned a constitutionally perverse sexual status, which presumed that civilized sexuality was accessible only to white people. Yet if this framing made perversions like homosexuality typical of people of color, requiring little explanation beyond their primitivity, their appearance among white people threatened to put whiteness into crisis. Scholars show that sexologists pursued white subjects in order to explain how a primitive sexuality could arise in them and, in the process, associated syndromes like homosexuality with the racial degeneration of a civilized body. Siobhan Somerville and Kevin Mumford trace how notions of racial mixture defined early twentieth-century scientific, legal, and popular stories of homosexuality, which was thought to reflect or to be precipitated by miscegenation or multiracial socializing. Yet as vice squads targeted white perverts who slummed in urban mixed-race sex districts, and analysts read homosexuality as a failure of whiteness to sustain sexual normality, subjects marked by such stories began to reverse the discourses assigned them and to claim as "sexual minorities" that they were normal and deserved full membership in society. Their claims implicitly addressed white subjects, as those for whom ending sexual oppression would result in belonging to a white-dominated society. But scholars including Scott Morgensen and Kenyon Farrow show that their sexual politics also explicitly invoked racial narratives. Sexual minorities could invoke their association with primitive sexuality to claim an ancient sexual nature, one that carried a collective integrity (analogous to racial or national groups) and made their constituencies seem inherently global, transhistorical, and multiracial. Such claims let white sexual minorities **"pass"** as more racially marginal than they were, while fostering a single-issue sexual politics. In these ways, queer studies scholars join LGBTQ activists of color in arguing that histories of sexuality and of whiteness are incomplete until their mutual production is explained. Their work directs whiteness studies to foreground the interdependence of sexuality and race in order to explain how both arise together.

Further Reading

Berubé, Allan. 2001. "How Gay Stays White and What Kind of White It Stays." In *The Making and Unmaking of Whiteness*, ed. Birgit Brander Rasmussen, Irene J. Nexica, Eric Klinenberg, and Matt Wray, 234–65. Durham, NC: Duke University Press.

Duggan, Lisa. 2003. *The Twilight of Equality: Neoliberalism, Cultural Politics, and the Attack on Democracy*. Boston: Beacon Press.

Morgensen, Scott. 2005. "Rooting for Queers: A Politics of Primitivity." *Women and Performance: A Journal of Feminist Theory* 15 (1): 251–89.

Shah, Nayan. 2003. "Perversity, Contamination, and the Dangers of Queer Domesticity." In *Queer Studies: An Interdisciplinary Reader*, ed. Robert J. Corber and Stephen Valocchi, 121–41. Malden, MA: Blackwell.

Somerville, Siobhan. 2000. *Queering the Color Line: Race and the Invention of Homosexuality in American Culture*. Durham, NC: Duke University Press.

Scott Morgensen

Wicca and witches

Wicca is the modern revival of the earth-based spiritual traditions of pre-Christian Europe, drawing additional inspiration from ceremonial magicians and indigenous tribal cultures; it is but one of many varied modern **religions** classified as neopaganism. Wiccans often identify as witches and practitioners of witchcraft. With no centralized hierarchy, but groupings of small covens of 3 to 13 practitioners or solitary practitioners, beliefs vary and ceremonies are very personal. Within Wicca there are many subtraditions. Common beliefs and practices include belief in the divinity as male and female—god and goddess—with an emphasis on the goddess; belief in four elemental forces—fire, water, air, and earth; rituals performed in a circle; celebration of the full moons and eight seasonal holidays; meditation; reincarnation; karma; ancestor reverence; sacred sexuality; and magic spells. Rituals, tools, candles, herbs, oils, and chants are a part of spell casting, and the four common ritual tools are the blade, wand, cup or cauldron, and pentacle, the upright five-pointed star in a circle that has become the emblem of this religion. Wiccans believe in the Wiccan Rede, summed up as "An' ye harm none, do as ye will," emphasizing personal responsibility for all actions. Initially seen as a "fertility cult" emphasizing heterosexual partnering, modern witchcraft has evolved to welcome LGBT people increasingly for their unique blend of gender qualities and their contribution in ancient pagan cultures and mythology. Formal Wiccan traditions focusing on homosexual mysteries, like the Minoan Brotherhood/Sisterhood, have formed. The LGBT witchcraft community continues to add to the diversity and practices of the tradition.

Further Reading

Cunningham, Scott. 1998. *Wicca: A Guide for the Solitary Practitioner*. Woodbury, MN: Llewellyn Publications.

Evans, Arthur. 1978. *Witchcraft and the Gay Counterculture*. Boston: Fag Rag Books.

Ford, Michael Thomas. 2005. *The Path of the Green Man*. New York: Citidel Press.

Penczak, Christopher. 2003. *Gay Witchcraft*. Newburyport, MA: Weiser Publication.

Starhawk. 1999. *The Spiral Dance*. San Francisco: HarperCollins.

Christopher Penczak

Jonathan Williams (1929–2008)

Jonathan Williams, born in Asheville, North Carolina, studied art at Princeton, Phillips Memorial Gallery, Atelier 17, and the Chicago Institute of Design and writing at Black Mountain College. His appointment as the publisher of *Black Mountain Review* established Williams as a publisher/designer. Williams's budding Jargon Society, now known as one of the most important small presses, began in earnest around that time and led to Williams's recognition as one of the most influential, astute publishers and designers of the twentieth century.

For over 50 years the Jargon Society jump-started or consolidated the careers of many major poets, experimental fiction writers, photographers, and outsider artists in America and England including Thomas Clark, Robert Creeley, Simon Cutts, Guy Davenport, Denise Levertov, Elizabeth Matheson, John Menapace, Paul Metcalf, Lorine Niedecker, Charles Olson, and Kenneth Patchen; the gay cookbook author of *White Trash Cooking*, Ernie Mickler; gay visionary artist ST. EOM; as well as major and lesser-known gay writers **Jeffery Beam,** James Brougthon, CA Conrad, Robert Duncan, **Lou Harrison,** Ronald Johnson, **Thomas Meyer,** and **Harold Norse.**

Williams's 100-plus works of his own poetry and photography express vast interests through an unconventional synesthetic panache, commanding economy, and vinegary wit. Even the titles of his works exemplify his playful blend of polish and earthiness. *A Palpable Elysium: Portraits of Genius and Solitude* offers a select view of Williams's photographs of unique places and people accompanied by pithy, revealing miniessays. *The Magpie's Bagpipe* and *Blackbird Dust* collect his spicy essays on art and culture. *Jubilant Thicket: New and Selected Poems* contains a selection of the more than 1,000 poems Williams has written.

These works and others such as *gAy BCs* (with drawings by Joe Brainard) project Williams's gay identity without apologies, long before it was fashionable. His works equally capture the charmed and unpretentious nuances of country speech and the refinement of the "aristocracy," as well as the sometimes-dumb misapprehensions of each. His letters, slide collections, and photographs alone, when finally collected, will provide bountiful insight into twentieth-century culture and gay history, sensibility, and community.

Further Reading

Beam, Jeffery. *A Snowflake Orchard and What I Found There—The Jargon Society: One Village Idiot's Oh-So Personal Appraisal.* Highlands, NC: The Jargon Society. Available at: http://jargonbooks.com/snowflake1.html. Accessed July 15, 2008.

Beam, Jeffery. *Tales of a Jargonaut: An Interview with Jonathan Williams.* Minneapolis, MN: Rain Taxi. Available at: http://www.raintaxi.com/online/2003spring/williams.shtml. Accessed July 15, 2008.

Jeffery Beam

Tennessee Williams (1911–1983)

Tennessee Williams is regarded as one of the most celebrated American **playwrights** of the twentieth century, recognized for works such as *The Glass Menagerie* (1944), *A Streetcar Named Desire* (1947), and *Cat on a Hot Tin Roof* (1955). Born Thomas Lanier Williams III, he adopted the nom de plume of "Tennessee" during his early college years because of his accent and ties to the South. Williams's family history is as widely known as his writings. He was born in Mississippi, but by 1918 the family had moved to St. Louis. In 1943 Williams's parents authorized a prefrontal lobotomy to be performed on his sister Rose in effort to alleviate her schizophrenia. The operation was not a success, however, and Rose remained in a weakened state until her death. Rose's illness and death plagued Tennessee Williams throughout his entire life. He blamed his parents for her demise and developed a personal fear that his own mental state would debilitate.

Many critics view the strong female leads in his plays as patterned after Williams's own mother, Edwina Dakin Williams. One of the strongest associations compares Edwina to Amanda Wingfield in *The Glass Menagerie*. Williams's sister Rose also factored into the same work as Laura Wingfield; the motif of absent or abusive male figures featured largely in Williams's works. Characters in his plays were often ambiguous about their sexual histories and ties to other characters. His late works, especially plays that have been discovered in the twenty-first century, address homosexuality and other nonheterosexual alternatives in an overt manner, often with a **camp** perspective.

Tennessee Williams. Courtesy of the Gay, Lesbian, Bisexual, Transgender Historical Society, San Francisco.

Williams's longest relationship was with Frank Merlo, a man he met during one of his stays in New Orleans. The two became lifelong lovers, and Williams wrote *The Rose Tattoo* (1951) as a result of their relationship. Williams and Merlo were together from 1947 until 1963 when Merlo died from cancer complications.

Williams was awarded the Pulitzer Prize for Drama in 1948 for *A Streetcar Named Desire*. In 1952 he was presented the Tony Award for his play *The Rose Tattoo*. Williams won the distinction of the Pulitzer Prize for Drama a second time in 1955 for *Cat on a Hot Tin Roof*. His awards also include the New York Drama Critics' Circle Awards for *The Glass Menagerie* in 1945 and *The Night of the Iguana* in 1961.

Tennessee Williams wrote in an aesthetic he called plastic theater, based on his use of multiple stage elements available for theatrical productions. In *Menagerie's* initial script, Williams called for the use of slide projectors, background music, and intricate lighting effects. Williams's plastic theater made his productions multimedia, crossing the boundaries of playwriting, poetry, visual art, and more. It was only fitting for the plays to transcend the stage and enter a new medium. Many of the plays were adapted from the stage to the motion picture screen in various remakes and revisions, as continues to occur each year. These film representations of Williams's work have been nominated for and awarded recognition with Academy Awards, Golden Globes, Grammys, and much more.

Williams's works continue to be celebrated in the twenty-first century. In 2005, *Mister Paradise and Other One-Act Plays by Tennessee Williams* was published, offering up material that had never before been made available to the public. His plays are also receiving first-time productions on large and small stages. *And Tell Sad Stories of the Deaths of Queens*, a one-act play constructed over 30 years ago was first presented to a public audience in 2004 by the Shakespeare Theatre in Washington, D.C. *The Parade or Approaching the End of Summer* was written in 1940 but was recently performed for the first time in Provincetown, Massachusetts, by the Shakespeare on the Cape theater company in October 2006.

Further Reading

Leverich, Lyle. 1995. *Tom: The Unknown Tennessee Williams*. New York: Crown Publishers.

James Francis Jr.

Doric Wilson (1939–)

Doric Wilson launched a rich career in the early days of the off-off-Broadway scene through involvement in Caffe Cino and as a founding member of TOSOS (The Other Side of Silence, considered by some to be the first professional theater company to deal openly with the gay experience) and other theater groups. It was at Caffe Cino that Wilson staged his first play, *And He Made a Her*, in 1961. His satires address the attitudes and mores of gay life: *Now She Dances!* (1975); *The West Street Gang* (1977), which presents stock characters—the leather guys, the transvestite, the cowboy—who capture a gang leader suspected of gay bashing; *A Perfect Relationship* (1978), which is set in a Christopher Street apartment and features Greg and Ward, roommates who discover through a variety of tests that they might have a promising future together; *Forever After* (1980), in which the muses of comedy and tragedy compete to determine the future of couple Tom and David; and, finally, *Street Theater* (1982), which revisits the moments before the **Stonewall Riots** as stock characters **cruise** and exchange catty bantering before uniting against the police. Wilson received the Robert Chesley Award for Lifetime Achievement in Gay Theater in 1994 and revived *Street Theater* at the 2001 resurrection of TOSOS as TOSOS II.

Further Reading

Bottoms, Stephen J. 2004. *Playing Underground: A Critical History of the 1960s Off-Off-Broadway Movement*. Ann Arbor: University of Michigan Press.

Crespy, David A. 2003. *Off-Off-Broadway Explosion: How Provocative Playwrights of the 1960s Ignited a New American Theater*. New York: Back Stage.

John Pruitt

Lanford Wilson (1937–)

Openly gay, Pulitzer Prize–winning playwright Lanford Wilson was born in Lebanon, Missouri. After his parents divorced, Wilson spent his childhood living throughout Missouri with his mother and later with a stepfather as well. He graduated from high school and moved to San Diego to be with his father and attend San Diego State. This would prove to be an unsuccessful reunion, and Wilson soon left his father and school to move to Chicago where he began work for an advertising firm. While there, he took extension courses through the University of Chicago in the area of playwriting. After some years, he moved to New York in 1962 and enmeshed himself in the thriving theater scene of Greenwich Village.

The theatrical arena of Greenwich Village allowed for new ideas and creative ways of conceptualizing theater. Wilson's early plays were produced by various theater groups throughout the Village. In 1969, he and several other artists combined efforts to begin their own theatrical group, Circle Repertory Company. This would prove to be an amazing and artistically fruitful venture that would continue as a staple of New York's off-off-Broadway theater community; in many ways it was its birth. Circle Rep and others like it produced theater that pushed against the mainstream and questioned not just theatrical assumptions but larger societal issues, as well.

As a playwright, Wilson has continually developed thought-provoking subject matter and characters. Whether through the gay men in his plays or the estranged family members, he has consistently given each play its own essence and form. Some would note that stylistically he is best described as a realist who portrays situations just as they are. Many of his works, though, are anything but realist in form; instead, he scrambles the narrative so that the audience must wait until the second act to be given the key that allows them to actually understand the first. In fact, Wilson's first full-length play, *Balm in Gilead* (1965), with its massive cast of diverse characters and overlapping dialogue and scenes, is a singular example of his ability to create innovative works.

While not all of Wilson's works revolve around gay themes, a number of his plays do include gay characters and plotlines. His play *Balm in Gilead* had a number of gay, lesbian, bisexual, and transsexual characters, while his earlier one-act play *The Madness of Lady Bright* (1964) follows the fall of an unloved **drag** queen. "Lemon Sky" (1970), Wilson's autobiographical story of a father and son being reunited, focuses on the strain that the son's homosexuality puts on the relationship. Even some of Wilson's heterosexual characters can be seen to represent gay persons, as they struggle with fluid sexuality, power displacement, and bigoted oppression. Matt and Sally from *Talley's Folly* (1979) and Chad Jasker from *The Mound Builders* (1975) are primary examples of such persons.

Among Wilson's other gay-themed works is *The Gingham Dog*. Written in 1968 it was Wilson's first play to be produced on Broadway. Never naming its main character as gay, the play leads the audience to the rather obvious conclusion. In 1987, Wilson published two plays dealing directly with gay subject matter. *Burn This* is a full-length exploration of the homosexual main character, and the one-act play *A Portrait of the Cosmos* forces the audience to grapple with the interrogation of a man for the murder of his gay lover.

Arguably Wilson's best-known work, the Talley trilogy is a series of three full-length plays that follow several generations of the same family. The plays are set in Wilson's birthplace of Lebanon, Missouri, and revolve around this family's disillusionment with America following the Vietnam War. *Fifth of July* (1978) introduces the family that would be the staple of this literary and theatrical venture. The first installment won Wilson not only the New York Drama Critics Award but also the Pulitzer Prize and a Tony nomination. Wilson penned *Talley's Folly* in 1979, which earned him a second Tony nomination. *Talley and Son*, originally titled *A Tale Told*, was completed in 1981. The trilogy has become a staple of local, educational, and regional theaters throughout America and appears to be in constant rotation.

Wilson's *Book of Days* (1998) has found success in these same venues. Originally commissioned and produced by Jeff Daniels's Purple Rose Theatre in Michigan, it has since found success in local and regional theater. Similar to his first play, this work has a large cast that functions as a Greek chorus. Wilson's other plays include *Rimers of Eldritch* (1965), for which he won the Vernon Rice Award; *Hot L. Baltimore* (1973), which won him an Obie Award, an Outer Circle Award, and a New York Drama Critic's Circle Award; and *The Mound Builders* (1975), for which Wilson earned another Obie Award. Wilson also received his third Tony nomination in 1981 for *Angels Fall*.

His contributions to the world of theater and the arts are innumerable and reach beyond his abilities as a playwright. He has penned many highly regarded translations of the works of Anton Chekov and provided the libretto for an opera based on a work by **Tennessee Williams,** proving himself as a multifaceted artist. The sheer fact that he has consistently been an out artist, in times and places where others were not, provided an example for others and a voice for those unseen. His creation of queer characters and plots allowed audiences to see people just like themselves yet also completely different from themselves, thus providing an opportunity for them to discover their own self-worth and bias. Wilson's strength also lies in showing that gay writers can create more than gay work and be successful in doing so.

Further Reading

Bryer, Jackson. 1993. *Lanford Wilson: A Casebook.* New York: Garland.

Fink, Larry. 1995. "From 'Madness' to 'The Cosmos': Gay/Lesbian Characters in the Plays of Lanford Wilson." *Journal of American Drama and Theatre* 7: 57–65.

Ryzuk, Mary S. 1989. *The Circle Repertory Company: The First Fifteen Years.* Ames: Iowa State University Press.

Schultz, Ray. 2002. "When the 'A' Word Is Never Spoken: Fear of Intimacy and AIDS in Lanford Wilson's *Burn This.*" *Journal of American Drama and Theatre* 14: 44–63.

Williams, Phillip M. 1993. *A Comfortable House: Lanford Wilson, Marshall W. Mason, and the Circle Repertory Theatre.* Jefferson, NC: McFarland.

Needham Yancey Gulley

Fran Winant (1943–)

Francine Ellen Winant was born in Brooklyn and in early childhood demonstrated advanced ability in artistic expression. Her emotions emerged in poetic, sketch, and prose forms as vast thought evolved in her young mind. To thwart discovery of forbidden feelings about the female body, she conceived a cryptic articulation: a synthesis of numeric and ancient symbols. This protective "secret language" is foreshadowed in the 1817–1824 diaries of Anne Lister, who used a secret language to record her erotic experiences with other women (Rando 1996). Winant described this process as "a metaphor for an inner language of the socially inexpressible, and on another level, the secret language of nature" (Pettis 2005). The forthcoming **gay liberation movement** provided the medium for the actualization of this remarkable girl.

Winant was a founder of the 1969 gay liberation movement that developed in the aftermath of the **Stonewall Riots.** Consequently, she and fellow founding members of the movement were featured the following year on Peter Hujar's "**Come Out**" poster declaring the inceptive gay pride march. Winant penned the passionate, ceremonious anthem that marked the milestone: "Christopher St. Liberation Day, June 28, 1970": "our banners are sails/pulling us through the streets/where we have always been/as ghosts/now we are shouting our own words" (Rando 1996).

Winant embraced her inherent creative forces and exemplified the concept of lesbian and homosexual culture during the 1970s and early 1980s. Impassioned, Winant and her companion at the time, Judy Grepperd, established Violet Press (early 1970s) to publish their written works and those of sister lesbians who had languished too long in visible invisibility. Included in Violet Press Publications are Winant's *Looking at Women: Poems* (1971), *Dyke Jacket* (1976), and *Goddess of Lesbian Dreams* (1980), and Winant's and Grepperd's anthology of lesbian poetry, *We Are All Lesbians* (1980).

An award-winning artist, Winant exhibited her work throughout the metropolitan area for many years. She first exhibited her paintings in 1974 as a member of the Feminist Lesbian Art Collective. Her perception of human interconnectedness and sentiment for animals is revealed in her art. Expressing her belief that both animal kingdom and gay culture are deemed a lesser order (by society), her paintings are symbolic and often incorporate the protective, secret language of her youth.

At 32 years of age, Winant was a nontraditional student when she received her BA in studio art from Fordham University in 1975. To complement her work she pursued additional training at the School of Visual Arts in New York City. She is a member of the National Association of Women Artists. "Using the figure for reference, I take the form and manipulate scale and space" (Rando 1996). Her work is in the permanent collections of FAMLI and C. W. Post College.

Further Reading

Boffin, Tessa. 1992. *Stolen Glances: Lesbians Take Photographs.* United Kingdom: Pandora Press.

Broude, Norma, and Mary D. Garrard. 1994. *The Power of Feminist Art.* New York: Harry N. Abrams Publishing.

Pettis, Ruth M. 2005. "Fran Winant." Available at: http://www.glbtq.com/arts/winant_f_art.html. Accessed July 15, 2008.

Rando, Flavia. 1996. "We're Here: Gay and Lesbian Presence in Art and Art History." *Art Journal* 55.4. 8–10. (December 22). Available at: http://www.questia.com/googleScholar.qst;jsessionid=L9JfBQjqJL2vDDfn94XJJsc8FMHPp3BXvQTvgV17dJ6wJFmDRGCl!-1596093884?docId=5000447119. Accessed July 15, 2008.

Vicki Lynn White

Donald Windham (1920–)

One frequently first encounters the name Donald Windham when engrossed in the (auto)biographies of other writers. Windham, born in Atlanta, moved to New York with his first partner in 1938. He rapidly formed more or less close friendships with a collection of gay and gay-friendly writers, often Southerners like him, such as **Tennessee Williams, Truman Capote,** or Carson McCullers. His own personal tragedies were that he never became as successful as any of them and that they always eventually forsook him. With Tennessee Williams he wrote an adaptation for the theater of D. H. Lawrence's story *You Touched Me.* His first novel, *The Dog Star* (1950), a bildungsroman that shares traits with the fiction of Capote and Mc-Cullers and even Harper Lee (or Graham Greene, for that matter), never quite matches those of his contemporaries. A slow yet prolific author, Windham writes beautifully but lacks the flamboyance of his "travel companions" (he spent a lot of time in places like Italy with them). Windham never mastered the art of selling himself, which partly accounts for his usual lagging-behind. His short stories (collected in *The Warm Country*) and novels are pleasant reads, especially *The Hero Continues* (1960), but his nonfiction is altogether much more entertaining. His account of childhood and adolescence in Atlanta, *Emblems of Conduct* (1963), is moving without being sentimental. *Lost Friendships: A Memoir of Truman Capote, Tennessee Williams, and Others* (1983) is fascinating to aficionados of the writers it chronicles, while heartbreakingly sad for the picture of the loyal, mistreated, truth-telling friend it draws. His famous edition of Tennessee Williams's letters to him is absolutely indispensable for any admirer of Williams. Generally speaking, Windham's writing—his fiction, at any rate—has been better received in the United Kingdom and continental Europe than in the United States.

Further Reading

Forster, E. M., and Donald Windham. 1975. *E. M. Forster's Letters to Donald Windham, with Comment by the Recipient.* Verona, Italy: Sandy Campbell.

Kellner, Bruce. 1991. *Donald Windham: A Bio-Bibliography.* Bio-Bibliographies in American Literature. Westport, CT: Greenwood Press.

Williams, Tennessee, and Donald Windham. 1977. *Tennessee Williams' Letters to Donald Windham, 1940–1965.* New York: Holt, Rinehart and Winston.

Georges-Claude Guilbert

Terry Wolverton (1954–)

Lesbian writer, performance artist, and editor, Terry Lynn Wolverton was born in Cocoa Beach, Florida. She attended high school in Detroit, where she studied performing arts. Wolverton attended the University of Detroit, the University of Toronto, Sagaris Institute, and Thomas Jefferson College, where she earned a BA in 1977. She has lived in Los Angeles since 1976. In 1988, Wolverton began teaching a writing workshop for people living with HIV/AIDS. In 1997, she founded Writers at Work, a center for creative writing in Los Angeles where she teaches a number of creative writing workshops.

She has published three collections of poetry, *Black Slip* (1992), *Mystery Bruise* (1999), and *Shadow and Praise* (2007) and two novels, *Bailey's Beads* (1996) and *The Labrys Reunion.* Wolverton also wrote an autobiographical poetic novel,

Embers, based on her troubled family. She edited two volumes of *Blood Whispers: L.A. Writers on AIDS*. Wolverton has also coedited several popular volumes of gay and lesbian writing. She has been nominated for the Lambda Literary Award for several of her works.

Further Reading

Rosen, Deena. 1994. "Terry Wolverton: Writing to Live." *High Performance* 17 (3): 52–53.

Wolverton, Terry. 2002. *Insurgent Muse: Life and Art at the Woman's Building*. San Francisco: City Lights.

Erica Reichert

womanist

Due to the persistent presence of white supremacy and patriarchy in American society, African American women and their issues were often excluded from the agendas of both the male-dominanted civil rights and white-oriented women's movements of the twentieth century. Out of this gap in social and political vision, womanist thought and practice were born.

In 1983, Alice Walker coined the term *womanist* as an alternative label for feminists of color. Defined by Walker in an epigraph to her essay collection *In Search of Our Mother's Gardens: Womanist Prose*, womanist practice contains an impulse toward restorative justice in gender and race relations. Womanism seeks to heal the damage done by white racism and patriarchy to men and women of color. Walker traces the etymology of the word back to a black vernacular expression for women who challenge conventional notions of behavioral and intellectual appropriateness.

Womanist analysis begins with the social location of black women. This serves as the primary interpretive lens through which womanists view the world. A womanist concerns herself with preserving black women's culture, protecting and restoring the integrity of the black family and fighting sexual and racial oppression in collaboration with men. Womanists do not view men as enemies, but they also do not tolerate or remain silent in the face of gendered violence inside the black community. Womanists struggle for the creation of a more economically and socially sustainable world for all people, while maintaining a dedication to the ideal of racial and collective self-determination in social change movements.

Alice Walker. Courtesy of the Gay, Lesbian, Bisexual, Transgender Historical Society, San Francisco.

Further Reading
hooks, bell. 1984. *Feminist Theory: From Margin to Center*. Boston: South End Press.
Walker, Alice. 1983. *In Search of Our Mother's Gardens: Womanist Prose*. New York: Harcourt/Brace.

TJ Geiger II

women's and gender studies in universities

The study of women and gender (also known as women studies or feminist studies) has evolved as an interdisciplinary academic field, growing in size, influence, and impact on the American college campus since its beginnings in the early 1970s. Women's studies, as a discipline, is diverse in its reach and breadth. Topics explored through the lens of women's studies include **feminism,** women's social movements, girls' and women's development, feminist legal studies, public policy related to women (in areas including reproductive rights, economic policy, and education), women in science, literature by women, and virtually every other field of study. Women's studies takes as its principle unit of analysis women's lives in context (including identities of race, nationality, ability, sexuality, and socioeconomic class). Based on the premise that traditional academic inquiry has been characterized by sexism and thus has silenced, marginalized, or erased the experiences and perspectives of women, the field seeks to reconstitute what is understood to be knowledge as well as to pose new questions emanating from the particulars of women's individual and collective struggles. Inherent in the study of women and gender is a commitment to social change through praxis and the integration, testing, and reformation of theory resulting from feminist action in the world. Following in the ideological footsteps of previously established black and Chicano studies programs, women's studies has been heavily influenced by social theories including Marxism, socialism, **queer theory,** and postcolonial critiques of Western culture and has sought to both deconstruct and interrupt hegemonic power structures curtailing women's free expression and agency.

Women's studies' emphasis on deconstructive social change has been criticized heavily by conservative scholars (such as Alan Bloom, E. D. Hirsch, and Daphne Patai) who assert that contemporary women's studies' focus on feminist interdisciplinarity and social change detracts from the preservation of Western cultural norms and lacks both the rigor and coherence of the traditional canon. Theorists whose work comprises the alternative canon of women's studies include authors such as **Audre Lorde, Dorothy Allison, Alice Walker,** and Toni Morrison; feminist legal theorists Catharine Mackinnon, Kimberly Crenshaw, and Martha Nussbaum; literary critics Gayatri Spivak, Elaine Showalter, Susan Gubar, and Annette Kolodny; feminist philosophers Uma Narayan, Chandra Mohanty, and Luce Irigiray; and sociologist Patricia Hill Collins.

Women's studies in the United States originated during the early years of second-wave feminism in the late 1960s. The social turbulence of this era was sparked by the simultaneous emergence of three interrelated American social movements: the civil rights movement for black voting rights and educational integration, protests against the war in Vietnam, and second-wave feminist activism, resulting from women's newly raised consciousness regarding ongoing discrimination in employment and education, oppressive family structures, and a growing awareness of the individual and collective lack of fulfillment found in traditional female roles. Publications including grassroots newsletters, popular nonfiction (such as Betty Friedan's *Feminine Mystique*), and academic treatises on the deconstruction of women's roles (such as Simone de Beauvoir's *Second Sex*) contributed to the establishment of women's studies as a discipline. During the 1970s, stand-alone women's studies classes were forming in state and private higher education institutions across the country, as well as being informally organized in campus women's centers. The first women's studies program in the United States was established in 1970 at San Diego State College (now San Diego State University) following a period of extensive organizing on the part of women students and faculty. Following the founding of this department, many other universities followed suit, including New York University, University of California at Santa Cruz (1974), Barnard College (1977), the State University of New York at Albany (1978), and the University of California at Berkeley (1991). Today, more than 700 institutions in America offer an undergraduate major, minor, or certificate in women's studies, and approximately 50 offer a master's or doctorate in the interdisciplinary study of women. In addition to having a strong presence in American colleges and universities, women's studies courses and departments can be found in universities across the world, including in Australia, Canada, China, England, Hungary, Israel, Kenya, and the Netherlands. The National Women's Studies Association, founded in 1977, is the professional association dedicated to the support of women's studies programs and departments in the United States. In 2007, 395 institutions belonged to the association, comprising 2,000 individual members. In addition to holding an annual conference, the association produces an online newsletter (NWSAction) and a peer-reviewed journal of interdisciplinary women's studies scholarship, the *NWSA Journal*, and enlists its membership regularly in taking unified activist stances related to feminist social causes.

While women's studies has been, from its beginnings, populated by scholars and students of all racial and ethnic backgrounds, cultural traditions, nationalities, and sexual orientations, in practice it has been accused of replicating white supremacist norms, as well as focusing solely on the concerns of women who identify as heterosexual. Women of color, feminists outside of the United States, and lesbians of all races have provided especially insightful critiques of women's studies as it is practiced in the United States, asserting that the priorities of women's studies scholarship, the criteria for acclaim and advancement within the discipline, and the anointing of leaders within the academic arm of the women's movement continue to reify racist, colonial, and heteronormative values. Women of color, transnationally focused feminists, and lesbians have demonstrated resistance to these practices through active dissent during activist gatherings and conferences as well as in their writing. Recently, **transgender activists** have also acknowledged the transphobic features of women's studies (and feminism more generally), challenging the exclusion of transfeminist concerns from the larger discourse among academic feminists and other practitioners of women's studies.

Lesbian scholars have additionally been proactive in the development and dissemination of academic work dedicated to the study of lesbian lives and culture. In 1996, the *Journal of Lesbian Studies*, edited by Esther Rothblum (professor at San Diego State University), was created. This journal, developed in direct response to the lesbian invisibility encountered in both mainstream women's studies and LGBT studies, affirmed that "when lesbian issues and interests overlap with queer issues, the unique needs, concerns, and interests of lesbians can get lost in the shuffle. The *Journal of Lesbian Studies* helps sort through the confusion, fostering new lesbian scholarship without cutting ties to grassroots activism. The journal gives the lesbian experience an international and multicultural voice, presenting book reviews, poetry, letters to the editor, debates, and commentaries" (*Journal of Lesbian Studies* Web site).

These ideological fissures of race, class, and sexual identity have certainly contributed to the expansion, or in some cases revisioning, of women's studies into the newer field of gender studies. The emergence of gender studies occurred in the 1990s as a result of increasing attention to the fact that women's studies had historically limited the analysis of gender to the experiences of women, tacitly acknowledging that feminism is not the only theoretical lens through which to understand and analyze gender. In addition to studying women's lives, the study of masculinity, men's studies, and studies of transgender and transsexual people's lives all fall under the rubric of gender studies, rendering the study of gender more complex and rich. This shift to considering gender more broadly results from the work of highly influential gender theorists including Judith Butler, Michel Foucault, **Kate Bornstein,** and others. Butler, in particular, has contributed greatly to the shift in studying gender with her seminal work *Gender Trouble*, which posits that gender is not biologically ordained nor simply socially sanctioned by powerful institutions but is systemically recreated daily through acts of gender performance. This performance, through what Butler terms "stylized acts," entails mimicking social norms of masculinity and femininity and is regulated through social approval and/or rebuke, depending on the individual's ability and willingness to adhere to these gender norms. Likewise, Butler asserts that biological sex itself is established, encoded, and reified through performative practices, noting the fact of the diversity and array of biological expressions of sex. Feminism, Butler asserts, has "performed an unwitting regulation and reification of gender relations" (Butler 1997, 411) in its traditional analysis of, without willingness to abandon, the binary gender system. The answer, to Butler, lies in a freeing of personal choice, not only around one's gender expression and sexual identity, but also in the expression of desire, creating possibilities for sexual and relational configurations that are not then typified as "abnormal" with reference to the heterosexual "normal."

In the same way that women's studies programs were preceded by black and Chicano studies, women's studies is intricately connected to the emergence of LGBT and queer studies programs. LGBT studies, also emerging in the 1990s, inherited women's studies' commitment to interdisciplinarity and seeks to examine the particularities of minority sexual orientations and gender identities/expression. LGBT studies, now present as a minor or major in 40 colleges and universities in America, focuses on naming and deconstructing the effects of oppression of lesbian, gay, bisexual, and transgender people's lives. Women's studies, in turn, has contributed to documenting the lives of lesbians and other queer-identified women, as well as analyzing social phenomena at the intersection of feminism and LGBT identity, including ongoing debates about the merits of assimilation into the dominant culture versus practices of resistance, the AIDS crisis and activist responses to it, reproductive rights of queer people, gay marriage, transgender rights, and the impact of religious fundamentalism on women's and queer people's agency.

While LGBT studies has sought to examine and reconstruct categories of normal and abnormal solely with respect to gay, lesbian, bisexual, and transgender people's existence, the theoretical evolution of LGBT studies has led to queer theory, which, while a distinct theoretical approach, shares particular epistemic markers with women's studies as well. In many respects, queer theory functions as a bridge between women's studies and LGBT studies, with its interest in analyzing categories of identity for the implicit power dynamics laden in particular sexual and gender identities and the behaviors (normative as well as transgressive) within them. Queer theory interrogates the relationships between and among identities of gender and sexuality, focusing on the dynamism it views as inherent to identity formation. Queer theory examines the specifics of what are termed discursive practices, practices that are constantly negotiated within the confines of the values of those in power in a given society and thus are never fixed for either an individual or a collective. In this sense, then, queer theory negates women's studies' insistence on either a fixed individual or a collective category of "woman." According to queer theorists, the category woman and the norms of behavior, expression, and identity associated with the name woman are constantly shifting in response to the machinations of those in power coupled with the resistant practices of those who are oppressed. Culture, era, political activities, and even climate contribute to the shifting nature of the category woman. In this sense, queer theory borrows the tools of women's studies—namely, deconstruction of terms and their implicit organizing properties, an emphasis on interrogating relations of power, and a reclamation of lost or marginalized histories and narratives—and uses them to rebuild an alternative paradigm for understanding self and society. Theorists such as Butler, Foucault, Jacques Derrida, and Judith Halberstam form the cornerstone of required reading in queer theory.

Women's studies programs, courses, and departments thus share much of their history, focus, and theoretical techniques with lesbian studies, LGBT studies, and queer theory. In the same manner, but with differing tactics and spokespersons, academic feminism and the study of gay, lesbian, bisexual, and transgender identities have resulted in new paradigms of power sharing and connection as well as invoking newly contested areas of definition and strategy. The unity of mission—the liberation of those oppressed by rigidly prescribed heteronormativity and forced-choice binary gender identity, toward freedom of self-expression and agency—means that women's studies and LGBT studies have historically shared, and will continue to share, a steadfast commitment to understanding the individual and community in ways that affirm alternative ways of knowing, living, and loving.

Further Reading

Butler, Judith. 1997. "Performative Acts and Gender Constitution: An Essay in Phenomenology and Feminist Theory." In *Writing on the Body: Female Embodiment and Feminist Theory*, ed. K. Conboy, N. Medina, and S. Stanbury, 401–17. New York: Columbia University Press.

Howe, Florence. 2000. *The Politics of Women's Studies: Testimony from Thirty Founding Mothers*. New York: The Feminist Press at the City University of New York.

Journal of Lesbian Studies Web site. Available at: http://www.haworthpress.com/store/product.asp?sid=XVC9RPQPPH0E9NGCXDKCB9ELVXDN6QLC&sku=J155&detail=AbThJrn#AbThJrn. Accessed July 15, 2008.

Kennedy, Elizabeth Lapovsky, and Agath Beins. 2005. *Women's Studies for the Future: Foundations, Interrogations, Politics*. New Brunswick, NJ: Rutgers University Press.

Lovaas, Karen, John P. Elia, and Gust A. Yep. 2007. *LGBT Studies and Queer Theory: New Conflicts, Collaborations, and Contested Terrain*. New York: Harrington Park Press.

Weed, Elizabeth, and Naomi Schor. 1997. *Feminism Meets Queer Theory*. Bloomington: Indiana University Press.

Susan Marine

women's music

Women's music is broadly defined as music by women, for women: women's music is not associated with a particular sound but with a concern for women's culture and empowerment. This concern is realized through a close-knit community of artists who ensure that women dominate all levels of music production, from the fans and bookies to producers and label owners. Women's music is popular with feminists, especially **lesbian feminists** who prefer to support lesbian or queer-friendly singer-songwriters and bands over heterocentric music that they say excludes them. Separation from these male-dominated music scenes was accelerated by the formation of women's music festivals, some of which exclude male participation entirely.

Noting the lack of critical acknowledgment, chart success, and respect for women (compared to no shortage of talent), female musicians involved in the social protest movements of the 1960s and 1970s decided that the time was ripe for a particular brand of music geared toward women. Thus, while women have been involved in music entertainment throughout much of America's history, they did not begin to produce and consume music as a collective group until the 1970s. The history of women's music grew out of the songs that borrowed rock 'n' roll rebellion and folk roots to express dissatisfaction with the Vietnam war. The first rumblings of women's music began with the artist Holly Near. "Holly Near," writes Pamela Murray Winters, "practically gave birth to the genre known as 'women's music'" (quoted in Walters and Mansfield 1998). Near attended the University of California, Los Angeles, where she participated in anti-Vietnam protests and vigils. Inspired by the Kent State shootings in 1970, she wrote the song "It Could Have Been Me," which marked the beginning of a long career in protest music. She joined the *Free the Army Tour,* a music/comedy road show that was designed as an anti-Vietnam response to Bob Hope's United Service Organizations tour. She was likely one of the first women to start her own record company, Redwood Records (now defunct), which she founded in 1972. Near's first album, *Hang in There* (1973), contained songs with feminist themes. In 1976, Near began a re-lationship with Meg Christian, a fellow women's music pioneer. A performer in Washington, D.C.'s nightclubs, Christian found her feminist consciousness when she wrote an angry letter to the *David Frost Show,* during which the host maligned his feminist guests. Christian later discovered fellow musician Cris Williamson and began performing Williamson's songs along with her own. With other radical women from the group the Furies, Williamson and Christian founded Olivia Rec-ords in 1973. Their first record was a single featuring Williamson and Christian. Olivia went on to put out Williamson's hit record *The Changer and the Changed* (1973). It was the first record written, produced, and engineered exclusively by women; it became Olivia records' best seller and is now considered canonical for women's music. Williamson's albums are often considered rich enough for inclu-sion in both spiritual and academic settings, and her songs are frequently used in women's studies courses (Cris Williamson Biography). Today Williamson has a new label, Wolf Moon Records, which distributed her latest release *Real Deal* (2005). Williamson has collaborated with Holly Near, Bonnie Raitt, Vicki Randle, and Laurie Lewis. Other women linked to women's music include Tret Fure, Fer-ron, Margie Adam, Kate Wolf, Bernice Johnson Reagon, and Sweet Honey in the Rock. Some are heterosexual feminists (like Reagon); some eschew the folk singer-songwriter approach (Sweet Honey); and others are not necessarily allied with the feminist movement (Wolf).

Most of these artists thrived on independent labels and were passed around by word-of-mouth, feminist bookstores, or mail-order catalogs. However, the backlash against the women's movement and feminism in general spilled over into the music world, as some artists in women's music came under attack for their separatist ten-dencies. Lesbian feminist Arlene Stein claims that women's music embodies a lim-ited conception of femininity and declares "power chords, teenage angst, and even gender ambiguity off-limits" (Stein 2006, 66). The genre's separatism from male rock like the Rolling Stones, then, has come under critique for creating a stereo-type of the female folksinger who by her very existence *must* be a part of women's music. These politics of the past affect artists in the present, as some women like Kate Bush, Björk, and PJ Harvey work hard to resist such labeling—despite creat-ing songs that can be read as covertly feminist.

Women's festivals during the 1970s ensured that women's music was more than a passing fad. The first women's music festival took place in 1973 at Sacramento

State University. The following year saw the creation of the National Women's Music Festival at the University of Illinois at Champaign-Urbana, which today still bills artists like Melissa Ferrick, Ferron, and Jamie Anderson. Perhaps the best known is the Michigan Womyn's Festival, or Michfest, created in 1976 by Mary Kindig and Lisa and Kristie Vogel. It is primarily a lesbian-centered festival, with some 3,000–10,000 lesbian-identified women attending each year. The gender of participants makes the festival unique: attendees must be women-born-women, a policy that excludes men from attending (no males over the age of four may enter). This policy has received criticism, especially from the trans community, who call the festival's planners transphobic. This group believes that the policy purposefully excludes male-to-female transsexual and transgender individuals. Members of the trans community protested by organizing Camp Trans next door to Michfest. Nevertheless, this controversy has not swayed the festival's owners, who stress the importance of a community of women who are united by their unique experiences of girlhood and growing up in women's bodies.

These critiques of women's music have not disappeared but have continued to trouble female artists of the 1990s. As marketing music became tied to the highly visible and apolitical face of MTV, artists who espoused a loud feminist or lesbian sensibility became a hard sell. The changing dynamics of the industry ensured that women's music would stay underground permanently, despite the fact that women's music was still being produced without a direct link to the feminist movement. Indeed, women's music has adapted as artists in the late 1980s and early 1990s replaced the old artists from the 1960s and 1970s. With the 1990s, therefore, came a resurgence of woman-centered music, some of which came packaged with third-wave feminist activism. Five artists—**k. d. lang, Ani DiFranco,** Sarah McLachlan, **Melissa Etheridge,** and the **Indigo Girls**—represented the "new school" of women's music. Lilith Fair signified mainstream recognition of new artists. Founded by McLachlan in 1997, Lilith Fair was a touring women's music festival that originated with a performance by McLachlan, Paula Cole, and Lisa Loeb in 1996. In the following year, McLachlan decided to take the show on the road with Sheryl Crow, Jewel, and Emmylou Harris, among others. Lilith Fair was the top-grossing festival tour in 1997 (Stein 2006). There were criticisms that the festival was biased toward white acoustic rock, but by 1998 it had incorporated women from hip-hop and R&B (O'Brien 2002). By the time Lilith Fair ended in 1999 (because organizers said "it was time for a break"), more than 130 shows had taken place across America and over 100 artists had appeared on the bill (Lilith Fair Web site). Overall, Lilith Fair was a milestone for women in music in the late 1990s, and a touring festival of its size, scale, and gender has not been developed since.

The Riot Grrl movement of the early 1990s is also lumped into the category of women's music, although its sound was qualitatively different from the traditional folk/rock/pop sound coming out of the women's music canon. Patti Smith, the Slits, Exene Cervenka, X-Ray Spex, Yoko Ono, and Kim Gordon (of Sonic Youth) are cited as some of the foremothers of Riot Grrl. Unlike the soothing sounds coming from Near and Christian, Riot Grrl directly challenged male rock on its own turf by crafting loud, offensive punk noise while simultaneously cultivating safe spaces for women. The ethics behind Riot Grrl are similar to women's music in that the feminist message was just as important as (if not more so than) the music (Reynolds and Press 1995, 327). Riot Grrl, moreover, extended beyond the music to include fanzines and workshops devoted to ending violence, **homophobia,** and sexual double standards. Riot Grrl worked with straight or gay men who were allies, most notably through their record labels Kill Rock Stars, Mr. Lady, Alternative Tentacles, and K Records. While men played a part in creating or listening to their music, Riot Grrls took the separatism of women's music one step further by sending men to the back of the crowd to create spaces for women at the front. This was later a controversial decision that has fueled a litany of media misconceptions about the movement. For example, Corin Tucker of Sleater-Kinney said that the media refused to take them seriously and saw them as "ridiculous girls...parading around in their underwear" (YouTube.com: http://www.youtube.com/watch?v=Vw3aIijPXws). Bikini Kill, Huggy Bear, and Bratmobile are classic Riot Grrl bands, but other artists like Team Dresch, Tribe 8, and Excuse 17 also fit the Riot Grrl ethic (albeit as part of a separate movement called queercore or homocore).

In 1991, K Records organized a festival called the International Pop Underground convention, a string of concerts that brought many of these artists together for the first time. Other artists have not necessarily identified themselves as producing "women's music" but are nonetheless classified as feminist-friendly because of their high-profile status as women in music. These artists include Courtney Love, Tori Amos, Fiona Apple, Regina Spektor, Aimee Mann, India Arie, Erykah Badu, Liz Phair, Lauryn Hill, Alanis Morissette, and Cat Power. While women's music and Riot Grrl both have separate histories, they epitomize the second- and third-wave feminist movements, respectively. As the third-wave feminist movement matured, lesbians, feminists, and gay men continued to make music in the new millennium. To date, few women's festivals have made headlines on a national scale like Lilith Fair, but this has not stopped activists from continuing to center their queer and feminist organizing around women in music.

Further Reading

Cris Williamson Biography. *Cris Williamson.com.* Available at: http://www.criswilliamson.com/about/biography.html. Accessed July 17, 2008.

Freydkin, D. 1998. "Lilith Fair: Lovely, Lively and Long Overdue." *CNN.* July 28. Available at: http://www.cnn.com/SHOWBIZ/Music/9807/28/lilith.fair/. Accessed July 17, 2008.

Lilith Fair 1999. Available at: http://www.lilithfair.com/. Accessed July 17, 2008.

O'Brien, L. 2002. *She Bop II: The Definitive History of Women in Rock, Pop, and Soul.* London: Continuum.

Reynolds, S., and J. Press. 1995. *The Sex Revolts.* Cambridge University Press.

Stein, A. 2006. *Shameless: Sexual Dissidence in American Culture.* New York: New York University Press.

Walters, N., and B. Mansfield. 1998. *MusicHound Folk.* Visible Ink. Available at: http://www.musicianguide.com/biographies/1608004306/Holly-Near.html. Accessed July 17, 2008.

Meggan Jordan

workplace issues

Many unique challenges face LGBTQ individuals in the workplace. While it is far easier for a person to be open on the job than in the past, queer employees have to face a wide array of obstacles from which their nonqueer counterparts are exempt.

ANTIDISCRIMINATION POLICIES

A major fear faced by many queer individuals is whether their employer's equal opportunity statement includes sexual orientation and/or gender identity. Over the past 10 years, more and more organizations include such policies: more than 430 of the Fortune 500 companies include sexual orientation in their antidiscrimination policies, and 118 include gender identity and expression. This reflects a 10-fold increase since 2001.

Given that no federal law prohibits employment discrimination based on sexual orientation and gender identity, and fewer than 20 states prohibit such discrimination (17 states plus the District of Columbia prohibit antigay discrimination; 7 states plus the District of Columbia prohibit antitransgender discrimination), workplace antidiscrimination policies are an important consideration for queer employees. Aside from the issue of fairness, the existence of a comprehensive antidiscrimination clause makes it more likely that an organization will be amenable to domestic partnership benefits.

DOMESTIC PARTNERSHIP BENEFITS

Fringe benefits, such as health and life insurance and pension plans, are a common way for employers to compensate their workers and maintain a competitive edge. Most employers automatically extend benefits such as health insurance and dental plans to the spouses and dependents of their employees; offering them to domestic partners, however, is a very new concept. The *Village Voice*, a New York City alternative weekly, became the first company to offer domestic partnership benefits in 1982. By 1990 fewer than 22 companies offered "spousal equivalent" benefits to the same-sex partners of their employees. In 1992, Lotus Development Corporation became the first publicly traded company to extend domestic partnership benefits.

Today, the number of organizations offering domestic partnership benefits stands at over 5,400, according to a survey conducted by the **Human Rights Campaign (HRC).** At least 263 of the Fortune 500 companies offer domestic partnership benefits for queer employees in same-sex partnerships. Domestic partnership benefits can include medical and dental insurance, disability and life insurance, pension benefits, family and bereavement leave, education and tuition assistance, credit union membership, relocation and travel expenses, and inclusion of partners at company events. LGBTQ advocates usually recommend presenting managers with a business case for offering domestic partnership benefits. Often, complex tax, insurance, and legal issues must be hashed out.

FEDERAL RECOGNITION

Federal law prohibits employment discrimination based on non–job-related traits such as race, religion, sex, and marital status. Under the Defense of Marriage Act, the federal government does not recognize same-sex marriages or domestic partnerships. Furthermore, no federal law mandates that same-sex domestic partners of employees be entitled to the benefits often guaranteed opposite-sex spouses.

REASONS FOR OFFERING DOMESTIC PARTNERSHIP BENEFITS

Aside from the issue of fairness, there are business reasons for an organization to offer domestic partnership benefits. A comprehensive benefits program will help alleviate personal stress that may keep employees from focusing fully on work. The Human Rights Campaign has worked out a formula purporting to measure the dollar amount of increased productivity created by offering domestic partnership benefits. The formula conservatively assumes the number of LGBTQ employees in any workplace to be 5 percent and the amount of productivity associated with a safe and equitable workplace to be 10 percent. Using these figures, HRC illustrates how much money a company might lose by not providing a safe and equitable workplace. (For example, a company with a workforce of 1,000 employees would have 50 LGBTQ employees [1,000 x 0.05 = 50]. If the average salary is $40,000, the average loss in productivity per LGBTQ worker per year is $4,000 [$40,000 x 0.10 = $4,000]. Thus, the total annual loss to the company in productivity would be $200,000 [50 x $4,000 = $200,000].)

Domestic partnership programs can also have a positive effect on hiring and retention. These benefits are a cost-effective bolster to an overall compensation package and are quickly becoming a hallmark of progressive companies. For LGBTQ executives, the presence of a comprehensive domestic partnership benefits program was ranked as the number one incentive; for line workers and managers, it was ranked number three. As LGBTQ individuals and families are becoming a larger part of the American workforce, these are very auspicious factors to take into account; the 2000 Census counted 601,209 LGBTQ families. This is a 314 percent increase from 1990.

BUSINESS DEFINITION OF DOMESTIC PARTNERS

Many employers that offer domestic partnership benefits require employees and their partners to file an "affidavit of domestic partnership" in order to obtain coverage, although businesses do not require employees in heterosexual marriages to do this. Companies are free to draft the affidavit as they see fit, but generally they follow the following format and require that the partners have lived together for a specified period (usually at least six months), are responsible for each other's financial welfare, are not blood relatives, are at least 18 years of age; are mentally competent, are life partners and would marry legally were the option available, are registered as domestic partners if there is a local domestic partnership registry, are not legally married to anyone, and agree to inform the company in the event the domestic partnership terminates (typically this involves filling out an "affidavit of dissolution of domestic partnership"). In addition to the affidavit, the company may require proof of coresidence and financial interdependence. For example, a workplace may stipulate that the employee provide proof of a joint checking account, mutual powers of attorney, drivers' licenses, leases, mortgages, or utility bills.

It bears mentioning that signing an affidavit may have legal consequences. Should the employee violate any portion of the affidavit, she or he may be required to reimburse the company for the cost of benefits received. To date, there has been no evidence of fraud on the part of employees.

TAX IMPLICATIONS

The Internal Revenue Service has ruled that domestic partners cannot be viewed as legal spouses for tax purposes. Employers are therefore obligated to withhold taxes on the fair market value of the domestic partnership coverage. This is not true for legal spouses. If a partner meets the definition of a legal dependent, they may be itemized as a deduction for the employee. Some employers have chosen to offset this taxation by paying the difference ("grossing up").

FAMILY AND MEDICAL LEAVE ACT (FMLA)

The Family and Medical Leave Act (FMLA) was signed into law by President Clinton on February 5, 1995. Under FMLA, eligible employees are granted up to 12 weeks of unpaid leave during any 12-month period for one of the following reasons: birth and care of a newborn child, placement of a son or daughter with the employee for adoption or foster care, care for an immediate family member (spouse, child, or parent), and necessary leave for a serious health condition. At the time of this writing, same-sex spouses or partners are not guaranteed coverage under FMLA.

There are reasons why an organization might or might not want to offer FMLA benefits to their queer employees. Some may fear a negative backlash from anti-queer organizations such as Focus on the Family and the American Family Association (much like the 2005 Ford boycott), while others believe that extending FMLA benefits to same-sex partners is a viable way to retain valued employees. At the time of this writing, 60 of the Fortune 500 companies extend FMLA-like leave to their queer employees.

THE CONSOLIDATED OMNIBUS BENEFITS RECONCILIATION ACT OF 1995 (COBRA)

The Consolidated Omnibus Benefits Reconciliation Act of 1995 (COBRA) mandates that most employers offer employees and their spouses the ability to pay for continued health insurance coverage in the event that coverage ends due to divorce or termination. Again, because of the federal government's nonrecognition of same-sex partnerships, COBRA does not require the extension of these benefits to domestic partners. While some employers do opt to extend these protections to their queer employees and their partners with the approval of their health maintenance organizations (HMOs), until the federal government opts to recognize same-sex partnerships there is no guarantee that these employees and partners will receive coverage. Currently, 77 of the Fortune 500 companies offer COBRA-like coverage for their queer employees.

SPOUSAL EQUIVALENCY

At the time of this writing, the only state where same-sex couples can legally marry is the Commonwealth of Massachusetts (the state of New Jersey has not yet outlined whether same-sex couples will be granted marriage or civil union rights). The states of Vermont and Connecticut permit civil unions. Because certain tax benefits are regulated by state agencies and others by the federal government, benefits administration can be extremely complicated. It is advisable to consult with a benefits specialist in order to ascertain limitations governing their benefits plan and to obtain detailed information regarding state- and federal-level regulatory permissions. Considering that little thought is usually given to the particular issues faced by transgender individuals in the workplace, particular obstacles unique to transitioning employees will be discussed below.

SPECIFIC ISSUES FACED BY TRANSGENDER EMPLOYEES

Up until the 1990s, little attention was given to the challenges faced by transgender employees in the workplace. This is rather unfortunate, as employees who are transitioning—that is to say, moving outside the socially accepted norms of dress, behavior, and physiology of their birth sex—often cannot help but challenge what is considered standard gender-appropriate self-identification, appearance, or expression. Furthermore, even fewer legal protections exist covering gender nonconformity than covering sexual orientation.

GENERAL OVERVIEW OF TRANSITIONING

Transitioning occurs with the help of medical professionals in accordance with standards of care that have been in place since the 1960s. Typically, a person who wishes to transition undergoes the following procedures: initial psychiatric evaluations to rule out other diagnoses; psychiatric monitoring and counseling over the next several months to examine the extent of the condition and to ensure that the patient fully understands all consequences; health evaluation for hormone therapy and how the patient may respond; administration of hormones; continued monitoring to assess effects of hormones, trial living period of one year to ascertain level of comfort living in the reassigned sex (typically this is the period during which the patient's employer is notified of the patient's condition and intentions); if transitioning individual decides to continue the process, continued application of hormones and life in the reassigned sex, sometimes (but not always) accompanied by surgical reconstruction of primary and secondary sex characteristics, facial structure, and so on. This process renders a hasty and uninformed decision virtually impossible. In the overwhelming majority of cases, the treatment is successful and the transitioning individual goes on to live a fully functioning life in the reassigned sex. The degree of success can be greatly influenced by whether or not (1) the person is able to maintain a steady job and income during the transition process (the procedure can be prohibitively expensive, making insurance coverage important) and (2) whether a supportive work environment exists. As mentioned above, 118 of Fortune 500 companies include gender identity and expression in their antidiscrimination policies. In addition to discrimination, however, employees who transition on the job face unique obstacles.

COMING OUT AND TRANSITIONING IN THE WORKPLACE

Before transitioning, a transgender individual must consider the following:

- Legal factors. An "at-will" transitioning employee (noncontract, nonunion) working in a jurisdiction lacking legal protection for transgender employees can be terminated for any reason not forbidden by an antidiscrimination law, even if unrelated to job performance. As mentioned above, few legal resources exist to protect gender nonconformity.
- Job value. Transitioning employees should take into account how much they value their job: whether it is the "world's greatest job" or merely an income stream. Likewise, they should consider how irreplaceable they are or are not.
- Job sector. Do transitioning employees work in a more tolerant field such as academia or software design, or a more corporate environment? Do they work in a field where gender conformity is actually promoted as a value by their employer, such as a parochial school, or in an environment that emphasizes regimentation and conformity, such as the military or a police precinct?
- Insurance. Transitioning employees should find out how their insurance and medical coverage will be affected by the procedure. Will coming out affect their employer's insurance premiums or their own premiums and copayments? What will the insurance company itself do with the employee's medical information? This will (at least in part) depend on the employer's perception of how the transitioning process will affect their health care costs. Furthermore, insurance coverage usually does not extend to modification of fully functioning organs.

PREPARING MANAGEMENT AND COWORKERS

Many transgender advocacy organizations, such as the National Center for Transgender Equality, encourage transitioning employees to inform and educate management. This will involve giving notice of your plans and how you will implement them. Suggested topics could include issues of timing, responding to harassment, job responsibilities, pronouns, and, possibly most importantly, bathroom use.

THE BATHROOM ISSUE

One of the most sensitive issues for transgender employees is which bathroom to use. Female employees, for example, may feel uncomfortable sharing a restroom with a coworker undergoing a transition from male to female. Employers such as IBM, Apple Computers, and Lucent Technologies have managed to find workable solutions with their transgender employees, such as: (1) Employees may use any restroom that corresponds with their full-time gender presentation. Management requires only that, after notifying the human resources department of their intent to transition, a transitioning employee should present according to her or his gender identity thereafter. This is the policy recommended by most transgender advocacy organizations. (2) A transitioning employee may use a unisex bathroom, if one is available and accessible, for some period during the transition period. (3) Employees may use a restroom that corresponds with their biological sex; employees who have completed sex-reassignment surgery may use restrooms that correspond with the biological sex to which they transitioned. Generally, transgender advocacy organizations do not recommend this as an appropriate response to the restroom access needs of their transgender employees. Employers should also note that new Health Insurance Portability and Accountability Act regulations reinforce the confidentiality of employee medical information. As a result, unless an employee tells management directly, management may not know whether or when an employee has had sex-reassignment surgery and therefore may have difficulty implementing a policy based on this standard.

Until the federal government recognizes same-sex partnerships and civil rights protections for sexual orientation and gender identity, the plight of queer Americans in the workplace will be very difficult.

Further Reading

Out and Equal Workplace Advocates. Available at: http://www.outandequal.org/. Accessed July 15, 2008.

Human Rights Campaign Workplace Project. Available at: http://www.hrc.org/issues/workplace. as. Accessed July 15, 2008.

National Center for Transgender Equality. Available at: http://www.nctequality.org/2005Archives. asp. Accessed July 15, 2008.

Jonathan G. Turbin

World Professional Association for Transgender Health, Inc.

Formerly known as the Harry Benjamin International Gender Dysphoria Association, the World Professional Association for Transgender Health, Inc. consists of international professionals who are committed to advancing understanding and treatment in regards to transgender health. Transgender identity has historically been referred to as gender dysphoria, gender identity disorder, or transsexualism. Gender dysphoria is a term that the association used to articulate a discrepancy between anatomy and sexual self-identification. The *Diagnostic and Statistic Manual of Mental Disorders* published by the American Psychiatric Association added Gender Identity Disorder as a diagnosis in 1979. In the same year, the Harry Benjamin

International Gender Dysphoria Association was founded to honor the work of Dr. Harry Benjamin, who was one of the first physicians to work with and advocate for transsexual people.

Harry Benjamin (1885–1986), born in Berlin, popularized the term transsexualism beginning in 1954. He published the first major work about transsexual experiences, *The Transsexual Phenomenon*, in 1966. Benjamin worked as a sexologist and endocrinologist. He was acquainted with people such as Eugene Steinach, Magnus Hirschfeld, Havelock Ellis, Albert Moll, Sigmund Freud, and Alfred Kinsey. Sexologist Magnus Hirschfeld was the first to coin the term transvestite in 1910 to describe people who cross-dressed. Expanding Hirschfeld's work, Benjamin distinguished those who were transsexuals from transvestites and assisted the former with accessing medical treatments.

The association is governed by an executive committee and board of directors. There are 11 different committees focusing on issues such as advocacy and liaison, archives, ethics, intersexuality, and legal issues. Ethical guidelines exist for professionals and apply to members of this association.

The Harry Benjamin International Gender Dysphoria Association created internationally accepted standards of care that are used by professionals encountering transsexual/transgender patients. These standards of care are designed to promote the health and well-being of a transgender person. They articulate a professional consensus about suggested treatment directions and offer professionals a course of action when providing services for transgender people. The standards of care also assist transgender persons, family members, and social institutions in understanding current professional thinking about transgender concerns.

The association sponsors a biannual symposium, celebrating 20 years in 2007, that attracts and brings together professionals from around the world who are researching and shifting trends in the field of transgender health. The association creates a biannual newsletter and bimonthly updates to inform members of recent activities within the organization. An annual membership directory is available for members to maintain contact with people working on transgender health.

For eight years, the association has generated the *International Journal of Transgenderism* online, and it is currently being published by Hawthorne Press. The journal is a way for furthering understanding about transgender health, advancements in treatments, acceptance in social and legal spheres, and development in educating professionals and the public about transgender.

Further Readings

Benjamin, Henry 1966. *The Transsexual Phenomenon*. New York: Julian Press.
International Journal of Transgenderism. Hawthorne Press.
The World Professional Association for Transgender Health, Inc. Available at: http://www.wpath.org/. Accessed July 15, 2008.

Jordon L. M. Johnson

Mark Wunderlich (1968–)

Mark Wunderlich is the author of two well-received books of poetry, *The Anchorage* (1999) and *Voluntary Servitude* (2004). Strongly influenced by the work of **Mark Doty** and Greek poet Constantine Cavafy, much of Wunderlich's poetry focuses on the workings of desire and identity in contemporary gay male life. *The Anchorage* evokes the cityscape of bars, bathhouses, and back rooms, clubs and one-night stands, and adeptly conjures up and questions the fantasies and mythologies urban gay men often weave around their temporary sexual encounters, both in anticipation and in retrospect. Some of the poems also deal with growing up in rural Wisconsin, treated as the opposite of that urban lifestyle; the poems draw energy from the juxtaposition of such different worlds.

The interplay of memory, imagination, and immediate experience is key to *Voluntary Solitude*, which is less centered on the apparently autobiographical narratives of *The Anchorage*. Indeed, many of the poems take place in an almost mythic landscape of the mind. In this book, sexuality is a kind of voluntary servitude, the mind submitting to the body, binding itself to the will of the flesh, the body submitting to another body, to the mind that both rules and is ruled by that other's body. The games of domination and submission the poems engage make this servitude explicit, embodying and enacting through particulars this general truth.

Further Reading

Wunderlich, Mark. 2007. "Openhearted: Stanley Kunitz and Mark Wunderlich in Conversation." *Poets.org from the American Academy of Poets*. Available at: http://www.poets.org/view media.php/prmMID/15893. Accessed February 28, 2007.

Reginald Shepherd

Y

Chay Yew (1965–)

Asian, Singaporean, American, Chinese, gay, Asian American playwright, Los Angeles–based Singapore director: these are just a few of the identities, cultural markers, and political constituencies that interface with Chay Yew's professional work as a theater director, playwright, and producer. The transnational and multifaceted dimensions of Yew's oeuvre point to the ways in which conceptions of home, kinship, and sexual identity are inflected by histories, memories, and queer imaginations that confound national and heterosexist boundaries. A typical biographical sketch on Yew highlights his diasporic formation: he was born and raised in Singapore, and his family emigrated to the United States, where he attended Pepperdine University and Boston University. Yew's career as a theater artist is similarly transnational, most obviously in playwriting; he has won a number of awards for his original plays, including the "Whitelands" trilogy: *Porcelain* (1992), *A Language of Their Own* (1994), and *Wonderland* (1996); as well as his other plays *A Beautiful Country* (1998); *Red* (1998); and *Scissors* (2000). Yew is also an accomplished director of numerous productions that cut across various genres, from one-man shows, musicals, operas, and Broadway drama to his own intercultural adaptations of Western classics such as *A Winter People* based on Chekhov's *The Cherry Orchard* and set in China, Lorca's *The House of Bernada Alba*, and *Distant Shore*, which used the framework from another Lorca play, *Blood Wedding*. Yew's prominence can be gleaned from the numerous national and international fellowships, appointments, and accolades he has received. He has been artistic director at the Asian Theater Workshop at the Mark Taper Forum in Los Angeles and the artistic director of the Northwest Asian American Theater in Seattle. He is currently serving on the executive board of the Society of Stage Directors and Choreographers and the Theater Communications Group Board of Directors.

Shay Youngblood (1959–)

Further Reading
Cho, Nancy. 2005. "Beyond Identity Politics: National and Transnational Dialogues in Anna Deavere Smith's *Twilight: Los Angeles, 1992* and Chay Yew's *A Beautiful Country*." *Journal of Dramatic Theory and Criticism* 20 (1): 65–81.
Diehl, Heath A. 2004. "Beyond the Silk Road: Staging a Queer Asian America in Chay Yew's *Porcelain*." *Studies in the Literary Imagination* 37 (1): 149–67.

Eng-Beng Lim

Shay Youngblood (1959–)

Shay Youngblood is a poet, playwright, and fiction writer and has also written, produced, and directed two short films. She won a Pushcart Prize for her short story "Born with Religion." Other awards include the Lorraine Hansberry Playwriting Award, the Astaea Writes' Award, and several National Association for the Advancement of Colored People Theater Awards. Born in Columbus, Georgia, she now lives in New York. Among her works are the books *Black Girl in Paris* (2000, a finalist for lesbian fiction for the Lambda Literary Award), *Soul Kiss* (1997), *One Red Shoe* (1990), and *Big Mama Stories* (1989); and the plays *Shakin' the Mess Outta Misery* (1988, film version in 1992), *There Are Many Houses in My Tribe* (1996, first published in *Gay and Lesbian Plays Today*, edited by Terry Helbing), *Amazing Grace* (1995), *Square Blues* (her dissertation, 1994, about lesbian art activists, among other things), *Black Power Barbie in Hotel de Dream* (1992), *Communism Killed My Dog* (1991), and *Talking Bones* (1992). According to Youngblood, *Big Mama Stories*, her first published text, is the closest to autobiographical of all of her works.

Teaching since 1987, Youngblood has instructed in black women's literature and put on workshops in creative writing, fiction, and playwriting at the following institutions: University of Mississippi; New York University; New School University, Eugene Lang College; Wheaton College; Brown University; Rhode Island Prison Program, Adult Correctional Institution for Women; American University; Boston College; Bronx Community College; Chicago Art Institute; Columbia University; Dartmouth College; Emory University; and Spelman College, as well as in elementary and high schools, at national and regional Conferences, and in senior centers and libraries.

Further Reading
Danquah, Ama. 2003. *Shaking the Tree: A Collection of New Fiction and Memoir by Black Women*. New York: W. W. Norton and Company.
Moore, Lisa C., ed. 1997. *Does Your Mama Know?: An Anthology of Black Lesbian Coming Out Stories*. Decatur, GA: RedBone Press.
Waugh, Debra Riggin. 1997. "Delicious, Forbidden: An Interview with Shay Youngblood." *Lambda Book Report: A Review of Contemporary Gay and Lesbian Literature* 6 (2): 1, 6–7.

Natalia Fior

youth and youth groups

Young people who identify as lesbian, gay, bisexual, transgender, or queer (LGBTQ) are estimated to account for nearly 5 percent of the U.S. youth population, or approximately three million people age 14–24. Studies indicate awareness of sexual orientation and gender identity happen early. The average age for LGBQ self-identification is about 16 years, and the first awareness of same-sexual attraction occurs at about age 9 for males and 10 for females. Regarding gender identity, transgender people report experiencing conflict over their gender assignment throughout their childhood and adolescence.

In addition to **coming out,** a number of challenges affect LGBTQ youth today. **Homophobia** (fear or contempt of lesbians and gay men), transphobia (aversion and expression of hatred toward transgender people), and heterosexism (often-unconscious prejudice against LGBT people exhibited primarily in language) greatly contribute to high rates of attempted and completed suicide, violence, substance abuse, teenage pregnancy, lack of adequate and specific health care, and risky sexual behaviors. The National Mental Health Association reports that LGBTQ youth are three times more likely to attempt suicide than other youth. The violent murders of Matthew Shepard, Gwen Araujo, and Sakia Gunn are a few examples of the impact of hate crimes on LGBTQ youth.

Transgender and LGBTQ youth of color face additional challenges, often including experiencing harassment due to racial or gender identity as well as sexual orientation. Many LGBTQ young people, however, create and access resources and support needed to address the myriad of concerns. In addition, LGBTQ youth have a long history of political organizing. The first LGBTQ youth organizing group was established before the **Stonewall Riots** in 1969.

Often, LGBTQ youth are afraid to come out to friends and family for fear of negative consequences. According to a recent report issued by the **National Gay and Lesbian Task Force,** half of LGBTQ teenagers experience negative reactions from their parents or guardians upon coming out, and 26 percent of LGBTQ youth are forced to leave home because of conflicts over their sexual orientation or gender identity/expression. A disproportionate percentage (between 20 and 40 percent) of homeless youth are LGBTQ. Most homeless LGBTQ youth have been kicked out of or have run away from home, frequently cycling through child welfare and foster care systems. For transgender youth, who often must navigate single-sex facilities, temporary and homeless shelters pose a number of particular challenges.

Some LGBTQ youth advocates provide services to address these issues, including drop-in hours, street outreach, and education and advocacy. In addition, organizations like **Parents, Families, and Friends of Lesbians and Gays (PFLAG)** offer support for parents of LGBTQ youth and adults through local chapters, as well as online and print publications.

Lyric, a group for LGBTQ youth in San Francisco. Courtesy of the Gay, Lesbian, Bisexual, Transgender Historical Society, San Francisco.

Currently, there are dozens of local groups, whether LGBTQ youth centers or youth programs affiliated with LGBT centers, that provide a range of services, including psychological counseling, safer-sex education, and legal assistance, for LGBTQ youth and young adults. Some programs and centers include high school facilities or a residential component for homeless LGBTQ youth.

The Hetrick-Martin Institute (HMI) in New York City, established in November 1979, is the oldest and largest nonprofit agency created to serve LGBTQ youth. Initially called the Institute for the Protection of Lesbian and Gay Youth (IPLGY), doctors Emery Hetrick and Damien Martin founded the organization after hearing the heartbreaking story of a homeless 15-year-old boy who had been beaten up and kicked out of his emergency shelter because he was gay. In 1988, the institute was renamed the Hetrick-Martin Institute in honor of Hetrick and Martin's lifelong commitment to serving the needs of LGBTQ youth.

According to the Gay, Lesbian, Straight Education Network's National School Climate Survey, a biennial survey of LGBTQ youth, 97 percent of LGBTQ public high school students report regularly hearing homophobic remarks from their peers, and 53 percent of students report hearing homophobic comments made by school staff. Approximately 28 percent of LGB youth drop out of high school because of discomfort resulting from verbal and physical abuse in the school environment.

For LGBQ youth of color, almost half report being victimized in school because of both their sexual orientation and race or ethnicity. According to the same study, harassment or assault because of one's race or ethnicity was more common in schools where the students are a racial minority. Harassment or assault because of one's sexual orientation, however, was more common when the student population was of the same race or ethnicity as the student.

Transgender high school students tend to experience higher frequencies of harassment and assault than their LGBQ classmates, as do students with other gender identities as well, such as genderqueer—which describes a person who identifies as neither male nor female.

Student-led clubs aimed to address bullying and harassment in schools, most commonly known as gay-straight alliances (GSAs), have sprung up in secondary schools across the country. Today the **Gay, Lesbian, and Straight Education Network (GLSEN),** a national organization that, among other programs, aims to support GSAs around the country, estimates that at least 3,000 clubs exist in high schools nationally.

Founded by educator Virginia Uribe, Los Angeles's Project 10 is widely acknowledged as the first systematic effort to provide support and education for LGBTQ youth in American public schools and is among the earliest instances of LGBTQ student groups. Established in 1984 at Fairfax High School of the Los Angeles Unified school district, Project 10 was named after sexologist Alfred Kinsey's now-disproved estimate that 10 percent of the general population was gay. Support groups aimed at LGBTQ youth focus on preventing or reducing alcohol and drug abuse and risky sexual behaviors among youth.

The first high school–based groups to call themselves GSAs were formed in 1989 at two private schools in Massachusetts, the Phillips Academy in Andover and the Concord Academy in Concord. Kevin Jennings, the faculty advisor for the Phillips Academy group, conducted workshops about the gay-straight model throughout Massachusetts, which led to the adoption of the gay-straight group model by the Governor's Commission for Gay and Lesbian Youth in Massachusetts as the preferred model for their Safe Schools Program. The adoption of the GSA model by the State of Massachusetts Safe Schools Program and the affirmative decision in the 1999 federal court ruling in Utah—*East High Gay/Straight Alliance v. Board of Education Salt Lake City School District,* 81 F. Supp. 2d 1166, 117 (D. Utah 1999)—in which high school student Kelli Peterson sued her school for denying her the right to create a GSA, served as two major catalysts in the GSA movement.

GSAs and other student clubs that address LGBTQ issues often engage in peer education by participating in a series of nationally orchestrated events throughout the school year. Most notably, many student groups take part in an annual action called the Day of Silence, in which students take a vow of silence to protest the ways that LGBTQ students are silenced every day. Students often hand out "speaking cards" that read:

> Please understand my reasons for not speaking today. I am participating in the Day of Silence, a national youth movement protesting the silence faced by lesbian, gay,

bisexual and transgender people and their allies. My deliberate silence echoes that silence, which is caused by harassment, prejudice, and discrimination. I believe that ending the silence is the first step toward fighting these injustices. Think about the voices you are not hearing today.

The Day of Silence was created by two University of Virginia students, Maria Pulzetti and Jessie Gilliam, in 1996 and became a national event in 1997. In 2001 GLSEN became a national sponsor of the initiative. Participation in the Day of Silence grows each year with hundreds of thousands of students taking part at secondary schools, colleges, and universities. Other secondary school–based actions that have been initiated by student clubs include Transgender Day of Remembrance, which seeks to bring awareness to antitransgender murder; Ally Week, which encourages all members of the school community to pledge to be an ally to the LGBTQ community; and Martin Luther King Jr. Organizing Weekend, in which student clubs work with local community groups on broader issues of social justice.

At colleges and universities, incidences of bullying and harassment of LGBTQ students persist, with verbal harassment noted as the most prominent form. According to one study, 90 percent of college students observe derogatory or homophobic remarks on campus. LGBT centers, departments, and student clubs serve to support LGBTQ college students.

The first formally recognized gay student organization at a college or university was established in the late 1960s; however, LGBTQ students created informal networks and meetings as early as the turn of the twentieth century. LGBTQ groups proliferated across campuses, bolstered by the visibility and momentum of the Stonewall Riots, throughout the 1970s. These groups tended to be male-dominated and predominantly white; lesbians, transgendered people, and LGBTQ people of color often formed their own groups as a result of feelings of exclusion. Universities in the late 1970s and early 1980s began to address LGBTQ school climate issues by implementing LGBT centers, and, in the 1990s, college curriculum began to include more LGBTQ issues.

In addition to the Day of Silence, LGBTQ students and student groups on college and university campuses often observe National Coming Out Day. Established by the **Human Rights Campaign (HRC)** in 1987, National Coming Out Day is celebrated annually on October 11, urging LGBTQ people on that day to declare their sexual orientation and gender identity to others. It has become a form of political activism to increase visibility and support for LGBTQ rights. Colleges and universities also often celebrate LGBT Month, inviting artists, activists, and scholars to discuss the current challenges and victories for LGBTQ people. In addition, the Lambda 10 Project, founded by Shane L. Windmeyer, is an initiative that aims to provide support to prospective and current LGBTQ sorority and fraternity members.

A number of legal cases demonstrate that school districts can be held liable under existing federal law for failing to protect LGBTQ students from harassment based on sexual orientation and gender nonconformity. However, without clear directives from federal and state legislatures, many school districts have failed to protect students from harassment and discrimination, putting themselves at risk for potential legal liability. In all of the cases brought to date, the student either prevailed after trial or achieved a settlement. Currently, nine states have antibullying policies that explicitly protect LGBTQ students. Generic antibullying policies that do not enumerate specific categories of protection have been found to have the same effect on bullying and harassment as no policy at all. At present, no federal antibullying legislation specifically protects LGBTQ students.

Numerous books, films, and online resources address LGBTQ youth issues directly. Some works of fiction include *The Snow Garden: A Novel*, by Christopher Rice, *Rainbow Boys*, by Alex Sanchez, *Coffee Will Make You Black*, by April Sinclair, *Stone Butch Blues*, by Leslie Feinberg, and *Go Tell It on the Mountain*, by James Baldwin. Nonfiction works include *Two Teenagers in Twenty: Writings by Gay and Lesbian Youth*, edited by Ann Heron, *My Gender Workbook*, by Kate Bornstein, *Becoming Visible: A Reader in Gay and Lesbian History for High School and College Students*, by Kevin Jennings, and *Sister Outsider*, by Audre Lorde. LGBTQ youth-related films include *The Incredibly True Adventure of Two Girls in Love*, *All Over Me*, *Billy Elliot*, *Ma Vie en Rose*, and *But I'm a Cheerleader*.

Online sites and publications are perhaps the most often utilized resources for LGBTQ youth, particularly for those who live in suburban and rural areas. *Oasis*, an online magazine created by and for LGBTQ youth, provides a virtual space for student reporting, poetry, and journaling. Many LGBTQ youth organizations and programs offer online resources, including GLSEN, Advocates for Youth, and U.S. Students Association.

Further Reading

Barry, Richard. 2000. "Sheltered 'Children': The Self-Creation of a Safe Space by Gay, Lesbian, and Bisexual Students." In *Construction Sites: Excavating Race, Class, and Gender among Urban Youth*, ed. Lois Wise and Michelle Fine, 84–99. New York: Teachers College Press.

Blumfled, Warren J. 1994. "Gay/Straight Alliances: Transforming Pain to Pride." *The High School Journal* 77 (1–2): 113–21.

Cass, Vivienne. 1979. "Homosexual Identity Formation: A Theoretical Model." *Journal of Homosexuality* 4: 219–35.

Dennis, Jeffrey P. 2006. *Queering Teen Culture: All-American Boys and Same-Sex Desire in Film and Television*. Binghamton, NY: Harrington Park.

Dupree, Jeffery, dir. 1998. *Out of the Past: The Struggle for Gay and Lesbian Rights in America*, DVD Video. USA: Allumination.

Gay, Lesbian, and Straight Education Network (GLSEN). 2003. *The 2003 National School Climate Survey: The School-Related Experiences of Our Nation's Lesbian, Gay, Bisexual and Transgender Youth*. New York: GLSEN.

Gay, Lesbian, and Straight Education Network (GLSEN). 2003. *School-Related Experiences of LGBT Youth of Color: Findings from the 2003 National School Climate Survey*. New York: GLSEN.

Gay, Lesbian, and Straight Education Network (GLSEN). 2006. "FAQs: Top 5 Frequently Asked Questions from the Media." November 20. Available at: http://www.glsen.org/cgibin/iowa/all/library/record/863.html. Accessed July 15, 2008.

Gay, Lesbian, and Straight Education Network (GLSEN) and the National Center for Lesbian Rights. 2005. *Fifteen Expensive Reasons Why Safe Schools Legislation Is in Your State's Best Interest*. New York: GLSEN.

Harbeck, Karen M. 1994. "Invisible No More: Addressing the Needs of Gay, Lesbian and Bisexual Youth and Their Advocates." *School Journal* 77 (1–2): 169–76.

Harris Interactive and Gay, Lesbian, and Straight Education Network (GLSEN). 2005. *From Teasing to Torment: School Climate in America, A Survey of Students and Teachers*. New York: GLSEN.

Henry J. Kaiser Family Foundation. 2001. *Inside-OUT: A Report on the Experiences of Lesbians, Gays, and Bisexuals in America and the Public's Views on Issues and Policies Related to Sexual Orientation*. Publication No. 3193. Menlo Park, CA: Henry J. Kaiser Foundation.

Human Rights Watch. 2001. *Hatred in the Hallways: Violence and Discrimination against Lesbian, Gay, Bisexual, and Transgender Students in U.S. Schools*. New York: Human Rights Watch.

Kosciw, J. G., and E. M. Diaz. 2006. *The 2005 National School Climate Survey: The Experiences of Lesbian, Gay, Bisexual and Transgender Youth in Our Nation's Schools*. New York: GLSEN.

Lipkin, Arthur. 1992. "Project 10: Gay and Lesbian Students Find Acceptance in Their School Community." *Teaching Tolerance* 1 (2): 24–27.

National Gay and Lesbian Task Force (NGLTF). 2007. *Lesbian, Gay, Bisexual and Transgender Youth: An Epidemic of Homelessness*. New York: NGLTF.

Russell, Stephen T., and Kara Joyner. 2001. "Adolescent Sexual Orientation and Suicide Risk: Evidence from a National Study." *American Journal of Public Health* 91 (8): 1276–81.

Savin-Williams, Ritch C. 1994. "Verbal and Physical Abuse as Stressors in the Lives of Lesbian, Gay Male, and Bisexual Youths: Association with School Problems, Running Away, Substance Abuse, Prostitution, and Suicide." *Journal of Consulting and Clinical Psychology* 62 (2): 261–69.

Savin-Williams, Ritch C. 1998. "The Disclosure to Families of Same-Sex Attractions by Lesbian, Gay, and Bisexual Youths." *Journal of Research on Adolescence* 8: 49–68.

Snively, Carol A. (n.d.) "Gay-Straight Alliances." Available at: http://www.glbtq.com/social-sciences/gay_straight_alliances,2.html. Accessed July 15, 2008.

The Facts: GLBT Youth. Available at: http://members.aol.com/outhealth/topics/youth2.htm. Accessed July 15, 2008.

Uribe, Virginia. 1994. "Project 10: A School-Based Outreach to Gay and Lesbian Youth." *High School Journal* 77 (1–2): 108–12.

Uribe, Virginia, and Karen M. Harbeck. 1992. "Addressing the Needs of Lesbian, Gay and Bisexual Youth: The Origins of PROJECT 10 and School-Based Intervention." In *Coming Out of the Classroom Closet: Gay and Lesbian Students, Teachers and Curriculum*, ed. Karen M. Harbeck, 9–28. Binghamton, NY: Harrington Park Press.

Zera, Deborah. 1992. "Coming of Age in a Heterosexist World: The Development of Gay and Lesbian Adolescents." *Adolescence* 27: 849–54.

Riley Snorton

Z

David Zamora Casas is a gay Chicano artist living in San Antonio, Texas. He is very well known there for his art, which not only uses traditional oil painting but also incorporates various objects right onto the canvas, such as bone, magazine clippings, ribbons, and various types of plant components, among other objects. Though his love of painting developed after he had been inspired by a male lover, Casas has not stopped only at paintings. He is also a performance artist and has done a one-man show that incorporates his homosexuality, his Chicano heritage, and religion. One of his favorite themes is **identity,** specifically **androgyny,** which can be seen in his self-portrait, "Portrait of a Burnout," which shows him wearing a blue skirt, a striped shirt, and pink wings in addition to a giant red sombrero. Another piece, "Love Has No Gender," incorporates many materials, including tin and cacti, its major theme being gender and the body, with the drying and decaying cacti emphasizing the transitory and renewing nature of life. His art has been exhibited, singly and as part of a group, most notably at the San Antonio Museum of Art, the University of Oklahoma Tulsa campus, and many other galleries. He is the recipient of several prestigious grants, including one from the Andy Warhol and Rockefeller Foundation in 1992. He is also an activist, focusing most of his attention on AIDS and LGBTQ issues. He currently sits on the Board of Directors for the Esperanza Peace and Justice Center in San Antonio, Texas. Casas works on his art in his studio, called The Anti-Oppression Church of Hardcore Folk Art in San Antonio.

Further Reading

Latinalo Art Community. Available at: http://latinoartcommunity.org/community/ChicArt/ArtistDir/DavCas.html. Accessed July 4, 2008.

Katherine J. J. Pionke

General Bibliography

Abelove, Henry. 1993. *The Lesbian and Gay Studies Reader*. New York: Routledge.

American Academy of HIV Medicine. 2007. *AAHIVM Fundamentals of HIV Medicine for the HIV Specialist*. Washington, DC: American Academy of HIV Medicine.

Armstrong, Elizabeth. 2002. *Forging Gay Identities: Organizing Sexuality in San Francisco, 1950–1994*. Chicago: University of Chicago Press.

Bernstein, Robert A. 2003. *Straight Parents, Gay Children: Keeping Families Together*. Rev. ed. Cambridge, MA: Da Capo Press.

Blake, Nayland, Lawrence Rinder, and Amy Scholder, eds. 1995. *In a Different Light: Visual Culture, Sexual Identity, Queer Practice*. San Francisco: City Lights.

Borden, Audrey. 2006. *The History of Gay People in Alcoholics Anonymous: From the Beginning*. Philadelphia: Haworth Press.

Borhan, Pierre, Olivier Saillard, Gilles Mora, and Jose Villarrubia. 2007. *Man to Man: A History of Gay Photography*. New York: Vendome Press.

Bornstein, Kate. 1994. *Gender Outlaw: On Men, Women, and the Rest of Us*. New York: Routledge.

Boykin, Keith. 2005. *Beyond the Down Low: Sex, Lies, and Denial in Black America*. New York: Carroll & Graf.

Boylan, Jennifer Finney. 2003. *She's Not There: A Life in Two Genders*. New York: Broadway Books.

Brett, Philip, Elizabeth Wood, and Gary C. Thomas, eds. 1994. *Queering the Pitch: The New Gay and Lesbian Musicology*. New York: Routledge.

Brill, Stephanie. 2006. *The New Essential Guide to Lesbian Conception, Pregnancy, and Birth*. New York: Alyson Books.

Brown, Mildred L., and Chloe Ann Rounsley. 2003. *True Selves: Understanding Transsexualism—For Families, Friends, Coworkers, and Helping Professionals*. Hoboken, NJ: Jossey-Bass.

Burleson, William. 2005. *Bi America: Myths, Truths, and Struggles of an Invisible Community*. New York: Routledge.

Butler, Judith. 2006. *Gender Trouble: Feminism and the Subversion of Identity*. New York: Routledge.

Clifford, Denis, Frederick Hertz, and Emily Doskow. 2007. *A Legal Guide for Lesbian and Gay Couples*. 14th ed. (book with CD-ROM). NOLO.

Clum, John M. 1999. *Something for the Boys: Musical Theater and Gay Culture*. New York: St. Martin's.

Clum, John M. 2000. *Still Acting Gay: Male Homosexuality and Modern Drama*. New York: Palgrave.

Clunis, D. Merilee, and G. Dorsey Green. 2004. *Lesbian Couples: A Guide to Creating Healthy Relationships.* 4th ed. Berkeley, CA: Seal Press.

Deitcher, David, ed. 1995. *The Question of Equality: Lesbian and Gay Politics in America since Stonewall.* New York: Scribner.

D'Emilio, John. 1998. *Sexual Politics, Sexual Communities: The Making of a Homosexual Minority in the United States, 1940–1970.* Chicago: University of Chicago Press.

Dreger, Alice Domurat, ed. 1999. *Intersex in the Age of Ethics.* Hagestown, MD: University Publishing Group.

Duberman, Martin. 1994. *Stonewall.* New York: Dutton/Plume.

Eisenbach, David. 2006. *Gay Power: An American Revolution.* New York: Carroll & Graf.

Eskridge, William E. 1996. *The Case for Same-Sex Marriage.* New York: The Free Press.

Eskridge, William N., and Nan D. Hunter. 2003. *Sexuality, Gender and the Law.* 2nd ed. Westbury, NY: Foundation Press.

Faderman, Lillian. 1991. *Odd Girls and Twilight Lovers: A History of Lesbian Life in Twentieth-Century America.* New York: Columbia University Press.

Fausto-Sterling, Anne. 2000. *Sexing the Body: Gender Politics and the Construction of Sexuality.* New ed. New York: Basic Books.

Feinberg, Leslie. 1996. *Transgender Warriors: Making History from Joan of Arc to RuPaul.* Boston: Beacon.

Fellows, Will. 1996. *Farm Boys: Lives of Gay Men from the Rural Midwest.* Madison: University of Wisconsin Press.

Flowers, Charles. 2000. *Golden Men: The Power of Gay Midlife.* New York: Harper.

Gates, Gary J., and Jason Ost. 2004. *Gay and Lesbian Atlas.* Washington, DC: Urban Institute Press.

Green, Jamison. 2004. *Becoming a Visible Man.* Memphis, TN: Vanderbilt University Press.

Greenwood, David Valdes. 2008. *Homo Domesticus: Notes from a Same-Sex Marriage.* New York: Da Capo Press.

Griffin, Carolyn W., and Marian J. Wirth. 1997. *Beyond Acceptance: Parents of Lesbians and Gays Talk about Their Experiences.* Rev. ed. New York: St. Martin's Griffin.

Halperin, David. 2007. *What Do Gay Men Want?: An Essay on Sex, Risk, and Subjectivity.* Ann Arbor, MI: University of Michigan Press.

Hammond, Harmony. 2000. *Lesbian Art in America.* New York: Rizzoli.

Hardin, Kimeron N., and Marny Hall. 2001. *Queer Blues: The Lesbian and Gay Guide to Overcoming Depression.* Berkeley, CA: New Harbinger Publications.

Hogan, Steve, and Lee Hudson. 1998. *Completely Queer: The Gay and Lesbian Encyclopedia.* New York: Macmillan / Holt.

Holleran, Andrew. 2008. *Chronicle of a Plague, Revisited: AIDS and its Aftermath.* Cambridge, MA: Da Capo Press.

Jacobs, Sue-Ellen, Wesley Thomas, and Sabine Lang, eds. 1997. *Two-Spirit People: Native American Gender Identity, Sexuality, and Spirituality.* Urbana: University of Illinois Press.

Johnson, Troy. 2008. *Family Outing: What Happened When I Found Out My Mother Was Gay.* Baltimore: Arcade Press.

Johnston, Jill. 1973. *Lesbian Nation: The Feminist Solution.* New York: Simon and Schuster.

Kaiser, Charles. 1997. *The Gay Metropolis, 1940–1996.* Boston: Houghton Mifflin.

Katz, Jonathan [Ned]. 1976. *Gay American History: Lesbians and Gay Men in the U.S.A.: A Documentary.* New York: Crowell.

Kaufman, Gershen. 1996. *Coming Out of Shame: Transforming Gay and Lesbian Lives.* New York: Main Street Books.

Kennedy, Elizabeth Lapovsky, and Madeline D. Davis. 1993. *Boots of Leather, Slippers of Gold: The History of a Lesbian Community.* New York: Routledge.

Kilmer-Purcell, Josh. 2006. *I Am Not Myself These Days.* New York: Harper Perennial.

Kristal, Nicole, and Mike Szymanski. 2006. *The Bisexual's Guide to the Universe: Quips, Tips, and Lists for Those Who Go Both Ways*. New York: Alyson Books.

Lev, Arlene Istar. 2004. *The Complete Lesbian and Gay Parenting Guide*. New York: Berkley Trade.

Link, Aaron, and Hilda Raz. 2008. *What Becomes You*. Omaha: University of Nebraska / Bison Books.

Loughery, John. 1998. *The Other Side of Silence: Men's Lives and Gay Identities: A Twentieth-Century History*. New York: Henry Holt.

Love, Heather. 2007. *Feeling Backward: Loss and the Politics of Queer History*. Cambridge, MA: Harvard University Press.

Luibhéid, Eithne, and Lionel Cantú Jr., eds. 2005. *Queer Migrations: Sexuality, U.S. Citizenship, and Border Crossings*. Minneapolis: University of Minnesota Press.

Lustig, Harold L. 1999. *Four Steps to Financial Security for Lesbian and Gay Couples*. New York: Ballantine.

Lyon, Phyllis, and Del Martin. 1972. *Lesbian/Woman*. San Francisco: Glide Publications. Rev. ed. Volcano, CA: Volcano Press, 1991.

Makadon, H., K. Mayer, J. Potter, and H. Goldhammer, eds. 2008. *Fenway Guide to Lesbian, Gay, Bisexual, and Transgender Health*. Philadelphia: American College of Physicians.

Malinowski, Sharon, and Christa Brelin, eds. 1995. *The Gay and Lesbian Literary Companion*. Detroit: Visible Ink.

Marcus, Eric. 1992. *Making History: The Struggle for Gay and Lesbian Equal Rights, 1945–1990: An Oral History*. New York: HarperCollins.

McGarry, Molly, and Fred Wasserman. 1998. *Becoming Visible: An Illustrated History of Lesbian and Gay Life in Twentieth-Century America*. New York: New York Public Library/Penguin.

Meyer, Richard. 2001. *Outlaw Representation: Censorship and Homosexuality in Twentieth-Century American Art*. New York: Oxford University Press.

Meyerowitz, Joanne. 2002. *How Sex Changed: A History of Transsexuality in the United States*. Cambridge, MA: Harvard University Press.

Moraga, Cherríe, and Gloria Anzaldúa, eds. 1983. *This Bridge Called My Back: Writings by Radical Women of Color*. New York: Kitchen Table: Women of Color Press.

Murdoch, Joyce, and Deb Price. 2001. *Courting Justice: Gay Men and Lesbians v. the Supreme Court*. New York: Basic Books.

Murphy, Timothy F., ed. 2000. *Reader's Guide to Lesbian and Gay Studies*. Dearborn, MI: Fitzroy.

Murray, Stephen O. 1996. *American Gay*. Chicago: University of Chicago Press.

Nelson, Emmanuel S. 1993. *Contemporary Gay American Novelists: A Bio-Bibliographical Critical Sourcebook*. Westport, CT: Greenwood.

Nelson, Emmanuel S. 2003. *Contemporary Gay American Poets and Playwrights: An A-to-Z Guide*. Westport, CT: Greenwood.

Nelson, Emmanuel S., ed. 1992. *AIDS: The Literary Response*. New York: Twayne.

Nestle, Joan, ed. 1992. *The Persistent Desire: A Femme-Butch Reader*. New York: Alyson.

Newman, Felice. 2004. *The Whole Lesbian Sex Book: A Passionate Guide for All of Us*. 2nd ed. San Francisco: Cleis Press.

Polikoff, Nancy D. 2008. *Beyond (Straight and Gay) Marriage: Valuing All Families under the Law*. Boston, MA: Beacon Press.

Pollack, Sandra, and Denise D. Knight, eds. 1993. *Contemporary Lesbian Writers of the United States: A Bio-Bibliographical Critical Sourcebook*. Westport, CT: Greenwood.

Preves, Sharon E. 2003. *Intersex and Identity: The Contested Self*. New Brunswick, NJ: Rutgers University Press.

Rauch, Jonathan. 2004. *Gay Marriage: Why It Is Good for Gays, Good for Straights, and Good for America*. New York: Holt.

Roscoe, Will. 1998. *Changing Ones: Third and Fourth Genders in Native North America*. New York: St. Martin's Press.

Rupp, Leila J. 1999. *A Desired Past: A Short History of Same-Sex Love in America*. Chicago: University of Chicago Press.

Sears, James T. 1997. *Lonely Hunters: An Oral History of Lesbian and Gay Southern Life, 1948–1968*. Boulder, CO: Westview.

Sedgwick, Eve Kosofsky. 2008. *Epistemology of the Closet*. 2nd ed. Berkeley: University of California Press.

Sheff, Nic. 2008. *Tweak: Growing Up on Methamphetimines*. New York: Simon and Shuster/ Atheneum / Ginee Seo Publishing.

Shilts, Randy. 1982. *The Mayor of Castro Street: The Life and Times of Harvey Milk*. New York: St. Martin's Press.

Shilts, Randy. 1987. *And the Band Played On: Politics, People, and the AIDS Epidemic*. New York: St. Martin's Press.

Shilts, Randy. 1993. *Conduct Unbecoming: Gays and Lesbians in the U.S. Military: Vietnam to the Persian Gulf*. New York: St. Martin's Press.

Signorile, Michelangelo. 1993. *Queer in America: Sex, the Media, and the Closets of Power*. New York: Random House.

Snow, Judith. 2004. *How It Feels to Have a Gay or Lesbian Parent: A Book by Kids for Kids of All Ages*. New York: Routledge.

Spinelli, Frank. 2008. *The Advocate Guide to Gay Men's Health and Wellness*. New York: Alyson Books.

Stein, Edward, ed. 1992. *Forms of Desire: Sexual Orientation and the Social Constructionist Controversy*. New York: Routledge.

Stein, Marc, ed. 2003. *Encyclopedia of Lesbian, Gay, Bisexual and Transgender History in America*. New York: Scribner's.

Stevens, Tracey. 2002. *How to Be a Happy Lesbian: A Coming Out Guide*. Asheville, NC: Amazing Dreams Publishing.

Stewart, Chuck. 2003. *Gay and Lesbian Issues: A Reference Handbook*. New York: ABC Clio.

Streitmatter, Rodger. 1995. *Unspeakable: The Rise of the Gay and Lesbian Press in America*. Boston: Faber and Faber.

Stryker, Susan. 2008. *Transgender History*. Berkeley, CA: Seal Press.

Stryker, Susan, and Jim Van Buskirk. 1996. *Gay by the Bay: A History of Queer Culture in the San Francisco Bay Area*. San Francisco: Chronicle.

Sullivan, Andrew. 1995. *Virtually Normal: An Argument about Homosexuality*. New York: Knopf.

Sullivan, Andrew, ed. 1997. *Same-Sex Marriage: Pro and Con, A Reader*. Rev. ed. 2004. New York: Vintage.

Summers, Claude, ed. 2002. *The Gay and Lesbian Literary Heritage: A Reader's Companion to the Writers and Their Work, from Antiquity to the Present*. New York: Routledge.

Summers, Claude J., ed. 2004. *The Queer Encyclopedia of Music, Dance and Musical Theater*. San Francisco: Cleis.

Summers, Claude J., ed. 2004. *The Queer Encyclopedia of the Visual Arts*. San Francisco: Cleis.

Summers, Claude J., ed. 2005. *The Queer Encyclopedia of Film and Television*. San Francisco: Cleis.

Thompson, Mark, ed. 1994. *Long Road to Freedom: The Advocate History of the Gay and Lesbian Movement*. New York: St. Martin's Press.

Tyrkus, Michael J., ed. 1997. *Gay and Lesbian Biography*. Detroit: St. James.

Vaid, Urvashi. 1995. *Virtual Equality: The Mainstreaming of Gay and Lesbian Liberation*. New York: Anchor/Doubleday.

Valentine, David. 2007. *Imagining Transgender: An Ethnography of a Category*. Durham, NC: Duke University Press.

Weinberg, Martin S., Colin J. Williams, and Douglas W. Pryor. 1995. *Dual Attraction: Understanding Bisexuality*. New York: Oxford University Press.

Zimmerman, Bonnie. 1990. *The Safe Sea of Women: Lesbian Fiction, 1969–1989*. Boston: Beacon Press.
Zimmerman, Bonnie, and George E. Haggerty, eds. 2000. *The Encyclopedia of Lesbian and Gay Histories and Cultures*. New York: Garland.

WEB SITES

American Civil Liberties Union Lesbian Gay Bisexual Transgender Project. http://www.aclu.org/lgbt/index.html. Accessed July 25, 2008.
Advocate. http://www.advocate.com/ExclusiveCategory.asp?Category=Commentary. Accessed July 25, 2008.
CenterLink, the Web site for the Community of LGBT Centers. http://www.lgbtcenters.org. Accessed July 25, 2008.
Gay and Lesbian Association of Retiring Persons. http://www.gaylesbianretiring.org. Accessed July 25, 2008.
Gay and Lesbian Review Worldwide. http://www.glreview.com. Accessed August 24, 2008.
Gay, Lesbian, Bisexual, Transgender Historical Society. http://www.glbthistory.org. Accessed July 25, 2008.
Halsall, Peter, site maintainer. *People with a History: An Online Guide to Lesbian, Gay, Bisexual, and Trans History*. http://www.fordham.edu/halsall/pwh/index.html. Accessed July 25, 2008.
International Gay and Lesbian Travel Association. http://www.iglta.org. Accessed July 25, 2008.
Lesbian and Gay Archives and Libraries. http://www.glinn.com/news/lar1.htm. Accessed July 25, 2008.
National Gay and Lesbian Chamber of Commerce. http://www.nglcc.org. Accessed July 25, 2008.
National Gay and Lesbian Task Force. http://www.thetaskforce.org. Accessed July 25, 2008.
National Gay and Lesbian Task Force Issues. http://www.thetaskforce.org/issues. Accessed July 25, 2008.
Planet Out Gay Lesbian Queer community. http://www.planetout.com. Accessed July 25, 2008.
Resources for Queer and Questioning Youth. http://www.outproud.org. Accessed July 25, 2008.
Sexuality Information and Education Council of the United States. http://www.siecus.org. Accessed July 25, 2008.
Summers, Claude, ed. *glbtq: An Encyclopedia of Gay, Lesbian, Bisexual, Transgender, and Queer Culture*. Available at: http://www.glbtq.com/. Accessed July 25, 2008.
365 Gay: Daily gay news. http://www.365gay.com. Accessed July 25, 2008.

Index

Page numbers in **bold** indicate the main article on a topic.

Index

American Family Association, 880, 982

American Friends Service Committee, 5

American Gamelan movement, 516, 517

American Ghosts (Plante), 893

American Historical Association (AHA), 249, 250–51, 252. *See also* Committee on Lesbian and Gay History

American Idiom, The (Williams and Norse), 820

American Law Institute, 196

American Library Association. *See* Gay, Lesbian, Bisexual, and Transgendered Round Table of the American Library Association

American Medical Association (AMA), 434, 435, 526

American Philosophical Association, 1145

American Primitive (Oliver), 836

American Psychiatric Association (APA): Association of Gay and Lesbian Psychiatrists and, 75; Fryer, John E., and, 415–16; protests and actions, 953; psychiatry and homosexuality, 961–64; science and medicine of homosexuality, 1091, 1092; transgender studies and, 1225; Transsexual Menace and, 1231. See also *Diagnostic and Statistical Manual of Mental Disorders;* Psychiatry and homosexuality

American Psychological Association, 851, 1029, 1092

American Shore, The (Delany), 1084

American Sign Language, 294, 295

Americans with Disabilities Act (1990), 46, 525–26, 531, 1218

American Woman in the Chinese Hat, The (Maso), 730

America Online (AOL), 1104

America's Next Top Model, 1189

Amistad, La, 653–54

Ammiano, Tom, 7

Amnesty International Members for Lesbian & Gay Concerns, 50

Amnesty International OUTfront, **48–50**

Amnesty International USA, 50

Among Women (Rabinowitz and Auanger), 569–70

Amyl nitrite, 37, 410

Anal sex, 46, **51**, 1148, 1149. *See also* Barebacking; Sodomy; Sodomy laws

Anatomic and neurophysiological studies, 475–76

Anchorage, The (Wunderlich), 1289

Andersen v. King County (2006), 723

Anderson, Cora, 85

Anderson, Laurie, 175, 1027

And He Made a Her (Wilson), 1268

Andre's Mother (McNally), 739

Andringa, Mel, 860–61

Andriote, John-Manuel, 528

Androgen insensitivity syndrome, 595

Androgyny, **51–53,** 177–78

Andros, Phil, 374, 889

Androzine, 1005

And Tell Sad Stories of the Deaths of Queens (Williams), 1267

And the Band Played On (film), 399

And the Band Played On (Shilts), 698, 699, 1129

Angelic Rebels (Boffin), 885

Angel on My Shoulder, 388

Angelou, Maya, 15, 78

Angels in America (film), 400

Angels in America (Kushner), 9, 608, 641, 642, 696, 897

Anger, Kenneth, 381–82, 395

Anglican Communion, 230, 334–35, 337

"Angouleme" (Disch), 1084, 1085

Angus, Patrick, **53–54**

"Animals" series (Carlson), 217

Anna's Country (Lang), 297

Annie on My Mind (Garden), 369

Annotations (Ligon), 693

Annual Reminder, 560–61

Annual Transgender Day of Remembrance, 1143

Annunciation (Plante), 893

Another Country (Baldwin), 91, 825

Another Mother Tongue (Grahn), 497

"Another Traditional Family" (Atkins), 885

Answered Prayers (Capote), 191

Answer Song (Trinidad), 1235

Antes que anochezca (Arenas), 58

Antibullying policies, 1297

Anti-Defamation League, 521

Anti-Semitism, 606, 607

Anti-Violence Project, 794–95

Antler, **54**

Antony and Cleopatra (Barber), 96

Anvil, 112

"Any Old Place with You" (Rodgers and Hart), 518

Anzaldúa, Gloria Evangelina, **54–55,** 87, 209–10, 802, 876, 906

AOL. *See* America Online

"Aphrodisiac" (Bram), 164

API Family Pride, 73

Appalachian Spring (Copland), 264

Appearance-based covering, 270

Applause, 770, 771

Apple Computers, 1287

Apples and Oranges (Clausen), 229

Applied ethics, 875

Apprentice of Fever, The (Tayson), 1182, 1183

Araki, Gregg, 72, 399, 405, 406

Araujo, Gwen, 431, 520, 567

ARC/AIDS Vigil, 1074

Archer, Nuala, **55–56**

Architects, **56–57.** *See also* Art and photography

Archives. *See* Lesbian Herstory Archives; Libraries and archives

Arc of Light, An (deVries), 302

Arc of Love, The (Coss, ed.), 269

Arden Eversmeyer Old Lesbian Oral Herstory Project, 835

Arellano, Cathy, **57**

Arenas, Reinaldo, **58–59**

Ariston baths, 107

Arkansas (Leavitt), 660

Arnett, Chuck, 61, 1066

Arnold, June, **59–60**

Arpino, Gerald, 610

Art and photography, **60–62,** 497, 541–42, 558. *See also* Artists, men; Artists, women; Artists and photographers, early trailblazers; Photographers, men; Photographers, women; *specific artists and photographers*

Index

Index

Index

Burger, Warren Earl, 1151
Burning Bridges (Dean), 297
Burns, John Horne, **172–73**
Burns, Randy, 804
Burns, Sean, 1161
Burnt Offerings (Liu), 700
Burnton Widows, The
    (McConnell), 736
Burroughs, Augusten, **173**
Burroughs, William Seward, **174–
    75,** 206, 825–26
Burroughs Wellcome, 11–12
Burston, Paul, 406
Burton, John, 1072
Busch, Charles, **175–76,** 314–15
Bush, George H. W., 531, 577, 797
Bush, George W., 260, 702, 943
Bush v. Gore (2000), 46–47
Butch–femme, **176–79;** bars,
    lesbian, and, 104; class and, 225;
    fashion, style, and clothing and,
    360, 362; granola lesbian and,
    694; heteronormativity and,
    536; Hollibaugh, Amber,
    and, 556–57; sex wars of the
    1980s and, 1124; stereotypes,
    1163. *See also* Femme Mafia
Butchies, The, 768
Butler, Judith: butch-femme, 177;
    camp, 187; drag, 312; identity,
    586; Judaism, 608; lesbian
    identity, 664; passing, 854–55;
    performativity, 251, 316–17,
    468, 865–66, 867, 868, 869–70;
    queer studies, 990, 991, 992;
    queer theory and social science,
    1002; sexualities, 1115;
    stereotypes, 1167; women's and
    gender studies in universities,
    1276, 1277
Butler, Octavia E., 1087
Butterfly, The (Rumaker), 1058
Button, John, 61
BWMT. *See* National Association
    of Black and White Men
    Together
Byron and Greek Love (Crompton),
    274

C

"C33" (Crane), 273
Cabaret, 392, 598, 781

Cabinet of Dr. Caligari, The, 403
Cabranes-Grant, Leo F., **181–82**
Cade, Cathy, 883
Cade, Toni, 15
Cadge, Wendy, 944
Cadmus, Paul, 63
Cady, Joseph, 695–96
Caffe Cino, 894, 1192–93, 1268
Cage, John, **182–84,** 516
Cage, Xenia, 182, 183
Cage aux Folles, La, 655, 770, 773,
    775, 895
Calamus Books, 753
Cale, John, 1027
Calhoun, Cheshire, 235, 1021–22
Califia, Patrick, **184,** 1066
California: age of consent, 26; bars,
    gay, 1069; family law, 354; gay
    rodeo, 458; homosexual panic,
    567–68; marriage, same-sex,
    and domestic partnerships, 455,
    456, 717, 723; Proposition 6,
    70, 462, 702; Proposition 187,
    654; protests and actions, 956;
    sodomy laws, 1072. *See also*
    Los Angeles; San Francisco
Call, Hal, 618
Callahan, Timothy (fictitious
    character), 373
Callen, Michael, 530, 539, 540
"Call for Dissonance" manifesto, 144
Callis, Charles A., 762
Calvin Klein products, 638
Camera Query, 886
Cameron, Barbara, 804
Cameron, Loren, 880–81, 1214
Camp, **184–89;** bars, gay, and,
    103; comedians and, 241; drag
    and, 313–16; fashion, style,
    and clothing and, 359; musical
    theater and films and, 779–80;
    poets, gay, and, 900; theater
    companies, 1192, 1193
Campaign for Homosexual Equity,
    592
Campbell, Bobbi, 539, 540, 1073
Camp Concentration (Disch), 1085
Campo, Rafael, **189–90**
"Campo" (Muñoz), 1135
Camp Trans, 956, 1231, 1280
Campus Organizing Project, 796
Cam-to-cam cybersex, 1103

Canadian Lesbian and Gay
    Archives, 684–85
Canary (Aldyne), 373
Cancer, 673–74, 743
Candida albicans, 547
Candy-Ass Records, 768
Cannabis, 38
Can't Stop the Music, 781, 1243
Cantú, Lionel, 486–87
Cape Cod (Woods), 957
"Capitalism and Gay Identity"
    (D'Emilio), 100–101, 586
Capote, Truman, 66, **190–92,** 372,
    825, 1272
Captain Swing (Duplechan), 321
Carangi, Gia, 400
Card, Claudia, 876, 1145
Cardiovascular diseases, 674
CARE Act. *See* Ryan White
    CARE Act
Carlson, Ann, 217
Carlyle Simpson (Osborne), 839
Carmichael, Stokely, 442
Carnivorous Saint (Norse), 820
Caroline (Kushner), 642
Carpenter, Scott (fictitious
    character), 375
Carroll, Lewis, 298–99
Carruthers, Mary J., 905
Carter, Jimmy, 794
Carter, Julia. *See* Blackwomon,
    Julie
Casal, Mary, 86
Case, Luella J. B., 85
Case, Sue Ellen, 1195
Casid, Jill, 886
Cass, Vivian, 245–46, 247
Cassady, Marshall "Marsh," **192**
Cassells, Cyrus, **192–93**
Cassera, Maryanne, 316
Castro, Fidel, 58, 59
Castro (San Francisco
    neighborhood), 7, 10, 101, 155,
    954, 1071–72
Catacombs, 1066
Catching Saradove (Harris), 514
Catechism of the Catholic Church,
    1050, 1052
Catenary series (Johns), 611
Cather, Willa, 823, 829
Catholic, The (Plante), 893
Catholic Adoption Services, 355

Index

Index

Index

Index

Index

James, Jimmy, 313–14

James C. Hormel Gay and Lesbian Center, 1075

James White Review, 617, 624

Jamie Is My Heart's Desire (Chester), 206

Jamison, Judith, 31

Jane Chambers Playwriting Award, 203

Janus Society, 619

Jargon Society, 1265–66

Jarman, Derek, 396, 399, 405

Jay, Karla, 668, 670

J.D.s, 979–80

Jean, Lorri, 797

Jeanne Dielman, 394

Jeffrey (Rudnick), 696, 1055

Jenkins, Walter, 909

Jennings, Dale, 560, 618

Jennings, Kevin, 439, 440, 1295

Jenny Jones, 567

Jerker (Chesley), 205, 897

Jerome Robbins Broadway, 1044

Jerome Robbins Foundation, 1044

Jessie's Song and Other Stories (Villanueva), 1244

Jett, Joan, **603**

Jewell, Terri L., **604**

Jewish Anti-Defamation League, 607

"Jewish Food, Jewish Children" (Kaye/Kantrowiz), 1134

Jews and Judaism, 562, 563, **604–9**, 819, 1036

Joan Heller-Diane Bernard Fellowship, 200

Joan Jett and the Blackhearts, 603

Joan Nestle Prize, 250

Job's Year (Hansen), 372

Joe Goode Performance Group, 489, 490

Joffrey, Robert, **609–10**

Joffrey Ballet, 610

John Boswell Prize, 250, 251

John Bush Gerald Mallon Institute for Social Justice, 790

John E. Fryer Award, 416, 964

Johns, Erik, 263, 264

Johns, Jasper, **611**, 612–13, 1024, 1025

Johnson, Anthony Godby, 1261

Johnson, Cary Alan, 20

Johnson, David K., 493

Johnson, Fenton, **611–12**

Johnson, Jeff, 230

Johnson, Lyndon Baines, 909, 1242

Johnson, Magic, 540

Johnson, Marsha P., 953, 1224

Johnson, Philip Cortelyou, 56

Johnson, Sarah East, 218

Johnson, Steve, 375

Johnson, William, 230, 462, 946–47, 1240

Johnston, Georgia, 78

Johnston, Jill, 87, **612–13,** 830

Joint adoption, 850, 851

Jones, Bill T., and Arnie Zane, **613–14**

Jones, Cherry, 2

Jones, Cleve, 784, 1074, 1130

Jones, G. B., 979

Jones, Randy, 1243

Jones, Rosie, 1158–59

Jones v. Hallahan (1973), 718, 719

Jordan, June, 14, **614–15**

Jordan, Mark, 1047

Jorgenson, Christine, 366, 1114, 1209, 1213, 1222, 1228

Joseph, Gloria, 239, 706

Joseph and the Old Man (Davis), 293

Journalism, academic, **615–18.** *See also specific publications*

Journalism, popular, **618–25;** Cornwell, Anita, 266; Ford, Charles Henri, 411; Preston, John, 925; protests and actions coverage, 953; Shilts, Randy, 1128–29; Signorile, Michelangelo, 1139–40; Sullivan, Andrew, 1174–75; Tinney, James, 1202; Vincent, Norah, 1244–45. *See also* Magazines; *specific publications*

Journal of Homosexuality, 616

Journal of Lesbian Studies, 1276

Journal of Sexuality, 616

Journal of the Plague Years, A (Holland), 556

Journey of the Souls (Snyder), 1144

Journeys from Berlin/1971, 387

Journey to a Woman (Bannon), 94, 973

Joyce, James, 45, 194

Joyful Blue Book of Gracious Gay Etiquette, The (Curzon), 286–87

"Joy" (Hughes), 512

Joy of Lesbian Sex, The (Sisley and Harris), 514

Jubilant Thicket (Williams), 1266

Judaism. *See* Jews and Judaism

Judge, Mychal, 229–30

Judson Dance Theater, 216

Judy Grahn Award, 965–66

Juillerat, Martha, 947

Julien, Isaac, 511

Junglee Girl (Kamani), 627

Junkie (Burroughs), 174

Juno, Andrea, 890

Just Above My Head (Baldwin), 91, 825

Justice, Benjamin (fictitious character), 376

Justice Weekly, 1065

Just Say Yes (McDaniel), 737

K

Kaddish (Bernstein), 123

"Kaddish for Naomi Ginsberg (1894-1964)" (Ginsberg), 1076

Kadi, Joanna, 227

Kaleidoscope (Corigliano), 265

Kalin, Tom, 405, 407

Kamani, Ginu (Gaurangi), **627–28,** 1179

Kameny, Frank: gay rights movement, 450, 451; homophile movement, 561; journalism, popular, 619; National Gay and Lesbian Task Force and, 792, 793; protests and actions, 950; psychiatry and homosexuality, 416, 962, 964

Kansas rape, sexual assault, and domestic violence laws, 1018–19

Kanshou, The (Gearhart), 462

Kantrowitz, Arnie, 79, 427

Kaposi's Sarcoma Clinic at the University of California-San Francisco, 529

Kaposi's Sarcoma Foundation, 530

Kaposi's sarcoma (KS), 545, 546, 547, 552

Index

Index

Matthew Shepard (Del Tredici), 299
Matthiessen, Francis Otto, **732**
Maud's Study, 1071
Maupin, Armistead, 542, 1247, 1261. See also West Coast New Narrative Movement, The
Mautner Project for Lesbians with Cancer, 532
Mawrdew Czgowchwz (McCourt), 826
Max Robinson Center, 531
Maye, Michael J., 845
Mayne, Xavier, 824
Mayor of Castro Street, The (Shilts), 1129
McBride, Dwight, 558
MCC. See Metropolitan Community Churches
McCann, Richard, **732–33**
McCarthyism, **733–34;** Blitzstein, Marc, 148; Copland, Aaron, 264; gay liberation movement, 441; government and military prosecution, 493, 494; House Un-American Affairs Committee, 733; Mattachine Society, 731; political scandals, 908; privacy and privacy rights, 935; Robbins, Jerome, 1044. See also Communist Party
McCauley, Stephen, **734–35**
McClatchy, Joseph Daniel, **735–36,** 901
McConnell, Michael, 718, 725
McConnell, Vicki P., **736**
McCormack, Tom, 432
McCourt, James, 826
McCullers, Carson, 825
McCusker, Mark, 861
McDaniel, Judith, **737**
McDowell, Michael, 373
McFeeley, Tim, 577
McGehee, Peter, **737–38**
McGillin, Howard, 770, 777
McGowan, Jeffrey, 80–81
McGreevey, James Edward, 841, 909–10
McHugh, Maureen, 1087
McIlvenna, Ted, 1035
McIntosh, Mary, 1003
McIntyre, Doug, 568
McKay, Claude, 511–12, 513

McKechnie, Donna, 121
McKenna, Wendy, 1227
McKinney, Aaron, 567, 1033
McKinney, Stewart, 531
McKuen, Rod, 6–7
McLachlan, Sarah, 1280
McLaughlin, Sheila, 388
McLeod, R. W. Scott, 908–9
McNally, Terrence, 533, **738–40,** 766, 895, 898
McPherson, Scott, **740–41**
McRobbie, Angela, 867
McRuer, Robert, 307, 994–95
McVeigh, Timothy, 1104
McWilliams, Danny, 242
Mead, Margaret, 1004, 1113
Meaker, Marijane, 972
Medhurst, Andy, 244
Medical Expertise Retention Program, 435
Medical power of attorney, 525, 672
Medicine of homosexuality. See Science and medicine of homosexuality (history)
"Meditations in Zürich" (Huston), 580
Meditations on the Rainbow (Sapphire), 1080
Meehan, Martin, 1098
"Melanctha, or Each One As She May" (Stein), 85
Mel Brooks' The Producers, 769–72, 775
Mellis, Miranda F., 169–70
Melrose Place, 1186
Melville, Herman, 823
Memoir, 77, 697–98. See also Autobiography, gay; Autobiography, lesbian
Memoir (Moore), 758
Memoirs of a Woman of Pleasure (Cleland), 197
Memoirs of Margaret Fuller Ossoli (Fuller), 84
Memorial (Bleckner), 147
Men from the Boys, The (Crowley), 280–81
Men of All Colors Together (MACT), 789
Men on Men series, 122
Men on the Verge of a His-Panic Breakdown (Reyes), 1036

Menotti, Gian Carlo, 95–96, 555
Men's Associated Exchange, 1100
Mental health issues, 526, 583, 675, **741–45**
Men with Their Hands (Luczak), 710
Menzel, Idina, 779
Meredith, William, **745–46**
Meritor Savings Bank v. Vinson (1986), 1108
Merlo, Frank, 1267
Merrill, James, 236, 735–36, **746–48**
Mesrobian, Michael, 375
Messiah (Sherman), 1127
Messner, Michael, 569
Metaethics, 875
Metatextuality, 1135, 1260
Metropolitan Community Churches (MCC), 229, 1029, 1035–36, 1198
Metrosexuality, 52
Mexican-American, as term, 211
Meyer, Thomas, **748**
Michael Callen Achievement Award, 432
Michaels, Dick, 620
Michaels, Duane, 878
Michaels, Grant, 375
Michigan: adoption, 354; sodomy laws, 1147
Michigan Womyn's Music Festival, 586, 767, 1280
Mic to mic phone sex, 1103
Middle Sister (Goodman), 490–91
Midler, Bette, 189
Midlife Queer (Duberman), 79, 320
Midnight Robber (Hopkinson), 572
Midnight Salvage (Rich), 1039
Midtowne Spas, 108, 109
Midwest, **749**
Midwest Bisexual Gay College Conference, 749
Midwest Bisexual Lesbian Gay Transgender Ally College Conference, 749
Midwest Gay Pride Conference, 4
Migrant Souls (Islas), 601
Milan, Amanda, 520
Mildred Pierce, 188
Military, gays in the: African American attitudes toward, 19; autobiography, gay, 80–81, 82;

Index

Index

Index

Index

Index

Index

Index

About the Editor, Advisory Board, and Contributors

EDITOR

John C. Hawley is a professor in and chair of the English Department at Santa Clara University, where he is recent past president of the faculty senate. He is the author of *Amitav Ghosh: An Introduction* (Cambridge University Press, New Delhi [2005]) and the editor of 10 books, including two for Greenwood (*Encyclopedia of Postcolonial Studies* [2001]; *Postcolonial and Queer Theories: Intersections and Essays* [2001]). Entries: acting; artists and photographers, early trailblazers; Frank Bidart; Sanford Friedman; hanky code; Phyllis Lyon and Del Martin; transgender; Luz María Umpierre-Herrera.

ADVISORY BOARD

S. Bear Bergman is a writer, theater artist, and storyteller. Ze is also the author of *Butch Is a Noun* (Suspect Thoughts Press, 2006) and three award-winning solo performances, as well as a frequent contributor to anthologies on all manner of topics from the sacred to the extremely profane. Entries: Nayland Blake; transgender health.

Judith Butler is Maxine Elliot Professor in the Department of Rhetoric at the University of California at Berkeley; she is author of *Subjects of Desire: Hegelian Reflections in Twentieth-Century France; Gender Trouble: Feminism and the Subversion of Identity; Bodies That Matter: On the Discursive Limits of "Sex"; The Psychic Life of Power: Theories of Subjection; Excitable Speech; Antigone's Claim: Kinship between Life and Death*; and other works.

Eli Coleman is director of the Program in Human Sexuality at the University of Minnesota; past president of the Harry Benjamin International Gender Dysphoria Association; author of *Sexual Offender Treatment: Biopsychosocial Perspectives; Masturbation as a Means of Achieving Sexual Health; Chemical Dependency and Intimacy Dysfunction; John Money: A Tribute*; and other works.

Paul G. Crowley is chair of the Department of Religious Studies at Santa Clara University and author of *Unwanted Wisdom: Suffering, the Cross, and Hope*. Entry: Roman Catholicism.

Judith Halberstam is in the Department of English at the University of Southern California; she is author of *Female Masculinities; Skin Shows; The Butch Anthropologist Out in the Field*, and others.

Michael Horberg, MD, is director of HIV/AIDS policy, quality improvement, and research for The Permanente Federation. He has presented his research at the Infectious Diseases Society of America, the Conference on Retroviruses and Opportunisitc Infections, the Interscience Conference on Antimicrobial Agents and Chemotherapy, and World AIDS Conferences; he is chairperson of the Central Research Committee for all of Kaiser Permanente Northern California (KPNC); member of the KPNC Health Services Institutional Review Board; cochair of KPNC's HIV Provider and Therapeutics Committee; secretary of Kaiser Permanente Northern California Region HIV Steering Committee; past president of the (national) Gay and Lesbian Medical Association (GLMA); and one of the principal writers of the Kaiser Permanente *LGBT Cultural Competency Handbook*.

Karen C. Krahulik is associate dean at Brown University, chair of the Gay and Lesbian History Association, and author of *Provincetown: From Pilgrim Landing to Gay Resort*.

Edward Stein is professor of law and codirector of the Program for Family Law, Policy, and Bioethics at the Cardozo School of Law; he is also author of *The Mismeasure of Desire: The Science, Theory and Ethics of Sexual Orientation* and *Without Good Reason: The Rationality Debate in Philosophy and Cognitive Science*. Entry: marriage, same-sex, and domestic partnerships.

Claude J. Summers is William E. Stirton professor emeritus in the humanities and professor emeritus of English at the University of Michigan-Dearborn. He has published widely on seventeenth- and twentieth-century English literature, including book-length studies of E. M. Forster and Christopher Isherwood, as well as *Gay Fictions: Wilde to Stonewall* and *Homosexuality in Renaissance and Enlightenment England: Literary Representations in Historical Context*. He is general editor of *The Gay and Lesbian Literary Heritage: A Reader's Companion to the Writers and Their Work, from Antiquity to the Present; The Queer Encyclopedia of Film and Television; The Queer Encyclopedia of the Visual Arts; The Queer Encyclopedia of Music, Dance, and Musical Theater*.

Yvonne Yarbro-Bejarano is professor in the Department of Romance Studies at Stanford and chair of the Chicana/o Studies Program in Stanford's Center for Comparative Studies in Race and Ethnicity; author of *Feminism and the Honor Plays of Lope de Vega; The Wounded Heart: Writing on Cherríe Moraga*; and coeditor of *Chicano Art: Resistance and Affirmation*. Since 1994, Yarbro-Bejarano has been developing "Chicana Art," a digital archive of images focusing on women artists.

CONTRIBUTORS

Jeff Abell is a composer, writer, and performance artist in Chicago. Active as a critic and editor, he has been writing about the visual and performing arts for 25 years. He is a professor of interdisciplinary arts at Columbia College Chicago. Entries: John Cage; Aaron Copland; Music; Virgil Thomson.

Susan Abraham is assistant professor of women and ministry studies at Harvard Divinity School. Her research and publications deal with Roman Catholic theology, postcolonial theory, and feminist theory. Her current research focuses on Christianity between colonialism and postcolonialism. Entry: queer theology and spirituality.

Jorge Abril-Sánchez is a PhD candidate in the Department of Romance Languages and Literatures of the University of Chicago. Entries: Marshall "Marsh" Cassady; Clare Coss; Fred Hersch.

J. G. Adair is currently a PhD candidate at Northern Illinois University. His current research focuses on the formation of gay space in the literature of the World Wars. Entries: David Plante; Joe Ashby Porter; Jonathan Strong; Peter Weltner.

Joel C. Adams is a university library associate with the School of Information at the University of Michigan. Entry: Throw Shade.

Jon Robert Adams is associate professor of modern and contemporary American literature at Western Michigan University and author of *Male Armor*. Entries: John Horne Burns; Mark Doty; David Rabe.

Mark Adnum is the editor of Outrate.net. Entry: film, New Queer Cinema.

Jennifer L. Ailles is a visiting assistant professor of English at Rollins College. Entries: Samiya Bashir; Black Triangle; Boston marriage; Judy Chicago; Judy Grahn; Indigo Girls; Willyce Kim; k. d. lang; pomosexual.

Frederick Luis Aldama is professor of English and comparative studies at the Ohio State University. He is the author and editor of seven books, including the Modern Language Association Award–winning *Dancing with Ghosts: A Critical Biography of Arturo Islas*. He sits on the editorial boards of *Narrative*, *Journal of Narrative Theory*, and *Narrative and Image*. Entry: Arturo Islas, Jr..

Jacob Anderson-Minshall, Trans author, pens the nationally syndicated column *TransNation*, writes for *Bitch*, coauthors the Blind Eye mysteries, and cofounded *Girlfriends* magazine. He has an MA in speech communication. Entries: Mariette Pathy Allen; drag, drag queens, drag kings; Lee Lynch; Queer Nation.

Amy André is a sexuality educator and published author. Her writing focuses on the bisexual community; visit her online at www.amyandre.com. Entries: BiNet USA; bisexual health; Bisexual Resource Center.

Gabriel Arkles is staff attorney at the Sylvia Rivera Law Project in New York City, where he provides free legal services to low-income transgender, intersex, and gender-nonconforming people of color. Entry: hate crime law and policy.

Katherine Arnup is a historian, professor, and interdisciplinary scholar at Carleton University in Ottawa, Canada. She has published many articles on lesbian and gay families, a book on the history of motherhood, and an edited collection of essays (*Lesbian Parenting: Living with Pride and Prejudice*, gynergy, 1995). Entries: Jan Clausen; Joan Larkin; parents, LGBT.

Ben Aslinger is a doctoral candidate in the Department of Communication Arts, media and cultural studies division, at the University of Wisconsin–Madison. Entries: Ani DiFranco; film directors and producers, men; rappers and hip hop; Rufus Wainwright.

M. Jay Asplan teaches art history at Cincinnati State College. He has a master's degree in art history from the University of Cincinnati and is completing a master's degree in English at Xavier University in Ohio. He has published in *School Arts* and other art journals. Entry: Félix González-Torres.

Tommi Avicolli-Mecca is a radical, southern Italian (in the tradition of Sacco and Vanzetti), working-class, queer performer, activist, and writer living in San Francisco. Entries: activists; Joseph Beam.

Marlon M. Bailey is assistant professor of gender studies and African American and African diaspora studies at Indiana University. Entry: ballroom culture (house culture).

Kelly Hudgins Ball is a graduate student in the Department of Women's Studies at the Ohio State University. Her research interests include continental philosophy, sexuality, and trauma. Entry: Society for Lesbian and Gay Philosophy.

Mary Barber, MD, is medical director/clinical director at Ulster County Mental Health Department in Kingston, New York. Entries: Association of Gay and Lesbian Psychiatrists (AGLP); John E. Fryer.

About the Editor, Advisory Board, and Contributors

Alexandra Barron is a visiting assistant professor in the Feminist Studies Program at Southwestern University. Her latest research focuses on the growing prevalence of transnational films at gay and lesbian film festivals. Entries: Jim Grimsley; Ginu (Gaurangi) Kamani; Lesbian Avengers; South Asian Lesbian and Gay Association (SALGA); Dean Spade.

Chris Bell is a doctoral student in English at Nottingham Trent University in England. His research examines cultural responses to the AIDS crisis in the United States. He is editor of the forthcoming anthology *Remember AIDS?* Entries: Melvin Dixon; E. Lynn Harris; Essex Hemphill.

Jeffery Beam is poetry editor of *Oyster Boy Review* and a botanical librarian at the University of North Carolina at Chapel Hill. He is the author of nine books of poetry including the award-winning *What We Have Lost*. Entries: Antler; Lee Hoiby; Thomas Meyer; Jonathan Williams.

Melanie Beaudette is pursuing her doctorate in twentieth-century urban and queer history at Ohio State University in the Women's Studies Department. Entries: bookstores; censorship, obscenity, and pornography laws; passing.

Rebecca Beirne is the editor of *Televising Queer Women*. Her research interests include queer television and film, the sex wars, and contemporary lesbian culture. Entries: sex wars of the 1980s; television shows.

Corinne E. Blackmer is professor of English at Southern Connecticut State University. Entries: Judith Barrington; Melinda Goodman; Jews and Judaism; Andrea Freud Loewenstein; poets, lesbian; rape, sexual assault, and domestic violence laws.

Ralph Blair has been a New York City psychotherapist in private practice, mainly with gay men, since 1972. He founded Evangelicals Concerned in 1975. Entries: Exodus Ministries and reparative therapy; Protestants, evangelical.

Dan Bloom has been a psychotherapist in private practice in New York since 1976. He was a clinical director of Identity House, an LGBT counseling center and, in the 1980s, a volunteer with the Gay Men's Health Crisis (GMHC). He was a codesigner of GMHC's early safer-sex community education program. Dan is a licensed clinical social worker in the state of New York, an attorney, and a charter member of The Saint. He has never missed a black party. Entry: dance club culture.

Sarah Boslaugh is a performance research analyst for BJC Health Care, an instructor at the Washington University School of Medicine, producer of *Reality Now* (KDHX radio in St. Louis, Missouri), and a theater critic for KDHX radio and talkinbroadway.com. She is the author of *Secondary Data Sources for Public Health* and editor of *The Encyclopedia of Epidemiology*. Entries: architects; Ann Bannon; Christopher Isherwood; pulp fiction, lesbian.

Beth M. Bouloukos is a PhD candidate in Romance studies at Cornell University. Her research focuses on twentieth-century Latin American literature and film. Entries: Cathy Arellano; Rafael Campo.

Tom Bourdon is the assistant director of the LGBT Center at the University of California at Los Angeles. Entry: college and university LGBTQ organizations.

Stacy C. Brand is in the MFA program at California State University, Fresno. Entry: Dorothy Allison.

Matthew Brim is a Mellon Fellow in the Duke University Writing Program. Entry: short stories.

Catherine Burriss is assistant professor of performing arts at California State University, Channel Islands, and has published in *Theatre Journal*. Entries: theater and performance; Paula Vogel.

Patricia Cain is the Inez Mabie distinguished professor of law at Santa Clara University. She teaches and writes about federal tax law, feminist legal theory, and gay and lesbian legal issues. Entry: gay rights in the United States.

Russell Cambron is an MA/PhD student in religious studies at the University of California, Santa Barbara, where he studies evangelical Christianity and sexual identity. Entry: Southern United States.

Kristopher L. Cannon is a PhD candidate in moving image studies at Georgia State University. His research explores queerness and bodies in new media and film. Entry: Kathryn Bond Stockton.

Dale Carpenter is the Julius E. Davis professor of law at the University of Minnesota Law School. Entry: rights of association and assembly.

Edward Chamberlain lectures about representations of medicine in film and literature. He is a PhD student in the Department of Comparative Literature at Indiana University. Entry: film, HIV/AIDS impact on.

Karma R. Chávez conducts communication research in the areas of queer and feminist theory, social movement, and immigration. Entry: Sally Miller Gearhart.

Megan Chawansky is a doctoral candidate in sport and exercise humanities at the Ohio State University. Entry: sports.

Howard Hsueh-Hao Chiang is a PhD student in the history of science program at Princeton University. Entries: anal sex; circuit parties; queer theory and social science; science and medicine of homosexuality (history); sexualities.

Kimberly Christensen is associate professor of economics and women's studies and former director of gender studies (women's studies/LGBT studies) at State University of New York/Purchase College. Entries: bisexuality; economics.

Mária I. Cipriani, MA, LCSW, a holistically oriented psychotherapist in private practice in New York City, works extensively with lesbian and gay individuals and couples. She teaches shamanic healing and diversity awareness as part of basic psychotherapy skills. Her psychotherapy practice includes psychospiritual transformation, shamanic healing, and imaginal work. Entries: Center for Lesbian and Gay Studies (CLAGS); Katherine V. Forrest; heteronormative, heteronormativity; lesbian bed-death syndrome; mental health issues; Native American spiritualities; Pauline Oliveros; prostitution.

Damion Clark is a PhD candidate in English at the University of Maryland. Entry: fiction, coming of age.

John Lee Clark runs the Tactile Mind Press, which produces books and DVDs of signing community literature. Entry: Raymond Luczak.

Billy Clem is a doctoral candidate in English and women's studies at Northern Illinois University and teaches composition and multicultural literatures at Waubonsee Community College. Entries: Christopher Davis; John Fox; Native American feminism.

Amber R. Clifford-Napoleone is an instructor in anthropology at the University of Central Missouri. She holds degrees in American history, museum studies, and American studies and is researching the history of female impersonation in the Kansas City jazz scene. Entries: class; Esther Newton.

Keith E. Clifton, associate professor of musicology at Central Michigan University, is active as a researcher, classical singer, and pianist. His numerous publications appear in *Notes*, the *Opera Journal*, the *Journal of Musicological Research*, and elsewhere. Entry: Jake Heggie.

John M. Clum is professor of theater studies and English and chair of the Department of Theater Studies at Duke University. He is the author of *Still Acting Gay: Male Homosexuality in Modern Drama; Something for the Boys: Musical Theater and Gay Culture*, and *He's All Man: Learning Masculinity, Gayness and Love from American Movies* and editor of the anthologies *Staging Gay Lives* and *Asking and Telling*. He has written numerous articles on twentieth-century British and American drama. Entry: playwrights.

Sue Coffee is artistic director of Sound Circle and Resonance Women's Chorus in Boulder, Colorado, and former artistic director of the Denver Gay Men's Chorus. She received the 2004 GALA Choruses Legacy Award for service to the LGBT choral movement. Entry: choruses.

Bertram J. Cohler is the William Rainey Harper professor of social sciences and professor in the departments of Comparative Human Development and Psychiatry at the University of Chicago. Cohler is also a graduate psychoanalyst on the faculty of the Institute for Psychoanalysis (Chicago) and former board member and presently a volunteer therapist at the Center-on-Halsted, Chicago's LGBTQ community center. Entry: bathhouses and sex clubs.

David Coon is a PhD student in the Department of Communication and Culture at Indiana University. Entries: suburbs; tourism, cruises, and resorts.

Michael G. Cornelius is the chair of the Department of English and Mass Communications at Wilson College. His novel is *Creating Man* (2000), and he can be found on the Web at michael-gcornelius.com. Entries: Alfred Corn; David Drake; James Earl Hardy; Walter Holland; pulp fiction, gay; Joan Snyder.

Will Curl is lecturer in English at University of Wisconsin–Fox Valley. Entries: Jeff Baron; Ricardo Bracho; Robert Chesley; Nancy Dean; Harry Kondoleon; Robert O'Hara; Peter Parnell; Hubert Selby; Joel Tan.

Rita B. Dandridge is a professor at Virginia State University where she teaches courses in women's studies and British literature. Entries: SDiane A. Bogus; Michelle Cliff; Alexis DeVeaux; Randall Kenan.

Jodi L. Davis currently lives and teaches women's studies in southern California. She holds a BA in women's studies from California State University Fullerton, as well as an MA in applied women's studies from Claremont Graduate University. Entries: Lisa Alther; lesbian feminism.

Khytam Dawood is director of the Child and Adolescent Gender Identity Clinic in the Department of Psychiatry at the University of Chicago. She received a Ford Foundation Sexuality Research Fellowship Award to conduct the first family study of children with Gender Identity Disorder and is beginning a new study of epigenetic factors in the development of sexual orientation using identical twins discordant for sexual orientation. Entry: genetics and the development of human sexual orientation.

Lewis Brian Day is technical services librarian at the Houghton Library of Harvard University. Entry: journalism, popular.

tatiana de la tierra is a Colombian American writer and librarian in southern California. She is the author of *For the Hard Ones: A Lesbian Phenomenology*. Entry: Jaime Manrique.

Danielle M. DeMuth is assistant professor of women and gender studies at Grand Valley State University in Michigan; she works in lesbian literature and Arab feminism. Entries: Alice Bloch; Furies; Camarin Grae; Noretta Koertge; Judith McDaniel; Nancy Toder.

Aureliano Maria DeSoto is assistant professor of ethnic and religious studies at Metropolitan State University in Saint Paul, Minnesota, and has published in *MELUS* and elsewhere. Entries: ghettoes, gay; Ethan Mordden.

Leah DeVun is an assistant professor of history at Texas A&M University. Her work focuses on contemporary and historical understandings of gender and sexuality. She is currently a fellow at the Institute for Research in the Humanities, University of Wisconsin–Madison. Entries: Tisa Bryant; Rachel Guido deVries; Victoria Lena Manyarrows.

Cy Dillon has been director of the Stanley Library of Ferrum College since 1985. Coeditor of *Virginia Libraries,* he is also a founding editor of the *Nantahala Review.* Entry: Jeffrey Beam.

Joanna Di Mattia has a PhD in women's studies from Monash University (Australia) and is currently an independent scholar. She has published widely in the field of gender and popular culture, including essays on *Sex and the City, Six Feet Under, Seinfeld, Angels in America,* and *Queer as Folk.* Her current research explores the importance of images of sexual practice and pleasure in debates about queer visibility. Entries: Gay and Lesbian Alliance against Defamation (GLAAD); Larry Kramer.

Martin Dines has recently been awarded a PhD for his thesis on gay suburban narratives in British and American film and fiction from Kingston University in the United Kingdom, where he currently teaches English literature and media studies. Entries: conservatism, LGBTQ; Michelangelo Signorile; Andrew Sullivan.

Kate Drabinski received her PhD from the University of California at Berkeley in rhetoric and women's studies. She currently teaches gender studies at Lewis and Clark College and Portland State University. Entries: closet; homosexual panic; trade.

Jack Drescher, MD, is an adjunct faculty member at New York University and New York Medical College. He is a training and supervising analyst at William Alanson White Psychoanalytic Institute and is the author of *Psychoanalytic Therapy and the Gay Man.* Entries: coming out; psychiatry and homosexuality.

Steve Du Bois is a PhD student in clinical psychology at the University of Illinois at Chicago, researching LGBT sexual health. His work can be found in *VIVA Magazine* and *Newsweek.* Entries: Eli Clare; T. Cooper.

Sally Eckhoff is a working artist. Entries: Blanche McCrary Boyd; Camille Paglia.

Michael J. Emery is professor of English at Cottey College, where he teaches writing, literature, and film. He has published essays on Samuel R. Delany and Robert Chesley. Entry: Kenneth Pobo.

Julie R. Enszer is a poet, writer, and activist living in Maryland. You can read more about her work at www.JulieREnszer.com. Entries: Robin Becker; community-based organizing; Human Rights Campaign (HRC).

Gabriel S. Estrada is an assistant professor in American Indian Studies at California State University, Long Beach. He is Nahuatl, Raramuri, and Mestizo. Entries: Los Angeles; Native Americans and LGBTQ issues; Proyecto contra SIDA por Vida; Ryan White CARE Act.

Victor Evans is an assistant professor of communication at Thiel College, where he teaches mass communication courses and oversees the campus student television station. Entry: African Americans and LGBTQ issues.

Breanne Fahs is assistant professor of women's studies at Arizona State University. She has published in *Feminist Studies, Journal of Divorce and Remarriage,* and *Michigan Feminist Studies* and has several forthcoming articles and chapters on topics ranging from purity balls to Valerie Solanas. Entries: Leah Lakshmi Piepzna-Samarasinha; Carol Queen.

Kate Falvey holds a PhD in English and American literature from New York University where she taught for many years. She currently teaches at New York City College of Technology of the

City University of New York. Her published work includes articles on women writers such as Grace King and Sui Sin Far. Entry: James Merrill.

Paul Falzone is an experimental and documentary filmmaker, radical ethnographer, activist, and academic. A graduate of the University of Pennsylvania, his research focuses on the theory and production of media for social and political change. Entries: film; Robert Rauschenberg; George Segal.

Amy Farrell is professor of American studies and women's studies at Dickinson College in Carlisle, Pennsylvania. She is currently working on *Fat Shame*, a history of fat denigration and fat activism in the United States. Entries: fat acceptance; Susan Stinson.

Erika Feigenbaum is actively involved in organizing around issues of equity with several community groups. She teaches women's studies at Cleveland State University, and her creative work has appeared in *Off Our Backs Feminist NewsJournal, Sinister Wisdom, Creative Woman*, and *Hypatia*. Entries: Chrystos; philosophy and ethics; Minnie Bruce Pratt.

Susan Feldman is a lecturer in the English Department at the University of Tennessee, Knoxville. Entries: James Purdy; Joanna Russ.

Douglas Field is a lecturer at Staffordshire University in the United Kingdom. He is the editor of *American Cold War Culture* and has published on African American literature, religion, film, and music. Entries: Harold Norse; James Tinney.

Natalia Fior is pursuing her PhD in English literature and cultural studies at Claremont Graduate University. Entries: Louis Crompton; Paula Martinac; Shay Youngblood.

James Fisher, professor of theatre and head of the Department of Theatre at the University of North Carolina at Greensboro, is author of *The Historical Dictionary of the American Theatre: Modernism* (Scarecrow, 2007), coauthored with Felicia Hardison Londré. He is the recipient of the 2007 Betty Jean Jones Award for Excellence in the Teaching of American Theatre from the American Theatre and Drama Society. Entry: Tony Kushner.

Charles H. Ford is associate professor and chair of jistory at Norfolk State University in Norfolk, Virginia. He has also served on the board of the Tidewater AIDS Community Taskforce (TACT) since August 1994. Entries: Samuel Osborne Barber; Martin Duberman; health organizations and regional health centers.

James Francis Jr. has a doctorate in children's literature and film from Middle Tennessee State University and is the associate editor of *Slayage: The International Journal of Buffy Studies*. Entries: film, horror and noir; outing; trick; water sports; Tennessee Williams.

Meredith Frederich is currently pursuing a PhD in American literature at Northern Illinois University. Entry: fiction, mystery and detective.

Christianne Anastasia Gadd graduated from Sarah Lawrence College in 2002 and holds a master's degree in American studies from Lehigh University, where she is currently enrolled in the PhD program in history. Entries: Committee on Lesbian and Gay History (CLGH); Music, Indie; queercore movement; .

Merry Gangemi holds a BA from New York University and an MA in comparative literature from San Francisco State University. She lives and writes in Woodbury, Vermont, and is the producer and host of Woman-Stirred Radio, a queer cultural journal. Her blog can be found at www.merrygangemi.org. Entries: Alison Bechdel; Suzanne Gardiner; Doris Grumbach; Eloise Klein Healy; theology, ethical.

Linda Garber is director of women's and gender studies at Santa Clara University. She is the author of *Identity Poetics: Race, Class, and the Lesbian-Feminist Roots of Queer Theory* and

Lesbian Sources: A Bibliography of Periodical Articles, 1970–1990, and editor of *Tilting the Tower: Lesbians/Teaching/Queer Subjects*. Entry: Irena Klepfisz.

TJ Geiger II is a graduate assistant in English at Texas Woman's University. Entries: African American feminism; womanist.

Joseph Gelfer teaches at Monash University in Australia and is managing editor of the *Journal of Men, Masculinities and Spirituality*. Entries: Buddhists and Buddhism; Mormons.

Jeremie Giacoia recently received his master of theological studies from Harvard Divinity School. His research interests lie primarily in the intersections of gender fluidity and Christian theology. Entry: Kate Bornstein.

Suzanne B. Goldberg is a clinical professor of law at Columbia Law School and director of Columbia Law School's Sexuality and Gender Law Clinic. She is coauthor of *Strangers to the Law: Gay People on Trial*. Entry: sexual harassment law and policy.

A. Cassandra Golding is a clinician in clinical psychology and doctoral student at the University of Rhode Island. Her work around resiliency in lesbian families has been published in the *Journal for Feminist Family Therapy*. Entries: butch–femme; Marilyn Hacker.

Dustin B. Goltz is a doctoral student at Arizona State University in performance studies. He received his MFA in performance art from the School of the Art Institute of Chicago. Entry: performance artists.

Deena J. González is Professor and Chair of the Department of Chicana and Chicano Studies at Loyola Marymount University in Los Angeles. She is the author of *Refusing the Favor: The Spanish-Mexican Women of Santa Fe, 1820–1880* and was editor-in-chief of the four-volume, *Oxford Encyclopedia of Latinos and Latinas in the U.S.* Entry: Latino/Latina Americans and LGBTQ issues.

Dr. Julio González-Ruiz is an assistant professor of Spanish at Spelman College and is completing his book manuscript on Spanish playwright Lope de Vega. Entry: Reinaldo Arenas.

Georges-Claude Guilbert is professor of American studies at the University of Tours in France. He has published books on Carson McCullers, Madonna, Billy Wilder, and gender. Entries: Alfred Chester; Stephen McCauley; Peter McGehee; Matthew Stadler; Donald Windham.

Needham Yancey Gulley is a graduate student at California State University in Long Beach. Entries: Christopher Durang; Joe Keenan; Mattachine Society; Reynolds Price; Lanford Wilson.

Alexis Pauline Gumbs is a doctoral student in English, women's studies, and African and African American Studies at Duke University. She is also the founder of BrokenBeautiful Press (brokenbeautifulpress.blogspot.com). Entries: Cheryl Clarke; Combahee River Collective; June Jordan; Audre Lorde.

T. Chandler Haliburton works in Great Britain. Entries: Steve Abbott; Bruce Boone; Clayton R. Graham; Bo Huston; Kevin Killian; Michael Klein.

Zennia D. Hancock is assistant professor of Spanish at St. Bonaventure University, where she is a faculty advocate for Spectrum, a gay-straight alliance. Her scholarship explores medieval and Golden Age narrative, Latino studies, feminist theory, and foreign language pedagogy. Entry: Chicana feminism.

Reginald Harris, librarian and author, is co-compiler of *Carry the Word: A Bibliography of Black LGBTQ Books*. Entries: Donna Allegra; Becky Birtha; Christopher Coe; Rosa Guy; Michael Lassell; National Black Justice Coalition (NBJC); Kate Rushin; Assotto Saint (Yves Francois Lubin); Reginald Shepherd.

Kylo-Patrick R. Hart is chair of the Department of Communication and Media Studies at Plymouth State University. He is author of the book *The AIDS Movie: Representing a Pandemic in Film and Television* and editor of the anthology *Film and Sexual Politics*. Entries: androgyny; Harvey Fierstein; Key West; Liberace; Village People.

Stacey Zwald Hegarty has worked as a curatorial aide/researcher at the Oakland Museum of California since 2002. Entries: Anita Cornwell; gay liberation movement; Daphne Gottlieb.

Bruce Henderson is professor of speech communication at Ithaca College, where he also coordinates the programs in culture and communication and health communication. He has PhDs from Northwestern University in performance studies and the University of Illinois at Chicago in disability studies. He was editor of *Text and Performance Quarterly* from 2007 to 2009 and is coauthor with Carol Simpson Stern of *Performance: Texts and Contexts*. Entry: musical theater and films.

Christopher Hennessy is the author of *Outside the Lines: Talking with Contemporary Gay Poets*. He is associate editor for *Gay and Lesbian Review-Worldwide*. Entries: Richard Howard; Rudy Kikel.

María Henríquez Betancor has been teaching at the University of Las Palmas de Gran Canaria (Spain) since 1996 and has published on Gloria E. Anzaldúa. Entries: Gloria Evangelina Anzaldúa; Alicia Gaspar de Alba.

Imani Henry has been a staff organizer at the International Action Center (IAC), where his work has focused on national organizing of communities of color and the lesbian, gay, bisexual, and transgender movement toward broader social justice and antiwar campaigns. He tours with his theater piece *B4T (before testosterone)* and is a journalist for the progressive weekly *Workers' World*. Entry: Robert Kohler.

Liz Highleyman is a San Francisco–based freelance journalist who has written widely on health, sexuality, and politics. She is author of *Past Out*, Q Syndicate's biweekly LGBT history column. Entries: HIV/AIDS impact on LGBTQ culture in the United States; piercings, tattoos, and scars; protests and actions.

Elizabeth L. Hillman, professor of law, Rutgers University School of Law, Camden, studies gender, sexuality, and law in the military and is the author of *Defending America: Military Culture and the Cold War Court-Martial*. Entries: government and military prosecution; Servicemembers Legal Defense Network (SLDN).

Katie Hladky is a doctoral student and college teaching fellow in the Department of Religion at Florida State University. Entries: colleges and universities, religiously affiliated; gay; Islam and Muslims; Queers United against Straight-Acting Homosexuals (QUASH); religion; sissyphobia and femiphobia.

Jon Hoffman is a PhD student in the Department of Communication Studies at the University of Minnesota. Entries: Amnesty International OUTfront; faggot.

Debra Hoffmann is information literacy coordinator for the Broome Library at California State University, Channel Islands, in Camarillo, California. Entry: Lou Harrison.

Cleo House Jr. is a professional actor (theater and film) and has performed at regional theaters across the country. Currently he serves as program coordinator for theater at Pennsylvania State University in Berks. Entry: theater companies.

Yetta Howard is a PhD candidate in the Department of English at the University of Southern California. She is completing a dissertation on ugliness and contemporary cultural productions of lesbianism. Entry: lesbian.

Neil Hultgren is completing his dissertation on melodrama, imperialism, and Victorian fiction at the University of Virginia, where he served on the LGBT Resource Center Board. Entry: camp.

Ski Hunter, MSW, PhD, is a professor at the School of Social Work at the University of Texas at Arlington. She has published three books on LGBT youth and adults, and another book is in progress. Entries: Alice B. Toklas Lesbian Gay Bisexual Transgender Democratic Club; Gay and Lesbian Medical Association (GLMA); Log Cabin Republicans.

Sue Hyde has worked for the National Gay and Lesbian Task Force since 1986 and directs the annual Creating Change Conference, the movement's preeminent LGBT skills and strategy conference. Entry: National Gay and Lesbian Task Force.

Mikel Imaz graduated from the University of Deusto and received a doctorate in Latin American literature from Arizona State University. His dissertation analyzed questions regarding homoerotic masculinities in contemporary Argentine narrative. He currently teaches at the State University of New York at Plattsburgh. Entry: Bears.

Andy Inkster is a transplanted Canadian currently making his home in Northampton, Massachusetts. His research interests are centered on transmasculinity, and he is at present a PhD student in sociology at the University of Massachusetts at Amherst. Entries: John Preston; Gwendolyn Ann Smith; Tim'm T. West.

Mark John Isola earned his BA in gerontology from Quinnipiac University, an MA in English from Simmons College, and a PhD in literature from Tufts University. His interests include American literature and LGBT/AIDS studies, and his work has appeared in *Bad Subjects, eSharp,* and the *Nordic Journal of English Studies.* Entries: Harlan Greene; Reginald Harris; HIV/AIDS impact on literature; Paul Reed; The Violet Quill.

Daniel M. Jaffe currently teaches creative writing workshops online and in-person for the University of California, Los Angeles, Extension Writers' Program. More than 100 of his short stories, essays, and articles have appeared in anthologies, literary journals, and newspapers such as *The Forward, Jewish Currents, Response: A Contemporary Jewish Review, The Greensboro Review, The Florida Review, Found Tribe,* and M2M: *New Literary Fiction.* Entry: Leo F. Cabranes-Grant.

Amy Jamgochian is a doctoral candidate in the Department of Rhetoric at the University of California, Berkeley. Entries: sex-positive movement; stereotypes.

Courtney Denine Johnson is a PhD candidate in English at the University of California, Los Angeles, specializing in black women's literature, prison literature, and sexuality studies. Entry: Helen Elaine Lee.

Jay Emerson Johnson, an Episcopal priest and theologian, teaches courses in LGBTQ studies and theology at Pacific School of Religion and directs programming for the school's Center for Lesbian and Gay Studies in Berkeley, California. He is also the cochair of the Gay Men's Issues in Religion Group of the American Academy of Religion. Entries: clergy; Episcopal Church.

Jordon L. M. Johnson, MA, MSW, is a national consultant on transgender issues. His research focuses on transgender interactions with health care systems in New Mexico. Entries: National Transgender Advocacy Coalition (NTAC); World Professional Association for Transgender Health, Inc.

Lisa Johnston is associate director of the Sweet Briar College Library, where she is a humanities specialist with emphasis on literature, film studies, and art history. She is active in the American Library Association's Gay, Lesbian, Bisexual, and Transgendered-Round Table. Entry: Jane (Auer) Bowles.

Jordy Jones is a PhD candidate in visual studies and critical theory at the University of California at Irvine where he is a University of California Chancellor's Fellow. Entry: photographers, men.

Meggan Jordan is a doctoral student in sociology at the University of Florida. Entry: women's music.

About the Editor, Advisory Board, and Contributors

Alison Kafer is an assistant professor of feminist studies at Southwestern University and the 2006–2007 Ed Roberts Visiting Scholar in Disability Studies at the University of California, Berkeley. Entry: disability studies and LGBTQ issues.

Kristian T. Kahn is a doctoral research student in English and comparative literary studies at the University of Warwick. Entries: Carole Maso; Aaron Shurin.

Beth Kattelman is currently the associate curator of the Lawrence and Lee Theatre Research Institute at the Ohio State University. She also is a member of the advisory board for the Columbus National Gay and Lesbian Theatre Festival. Entries: Edward Albee; Jane Chambers; William Finn; Scott McPherson.

John Keene is the author of a novel and, together with a visual artist, of a poetry collection. He teaches at Northwestern University. Entry: Cyrus Cassells.

Cynthia Keiken received her BA in creative writing from the State University of New York at New Paltz and her MA in English from Buffalo State College. Entry: Jane Rule.

Jodi Kelber-Kaye is a lecturer in the Gender and Women's Studies Program at the University of Maryland, Baltimore County. She also directs their Women Involved in Learning and Leadership Program. Entries: Gran Fury; lesbian health issues.

Jim Kellogg has been an attorney for the American Civil Liberties Union of Louisiana and the Lambda Legal Defense Fund, has also served on the boards of both organizations, and was a civil rights and civil liberties litigator in New Orleans for over 20 years. He is one of the moderators of the Same Sex Marriage mailing list. Entries: American Civil Liberties Union (ACLU); Lambda Legal Defense and Education Fund (LLDEF); sodomy laws.

Robin Kemp is a doctoral student in poetry at Georgia State University, with poems in *Letters to the World: Poems from the WOM-PO Listserv*; *Maple Leaf Rag III*; *Verse Daily*; and *Texas Review*. Entry: Elizabeth Bishop.

Holly M. Kent is a doctoral candidate in the History Department at Lehigh University. Entries: Lillian Faderman; Kathleen Fleming; Susan Griffin; Vicki P. McConnell; Kate Millett; Valerie Miner; Robin Morgan; Elisabeth Nonas; Sapphire; Chea Villanueva.

Kelly Kessler teaches media studies in and around New York City. Her work appears in *Film Quarterly*, *The New Queer Aesthetic on Television*, and the *Encyclopedia of Men and Masculinity*. Entries: Lorenz Milton Hart; Homosexuals Anonymous; political scandals; Jerome Robbins; Tommy Tune.

Bryan Kim-Butler is a student at Vassar College studying women's studies and philosophy. Entries: Asian Americans and LGBTQ issues; Paul Russell.

Aimee Klask is an associate curator of history at the Oakland Museum of California and history instructor at Diablo Valley College. She is a specialist in California history. Entries: Jaime Cortez; Daughters of Bilitis; Alma Lopez; Parents, Families, and Friends of Lesbians and Gays (PFLAG); photographers, women.

Beth Kling is a freelance writer and editor who lives in New York City. Entry: Services and Advocacy for GLBT Elders (SAGE).

Harold Kooden is a fellow of the American Psychological Association (APA) and a founder and board member of the National Gay and Lesbian Health Foundation, APA's Division 44, The Society for the Study of Lesbian and Gay Issues and the Association of Lesbian and Gay Psychologists. Since 1985, he has worked extensively with the International Lesbian and Gay Association. Entry: Ageism.

Mandy Koolen is a PhD candidate at McMaster University. Her dissertation, entitled *Qu(e)erying History: Lesbian, Queer and Trans Historical Fiction and the Construction of Contemporary Pasts*, examines the ability of historical identifications to challenge homophobia, biphobia, and transphobia. Entry: fiction, historical.

Gerard Koskovich is a San Francisco–based editor, writer, and dealer in rare LGBT print materials who has published and presented widely on queer historical and cultural topics since the mid-1980s. He serves on the board of directors of the GLBT Historical Society in San Francisco and the Mémorial de la Déportation Homosexuelle in Paris, and he holds a lifetime membership in the Committee on Lesbian and Gay History. Entry: libraries and archives.

Robert Kulpa is pursuing a doctorate at University College London. Entry: Names Project AIDS Memorial Quilt.

Sheela Lambert is the founder of the Bi Writers Association, cofounder of Bi Women of All Colors, founder of the Bi Mental Health Professionals Association, cofounder of the Coalition of Unity and Inclusion, and organizer of the Bisexual Speakers Bureau of New York. Entries: biphobia; bisexual; bisexual Erasure.

Brad Houston Lane is a PhD student in the nation's first doctoral program in gender studies, at Indiana University. Entries: Gay, Lesbian, and Straight Education Network (GLSEN); International Foundation for Gender Education (IFGE); International Lesbian and Gay Association (ILGA); North American Man/Boy Love Association (NAMBLA); Tri-Ess Society (The Society of the Second Self).

Jennifer Burns Levin is at the University of California, Irvine (UCI), writing a dissertation on literary representations of masochism in modern fiction. She is the 2006–2007 James J. Harvey fellow for gay/lesbian studies at UCI. Entries: Natalie Clifford Barney; fisting; sadomasochism, sadists, masochists, and BDSM.

Eng-Beng Lim is assistant professor of English at Michigan State University. His work has appeared in *Theatre Journal, Asian Theater Journal,* and *Modern Drama*. Entries: Charles Busch; Chay Yew.

Bill Lipsky lives in San Francisco with his partner of 28 years and with Hillary Rodham Kitten and Scarlett O'Hairball (who will never be hungry again). He works at the GLBT Historical Society. Entry: San Francisco.

Marc Lombardo is a faculty associate in the Department of Communication Studies at Arizona State University. His interests include American pragmatism, rhetoric, and African American intellectual history. Entry: Cecil Taylor.

Thomas Lawrence Long is professor of English at Thomas Nelson Community College (in Hampton, Virginia) and the author of *AIDS and American Apocalypticism*. He is editor-in-chief of *Harrington Gay Men's Literary Quarterly*. Entries: Christopher Bram; journalism, academic; novelists, gay.

Frederick Lowe is a practicing psychotherapist, poet, and freelance essayist. His writing has appeared in numerous journals and on the Web. Entries: David Leo Diamond; Maurice Kenny.

Jamie Lowe currently works as a health educator at the Ruth M. Rothstein CORE Center. She is pursuing graduate studies in public health, human sexuality, and lesbian, gay, bisexual, and transgender studies. Entry: Jenifer Levin.

Sassafras Lowrey has a bachelor's degree with an emphasis on queer media studies and works as a freelance journalist for LGBTQ publications. Hir first book, *GSA to Marriage: Stories of a Life Lived Queerly*, is scheduled for release in summer of 2008. Ze is also the editor of *Kicked Out*, an anthology about queer youth homelessness from Homofactus Press. Entries: art and photography; bars, lesbian; privacy and privacy rights; queer gaze.

Christopher Lozensky holds a BA in English from Minot State University, North Dakota, with minors in history and gender/women's studies. In 2006 he served as the assistant editor of the *Medieval Feminist Forum*, and he has several essays forthcoming in *The Facts on File Companion to British Poetry before 1600*, edited by Michelle M. Sauer. Entry: sex over cyberspace.

Raymond Luczak has written and edited eight books, including *Assembly Required: Notes from a Deaf Gay Life* and *Eyes of Desire 2: A Deaf GLBT Reader*. Entries: Victor Bumbalo; Deaf Culture; William M. Hoffman; Honor Moore; Norah Vincent.

Jimmie Manning is an assistant professor in the Graduate Program of Communication at Northern Kentucky University. He has authored over 20 book chapters and journal articles exploring gender, sexuality, and the rhetoric of relationships. Entries: marriages, mixed-orientation; Midwest.

Veronica Marian has a MA in English from Claremont Graduate University. Entry: John Corigliano.

Susan Marine is a doctoral candidate in higher education at Boston College and is the director of the Harvard College Women's Center at Harvard University. Entry: women's and gender studies in universities.

Krista L. May is associate editor of the *World Shakespeare Bibliography Online* at Texas A&M University. She has written CD and concert reviews for *Popular Music and Society* and the online magazine *Popmatters*. Entries: William Seward Burroughs; queer skinheads; Lou Reed; Andy Warhol.

Craig W. McClain majored in lesbian, gay, and bisexual studies at Hobart College and received his master's degree in American studies from the University of New Mexico. Entry: gay rodeo.

Jeffrey McCune is assistant professor of American studies and women's studies at the University of Maryland. Entry: Down Low.

Lena McQuade is a doctoral candidate in the American studies program at the University of New Mexico. Entries: Leslie Feinberg; Emma Pérez.

Tey Meadow is a lawyer and doctoral candidate in sociology at New York University. Her work explores the legal regulation of gendered identities and behaviors. Entry: transgender studies.

G. Douglas Meyers is a professor of English at the University of Texas at El Paso. Entries: Daniel Curzon; Allan Gurganus.

Louis M. Miranda lives in Minneapolis, Minnesota. Entry: Norah Vincent.

Omar A. Moran teaches English at California State University, San Bernardino. Entries: Gary Glickman; Karen Lee Osborne.

Scott Morgensen teaches women's and gender/sexuality studies at Macalester College in St. Paul, Minnesota. Entries: globalization; radical faeries; whiteness studies.

Sara Munoz is a graduate student at Arizona State University. Entries: rainbow flag; religion and HIV/AIDS; sodomy.

JoAnne Myers teaches political science and women's studies at Marist College in Poughkeepsie, New York. She is the author of *The Historical Dictionary of the Lesbian Liberation Movement: Still the Rage* and numerous book chapters and articles. Entries: Bertha Harris; Isabel Miller.

James Najarian is an associate professor of English at Boston College and the author of *Victorian Keats: Manliness, Sexuality, and Desire*. Entries: David Bergman; Henri Cole; Charles Demuth; Joseph Daniel McClatchy; William Meredith.

Vani Natarajan works as a reference librarian at the University of Pittsburgh and as a volunteer journalist for Rustbelt Radio. Entry: Linda Besemer.

Emmanuel S. Nelson is professor of English at the State University of New York at Cortland. Most recently he is the editor of *The Greenwood Encyclopedia of Multiethnic American Literature* (Greenwood Press, 2005). Entries: James Baldwin; Larry Duplechan; David B. Feinberg; John Rechy.

Robyn Ochs is editor of the anthology *Getting Bi: Voices of Bisexuals around the World*. Her writings have been published in numerous bisexual, women's studies, multicultural, and LGBT anthologies. She lives in Massachusetts, and on May 17, 2004—the first day it was legal—she married Peg Preble, her longtime partner. Entry: bisexual movement.

Andrew O'Day is coauthor (with Jonathan Bignell) of *Terry Nation* and lectures in media and film at the University of Winchester in the United Kingdom. Entries: autobiography, gay; New York City; poets, gay; The West Coast New Narrative Movement.

Jessica Elise O'Keefe, theater and women's studies scholar at the University of California, Santa Barbara, writes about American transgender theater as a method of achieving social justice. Entry: Imani Henry.

Connie G. Oxford is an assistant professor of women's studies at the State University of New York at Plattsburgh. Entry: Gay and Lesbian Advocates and Defenders (GLAD).

David W. Pantalone is a doctoral candidate in clinical psychology at the University of Washington where his research is funded by the National Institutes of Health. Entries: barebacking; oral sex; serosorting.

Ilya Parkins is assistant professor of women's studies at Trent University. Entry: fashion, style, and clothing.

Christopher Penczak is a modern witch serving the gay and pagan communities as an author, teacher, healing facilitator, and minister. His books include *Gay Witchcraft, The Inner Temple of Witchcraft*, and *The Mystic Foundation*. Entry: Wicca and witches.

Bryan Peters is a visiting instructor at Miami University. Entry: Cherríe Moraga.

Anthony Petro is a graduate student in the Department of Religion at Princeton University. His academic interests include the ethnographic study of religion, feminist theory, and the AIDS crisis in the 1980s. He previously worked as the program associate for the Feminism and Legal Theory Project at Emory University Law School. Entry: Protestants, mainline.

Daniel F. Pigg is a professor of English at the University of Tennessee at Martin, where he teaches courses in medieval literature. He has a number of publications examining the gendered representation of masculinity in historical context. Entries: homoeroticism; homosociality; queer studies.

Katherine J. J. Pionke teaches English at two colleges in Illinois. Entries: David Zamora Casas; Nalo Hopkinson; Barbara Seyda; Paul Taylor.

Thomas Piontek is visiting assistant professor of English at Otterbein College in Westerville, Ohio, and the author of *Queering Gay and Lesbian Studies*. His work has also been published in journals such as *Discourse* and the *Journal of Homosexuality,* as well as in several recent anthologies. Entries: John Champagne; homophile movement; Richard McCann; Stonewall Riots.

Kenneth Pobo teaches at Widener University. His essays appear in *A House of Gathering: Poets on May Sarton's Poetry, Asylum,* and *Poet and Critic*. Entry: Edward Field.

Milan Pribisic holds a PhD in theater studies and teaches in the Department of Communication at Loyola University Chicago. His research interests include queer representations, film adaptation, and "theater film." Entries: film, American and non-American influences; pornography stars.

John Pruitt is assistant professor of English at the University of Wisconsin–Rock County. Beyond teaching writing and literature courses, he is completing a project on teaching LGBT literature in survey courses. Entries: Mart Crowley; David Groff; Moisés Kaufman; Paul Rudnick; Martin Sherman; Gore Vidal; Doric Wilson.

David Puts is a postdoctoral fellow in the neuroscience program at Michigan State University and author of *Human Sexuality: A Holistic Approach.* In 2004, he received the New Young Investigator Award from the Human Behavior and Evolution Society. His research has been featured on the National Public Radio program *All Things Considered,* and has also been covered by *Pravda, The Guardian, derStandard,* Associated Press, Fox News, MSNBC, and *USA Today.* Entry: genetics and the development of human sexual orientation.

Jennifer Randall, MSW, LICSW, is a medical social worker with specializations in chronic illness and end of life. She is currently pursuing a PhD in social work at Boston College. She lives in Boston with her wife, Anne. Entry: health care laws.

Sharon M. Raphael is professor emeritus at California State University Dominguez Hills (CSUDH). A lesbian activist since 1971 in Los Angeles, she founded the Gerontology Graduate Program at CSUDH and received the Christopher Street Pride Parade Steve Berman Humanitarian Award in 1993, together with life partner Mina K. Meyer. Entry: Old Lesbians Organizing for Change (OLOC).

Jennifer Reed teaches women's studies at California State University Long Beach and writes about gender and sexuality in mass media. Entries: comedians; radicalesbians.

Jackie Regales is an instructor in American studies at Anne Arundel Community College in Arnold, Maryland. Her work on transgender zine writers appears in *Queer Youth Cultures.* Entries: queer zines; Transgender Nation; Transsexual Menace.

Mark Reger is the dean of the College of Arts and Sciences and director of the University Honors Program at Mississippi Valley State University, as well as professor of English in the Department of English and Foreign Languages. He has served as the associate editor of the *Journal of Social and Behavioral Sciences* and coedited the letters of Sir Leslie Stephen. Entry: cross-dressing and transvestism.

Erica Reichert is completing her MA in sociology at Indiana University. Entries: Michiyo Fukaya; Ruth Geller; Ifti Nasim; Margaret Randall; Muriel Rukeyser; Terry Wolverton.

Robert Ridinger is an electronic information resources librarian and anthropologist at Northern Illinois University. He is the editor of *Speaking for Our Lives.* Entries: African American LGBTQ organizations; Asian Pacific Lesbian Bisexual Network; Black Took Collective; Deaf Queer Resource Center; David Del Tredici, ; Fenton Johnson; National Association of Black and White Men Together; National Organization of Gay and Lesbian Scientists and Technical Professionals; OutRage!; Sisters of Perpetual Indulgence; Michael Tilson Thomas; transgender life stories; Trikone.

Damien W. Riggs is an Australian Research Council postdoctoral fellow in the School of Psychology at the University of Adelaide. He is the author of two books: *Priscilla, (White) Queen of the Desert: Queer Rights/Race Privilege* and *Becoming Parent: Lesbians, Gay Men, and Family.* Entry: essentialist and constructionist positions.

Jeannette E. Riley is associate professor of English and director of women's studies at the University of Massachusetts at Dartmouth. Entries: Paula Gunn Allen; Nuala Archer; Olga Broumas; Rita Mae Brown; Janice Gould; Mary Oliver; Pat Parker; Adrienne Rich.

Christopher Rivera is completing an interdisciplinary PhD in comparative literature and women's and gender studies at Rutgers University and serving as an adjunct professor at the College of New Jersey. Entries: bars, gay; gyms.

Jean Roberta teaches English in a Canadian university and writes in several genres including erotica, reviews (mostly on LGBT subjects), and research-based articles. Entries: choreographers, women; Amber Hollibaugh; Sharon Isabell.

Margaret Robinson is a feminist scholar and bisexual activist. She holds an MA in theology and is currently writing her dissertation, a qualitative study of polyamory and monogamy among bisexual women in Toronto. Entries: monogamy; non-monogamy; polyamory; promiscuity.

Nancy McGuire Roche studied writing with Allen Ginsberg, William S. Burroughs, and Diane Di Prima and with the two cofounders of the Poetry Project at Saint Mark's Church, Anne Waldman and Bernadette Mayer. She is currently an adjunct professor at Fisk University. Entry: San Francisco Bay Area Poets.

Matthew Rohweder is a graduate student at Simon Fraser University. Entries: James Barr; Michael Cunningham; Kenny Fries.

Carol Rosenfeld is a New York City–based poet, writer, and aspiring performance artist. Entry: Publishing Triangle.

Yvette Saavedra has taught history at Santa Monica College. Entry: Latino/Latina Americans and LGBTQ issues.

Gayle Salamon is the Cotsen LGBT postdoctoral fellow at Princeton University. Entries: identity and identity politics; performativity.

Cy-Thea Sand cofounded *The Radical Reviewer* in 1980 in Vancouver and corresponded with Elsa Gidlow about the publication, especially its overt and celebratory lesbianism, which the poet deeply appreciated. Entry: Elsa Gidlow.

Ronni Sanlo is the director of and a professor for the University of California, Los Angeles (UCLA), master's of education program in student sffairs as well as director of the UCLA Lesbian Gay Bisexual Transgender Campus Resource Center. Entries: Lavender Graduation; National Consortium of Directors of LGBT Resources in Higher Education.

Jeffrey A. Sartain teaches literature and composition at Indiana University. He is currently editing an anthology about Chuck Palahniuk's work. Entries: Chuck Palahniuk; Tom Spanbauer.

Michelle M. Sauer is managing editor of *Medieval Feminist Forum and* associate professor of English at the University of North Dakota. She is the winner of the first LGBT Religious Archives Network Award. Entries: Gay and Lesbian American Music Awards (GLAMA); intersex; Lesbian Herstory Archives.

John Sauvé, PsyD, is a senior clinical psychologist in counseling and psychological services (CPS) at the University of California, Berkeley, where he is the coordinator of group programs and CPS liaison with LGBTQ communities on campus. Previously he worked in adult psychiatry and chemical dependency recovery clinics at Kaiser Permanente in Oakland and South San Francisco, California. Entries: alcohol and drugs; queer hotlines.

Ann M. Savage is an associate professor of media and cultural studies at Butler University, Indiana. Publications include *They're Playing Our Songs: Women Talk about Feminist Rock Music* (Greenwood). Entries: Judie Bamber; Melissa Etheridge; film directors and producers, women; Joan Jett.

Lindsey E. Schell is bibliographer for English literature, women's and gender studies, and youth literature for the libraries at the University of Texas at Austin. Entry: book publishers.

Christopher Schmidt is a PhD candidate in English literature at the City University of New York's Graduate Center. His poems and essays can be found in *Tin House, Court Green 3,* and

About the Editor, Advisory Board, and Contributors

Canadian Poetry. Entries: Mark Bibbins; Wayne Koestenbaum; New York School of Poets The May Swenson; David Trinidad.

Andrew Schopp is assistant professor of English at Nassau Community College in New York. Entries: Michael Bennett; pornography in film.

A. B. Christa Schwarz was educated at Bonn University (Germany), Queen Mary and Westfield College (England), and at the University of Sussex (England). She is an independent scholar and author of *Gay Voices of the Harlem Renaissance* (2003). Entries: Charles Henri Ford; Harlem Renaissance; pink triangle.

Jo Scott-Coe is a Pushcart-nominated essayist who writes and teaches in California. Her interview with Richard Rodriguez appeared in *Narrative* magazine, and other nonfiction has been published in *Fourth Genre, Ninth Letter,* and the *Los Angeles Times.* Entries: age of consent; Richard Rodriguez; Randy Shilts.

Mary Shearman is a doctoral student in the Department of Women's Studies at Simon Fraser University in Vancouver, Canada. She has worked on feminist theater for young audiences, Canadian legislation governing sexual behaviors, and historical and contemporary manifestations of feminist theater in burlesques and cabaraet performances. Entries: Patrick Califia; Tristan Taormino.

Reginald Shepherd is the editor of *The Iowa Anthology of New American Poetries* and of *Lyric Postmodernisms.* His five volumes of poetry are *Fata Morgana; Otherhood* (a finalist for the 2004 Lenore Marshall Poetry Prize); *Wrong; Angel, Interrupted;* and *Some Are Drowning* (winner of the 1993 Associated Writing Programs' Award in Poetry). He is also the author of *Orpheus in the Bronx: Essays on Identity, Politics, and the Freedom of Poetry.* Entries: Donald Britton; Hart Crane; Tim Dlugos; Timothy Liu; Carl Phillips; D. A. Powell; Brian Teare; Mark Wunderlich.

Clarence R. Slavens teaches English at Dana College in Blair, Nebraska. Entry: John Gilgun.

Graham Sleight is editor of *Foundation: The International Review of Science Fiction,* a contributing editor for *Locus,* and a writer for *The New York Review of Science Fiction, Strange Horizons,* and *Interzone.* His Web site is www.gsleight.demon.co.uk. Entry: science fiction, fantasy, and horror.

Leverett T. Smith taught at North Carolina Wesleyan College. Entry: Michael Rumaker.

Helen Smith has a master's degree in human sexuality studies from San Francisco State University. She is currently involved in LGBT public health research. Entries: interracial couples; sex toys.

Liberty Smith researches U.S. and Latin American queer collaborative writing, art, and political engagement. She pursues issues of civic engagement as the program manager of the National Service-Learning Clearinghouse. Entries: autobiography, lesbian; McCarthyism; Guillermo Reyes.

Tom Smith is a playwright and associate professor of theater arts at New Mexico State University; he has published articles and reviews for *Theatre Topics, Theatre Journal,* and Salem Press's *GLBT History.* Entries: Daryl Hine; Craig Lucas; Charles Ludlam; Terrence McNally; Ron Mohring; Mark Morris; Richard Tayson.

Riley Snorton is a Fontaine fellow and doctoral student at the University of Pennsylvania. He is a student of communications with a focus on Africana and gender and sexuality studies. He received his AB from Columbia University in women and gender studies and worked as a media relations manager for the Gay and Lesbian Alliance against Defamation (GLAAD) and Gay, Lesbian, and Straight Education Network (GLSEN). Entry: youth and youth groups.

Steve Stratton is associate professor and head of collections and technical services at California State University, Channel Islands, in Camarillo, California. Entries: HIV/AIDS, medical history; sexually transmitted infections; Dean Spade; Marvin K.White.

Elnora Tayag is librarian at California State University, Channel Islands. Entry: Ross Bleckner.

Anne Thalheimer received her PhD from the University of Delaware in 2002 with a dissertation on lesbian comix and is currently a chief reader in the Hadley, Massachusetts, office of NES/Pearson. Entries: Jean-Michel Basquiat; Justin Chin; comics and graphic novels; Keith Haring; Morrissey.

Shari Thurer is a psychoanalytically trained psychologist in private practice in Boston, a long-time professor at Boston University and now an adjunct, and the author of *The End of Gender: A Psychological Autopsy* and *The Myths of Motherhood: How Culture Reinvents the Good Mother*. Entry: gender studies.

Matthew Tiritilli is a scholar, writer, artist, and performer. He lives in Illinois. Entries: Leonard Bernstein; Marc Blitzstein; Elana (Nachman) Dykewomon; Lorraine Hansberry; Jasper Johns; Arthur Laurents; Aleida Rodríguez.

Andrea Tucker received her Master of Theological Studies from Emory University and is a board member of the Femme Mafia. Entries: Femme Mafia; lipstick lesbian and granola lesbian; religion and politics.

Jonathan G. Turbin is a freelance writer and copyeditor pursuing a doctorate in global health. He holds a masters in public administration and has worked for the Human Rights Campaign's Workplace Project, where he evaluated LGBTQ-friendly policies for Fortune 500 companies. Entry: workplace issues.

Douglas Turnbaugh is a biographer of Duncan Grant, Serge Diaghilev, and others and is a documentary filmmaker (*Ballet Russes*; forthcoming: *Mia Slavenska, Ballerina; Stardust Melody*). Entries: Patrick Angus; Delmas Howe; Robert Joffrey; Robert Patrick.

Jack Turner recently retired from teaching at Humboldt State University. Although his field was Shakespeare, he has taught many other courses, including several in LGBTQ literature. Entries: Frederick Newton Arvin; Paul Bowles; Alan Bowne; John Cheever; William Inge; David Leavitt; Francis Otto Matthiessen; Paul Monette.

Jennifer Tyburczy is a doctoral candidate in critical studies in performance at Northwestern University. Entries: AIDS History Project; leather; Perverts Undermining State Scrutiny (PUSSY).

Marcus C. Tye is an associate professor and chair of the Psychology Department at Dowling College in Oakdale, New York, and a clinical psychologist who researches in the area of law and psychology, including custody evaluations with LGBT parents and confidentiality in psychotherapy. cruising; family law, adoption, and custody; homophobia; tearooms.

Lindasusan Ulrich is a writer and musician. Entry: Horizons Foundation.

Mimi Iimuro Van Ausdall is a visiting assistant professor of English at the University of Iowa. She is working on a book entitled *Novel Contributions: Reframing the 1970s through the Lesbian Novel*. Entries: June Arnold; Jill Johnston; Ann Allen Shockley.

Jim Van Buskirk is program manager at the James C. Hormel Gay and Lesbian Center at the San Francisco Public Library. Entry: Frederic Allen Sawyer.

Emily van der Meulen is a PhD candidate in women's studies at York University in Toronto, Canada. Entry: Ronald K. Brown.

Yarma Velázquez Vargas is a graduate student at the Florida State University, Tallahassee, working on media representation and sexuality. Entries: Gay Latino Alliance (GALA); queer; Sheila Ortiz-Taylor.

Christopher H. Walker is a cataloging librarian at Pennsylvania State University. His research interests include the history of libraries in their cultural contexts and general historical trends as reflected in opera repertoire. Entries: Truman Capote; Ned Rorem; Conrad Susa.

Jeff Walker is a public health professional, poet, fiction writer, artist, and justice of the peace who lives and works in both Cambridge and Provincetown, Massachusetts. Walker has been a part-time resident of Provincetown since he was a teenager 30 years ago. Entry: Provincetown.

Kristen Warder is an instructor at the University of Western Ontario, who specializes in Canadian literature, queer theory, and cultural geography. Entry: Terry Baum.

Linda S. Watts is professor of American studies in the Interdisciplinary Arts and Sciences Program at the University of Washington, Bothell. Entry: pride parades and festivals.

Jillian T. Weiss is assistant professor of law and society, Ramapo College, where her area of research is transgender workplace policies. Entries: employment law; transgender rights.

Milton W. Wendland is a practicing attorney as well as a doctoral student in American studies at the University of Kansas. He teaches courses in American cultures, gender studies, and LGBT history. Entries: May Sarton; Sylvester.

Lorna Wheeler teaches at Metropolitan State College of Denver. Entries: ACT UP (AIDS Coalition to Unleash Power); Mae V. Cowdery.

Vicki Lynn White has completed a double major in psychology and rhetoric at the University of Arkansas-Fort Smith. She is in the graduate program in rehabilitation counseling at the University of Arkansas-Fayetteville. Entries: Don Bachardy; Julie Blackwomon; Martha Courtot; doris davenport; Terri L. Jewell; Jacqueline Lapidus; Hawk Madrone; Susan Sherman; Kitty Tsui; Fran Winant.

Claire Williams is a master's degree candidate in sport and exercise humanities at the Ohio State University. Entry: sports.

Howell Williams is writing her dissertation in American religious history at Florida State University. Entries: John Boswell; religious groups and movements, LGBTQ; United Church of Christ (UCC).

Brian Willoughby is a doctoral candidate in the Department of Psychology at the University of Miami. Entry: children, LGBTQ.

Brandy T. Wilson is a PhD candidate at Florida State University. She was recently named as finalist in fiction for the Astraea Lesbian Writers Fund Award. Her work is featured in Robert Olen Butler's *From Where You Dream: The Process of Writing Fiction, Feeling Our Way* and is forthcoming in *Ninth Letter*. Entries: novelists, lesbian; Sarah Schulman.

Dagmawi Woubshet is assistant professor of English at Cornell University. Entries: Alvin Ailey; Audre Lorde Project (ALP); Thomas Glave; Bill T. Jones and Arnie Zane; Glenn Ligon.

Katheryn Wright is a PhD candidate in the Interdisciplinary Humanities Department at Florida State University. Entry: politics and activism.

Nicholas Wright received an MA from the State University of New York at New Paltz this spring. His major literary interests are Victorian, modernist, and Holocaust literatures with focus on queer theory. Entries: Sarah Anne Dreher; Larry Mitchell.

Nolana Yip has taught at the George Washington University and teaches at the Corcoran College of Art and Design and Georgetown University. Entry: Asian American feminism.

Kenji Yoshino is Guido Calabresi Professor of Law at Yale Law School. His book, *Covering,* was in 2006. Entry: covering.

Lee Zevy is one of the founders of Identity House, a past president of the New York City Coalition for Women's Mental Health, and a past president of her psychotherapy training institute, the New York Institute for Gestalt Therapy. Entries: Identity House; *Lesbian Psychologies*.

Ger Zielinski is a doctoral candidate at McGill University, writing on the cultural politics of LGBTQ film festivals and lecturing on media theory and sexuality. Entries: Robert Indiana; queer film festivals.